Fourth Edition

Social Welfare in Canada

Inclusion, Equity, and Social Justice

DEDICATION

Katherine McParland (1987-2020)

This book honours all those whose advocacy, dedication, and perseverance creates and improves the social welfare of people in Canada and around the globe. One such charismatic woman was Katherine McParland (1987-2020), a social worker who was awarded the Champion of Child and Youth Rights Award in 2021. Katherine's lived experience of aging out-of-care and youth homelessness fuelled her passion and created her national and international legacy as a "fierce warrior" who was transforming "the superhighway to homelessness" for youth-in-care everywhere.

Fourth Edition

Social Welfare in Canada

Inclusion, Equity, and Social Justice

Steven Hick, Carleton University
Jackie Stokes, Thompson Rivers University

THOMPSON

Information on how to obtain copies of this book is available at:
www.thompsonbooks.com

ISBN 978–1–55077–281–4 (Print Edition)
ISBN 978–1–55077–282–1 (Online Edition)

Previous editions of this work were published under the title *Social Welfare In Canada: Understanding Income Security.*

Cover Design: Gary Blakeley, www.blakeleyblakeley.com

Library and Archives Canada Cataloguing in Publication

Title: Social welfare in Canada : inclusion, equity, and social justice / Steven Hick, Carleton University ; Jackie Stokes, Thompson Rivers University.

Names: Hick, Steven, 1959- author. | Stokes, Jackie, author.

Description: Fourth edition. | Previous edition has subtitle: Understanding income security. |

Includes bibliographical references and index.

Identifiers: Canadiana (print) 20210132469 | Canadiana (ebook) 20210132485 | ISBN 9781550772814 (softcover) | ISBN 9781550772821 (HTML)

Subjects: LCSH: Social security—Canada—Textbooks. | LCSH: Income maintenance programs—Canada—Textbooks. | LCSH: Poverty—Canada—Textbooks. | LCGFT: Textbooks.

Classification: LCC HV105 .H5 2021 | DDC 362.5/820971—dc23

Canada

We acknowledge the support of the Government of Canada.
Printed in Canada.
1 2 3 4 5 6 7 30 29 28 27 26 25 24 23 22 21

Contents

Table of Contents

Acknowledgements

In this fourth edition, we have brought together a group of authors with a wealth of experience to ensure that readers and learners are introduced to contemporary ideas about social welfare in Canada. This requires attention to the past, to the present national and global context, and to considering social policies that are required for the well-being of future generations.

The team contribution to any textbook is enormous. This book has been reviewed by multiple anonymous reviewers over the years, and without the exceptional contributions and ideas of the editorial and production team the book could not have been completed.

This edition builds on the work of previous authors who have made outstanding achievements in social work and social welfare policy. This includes Allan Moscovitch who initiated the ideas for the first edition; Roy Hanes who has contributed to each edition of the book; and Alvin Finkel who was instrumental in describing the historical themes of social welfare. This book also builds on the suggestions and contributions to previous editions of Sarah Todd at Carleton University, Purnima Sundar (previously at Carleton), and Peter Graefe at McMaster University. Throughout each edition, Keith Thompson has been a guiding presence to ensure the book provides the best materials and resources for learners, and that the work, the ideas and the publication continues to get better.

This edition marks a major shift away from describing the workings of the income security system in Canada toward understanding the importance of social welfare policies to ensure equitable opportunities for all people living in Canada to income and social well-being. As the subtitle indicates, throughout the book, the dominant themes are:

- Inclusion — ensuring that all voices participate in decision making and that policies reflect multiple histories and circumstances
- Equity — providing additional support and opportunities to those who are susceptible to hardship and vulnerability
- Social justice — removing systemic barriers to ensure everyone has opportunities regardless of their social location

The co-authors and contributing authors hope that this book will provide a strong foundation for all those interested in playing their part in bringing about a fair and just society for everyone.

Steven Hick and Jackie Stokes

The Author Team

Lead Authors

Steven Hick, School of Social Work, Carleton University (Retired)

Steven is an award-winning professor of social work and the author of the companion text, *Social Work in Canada: An Introduction*. He has practised at home and abroad as a human rights worker, social services worker, and social policy analyst. He is the co-founder of War Child Canada. Recently retired from the School of Social Work at Carleton, Steven currently teaches insight meditation and mindfulness-based interventions.

Jackie Stokes, Faculty of Education and Social Work, Thompson Rivers University

Jackie holds an MSW from the University of Northern British Columbia and an EdD from Simon Fraser University. She has practised social work in northern British Columbia for more than twenty years, primarily in the areas of substance use and child protection. She is a co-author with Steven Hick of *Social Work in Canada: An Introduction* (Fourth Edition) and author of her own separate work, *Social Work Practice: Knowledge, Values, and Skills.*

Contributing Authors

Mary Holliday Bartram, Mental Health Commission of Canada

Mary has extensive experience in mental health and substance use policy development with federal and territorial governments, Indigenous organizations, and NGOs, including as the Director of Policy with the Mental Health Commission of Canada. She is an RSW and holds an MSc in Family Therapy from Purdue University. She completed her PhD in Public Policy at Carleton University, where she teaches mental health and substance use policy as an Adjunct Professor. Her research has focused on access to psychotherapy, recovery, and the mental health workforce.

Roy Hanes, Carleton University

Roy retired as an Associate Professor in the School of Social Work at Carleton University in 2020. Known for his disability activism throughout Canada. Roy is a member of the Social Policy Committee, Council of Canadians with Disabilities, and he was a founding member of both the Persons with Disabilities Caucus of the Canadian Association for Social Work Education and the Canadian Disability Studies Association. His research interests include disability histories, social construction of disability, disability and immigration policy, disability rights and violence toward people with disabilities.

Damien Lee, Ryerson University

Damien is a cis-gendered racially-white man who belongs with Anishinaabeg of the northern shore of Lake Superior. He was adopted as an infant into Fort William First Nation in accordance with Anishinaabe law, and raised as Anishinaabe by his family. He was mentored by Anishinaabe knowledge holders Doug Williams and Marlene Pierre, and holds the Canada Research Chair in Biskaabiiyang and Indigenous Political Resurgence based at Ryerson University. Damien is an Associate Fellow with the Yellowhead Institute and Assistant Professor in Ryerson's Department of Sociology.

David Macdonald, Canadian Centre for Policy Alternatives

David joined the Canadian Centre for Policy Alternatives as its Senior Ottawa Economist in 2011, although he has been a long-time contributor as a research associate. Since 2008, he has coordinated the Alternative Federal Budget, which takes a fresh look at the federal budget from a progressive perspective. He has also written on a variety of topics, from Canada's real estate bubble to Indigenous income inequality, and he is a regular media commentator on policy issues. David received his BA from the University of Windsor and his MA from the University of Guelph.

Beth Martin, Carleton University

Beth is an Assistant Professor in the School of Social Work at Carleton University. She holds a PhD in Policy Studies from Ryerson University and a MSW from McGill University. Her areas of interest include migration policies and social work with immigrants and refugees, international social work and global social justice, and mixed methods for social work research.

Shiri Pasternak, Ryerson University

Shiri is Assistant Professor in Criminology at Ryerson University in Toronto and the co-founder and Research Director of the Yellowhead Institute, based at Ryerson University. Shiri teaches courses in the Indigenous Justice stream and her research involves interdisciplinary approaches to Indigenous jurisdiction, resource economies, and Crown–First Nations' relations. She publishes in the fields of legal and historical geography, settler colonial studies, political economy, and critical legal studies.

Katherine Scott, Canadian Centre for Policy Alternatives

Katherine is the director for gender equality and public policy work at the Canadian Centre for Policy Alternatives. She has worked as a researcher, writer, and advocate over the past 20 years, writing on a range of issues from social policy to inequality to funding for nonprofits. Katherine has served as Vice President of Research at the Canadian Council on Social Development and, more recently, produced research and analysis for organizations such as Prosper Canada, Volunteer Canada, Capacity Canada, Pathways to Education Canada, and the Federation of Canadian Municipalities. Katherine holds degrees in political science from Queen's University and York University.

Richard Shillington, Social Policy Consultant and Researcher

Richard holds post-graduate degrees in statistics from the University of Waterloo. He has been engaged in the quantitative analysis of health, social and economic policy for the past 30 years. His research has covered several policy fields: health manpower planning, program evaluation, income security, poverty, tax policy, and human rights. He has worked for several provincial and federal departments, as well as commissions studying the economy, unemployment insurance, human rights, and tax policy. Richard appears regularly before committees of the House of Commons and the Senate. He also provides commentaries regularly for television, radio, and newspapers on issues of taxation, human rights, and social policy.

Tracy Smith-Carrier, King's University College, Western University

Tracy is an Associate Professor in the School of Social Work at King's University College at Western University and an Adjunct Research Professor in the Arthur Labatt Family School of Nursing at Western University. Her research touches upon a number of fields in the social policy arena, including access to social welfare benefits, social assistance receipt, food in/security, homelessness, caring, labour, and basic income. She has extensive experience in social planning and in non-profit organizations, government, academic, and hospital settings. Tracy is currently the Research Coordinator of the Ontario Basic Income Network.

What's New in this Edition?

Inclusion, Equity, and Social Justice

The social welfare policies and programs created after World War II in Canada were primarily designed to protect working people and to strengthen Canadian society. The postwar welfare state was not perfect, but it pointed in the right direction. However, under the pressures of neoliberal economic policies starting in the 1980s, many of these social welfare policies and programs were systematically eroded.

Then, in 2020, the COVID–19 pandemic hit.

The pandemic exposed multiple gaps and systemic weaknesses. It became clear that some populations were affected more harshly by the virus itself and by the various public health measures designed to deal with it. Racialized minorities, young people, and women lost jobs and incomes at a much higher rate due to their disproportionate labour market involvement in low-pay, low-benefit, and precarious jobs. Children, particularly vulnerable children, suffered as their visibility, socialization, and access to additional supports were removed when schools were closed. The atrocious conditions for some older Canadians in long-term care facilities were exposed, and many people with disabilities lost their access to programs that were not deemed essential services.

Transformative Social Policies

The post-pandemic recovery calls for transformative policies that address not only economic concerns but also social justice in all of its dimensions. This requires a commitment to individual and social well-being, to improving opportunities for vulnerable populations, and to environmental sustainability.

The themes of this new edition are as follows:

(1) A Focus on Individual and Social Well-being

A recurring theme is individual and social well-being. Social welfare is more than a reactive set of income and social service programs. It is a vast network of programs that ensures that everyone has access to a full range of opportunities to attain early childhood learning, educational achievement, economic and personal security, a clean environment, and social and health equity. Social well-being is holistic. It means having a voice in democratic processes, having housing and food security, having access to leisure and cultural activities, and having a lifestyle that contributes to physical and mental well-being.

Fundamentally, social welfare policies are mechanisms to provide resources and services to ensure that everyone has access to opportunities, regardless of their social location. In some cases, this means universal programs; in others, targeted programs may be needed in order to ensure equity.

(2) A Focus on Opportunities for Less Privileged Populations

Many of the people who gained from welfare state programs and the neoliberal policies of the late twentieth century belonged to populations that are considered dominant in Canadian society. This largely unearned privilege provided them more opportunities to increase their individual well-being. A central message in this new edition is to give voice to populations who do not have unearned privilege and to describe and highlight their voices and experiences. This includes people with precarious work, people in poverty, women and families, children whose early lives are lived through abuse and neglect, those whose lives are affected by mental health and substance use disorders, immigrants and temporary residents, racialized and older people, and people with disabilities.

(3) A Focus on Truth and Reconciliation

Perhaps the most important agenda for all social workers embarking on their career in the twenty-first century is Truth and Reconciliation with Indigenous people across Canada. This requires acknowledging multiple histories and voices, and ensuring that each nation is respected for their unique history, culture, and healing journeys. Social workers have an additional responsibility to acknowledge past colonial practices within the profession, including within residential schools and child welfare. As social workers work to redress the harms and find new paths, it is especially important to ensure that practices of today both address the intergenerational trauma of yesterday and support healing for future generations.

(4) A Focus on Empowerment and Universal Human Rights

Social welfare in Canada will always be evolving and changing as the political, environmental, social, and global context changes. The social safety net of the mid-twentieth century will not work for the twenty-first century. Rather than protections alone, the focus has to be on empowerment and access to opportunity, with decision making that is inclusive of multiple voices and histories. These perspectives are consistent with universal human rights which promote social and economic equality, promote the dignity and worth of people, and recognize the importance of human relationships.

(5) A Focus on Environmental Justice

Social workers have long insisted that individual and community well-being can only occur within a context of a healthy environment. Among large sections of the Canadian population and policymakers, the need to proactively protect our environment and ensure environmental justice and sustainability is taking on a new urgency. The coronavirus pandemic, which cruelly exposed the effects of deep-seated social inequalities for all to see, has underscored that urgency. The possibility of catastrophic climate change, future pandemics, and natural disasters — indeed, their likelihood — has underlined the need to redouble our efforts to advance inclusion, equity, and social justice if we are to secure a safe, equitable, and prosperous future for generations to come.

The COVID–19 Pandemic Changes Everything

The Six Principles of a Just Recovery

COVID–19 underscores the need to eliminate systemic inequity

The COVID–19 recovery must not entrench outdated systems that jeopardize health and well-being, worsen the climate crisis, or perpetuate the oppression of racialized and marginalized people.

As governments and institutions began to make plans to "recover" from the COVID–19 emergency, civil society groups across Canada came together to demand that our recovery plans build the resilient future we need for all people and ecosystems.

These six principles stretch us beyond immediate, emergency responses to consider how we might "build back better" so that our economy supports all people, instead of people working to support the economy. Instead of sacrificing people or the planet for short-term profits, these principles guide us to a society that prioritizes resilience and well-being.

For years, we have witnessed the results of chronic underinvestment and inaction in the face of the ongoing, pre-existing crises of colonialism, human rights abuses, social inequity, ecological degradation, and climate change. This moment is a reminder that the status quo can and must be disrupted. We are standing on the threshold between the old world and the next and we must choose to build the future we want.

Put people's health and well-being first. No exceptions

Health is a human right and is interdependent with the health and well-being of ecological systems. Recognizing this, ensure that all policies and programs address the social, economic, and environmental determinants of health and are responsive to the climate emergency, which is, in itself, a health crisis. Learn from the pandemic: develop policies and make investments that keep communities and workplaces, particularly those on the front lines, safe.

Increase the resilience of our health and social systems — expand and invest in health services, social services, and frontline services everywhere. Ensure services are public, culturally safe, linguistically appropriate, and accessible to all without discrimination based on status, location, or circumstance — including to Indigenous peoples living on- and off-reserve, people in remote communities, migrants, and undocumented people.

Strengthen the social safety net and provide relief directly to people

Focus relief efforts on people — particularly those who are structurally oppressed by existing systems. Prioritize redistributive policies and social services that meet the immediate and long-term needs of all people and eliminate social, economic, and wealth inequalities. Rebuild a single-tier immigration system with permanent resident status for all.

Prioritize the needs of workers and communities

Support must be distributed in a manner consistent with Indigenous sovereignty, a climate-resilient economy, and worker rights, including safe and fair labour standards and a right to unionize. Improved conditions for essential service workers must be maintained beyond this crisis.

Bailout packages must not encourage unqualified handouts, regulatory rollbacks, or regressive subsidies that enrich shareholders or CEOs, particularly those who take advantage of tax havens. These programs must support a just transition away from fossil fuels that creates decent work and leaves no one behind.

Build resilience to prevent future crises

We cannot recover from the current crisis by entrenching systems that will cause the next crisis. We must invest in sustainable infrastructure and build resiliency within communities, ensuring that people can access public essential services, meet their basic needs, and engage in cultural and artistic expression.

Recovery plans should move us toward a diversified economy and systems that reduce social and economic inequity; respect the limits of the planet; protect land, water, and air; uphold human rights and rights of Indigenous peoples; support people who are not in the workforce to thrive; create decent jobs; and foster social, emotional, and cultural health and resiliency from infants to elders.

Build solidarity and equity across communities, generations, and borders

In a globalized world, what happens to one of us matters to all of us. A Just Recovery must be guided by the principles of equity, solidarity, and sustainability across domestic and international relations. Recovery plans must honour and expand human rights, including the rights of Indigenous peoples, and advance gender equity while opposing authoritarian regimes and oppressive systems.

Emergency expenditures and measures must not be used as an excuse to subvert or suspend human rights, to centralize or reduce checks and balances on power, or to revert to austerity, protectionism, xenophobia, racism, ableism, or pre-pandemic systems that sustain structural inequalities. Canada has the historical obligation and the resources to ensure that, both domestically and internationally, funding and resources are provided to enable individuals and communities to thrive, engage in democratic institutions, and assert their rights and live with dignity.

Uphold Indigenous rights and work in partnership with Indigenous peoples

A Just Recovery must uphold Indigenous Rights and include the full and effective participation of Indigenous Peoples, in line with the standard of free, prior and informed consent.

Indigenous Peoples require sustained resources and investments that stimulate Indigenous economies, create healthy communities, and protect the lands and waters. Indigenous communities need investment in infrastructure, along with social and health services.

In recognizing Indigenous sovereignty, communities must have control over their housing, water, food, and energy. A Just Recovery must include robust renewable energy policy that ensures Indigenous ownership and equitable partnership of renewable energy projects in Indigenous homelands.

Indigenous laws, values, customs, and traditions must be recognized and upheld, including the need for the implementation of the United Nations Declaration on the Rights of Indigenous Peoples in all jurisdictions.

Just Recovery Coalition. www.justrecoveryforall.ca / www.relancejuste.ca
Artist: Corrina Keeling. Reproduced by permission.

Social Welfare and Social Well-Being in Canada

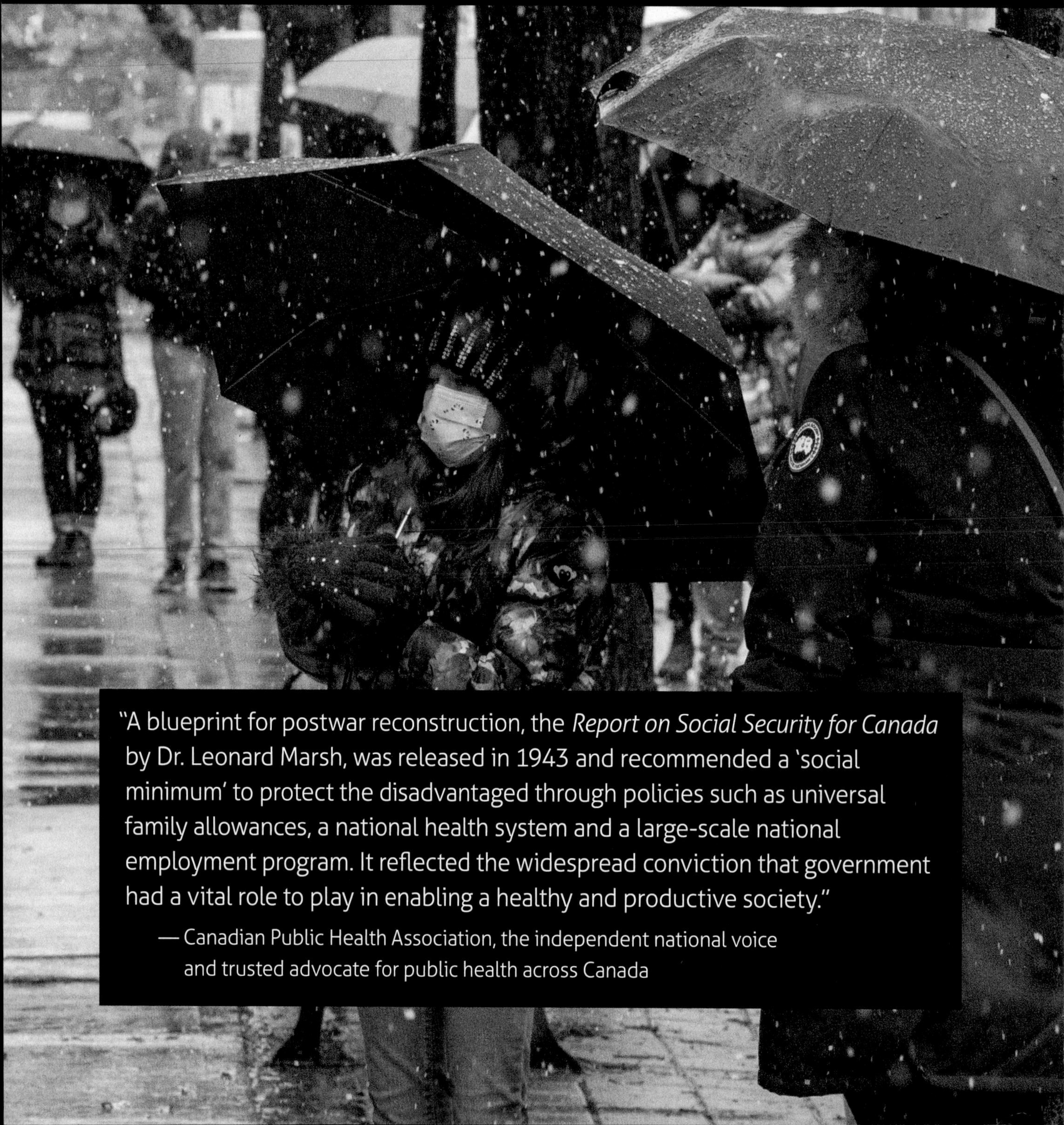

"A blueprint for postwar reconstruction, the *Report on Social Security for Canada* by Dr. Leonard Marsh, was released in 1943 and recommended a 'social minimum' to protect the disadvantaged through policies such as universal family allowances, a national health system and a large-scale national employment program. It reflected the widespread conviction that government had a vital role to play in enabling a healthy and productive society."

— Canadian Public Health Association, the independent national voice and trusted advocate for public health across Canada

Inclusion, Equity, and Social Justice

COVID–19 has focused public attention on the need to eliminate socioeconomic inequities.

Social work is primarily focused on advancing the well-being of individuals, families, and communities. Recognizing that many personal problems are rooted in broader social and economic inequities, social workers apply a macrosystems approach. This involves formulating and implementing public policies that promote inclusion, equity, and social justice for all.

But not everyone agrees about the extent to which the state should intervene in people's lives. The debate revolves around which problems are private troubles and which are public issues. For example, it was not always the case, but nowadays intimate partner violence is understood to be a public issue, not simply a private trouble. To address the problem as a public issue, social policies have been developed in areas such as criminal justice, child protection, and the funding of transition houses.

Clearly, social policy of this kind can make a big difference to citizens' well-being. But are there limits? What role should the state play in advancing the welfare of individuals, families, and communities? How proactive should governments be?

Key Concepts

- Welfare state
- Income security
- Social services
- Canadian Index of Wellbeing (CIW)
- Social investment model
- Residual approach
- Institutional approach
- Public welfare
- Private welfare
- Welfare pluralism
- Universal programs
- Targeted programs
- Universality
- Fiscal transfers
- Canada Health Transfer (CHT)
- Canada Social Transfer (CST)

Inclusion, Equity, and Social Justice

This chapter describes the main components of social welfare in Canada today and looks at some of the underlying debates and issues associated with enhancing people's overall well-being.

After completing this chapter, you should be able to:

- Define "welfare state" and its relationship to social well-being;
- Describe the different types of programs available to people in Canada;
- Explain the distinction between public and private welfare, and the mix of models that contribute to welfare pluralism;
- Make the case for and against universality;
- Describe the residual, institutional, and social investment approaches to social welfare, and explain the ideological foundations of each;
- Describe three contemporary fiscal transfers; and
- Outline the main frameworks, or lenses, through which social workers can assess social welfare policies.

1.1 Social Welfare and Social Well-Being

The central idea underpinning social welfare is that of citizenship rights. This idea was captured in sociologist T. H. Marshall's 1950 essay, *Citizenship and Social Class*, which has influenced social welfare thinking for decades.

In his essay, Marshall outlined the history of citizenship rights, arguing that the struggles over rights resulted in the acquisition of "civil rights" in the eighteenth century, "political rights" in the nineteenth century, and "social rights" in the twentieth century. This evolution culminated in the concept of "citizenship rights." According to Marshall (1950), citizenship rights are best fulfilled if the state plays an active and comprehensive role in ensuring and promoting the overall well-being of its citizens.

The term welfare state appears first to have been used in 1941 in a book by William Temple, the Archbishop of York, in England. It came to be used to describe societies where the power of the state is used to modify the play of market forces in order to help allay personal contingencies, such as sickness, poverty, and unemployment (Moscovitch, 2015).

To the outside world, Canada is still generally regarded as a welfare state. Many of the core institutions of the welfare state are still in place. However, the sheer scale of cutbacks to income security programs and social services under both Liberal and Conservative governments at all levels has led many to question whether Canada can still be designated as a welfare state.

The Unravelling of the Welfare State

Canadian social welfare programs up to World War II were essentially residual in nature. Social welfare, mostly in the form of modest income supports, was offered begrudgingly and only to those most in need. Social welfare was seen as a limited and temporary response to human need, implemented by governments only when all else failed.

The post–World War II period saw a tremendous expansion of social welfare, not only in Canada but also in the rest of the industrialized world. This expansion involved a shift from viewing social welfare as a form of stigmatizing charity to recognizing it as an important mechanism for ensuring social and personal well-being — not a privilege but a right of citizenship. Indeed, programs such as the Family Allowance, Employment Insurance, workers' compensation, and universal health care came to be regarded as the bulwarks of an institutional approach to social welfare in a democratic and caring society.

By the end of the twentieth century, however, the social welfare system in Canada was unravelling. Under both Liberal and Conservative governments, many programs were curtailed and many pre–World War II ideas of limited, temporary (residual) support came back into fashion. Programs that had been institutionalized and become a hallmark of the post–World War II period were under threat, seriously diminished, or terminated altogether. Bare minimums, means tests, and service cutbacks became the norm.

"Canada must modernize its social security system to meet the heavy demands of a changing economy, society and political system. Conceived in the 1930s and 1940s and built largely in the 1950s, 1960s and 1970s, our social programs require rethinking, reconstruction and (because some parts were never built) construction: We need a new "architecture" of social policy for the 21st century.

"Building sound social infrastructure is essential for a robust economy as well as social justice: Strong social programs contribute to a nation's economic strength, productivity and international competitiveness."

Battle, K. (2006). Modernizing the Welfare State. *Policy Options.*

Ken Battle is one of Canada's leading social policy thinkers. He co-founded the Caledon Institute of Social Policy in 1992 with Alan Broadbent and served as its president until 2017.

The Well-Being of Canadians

Today, the social welfare system in Canada consists of a vast network of income security and social service programs at the federal, provincial/territorial, and municipal levels. Laws, social policies, rules and regulations, strategies, and other directives set the framework.

Although it is not always easy to distinguish between an income security program and a social service, the distinction is a useful one.

- Income Security. Income security programs provide monetary or other material benefits to supplement income or maintain minimum income levels (e.g., Employment Insurance, social assistance, Old Age Security).
- Social Services. Social service programs help people by providing non-monetary aid (e.g., parent–child programs, child care centres, youth drop-in centres, women's shelters, mental health and substance use programs, child protection and family support services, and criminal justice services).

In general, under the Canadian constitution, income security programs are a federal responsibility, whereas social service provision falls under the jurisdiction of the provinces and territories and/or the municipalities.

The social welfare system is not perfect, and certainly it has detractors. However, for many decades it has provided a degree of income and social security for people in Canada. Appropriately, it is frequently referred to as "Canada's social safety net."

Government cutbacks and cost-saving measures in recent years have eroded the ability of the welfare state to advance the well-being of Canadians.

How Should We Measure Well-Being?

Broadly speaking, social welfare refers to a system of social policies and programs designed to ensure the well-being of people in Canada. However, as a concept, social welfare can be thought of in different ways. Traditionally, it has been viewed from a somewhat narrow economic perspective, using indicators such as gross domestic product (GDP), gross revenue, and unemployment rates (Carrasco-Campos et al., 2017). However, when Canadians go to bed at night, they might not be as worried about GDP as about things such as locating affordable housing, finding child care, dealing with rising tuition fees, and having time for leisure and balance in their lives.

Such additional, non-economic indicators of well-being have been emphasized in more recent research. For example, the Canadian Index of Wellbeing (CIW) provides a comprehensive assessment of how Canadians are really doing in those areas of their lives that matter most to them. Researchers at the University of Waterloo, where the CIW is housed, draw from almost 200 reliable data sources, primarily from Statistics Canada, that highlight 64 indicators in eight interconnected domains related to quality of life.

Figure 1.1

The Eight Dimensions in the Canadian Index of Wellbeing

Canadian Index of Wellbeing (2016).

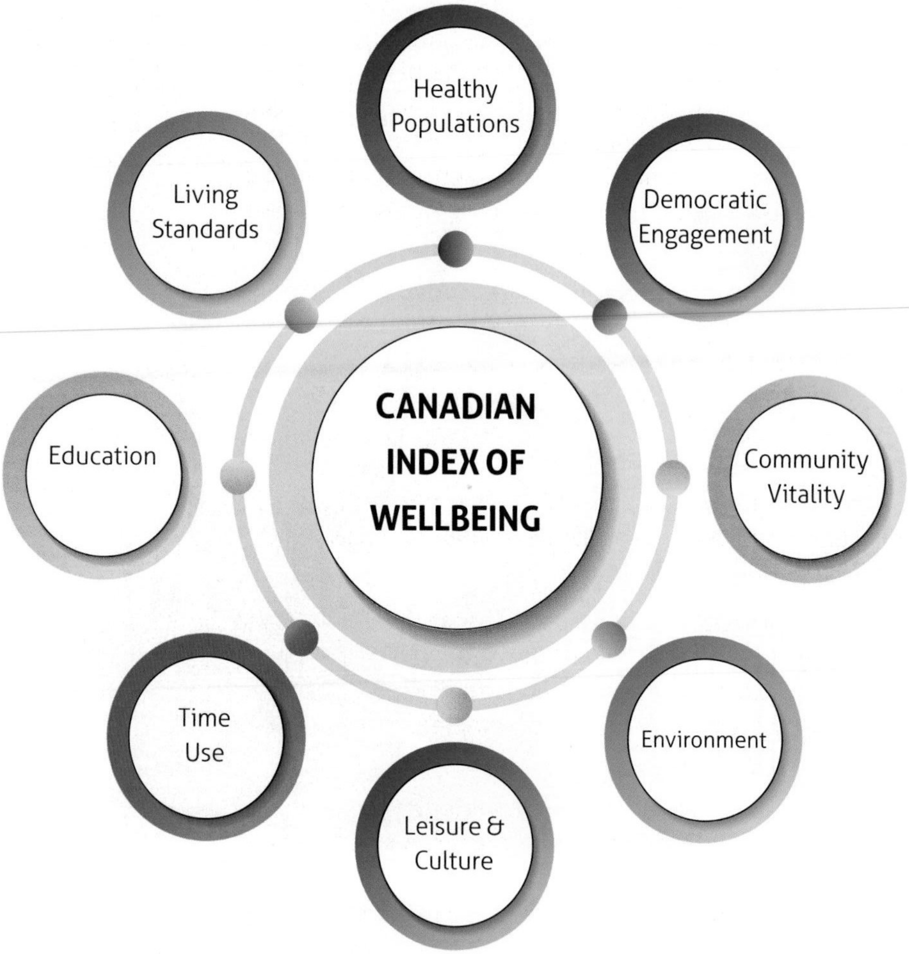

The Canadian Index of Wellbeing (2016).

The Purpose of Social Welfare: Inclusion, Equity, and Social Justice

A focus on economic security, narrowly conceived, underpinned the expansion of post–World War II welfare programs and services. The view was that "the state had a paramount role in ensuring, for its citizens, as a matter of right, a certain minimum standard of living, economic welfare and security" (Vaalavuo, 2013, p. 517). The traditional concerns were with protecting breadwinners (males, generally) from unforeseen events, such as unemployment and sickness. This model can be characterized as a passive protection system, and usually it was associated with cash benefits to the needy and the poor.

Today, among social workers and policymakers, while economic security remains a key focus, additional emphasis is being placed on people's overall well-being and new social risks (e.g., child and elder care responsibilities, and lack of education for today's jobs). This new emphasis identifies special risk groups, such as the young, the low-skilled, and women. At the same time, "family instability and difficult reconciliation of work and family life have become major policy issues as they increase the incidence of poverty for families with children, especially for lone-parents" (Vaalavuo, 2013, p. 514).

The twenty-first century approach to social welfare is more proactive, with a focus on eliminating poverty, promoting social inclusion, eliminating oppression, ending all forms of violence, increasing investments in health and education, and protecting and restoring environmental resources. It is a social investment model of social welfare. This renewed focus on overall well-being is consistent with the broader notions of citizenship engagement, equality of opportunity, and fairness. This idea is expressed in the first principle of the Canadian Association for Social Work Education (CASWE) standards, which states:

> Guided by the principles of fundamental human rights and responsibilities and respect for human diversity, social work seeks to facilitate *well-being* [italics added] and participation of people, promote social and economic justice, address structural sources of inequities, and eliminate conditions that infringe human and civil rights. Grounded in reflective practice and engaged in persistent inquiry into theoretical and research bases in the field, social work employs professional approaches and interventions to enhance individual, family, group, community and population well-being. (Canadian Association for Social Work Education, 2014, p. 2)

This social investment model of social welfare aims to integrate the economic and social objectives underlying social welfare. "Rather than reduce income inequality, new social-risk policies aspire to an active society with economic participation and social inclusion through the redistribution of opportunities and investment in human capital" (Vaalavuo, 2013, p. 516).

Income security remains important, to be sure, and existing income security programs need to be protected and expanded. However, for many social welfare activists today, income security is no longer the only focus. Rather, capacity needs to be built through healthy childhood education, strong families and communities, citizen participation, and lifelong learning.

Transformative Social Policies

The COVID–19 pandemic's disproportionate affect on women, racialized minorities, Indigenous peoples, and the working poor underlined the need for policymakers to think of well-being in a comprehensive way.

Transformative social policies and programs are needed that are designed to end poverty, promote social inclusion, eliminate oppression, and invest in health, education, and the environment.

Social Welfare in Perspective

Social Welfare and the Quality of Life

The Canadian Index of Wellbeing

The Canadian Index of Wellbeing (CIW) helps determine trends in our overall quality of life, providing a powerful tool for social and political action.

Canada lacks a single, national instrument for tracking and reporting on our overall quality of life. Gross domestic product (GDP) was never designed or intended to be a measure of social progress or quality of life. It is simply a calculation of the value of all goods and services produced in a country in one year. Even the "father of GDP," Nobel laureate Simon Kuznets, acknowledged that "the welfare of a nation can scarcely be inferred from a measurement of national income as defined by the GDP."

Over time, GDP has emerged as a surrogate for well-being. As the central measure of what we call productivity, GDP guides economic and social policies, but it does not necessarily result in us becoming better off as a country. That is a big problem.

As a measurement of national income, GDP does not distinguish between activities that are good and those that are bad for our society. Think of GDP as a giant calculator with an addition but no subtraction button. Activities such as smoking, drinking to excess, building jails and hiring police to deal with crime, destroying green lands to build sprawling subdivisions, over-harvesting our natural resources to the point of jeopardizing their sustainability, and using fossil fuels that pollute our air and heat up our planet propel GDP upward.

At the same time, GDP fails to include a host of beneficial activities such as the value of unpaid housework, child care, volunteer work, and leisure time, because they take place outside of the formal marketplace. Nor does it subtract detrimental activities. The notion of sustainability — ensuring that precious resources are preserved for future generations — does not enter the equation.

A Made-in-Canada Solution

In order for well-being to improve in this country, we first need to track and report on well-being indicators so that we can better understand the root causes of our current quality of life.

This is where the Canadian Index of Wellbeing (CIW) is useful. The CIW fills a large gap in the dialogue about public policy making in Canada. It helps build a dialogue that goes beyond what GDP, as a purely economic measure, can tell us about our well-being.

The CIW distinguishes between activities that are beneficial and harmful to our overall well-being. It treats beneficial activities as assets and harmful ones as deficits, thereby providing a more accurate accounting of the well-being of Canadians. In the CIW framework, "less is often (though not always) better." Less crime, less pollution, less tobacco, and living longer and better all drive the CIW upwards.

The CIW national index:

- Distinguishes between good things like health and clean air, and bad things like sickness and pollution
- Promotes volunteer work and unpaid caregiving as social goods, and overwork and stress as social deficits
- Puts a value on educational achievement, early childhood learning, economic and personal security, a clean environment, and social and health equity, and
- Values a balance between investment in health promotion and spending on illness treatment

The graph shows the gap between the focus on the economy alone (GDP) and the Canadian Index of Wellbeing. Over 20 years, GDP increased almost 40%, while CIW increased less than 10%.

Evidence-Based Policymaking

The CIW provides a revealing analysis of how we are really doing in the areas of our lives that matter most to us. Because of the way the multidimensional set of indicators connect and interact, improving well-being in one area has a positive impact on others.

The reality is that our well-being consistently lags behind economic measures such as GDP. This confirms what we already knew intuitively — namely, that the good life cannot be measured in terms of economic performance indicators alone.

The CIW amounts to an evidence-based approach to social policy formation. It enables policymakers to focus on what Canadians consider important in their daily lives and develop policies and programs to address any deficiencies.

This material has been adapted for this chapter by permission of the Canadian Index of Wellbeing from an overview on the CIW's website entitled "Wellbeing in Canada." www.uwaterloo.ca/canadian-index-wellbeing

The Eight Domains Included in the CIW

- DEMOCRATIC ENGAGEMENT. Involvement in the democratic process through political institutions and activities.
- EDUCATION. The availability of systematic instruction, schooling, or training for all.
- HEALTHY POPULATIONS. Lifestyle and behaviours that influence health and health care.
- COMMUNITY VITALITY. The extent to which there are strong relationships within the community.
- LIVING STANDARDS. A measure of income, poverty, economic volatility, housing, and food security.
- ENVIRONMENT. Trends in the availability and use of natural resources.
- LEISURE AND CULTURE. How leisure and cultural activities contribute to overall well-being.
- TIME USE. How personal time is used and how it affects physical and mental well-being.

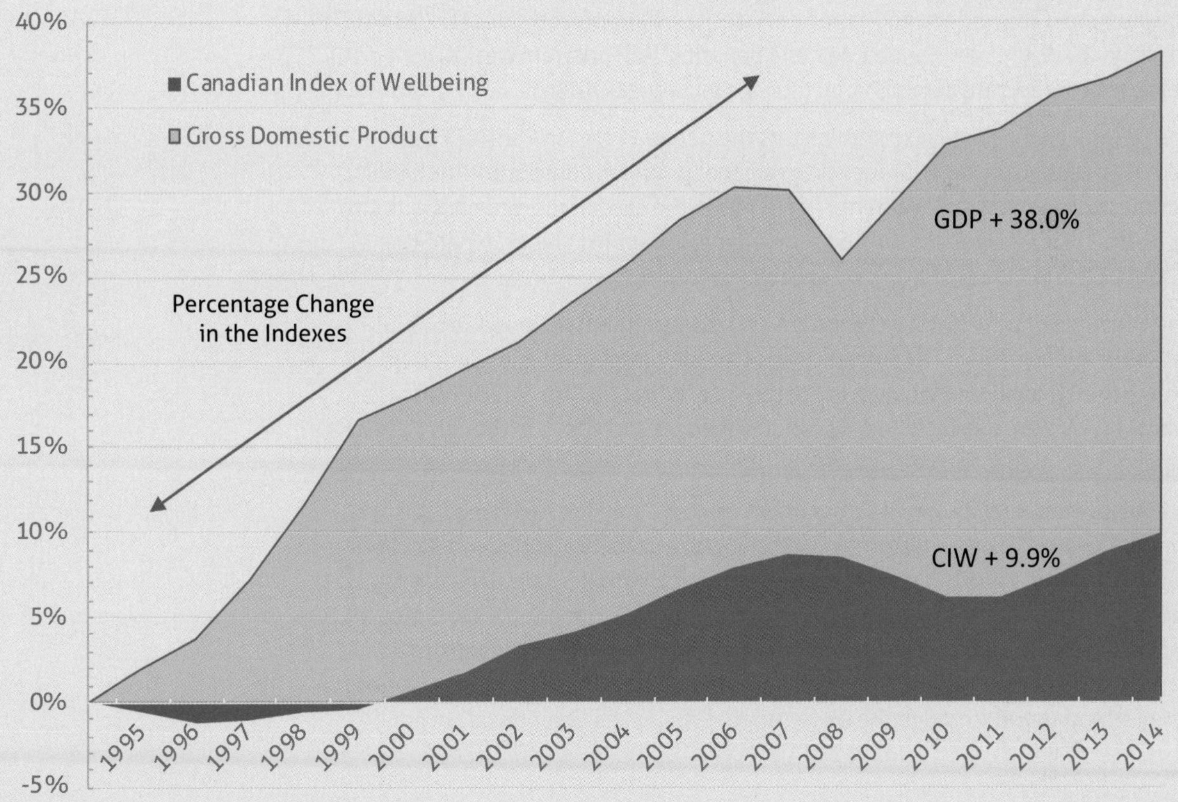

The Canadian Index of Wellbeing (2016).

1.2 Social Welfare in Canada Today: A Snapshot

The expansion of the social welfare system in the post–World War II period, in Canada and other industrialized countries, helped even out inequalities and provided much-needed services to vulnerable members of society. This postwar period was the heyday of the welfare state.

Many of the current social welfare programs and strategies have their roots in these welfare-state programs. However, as a result of neoliberal cutbacks beginning roughly in the early 1980s, many populations continue to experience significant inequities.

Below is a summary of key issues and social welfare programs associated with various populations of interest to social workers. The chapter noted in parentheses looks at each topic in detail.

The Welfare and Well-Being of People in Poverty (Chapter 4)

Poverty continues to be a central social welfare issue. In 2018, for the first time, Canada set the official poverty line using the Market Basket Measure (MBM). The MBM is a regional amount that is based on the cost of a basket of food, clothing, shelter, transportation, and other items for individuals and families that represent a modest, basic standard of living.

To help offset chronic poverty, the federal government administers income supplement programs such as the Canada Child Benefit, the Guaranteed Income Supplement (GIS), and the goods and services tax/harmonized sales tax (GST/HST) credit. In 2019, the new Canada Workers Benefit (CWB) program was launched. All of these programs are administered through income tax returns.

The federal government also administers the Canada Pension Plan (CPP), an earnings-related social insurance program that provides contributors and their families with partial replacement of earnings in the case of retirement, disability, or death. The CPP operates throughout Canada, except in Québec, where the Québec Pension Plan (QPP) provides similar benefits.

The Old Age Security (OAS) program is a secondary stream of Canada's public retirement income security system and is Canada's largest pension program. Unlike the CPP/QPP, individuals do not pay into it directly. The OAS pension is a monthly payment available to older adults aged 65 and above, although there is a clawback for higher-income Canadians.

Social assistance (also known as "income support," "income assistance," or simply "welfare") is administered provincially/territorially and has widely varying eligibility criteria and benefits across jurisdictions. Workers' compensation, the first income security program to be introduced in Canada (in 1918) is also a provincial/territorial responsibility and is funded by employers based on their payroll, industry sector, and history of injuries. Federal government employees are covered separately, through the Government Employees Compensation Act.

The Welfare and Well-Being of Women and Families (Chapter 5)

At the time of the 2016 census, there were 9.8 million families in Canada, 15 times as many as there were at the time of the first census in 1871 (Statistics Canada, 2017). Over this 150-year period, massive social changes have occurred. The purpose of family policy is to keep up with these changes, anticipate them, and, to an extent, influence them.

Massive changes have occurred in family dynamics in the last 50 years: the Divorce Act of 1968, technological advances related to reproduction, the growing participation of women in both paid work and higher education, and the legalization of same-sex marriage, to name just a few. Today, most parents work to earn income for their families. Yet a serious shortfall exists in areas such as the number of spaces and the affordability of child care, and adequate parental leave.

Progress in these areas has been made in certain jurisdictions (e.g., Québec), but the deficit across the country is a major concern. In addition, little effort has been made to address the economic insecurity of many families: even with two parents working, it is hard for many families to make ends meet. For lone parents, the difficulties are often overwhelming.

Family well-being is inextricably tied to women's well-being. Persistent gender income gaps and the disproportionate responsibilities of women to provide caregiving are resulting in income security initiatives such as the Canada Caregiver Credit and gender-based budgeting legislation.

The Social Welfare and Well-Being of Children (Chapter 6)

The welfare of Canadian children is by and large associated with the welfare of Canadian families — children in need typically live in families in need. According to UNICEF Canada, while many Canadian children are doing well, 9% fall below the official poverty line (UNICEF Canada, 2017). Dismally, on overall child and youth well-being, Canada ranks 25th out of 41 well-resourced (rich) countries.

> Canada performs well in indicators related to education, but the widest and most worrying gaps are in child health, violence experienced by children and their own sense of well-being. The inequalities between families in income and food security are alarming. (UNICEF Canada, 2017)

Child maltreatment continues to be major social issue. Although often considered a private family problem, child maltreatment has a strong association with socio-economic impoverishment and racialization. Indigenous children and Black Canadian children are disproportionately represented among children who are investigated for maltreatment.

Each province and territory has legislation on child maltreatment and a department or ministry in charge of child welfare. These agencies are responsible for investigations, family support, and alternative care programs such as kinship care, foster care, permanency programs, and adoption. In many provinces, distinct agencies are responsible for Indigenous children's care.

Social Welfare and Mental Well-Being in Canada (Chapter 7)

Universal, public health care is provided to all Canadian citizens, permanent residents, and certain temporary residents. To be eligible to receive full federal contributions for health care, each provincial/territorial health care plan must meet requirements specified in the Canada Health Act (1985). However, people may pay privately or have private insurance for medications, dental care, eye care, physiotherapy, etc. Private clinics also exist, offering specialized services.

Mental health is not fully integrated into the public health care system. The level of coordination between mental health services and physical health is unique to each province or territory. There is universal coverage for physician-provided mental health care, along with a fragmented system of allied services. Hospital mental health care is provided in specialty psychiatric residences and in general hospitals with mental health beds. The provinces and territories also provide community mental health and substance use services, including help for families and caregivers, community crisis services, and supportive housing. Psychiatrists generally are paid through medical plans, whereas psychologists typically work privately, although like social workers may be salaried in publicly funded organizations (Allin & Rudoler, 2016).

The Mental Health Commission of Canada, an organization operating at arm's length from the federal government, released the first Mental Health Strategy for Canada in 2012. Subsequently, a further Framework for Action (2017–2022) has been released. The federal budget in 2018–2019 set aside $5 billion to improve access to mental health services over the following 10-year period.

Inuit Children at Risk

Inuit in Canada are burdened with the highest hospitalization rates of children with severe lower respiratory tract infections in the world, suffer from an infant mortality rate three times that of the rest of Canada, and live with the highest levels of residential overcrowding in the country.

In 2019, the federal government reached a housing agreement with Nunavut that will create "thousands" of homes and help address the housing crisis across the territory.

Knotsch, C. & Kinnon, D. (2011). If not now ... when? Addressing the ongoing Inuit housing crisis in Canada. Ottawa: National Aboriginal Health Organization.

Photo: Inuit Celebration of Life on Parliament Hill in 2015 highlighting the need for action to address the high suicide rate among Inuit youth.

The Welfare and Well-Being of Indigenous Peoples (Chapter 8)

Canada was founded and built on the seizure of First Nations land and resources and the imposition of colonial rule. The federal government retains responsibility for First Nations programs on-reserve and matters pertaining to Indian status. As a direct result of these colonial policies, Indigenous peoples face enormous social and economic disadvantages: high rates of poverty, very poor housing, large numbers of children in government care, high rates of incarceration, high rates of violence, and contaminated water advisories on First Nations reserves, to name a few.

The legacy of colonialism can be understood through five enduring themes: (1) the struggle for treaty rights; (2) the discredited Indian Act; (3) the effects of the reserve system; (4) the experience of residential schools; and (5) the growing call by Indigenous peoples for self-government. The resistance and persistence of Indigenous groups provided the catalysts for recent federal government inquiries and policy initiatives in relation to Indigenous peoples.

While positive steps are welcome, many Indigenous leaders question the government's commitment to Indigenous rights, saying that the declarations made in public are not matched by policies and actions that would guarantee them in practice. They also maintain that the process of change has proceeded without adequate consultation or engagement, and especially that the core issues of treaties and land rights are not being addressed "nation to nation." Underlying all of this is the desire of Indigenous peoples for self-government — Indigenous control of Indigenous affairs.

"Before the arrival of Europeans in North America, Indigenous peoples were organized as sovereign nations with their own cultures, economies, governments, and laws. They owned the lands and resources within their territories, and so had property rights. They were subject only to the responsibilities placed on them by the Creator to care for the land and share it with the plants and animals who also lived there.

"The inherent right of self-government that Indigenous peoples have today under Canadian law comes from the sovereignty that they exercised prior to contact with Europeans."

Adapted from National Centre for First Nations Governance (2007). *A Brief History of Our Right to Self-Governance Pre-Contact to Present.*

The Welfare and Well-Being of Immigrants and Temporary Residents (Chapter 9)

Traditionally, Canada's immigration policy has been aimed at attracting immigrants with the expectation that, over a reasonable length of time, they would become full citizens. The difficulties encountered by newcomers to Canada are well-known: learning a new language, having credentials and experience recognized, securing employment, finding housing, dealing with racial discrimination, and integrating children and families in their new home and community.

Social welfare programs have been devoted to assisting immigrants in these respects, often with very good success. However, recent shifts in immigration policy toward favouring temporary immigrants (geared to filling immediate employment needs) has added generalized insecurity to the hardships already faced by newcomers. Despite the enormous implications of such a shift, it has happened largely without the influence of public debate.

For temporary residents in Canada, many language programs, income, and social supports are no longer available. The lives of temporary residents are unstable, and the road to citizenship is often unclear or non-existent. Temporary residents are a growing, vulnerable group in Canadian society. For a country largely built on immigration, policy work needs to ensure that all newcomers are welcome and provided the necessary assistance to prosper.

The Welfare and Well-Being of Older People (Chapter 10)

Dalhousie University economist Lars Osberg (2001) has referred to the reduction in poverty among older adults over the past three decades as "the major success story of Canadian social policy in the twentieth century" (p. 170). The critical parts of that policy were a universal component (Old Age Security), a negative income tax (Guaranteed Income Supplement), and an earnings component (CPP/QPP).

Nevertheless, today, poverty among older adults is increasing again as more people move into the over-65 demographic. In particular, there is a growing risk of poverty for pensionless cohorts of older adults, especially women. According to the European Centre for Social Welfare Policy and Research, "systematic reforms have changed the nature of pension provision from defined benefit type provisions to defined contribution type provisions" (Zaidi, 2006). Defined contribution plans can result in a greater risk of poverty in retirement for people who have earned less while working.

The number of Canadians over the age of 65 will increase to almost one-quarter of the total population by 2030 (Canada, 2014), which will create a significant demand on public pensions and Old Age Security. Going forward, developing income supports and services that preserve the gains older Canadians have made will be a major priority of Canadian policymakers.

The Welfare and Well-Being of Persons with Disabilities (Chapter 11)

About one in five people have one or more disabilities (Statistics Canada, 2018). Persons with disabilities are more likely to experience adverse life outcomes. The barriers to full inclusion include inaccessible physical environments, the unavailability of assistive devices, gaps in services and service delivery, and discrimination. Those who do not qualify for public or private income security programs rely on social assistance programs.

At the same time, there are some positive signs across the country, with many provinces and territories introducing proactive legislation to ensure social inclusion for people with disabilities. In addition, in October 2015, the federal government affirmed its commitment to legislation that would guarantee the rights of people with disabilities. The resulting Accessible Canada Act was passed in 2019 with unanimous support from both the House of Commons and the Senate. Nevertheless, critics continue to have concerns with the new federal legislation as it lacks firm timelines, allows exemptions, and only applies to organizations, services, and businesses under federal control.

Canadian social welfare policy seeks to advance and support the full participation and well-being of persons with disabilities. Despite programs such as CPP/QPP disability benefits, veterans' disability pensions, disability tax credits, and the registered disability savings plan, people with disabilities continue to experience income insecurity and multiple barriers to basic human rights and freedoms included in the Canadian constitution and UN Conventions.

Other Types of Social Welfare Programs and Services

Other social welfare programs and services may be talked about less, but are no less important. For example:

- Elementary and secondary education, which is delivered by the provinces and territories and is compulsory up to age 16, is essentially free to Canadians.
- Post-secondary schooling is not free, but it is subsidized by the federal and provincial/territorial governments, and student loans and bursaries are available.
- Regional programs provide support for economic development in the North and parts of the country where business investment may need a boost.
- The federal, provincial/territorial, and municipal governments provide grants and favourable tax programs for core industries and businesses.
- Cultural industries — music, television, film, and publishing — are also supported by the multiple levels of governments through grants and favourable tax programs.
- The Canadian Broadcasting Corporation (CBC/Radio-Canada), established in 1936, is a Crown corporation that serves as the national public broadcaster for both radio and television.

All of these areas contribute significantly to the overall well-being of Canadians today. It is hard to imagine Canada without the CBC or quality public schools. However, as circumstances and governments change, the programs and services will continue to evolve — hopefully to represent more social justice, equity, and inclusion.

Social Welfare in Perspective

Are We Obliged to Help Those in Need?

Three Different Approaches to Social Welfare

The "social investment" approach to social welfare is increasingly seen as being more effective. It is focused on eliminating systemic inequality and achieving inclusivity, equity, and social justice for all.

The idea of providing support to people in need is no longer controversial in Canada. Pretty well everyone concurs. Major disputes do arise, however, in determining which groups are in need and to what extent they need government assistance.

Successive Canadian governments have moved back and forth essentially between two approaches to social welfare: the residual approach and the institutional approach. Examples of residual programs today are income security (or social assistance) benefits and workfare programs.

More recently, social workers and policy analysts have begun to adopt a "social investment" focus, underlining not only income security but the importance of broader aspects of well-being.

Three different approaches to social welfare provision can be identified: (1) the residual approach, (2) the institutional approach, and (3) the social investment approach.

1. The Residual Approach

In the **residual approach**, social welfare is a limited, temporary response to human need, implemented only when all else fails. It is based on the premise that there are two "natural" ways through which an individual's needs are met: through the family and through the market economy. The state should only step in when these sources of support fail and individuals are unable to help themselves.

Residual social welfare is highly targeted to those deemed most in need. It tends to provide benefits at a low level to discourage use and make welfare undesirable. Canadian public social welfare programs, from early history up to at least the Great Depression of the 1930s, can be characterized as essentially residual in nature.

2. The Institutional Approach

In the **institutional approach**, social welfare is a necessary public response that helps people attain a reasonable standard of health and well-being.

People cannot always meet all of their needs through family and work, so it is legitimate to help people through a set of publicly funded programs and institutions. For those who hold this approach, these institutions are the bulwarks of a democratic and caring society.

The institutional approach attempts to even out, rather than promote, economic stratification or status differences. The period after World War II saw the beginning of the rise of the institutional view not just in Canada but throughout the industrialized world. There was an expansion of the welfare state during this period.

The most revered institutional approach to social welfare was the universal Family Allowance that began in 1945 (eliminated in 1992). Today, programs such as Old Age Security and medicare are considered institutional programs.

3. The Social Investment Approach

Social rights underpinned the development of post–World War II welfare states in Western industrialized countries, including Canada. The period was typified by a shift from a residual approach (seeing social welfare as a form of stigmatizing charity) to an institutional approach (seeing social welfare as an entitlement).

In the past few decades, social policy analysts have begun to view social welfare in a "social investment" framework — a "third way." The goal of social investment is inclusion, equity, and social justice. Therefore, it requires change at multiple levels — change that goes beyond meeting only basic economic needs.

This newer approach to policymaking recognizes the multidimensional nature of social issues. It focuses on all aspects of social well-being and investing in ways that alleviate the structural disadvantages faced by high-risk and vulnerable populations. These populations include Indigenous peoples, lone parents, homeless people, unemployed youth, women, children, people with disabilities, immigrants, and racialized minorities.

Social Investment Programs Today

Social investment programs are generally well established across Europe. The common themes of such programs include:

- Reduction in the duration of social assistance and unemployment benefits and levels
- Provision of various forms of assistance to obtain employment: personalized support, core skills training, and individual guidance
- Expansion of child care and parental leave options
- Pressure to either accept suitable job offers or participate in education
- Provision of wage subsidies to employers in the private sector
- Financial support for education and training (Walmsley, 2018, p. 46)

Canadian examples of social investment programs include grants and loans for post-secondary education — with larger grants to Indigenous students, lone parents, and people with disabilities — and increases in early childhood and kindergarten spaces.

1.3 The Provision of Social Welfare

When Canada was formed in 1867, social welfare was largely the private responsibility of the individual, family, and church. The British North America Act (1867) (also called "Constitution Act, 1867") said little about income security or social services. Subsequent political wrangling and non-stop constitutional amendments over decades eventually established the basis for today's social welfare system.

The outcome, broadly, was that income security (other than social assistance) would be an area of federal authority and the provinces and territories would be responsible for the delivery of social programs and services. However, the federal government was, and continues to be, responsible for services and programs under the Indian Act. At times, jurisdictions overlap, but essentially the federal government retains responsibility for the provision of social welfare to First Nations people on-reserve through the Indian Act.

The Spirit Level

In their book, *The Spirit Level: Why More Equal Societies Almost Always Do Better,* Richard Wilkinson and Kate Pickett (2009) describe in detail how greater equality contributes to the health and well-being of societies. Their research links inequality to a wide range of social issues, including mental and physical health, drug use, obesity, educational performance, teenage births, violence, imprisonment, and social mobility.

Their conclusion is that the greater the inequalities, the greater the stress on people all along the income spectrum, and the worse the outcomes are for a society overall — not just for those at the bottom of the income ladder.

Public and Private Welfare

There are different ways of categorizing social welfare provision. Perhaps the most important distinction is between "public" and "private" welfare.

- Public Welfare. Public welfare refers to monetary benefits and services that are provided directly by any of the three levels of government: the federal government, a provincial or territorial government, or a regional or municipal government. Typically, public welfare is associated with income security. Governments also enforce legislation and policy associated with labour standards, minimum wage legislation, and policies associated with social services such as housing, mental health, and child care.
- Private Welfare. Private welfare is delivered through non-profit organizations or for-profit organizations and individuals. Most often, such agencies provide social services. Some receive government funding and are accountable through funding mechanisms, others are governed by legislation (e.g., Societies Act or Canada Not-for-profit Corporations Act), and still others rely on private payments from individuals.

Any social welfare system consists of family and friends, and a mix of public, private non-profit, and for-profit provision. The size, roles, and relative importance of each of the four core institutions (the state, the market, family/household, and civil society) varies in relation to "a wide range of contextual factors (history, tradition, values, and norms) and contemporary challenges (population pressure, economic crisis, social chaos, and environmental degradation)" (Estes & Zhou, 2015, p. 348). For example, food banks, usually operated by non-profit or charitable organizations and heavily staffed by volunteers, first emerged in 1981. Initially, they were supported by churches and donations. Food banks now exist in virtually every community. Today, private and business donations are a major component of funding, with non-profit agencies such as the United Way also providing support. In some cases, they also receive direct government funding.

Welfare Pluralism

Canada's "social safety net" had been seriously eroded by the turn of the twenty-first century. Increasingly, neoliberal governments at all levels — federal, provincial/territorial, and municipal — had sought out market-based solutions to public social problems (Dunlop, 2006). The thinking was that the state should play only a limited role in addressing social problems (Dunlop, 2006). This approach resulted in what has sometimes been referred to as a "mixed-economy welfare" (Rice & Prince, 2000), or welfare pluralism.

In addition to public and private welfare, a myriad of organizations and groups — the voluntary sector, the commercial sector, public–private partnerships, and social entrepreneurs — all contribute to a complex network of social welfare services. Charity and philanthropy also continue to have an important role in the broader system aimed at well-being in Canada.

- **Voluntary Sector.** In 2017, an estimated 13 million people (almost 50% of the Canadian population) contributed more than 2 billion hours of volunteer time (Conference Board of Canada, 2018). Common volunteer activities include fundraising; sitting on committees or boards; collecting, serving, or delivering food; or providing health care and other social supports.
- **Commercial Sector.** The commercial and business sector offers a wide range of social services, including private child care, substance-use treatment, personal counselling, and services for people with disabilities. These services may be offered on a sliding scale that depends on the person's financial needs, or the government may subsidize the costs of services (Chappell, 2014). An example is services for people with autism.
- **Public–Private Partnerships.** Public–private partnerships are one aspect of a broader privatization strategy, which includes contracting out public services to the private sector and downsizing the government workforce (Dunlop, 2006). The move toward this type of arrangement is consistent with government cutbacks in social welfare funding. There are multiple examples of public–private partnerships in areas such as social housing development, employment training programs, and long-term care.
- **Social Entrepreneurship.** Social entrepreneurship focuses on creating social capital (the strengthening of social cohesion) by using entrepreneurial principles and market-based (business-plan) strategies to organize, create, and manage a venture to find sustainable solutions to social problems. Social entrepreneurs may be associated with voluntary or non-profit sectors, or the for-profit sector (Canadian Social Enterprise Fund, 2017). Examples include microfinance institutions and educational initiatives.
- **Charity and Philanthropy.** A study conducted by Imagine Canada (2018) estimates that Canadians donated approximately $14.3 billion to registered charities in 2014. This money supports work in a variety of areas, although the "big four" causes are religion, health, social services, and international aid. Other examples include donating to a food bank and donating toys to provide Christmas presents to children.

Welfare Pluralism

Concepts of "welfare pluralism" and "the mixed economy of welfare" have come to increasing prominence in social policy discussions.

The terms are used broadly to describe the multiple arrangements and public-private partnerships for the provision of social welfare.

Eligibility for Social Welfare Programs

Eligibility for social welfare programs differs across the country. Programs are typically distinguished as either "universal" or "targeted":

- Universal Programs. Universal programs are available to everyone in a specific category, regardless of income or financial situation. Although basic eligibility criteria (e.g., age or residency) may have to be met, no further test of need is required. The Family Allowance (Baby Bonus) that began in 1945 (and ended in 1992) was Canada's first universal program. Health insurance is still considered a universal program.
- Targeted Programs. Targeted programs provide benefits based on a means test (sometimes called an "income test" or a "needs test"). For example, to receive social assistance, one must prove that income and assets fall below a certain level. In provinces with workfare, such as Ontario, applicants must also comply with an employment or training placement.

Eligibility for Social Assistance

The specifics vary, but the basic structure of social assistance is much the same across the country.

In every jurisdiction, eligibility for social assistance is determined on the basis of a needs test, which takes into account a household's financial assets and income.

Many of Canada's income security programs are targeted programs with complex selection criteria based on income, work history, or the willingness to find a job. Some programs require the recipient to have contributed to them to be eligible to access them. For example, the CPP/QPP is an earnings-related social insurance program that requires employees to have contributed. Likewise, many health benefits plans require joint employer and employee contributions. By contrast, the Old Age Security program is universal in that it is accessible to all people 65 years of age or older who meet legal and residency requirements — although it is then clawed back for higher income earners.

Social assistance (income assistance) programs are targeted programs. To be eligible, individuals must pass a means test, proving that their income and assets fall below a certain level. Those wishing to access these programs must complete an application and possibly have an interview with a caseworker to prove that they are in need and do not have the means to meet their needs.

Affordable child care is often on political agendas and is an example of a program that has universal aims but some targeted aspects. The federal government has not yet been able to implement a national child care program. Paul Martin's Liberal government had provincial agreements to do so, but when his party lost to the Conservatives in 2005, the program was eliminated.

Québec introduced the first universal province-wide daycare program in 1997 at a $5.00 per day rate. The rate was increased to $7.00 per day in 2004, and a sliding scale tied to family income was introduced in 2014. Depending on how the service is provided (through the non-profit Centres de la petite enfance (CPEs), family-based caregivers, or for-profit private daycares), the benefit is either received as a direct subsidy or through a provincial refundable tax credit.

Canada continues to rank near the bottom of Organisation for Economic Co-operation and Development (OECD) countries when it comes to child care spending (OECD, 2006). Québec's child care program remains the envy of many parents across the country who have young families.

The Cases For and Against Universality

Supporters of universality maintain that universal programs promote a sense of citizenship, solidarity, and nationhood. They claim that targeted programs for those in need tend to be punitive and stigmatizing, are more susceptible to cutbacks, and lack necessary mass public support. If services are only for the poor, the argument goes, then the services are likely to be poor services. Many believe that universal income security programs can fulfill various economic functions, such as economic stabilization, investment in human resources, and development of the labour force.

The foremost objection to universal programs is the cost. Giving a benefit to everyone, regardless of income, means that even the wealthy get a benefit. On the other hand, universal programs tend to be less expensive to administer, as government workers are not required to scrutinize each individual situation.

Increasingly, social policy experts are seeing that some targeted programs are necessary to tackle poverty and inequality. Targeted programs are often viewed as more efficient and less costly in the long run, as the government provides benefits only to those individuals most in need. However, identifying eligible recipients using means or needs tests can be administratively complex and costly, which can remove money from the system that could be directed toward benefits. Increasingly, higher administrative costs are partially avoided by using the tax system as a method of determining eligibility and as a means of dispensing benefits.

What the COVID–19 pandemic has revealed ...

Political Ideology and COVID–19

National Leadership and Citizen Well-Being

To what extent should governments intervene with policies that protect and advance the well-being of citizens? This question took on great urgency during COVID–19.

Social welfare policies and programs are premised on political values and beliefs (ideologies). These beliefs describe how the world works, or at least how it is thought to work. Understanding these belief systems can throw light on the intention and direction of social welfare programs.

Generally, political ideologies are classified as "left-wing" or "right-wing," but it may be more helpful to put three main points on this continuum — socialism (left wing), conservatism (right-wing), and liberalism (centrism) in between. Other ideologies on, or slightly off, the continuum might include neoliberalism, neoconservatism, feminism, anti-racism, environmentalism, and populism (Armitage, 2003).

Collectivism vs. Individualism

A broad distinction can be made between "collectivist" and "individualist" ways of thinking.

- **Collectivism.** Associated with institutional social welfare approaches, it emphasizes citizen rights and the welfare of society as a whole.
- **Individualism.** Individualism, by contrast, is associated with residual approaches to welfare, which emphasize individual self-reliance and a reliance on the market to sort things out.

But keep in mind that political ideologies are very complex and there is much diversity within each viewpoint. Oversimplification, or simply associating an ideology with a political party, is hazardous.

The Ideological Spectrum

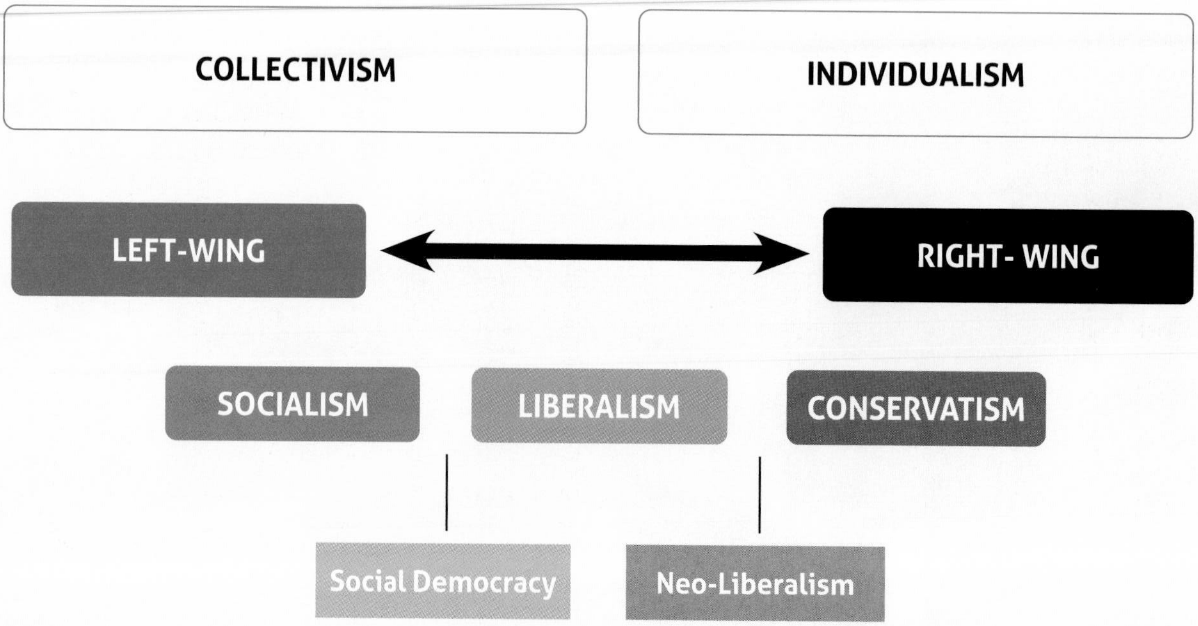

Responding to COVID–19

By March 2020, most governments around the world understood that COVID–19 could lead to immeasurable social and economic hardship. Some responses were collectivist in nature — that is, they prioritized government coordination and leadership at the national level, while others adopted a response that placed responsibility more on the local levels of government and on the mechanisms of supply and demand in the marketplace.

By and large, Canada took a collectivist approach to the COVID–19 pandemic. Although Canadian provinces and territories have jurisdiction over the delivery of health care, public health comes under federal oversight through the Canada Health Act. This is especially the case when it comes to infectious disease, as was the experience with the SARS virus in 2003 (McCarten, 2020).

All levels of Canadian government, and indeed all political parties, generally worked together to try to "flatten the curve" of the pandemic and support citizens economically and socially.

Contrasting Ideologies

A number of European countries also adopted a collectivist response to COVID–19. For example, although Denmark was one of the first countries to begin a national lockdown in response to the virus, the Danish government did not act unilaterally. Employer associations and trade unions were consulted to ensure wider societal support. This cooperation made it easier for Denmark to exit the lockdown in the end.

Canada's and Denmark's collectivist approach stands in stark contrast to that of the United States and even the United Kingdom. In both countries, the national response to COVID–19 followed a different playbook (Ornston, 2020).

In the US, the response was characterized by weak or non-existent national coordination under the administration of President Donald Trump that left individual state governors in critical moments of the crisis competing with each other to buy much-needed resources on the open market, including ventilators and protective gear (McCarten, 2020).

Citizens' Opinions on Their Government's Response to COVID–19

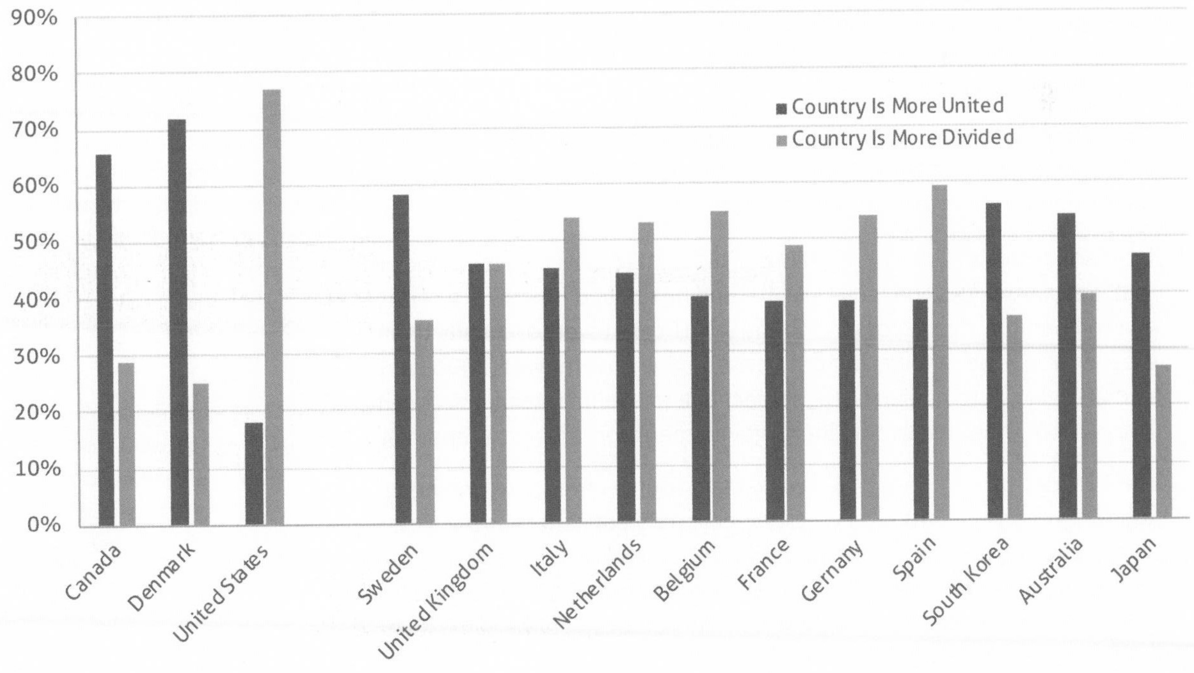

Pew Research Centre (2020).

1.4 Who Pays for Social Welfare?

The Constitution Act, 1867 assigns authority to the provinces to make and implement social policy in most areas. This provision reflects the nineteenth-century view that social policy is largely a local and private matter. However, in practice the federal government influences social policy in many ways in areas of immigration, labour force participation policies, pay equity legislation, parental leave, and compassionate care policy, to name just a few.

Federal Transfers and the Well-Being of Canadians

The federal government exercises its spending powers through fiscal transfers to provinces and territories, federal–provincial shared-cost programs, and direct spending in areas of provincial/territorial jurisdiction. These fiscal transfers address economic disparities among the provinces and territories.

There are three main fiscal transfer programs: (1) provincial equalization payments, (2) Territorial Formula Financing, and (3) health and social transfers.

- **1. Provincial Equalization Payments.** Equalization payments are unconditional per-capita grants to the provinces. Their purpose is to assist provinces in providing comparable services across the country. The payment is determined using a province's ability to generate revenues (its "fiscal capacity") compared with the average revenue of all 10 provinces. In 2018–2019, Newfoundland and Labrador, Saskatchewan, Alberta, and British Columbia were considered "have provinces" and did not receive equalization payments.
- **2. Territorial Formula Financing.** The territories do not have provincial powers or the same capacity for revenue generation, so the Territorial Formula Financing transfer provides federal funding to the three territorial governments to fund activities in a manner comparable to what is offered by the provinces.
- **3. Health and Social Transfers.** In addition to the two "equalization" payments, there are two per-capita transfers. These substantial amounts are provided to the provinces/territories to help finance health and social programs, child welfare, and post-secondary education.

  The Canada Health Transfer (CHT) is a cash transfer as well as tax adjustment that helps provinces and territories to fund health and health care services at a comparable level across the country. CHT cash levels originally had been growing at 6% per annum, but the Conservative government (2006–2015) tied CHT growth to nominal GDP, subject to a minimum rate of 3% starting in 2017–2018. The subsequent Liberal government continued this approach.

  The Canada Social Transfer (CST) is the main source of federal funding to support programs in the areas of post-secondary education, social assistance, social services, and programs for children. As such, the CST has far-reaching implications for the all-round well-being of people in Canada. Despite its role in ensuring people's well-being, the CST has not received the same level of funding or attention as the CHT.

Health Care Funding Shortfalls

The provinces and territories administer and deliver most of Canada's health care services with the assistance of federal cash and tax transfers. The exact amount of funding has long been a source of dispute between the federal and provincial/territorial governments.

The dispute became more heated during the COVID–19 pandemic with enormous pressures on the provinces/territories to deliver routine health care, urgently needed pandemic care, as well as all-out vaccination campaigns.

In a virtual meeting in March 2021, the premiers demanded that the federal government increase its share of health care spending to 35%. This would mean an additional $28 billion for health care funding in the next federal budget.

Under the original Medical Care Act of 1966, the federal government covered 50% of eligible hospital and physician expenses. That percentage has since dropped to 22%.

Federal Spending on Social Welfare

By any measure, the federal government spends a considerable amount on ensuring people's welfare and well-being. In 2019–2020, the federal budget included $76.9 billion in transfer payments to other levels of government (Canada, 2019a). Most of the transfer payments were assigned to the CHT ($40.4 billion), fiscal equalization ($19.8 billion), and the CST ($14.6 billion).

The 2019–2020 federal budget also included $100.4 billion of direct cash transfers for individuals. Most of this amount was for elderly benefits ($56.2 billion), Employment Insurance benefits ($19.9 billion), and the Canada Child Benefit ($24.3 billion) (Canada, 2019a). Demographic trends indicate that the older adult population in Canada will continue to grow in the years ahead, which will no doubt increase government income security expenditures.

It is important to note that these figures do not include mandatory private social benefits provided by employers, voluntary private social benefits provided by charities, or tax breaks for social purposes. Moreover, the federal government's social security statistics do not include data on the Registered Retirement Savings Plan (RRSP), which primarily benefits those who are more well off.

Table 1.1

Federal Transfers to People and to Other Levels of Government (Billions)

	2017/18	2018/19	2019/20	2020/21	2021/22	2022/23	2023/24
Major Transfers to People							
Elderly benefits	50.6	53.3	56.2	59.7	63.3	66.9	70.6
EI benefits	19.7	18.8	19.9	21.5	23.	24.0	24.8
Canada Child Benefit	23.4	23.9	24.3	24.6	25.1	25.6	26.1
Total	**93.8**	**96.0**	**100.4**	**105.8**	**111.4**	**116.4**	**121.5**
Major Transfers to Other Levels of Government							
Canada Health Transfer	37.1	38.6	40.4	41.8	43.3	44.9	46.6
Canada Social Transfer	13.7	13.2	14.6	15.0	15.5	15.9	16.4
Equalization	18.3	19.0	19.8	20.5	21.3	22.1	22.9
Territorial Formula Financing	3.70	3.8	3.9	4.2	4.3	4.4	4.6
Gas Tax Fund	2.10	4.3	2.2	2.2	2.3	2.3	2.4
Home care & mental health	0.30	0.9	1.1	1.3	1.5	1.2	1.2
Other fiscal arrangements	–4.70	–4.7	–5.1	–5.3	–5.5	–5.8	-6.0
Total	**70.5**	**76.0**	**76.9**	**79.6**	**82.6**	**85.0**	**88.1**

Canada (2019a). *Budget of Canada: Investing in the middle class 2019.*

Social Welfare in Perspective

Medicare — A Canadian Success Story

The Importance of Nationwide Standards

The Canada Health Transfer, unlike the Canada Social Transfer, is backed by legislation and stringent requirements. This has resulted in high-quality health care nationwide.

Medicare is Canada's publicly funded health care system. Under this system, all Canadian residents have reasonable access to medically necessary hospital and physician services without paying out-of-pocket.

Provincial/Territorial Responsibilities and Federal Oversight

The provincial and territorial governments are responsible for the management, organization, and delivery of health care services to residents. For its part, the federal government is responsible for the following:

- Setting and administering national standards for health care through the Canada Health Act
- Providing funding support for provincial and territorial health care services
- Supporting the delivery of health care services to specific groups
- Providing other health-related functions

Provincial/territorial health departments consult with their jurisdiction's physicians' colleges or health care services to decide which services are medically necessary for health care insurance purposes.

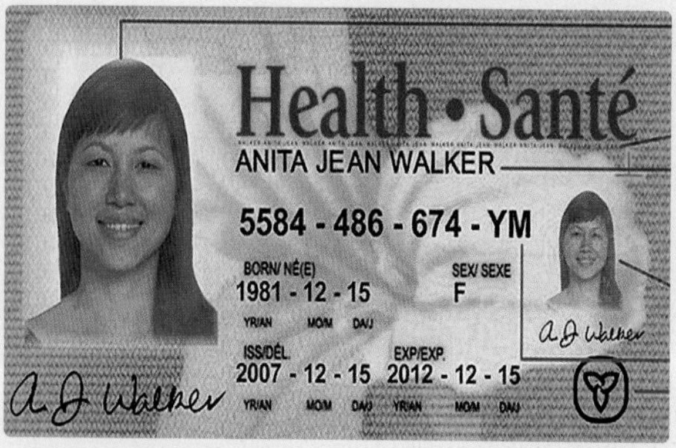

Canada Health Act

The Canada Health Act sets out the primary goal of health care policy, which is "to protect, promote and restore the physical and mental well-being of residents of Canada and to facilitate reasonable access to health services without financial or other barriers."

The Canada Health Act establishes criteria and conditions related to insured services and extended health care that the provinces and territories must fulfill to receive the full federal cash contribution under the Canada Health Transfer (CHT). The aim is to ensure that all eligible residents have reasonable access to health care services without charges at the point of service.

The Five Program Criteria of the Canada Health Act

Provinces and territories must meet the following five program criteria to qualify to receive full federal funding under the Canada Health Act:

- **Public Administration.** The administration of provincial health insurance must be carried out by a public authority on a non-profit basis, and records and accounts must be subject to audits.
- **Comprehensiveness.** All necessary health services, including hospitals, physicians, and surgical dentists, must be insured.
- **Universality.** All insured residents are entitled to the same level of health care.
- **Portability.** A resident moving to another province or territory is entitled to coverage from the home province during a minimum waiting period.
- **Accessibility.** All insured persons have reasonable access to health care facilities, and all physicians and hospitals must have reasonable compensation for services they provide.

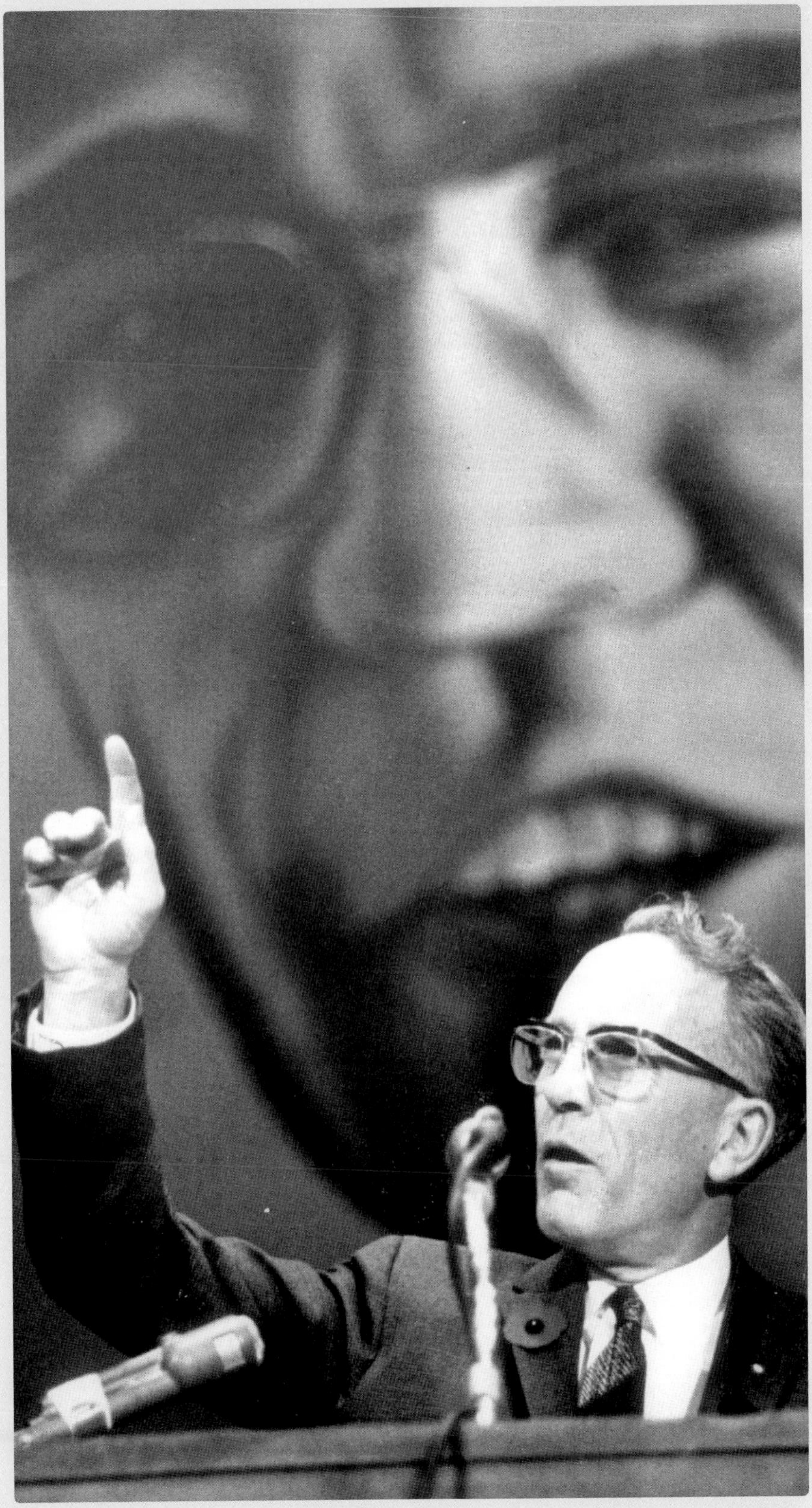

T. C. (Tommy) Douglas

Tommy Douglas (1904–1986), recognized as the father of Canadian Medicare, had a vision for the role of government and the welfare state.

Douglas believed that governments and their leaders had a primary responsibility to improve the lives of ordinary people through initiatives and well-funded programs that made a real difference to their everyday lives.

In a 2004 television series by the Canadian Broadcasting Corporation to determine who was the greatest Canadian of all time, the winner, after 1.2 million votes were cast, was Tommy Douglas.

Photo: The New Democratic leader speaking at Maple Leaf Gardens during party convention on November 4, 1965. Photo by Boris Spremo / *The Globe and Mail*. Reprinted by permission of The Canadian Press.

The Social Determinants of Health

The Correlates of Personal Well-Being in Canada

A health care system — even the best health care system in the world — will be only one of the ingredients that determine whether your life will be long or short, healthy or sick, full of fulfillment, or empty with despair.

— The Honourable Roy Romanow, 2004

The primary factors that shape the health of Canadians are not medical treatments or lifestyle choices but rather the living conditions they experience. These conditions have come to be known as the social determinants of health.

The importance to health of living conditions was established in the mid-1800s and has been enshrined in Canadian government policy documents since the mid-1970s. Recent reports from Canada's Chief Public Health Officer, the Canadian Senate, and the Public Health Agency of Canada continue to document the importance of the social determinants of health.

While it is based on decades of research and hundreds of studies in Canada and elsewhere, the idea of the "social determinants of health" tells a story that is unfamiliar to most Canadians. Canadians are largely unaware that our health and well-being are shaped by how income and wealth are distributed, whether or not we are employed, and if so, the working conditions we experience.

Furthermore, our well-being is also determined by the health and social services we receive and our ability to obtain quality education, food, and housing, among other factors. And contrary to the assumption that Canadians have personal control over these factors, in most cases these living conditions are—for better or worse—imposed upon us by the quality of the communities, housing situations, work settings, health and social service agencies, and educational institutions with which we interact.

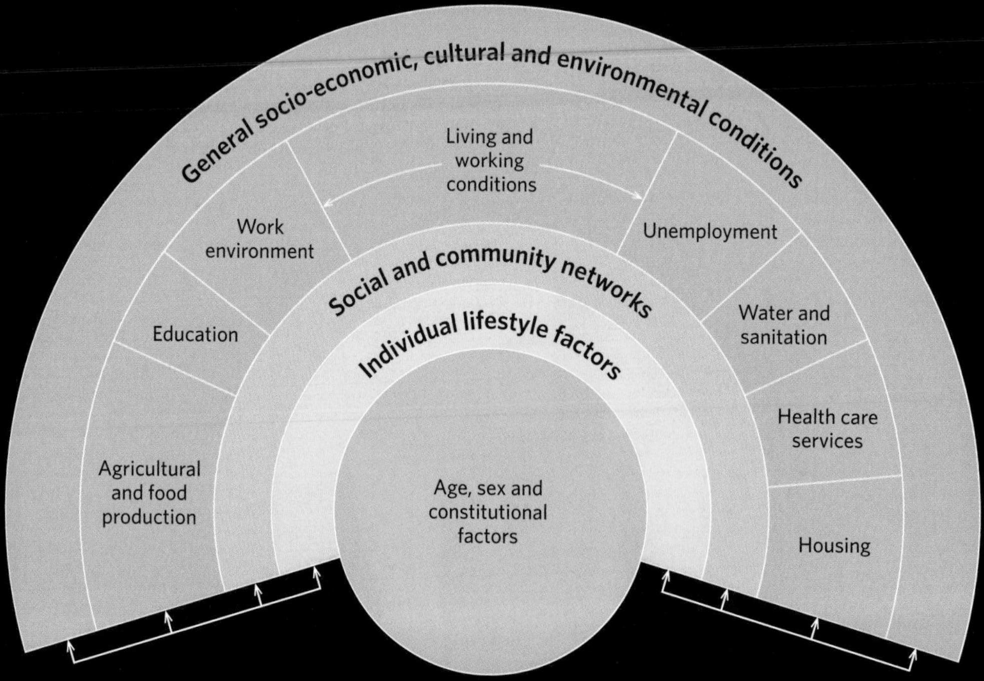

Dahlgren, G. and Whitehead, M. (1991). *Policies and Strategies to Promote Social Equity in Health.* Stockholm: Institute for Future Studies

There is much evidence that the social determinants of health help to explain the wide health disparities and inequalities that exist among Canadians. How long Canadians can expect to live and whether they will experience cardiovascular disease or adult-onset diabetes are very much determined by living conditions.

Social determinants also affect the health of Canadian children in terms of surviving beyond the first year of life, experiencing childhood afflictions such as asthma and injuries, and falling behind in school.

Research is also finding that the quality of these health-shaping living conditions is strongly influenced by public policy decisions that governments make. Governments at the municipal, provincial/territorial, and federal levels create policies, laws, and regulations that influence how much income Canadians receive, the quality and availability of affordable housing, the kinds of health and social services and recreational opportunities they can access, and even what happens when Canadians lose their jobs during economic downturns.

These experiences also provide the best explanations for how Canada compares to other nations. Canadians do not do as well compared to other nations that have public policies in place that strengthen the social determinants of health. The World Health Organization sees health-damaging experiences as resulting from a toxic combination of poor social policies and programs, unfair economic arrangements, and bad politics.

Moreover, there has been insufficient effort by Canadian governments and policymakers to improve the social determinants of health. Inequality and poverty rates are growing and public spending in support of families, persons with disabilities, older Canadians, and employment training is among the lowest of the developed nations. Improving the health of Canadians is possible but requires Canadians to think about health and its determinants in a more sophisticated manner than has been the case to date.

Mikkonen, J., & Raphael, D. (2010). *Social Determinants of Health: Canadian Facts*. Toronto, ON: York University School of Health Policy and Management.

A Model of the Social Determinants of Health

Among the variety of models of the social determinants of health that exist, one developed at a conference held at York University in Toronto in 2002 has proven especially useful for understanding why some Canadians are healthier than others. The 14 social determinants of health in this model are as follows:

Aboriginal status	Gender
Disability	Housing
Early life	Income and income distribution
Education	Race
Employment and working conditions	Social exclusion
Food insecurity	Social safety net
Health services	Unemployment and job security

Mikkonen, J., & Raphael, D. (2010). *Social Determinants of Health: Canadian Facts*. York University School of Health Policy and Management.

1.5 Assessing Social Welfare Policies

Social welfare policies provide the framework through which income security and social service programs are delivered (Chappell, 2014). In their daily practice, social workers are affected by social welfare policies directly. Policies determine who gets what, for what reasons, and under what conditions (Caputo, 2014). For that reason, social workers must be able to analyze how social welfare policies frame the social problems they are meant to address and whether policy development, implementation, and evaluation truly reflect the principles of inclusion, equity, and social justice.

Canada has no preferred or "best" model for assessing social welfare policies (Chappell, 2014). Figure 1.2 is based on Chappell's (2014) framework and represents one way of reviewing or assessing social welfare policies. These six steps form a framework for reviewing policies throughout this book:

1. How is the social problem understood?
2. How was the policy formulated?
3. What are the purpose and goals of the policy?
4. How does the policy reflect the values of inclusion, equity, and social justice?
5. How is the policy implemented?
6. What is the impact of the policy?

• 1. Identify How the Social Problem Is Understood

A social welfare policy is aimed at addressing a social problem in order to enhance people's well-being. For a social policy to be developed, the social problem must affect a large segment of the population and "create a measurable degree of economic or social hardship, psychological or physical injury, or other negative consequence that people want changed" (Chappell, 2014, p. 32). As an instrument of change, a social welfare policy can reduce or eliminate a particular issue that impacts at-risk and vulnerable populations. Conversely, of course, it can also exacerbate the vulnerability of certain populations.

When reviewing how the social problem is understood in a policy, key questions to ask include:

- How is the social problem understood within the economic, political, socio-cultural, environmental, and global context?
- What data and information are available to understand the extent and impact of the social problem?
- What are the social well-being indicators of the social problem?
- What evidence-based research and lived experiences can help understand how the problem developed and what can be done about it?

Figure 1.2

The Stages of the Policymaking Process

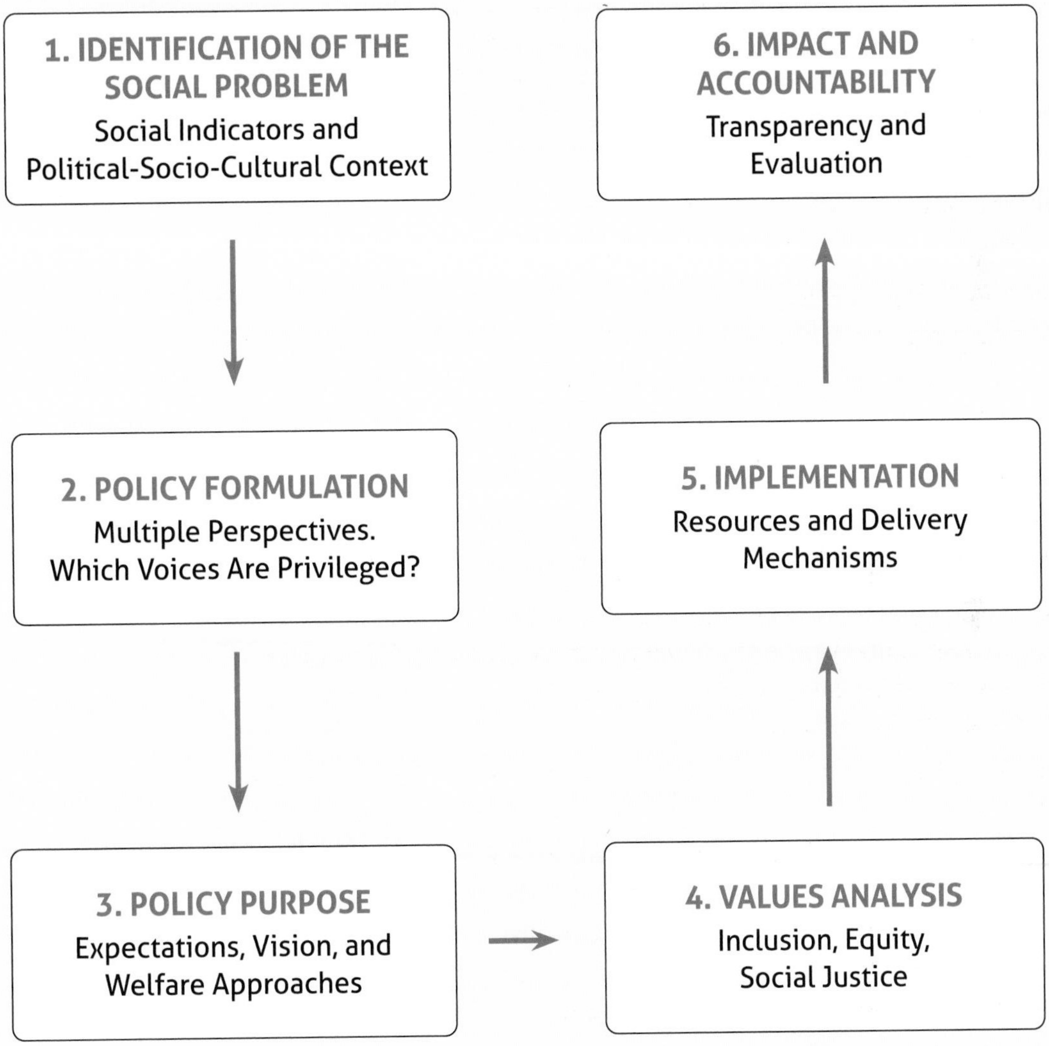

Adapted from Chappell, R. (2014). *Social Welfare in Canadian Society* (5th ed.). Nelson.

• 2. Consider How the Policy Was Formulated

Good policies require participation and collaboration among all relevant stakeholders. Citizen participation throughout all the phases of policymaking ensures that multiple voices and different conceptual understandings are clarified in order to develop better policies that have a positive impact on the people being served by them (OECD, 2017). Having participatory and meaningful citizen engagement processes encourages the public to speak out about decisions that affect them, helps renew relationships between policymakers and citizens, and increases trust in government policymaking. Active participation is considered a cornerstone in modern democracy and crucial to active citizenship (Shookner, 2002).

Traditionally, citizen engagement in policy development took place through public hearings, citizen polls, and other consultative methods. Today, meaningful participation in policy development extends beyond citizen engagement to include citizen empowerment. To ensure meaningful participation, structural and cultural barriers need to be recognized and addressed throughout the policy formulation process.

When reviewing how a policy was formulated, key questions to ask include:

- Whose lived experiences were included in its development?
- What mechanisms were used to ensure that multiple voices and perspectives were considered in its development?
- What processes ensured that it provides a foundation for social change rather than perpetuating dominant hegemony and historical inequalities?

• 3. Identify the Purpose and Goals of the Policy

A policy exists for a reason. Its purpose is often expressed in a vision statement. This statement is often future oriented and inspirational and describes the long-term desired state of affairs. Linked to the vision statement are a set of principles and goals. The goals are sometimes described as "elements" or "priority areas," and are generally more pragmatic and specific. At times, these goals may be written in a SMART (Specific, Measurable, Attainable, Realistic, Timely) format. Other times, they may be written more generally.

When reviewing the purpose and goals of a policy, key questions to ask include:

- What is it expected to "do" (what problem is it expected to alleviate)?
- What principles or values are expressed in it explicitly?
- What principles are missing and may cause barriers for some populations?
- What political ideology and social welfare approaches are implicit in it? Are they consistent or inconsistent with social work ideology and approaches?
- What is the pervasive understanding about the population experiencing the social problem? Is it consistent or inconsistent with the social work principles of dignity and respect?

- **4. Apply a Social Work Values Analysis**

Typically, a social policy is organized around the population it is designed to serve (e.g., children and families, youth, older adults, people with disabilities) or seeks to protect (e.g., neglected or abused children). When reviewing a policy, it is important to consider whether it incorporates core social welfare values.

Social Work Values Analysis

When assessing a social policy, social workers consider the three core values:

- Inclusion
- Equity
- Social Justice

(A) The Inclusion Lens

- How will the policy increase or decrease discrimination on the basis of gender, race, age, culture, or ethnicity?
- How will the policy increase or decrease personal income and resources available for people to participate in social and economic activity and promote income equity?
- How will the policy increase or decrease access to resources?
- How will the policy affect opportunities for participation in decision making?
- How will the policy add or remove barriers to common spaces, safe environments, and social interaction?
- How will the policy protect or compromise the rights of people?
- How will the policy increase or decrease opportunities for personal development and social support?
- How will the policy increase or reduce access to resources and programs for excluded groups? (Shookner, 2002)

(B) The Equity Lens

- Who is positively and negatively affected by the policy, and how?
- How are people differently situated to access the benefits of the policy?
- Are people traumatized/retraumatized by the policy decisions?
- How are environmental impacts and environmental justice included?
- How are public resources and investments distributed geographically?
- Are the communities most affected by inequities prioritized in the policy?
- Are there empowering processes in the policy? (Balajee, 2012)

(C) The Social Justice Lens

A social justice lens involves access, agency, solidarity action, and advocacy.

- **Accessibility.** What mechanisms exist for the inclusion of all points of view?
- **Agency.** How does the policy overcome systemic or hierarchical barriers to ensure that all points of view are considered?
- **Solidarity Action.** What processes are in place to include all members in identifying the impact of systemic change and the outcome?
- **Advocacy.** What mechanisms will ensure systemic change? (BC Teachers' Federation, 2019)

- **5. Implementation**

As the policy is implemented, analysis is needed to identify priority populations, distribution processes or sites, funding levels, and accessibility. Questions to ask may include:

- Are the people most at risk provided priority?
- Is the funding sufficient to meet the resource needs?
- Are there any barriers to accessibility?

- **6. Review the Impact of the Policy**

As citizen participation in social welfare policies has increased, so too has the demand for government accountability and transparency associated with the impact, or outcomes, of the policy. Often, policies have been based on the "big four" principles of economy, efficiency, effectiveness, and equity.

From a social welfare perspective, we broaden this view to include the effect of policies on populations, social equity, disadvantage, the social determinants of health, and social well-being.

When reviewing the measures for impact transparency of a policy, key questions to ask include:

- Could the policy have a negative impact on some populations or communities? If so, how can the negative/inequitable impacts be mitigated?
- Are the needs of disadvantaged individuals, communities, and priority populations considered?
- How will the policy address the social determinants of health?
- How will the policy address social well-being?
- What is the process of amending or changing initiatives and goals as the policy is implemented?

Criteria for Assessing Public Policy Proposals

When a public policy is being considered for development, it is evaluated based on a number of criteria, including the following (Caputo, 2014):

- **Political Feasibility.** Social welfare policies are developed through a political process. Some policies may carry a relatively low political risk (e.g., policies for low-income older adults or children, or vulnerable populations). By contrast, others may involve more divergent opinions and carry a higher political risk (e.g., medical assistance in dying, safe consumption sites, or a basic income strategy). Changing economic and political conditions, the climate of public opinion about related issues, and the election cycle all contribute to the acceptance or failure of a policy initiative. Often, policies associated with new program areas are initially conducted as a pilot program to reduce political risk.

- **Social Acceptability.** The degree to which the general public will accept or support a policy proposal is a consideration. The degree of social acceptability can sometimes be difficult to determine, as media headlines or social media can give the impression of greater public support or greater opposition than actually exists.
- **Administrative Feasibility.** It is important to consider whether the agency or department will be able to implement the policy and deliver the associated program well. This often requires an assessment of the available resources and capacity within the administrative unit.
- **Technical Feasibility.** Other considerations are the availability, reliability, and costs of the technology and associated systems needed to implement the policy.

Other Criteria for Assessing Social Welfare Policy

As stated earlier, there is no single model for assessing social welfare policies. Criterion frameworks for use in the development or evaluation of social welfare policy have been developed by various organizations and researchers.

Examples of these frameworks include:

- The Canada Health Act (1984), a cornerstone of the health care system, sets out the principles it uses to guide health funding: public administration, comprehensiveness, universality, portability, and accessibility.
- The Social Union Framework Agreement (SUFA) of 1999 builds on the Canada Health Act's principles and also includes accountability, citizen engagement, and results-based accountability (Phillips & Echenberg, n.d.).
- The Canadian Association of Social Workers (CASW) uses the following principles to guide its evaluation of policies: dignity and respect, equality, equity, comprehensiveness, quality services, constitutional integrity, subsidiarity, and social dialogue.

Canadian Association of Social Workers (CASW)

Founded in 1926 to monitor employment conditions and to establish standards of practice within the profession, the Canadian Association of Social Workers (CASW) has evolved into a national voice. The CASW Federation is comprised of 9 provincial and territorial partner organizations.

The CASW Board of Directors determines and oversees general and financial policies. With each provincial/territorial partner organization appointing one member to the Board, a unified voice for the Canadian social work profession is assured. The Board of Directors works from a national and, indeed, an international perspective to benefit the social work profession.

CASW (2020). *CASW Represents Canadian Professional Social Workers.* Canadian Association of Social Workers. https://www.casw-acts.ca/en/about-casw/about-casw

Social Welfare Policy in Action

Canada's Youth Policy

Improving Prospects for Young People

Canada's youth want to be included in decision making about their future. Investing in Canadian young people provides leadership for the future.

In May 2019, Prime Minister and Minister of Youth Justin Trudeau launched Canada's first-ever youth policy.

Canada's Youth Policy was developed after the formation of the Prime Minister's Youth Council and Constituency Youth Councils across the country. In addition, young people in Canada had access to an interactive online platform (youthaction.ca), where they could share their ideas and perspectives on what a youth policy should look like.

The focus of the youth-led dialogue was as follows:

- To identify issues that are important to youth and have an impact on their daily lives and futures
- To examine the type of support that enables all youth — regardless of their background — to be the leaders of today and tomorrow
- To assess initiatives that are already in place — and identify new actions that can be taken — to improve the lives of young Canadians

The Policy's Value Statement

Consistent with many governmental policies, which are inherently political, Trudeau prefaced the policy with a value statement about young Canadians:

> Young Canadians are the most educated, connected and diverse generation this country has ever seen. They are changing our communities, challenging the status quo, and taking the lead on building a better, fairer, and more sustainable future. ...
>
> ... This policy reflects the values and priorities of young Canadians, gives young people a voice in matters important to them, and creates more opportunities for young people to build a stronger and more inclusive Canada. (Canada, 2019b, p. 2)

The Policy's Preamble, Vision Statement, and Guiding Principles

The policy's preamble is as follows:

> Young Canadians are one of Canada's most important resources. Youth represent one third of the Canadian population and reflect Canada's entire diversity. ...
>
> Adolescence can be a period of vulnerability as young people transition from the dependence of childhood to the independence of adulthood. ... Young people's experiences can have lasting impacts on their future health, social and economic outcomes. ...
>
> Investing in youth is in Canada's social and economic interest. ... Canada's economy depends on the participation of young people and empowering them to take part will diversify our economy, making it more competitive and sustainable. (Canada, 2019b, p. 3)

The policy's vision statement is as follows:

> The Government of Canada's vision is that young people be equipped to live healthy and fulfilling lives and feel empowered to create positive change for themselves, their communities, and their world. (Canada, 2019b, p. 6)

The following guiding principles are to be used in the implementation of youth policy objectives:

- Youth have the right to be heard and respected.
- Youth have the right to equal access to opportunities and supports.
- When youth reach their full potential, it benefits all Canadians.

Indigenous youth are identified as a particularly vulnerable sector with unique challenges:

- Lack of access to clean drinking water, affordable food, adequate housing, health, and education services
- Racism, discrimination, and the intergenerational trauma of Canada's colonial history

Areas Prioritized under the Policy

- **Leadership and Impact.** This area includes participation in civic life and opportunities to assume leadership roles in their communities. Program example: Canada Service Corps.
- **Health and Wellness.** When young people are physically, mentally, and emotionally well, they are better equipped to handle life's challenges and opportunities. Mental health is a top priority. Budget 2019 committed to supporting a Pan-Canadian Suicide Prevention Service.
- **Innovation, Skills, and Learning.** A foundation in education and learning is a significant protective factor against negative outcomes and is essential for young people to reach economic empowerment. Young people have innovative ideas to solve global challenges and are eager to transform their ideas into reality. Program example: Youth Employment and Skills Strategy.
- Employment. Young people need work experience and work-integrated learning experiences to find long-term quality employment and job security. Youth employment is particularly important to Canada's economy as the aging population transitions into retirement. Program example: The Federal Student Work Experience Program, which has specific inventories for Indigenous youth, young women, and youth with disabilities.
- **Truth and Reconciliation.** Many young Canadians want to be the generation that mends the relationship between Indigenous peoples and non-Indigenous Canadians. Young Canadians believe reconciliation can be grounded in truth, respect, and healing. Budget 2019 committed to investing in a pilot program, delivered by Canadian Roots Exchange, to advance reconciliation by bringing together Indigenous and non-Indigenous youth to promote mutual understanding and respect.
- **Environment and Climate Action.** This area is a top priority for many young Canadians, as they are concerned about doing more to protect and conserve the environment. They want a Canada that protects its natural environment and addresses climate change in a process that emphasizes reconciliation with Indigenous peoples. Program example: Science Horizons Youth Internship Program, which supports green jobs for youth.

Budget 2019 Commitments

- $314.8 million over five years and $83.8 million per year ongoing to make the Canada Service Corps a signature national youth service program
- $49.5 million over five years to modernize the government's Youth Employment Strategy and improve services and supports for young people facing barriers to employment

Questions for Reflection

Canada's Youth Policy is available here: www.canada.ca/en/youth/programs/policy.html. Once you have reviewed the policy, consider the following questions:

- What indicators were used to determine the need for a national youth policy?
- Which political ideology and social work approach are apparent in this youth policy?
- Are the concerns of Indigenous youth addressed throughout the policy goals?
- Does the policy reflect inclusion, equity, and social justice?
- Is it clear how the implementation of this policy is likely to flow to the provinces and territories?
- Are there mechanisms in place to evaluate the success of the policy?
- What can you do to support, advocate for, improve, and/or implement Canada's first youth policy?

A Moment in Time, March 11, 2020

WHO Declares COVID–19 a Global Pandemic

"It is a crisis that will touch every sector."

In the winter of 2019–2020, everyone's lives changed. Almost no one living had experienced a global pandemic. Governments around the world responded in differing ways.

On December 31, 2019, the World Health Organization noticed a "viral pneumonia" in Wuhan, People's Republic of China. By January 10, WHO had published guidance documents related to the management of an outbreak of a new disease. On January 25, 2020, Canada reported its first presumptive case of COVID–19.

On March 11, the WHO declared COVID–19 a pandemic, pointing to over 118,000 cases around the world and the risk of further global spread.

"This is not just a public health crisis, it is a crisis that will touch every sector," said Dr. Tedros Adhanom Ghebreyesus, WHO director-general, at a media briefing. "So every sector and every individual must be involved in the fights."

Canada Responds

As a start, the Canadian federal government announced a $1 trillion response fund ($500 million for each of the provinces and territories, a $50 million contribution to WHO, and an additional $275 million to fund COVID–19 research). Starting March 16, 2020, border restrictions began and on March 18 the US border was closed for non-essential travel.

On March 24, the COVID–19 Emergency Response Act was enacted. The following day, the Canada Emergency Response Benefit (CERB) was announced to "help Canadians and businesses facing hardship as a result of the COVID–19 outbreak." A host of other income support programs followed over the following months.

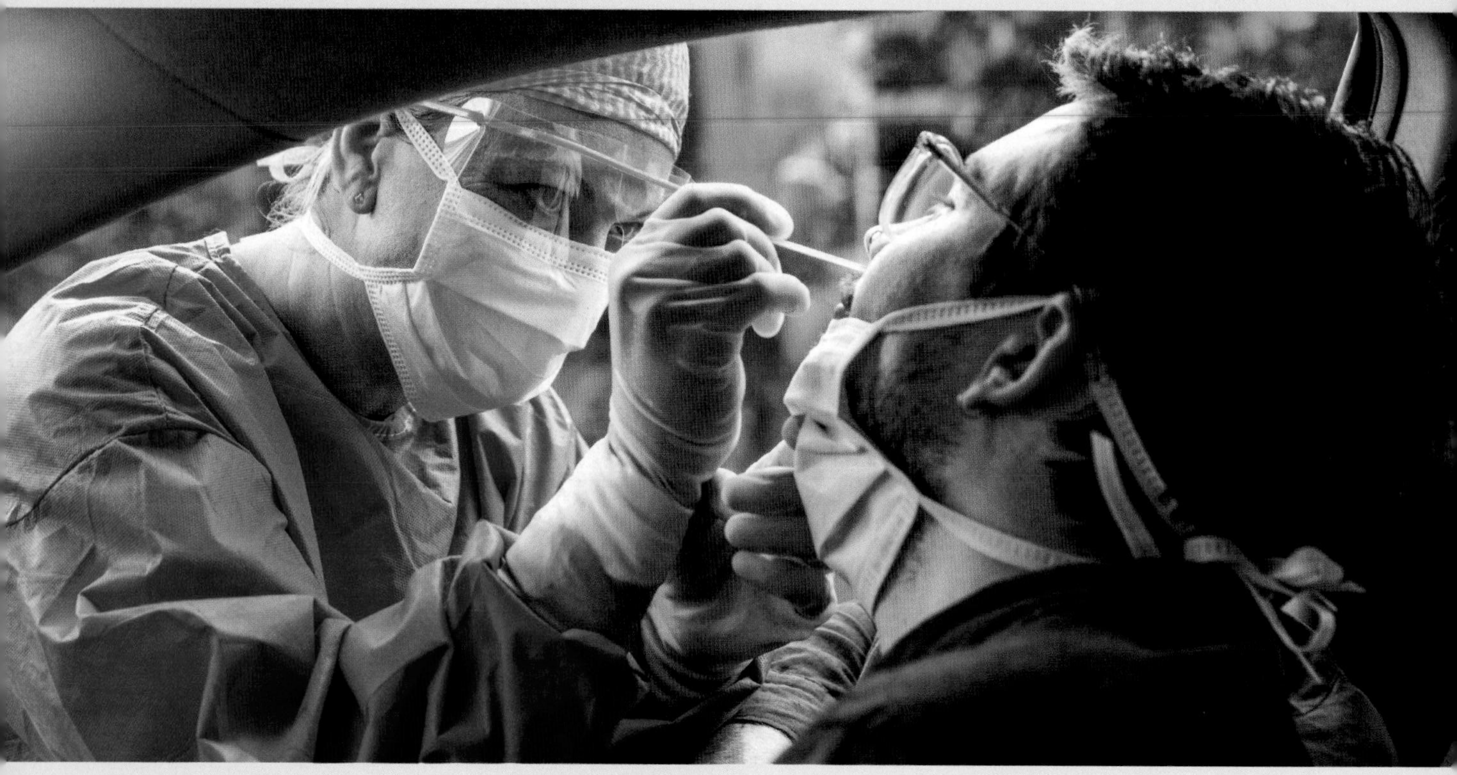

Chapter Review

Questions

1. What key ideas underlie the notion of a social welfare state?
2. The Canadian Index of Wellbeing can serve as a guide to policymakers. Describe the eight domains included in the Canadian Index of Wellbeing.
3. What is an ideology? What political ideologies exist in Canada, and how do they differ in their views on social welfare?
4. Make the cases for and against the idea that social welfare programs should be universally available to all people living in Canada.
5. What is the social investment approach to social welfare provision? How does this approach differ from the residual and institutional approaches?
6. When assessing (or crafting) a social welfare policy or program, it can be helpful to have a sequence of steps in mind. What are these steps?

Exploring Social Welfare

1. Each political party in Canada has a unique platform in relation to social welfare and income security. Pick one federal or provincial/territorial political party. On its website, locate its views on social welfare. How does the party's platform on social welfare relate to the political ideologies discussed in this chapter?
2. In May 2019, Prime Minister and Minister of Youth Justin Trudeau launched Canada's first-ever youth policy. Canada's Youth Policy is introduced in a separate section of this chapter. Investigate how this federal strategy is being implemented by the province or territory you live in. Are there examples of community programming that reflect the principles inherent in Canada's Youth Policy?

Websites

Canadian Association for Social Work Education (CASWE)
www.caswe-acfts.ca
CASWE-ACFTS is a voluntary national charitable association of university faculties, schools, and departments offering professional education in social work at the undergraduate, graduate, and post-graduate levels. Its website offers research reports, news, and school information.

Canadian Association of Social Workers (CASW)
www.casw-acts.ca
Founded in 1926, CASW is the national voice for Canadian social workers. It produces and distributes timely information for its members and initiates and sponsors special projects on their behalf. A code of ethics for the profession, a series of national policy and position papers, research projects, reports, and selected books are also available from CASW.

Canadian Index of Wellbeing
https://uwaterloo.ca/canadian-index-wellbeing
The Canadian Index of Wellbeing (CIW) is a composite index composed of eight domains that measure stability and change over time. It is part of a global well-being movement that recognizes the importance of taking into account the many domains of life. When partnered with traditional measures (e.g., GDP), the CIW provides the evidence needed to help Canadians build a society that responds to the call for greater equity and fairness.

International Council on Social Welfare (ICSW)
www.icsw.org
The International Council on Social Welfare (ICSW) was founded in Paris in 1928. The council gathers and disseminates information, undertakes research, convenes conferences, draws on grassroots experiences, develops policy, and works with policymakers and administrators. The council represents national and local organizations in more than 70 countries throughout the world.

The Rise and Fall of the Welfare State

"People must know the past to understand the present and face the future."

– Nellie McClung, (1873–1951), Canadian writer and early women's rights activist

Jackie Stokes

A History of Social Welfare in Canada

2

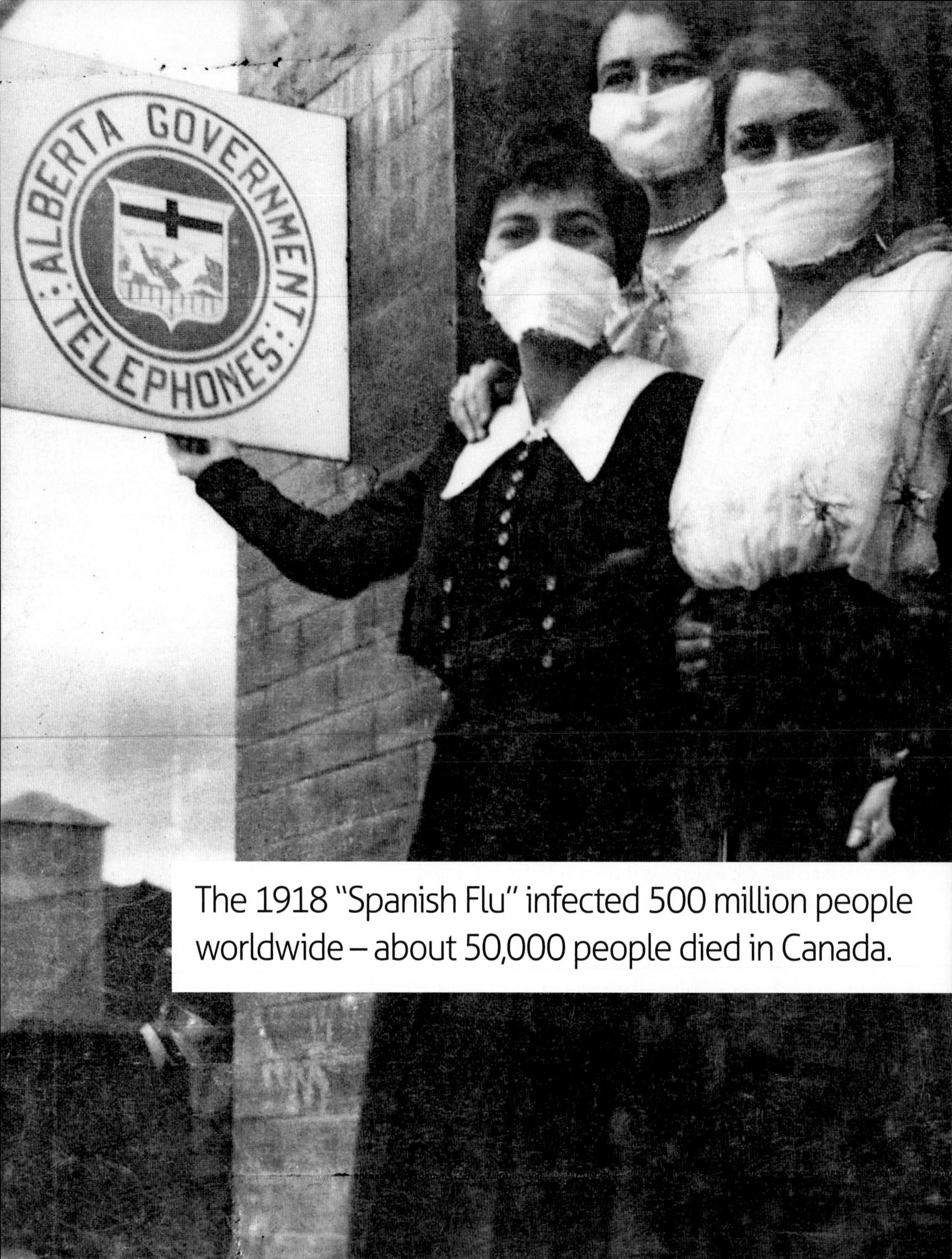

The 1918 "Spanish Flu" infected 500 million people worldwide – about 50,000 people died in Canada.

The Canadian social welfare system historically was based largely on the British model. In Canada, social welfare evolved gradually but progressively during the twentieth century as a response to the demands of workers and farmers for a share of the country's wealth. Following the Great Depression and World War II, a consensus was reached that led to an extensive social welfare system that aimed to ensure a minimum income and provide social services for people in Canada.

The evolution of social welfare in Canada can be divided into different phases that coincide with major political, social, and economic changes in the country:

- Phase 1: the colonial period, 1600–1867
- Phase 2: the industrialization period, 1868–1940
- Phase 3: the welfare state period, 1941–1974
- Phase 4: the rise of neoliberalism, 1975–2005
- Phase 5: retrenchment and recovery, 2006–present
- Phase 6: COVID times

A History of Social Welfare in Canada

This chapter provides an overview of the history of social welfare in Canada from the earliest days to the present. Subsequent chapters focus on more contemporary considerations associated with particular issues or populations.

After completing this chapter, you should be able to:

- Understand the origins of social welfare;
- Describe the Elizabethan Poor Law;
- Understand the underlying themes that have influenced the development of social welfare in Canada;
- Explain the significance of the 1929 economic crash and its effect on the development of social welfare in Canada;
- Explain the significance of the Beveridge Report and the Marsh Report, which were published in 1943;
- Trace the rise and decline of the welfare state in Canada and other industrialized countries after World War II; and
- Understand the contrasting visions and social policies pursued under the federal leadership of Stephen Harper and Justin Trudeau.

Key Concepts

- Elizabethan Poor Law (1601)
- Deserving poor
- Undeserving poor
- Less eligibility
- Workhouses
- Workers' compensation
- Mothers' allowance
- Old Age Pensions Act (1927)
- Great Depression
- On to Ottawa Trek
- Unemployment Insurance Act, 1940
- Family Allowance Act (1944)
- Old Age Security Act (1951)
- Canada Pension Plan (1965) and Québec Pension Plan (1966)
- Canada Assistance Plan (1966)
- Canada Health and Social Transfer
- Canada Health Act (1984)
- Report of the Special Senate Committee on Poverty (1971)
- Beveridge report (1943)
- Marsh Report (1943)
- Canada–United States Free Trade Agreement (CUSFTA) (1989)
- North American Free Trade Agreement (NAFTA) (1994)
- Canada–United States–Mexico Agreement (CUSMA)

2.1 Phase 1: The Colonial Period, 1600–1867

In Britain, by the early 1600s, the system referred to as "feudalism" (centring on the nobility, the clergy, and the peasantry) had largely disappeared in favour of a new system of relations based on wage labour (capitalism). This change came about over time as result of three factors that started in the 1300s: international demand for wool, soil erosion, and population decline.

Under the feudal system, peasants farmed land owned by a lord, and owed a portion of their production to that lord. The lords' returns were restricted by how much the peasants could produce beyond their own subsistence needs. Soil erosion in England resulting from poor farming methods made subsistence difficult and reduced the lords' returns as early as the 1300s. In addition, the Black Death of 1348–1349 reduced the population of Europe by as much as one-half, dramatically reducing the number of peasants that English lords could exploit. Their income in long-term decline, lords looked for ways to make their lands more productive and reduce their dependence on the number and productivity of peasants.

Origins of Social Welfare

As international demand for wool began to increase, English landowners saw an opportunity to end the system of mutual obligations between lord and peasant. The feudal ethic gave way to an emphasis on "improving" one's lands. Lords no longer allowed all peasants the right to farm plots of land; English landowners "enclosed" subsistence plots of land from hundreds of thousands of peasants, giving much of the land over to sheep and small numbers of hired shepherds. The remaining land, instead of being left as small peasant plots, was allotted as larger plots to those peasants who made the land as productive as possible. The remaining peasants, branded as surplus and lazy, lost their land and livelihood and moved to towns and cities to find work. Their labour, extracted by strict entrepreneurial employers, become another means to increase national income.

In the wake of the Black Death, many serfs and town labourers who survived the pestilence attempted to take advantage of the labour shortage by taking to the roads and demanding decent wages from potential employers. In response, the king and Parliament passed the Statute of Labourers in 1351, which required workers to return to their former feudal masters whenever possible; if their former master had died, leaving no heir to employ them, they were required to take whatever employment others offered.

Wages were frozen at 1346 rates for all forms of work. For good measure, to emphasize that no one had a right to avoid work or to refuse whatever work was offered to them regardless of wages or working conditions, the provision of alms to individuals deemed capable of seeking employment became a legal offence punishable by imprisonment.

The Elizabethan Poor Law

The Statute of Labourers and similar legislation temporarily maintained, however shakily, feudal relations. As population levels were restored and landlords shed unnecessary labourers, the concerns of the king and Parliament turned from merely forcing workers to stay with a particular employer toward dealing with the new phenomenon of mass unemployment.

Many of the expelled farm labourers who flooded into towns were unable to find work, particularly when market conditions were weak. They often resorted to riots to gain the attention of the authorities. The latter used force to suppress the riots and even executed many rioters. The authorities recognized that the long-term maintenance of law and order required some means of satisfying those unable to find work during periods of economic crisis, while at the same time reinforcing earlier laws that required all able-bodied workers to take whatever work was offered to them.

The result was the Elizabethan Poor Law of 1601. The **Elizabethan Poor Law** refined earlier versions of the Poor Law and defined the principles for worthiness of state aid. The law was passed in Britain at a time when poverty was considered necessary and inevitable since, it was believed, only fear of poverty would make people look for work The principles behind the Elizabethan Poor Law remained in place in Britain until the early 1900s. The underlying principles were applied not only in Britain itself but also in Britain's former colonies, including Canada.

"Careful, or you'll end up in the poorhouse."

There was a time when the threat of landing in the poorhouse wasn't just a metaphor for being broke. To the people of Ireland who lived during the great potato famine of the mid-1800s, the poorhouse was a real place and the prospect of ending up there was a very scary one.

Photo: An illustration of an Irish workhouse, published in 1901. Artist unknown.

The "Deserving Poor" and "Undeserving Poor"

The Elizabethan Poor Law distinguished between the "deserving poor" and "undeserving poor" and set out provisions for deciding on the worthiness of state aid:

1. The **deserving poor** were those unable to work, and those who were fit for work and willing to take any job on offer at rates determined by the employer. The **undeserving poor** were those who were deemed able to work but did not do so for whatever reason. They were thought to be of bad moral character and not deserving of help.
2. The state recognized no responsibility for the undeserving poor and made provision to place them in Houses of Correction that would attempt to change their attitude toward work, or in prisons if they appeared unruly.
3. The state recognized only limited responsibility for the deserving poor. The thinking was that to provide the deserving poor with more aid would discourage them from ever seeking work again and would encourage others not to take jobs that offered low pay and unsafe or otherwise unbearable working conditions.
4. In determining the bare minimum that poor relief recipients could receive, the state would always ensure that the minimum was lower than the minimum wages that day labourers were receiving. This principle of **less eligibility** ensured that those in work would always be terrified to lose their employment and forced to live an unspeakably miserable life.
5. Local authorities were empowered to build workhouses for recipients of aid. They were empowered to offer "indoor relief," which involved forcing poor individuals and families into a workhouse. Individuals were expected to earn their aid by working in the workhouse or by working for employers with whom the workhouse had contracts. Local authorities could also provide "outdoor relief" (e.g., money, food, clothing) to those who remained in their own homes. In practice, outdoor relief was common because it was cheaper than building more workhouses.
6. Families, regardless of income, were made responsible for the care of indigent parents or children so as to relieve the state of that responsibility. That meant the state only had responsibility for those without blood relations who could be forced to help out.
7. The parish had the right and the duty to separate children aged five to fourteen from destitute parents and find jobs or apprenticeships for them.
8. Tax collection and administration of poor relief occurred at the parish level, with overseers of the poor appointed to weed out deserving from undeserving applicants for relief.

Despised by all, and pitied by none

In 1834, the UK's new Poor Law created a system of workhouses, the likes of which Charles Dickens described in his 1838 novel *Oliver Twist*.

The new Poor Law required that the destitute could receive welfare assistance only while inside a workhouse. The residents were, in Dickens' words, "despised by all, and pitied by none."

The Industrial Revolution and Growing Social Needs

The Industrial Revolution (from about 1760 to 1840) produced a great deal of social dislocation and a higher number of poor people. At the time, the purpose of social welfare was to provide the minimum assistance necessary to keep the non-dissolute unemployed alive. The unemployed were tacitly blamed for their failure to find work, and maximum pressure was placed on them to take whatever jobs became available. Only members of society deemed unemployable and without relatives to support them were exempted from such pressure. However, they too received only modest state aid and were often placed in institutions. Until the late 1800s, such state institutions were generally undifferentiated; that is, the mentally ill, orphans, the unemployed, and the frail elderly were often placed under one roof.

The dominant beliefs at the time were anchored in Reformation Protestant theology. Pauperism was thought to be a result of family defects, and individuals were considered to be responsible for their own poverty. Idleness, worldly temptations, and moral decline resulted in poverty. The thinking was that people could lift themselves out of poverty through discipline and hard work. Meanwhile, more workhouses were built, and their inmates were required to perform labour within and outside of workhouses, often dying because they were already weakened by hunger.

The Elizabethan Poor Law model became the basis for the social welfare system adopted by British North American colonies.

Photo: Completed in 1841, the Union Workhouse in Litchfield, UK (shown below in 2007), was to hold 200 paupers under the strictest of discipline. The length of time an inmate was resident in the Workhouse varied depending on their circumstances. If inmates were able to find work and provide for themselves, or a family member was able to provide for them, they would be discharged. After World War II, the Union Workhouse became a community hospital under the auspices of Britain's National Health Service.

Social Welfare in the Colonial Period

The first phase in the emergence of social welfare in Canada spans the arrival of settlers to New France and English colonies to Confederation and the signing of the British North America Act of 1867 (also called the Constitution Act, 1867). In this era, social welfare was local and private, and economic security was a matter for the family first and the community second.

The state's role, whether or not a Poor Law was in place in a given colony, was initially limited to supporting charities. However, it gradually expanded to include building workhouses and implementing public health measures. Both the state and charities approached poverty by regulating and providing aid to the poor rather than by addressing the causes of poverty.

French and English Models

Before and after Confederation, two different but often parallel models were used to provide aid to the poor: the French and English models. Québec adopted a church-based model that had its origins in France. English Canada adopted the English Poor Law model supplemented by private charity.

The Québec model, in which the church rather than the state provided social services, included an array of institutions, from schools to hospitals to shelters for the poor, orphans, prostitutes, and elderly. However, it had a Poor Law ideology to a large degree and placed more importance on the cause of need than the fact of need.

The church, which had owned a significant portion of the land in New France and benefited from land sales after the British conquest of the French colony, defended inequalities in the distribution of wealth and property. Funds and services were denied to able-bodied individuals even when unemployment was rife, particularly if those individuals were judged as dissolute and sporadic in their church attendance. Single mothers were forced to give up their babies to the nuns. By contrast, the Soeurs Grises (Grey Nuns), beginning in 1858, opened daycares in working-class areas to care for children of working or ill mothers. The church, while its shelters often seemed similar to workhouses and poorhouses, always provided a portion of its help as outdoor relief.

In English Canada (which, like Québec, was mainly rural), local charities took on many of the same responsibilities that the church assumed for Catholics in Québec. Although Nova Scotia introduced a Poor Law in 1758 and New Brunswick introduced a Poor Law in 1786, charities rather than the state provided most of the assistance for those in need. Villages and small towns often proved generous in helping local families who fell on hard times, but outsiders who arrived at the town gates were jailed or even publicly auctioned to the lowest bidder in an effort to prevent strangers from taking advantage of whatever charitable instincts existed in the area.

Workhouses

In the colonies, population increases and immigration created a growing underclass dependent on wages. The rise of industry created many of the same problems that had occurred earlier in Europe: charities were overwhelmed, and the state (which often provided subsidies to charities) was forced to play a bigger role.

As in Britain, the state's role in the colonies involved the establishment of workhouses. Saint John opened the first in 1835, and Montréal, Québec City, Toronto, and Kingston opened workhouses within the next two years. Families were often separated in a workhouse. There was no supervision to ensure that the children were safe at work, not overworked, and free of physical and sexual abuse. At times, children were hired out to whatever employer was willing to provide room and board in return for work. In a workhouse, all men had to perform a "workhouse test": physical labour that proved that they were not in the workhouse as a means of avoiding the search for paid work.

Up until the Second World War, waves of newcomers migrated to Toronto — Irish, Jewish, Italian, Black American, and Chinese, among others. Many landed in "The Ward," an area crammed with rundown housing and immigrant-owned businesses (Héroux, 2015). Fearing that UK-style workhouses would be introduced in Toronto, in 1837 a group of reformers and dissenting ministers founded the "House of Industry," modelled on somewhat more humanitarian principles.

The House of Industry provided lodging to the needy and assisted abandoned or orphaned children, often placing them as indentured servants in homes and farms. The House of Industry provided both temporary and permanent accommodations. Residents were often required to do chores in return for help — similar to the old Dickensian workhouses of England. Unemployed men were given food and shelter for the night and expected to move on. To deter "casuals" from taking advantage of the system, trustees introduced a new law: breaking "two yards" of stone in order to qualify for relief (Héroux, 2015).

Over time, the cost of building and maintaining traditional workhouses, along with a growing unease about large institutions, eventually caused both Ontario and Québec to rely more on outdoor relief (Guest, 1980). The workhouse test was replaced by the work test, which meant that an applicant, unless he had a medical exemption, could stay at home but would be required to cut wood or break rock in order to receive financial aid (Guest, 1980).

New Brunswick and Nova Scotia, which experienced slow economic growth after the 1850s, resisted the move to outdoor relief. They did not shut down their workhouses until the second half of the 1950s.

The House of Industry

In 1848, a building for the House of Industry was erected at the corner of Elm Street and Elizabeth Street, in the middle of a downtown Toronto district that housed a dense slum populated by successive waves of immigrants.

One hundred years later, the clients of Ontario's houses of industry had become predominantly the elderly poor. The Toronto House of Industry building was converted into a home for the elderly and renamed Laughlen Lodge after Arthur and Frances Laughlen.

Photo: The Toronto House of Industry building in 2009.

Social Welfare in Perspective

Indigenous Peoples before European Contact

Distinct Systems and Community Well-Being

Prior to the arrival of colonial settlers and the formation of Canada itself, Indigenous peoples held shared egalitarian and social values along with a deep respect for nature and spirituality.

Prior to colonization, more than 500 identifiable Indigenous groups existed, representing tremendous diversity in terms of languages spoken, artistic techniques used, song and dance styles performed, and systems of governing (Belshaw, 2015). Canada's First Peoples developed complex cultures, living in harmony with the land and creating a distinct culture as a result of adaptation to different Canadian environments (Goldi Productions, 2007). While there was, and is, no single monolithic Indigenous culture, common features across North America indicated shared economic and cultural characteristics (Belshaw, 2015).

While Indigenous societies precontact can be described as "subsistence cultures, meaning that their diet, daily nourishment and medicines were provided by the resources of their local ecosystems" (Richmond & Cook, 2016, p. 3), the reliance on the ecosystem nurtured a deep cognitive, spiritual, and physical relatedness to the land and its resources. This cornerstone of the Indigenous way of life maintained local and distinct knowledge systems that seeded the roots for Indigenous societies to flourish in their social, political, cultural, economic, and spiritual systems (Richmond & Cook, 2016).

First Nations Government and Economy

First Nations in Canada had complex social systems with several levels of government based on the family, the band or clan, and the nation or tribe (Goldi Productions, 2007).

People with special leadership qualities were identified as leaders or Chiefs. In most First Nations, the Chief was advised by a council of Elders, and decisions on matters of importance were agreed on by consensus (Goldi Productions, 2007).

Each First Nation was self-governing and developed a unique system for social and economic organization. Each First Nation recognized the sovereignty of other First Nations (Goldi Productions, 2007). Socio-economic systems for ensuring tools, clothing, shelter, and transportation were provided were associated with seasonal migration and communal caring. "The only farming people were the Iroquois and Hurons, and related tribes, in what is now southern Ontario" (Goldi Productions, 2007, para. 6).

Canada's First Peoples "survived very well in a harsh environment, making everything they needed without polluting the water, or air, and without destroying the land or decimating the animal populations" (Goldi Productions, 2007, para. 2).

First Nations Health, Precontact

Precontact, First Nations had a complex system of social and cultural Indigenous practices that ensured good health, although they varied based on region and culture (First Nations Health Authority [FNHA], 2020). Precontact lifestyles included many health-protecting characteristics, including an active lifestyle associated with a mix of hunting, fishing, and gathering food; low population density; mobility on land and water; environmentally friendly subsistence practices; and the availability of a variety of food (FNHA, 2020).

The FNHA (2020) describes how oral histories suggest that staying healthy and attaining longevity were associated with the following: ceremonial, spiritual, and physical elements; access to healers such as midwives, herbal healers, and shamans; and the existence of customary laws regarding food and hygiene.

Although there were some health problems, such as abscessed jaw sockets and a limited number of infectious diseases and dermatological problems, First Nations people precontact experienced virtually no diabetes or dental cavities (FNHA, 2020).

Communities and families valued preventive and holistic approaches to health care, and a sense of place and belonging was recognized as one of the factors affecting health (FNHA, 2020). Traditional healing included spiritual healers (shamen) who "developed intimate understandings of their environment and the healing qualities of many plants, some of which are also used during ceremonies and for other spiritual reasons" (FNHA, 2020, para. 7).

Family Caring

Kinship and the trust and closeness of family relationships were key to traditional First Nations and Inuit social organization. Kinship systems carried particular roles and obligations to ensure that day-to-day tasks were undertaken and individuals were cared for (Government of Alberta, n.d.). Similar to today, the family and community would provide support and comfort when a member fell ill or was in need. Everyone contributed to the overall well-being of the group (FNHA, 2020, para. 8).

Child rearing was commonly understood as a responsibility of not only parents but also the extended family (FNHA, 2020). Children often spent time with their extended families learning lessons about the natural world and the importance of respect for the land from the shared stories of older generations (Government of Alberta, n.d.).

Traditional teachings about disabilities tended to reflect special gifts or powers that enabled people to communicate with the spiritual world (Dion, 2017). Here is an example from the traditional teaching of the Cree First Nations:

> The old man said, to have been born imperfect was a sign of specialness. ... The old man explained carefully that in the old days, if a child came with a hare-shorn lip, it wasn't a terrible thing or a hurtful thing; it meant the child's soul was still in touch with the Spirit World. (Dion, 2017, p. 5)

The arrival of European settlers ultimately led to the conquest of traditional lands and a disruption of traditional ways of life. Land treaties were entered into or imposed, often with little compensation.

Photo: Children take part in the Annual Echoes of a Proud Nation Pow Wow in Kahnawake, one of several Kanien'kehá:ka territories of the Mohawk Nation located at the southwest shore where the Saint Lawrence River narrows.

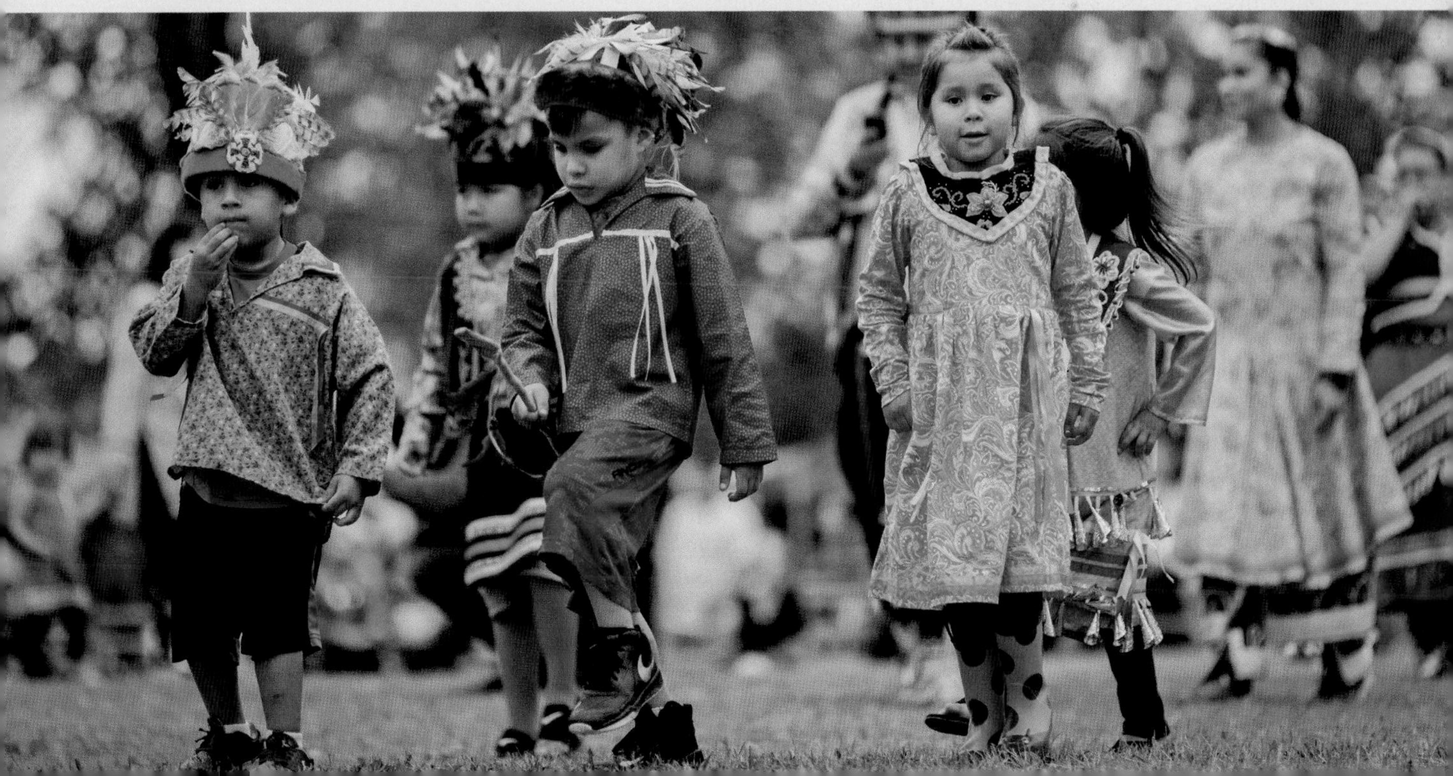

2.2 Phase 2: The Industrialization Period, 1868–1940

After 1867, Canada industrialized rapidly. This drew both people from abroad and people from rural communities into towns and cities. Many people left the security of the family to look for greater economic opportunities, sometimes ending up with insecure factory or mining jobs. The second phase of the history of social welfare in Canada covers the post-Confederation period roughly until the beginning of World War II.

During this time, popular sentiment still favoured a residual approach in which charity and local volunteer decision making closely scrutinized the allocation of aid to the help-worthy. Most poverty was still seen as the product of individual failings, and relief was minimal and carried stigma. The numbers of both reformers and socialists grew, but conservative ideology largely held sway until the severity of the Great Depression caused a massive shift away from the idea that individuals were the cause of their own poverty.

Workers' Compensation

Industrialization brought with it concerns over the mounting toll of workplace injury and death, the need for safety equipment, and the limiting of children's employment (Guest, 1980). Although Factory Acts were established to improve the conditions for children, they did not address the financial insecurity associated with workplace accidents. The Québec Workers' Compensation Act (originally called "Workmen's Compensation Act") was established in 1909. However, this Act was not compulsory and did not have an independent administrative board.

Workers' compensation was supported by many employers and by the rising labour movement. It was paid for by employers' contributions and provided both short- and long-term financial support to injured workers and their families without assessing blame for injuries on the job. Previously, workers who were injured on the job had to depend on charity or attempt to sue the employer in court for liability for the injury. The occasional generosity of courts in awarding huge damages to injured workers caused many employers to prefer a no-fault, state-run system of compensation.

In 1914, Ontario introduced its first workers' compensation legislation. It embodied the doctrine of no-fault liability and ensured that workers would receive benefits regardless of their employer's financial position. In contrast to the prevailing residual system of poor relief, the benefits would be paid in cash and as a right (Guest, 1980).

Six provinces had legislated workers' compensation programs based on the Ontario model by 1920. Québec followed in 1928 (to mandate employers and to establish an independent board), Saskatchewan in 1930, and Prince Edward Island in 1949. In 1950, one year after joining Canada as a province, Newfoundland and Labrador also legislated workers' compensation. Yukon did so in 1958. The Northwest Territories joined the Association of Workers' Compensation Boards of Canada in 1974 and in 1999 created a joint board with Nunavut.

The Social Gospel and Reform Movement

Post-Confederation industrialization in Canada created harsh conditions that called out for reform. Into this mix stepped the group of "social gospel" reformers who were less concerned with personal redemption than with bringing about urgent, society-wide change.

Prominent among this group of reformers was J. S. Woodsworth (1874–1942). Woodsworth broke with the conventional role of clergy and devoted himself to social action around issues of justice, peace, and equality.

The legacy of the early reformers continues today in the form of public entitlements such as the Canada Pension Plan and Employment Insurance, as well as Canadian political traditions based on equity, social obligation, and civic responsibility.

Mothers' Allowance and Pensions

Originally, workers' compensation programs were designed mainly for men. Shortly after several provinces had instituted workers' compensation programs, a number of provincial governments responded to campaigns from women's rights activists by introducing mothers' allowance legislation. The purpose of this legislation was to aid women who were raising children alone and without an adequate income. Manitoba acted first in 1916, followed by Saskatchewan in 1917, Alberta in 1919, and British Columbia and Ontario in 1920. Other provinces did not follow suit until later: Nova Scotia in 1930 and Québec in 1937. New Brunswick enacted legislation in 1930 but did not implement it until 1944.

Unlike workers' compensation, which applied universally and did not make moral judgments, mothers' allowances were infused with conventional judgments of "good women" versus "fallen women." Widows, wives with husbands too ill to work, and sometimes deserted wives were eligible for a mothers' allowance. However, all provinces excluded single mothers from receiving a mothers' allowance. Moreover, each province hired workers to make inquiries about how well the mothers receiving the allowance were running their homes, cutting off women who appeared to have a man in their lives or who were judged to be lacking in virtue.

The campaign for mothers' pensions picked up during World War I. The federal government extended pensions to the widows and children of soldiers who lost their lives.

In practice, the amount provided to women through mothers' allowances and pensions was low, and most recipients needed to work, at least part-time, to make ends meet.

Women and the Right to Vote

The focus on respectable motherhood reflected the conservative values of early twentieth-century feminists. A mostly middle- and upper-class movement at the time, its activists and the movement emphasized motherhood as they campaigned to end women's political and social inferiority.

Questioning the gender division of labour as such would have led to a backlash and to a smaller movement for incremental changes of benefit to women. The first priority of the movement at the time was women's suffrage, and from that standpoint the movement proved to be successful.

Women's right to vote was exercised for the first time nationally in the federal election of 1918. Between 1916 (Manitoba, Saskatchewan, Alberta) and 1940 (Québec), all provinces extended voting rights to some women. However, many women continued to be excluded from the right to vote based on race or Indigeneity. This first wave of feminist activism continued to campaign for equal rights in public life.

NEWS BULLETIN
INSTABUL, TURKEY, —FOR THE FIRST TIME IN TURKISH HISTORY WOMEN WILL VOTE AND BE ELIGIBLE FOR ELECTION TO PUBLIC OFFICE IN THE GENERAL ELECTION WHICH TAKES PLACE THIS WEEK.

Canadian political cartoon of a woman in Quebec reading a sign that reads: "News bulletin: for the first time in Turkish history women will vote and be eligible to the public office in the general election which takes place this week."

Women were granted the right to vote in Turkey in 1930, but the right to vote was not extended to women in provincial elections in Quebec until 1940.

Photo: A cartoon from Bibliothèque et Archives nationales du Québec by Arthur G. Racey (1870-1941), a cartoonist at the *Montreal Star.*

Income Security for the Elderly

The Government Annuities Act of 1908 provided Canadians with private funds as an investment opportunity to prepare financially for their old age. The Act allowed individuals to purchase government annuities on a voluntary basis. After retirement, individuals would receive government payments made up of the principal invested plus accumulated interest. The federal government offered this program as an alternative to the across-the-board old age pensions introduced in New Zealand and several Australian states in the decade before 1908. However, between 1908 and the passage of the Canadian federal Old Age Pensions Act in 1927, only 7,713 annuities had been issued (Guest, 1980).

Despite recommendations for old age pensions in several postwar reports on labour unrest in Canada, neither Liberal nor Conservative governments of the time seemed keen to pursue federal income security programs. In the 1921 federal election, the first two Labour members of Parliament were elected: J. S. Woodsworth, a former Methodist minister and social worker in Winnipeg, and William Irvine, a Unitarian minister in Calgary. Working with a subset of radical Progressive Party members, the Labour members formed a "Ginger Group" in the House of Commons who pushed for progressive reforms. Led by Woodsworth, the Ginger Group created the Co-operative Commonwealth Federation (CCF) in 1932, the forerunner of today's New Democratic Party (NDP).

When Prime Minister William Lyon Mackenzie King was left with a minority government after the 1925 federal election, he met with the Progressive and Labour members of Parliament to learn their price for supporting his government. Woodsworth demanded old age pensions, and Mackenzie King conceded. His government fell anyway, but when his Liberals received a majority in 1926, he kept his promise to Woodsworth.

The Old Age Pensions Act, 1927 was the first foray by the federal government into the provision of a minimum income program. The Act provided federal funds of up to $10 per recipient per month to provinces that were prepared to set up a public pension and match the federal donation. However, this pension had eligibility restrictions. Only Canadian citizens over 70 who had been British subjects for at least 20 years, and who could pass a means test that demonstrated that they had almost no other means of support (the maximum allowable annual income was $365) were eligible. First Nations and Inuit people were ineligible, although Métis people were eligible.

Led by British Columbia in 1927, the five most westerly provinces had all implemented provincial pension programs before the Great Depression started. Québec and the Maritime provinces followed only after the federal government increased its contribution to 75% of the pension in 1931, but these provinces set the pension well below the maximum $20 per month. Like mothers' allowances, Canada's first old age pensions supplied too little income to allow recipients to survive unless they had some other source of income. However, they helped keep many people out of poorhouses and workhouses.

Canadian Prime Ministers 1867–1940

- Sir John Alexander Macdonald (1867–73)
- Alexander Mackenzie (1873–78)
- Sir John Alexander Macdonald (1878–91)
- Sir John Abbott (1891–92)
- Sir John Thompson (1892–94)
- Sir Mackenzie Bowell (1894–96)
- Sir Charles Tupper, 1st Baronet (1896)
- Sir Wilfrid Laurier (1896–1911)
- Sir Robert Laird Borden (1911–20)
- Arthur Meighen (1920–21)
- W. L. Mackenzie King (1921–26)
- Arthur Meighen (1926)
- W. L. Mackenzie King (1926–30)
- Richard Bedford Bennett (1930–35)
- W. L. Mackenzie King (1935–48)

The 1929 Economic Crash

In 1929, the American stock market crashed, and this, along with other economic problems, led to a complete collapse of economies across the world, including in Canada. The Great Depression was a time of economic stagnation, and many people lived in severe poverty. The Prairie provinces were also affected by a widespread drought that left many farmers without crops.

In 1930, R. B. Bennett's Conservatives defeated the Mackenzie King government, promising to spend lavishly on relief. However, Bennett shared the view common at the time that deficit spending would drag down the economy. Protests against government inaction became widespread. In 1932, the government announced that single, homeless, unemployed men would only receive relief if they moved to relief camps under the authority of the Department of National Defence. In the camps, inmates were paid only 20 cents per day for mandatory work such as clearing bush, building roads, and planting trees.

On to Ottawa Trek

In the United States, by contrast, President Franklin D. Roosevelt's New Deal was putting people to work in public works projects. Taking a cue from this program and growing Canadian social unrest, Prime Minister Bennett went on the radio in January 1935 and told Canadians he would bring in his own New Deal, which would include unemployment insurance. The unemployed were not impressed.

The On to Ottawa Trek in June 1935 and the Regina riot on July 1 that brutally ended the trek made Bennett appear more interested in repression than reform. The trek was prompted by the poverty, dismal working conditions, and poor benefits in the unemployment relief camps — and by the federal government's inaction in getting people back to work. Bennett was unwilling to yield to the trekkers' demands that he close the camps and provide either work or compensation equivalent to relief camp wages. He ordered the RCMP to stop the trekkers when they reached Regina.

The trekkers had gained adherents as they moved eastward from Vancouver, and Bennett feared that their numbers would swell when they reached "radical" Winnipeg, home of the country's most famous general strike in 1919. RCMP arrests of trek organizers in Regina on July 1 led to an all-out battle with unarmed trekkers that the armed Mounties eventually won, but not before one man was killed and hundreds were injured. The Mounties then ordered the trekkers to return to their camps, providing transportation to get them there.

The On to Ottawa Trek and the support it gained from Canadians laid the foundation for labour reforms that were introduced in the following years. In August 1940, the federal government instituted a national public system of Unemployment Insurance (now called Employment Insurance [EI]), financed through contributions by employees, employers, and the Government of Canada. The EI program, albeit modified, continues today due to pioneering social activism in 1930s by the Ottawa trekkers and the Canadian labour movement at the time.

Depressions and Recessions

Policymakers and economists typically distinguish between depressions and recessions based on the length and severity of an economic downturn.

There is no clear-cut distinction. A depression is a long period of widespread unemployment, falling prices, and low incomes. If an economic downturn lasts longer than a year, and it is severe, it usually is referred to as a depression.

A persistent lack of confidence in the ability of the economy to provide for its citizens also is associated with what is commonly referred to as a depression.

Employment and Social Insurance Act, 1935

Bennett did get Parliament to pass the 1935 Employment and Social Insurance Act. However, Mackenzie King's government referred the legislation to the courts, which struck it down in 1937 because it represented federal intervention in the broad area of civil rights that the British North America Act reserved for the provinces. Mackenzie King's Liberal government quickly responded by forming the Royal Commission on Dominion–Provincial Relations to inquire whether the division of powers entrenched in 1867 when Canada was a predominantly rural society needed changes. Among its conclusions was that provincial governments should retain responsibility for unemployed people who were unemployable, seniors, single parents, and people with disabilities, and that the federal government should take responsibility for employable people.

By the time World War II had begun, the hardships of the Great Depression remained, and the federal government initiated negotiations with the provinces to expand its powers in relation to unemployment insurance. Mackenzie King was able to obtain the necessary provincial agreement that led to an amendment of the British North America Act in 1940, paving the way for a federal unemployment insurance system.

With the Unemployment Insurance Act, 1940, Canada became the last industrialized country to adopt a contribution-based unemployment insurance program. Yet, at its inception, the program excluded seasonal workers along with most women workers and Indigenous peoples from benefits.

The Great Depression

The Great Depression — beginning on "Black Tuesday" (October 29, 1929) — was a time when Canadians suffered unprecedented levels of unemployment. The unemployment rate was 30% and one in five Canadians depended on relief for their survival.

Changing Perceptions: The Great Depression and Its Aftermath

The Great Depression was so financially devastating that people were shocked into changing long-held beliefs about why people were poor and what the state should do to help out. People began to see that poverty and unemployment were not the results of individual inadequacy or laziness, but common and insurable threats to everyone's livelihood. Public perception of the poor gradually began to shift.

Massive numbers of people were unemployed during the Great Depression. Canadians began to see that this could not possibly be due to individual fault but had more to do with a lack of government policies to correct for the ups and downs of a market economy. As families became destitute and municipalities went broke trying to cope with severe unemployment, the idea that help for the poor should be a local or family responsibility was replaced with the idea that the provincial or federal government should be responsible for providing relief to the unemployed.

The Limits of a Market Economy

Mackenzie King's Liberals remained in power after the 1945 election. Mackenzie King remained a fiscal conservative and made what could be interpreted as a half-hearted attempt to implement his campaign promises. He proposed a comprehensive set of federally funded social programs to the provinces at a federal–provincial conference shortly after his government's re-election. However, though he knew that it was a deal breaker, he proposed that the provinces give the federal government the exclusive right to levy income and corporate taxes. That way, the reasoning went, the federal government would have sufficient funds to finance its new programs and ensure that neither individuals nor companies would be overtaxed.

The provinces, as Mackenzie King expected, indicated that they needed sources of funding to fulfill their own obligations to their voters. However, Mackenzie King, who privately did not want to implement a large number of new social programs, would not budge (Finkel, 2006a). Federal–provincial disputes would continue to plague efforts to achieve social reform in the years that followed, with each side blaming the other for lack of progress.

Supporters of comprehensive social programs tended to be adherents of the ideas of British economist John Maynard Keynes. Keynes's theory provided the foundation for demand management through government spending and other fiscal and monetary policies. While Mackenzie King remained largely unconvinced by Keynes's ideas, the Department of Finance and the Bank of Canada were persuaded that a modest application of Keynes's theory was acceptable for Canada. The government, they believed, could use a combination of tax policy, social programs, and the timing of public works to correct problems inherent in a market economy and to ensure that all citizens received at least a minimally adequate income.

Keynesian Economics

Keynesianism is an approach to economic policy first elaborated by the British economist John Maynard Keynes (1883–1946) during the Great Depression of the 1930s.

Keynesian economics is considered a "demand-side" theory. At the time, Keynes advocated for increased government expenditures and lower taxes to stimulate demand and pull the economy out of the depression.

From a policy standpoint, modern followers of Keynesian economics focus on using active government intervention in order to stimulate and manage "aggregate demand" in order to address or prevent economic downturns.

Social Welfare in Perspective

Democratic Inclusion: Women's Suffrage

First the Vote, Then Access to Elected and Appointed Offices

Non-Indigenous and non-racialized women in Canada first gained the right to vote during World War I. However, to be appointed to a seat in the Senate, women had to first become "persons."

Democratic engagement is one of the indicators in the Canadian Index of Wellbeing. However, it wasn't until 1960 that inclusive suffrage occurred. In the early days of Confederation, elections were tumultuous, and the right to vote was tied to property- or income-based eligibility. The 1885 Electoral Franchise Act identified three conditions common to all provinces for voter eligibility: being a male, 21 or over, and a British subject by birth or naturalization. Then Prime Minister John A. Macdonald had a "profound aversion to universal suffrage, which he considered one of the greatest evils that could befall a country" (Elections Canada, 2020, para. 34). Following Confederation, only First Nations people who renounced their "Indian" status could vote. However, as demographics changed and urbanization and industrialization progressed, the enfranchisement of workers, women, and Indigenous peoples slowly evolved.

When World War I began in 1914, Sir Robert Borden's Conservatives (later known as the Unionist Party) were in power at the federal level. Borden's government was under mounting pressure and in serious trouble as conscription became a central issue. The Military Voters Act (1917) was designed to increase the number of voters favourable to conscription — and the existing government. Also, it extended the vote to "Indian" persons and women in the military (Elections Canada, 2020). A full 2,000 military nurses — known as the "Bluebirds" — became the first Canadian women to vote. Another law, the Wartime Elections Act (1917), increased the number of voters to include "spouses, widows, mothers, sisters and daughters of any persons, male or female, living or dead who were serving or had served in the Canadian forces," provided they met the age, nationality, and residency requirements (Elections Canada, 2020, para. 66).

Statues of The Famous Five in Calgary, Alberta [public domain].

Although the Wartime Elections Act had extended the vote to women connected to the military, the momentum to full women's suffrage was well underway under the activism of Nellie McClung. The government also began to recognize that women had earned the right to vote through their war work. On May 24, 1918, federal suffrage was given to women — however, not all women. Asian women (and men) were not granted suffrage until 1948, Inuit women (and men) were not granted suffrage until 1950, and it was not until 1960 that suffrage in federal elections was extended to status Indians (Courtney, 2007).

In July 1919, enfranchised women gained the right to stand for the House of Commons. Agnes Macphail became the first female member of Parliament in the general election of 1921. However, women from minorities, including Indigenous women, still were not granted the right to run for office in Parliament, and appointment to the Senate remained out of reach for all women until after the Persons case of 1929.

The Persons Case and the "Famous Five"

While non-Indigenous and non-racialized women first gained the right to vote during World War I, they were still not considered "persons" under the law until the "Famous Five" took their case to the Privy Council in England, Canada's highest court at the time.

In 1928, the Supreme Court of Canada had decided that the word "person" in the British North America Act did not include women, and women therefore were not eligible to be appointed to the Canadian Senate. The "Famous Five" — Emily Murphy, Nellie McClung, Irene Parlby, Louise McKinney, and Henrietta Muir Edwards — took their fight to the Privy Council in England.

The Persons case was a ruling by the Privy Council of England in 1929 that reversed the Supreme Court's decision and established the right of women to be appointed to the Senate. The case (officially, *Edwards v. A.G. of Canada*) was presided over by Lord Sankey, who delivered the judgment. In his remarks, he noted: the "exclusion of women from all public offices is a relic of days more barbarous than ours [...] and to those who ask why the word [persons] should include females, the obvious answer is why should it not" (Canada, 2018).

The Persons case was a significant moment in the history of women's rights, even though the struggle for equality continues almost 100 years later.

Women's Right to Vote Provincially

In May 2018, Canada celebrated the 100th anniversary of women winning the right to vote in federal elections. As Prime Minister Justin Trudeau noted at the time, countless women have transformed politics and shaped a better country for all of us. However, he also noted that although social activists and feminists worked hard to win the right to vote and it was a turning point for women's participation in Canadian democracy, not all women benefited from this progress (Trudeau, 2018).

While the federal franchise for the majority of women occurred in 1918, provincial franchise occurred disparately across the country:

1916	Manitoba
1916	Saskatchewan
1916	Alberta
1917	British Columbia
1917	Ontario
1918	Nova Scotia
1918	Canada
1919	New Brunswick
1919	Yukon
1922	Prince Edward Island
1925	Newfoundland and Labrador
1940	Québec
1951	Northwest Territories

Indigenous women covered by the Indian Act could not vote for band councils until 1951, and they could not vote in federal elections until 1960.

It was not until 1960 that all Canadian women finally had the right to vote!

2.3 Phase 3: The Welfare State Period, 1941–1974

The depth of the Great Depression haunted policymakers as World War II endured. Politicians feared that if a recession occurred at the end of the war, ordinary people would revolt. The success of the Co-operative Commonwealth Federation (CCF) in opinion polls and in forming the government of Saskatchewan in 1944, plus militant unionization campaigns, drove home the point that a return to pre-1939 economic and social norms was not feasible.

Though many politicians and business people remained deeply conservative and created organizations to return to prewar values, a consensus was emerging for a coherent package of social policies that would come to be referred to as the "welfare state."

The Era of Social Welfare Program Expansion

After World War II, the notion held that economic growth and social programs could be partner policies rather than enemies. In fact, the redistribution of wealth that socialists proposed could be avoided by simply growing the economic pie and ensuring, via state policies, that shares of the bigger pie remained similar to shares of the previous smaller pie. That would allow those at the bottom of the income scale to achieve a bit more prosperity, but not at the expense of the wealthy. The state's role, then, was not to redistribute existing wealth. Instead, it was to help industry increase overall wealth and ensure that the tendency of unregulated markets to create ever greater wealth inequality was checked by government programs.

Thus, the welfare state became the successor to the warfare state, in which the Canadian government had become the largest employer and created large Crown corporations to deal with both military and domestic needs. Much of the population had hoped to see the wartime economic model applied in peacetime.

By 1971, social programs had reached a point where they touched the lives of most Canadians. However, major business and professional interests fought the implementation of many of these programs, including universal medicare and the Canada Pension Plan/Québec Pension Plan (CPP/QPP). Before the 1970s, most Canadians rejected the arguments of these special interests as the product of greed and old-fashioned ideological thinking. By the mid-1970s, many changes affected Canada: inflation and unemployment grew, oil prices went up, and the global economy changed. As government revenues were in a downward spiral, sophisticated campaigns railed against universal social programs and promoted a resumption of Poor Law ideology.

By simply looking through a list of social welfare programs, one can see how important this period was in establishing the Canadian welfare state. Total expenditures on social welfare, health care, and education grew from 4% of gross domestic product (GDP) in 1946 to 15% of GDP by 1976 (Moscovitch & Albert, 1987).

The Family Allowance

The first piece of social welfare legislation in the postwar period was the Family Allowance Act, 1944 (which came into effect in 1945). It was the first federal universal (i.e., not means tested) income security program in Canada. When it was first introduced, considerable debate took place over the desirability of a universal program.

The goals of this important piece of legislation were to maintain purchasing power when the war ended and demonstrate the government's commitment to the upcoming generation. The legislation also fit in with the government's efforts to send Canadian women, whom the government had encouraged to work during the war because of labour shortages, back home. Both economic and social conservative motives were at work here. The government was skeptical that work could be found for all who wanted it and hoped to ensure one job per household by excluding married women from most employment. Also, it believed that the traditional model of households in which women were dependent on men was worth preserving. Interestingly, the Family Allowance made a concession to married women who were going to lose their jobs after the war. It would be delivered in their names rather than those of their husbands, giving them some money in the household over which they alone could exercise discretion.

The Child Care Tax Benefit (CCTB), introduced in 1989 as a means-tested supplement to the Family Allowance for low-income and middle-income families, would replace the universal Family Allowance.

The Baby Bonus

In 1944, the Family Allowance was instituted. Beginning in 1945, the "Baby Bonus," as it came to be known, went to all families with children regardless of income. Over time, the benefit became geared to middle and low-income families. In 1993, the"Baby Bonus" was eliminated entirely.

Photo: The Government of Canada issued the first Family Allowance cheques to Canadian mothers on February 20, 1945.

EXPAND OUR CPP NOW!
AFTER A LIFETIME OF WORK RETIREMENT SECURITY for everyone
Retirement Security for Everyone!

Old Age Pensions and the CPP/QPP

In 1951, an amendment was made to the British North America Act to allow the federal government to operate a pension plan. Subsequently, the federal government passed the Old Age Security Act of 1951, which provided a pension (or demogrant) of $40 per month to Canadians beginning at the age of 70 (Guest, 1980). Pension payments, which began in 1952, were taxable. This universal program was extended to First Nations people, repealing the exclusion from the previous 1927 legislation.

At the same time, the Old Age Security Act of 1951 provided a means-tested benefit of $40 per month for those aged 65 to 69. This program was cost shared 50–50 by the federal and provincial governments. However, it was administered by provincial welfare departments who used a means test to determine eligibility. This residual program was viewed by the elderly as personally invasive and stigmatizing (Guest, 1980).

The Canada Pension Plan (1965) and Québec Pension Plan (1966) ("CPP" and "QPP," respectively) provided a wage-related supplement to Old Age Security and were the first programs to be indexed to inflation, or the cost of living allowance (COLA). The CPP/QPP provided wide coverage and advanced the concept of a social minimum.

The Canada Assistance Plan

The Canada Assistance Plan (1966), or "CAP," was instrumental in standardizing and funding income and social assistance across the country and was in effect between 1966 and 1996. This program was the consolidation of federal–provincial programs based on means tests or needs tests. Half the costs of all shareable items were assumed by the federal government, provided that a needs test was given. Assistance was possible for the working poor and was one aspect of the federal plan to eliminate poverty (Guest, 1980).

The historical debate concerning "fact of need" versus "cause of need" peaked when the CAP was introduced. The CAP was unequivocally a residual program intended to simply meet needs, regardless of the cause of need. While the adequacy of the assistance rates continued to be of great concern, the CAP introduced the idea that people had the right to appeal decisions (Guest, 1980).

The CAP was the basis for cost sharing, not only for income security programs but also for a wide range of social services and programs that included health care services, children's services, social assistance, disability allowances, old age assistance, services for the elderly, and institutional care. This program was the cornerstone of Canada's social service funding until 1996, when it was replaced by the Canada Health and Social Transfer.

The Canada Health and Social Transfer (CHST) was a system of block transfers from the federal to the provincial governments that was in place from the 1996 until 2004. In 2004, the CHST was split into the Canada Health Transfer (CHT) and Canada Social Transfer (CST).

The Fiscal Transfers

As with the CHST, its two successors (CHT and CST) are block transfers to the provinces to pay for health care and post-secondary education and welfare.

Cash transfers, as the name implies, consist of money transferred directly from the federal government to the provinces. In addition, because both the federal and provincial governments collect personal and corporate income tax, tax transfers involve the federal government reducing federal income tax rates, thereby allowing room for the provinces to increase their own rates.

The exact amount of transfer payments from the federal to the provincial governments is a matter of ongoing and often heated federal–provincial disputes, particularly in the area of health care funding.

Canadian Medicare

In the United States, public Medicare is essentially restricted to those who are elderly. By contrast, in Canada all citizens and permanent residents have access to high-quality medical services across the country, even when they travel or move from province to province.

The struggle for Canadian medicare was long and fractious. The devastation caused by the Great Depression was the spark. The first raucous steps toward public health care happened under the leadership of Tommy Douglas in Saskatchewan in 1947. Lester B. Pearson's government finally expanded this policy to universal health care with the Medical Care Act of 1966. The Canada Health Act (1984) amalgamated the 1966 Medical Care Act and the 1957 Hospital Insurance and Diagnostic Services Act. Today, there are 13 provincial and territorial plans, all funded through fiscal transfers and monitored by the federal government under the Canada Health Act.

Health care frequently tops public opinion polls as the main political concern for Canadians. Today's key issues include waiting lists, access to medical specialists, access to high-tech diagnostic equipment, privatization, and two-tier care. However, quality of care is not usually an issue. For most Canadians, public health care remains the defining characteristic of a caring society.

While Canadian medicare is not without limitations, it is held up as a model and has even figured prominently in political debates in the United States over single-payer, public health care. It remains to be seen whether the United States will follow the Canadian medicare example, or some variation of it.

Combatting Poverty

By pretty well any measure, Canada was a prosperous country at the end of the 1960s. Nevertheless, government reports of the time estimated one in five Canadians were living in poverty with close to 2 million people in 1967 considered "working poor" (Guest, 1980).

Notions of the causes and definitions of poverty were evolving in the late 1960s. The Senate appointed a Special Committee that held hearings across the country. The resulting 1971 Report of the Special Senate Committee on Poverty (known widely as the Croll Report), is considered a landmark report because it brought poverty out of the shadows (Senate of Canada, 2008).

The study of poverty in the 1960s and early 1970s revealed the extent of income inequality in Canada: that is, between the bottom fifth and top fifth of families on the income scale; from one province to another; between regions within a province; between rural and urban areas; between genders; and from one race to another (Guest, 1980).

Dissatisfaction with existing social security programs increased as numerous government reports highlighted systemic and structural inequities, particularly for vulnerable populations (such as Indigenous people, older adults, women, and lone mothers). The increased spending on social security programs (a growth of over

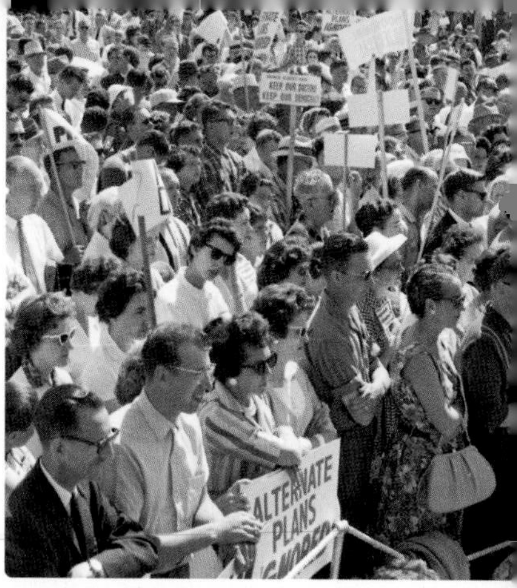

Socialized Medicine

Medicare was born in Saskatchewan on July 1, 1962. It would be the first government-controlled, universal, comprehensive medical insurance plan in North America. But it was a difficult birth.

The North American medical establishment and the entire insurance industry were determined to stop Medicare in its tracks. They feared it would become popular and spread, and they were right. Saskatchewan doctors went on strike.

Nevertheless, a compromise was reached and within 10 years all of Canada was covered by a medical insurance system based on the Saskatchewan plan, and no serious politician would openly oppose it.

Adapted from Brown, L. & Taylor, D. (2012, July 3). The birth of Medicare. From Saskatchewan's breakthrough to Canada-wide coverage. *Canadian DImension.*

$3.8 million in 1963 to over $11.2 million in 1972) was seen as out of hand because it was not eliminating poverty or even alleviating it (Guest, 1980). The prevailing view was to curb costs and to devise a method of funnelling the maximum number of welfare dollars to those in greatest need. Essentially, what was emerging was an attack on the principle of universality — and in effect a resurgence of the residual concept in social welfare policy (Guest, 1980).

The Social Security Review

In 1973, the federal government initiated a federal–provincial review of Canada's entire social security system. A Working Paper on Social Security in Canada was issued by minister of national health and welfare Marc Lalonde to provide a framework for the review. The report listed five strategies the government believed would create a better, more integrated system of social security:

- **Community Employment Strategy.** This strategy focused on improving both the job skills and the labour market for people with continuing difficulty in finding and holding employment.
- **Social Insurance Strategy.** Social insurance programs (i.e., CPP/QPP, EI, and workers' compensation) would be increased as a first line of defence against loss of income due to unemployment, sickness, or work accident. This strategy was also meant to improve the situation of people in retirement.
- **Income Support and Supplementation Strategy.** This strategy focused on meeting inadequacies of income through a guaranteed income for the working poor and those outside the labour force.
- **Social and Employment Services Strategy.** This strategy would make available a variety of employment assistance services such as counselling, rehabilitation, homemaking, and child care services to help people secure a foothold in the labour market.
- **Federal–Provincial Jurisdictional Strategy.** To address the provincial demands for autonomy and flexibility in tailoring programs to particular needs, this strategy focused on greater federal–provincial harmonization in the delivery of income and social supports (Guest, 1980; Johnson, 1975).

The social security review was born out of federal–provincial discord about shared-cost agreements and responsibilities for the nation's social security system (Johnson, 1975). It represented an attempt to establish a new social minimum income, particularly for the working poor. It was largely unsuccessful "primarily because conventional wisdom dictated that increases in social security spending must come from economic growth." (Guest, 1980, p. 204). However, it did contain proposals that led to a new Family Allowances Act in 1973 that increased the benefit per child as well as amendments to retirement benefits (CPP/QPP, OAS) that indexed these benefits to the consumer price index (Guest, 1980; Johnson, 1975).

Canadian Prime Ministers 1941–1974

- W. L. Mackenzie King (1935–48)
- Louis Saint Laurent (1948–57)
- John G. Diefenbaker (1957–63),
- Lester B. Pearson (1963–68).
- Pierre Elliott Trudeau, (1968–79)

Social Welfare in Perspective

The Beveridge and Marsh Reports

The Need for Universal Social Welfare

The Beveridge Report (Britain) and the Marsh Report (Canada), both released in 1943, established the baseline for the rapid expansion of universal social welfare.

Sir William Beveridge wrote a comprehensive report on postwar social security for Britain (called the Beveridge Report). It included recommendations for comprehensive health insurance and income security. This crucial report was followed by a Canadian equivalent, written by Dr. Leonard Marsh (pictured on the next page).

Marsh was born in England and attended the London School of Economics, graduating in 1928. After completing his schooling, Marsh studied wages and housing and spent some time conducting research for Sir William Beveridge. Marsh was also heavily influenced by the ideas of the British economist John Maynard Keynes.

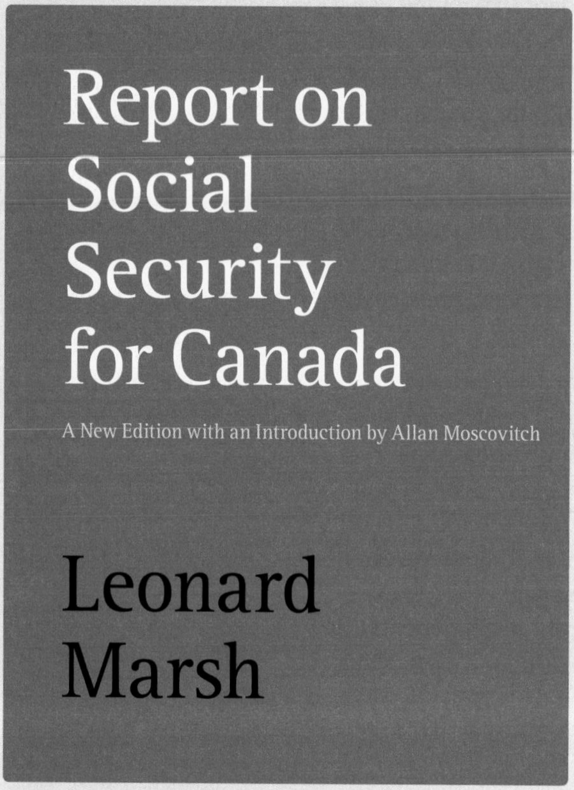

Report on Social Security for Canada
A New Edition with an Introduction by Allan Moscovitch
Leonard Marsh

Report on Social Security for Canada

In 1930, Marsh moved to Canada, where he had accepted the position of director of social research at McGill University. While at McGill, Marsh published several books on the state of employment in Canada.

In 1940, Marsh became the research director for the Committee on Post-War Reconstruction, and it was in this position that he would write his Report on Social Security for Canada, commonly known as the Marsh Report.

The report was written in just one month and received extensive media attention. In it, Marsh detailed the need for comprehensive and universal social welfare programs. His report sparked debate over universal income security benefits versus targeted income security benefits.

The report was presented to the committee for which Marsh was working and to the federal government, which at that time was led by William Lyon Mackenzie King. It was largely ignored at the time. However, many now consider the Marsh Report to be the most important report in the history of the Canadian social welfare state.

Marsh suggested that the country should establish a "social minimum" — a standard aimed at protecting the disadvantaged through policies such as social insurance and children's allowances. Despite initially being largely ignored, by 1966, most of his recommendations had become law.

Marsh's work served as the blueprint for the Canadian social welfare system. Marsh himself viewed his report as the natural outgrowth of the decade of social studies he had directed at McGill University.

The Beginning of a New Era for Social Welfare

In his report, Marsh established the concept of a desirable living minimum income. He went on to outline proposals that meet the principal types of contingencies that characterize industrial society, coining the three categories of contingencies that are still used today to describe social welfare.

Marsh proposed a two-pronged system of social insurance to cover both employment risks and universal risks: the first covered wage earners, and the second covered all persons for old age, disability, and death. He also proposed children's allowances and health insurance. Finally, he emphasized the importance of training and placement programs to help people, especially youth, prepare for employment.

The report made headline news as the media spoke about the proposed social spending of billions of dollars. People sensed the beginning of a new era in which they would have medical insurance coverage and protection from unemployment.

These were new ideas to most people, and they sparked debate about what this would mean for Canadian society. While some stressed the positive impacts on citizenship and responsibility for one another, others spoke of the onset of communism. Some social workers at the time, such as Charlotte Whitton, spoke negatively about the idea of social insurance. She advocated for social assistance, in which trained social workers supervised and counselled people needing assistance.

After writing the Marsh Report, Leonard Marsh would go on to work for the League for Social Reconstruction, act as a welfare adviser to the United Nations Relief and Rehabilitation Administration, and spend 25 years at the University of British Columbia's School of Social Work. Leonard Marsh retired and was named professor emeritus in 1972. Leonard Marsh died in 1983.

Sir William Beveridge, British Government [Public domain]

Leonard Marsh, City of Vancouver Archives

2.4 Phase 4: The Rise of Neoliberalism, 1975–2005

By the late 1970s the economic boom of the postwar decades was running out of steam. After-tax corporate profits were beginning to erode, and the rates of economic growth were slowing down. Conservative thinking at the time attributed the crisis in capitalism to alleged years of government overspending on social programs (Finkel, 2006b). By the 1980s, neoliberal ideas had taken hold in all of Canada's major federal and provincial political parties (Finkel, 2006b).

During this neoliberal period, the corporate sector placed a great deal of pressure on governments everywhere. They called for both fiscal (expenditures/taxes) policy and monetary (financial/money) policy to emphasize belt-tightening. In their view, Keynesian fiscal policy, with its focus on government spending, gave too little incentive to the private sector to address market issues. The corporate community in Canada was united by the late 1970s in demanding a reduced state presence and lower taxes, and they seemed to encounter a labour force that was less organized, or less prepared, to respond to these demands.

Pierre Trudeau's Liberal government (1968–1979 and 1980–1984) followed tight monetary policies after 1975 that ran counter to Keynes's prescription for expanding the money supply during periods of recession. It also made a number of cuts to social programs.

Canadian Prime Ministers 1975–2005

- Pierre Elliott Trudeau (1968–79)
- Joe Clark (1979–80)
- Pierre Elliott Trudeau (1980–84)
- John Turner (1984)
- Brian Mulroney (1984–93)
- Kim Campbell (1993)
- Jean Chrétien (1993–2003)
- Paul Martin (2003–06)

The Mulroney Years

Still bigger changes in social policy would take place during the prime ministership of Progressive Conservative Brian Mulroney, from 1984 to 1993.

During the 1980s, both the United Kingdom (Margaret Thatcher, 1979–1990) and the United States (Ronald Reagan, 1981–1989) had elected governments committed to rolling back the welfare state. However, Canada had a much more muted approach to reducing social expenditures than either Britain or the United States. Mulroney recognized that Canadians were not yet prepared to follow the American and British examples, so he focused his 1984 election appeal on a denunciation of Liberal cronyism rather than Liberal economic and social policies. He called Canada's social programs a "sacred trust" that he felt sworn to uphold. He even joined the leaders of both the Liberals and the NDP in promising a national daycare program. However, the ink was barely dry on the ballots before he attempted to reduce the value of old age pensions; although this was quickly retracted in the face of an unexpectedly militant response from seniors.

In the late 1980s, the Tories in Britain cut taxes and refused to reduce a budgetary surplus to increase the level of funding for social programs. By contrast, the Tories in Canada continued to run a large budgetary deficit and raised taxes to continue to fund federal social expenditures (Smardon, 1995). While certain areas of the federal welfare state were cut back and transfer payments to the provinces were eroded, Canada did not take the approach of privatizing major social programs or implementing wholesale market-oriented changes to existing programs that Britain and the US undertook (Smardon, 1995).

Free Trade and Its Aftermath

"Globalization" became a buzzword for neoliberal ideologues who believed that free markets, not governments, could be counted on to dispense economic justice (Finkel, 2006b). The Canada–United States Free Trade Agreement (CUSFTA) was the centrepiece of the Mulroney government's re-election bid in 1988, and it was implemented early in 1989. Supporters argued that protection of local industries kept alive uncompetitive firms while deterring the establishment of firms with a global reach. Opponents of free trade argued that it would worsen the problems Canada already faced from runaway firms looking for the cheapest place to operate and would result in downward pressures not only on wages but on social programs.

Mulroney denied a connection between social programs and free trade. However, once he had won the election, he argued that Canadians could not compete internationally if they taxed corporations and wealthy individuals too much.

In 1993, Jean Chrétien's Liberals had campaigned on a promise to renegotiate CUSFTA. After his Liberal government (1993–2003) was elected, it replaced CUSFTA with the North American Free Trade Agreement (NAFTA) in 1994. NAFTA resulted in the elimination or reduction of barriers to trade and investment between the United States, Canada, and Mexico. It also affected issues such as employment and the environment. In 2018, over 20 years later, NAFTA was replaced by a new Canada–United States–Mexico Agreement (CUSMA) during Donald Trump's US presidency.

NAFTA

NAFTA eliminated tariffs on more than half of the exports from Mexico to the US and Canada.

Photo: Union members with Unifor protest outside the sixth round of negotiations in Montréal on the revisions to the North American Free Trade Agreement in January 2018. NAFTA was subsequently replaced with the Canada–United States–Mexico Agreement (CUSMA).

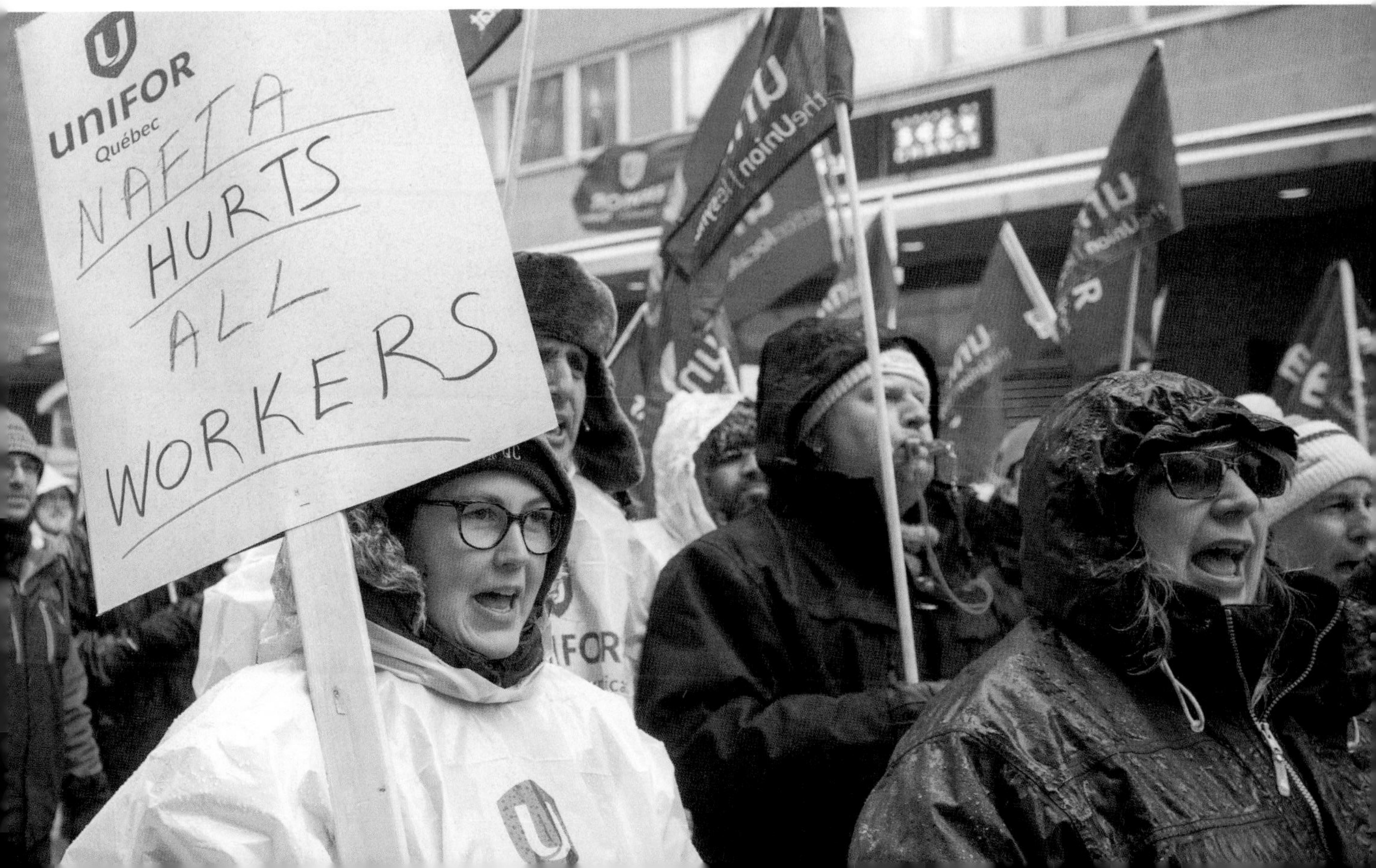

Neoliberal Social Program "Stealth" Cuts

While no federal party was interested in an extensive privatization or the market-oriented restructuring of social programs, the funding of existing programs became more selective throughout the late 1980s and early 1990s. In 1986, the Mulroney government began to cut transfer payments for health care and post-secondary education. By the 1990s, family allowances, the CAP, and federal financial support for social housing had all disappeared (Finkel, 2006b). Two-tiered medical care, in which some services could be purchased outside the public sector, had made some gains. In addition, "the percentage of unemployed people eligible to collect unemployment insurance had been eroded to levels unseen since the early 1950s" (Finkel, 2006b, p. 285). In the 1989 federal budget, the universality of old age pensions and family allowances was reduced through taxing the benefits back (Smardon, 1995).

The Child Care Tax Benefit (CCTB), introduced in 1989 as a means-tested supplement to the Family Allowance for low-income and middle-income families, would replace the universal Family Allowance. Daycare disappeared from the public agenda after the 1988 election (Finkel, 2006b).

In general, the Mulroney years were characterized by a significant retreat in government spending on social programs and income supports. "By the end of the Mulroney years in 1993, federal social spending accounted for 8.5 percent of the GDP, a decline from 10.5 percent in 1984" (Finkel, 2006b, p. 291).

"Starve the beast"

"Starving the beast" is a strategy minted by US conservatives under President Ronald Reagan. The idea was to deprive the government of revenue, largely by cutting taxes, thereby forcing the government to reduce spending on social programs.

The Liberals' Return to Power, 1993–2006

Paradoxically, the continued high deficits and debts caused a significant group of Progressive Conservatives to feel that the Mulroney government was insufficiently conservative. They formed a new party called the "Reform Party," which pledged to cut social programming far faster and to cut taxation at the same time, all while reducing deficits and debts. The Reform Party spoke about "starving the beast" (i.e., the welfare state) by depriving it of revenues and insisting on it breaking even. While the strength of the Reform Party helped reduce the once mighty Progressive Conservatives to a mere two seats in the 1993 federal election, the major benefactors of the split on the right were the federal Liberals, led by Jean Chrétien.

Yet, during their first term (1993–1997), the Chrétien Liberals were at least as neoliberal in their economic policies as their Tory predecessors. They continued to cut transfers to the provinces, refused to reverse the Mulroney government's decision to gut family allowances, and eliminated the CAP. Monies that had gone to the CAP for social assistance were combined with funds for medicare and post-secondary education and then shrunk to create the Canada Health and Social Transfer (CHST), which was implemented in 1996. Though the provinces would be receiving less money overall, their compensation was that the federal government would not tell them how to spend it. Notions of universality and federally supervised standards simply went out the window. Unlike under CAP, there was no mechanism for dealing with provinces that decided to exclude groups and individuals whom they wished to label as having caused their own poverty.

Federal funding for low-income housing, ended by the Mulroney government, was not revived by the Chrétien government. The Chrétien government renamed "Unemployment Insurance" as "Employment Insurance (EI)" in 1996. It also went well beyond the Mulroney government in toughening eligibility requirements for EI. While 96% of the unemployed were eligible to collect from the insurance program after the Trudeau reforms of 1971 and 85% were still eligible in 1989, only 41% of the unemployed were eligible to collect by 1997 (Finkel, 2006b). Those who did collect EI saw their rates reduced. However, EI premiums did not decrease, and the government used money from the program for retraining programs, which could have been funded from general revenues.

All of this cost-cutting predictably left low-income Canadians more vulnerable to falling into poverty. The national poverty levels had reduced from 27% in 1961 to 15.4% in 1975. However, following the recessions of 1982–1984 and 1990–1993, the rate of low-income families climbed to almost 20% (Finkel, 2006b). The economic boom in the late 1990s allowed the rate to drop to 16.2% in 1999. More and more, the vulnerable in Canadian society would be dependent on the ups and downs of a precarious economy rather than on social guarantees from the federal and provincial governments.

Growing Inequality

Government leaders who insisted on neoliberal policies claimed that they had no option. Canada, they claimed, was pricing itself out of world markets because of its allegedly Cadillac social services. Yet the numbers did not support this claim. Social expenditures as a percentage of GDP in 2000 were as follows: Canada, 17.3%; United Kingdom, 21.3%; France, 28.3%. The percentage point change in social expenditure as a percentage of GDP from 1990 to 2000 was as follows: Canada, −1.3%; United Kingdom, +1.8%; and France, +1.7% (Canadian Council on Social Development, 2005, p. 13).

For Canadians, the shortfall from the state's previous level of social involvement would result in a growing income gap between the wealthiest and the poorest. Income inequality measures how income is distributed. In the 1990s, income inequality was particularly evident, with the income share for the top 20% of the population jumping from 36.5% in 1990 to 39.1% in 2000 (Conference Board of Canada, 2011). During the same period of time, between 1989 and 1998, real average incomes among the poorest group fell by an average of 2.2% per year, due in part to the fact that average transfers from government fell over that period (Conference Board of Canada, 2011).

After making huge cuts to social programs in its first term, the Chrétien government, presiding over an economy that was on the upturn once again, was able to turn the former deficits into annual budget surpluses. However, apart from reinvesting in health care, it proved unwilling either to refinance social programs that had been cut or to introduce new programs. Instead, its focus was on tax cuts. During their bid for re-election in 2000, the Liberals campaigned on a program of income and corporate tax cuts that favoured the wealthy. In so doing, they knocked the sails out of the campaign of the latest installment of the Reform Party.

2.5 Phase 5: Retrenchment and Recovery, 2006+

The Liberals' success as a centrist party had been fuelled from 1993 onward by the split between the Reform Party and the Progressive Conservatives. In 2003, these two parties fused to form the Conservative Party of Canada, and in 2004 chose Stephen Harper, the former leader of the Canadian Alliance, as the leader of the merged party. By the fall of 2005, the NDP, whose support was rising in the polls, tired of supporting the Liberals. All three opposition parties voted against the Liberal government in a confidence vote, and an election was set for January 2006.

Canadian Prime Ministers 2006-

- Stephen Harper (2006–15)
- Justin Trudeau (2015–)

The Conservative Government of Stephen Harper

From 2006 until 2011, Stephen Harper led minority governments. The federal election in May 2011 gave Harper a parliamentary majority. During his years in power, there was a steady acceleration in cutbacks of social programs that were in place to limit the inequalities and social dangers that a marketplace economy creates. The Harper government's general orientation to decision making was to avoid consultation and democratic accountability (between elections) and to centralize power in the hands of the Prime Minister's Office (Healy & Trew, 2015).

The Harper government made deep cuts to government revenue, arguing that individual consumers and investors can make better decisions in almost every area of spending than governments. In the 2006 federal budget, 29 separate tax cuts were introduced, including lowering the Goods and Services Tax (GST) to 6% (Government of Canada, 2006). According to estimates by the Parliamentary Budget Office, tax cuts implemented by the Harper government from 2005 to 2013 resulted in a total revenue loss of $43.5 billion (Brooks & McQuaig, 2015). According to Brooks and McQuaig (2015), this meant that the federal government had $43.5 billion less to deal with the following:

> issues such as rising health care and post-secondary education costs, funding for early childhood education, education in First Nations communities, poverty reduction, replacement of decaying infrastructure, meat and railway inspectors, affordable housing, improving water supply and so on. (para. 5)

To a large degree, the government's philosophy was to "starve the beast"; that is, to cut taxes to the point where governments could argue that they simply lacked the revenues to fund major social programs. The cutbacks in program spending and rising family and child poverty levels angered many Canadians — those who relied on income assistance and those who did not. In the 2011 federal budget, conservative fiscal polices returned to an austerity agenda, dropping federal program spending by 16% in 2009–2010 and by a further 12.9% in 2015–2016 (Healy & Trew, 2015).

Like many leading political parties of the pre–World War II period, the Conservatives believed that the marketplace, left alone, would distribute goods and services to those who worked for them and motivate those who did not work hard or smart enough to do better. The Conservative government after 2006, and especially after 2011 when it gained a majority, took this philosophy to heart.

- **Indigenous Policies**

Indigenous peoples face significant earning and income disparities. In 2000, for example, more than half (55.6%) of urban Indigenous people lived below the poverty line (National Collaborating Centre for Aboriginal Health, 2009–2010). In 2005, at a meeting in Kelowna, British Columbia, a series of agreements between the federal government, provincial premiers, territorial leaders, and the leaders of five national Indigenous organizations was made to close the gap. These agreements, known as the Kelowna Accord, sought to improve the education, employment, and living conditions of Indigenous peoples through governmental funding and other programs. Although the accord was endorsed by Paul Martin's Liberal government, the Harper Conservatives did not proceed with it.

Meanwhile, programs for Indigenous peoples continued to be piecemeal and underfunded. More and more First Nations' reserves were unable to provide basic human services. While government reports suggest that about $3 billion needed to be spent to create parity between First Nations schools and provincial schools, the Harper government in 2012 committed only $275 million over a three-year period (Senate of Canada, 2012). Similarly, while federal reports suggested that $490 million per year needed to be spent over a 10-year period to provide clean water on reserves, the federal government committed only $165 million per year for two years in its 2011–2012 federal budget.

At the same time, the Harper government closed down the National Aboriginal Health Organization — whose task was to advise the government on culturally sensitive ways of delivering health programs — to save $5 million (Picard, 2012). It also terminated the Métis Health Funding Program.

- **Pension Reform**

In the 2012 federal budget, the age of eligibility for Old Age Security and the Guaranteed Income Supplement was raised from 65 to 67, to be implemented in 2023. The government argued that because Canadians were living longer and having fewer children, providing funding guarantees to all or most of them when they turned 65 would become prohibitive. These claims were challenged. However, the Harper government, having decided to reduce taxes on corporations and the wealthy and continue to cut taxes, had developed a notion of "sustainability" that required compressions in most social programs. The Trudeau government reverted the retirement age to 65 in 2016.

The Harper government also announced plans to cut the pensions of federal workers, partly by forcing them to pay a larger share toward their pensions. It also intended to impose "defined contribution" plans in which pensioners' earnings would be determined by the market value of the investments that the pension fund had made. Such plans would replace existing "defined benefit" plans in which the pensioner was guaranteed a fixed annual return. Efforts by the unions and the NDP to double CPP deductions, and thereby fund a doubling in CPP payments, were rejected. The Harper government's view was that individuals should make their own private arrangements to ensure that they had enough in retirement.

Stephen Harper

Stephen Harper was Canada's prime minister from 2006–2015. Harper succeeded in uniting the divided conservative movement at the time into the Conservative Party of Canada and then led it to three election victories.

Harper's tenure was not without controversy. His government's sweeping cutbacks affected programs and services in nearly every aspect of Canadian life. Harper's strict adherence to a brand of ideologically pure conservatism resulted in what the *Globe and Mail* called "Canada's first ever truly Conservative government."

However, during his time in office, Harper also apologized to Chinese Canadians for Canada's "head tax" and the subsequent exclusion of Chinese immigrants. He officially recognized the Québécois as a "nation" within Canada and offered an emotional apology to Indigenous people for the federal government's role in residential schools.

- **Employment Insurance**

During the recession of 2008–2009, the Harper government reluctantly agreed to the demands from the other parties in Parliament to extend EI benefits for about 190,000 recipients facing a cut-off of their benefits. However, with a majority in hand after the 2011 election, the Conservatives decided to limit expenditures on EI while forcing more workers to leave their home regions to seek employment in regions with labour scarcities. The 2012–2013 federal budget stated:

> Along with providing relevant and timely job information, the Government will introduce legislation to strengthen and clarify what is required of claimants who are receiving regular EI benefits and are looking for work. In the coming months, the Minister of Human Resources and Skills Development will announce fair and transparent guidelines for compliance, which take into account local labour market conditions and an individual's past history with the EI program. (Canada, 2012, p. 146)

The four Atlantic premiers quickly denounced what appeared to be a thinly veiled attack on seasonal workers unable to find work in their areas during the winter months. The concern was that they might pull up stakes altogether and leave many industries without a labour force. At the same time, the Employment Insurance Board of Referees, whose role was to hear people's EI decision appeals, was disbanded. It was replaced with a smaller Social Security Tribunal, which would hear appeals from CPP and OAS claimants as well. The Harper government's focus on cutting costs dominated its agenda not only on EI policy but also on immigration policy.

- **Immigration Policy**

With respect to immigration policy, the Harper government made aligning immigration with labour market needs a higher priority than family reunification. It also gave immigration priority to wealthy individuals who could invest in Canada over skilled tradespeople and professionals.

In addition, the government seemed to want to focus more on temporary foreign workers rather than landed immigrants with a chance of becoming citizens. The Temporary Foreign Worker Program allowed employers to bring in needed workers for jobs that Canadians allegedly could not fill. Between 1984 and 2012, the number of temporary foreign workers had more than tripled: from 65,000 in 1984 to 100,000 in 1998 and 213,000 in 2012 (McQuillan, 2013). While these workers do not have the right to remain in Canada permanently, it is becoming easier for them to apply for permanent residency.

The Harper government also made refugee admission much more difficult. Under the guise of reducing fraud, it introduced preadmission mandatory detention of so-called irregular arrivals. It also no longer permitted refugees access to health services while awaiting adjudication of their application (Lenard, 2015). Similarly, approved refugees lost access to supplementary coverage (e.g., medication, vision care, and dental care) that had been in place since the 1950s.

- **Environmental Programs**

The Harper government's cuts to environmental programs demonstrated its overall philosophy of government intervention in the economy when it benefited industry. In April 2012, Bill C-38 substantively changed federal environmental law. Sometimes referred to as the Conservatives' "war on science," Bill C-38 "stripped away environmental protections and cut funding at research institutes around the country" (Zhang, 2017, para. 2). For example:

- Funding cuts ended the Community Pasture Program, which managed more than 1 million acres of Prairie grasslands to help stop soil erosion, provide habitats for endangered species, and enable sustainable grazing.
- Funding was cut for the federal tree farm at Indian Head, which for 80 years had been growing millions of trees for Prairie farmers to use as windbreaks to keep topsoil from blowing away.
- Funding was severely reduced for Health Canada's Pest Management Regulatory Agency, which regulates things like neonicotinoid pesticides.
- Funding cuts to the Department of Fisheries and Oceans resulted in the end of the Habitat Management Program, which monitored the effects of harmful industrial, agricultural, and land-development activities on wild fish.
- The Polar Environment Atmospheric Research Laboratory in Nunavut, which monitored atmospheric data and the Arctic ozone hole, was closed.
- The Hazardous Materials Information Review Commission, which oversaw fracking firms, was eliminated (Nelson, 2013).

Environmental Cuts

In the 2011–2012 federal budget, Environment Canada's spending was cut by $222.2 million, which led to the elimination of 1,211 jobs (full-time equivalents) over the next three years. Some of the biggest cuts were in the areas of climate change, clean air, and water resources (Council of Canadians, 2011).

- **Federal Downloading to the Provinces**

Social welfare services are a tangle of federal, provincial, and territorial initiatives. In many cases, the provinces and territories depend on federal funding to implement local programs. Yet, after 2006 and beyond, the Harper government's program cuts affected the services that Canadians could expect from not only the federal government but also the provincial and territorial governments.

The Harper government's vision for federal–provincial relations has been described as "open federalism," meaning that much social and economic policy was a matter for provincial governments to deal with. The Harper Conservatives included using "every opportunity to displace public health care as a unifying national symbol and defined it instead as strictly a provincial matter" (Healy & Trew, 2015, p. 9). "In December 2011, the Harper government announced a major cut to the Canada Health Transfer (CHT) of $36 billion over 10 years beginning in 2017" (Newitt & Silnicki, 2015, p. 258). When the equalization portion of the CHT was eliminated in 2014, transfers were reduced by another $16.5 billion over five years (Newitt & Silnicki, 2015).

These decisions effectively shifted more federal debt to the provinces. They left the provinces to pick up the growing tab for health care expenditures and absolved the federal government of its ability to maintain its role as a guardian of national standards (Newitt & Silnicki, 2015).

Figure 2.1

A Political Map of Canada

In a number of important social policy areas, federal downloading to the provinces and territories jeopardized their ability to provide key services.

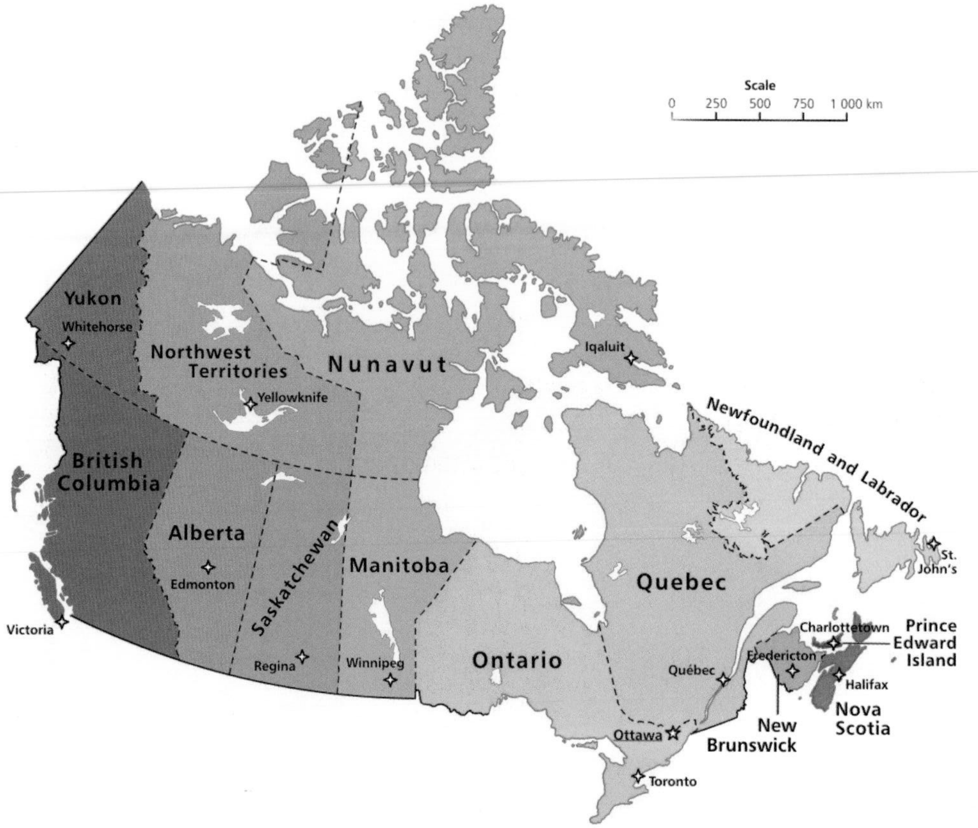

Wikipedia Creative Commons [public domain]

The First Liberal Government of Justin Trudeau, 2015–2019

After 1975, there was a marked erosion of the redistribution of wealth that Canadians had experienced during the welfare state period. The Conference Board of Canada (2020) reported most of the gains between 1976 and 2009 had gone to a very small group of "super rich," and that those gains were huge. The share of income earned by the richest 1% of Canadians had almost doubled during this period: from 7% to almost 14% (Campbell, 2011). In 2009, the average compensation of the top 100 CEOs was $6.6 million — 155 times the average worker's wage. The 61 Canadian billionaires that existed at the time were worth $162 billion in total, which was twice as much as the bottom 17 million Canadians (Campbell, 2011).

The idea of the welfare state era, however, was not totally dead. The election of the NDP as the official opposition in the federal election of 2011 suggested that many Canadians remained unconvinced by neoliberal arguments. In 2015, the federal Liberal Party interrupted the Conservative Party's reign of almost a decade with a stunning electoral victory. In his post-election victory speech, Justin Trudeau said, "I will be the prime minister of all Canadians. ... We beat fear with hope. We beat cynicism with hard work. We beat negative, divisive politics with a positive vision that brings Canadians together" (*CBC News*, 2015).

The Harper government had become known for being "tight-lipped" and secretive. Indeed, it was awarded the "Code of Silence Award" in 2018 by the Canadian Association of Journalists for the government's lockdown on information and for Harper's avoidance of news conferences and media questions (Hayward, 2012). Unlike his predecessor, Justin Trudeau argued for a more open, collaborative, and evidence-based government. Trudeau promised to scrap Harper's brand of politics, give more freedom to bureaucrats, and make himself and Cabinet ministers more accessible to journalists and the public (Bryden, 2014).

In policy matters, the new Liberal government expressed a desire to work to relieve family and child poverty, help support families with expanded parental leave and child care, address widespread mental health concerns, combat sexism and racism, help immigrants settle and succeed, redress long-standing injustices toward Indigenous peoples, help improve the lives of seniors and persons with disabilities, and combat climate change.

In the 2015 election campaign, many Canadians saw in Trudeau the chance of much-needed change for the better.

- **The Promise of Change**

The Liberals set an ambitious social reform agenda, marking a distinct break with the style of governing and social policies associated with the previous Conservative government under Stephen Harper. At the time of the 2019 election, its achievements included the following:

- **Reinstatement of Long-Form Census.** Citing a commitment to evidence-based policies as one of its first steps, the Liberals restored the mandatory long-form census (after former Prime Minister Stephen Harper had eliminated it in 2010). The reinstatement was heralded as a win for informed decision making and representation of the diversity in Canada (Aiello, 2019).
- **Appointment of First Gender-Balanced Cabinet.** In 2015, Trudeau presented the first ever gender-balanced federal Cabinet — 15 men and 15 women. As a self-identified feminist, Trudeau "moved to legislate pay equity in the federal sector, made the national anthem gender-neutral, enshrined in law protections for transgender people, and required gender-based analysis to be conducted on major policies" (Aiello, 2019). Although his commitment has come under question during his mandate, many of the changes made for gender equity may be hard for future governments to walk back.
- **Legalization of Marijuana.** The recreational use, possession, and sale of marijuana became legal on October 17, 2018. This places Canada as the world's largest country with legal cannabis sales. Legalization was complex and not without its critics, and there is a mixed bag of systems for each province. The legalization of edibles took place in winter 2019 (Aiello, 2019).
- **Resettlement of More Refugees Than Any Other Country in 2018.** With the infamous #Welcome to Canada tweet, a central focus of the four years of Trudeau government was immigration, with Canada resettling more refugees than any other country in 2018 (Aiello, 2019).
- **Prioritization of Climate Change.** Under the first Trudeau government, Catherine McKenna was named as the Minister of Environment and Climate Change — the first time climate change had been noted in a Cabinet title. Since then, the government has secured a pan-Canadian agreement on emissions and rolled out a carbon tax. The government also put money toward low-carbon infrastructure, protected more marine and coastal areas, and passed law to overhaul environmental assessment processes (Aiello, 2019).
- **Reconciliation with Indigenous Peoples.** Trudeau pledged to build a new relationship with Indigenous peoples. In the government's first four years, Indigenous leaders and policy experts say the prominence of reconciliation brought some positive changes, but also halting progress and disappointment. The National Inquiry into Missing and Murdered Indigenous Women and Girls was launched. Funding for Indigenous health care services, children's programs, and housing was increased by $21.4 billion over the four years. The Liberals also increased annual education funding for Indigenous children, funded an Inuit suicide prevention strategy, and started to tackle unsafe water supplies (Ballingall, 2019).

- **The Liberals' Return to Power with a Minority Government, 2019**

While, for many, the reforms of the first Liberal government of Justin Trudeau were too slow and piecemeal, there was a desire on the government's part to be more collaborative and inclusive. By contrast with the Conservatives, the Liberals' emphasis was on modernizing the policy activities of government, stripping away unnecessary bureaucracy, and collaborating across silos (Wernick, 2016). In 2019, Wernick's fourth report on the Public Service of Canada noted the Trudeau government's commitment to community engagement through inviting more voices to the table (Wernick, 2019). In 2019, the government launched a National Action Plan on Open Government.

However, the slow pace of change was frustrating for many Canadians. In the fall 2019 federal election, rather than opt for the Conservative Party led by Andrew Scheer, Canadian voters gave Trudeau's Liberals a second chance — but only barely. This time, the number of Liberal members of Parliament was drastically reduced (especially in Québec), and the new Liberal minority government would need to rely on tactical alliances with the NDP and the Green Party.

Challenges that were foreseeable for 2020 and beyond included implementing equity for Indigenous peoples through meaningful truth and reconciliation processes, maintaining climate and environmental agendas consistent with a land-locked oil and gas industry and federal government ownership of oil pipelines, developing trade agreements amid Trump's policies and Brexit changes, and reducing social and income inequities and uniting a divided country.

Pride Parade

Events like Pride parades are opportunities for political leaders to stand up for human rights and for communities that are marginalized.

Photo: The 35th Toronto Pride Parade in 2015 along Bloor and Yonge Streets.

2.6 Phase 6: COVID Times

Pandemics change everything. In the winter of 2019–2020, SARS-CoV-2, the novel coronavirus (COVID–19), hit Canada. In a few short months, little strands of RNA and DNA, otherwise inert, changed many aspects of socio-economic well-being in Canada and around the world. The impacts of COVID–19 will likely be long lasting and likely will change how social welfare is envisioned in Canada and around the world for some time to come.

Between March and early summer of 2020, provincial governments, working closely with federal leaders, locked down Canadian society in an effort to get the coronavirus under control. To the politicians' credit, they allowed health professionals to take the public health lead while they introduced income security programs as well as financial supports to businesses to mitigate the economic effects. The measures they took were largely successful in containing the worst economic outcomes over the spring and summer, but COVID–19 exposed deep-seated inequalities in Canadian society. Those most affected by COVID–19, including those who died from it, were the vulnerable to begin with — the working poor, racial minorities, immigrant workers, and especially older Canadians living in poorly staffed and poorly regulated care homes.

Containing the spread of the virus and getting the economy back on track necessitated addressing these underlying injustices, and that meant pouring resources into shoring up an already weakened welfare state.

Expanding Social Welfare

On April 1, 2020, Prime Minister Justin Trudeau, in his daily briefing to the country, announced a series of economic programs to augment the public health measures. He equated the government's approach to the welfare state measures implemented 80 years previously. In part, he stated:

> Canada hasn't seen this type of civic mobilization since the Second World War. These are the biggest economic measures in our lifetimes to defeat a threat to our health. These historic measures will support Canadians to stay home to defeat COVID–19. But the government alone cannot win this fight. We all have to answer the call of duty. This is service that most of us have never been called upon to do.
>
> We, each of us, have to live up to our end of the bargain. We must fulfill our collective responsibility to each other. Listening to public health rules is your duty. Staying home is your way to serve. So be smart about what you do, about the choices you make. That is how you will serve your country and how we will all serve each other. (Trudeau, 2020)

The federal government rapidly rolled out a series of measures that included emergency financial assistance, wage subsidies, increases to the Canada Child Benefit, mortgage payment deferrals, direct grants to businesses, and money to the provinces to top up pay for health care workers (Beattie, 2020). A parallel was drawn to the emergence of the welfare state itself in the immediate post–World War II period when there was a dramatic expansion of social programs in response to widespread risk and pervasive uncertainty (Sandher & Kleider, 2020).

Photo: A STM bus passenger wearing a mask during COVID–19 pandemic, Montréal, QC, May 2020.

A Perfect Storm — A Health Crisis, an Economic Crisis, and a Social Crisis

It was clear early on that there was a health crisis and an economic crisis, and that the two were intertwined. Containing the virus and getting the economy on track necessitated addressing both and that meant pouring financial resources into shoring up the health care system to meet the crisis and, at the same time, providing economic relief to Canadians.

Countries like Canada that had welfare state institutions in place, including a strong public health system, fared better in managing the fallout from COVID–19 than did countries with a more individualistic orientation (Hadas, 2020). However, by the time the pandemic hit, Canada's welfare state had been seriously eroded due to neoliberal economic thinking that began in the 1970s. The Mulroney government of 1980s, followed by the Chrétien government of the 1990s, had systemically cut federal spending through the reorganization of health and social transfers to the provinces (Marx, 2020).

This legacy of underfunding the welfare state (e.g., fewer hospital beds, lack of access to employment insurance and other social supports, and lack of social housing) exposed persistent inequalities across the country that surfaced during the COVID–19 pandemic (Marx, 2020). As a result, in addition to the health and economic crisis, there was an underlying social crisis. The burden of COVID–19 was being shouldered by Canadians who were already marginalized through, among other things, income inequality, ethnic discrimination, homelessness, Indigenous identity, and racism.

Black Lives Matter

The social crisis expressed itself most forcibly as a racial crisis. On May 25, 2020, George Floyd, a 46-year-old Black American, died in Minneapolis, Minnesota, while a white police officer knelt on his neck. The officer was later charged with second-degree murder and three other officers were charged with aiding and abetting. Around the world, massive protests under the umbrella of Black Lives Matter called for action against police brutality and systemic anti-Black racism.

While Canadian identity and values purport to be anti-racist, our history belies this mythology. Inequalities for non-white Canadians have existed since colonization, continued during the welfare state era, and persist today. Systemic racism and racial discrimination are part of Canada's contemporary history (O'Neill, 2020). Canada is perceived as having lower levels of racial discrimination but, since Canada does not collect race-based data on COVID–19 cases, this conclusion is not evidence based.

Certainly, there is evidence to the contrary. Patrick Denice and a research team, based at Western University assessed how racial and socio-economic factors shaped COVID–19 infection and death rates (Choi et al., 2020). They report that Black and immigrant communities are disproportionately affected. A one percent increase in the share of Black residents in a health region is associated with the doubling of infection rates. Their analysis underscores the need to include Black and immigrant groups in COVID–19 management plans.

Upirngasaq (Arctic Spring)

"Let's not wait for another virus, driven by climate change and environmental degradation, to terrify us, too late, into half-hearted action. There is no time for half measures. The values and knowledge of the Indigenous world, the survival of which utterly depends upon living within nature, not apart from nature, hold the answer to many of the global challenges we face today. Indigenous wisdom is the medicine we seek in healing our planet and creating a sustainable world. I truly believe this."

Watt-Cloutier, S. (2020). Upirngasaq (Arctic Spring). *Granta, Essays & Memoir*, Issue 153.

Sheila Watt-Cloutier is an Inuit activist and the author of *The Right to Be Cold*. She has been nominated for the Nobel Peace Prize and has received the UN Champion of the Earth Award, the Sophie Prize, the Jack P. Blaney Award for Dialogue and the Right Livelihood Award.

Photo: A Black Lives Matter protest in Montréal, QC, during the COVID–19 pandemic (May 31, 2020).

Combatting Systemic Inequality

A central question that remains is whether Canadian political leaders are willing and able to make the major investments that are necessary to overcome the social and economic fallout from the COVID–19 pandemic, restore a sense of security and confidence for ordinary citizens, and put in place public health measures that would prevent a similar crisis occurring in the future (Beattie, 2020).

For many social activists and some politicians this response must mean expanded social programs — such as universal pharmacare, paid sick leave, and more investments in public health, hospitals, and medical equipment. Arguments for funding such things as a nationwide child care program, introducing a universal basic income for all Canadians, and bringing long-term senior care facilities under the oversight of the Canada Health Act are discussions that are already moving into mainstream discourse (Beattie, 2020).

These are the kinds of social welfare programs that are urgently needed to address the health crisis, end income inequality, and support racialized and Indigenous communities across the country.

If anything, the COVID–19 pandemic has exposed the impossibility of a healthy economy without a healthy society. The main responsibility for advancing an agenda to overhaul and build a functioning social welfare system falls on the federal and provincial governments. Whether the mainstream political parties and their leaders are up to the task remains to be seen.

Social Welfare Policy in Action

Canada's Environmental Policy

A Pan-Canadian Framework

Environmental social work is founded on environmental justice principles that acknowledge the importance of access to safe and clean environments.

Integrating environmental justice principles into the social work discourse is increasingly important. This requires including the natural environment (both human and non-human) as a consideration in both social work policy and practice.

The International Federation of Social Workers clearly indicated that "protecting and improving the physical environment is intrinsic to improving the circumstances and well-being of everybody, including those living on the margins" (Truell & Jones, 2018). Of particular concern is that structural inequalities and environmental injustice leave some people disproportionately affected and more vulnerable to air and water pollution, and to greater impacts from natural disasters (Shajahan & Sharma, 2018).

Social workers advocating for social justice play a key role in addressing environmental justice to assist humanity through having a sustainable planetary ecosystem (Ramsay & Boddy, 2016).

Highlights of Canada's Environmental Movement

Canada's environmental movement began in the early 1900s with a focus on the conservation of natural resources. One of the oldest pieces of legislation in Canada is the Fisheries Act, which was enacted in 1868 to address the protection and conservation of fish and fish habitat. In 1917, the first international conservation act, the Migratory Birds Convention Act, was implemented to protect most species of birds in Canada.

By the 1960s, concerns moved beyond using resources wisely to concern about the effects of human activity on the environment. The focus on air and water pollution, hazardous waste, and pesticides led to the founding of Greenpeace in 1971, in Vancouver.

During the 1970s, environmentalists focused on major energy projects (e.g., the James Bay Project and the Mackenzie Valley Pipeline) and their impacts on the environment and Indigenous communities (Hummel, 2016).

Environmentalism in the late twentieth century continued to focus on issues of global concern. For example, the Canadian Coalition on Acid Rain (1981–1991) helped obtain agreements between Canada and the United States to reduce sulphur dioxide and nitrogen oxide emissions (Hummel, 2016). The Canadian Environmental Protection Act was enacted in 1999.

Also during this period, gains were made through multiparty agreements. For example, in 2006, the Great Bear Rainforest Agreement was signed by multiple First Nations groups and the BC government, laying out measures to protect the forest through sustainable logging practices.

The Green Party emerged in 1983, and since 2004 has run candidates in every federal riding (Hummel, 2016).

By the turn of the century, climate change had emerged as an overarching global and national concern. In 2002, under the Chrétien government, Canada ratified the Kyoto Protocol, an agreement to reduce greenhouse gas emissions. The Harper government enacted the Clean Air Act in 2006. However, in 2011, it withdrew from the Kyoto Protocol.

In 2015, Justin Trudeau made climate change a focus. In 2016, he signed the Paris Agreement, which outlines ways the international community will reduce global warming to 1.5°C above preindustrial levels. At the same time, "Environment Canada" was renamed "Environment and Climate Change Canada."

Pan-Canadian Framework on Clean Growth and Climate Change

In 2016, the Pan-Canadian Framework on Clean Growth and Climate Change (Canada, 2016) was developed. This framework was developed with working groups consulting with the public, businesses, and civil society across the country through interactive websites, in-person engagement sessions, and independent town halls. Indigenous peoples' representatives made recommendations to the working groups or to First Ministers directly.

A summary of some key points are included here.

- **The Vision**

According to the report:

> The Pan-Canadian Framework on Clean Growth and Climate Change presented here is our collective plan to grow our economy while reducing emissions and building resilience to adapt to a changing climate. It will help us transition to a strong, diverse and competitive economy; foster job creation, with new technologies and exports; and provide a healthy environment for our children and grandchildren. (Canada, 2016, p. 5)

- **The Framework's Pillars**
  - **Pricing Carbon Pollution.** This is an efficient way to reduce emissions, drive innovation, and encourage people and businesses to pollute less.
  - **Complementary Measures to Further Reduce Emissions across the Economy.** They include tightening energy efficiency standards and codes for vehicles and building and helping consumers save money by using less energy.
  - **Measures to Adapt to the Impacts of Climate Change and Build Resilience.** They include measures to adapt and build resilience to ensure that communities are adequately prepared for climate risks such as floods, wildfires, and extreme weather events.
  - **Actions to Accelerate Innovation, Support Clean Technology, and Create Jobs.** The focus is on being a global leader in clean technology innovation.

- **Protecting and Improving Health and Well-Being**

Climate change is increasingly affecting the health and well-being of Canadians (e.g., extreme heat, air pollution, allergens, Lyme disease, and food security). Indigenous peoples and northern and remote communities are particularly vulnerable. Section 4.3 of the framework report addresses climate change–related health risks and supporting healthy Indigenous communities.

- **Accountability**

The effectiveness of the plan will be assessed regularly (e.g., reducing greenhouse-gas [GHG] emissions). Performance will be reported publicly, through ongoing public outreach, including with youth and in accordance with international reporting obligations.

- **Budget 2019**

In the 2019 budget, the federal government committed $3 billion to support clean technology; $1.01 billion for energy- and cost-saving upgrades to buildings, including affordable housing developments; and $28.7 billion for the development and expansion of modern, reliable public transit.

Questions for Reflection

The Pan-Canadian Framework on Clean Growth and Climate Change is readily available online. Once you have reviewed the framework, answer the following questions:

1. According to the report, what social problem is being addressed?
2. How is climate change linked to social welfare and social well-being?
3. Which political ideology and social work approach are apparent in this framework?
4. Does the framework reflect inclusion, equity, and social justice?
5. Is it clear how this framework is to be implemented in the provinces and territories?
6. What mechanisms are in place to evaluate the success of the framework?

A Moment in Time: December 7, 1970

Royal Commission on the Status of Women

Ushering in an Era of Positive Change

The 1970 report of the Royal Commission on the Status of Women in Canada was a rallying point for women's rights in Canada.

The Royal Commission on the Status of Women in Canada was established in 1967 by the then Liberal government of Lester B. Pearson.

The postwar economic boom had resulted in a growing number of women choosing post-secondary education and paid employment over traditional roles. Women were also highlighting their double burden as income earners who continued to shoulder responsibility for caring work in the home.

Public hearings were held for more than six months, beginning in 1968. The Commission reviewed some 468 briefs and over 1,000 letters of testimony. Three years later, on December 7, 1970, the report was tabled. "The commission's 488-page report contained 167 recommendations to the federal government on such issues as pay equity, the establishment of a maternity leave program and national child care policy, birth control and abortion rights, family law reform, education and women's access to managerial positions, part-time work and alimony. A large section also addressed issues specific to Aboriginal women and the Indian Act" (Morris, 2006).

The Status of Women Canada

In 1971, the federal government established the Office of the Co-ordinator, Status of Women and the position of Minister Responsible for the Status of Women. In 2018, Status of Women Canada became a federal department, named Women and Gender Equality Canada (WAGE), which continues to promote gender equality and works to advance women's and girls' participation in Canadian life.

The commission did not fully address all issues of concern at the time. For example, it was criticized for not focusing on violence against women or on gay and transgender issues. Nevertheless, the Royal Commission on the Status of Women in Canada was a catalyst for social change. Notably, it helped to enshrine two important provisions on women's rights in the Constitution Act, 1982 — Sections 15 (equality rights) and 28 (gender equality).

Photo: Members of the Royal Commission on the Status of Women (The Bird Commission): left to right, John Peters Humphrey, Lola M. Lange, Jeanne Lapointe, Florence Bird, Jacques Henripin, Doris Ogilvie, and Elsie Gregory MacGill. Reproduced from: Virtual Museum.ca.

Chapter Review

Questions

1. What are the six phases in the history of social welfare in Canada? Map out these phases in a timeline, and include a list of the major developments in each period.
2. What were the main ideas behind the Elizabethan Poor Law? To what extent are they still prevalent today?
3. The economic crash of 1929 ushered in the Great Depression. Describe the effects of this period on the lives of Canadians at the time and on social welfare developments during and after the war.
4. There was a massive expansion of the welfare state after World War II. What were some of the programs that were generally considered successful during this period?
5. The period after 1974 began to see the dismantling of the welfare state. Draw up a timeline of historic developments during this phase.
6. As we enter the 2020s, how would you describe the welfare state in Canada?

Exploring Social Welfare

1. Many social welfare programs are premised on underlying ideas about why people become vulnerable and how they can best be helped. Select a social welfare program (e.g., Employment Insurance, the Canada Child Benefit, Old Age Security) and critically examine the underlying ideas of that program.
2. How are environmental justice and social well-being linked? Describe an example of environmental social work in your jurisdiction and its outcome.

Websites

Canadian Centre for Policy Alternatives

www.policyalternatives.ca

Founded in 1980, the Canadian Centre for Policy Alternatives is an independent, nonpartisan research institute concerned with issues of social, economic, and environmental justice. Focusing on public engagement, their findings are disseminated widely through research reports, fact sheets, infographics, and interactive multimedia.

Health Canada

www.hc-sc.gc.ca

Health Canada is the federal department responsible for helping Canadians maintain and improve their health, while respecting individual choices and circumstances. The Health Canada website provides information about the working of the department itself, a vast amount of information relevant to healthy living for Canadians, and information about legislation and commissions of inquiries.

Statistics Canada

www.statcan.gc.ca

Statistics Canada is the national statistical office. It produces statistics that help Canadians better understand their country — its population, resources, economy, society, and culture. In addition to conducting a census every five years, it conducts about 350 active surveys on virtually all aspects of Canadian life. Providing statistics is a federal responsibility. As Canada's central statistical agency, Statistics Canada is legislated to serve this function for the whole of Canada and each of the provinces and territories.

Policies and Programs

"Annual income twenty pounds, annual expenditure nineteen six, result happiness. Annual income twenty pounds, annual expenditure twenty pounds ought and six, result misery."

– Charles Dickens, *David Copperfield*

Investing in an Inclusive Labour Market

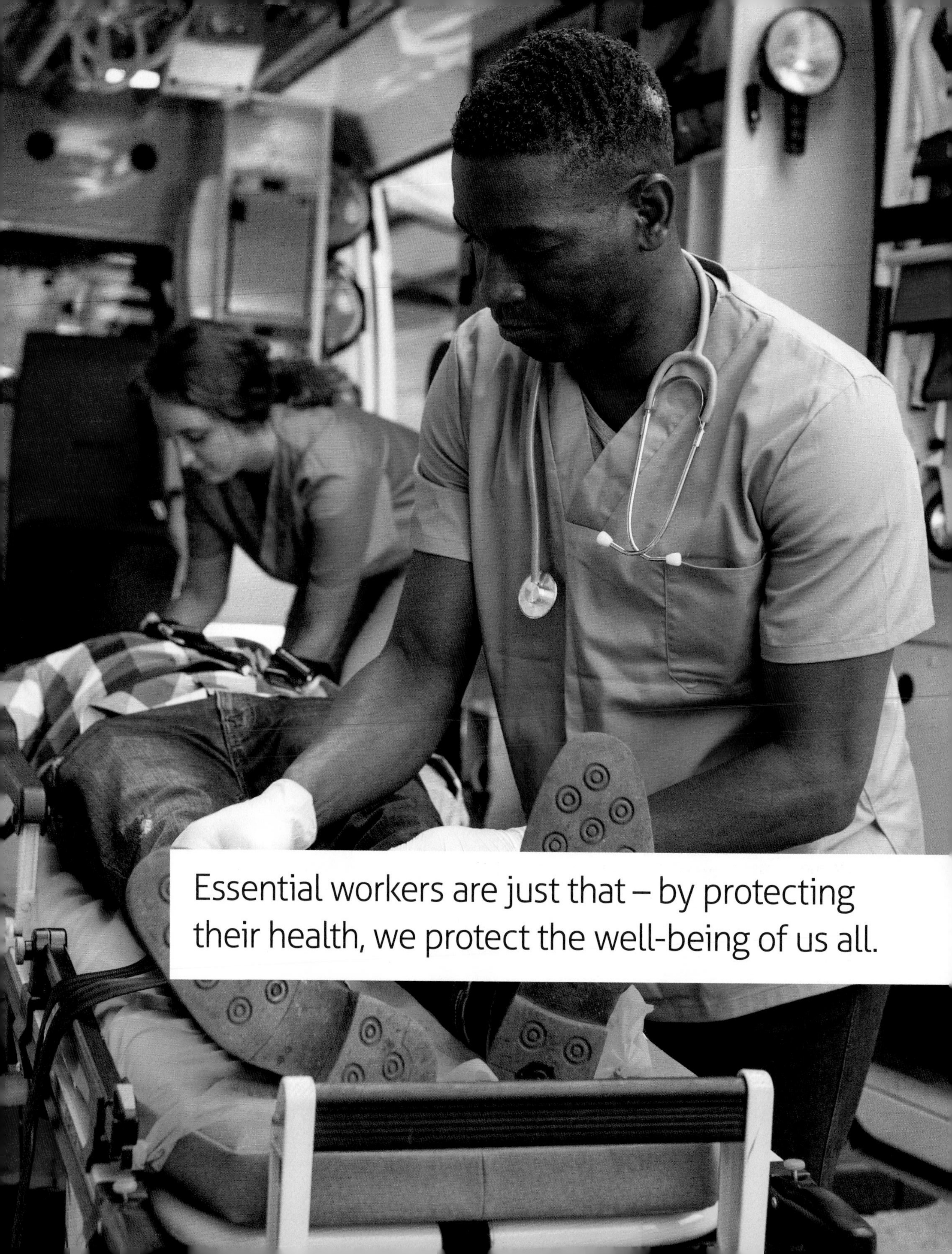

Essential workers are just that – by protecting their health, we protect the well-being of us all.

Many difficult social problems can be attributed to the repercussions of employment, underemployment, and low wages. Without a good job, a person faces the prospect of declining socio-economic status and, likely, personal distress. Being unemployed or underemployed is associated with poorer overall health and personal well-being.

Traditionally, policymakers have approached labour market policy from the point of view of minimizing economic risks, such as the loss of earnings associated with unemployment or injury on the job. More recently, policymakers have come to realize that this approach may not be proactive enough. Today, a social investment approach to the labour market and human resource development is also needed to foster greater social inclusion for vulnerable populations and to reduce overall social inequality.

Investing in an Inclusive Labour Market

This chapter examines the Canadian labour market in its broadest sense. It focuses on the need for policymaking that strengthens employment and income equality. As well, it addresses how the changing labour market enhances the personal well-being of all people in Canada.

After completing this chapter, you should be able to:

- Understand the impact and importance of Canada's labour market policies and programs;
- Appreciate the extent and depth of income inequality in Canada today;
- Describe the growth of precarious work in Canada;
- Define "underemployment" and the "working poor";
- Explain the state of youth unemployment in Canada;
- Describe the history of Employment Insurance and workers' compensation in Canada;
- Describe policies that can help health and social care professionals reduce workplace stress and minimize the risk of harassment and violence;
- Explain the emphasis and impact of a social investment approach to the labour market; and
- Describe the significance of the federal Pay Equity Act of 2018.

Key Concepts

- Inclusive labour market strategies
- Intersectional inequalities
- Racialized income inequality
- Precarious work
- Underemployment
- Working poor
- NEET generation
- Labour force participation rate (LFP)
- Unemployment rate (ER)
- Employment rate (EPR)
- Employment Insurance (EI)
- Workers' compensation
- Fellow servant rule
- Meredith principles
- Workplace health and safety

3.1 Canada's Changing Labour Market

Over the last 50 years, fundamental changes have occurred in the workplace. Computer-based technologies have helped automate workplaces. Globalization and the economic emergence of countries such as China and India have increased the volume of international trade and reshaped entire industries. The percentage of workers employed in unionized jobs, manufacturing jobs, or jobs covered by employer-sponsored pension plans has fallen dramatically. At the same time, Canadian workers have more formal education than ever before and are ready to take on the many challenges in front of them.

One of the most important changes to the Canadian labour market has been the increased labour force participation of women. In the early 1950s, about 25% of women aged 25 to 54 participated in the labour market. By 1990, their participation rate rose to 76%, and by 2014 their participation rate rose to 82% (with women making up 47% of the Canadian workforce) (Statistics Canada, 2018a).

Two additional recent trends are affecting the labour market. The first is the long-expected and unprecedented transition of baby boomers (those born between 1946 and 1964) from work to retirement. The second is the slow but steady return (before COVID-19) of the economy to full employment after the "Great Recession" of 2008 and 2009. Meeting large-scale labour market challenges such as these will require insight and foresight.

Responding to Labour Market Trends

Many problems of productivity and economic growth are deep seated and require radical economic and social policy solutions. In the last decade or so, governments have recognized that a different approach to labour market policy is required to respond to changing labour market conditions. For example, many governments in the European Union now approach social policy, economic policy, and employment policy not separately but as interrelated and mutually reinforcing.

Inclusive labour market strategies seek to address the shortcomings of the labour market, particularly as they affect racialized and marginalized people. They also seek to ensure that everyone of working age in Canada is part of the collective pursuit of economic and social development and that no one is left behind.

Inclusive labour market strategies go beyond welfare-to-work models and seek to expand "human capital" — that is, the knowledge, experience, and skills of workers. Such strategies focus on achieving labour market goals and stimulating economic growth based on the principles of inclusion, equity, and social justice (Perkins, 2010). The welfare and well-being of people are at the centre of these strategies.

Policies for a Changing Labour Market

Along these lines, Cliff Halliwell, a policy analyst and former director general of policy research at Human Resources and Skills Development Canada, has recommended a number of policy ideas to strengthen Canada's labour market over the coming years:

- Strengthening and formalizing the "second-chance" system to help Canadians upgrade their education or skills, or get better jobs over their careers
- Limiting temporary foreign worker programs to jobs that are truly temporary
- Reducing immigrant intake during recessions, and increasing investments in settlement supports to enhance the language and occupational skills of newcomers
- Modernizing labour market measures to discourage the frequent use of Employment Insurance, better support the needs of long-tenured workers, and more effectively target the skills development and training needs of the unemployed
- Improving labour market information and increasing the flexibility of post-secondary education so that students can more effectively select fields of study and have better access to trades, apprenticeships and occupations in demand (Halliwell, 2013, p. 1)

These and other policy ideas are aimed at addressing some of the current deeper-rooted problems in the Canadian labour market.

Economic Growth and Income Inequality

A major obstacle to economic growth in high- and middle-income countries is the extent of income and earnings inequality (Brückner & Lederman, 2015). The 1980s was a time of reduced income inequality in Canada. However, income and wealth inequality began to worsen in the 1990s. This mirrored trends across Organisation for Economic Co-operation and Development (OECD) countries, in which "the average income of the richest 10% of the population is about nine times that of the poorest 10%" (Organisation for Economic Co-operation and Development [OECD], 2015, para. 1). As a result of increasing income inequality, the standard of living of middle-income households has stagnated or declined. The OECD notes that a strong middle class is crucial for the economy for these reasons:

> The middle class sustains consumption, it drives much of the investment in education, health and housing and it plays a key role in supporting social protection systems through its tax contributions. Societies with a strong middle class have lower crime rates, they enjoy higher levels of trust and life satisfaction, as well as greater political stability and good governance. (OECD, 2019, p. 3)

Income inequality has risen in Canada because the number of higher-income earners has grown more rapidly than lower-income earners (Fang & Gunderson, 2019). Some groups are more vulnerable than others to income inequality and poverty. For example, Indigenous people, recent immigrants, and people with disabilities are more likely to experience **intersectional inequalities** and be poor (Government of Canada, 2016).

Per Capita Income as a Measure of Economic Well-Being

Per capita income, measured by gross domestic product (GDP) per capita, is often used to compare economic standing across countries and across population groups. It is an average measure — the total income of the country or population divided by the total population. In June 2019, Canada's GDP per capita reached US$45,410 (about C$62,780) (CEIC Data, 2019).

In terms of per capita income, Canada ranks well behind other OECD countries, such as Norway and the United States, although it stands ahead of the United Kingdom and Japan. According to the Conference Board of Canada (2019), the best way to increase the average per capita income is to boost productivity. That means fostering innovation, investing in machinery and equipment, and attracting foreign direct investment.

One has to be cautious about treating per capita income as a measure of quality of life. Economic growth alone does not translate into well-being (see Chapter 1). A social investment approach to the labour market emphasizes health and well-being, educational attainment, lifelong learning, and workplace training, which boost productivity and therefore average (per capita) income.

A measure of average income does not tell the whole story either, since averages are affected by high and low points. The median household income may be a more robust measure for income distribution, as it is not affected by high and low outliers.

Intersectionality

Writing for the minority in *Canada (A.G.) v. Mossop*, Madam Justice L'Heureux-Dubé of the Supreme Court of Canada remarked that "categories of discrimination may overlap, and that individuals may suffer historical exclusion on the basis of both race and gender, age and physical handicap or some other combination."

"Discrimination may be experienced on many grounds, and where this is the case, it is not really meaningful to assert that it is one or the other. It may be more realistic to recognize that both forms of discrimination may be present and intersect."

Madam Justice L'Heureux-Dubé. *Canada (A.G.) v. Mossop*, [1993] 1 S.C.R. 554 at 645–646.

Median and Mean Incomes as a Measure of Income Inequality in Canada

For an accurate assessment of income equality in Canada, both median income and mean (average) income should be considered. Median income is the point on the income distribution spectrum where half of the population earns more and half earns less. If the median and the mean are the same, then there is relative equality in income distribution. On the other hand, if mean (average) income is higher than median income, then the distribution of income is unequal (Manitoba Collaborative Data Portal, 2018).

According to Statistics Canada (2019b), in 2017 the average individual income in Canada was $46,700, compared with the median income of $35,000 (indicating that half of the population made less than $35,000). These numbers suggest that personal income in Canada is distributed highly unevenly. High-income earners skew the average income numbers upward.

This conclusion is supported by the data in Figure 3.1, which shows that income inequality in Canada is both deep and persistent. In 2017, the top 20% (the highest quintile) of income earners held 49% of household wealth, down only very slightly from about 50% in 2010 (Statistics Canada, 2018a). According to Statistics Canada (2018a), "wealth for households in the highest income quintile is 2.5 times higher than the overall average. The top 20% of income earners had a net worth of $1.8 million per household in 2017, compared with about $214,000 for the bottom 20%" (para. 2).

Figure 3.1

Distribution of Household Wealth by Disposable Income Quintile, 2010 and 2017

Statistics Canada (2018a). Distributions of household economic accounts for income, consumption, saving and wealth of Canadian households, 2017. *The Daily* (March 22). CANSIM Table 378–0310.

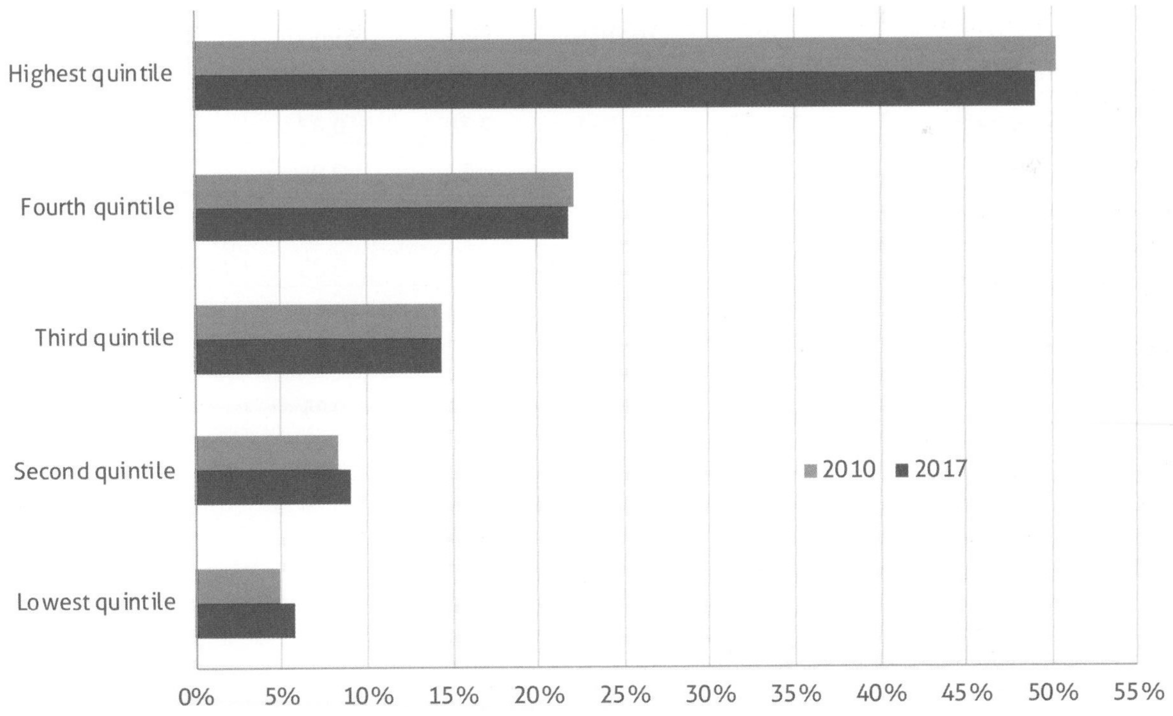

Social Welfare in Perspective

Colour-Coded Income Inequality

Racialized Discrimination in Employment and Income

Almost one-quarter of Canadians experience persistent racial discrimination in the labour market. Far-reaching anti-racism policies are needed to address this deep-seated inequality.

"The 2016 census counted 7.7 million racialized individuals in Canada. That number represented 22% of the population, up sharply from 16% just a decade earlier" (Block et al., 2019, p. 4). According to the report *Canada's Colour Coded Income Inequality* by Block, Galabuzi, and Tranjan (2019), the growth in the racialized population is not being matched by a corresponding increase in economic equality.

Labour Force Participation

The labour force participation rate measures the share of the population that is employed or actively seeking work. Racialized workers are more likely to be active in the labour force than non-racialized workers (66.5% versus 64.8%), and this is true for both men and women. However, despite high participation rates, racialized persons have a higher unemployment rate than their non-racialized peers.

Overall, in 2016, the racialized population had an unemployment rate of 9.2%, while the non-racialized population had a rate of 7.3%. Racialized women had the highest unemployment rate (9.6%), followed by racialized men (8.8%), non-racialized men (8.2%), and non-racialized women (6.4%).

Employment Income by Racialized Group in Canada, 2015

	Average Employment Income		Earnings Gap: Same Gender		Earnings Gap: Non-Racialized Men
	Men	Women	Men	Women	Women
Non-racialized	**56,920**	**38,247**	**1.00**	**1.00**	**0.67**
All racialized groups	**44,423**	**33,304**	**0.78**	**0.87**	**0.59**
South Asian	46,974	32,336	0.83	0.85	0.57
Chinese	49,470	37,785	0.87	0.99	0.66
Black	37,817	31,900	0.66	0.83	0.56
Filipino	41,563	34,065	0.73	0.89	0.60
Latin American	42,651	30,044	0.75	0.79	0.53
Arab	42,154	28,548	0.74	0.75	0.50
Southeast Asian	41,656	31,537	0.73	0.82	0.55
West Asian	40,405	28,982	0.71	0.76	0.51
Korean	41,229	29,765	0.72	0.78	0.52
Japanese	59,824	37,196	1.05	0.97	0.65
Visible minority	44,583	35,294	0.78	0.92	0.62
Multiple visible minorities	44,582	32,044	0.78	0.89	0.60

Adapted from Block et al. (2019, p. 23).

Income Inequality

A strong labour force participation rate does not result in better earnings outcomes for racialized workers. For example, in 2015, racialized men earned 78 cents for every dollar that non-racialized men earned. This earnings gap had remained unchanged since 2005.

Income discrimination continues to be gendered and racialized. In 2015, racialized women earned 59 cents for every dollar earned by non-racialized men. By contrast, non-racialized women earned 67 cents for every dollar earned by non-racialized men. Little progress was made in reducing this gap from 2006 to 2016, the period studied by Block et al. (2019).

Race, Immigration, and Employment Incomes

A common narrative revolves around the notion that the discrimination racialized workers face in the Canadian labour market is part of the immigrant experience and that it is common to all immigrants. Everyone who comes to this country struggles, the story goes, especially at first. However, the sacrifice is worth it because succeeding generations reap the benefits of that sacrifice and integrate rapidly — and with great success — into the labour market.

However, this narrative is not supported by the data. Non-racialized immigrants do better (and do better sooner) in the Canadian labour market than racialized immigrants. Moreover, income inequality between racialized and non-racialized Canadians extends to the second and subsequent generations. Clearly, immigration is not the only issue.

Among prime-age workers (25 to 54 years old), racialized immigrant men earned 71 cents for every dollar earned by non-racialized immigrant men. Racialized immigrant women earned 79 cents for every dollar earned by non-racialized immigrant women. These gaps continue into the second generation and beyond. Second-generation racialized men earned 79 cents for every dollar that second-generation non-racialized men earned. Second-generation racialized women earned 96 cents for every dollar that second-generation non-racialized women earned.

Further, there are distinct barriers in the labour market faced by different racialized groups. Both men and women who identified as Black had higher labour force participation rates than their non-racialized counterparts. However, they also had higher unemployment rates and bigger wage gaps than the average for all racialized workers.

Men who identified as Filipino had much lower unemployment rates than the average for racialized workers and yet had a larger earnings gap, while women who identified as Filipino had lower unemployment rates and a smaller earnings gap than the racialized average.

The Need for Anti-Racism Policies

Patterns of employment and income inequality along racial and gender lines persist in the Canadian labour market. Further, distinct barriers are faced by different racialized groups.

Addressing the labour market discrimination faced by racialized workers will require a deeper understanding of racism and the different ways it is manifested in the labour market. Labour market discrimination has many facets, and these need to be better understood so that anti-racism policies become more effective.

Economic inequality is not a passing socio-economic phenomenon. To the contrary, economic inequality tends to reproduce and entrench itself. The racialized labour market outcomes that Block et al. (2019) found point to an unequivocal pattern of **racialized income inequality**. In the absence of bold new policies aimed at combatting racism, this income inequality shows no signs of disappearing.

Note:

The above material was adapted for this chapter from *Canada's Colour Coded Income Inequality* by Sheila Block, Grace-Edward Galabuzi, and Ricardo Tranjan, which was published in 2019 by the Canadian Centre for Policy Alternatives (CCPA). It is reproduced here by permission of CCPA.

The full report and analysis can be downloaded from the CCPA website: www.policyalternatives.ca

3.2 Precarious Work

Precarious work refers to employment that may be insecure, have limited or no rights and protections, and is poorly paid. This includes jobs that are temporary, part-time, or subcontracted, as they can be added or removed from the labour force more easily. Some forms of self-employment are also considered precarious. These types of employment are precarious because they are associated with reduced financial security stemming from lower wages, less access to benefits (such as private pension plans and complementary health insurance), and greater uncertainty about future employment income (OECD, 2015). Figure 3.2 shows how the rate of growth of temporary work (seasonal, contract, casual) outpaced the growth of permanent work in Canada from 1998 to 2018.

According to the Law Commission of Ontario (2012), vulnerable workers — that is, those engaged in precarious work — are found across society, but in some populations more than others. Lone parents (usually women), racialized workers, and recent immigrants are most likely to find themselves in part-time, temporary work. Among part-time workers, women are more likely to be low paid.

In 2017, nearly one in five employed people in Canada, or 3.5 million people, worked part-time, with youth aged 15 to 24 being the most likely to work part-time (49% of employed youths), followed by workers aged 55 and older (23%). Canadian women were twice as likely as men to work part-time (26% versus 13%) (Patterson, 2018).

Figure 3.2

Index of the Number of Employees with a Permanent or Temporary Job, 1998–2018

Hardy, V., Lovei, M., and Patterson, M. (2018). Recent trends in Canada's labour market: A rising tide or a passing wave? Ottawa, ON: Statistics Canada; Labour Force Survey, Custom Tabulations (1998=100). June 1998 = 100.

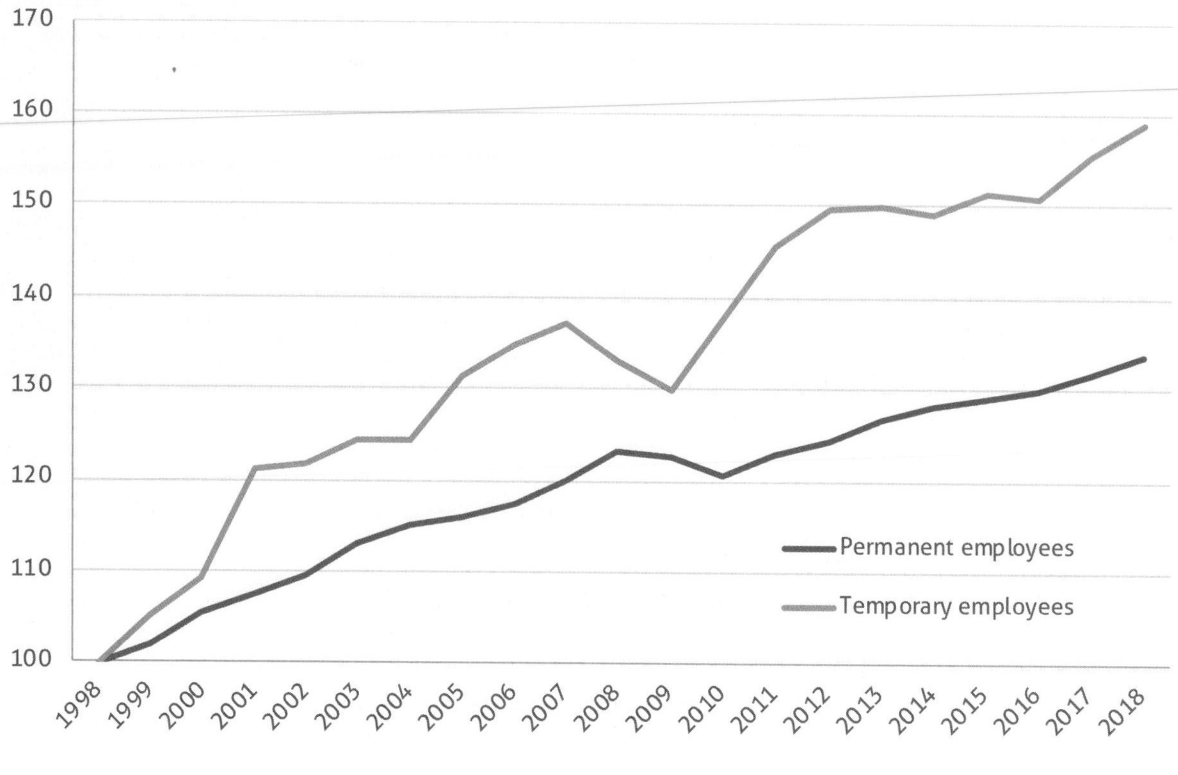

Negative Physical and Mental Health Outcomes

Studies consistently link precarious employment to negative physical and mental health.

- Precarious workers are more likely to experience health and safety risks due to lack of experience or training, lack of knowledge about occupational health and safety rights, and fear of losing one's job (or being deported).
- Precarious workers can experience significant stress due to job insecurity, the pressure of holding multiple jobs, irregular or long hours, insecure visa status, and a lack of legal protections.
- Precarious workers may also suffer health consequences as a result of their lower income. Low wages also affect workers' access to safe transportation and sufficiently nutritious food. Working more than one job and having long hours increases one's susceptibility to illness and injury and can have negative impacts on family life and communities.
- Due to low wages and a lack of benefits, precarious workers often have difficulty accessing medicine, particularly prescription drugs.
- Pregnant women engaged in precarious work are often not covered by statutory personal emergency leave provisions and, with insufficient time off, may not obtain necessary medical care.
- Precarious workers have limited opportunities to access training or education to upgrade their skills. This contributes to long-term economic vulnerability and a cycle of precarious work (Law Commission of Ontario, 2012).

The "Precariat"

Following the 2008–2009 financial crisis, many firms sought to restore profitability by cutting labour costs. Businesses shifted to part-time, hourly, gig, freelance, and contract work, instead of full-time work, thereby creating what some have loosely called the "Precariat" (a play on the word "proletariat").

Today, as part of the fall-out from the COVID–19 crisis, this segment of the labour force is growing again. In response to the uncertainty of the pandemic, businesses are slashing jobs to reduce labour costs, and re-hiring workers in more insecure, temporary positions.

Together with rising social inequality, many analysts see this trend as setting the scene for larger-scale unrest.

Underemployment

While many employed people are employed part-time (fewer than 30 hours per week) or have precarious work, others experience **underemployment** — that is, the education and training required for the job is less than the education and training of the worker who is doing the job. There are two types of underemployment.

- Visible underemployment describes individuals working fewer hours than is typical in their field and often working two part-time jobs to make ends meet.
- Invisible underemployment describes individuals in full-time jobs but whose jobs do not use all their training and work skills.

Neither of these indicators of underemployment are generally measured in Canada. However, based on Statistics Canada data, "B.C. has the lowest number of university graduates working in careers that utilize their bachelor's degree. The same data shows only 57% of workers with a university degree had jobs that required their respective undergraduate diploma" (Van Santvoort, 2017, para. 1).

Another category of underemployed people often omitted in the statistics are people who have actively looked for a job during the last year and would like to work and are available. Economists refer to this group as being marginally attached to the labour force. Within this group, there are those who have just given up looking altogether (for whatever reason) — the so-called discouraged workers.

Canada's Working Poor

To be complete, the category of underemployment should also include the working poor. The Public Health Agency of Canada (PHAC, 2018) defines the working poor as "individuals between 18 and 64 years who live independently, are not students, and earn at least $3,000 a year with an after-tax family income below the low-income threshold."

The PHAC estimates that 7.6% of Canadians between 18 and 64 years old are working poor. People who are considered working poor are more likely to have less stable jobs, unpredictable work hours, and fewer benefits (e.g., drug and dental plans, disability insurance). Living in poverty also affects overall health due to food insecurity and poor living conditions. Poverty also affects an individual's ability to access health care. In 2014, almost 13% of low-income Canadians (compared with 10% of middle- and high-income Canadians) had unmet health care needs. Notably, Indigenous people were more likely to have unmet health care needs than non-Indigenous people (Statistics Canada, 2016b).

Lower levels of education are associated with a higher proportion of working poor, and recent immigrants are twice as likely to be working poor compared with non-immigrants (see the infographic on the next page). Compared with white Canadians, Black Canadians are more than twice as likely to be working poor, and Asian and Arab Canadians are 1.5 times more likely to be working poor. First Nations people, both on-reserve and off-reserve, are 2.1 times more likely to be working poor compared with non-Indigenous people (PHAC, 2018). As the PHAC notes: "Reducing inequalities among the working poor requires providing access to education, safe working conditions, job security, a social safety net including pensions and benefits, and addressing discrimination."

Foreign Credential Recognition

Immigration has long been used as a driving force to meet Canada's labour market needs. However, newcomers to Canada often are unable to apply their education and professional experience toward meaningful employment and, consequently, have lower wages compared with people born in Canada.

In 2006, an estimated 62% of Canadian-born people were working in the regulated profession for which they were trained (i.e., a profession governed by a regulatory body and/or government), compared with only 24% of foreign-educated immigrants (Zietsma, 2010). The unemployment and underemployment of immigrants is estimated to cost more than $30 billion per year — or 2% of the GDP — in lost income for immigrants (RBC Economics, 2011).

Deficiencies in the foreign credential recognition program contribute significantly to underemployment for newcomers. A Vancity and Agnus Reid Global survey of 400 newcomers in British Columbia found the following: less than half (49%) of those seeking employment in their field found work at a level matching their credentials; and most newcomers said their home country work experience (70%), professional qualifications (67%), and education (66%) were less respected than their Canadian equivalents (Vancity, 2019).

Pan-Canadian Health Inequalities Reporting Initiative

Inequalities in Working Poor
Canadians

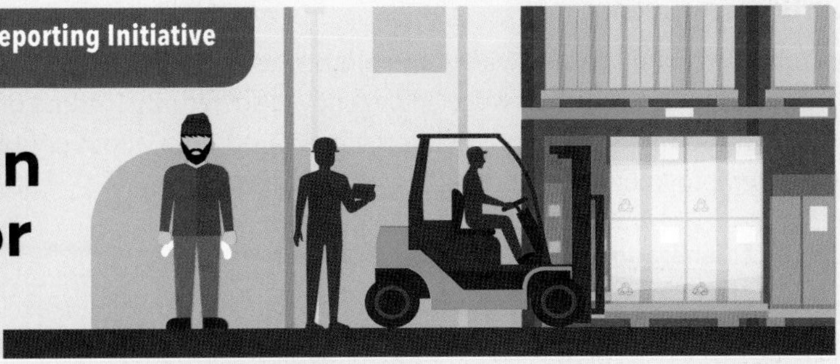

The working poor are Canadians who struggle to make ends meet.

7.6%* **of Canadians between 18 and 64 years old are working poor.****

The working poor are more likely to have:

- less stable jobs
- unpredictable work hours
- fewer benefits (e.g., drug and dental plans, disability insurance)
- greater health problems

Lower levels of education are associated with a higher proportion of working poor, particularly among women.

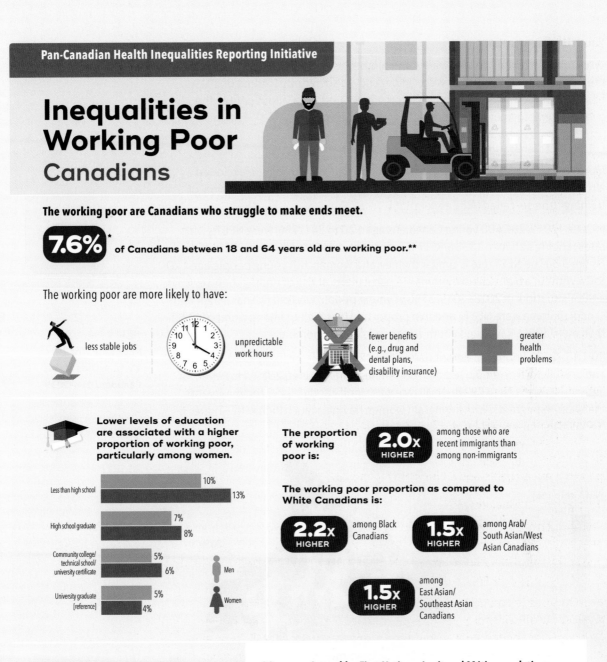

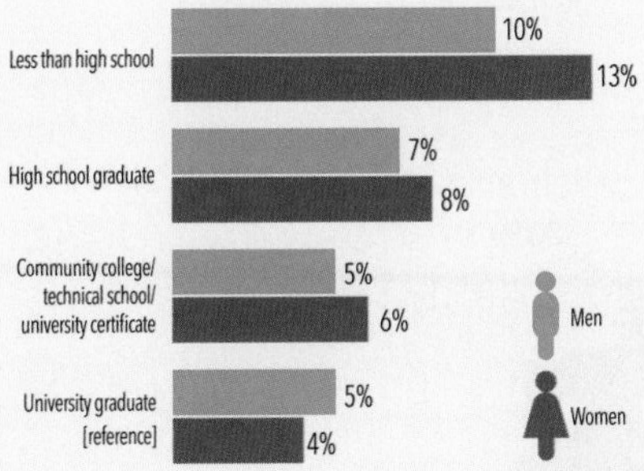

The proportion of working poor is: **2.0x HIGHER** among those who are recent immigrants than among non-immigrants

The working poor proportion as compared to White Canadians is:

- **2.2x HIGHER** among Black Canadians
- **1.5x HIGHER** among Arab/ South Asian/West Asian Canadians
- **1.5x HIGHER** among East Asian/ Southeast Asian Canadians

First Nations people, both on reserve and off reserve, have **2.1x HIGHER** proportion of working poor than non-Indigenous people

Inequities experienced by First Nations, Inuit and Métis populations are a direct result of colonial policies and practices that included massive forced relocation, loss of lands, creation of the reserve system, banning of Indigenous languages and cultural practices, and creation of the residential school system. Unaddressed intergenerational trauma adds to the ongoing challenges faced by Indigenous peoples.

Reducing inequalities among the working poor requires providing access to education, safe working conditions, job security, a social safety net including pensions and benefits, and addressing discrimination.

Public Health Agency of Canada (2018).

Youth Unemployment

Work provides young people with opportunities to gain valuable experience and life skills and to develop their voice and agency in society. By the end of 2019, however, the youth unemployment rate sat at around 11%, about double the overall unemployment rate (Trading Economics, n.d.).

- **The NEET Generation**

More concerning still is that many young people (aged 15 to 29) are excluded altogether from the labour market. They are "not in employment, education, or training" (the so-called NEET generation).

In 2018–2019, 287,400 young Canadians aged 20 to 24 (12%) were NEETs, with rates ranging between 10% and 17% across the provinces (Brunet, 2019). (See Figure 3.3.) The NEET rate is similar for men and women, but young people aged 20 to 24 without a high school diploma are particularly at risk of finding themselves in a NEET situation. In 2018–2019, 37% of young people who did not have their high school diploma were NEETs, and that proportion was higher among women (47%) than men (30%). Racialized youth were especially vulnerable.

In 2018–2019, young immigrants (aged 20 to 24) were more likely to be studying and less likely to be employed than non-immigrants (Brunet, 2019). However, for individuals aged 25 to 29, the NEET rate was significantly higher for immigrants than non-immigrants, with immigrant women having a much higher NEET rate (16%) than non-immigrant women (10%).

Figure 3.3

NEET Rates for 20- to 24-Year-Olds across Canada, 2018–2019

Statistics Canada, Labour Force Survey, September 2018 to April 2019.

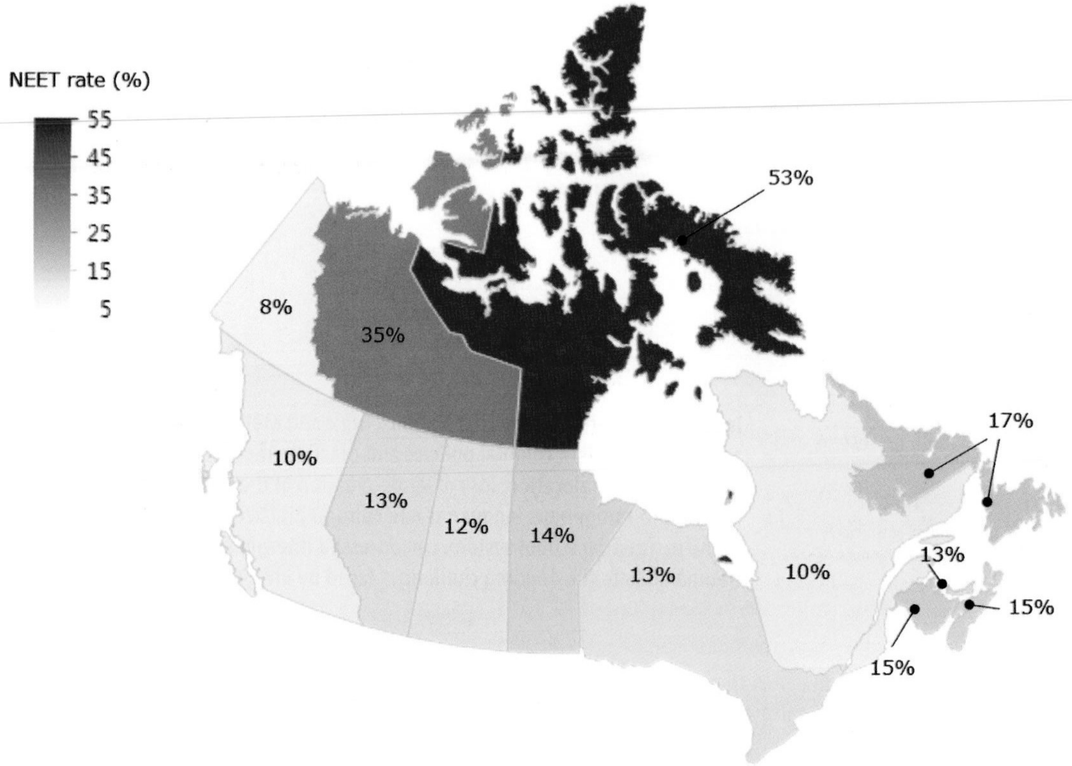

- **Indigenous Youth**

The unemployment and NEET situation for Indigenous youth is severe. Key contributors to this situation are colonial expropriation of land, the reserve system, the residential school system, child welfare policies (e.g., the Sixties Scoop), and systemic underfunding for Indigenous education, families, and children. Indigenous youth are more likely than their non-Indigenous counterparts to face difficulties in the labour market: their unemployment rates tend to be higher, and their labour participation rates tend to be lower than for non-Indigenous youth (Moyser, 2017).

The definition of "Aboriginal identity" used in Statistics Canada's Labour Force Survey is narrow. The Survey excludes persons living on-reserve and other Aboriginal (Indigenous) settlements in the provinces, as well as those living in the territories (Statistics Canada, 2018b). Nevertheless, it is possible to gain some insights from the Labour Force Survey. Aboriginal youth (men and women) who live off-reserve have higher NEET rates than youth overall (Brunet, 2019). In 2018–2019, the NEET rate for Aboriginal youth aged 20 to 24 was 23%, while for the national population of the same age the rate was 12% (Brunet, 2019).

The overall trend is not changing, either. From 2007–2008 to 2018–2019, year after year, Aboriginal youth have had significantly higher NEET rates than the national population of the same age (see Figure 3.4). Keep in mind that this analysis does not include persons on-reserve or those living in the territories, where the situation is likely much worse.

Figure 3.4

NEET Rates (Percentage) for the Off-Reserve Aboriginal Population and the Total Population by Age Group (Excluding the Territories), 2007–2008 to 2007–2019

Statistics Canada, Labour Force Survey, 1998 to 2019.

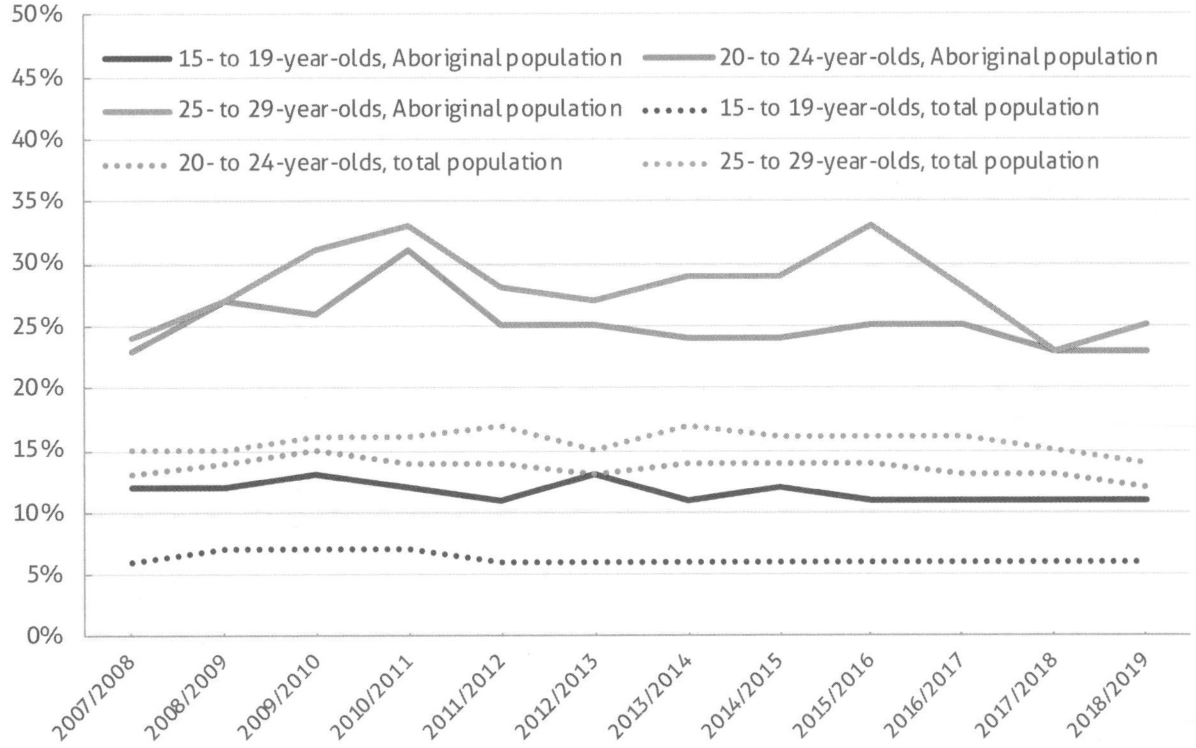

Social Welfare in Perspective

Understanding Employment Ratios

Making Sense of Labour Market Statistics

A number of measures are used to explain labour market activity in Canada. Three key indicators are the labour force participation rate, the employment rate, and the unemployment rate.

Labour market statistics provide a general indication of how well the Canadian economy is doing. However, statistics always have limitations and should be interpreted cautiously.

The labour force consists of the total adult population that is available for work at a particular time. It comprises employed people, unemployed people, and those seeking and available for work.

Labour market statistics are widely used in social policy formation, so it is important to understand what they mean. The three most common measures of labour market activity are the labour force participation rate, the employment rate, and the unemployment rate.

The Labour Force Participation Rate (LFP)

The **labour force participation rate** is the ratio of the labour force to the working-age population (people aged 15 to 64) (OECD, 2018b).

It is calculated as follows:

$$\text{LFP} = \frac{\text{Labour Force}}{\text{Working-Age Population}} \times 100$$

A high labour force participation rate means that a large proportion of the working-age population is either employed or actively seeking employment. This rate varies widely across the provinces and territories.

Labour Force Participation Rate and Employment Rate in Canada, January 2006 to 2019

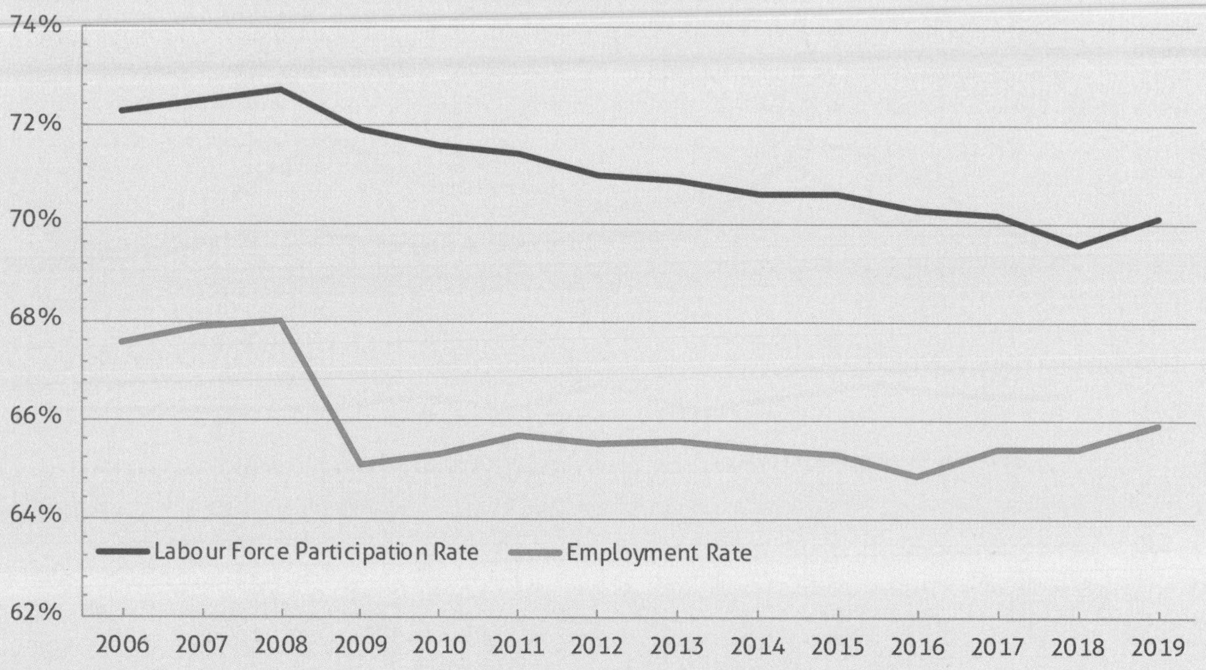

The Unemployment Rate (ER)

The **unemployment rate** is the statistic most frequently used to measure economic health. It represents the percentage of the labour force that is unemployed but is actively seeking employment and willing to work. It is calculated as follows:

$$ER = \frac{\text{Number of Unemployed People}}{\text{Number of People in the Labour Force}} \times 100$$

As noted, not all unemployed people are counted as unemployed. For example, individuals who are unemployed but have given up searching for work are not counted as "unemployed." As well, those who are outside the normal workforce for whatever reason are not included. These exclusions mean that this indicator alone does not provide a complete picture of those who are not employed in a particular jurisdiction.

The unemployment rate is typically higher for youth, women, people with disabilities, and Indigenous people.

The Employment Rate (EPR)

The **employment rate** (employment to population ratio) measures the extent to which available labour resources are being used. It is the ratio of the employed to the working-age population (aged 15 to 64) (OECD, 2018a). It is calculated as follows:

$$EPR = \frac{\text{Employed Persons}}{\text{Total Working-Age Population}} \times 100$$

The employment rate is a key indicator of the health of the labour market. The chart below, for example, tracks unemployment before, during, and after the recession of 2008–2009. The recovery period saw a decline in the unemployment rate, as might be expected. On the other hand, the employment rate (employed persons as a percentage of the working-age population) remains below levels prior to the recession. This suggests that more people have since stopped looking for work and are therefore no longer officially counted as "unemployed."

Unemployment Rate in Canada, January 2006–2019

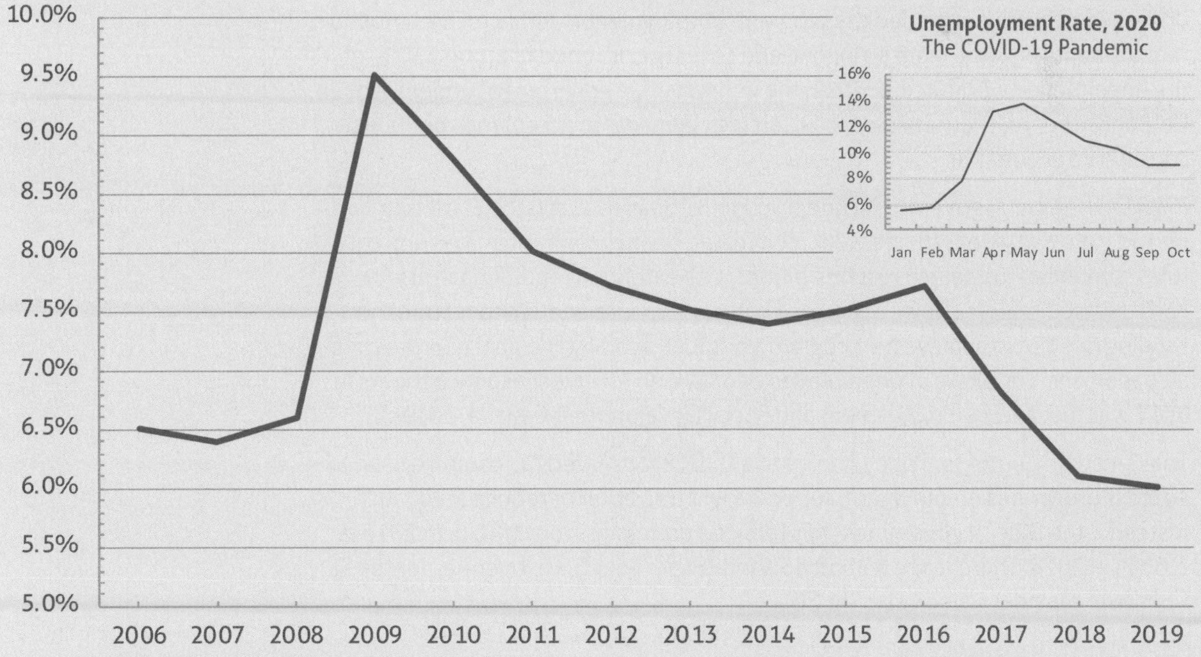

3.3 Employment Insurance

Employment Insurance (EI) is an income program that provides financial support to those who lose their jobs. This program was first introduced in Canada through the Unemployment Insurance Act, 1940. "Unemployment Insurance" (as it was then called) was the first national social insurance program in Canada.

A Brief History

The Great Depression was the primary catalyst for the creation of a national employment insurance program in Canada. The Unemployment Insurance Act of 1940 established a program based on wage-related financial benefits funded through employee, employer, and federal government contributions (Guest, 1980; Makarenko, 2009). Although it had shortcomings, the program provided a modest safety net for workers and their families. In 1971, a White Paper recommended an enhanced Unemployment Insurance program. In the same year, a new Unemployment Insurance Act was passed, which established a new program containing "substantial changes in coverage, contributions, and benefits and [...] a new sickness and maternity feature" (Weise, 1972, p. 31).

"Like Medicare, EI is highly valued by Canadians as part of our social safety net. It is an expression of our willingness to share risk and take care of each other during work disruptions."

Wood, D. (2019). *Employment Insurance: Next Steps on the Road to Renewal*. Atkinson Foundation.

By the 1990s, it was incurring billions of dollars in financial shortfalls each year. As a result, the federal government made changes to the program so that it would be self-financing, with costs shared between employees and employers (Makarenko, 2009). In 1990, Bill C-21 increased the number of workweeks required to receive benefits, reduced the maximum duration of benefits for most regions, and reduced the replacement rate from 60% to 50% of insurable earnings for those who declined suitable employment, quit without just cause, or were fired. In 1993, Bill C-113 cut the regular benefit rate from 60% to 57%, and benefits for workers who quit or were fired from their jobs were eliminated. In 1995, the Liberal government under Jean Chrétien renamed the program "Employment Insurance." EI eligibility requirements became more stringent, and coverage dropped to around 50% of the unemployed workforce. In 2012, the Conservative government under Stephen Harper further restricted access to EI, forcing claimants to accept jobs previously considered unsuitable.

In 2017, the Liberal government under Justin Trudeau reduced the EI waiting period from two weeks to one week, eliminated the new entrant and re-entrant rules, simplified job search responsibilities, and extended regular benefits for hard-pressed regions. However, these changes were not enough to restore the funding needed to achieve the program's original, overarching goal of protecting all Canadians. The share of unemployed people who received income benefits in 2017 was just 42.1% (Employment and Social Development Canada, 2019b).

The Canadian Centre for Policy Alternatives (2018) observed: "EI could be used to address precarious employment, support a just transition or reduce inequality. Instead ... the federal government has reduced premiums from 1.88% in 2015 to 1.66% in 2018. This change will cut $3.6 billion per year from revenues for the EI fund over the next seven years" (p. 50).

Employment Insurance: Three Facts and A Myth

1. FACT: EI is an insurance program.

EI is currently paid through mandatory contributions levied on workers and employers. It forces savings and shares the risk of unemployment across all contributors. It provides income security to individuals as opposed to families, making it different from programs such as child benefits financed from general tax revenues. It is also highly distinct from last-resort social assistance.

2. FACT: Employment insurance is critical in stabilizing incomes during economic downturns in any country.

Employment insurance has been an important macroeconomic adjustment tool. That means it speeds up the bounce-back after economic recessions. It played a vital role in stabilizing the incomes of Canadian workers during the downturns of the early 1980s, the early 1990s, and 2008 (Dungan & Murphy, 1995, 2012).

However, the reforms of the 1990s eroded the program's capacity to perform as a macroeconomic adjustment tool. In the early 1990s, 84% of the unemployed were eligible for UI/EI benefits. Today, that figure is only around 40%.

3. FACT: Constitutionally, EI is an exclusive federal responsibility.

Provincial governments have no veto over EI. When the program was established in 1940, responsibility for governance and costs were shared by business, labour, and government. Today, employers and workers pay 100% of program costs, but their voice in decision making has significantly diminished.

4. MYTH: EI mostly benefits rural Atlantic Canada.

EI promotes a more efficient labour market by allowing time for job searches to help all workers find jobs that meet their skills and experiences. That's true for all workers, not just those working in rural and remote communities or in seasonal industries such as agriculture, forestry, or the fisheries.

EI is one of Canada's most important poverty prevention tools. One national study compared the incomes of the unemployed before, after, and during a period on EI from the years 2000 to 2007. Without EI, the percentage of families below the low income cut-off would have doubled from 7% to 14% (Kapsalis, 2010).

The Road to Renewal

The EI program has been in decline since 1990, when the Government of Canada stopped contributing money to the program, leaving all costs to employers and workers. The reforms that occurred during the 1990s were designed to focus more resources on supporting "active" employment rather than "passive" support.

This shift in emphasis was captured in a change in the program's name — from Unemployment Insurance to Employment Insurance. The upshot was a series of deep cuts to income support benefits.

Three decades later, the benefits that unemployed workers receive from Employment Insurance are a pale shadow of what was available in the past.

EI's decline and the urgent steps needed for renewal are documented by Donna Wood in *Employment Insurance: Next Steps on the Road to Renewal*, a report released by the Atkinson Foundation in 2019.

The EI Coverage Gap

EI is a vital social program that contributes to the financial security of workers who have lost their jobs. The program has three main components:

- Regular benefits providing coverage for individuals who lose their job through no fault of their own (e.g., due to shortage of work, mass layoffs, or seasonal work)
- Special benefits providing coverage for individuals on maternity, parental, sickness, and compassionate care leave, and those caring for the critically ill
- Employment services providing essential training and other adjustment programs for unemployed workers

EI was expanded over the postwar years and, by and large, fulfilled its promise. However, as a result of policy changes since the 1990s, the EI program has been faltering (see Figure 3.5). EI did not hold up well in subsequent years, especially not after the "Great Recession" in 2008 or the COVID-19 pandemic in 2020. In 2009, coverage was about half of what it was in the early 1990s (Mendelson et al., 2009).

Many people also find themselves ineligible despite paying into the EI program. For example, "about 50% of temporary foreign workers and 100% of international students cannot access EI benefits" (Wood, 2019, p. 20). Students working in the summer contribute to EI but cannot collect when they return to school. Also, women in precarious work (which is often the case) and women who must quit their jobs because of working conditions or inadequate child care are ineligible.

Figure 3.5

The Share of Unemployed Covered by Employment Insurance, 1989–2016

Statistics Canada. Employment Insurance Monitoring & Assessment Reports; adapted from Donna E. Wood, *Employment Insurance: Next Steps on the Road to Renewal*. Atkinson Foundation, 2019.

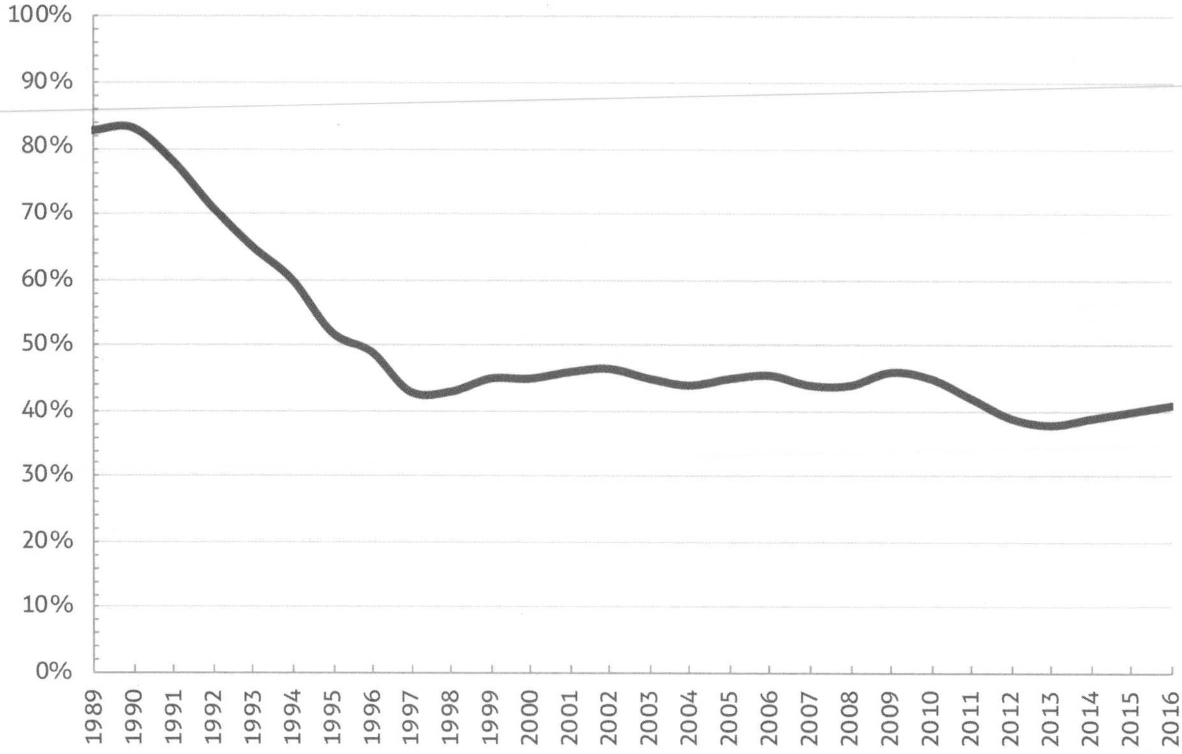

Structural Inadequacy of the EI System

ACORN Canada is an independent national organization of low- and moderate-income families. In a meeting with the EI Commissioner in 2017, ACORN's Action Group identified several issues with EI, based on their lived experiences:

- It is too hard to access benefits.
- It is too hard to keep receiving benefits that claimants are entitled to.
- It is too intrusive into workers' personal affairs.
- Payments are not enough.
- There is inadequate job training (ACORN Canada, 2017).

These were also the conclusions of a 2019 report by the Atkinson Foundation entitled *Employment Insurance: Next Steps on the Road to Renewal*. The author of the report, Donna Wood, who had worked many years in social services and was an adjunct professor at the University of Victoria, identified two policy changes that had significantly reduced the number of people who could claim EI benefits.

The first was the disqualification of people who quit their job voluntarily or who were fired for cause. The second was changing the eligibility criteria from the number of weeks worked to the number of hours worked. Donna Wood noted: "These access changes were particularly hard on women who, more than men, leave their jobs for family reasons or to avoid workplace sexual harassment. In addition, far more women work part time and therefore qualify for benefits less often under the new rules" (Wood, 2019, p. 9).

EI in COVID Times

The CERB was introduced in March 2020 to give money to people who had to stop working because of COVID–19.

In October, the federal government introduced two different programs to replace the CERB:

- An expanded EI system
- A new Canada Recovery Benefit for self-employed and "gig" workers who didn't qualify for EI

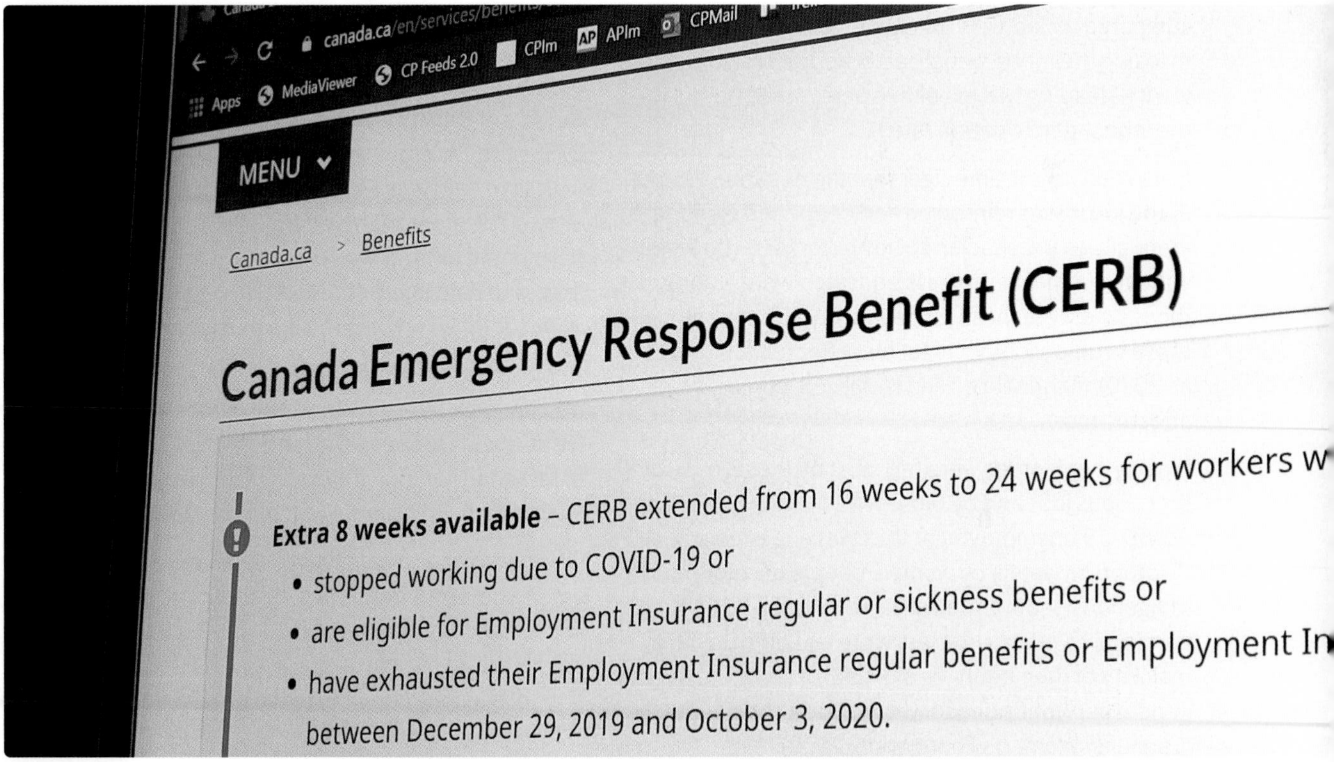

What the COVID–19 pandemic has revealed ...

Labour Market Policy and COVID–19

Addressing Long-Standing Inequities in the World of Work

Canada's economy requires focused efforts to fix long-standing problems in the labour market if there is to be a successful long-term recovery after COVID–19.

The COVID–19 pandemic resulted in a massive disruption of the Canadian labour market. The situation reached Depression-like levels of unemployment within weeks. By March 2020, 3,100,000 people in Canada were affected by either job loss or reduced hours (Statistics Canada, 2020).

In normal times, the social welfare response associated with labour market volatility is Employment Insurance (EI). But, as the scale of the COVID–19 crisis became clear, the EI program proved to be both insufficient and inadequate.

Inequity of Employment Loss and Job Safety

The immediate job losses in Canada due to the COVID–19 pandemic were staggering. The unemployment rate more than doubled in April 2020 compared to February (Beland et al., 2020). In addition to losing their jobs, people also stopped looking for work — leading to a fall of five percentage points in the labour participation rate.

It also quickly became clear that the negative effects of the job losses reinforced and deepened existing inequalities in Canadian society. Workers who were younger, unmarried, or less educated were among those who were the most negatively affected, while those in union jobs were far less affected (Beland et al, 2020). Marginalized and racialized workers were affected most.

Employment losses were felt most by those in precarious jobs and by those with the lowest earnings. COVID–19 unemployment thus was experienced disproportionately by women, people of colour, and Indigenous people. Almost six in 10 women (58%) earning $14 per hour or less were laid off or lost the majority of their hours, as did 45% of men. The overall gender gap continued to widen during the pandemic (Canadian Women's Foundation, 2020).

Inequities in Access to Paid Leave

Workers who had travelled to an infected area, who had been in contact with someone testing positive for COVID–19, and those experiencing symptoms were required to self-quarantine for two weeks before returning to work. While some workers continued to be paid while they were quarantining, most workers were not.

While quarantining and staying (or working) from home was promoted as an effective public health response, it simply wasn't realistic for many workers because it directly affected their ability to pay rent and put food on the table. In 2019, only 38% of workers had access to paid illness or disability leave (Macdonald, 2020).

Moreover, access to paid leave was disproportionate. in 2019. More than 65% of people earning more than $65,000 annually had access to paid leave compared to 14% of those earning less than $16,000 and 27% of those earning between $17,000 to $28,000. Access to paid leave also depended on the job type — in 2019, more than half (53%) of employees with permanent jobs (or who were self-employed) had access to paid leave compared to between 10% and 14% for those who were non-permanent.

Geographic inequities in paid leave also exist. Sixty percent of workers in some cities (for example, in Ottawa and Québec City) have paid leave compared to less than half of workers in cities such as Vancouver, Hamilton, or Edmonton (Macdonald, 2020).

Finally, in Canada paid leave is unevenly distributed among different industries. In accommodation and food services, for example, only 19% of the leave was paid leave. In the hard-hit travel industry, less than a third of the jobs had paid leave provisions.

More Can Be Done to Protect Canadian Workers

Employment Insurance along with universal health care are cornerstones of the Canadian social welfare system. However, EI is not well-suited to the gig economy of the 2020s, and it didn't measure up to the sudden surge of unemployment caused by COVID–19 (Dinan & Béland, 2020).

On March 11, 2020, the federal government put $5 million into EI to provide paid leave options when quarantining. The one-week wait period for EI and the medical certificate requirement were also waived. This was followed by the $2,000-per-month Canada Emergency Response Benefit (CERB) to individuals on March 25 and the 75% wage subsidy for employers on April 7. In June, the CERB was extended by eight weeks for an additional cost of $17.9 billion (Clemens et al., 2020). In September, those claiming the CERB were moved onto the EI program.

In September, the Liberal government indicated that it was prepared to keep borrowing and investing to support Canadians, even after the deficit had climbed up to $343 billion in response to COVID–19.

Do We Need a Universal Basic Income?

The severity of COVID–19 pandemic has increased calls for a universal basic income. The Parliamentary Budget Office (PBO) estimated that the cost of such a program for six months of 2020–21 (October-March) would be $47.5–$98.1 billion, with up to 20 million people receiving benefits. About $15 billion worth of existing tax measures could be "offset" by such a program (PBO, 2020).

According to an Angus Reid Poll in June 2020, 60% of Canadians favoured a universal basic income. Slightly more than half (55%) were concerned that such a program might be a disincentive to work, while 54% felt it would be too expensive. Women, younger people, and Liberal and NDP supporters were more likely to support a basic income (Angus Reid, 2020).

While many Canadians are fans of a basic income, there is debate about its merits (Vanzo, 2020). For example, Dinan & Béland (2020) argue that the basic income amount would likely be too low. Instead, they favour better targeting of benefits to low-income citizens, along with a more inclusive EI system.

Jobs or Majority of Hours Lost by Wage, February–April 2020

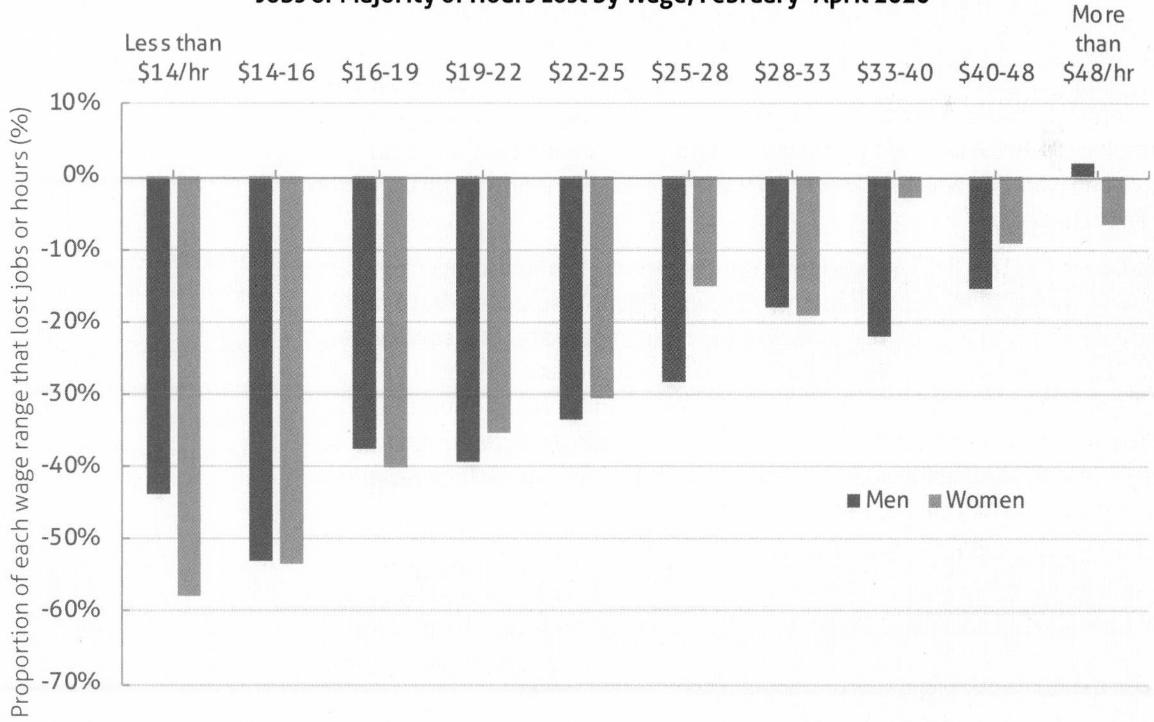

Statistics Canada (2020). Labour Force Survey, February and April. Excludes the self-employed.

3.4 Workers' Compensation

Workers' compensation is an insurance program designed to replace the tort system (the courts) in determining compensation for a work-related injury or illness. Workers' compensation provides no-fault compensation, which means that coverage is available to workers regardless of how a work-related injury or illness occurred. Under this program, workers give up the right to sue their employers in return for guaranteed compensation.

Workers' compensation covers the costs of rehabilitation from a work-related injury or illness. It also provides insurance against the interruption of income or the impairment of earnings capacity (whether temporary or permanent) that arises from a work-related injury or illness. It includes support for dependents in the case of the death of a worker at the workplace or arising out of work.

Every province and territory has its own workers' compensation program. Federal employees are covered under the Government Employees Compensation Act (GECA). Eligibility criteria, benefit levels, and coverage vary considerably across jurisdictions.

Some workers' compensation boards (WCBs) focus on workplace health and/or safety (e.g., British Columbia, New Brunswick, Newfoundland and Labrador, Ontario, Québec, and Yukon). Others tend to focus more on injury compensation (e.g., Alberta and Manitoba).

A Brief History

Workers' compensation originated in England in the late 1800s and in the United States in the early 1900s. Early laws in England made it extremely difficult for workers to sue an employer for negligence. Employers' defences were based on the assumption that the contract between a worker and employer was the same as the contract between two commercial parties of equal bargaining power. In other words, if workers did not like the employers' terms and conditions, they could simply find work elsewhere. However, by the late nineteenth century, this situation began to change.

In Canada in the 1880s, there was growing indignation and public concern over the rise in worker deaths and disablement (Guest, 1980). Unions were becoming more powerful, and the political parties of the day competed for the labour vote. Canadian governments passed legislation that slightly loosened the hold of employers' defences, and it became somewhat easier for workers to succeed in the courts. A spate of successful lawsuits by workers against dangerous factories of the era put many employers in a panic. Employers began to push for legislation that protected them from such lawsuits.

In 1909, Québec was the first province to establish a Workmen's Compensation Act, which spurred interest in Ontario (Guest, 1980). Initially, business interests in Ontario reacted negatively to the idea. After studying the implications of the Québec legislation, they recognized that supporting liability insurance with a form of accident insurance was a way to stabilize costs.

Principles of Workers' Compensation in Canada

Each province and territory regulates workers' compensation differently, but the underlying principles are the same:

- **No-Fault Compensation** Employees are compensated for injuries no matter who is at fault.
- **Collective Liability** Employers share the cost of workers' compensation through a common fund.
- **Security of Benefits** Payment comes from an independent fund, which ensures that it is always available.
- **Exclusive Jurisdiction** The compensation board is the only authority on workers' compensation claims.
- **Independent Administration** The compensation board is non-political and therefore is focused only on the needs of the employees and employer.

The Meredith Principles

In Ontario in 1910, a Royal Commission headed by William Meredith was established to study workers' compensation in other countries and to provide recommendations (International Insurance Society, n.d.). In his 1913 final report, Meredith rejected employers' defences, especially the **fellow servant rule**, which he considered a "relic of barbarism" (Risk, 2012, p. 460). Meredith recommended abolishing what he called "this nuisance of litigation" and proposed that the workers' compensation system be founded on principles that became known as the "Meredith principles" (Risk, 2012, p. 418). The **Meredith principles** were a "historic compromise": "workers forfeited their right to sue employers in exchange for a non-adversarial employer-funded compensation system" (Bedard, 2014a, para. 6).

Meredith's final report was the basis for Ontario's Workmen's Compensation Act of 1914. Similar legislation followed in all other provinces and territories over the next 40 years. In the 1960s, workers' compensation was expanded to include injuries that developed over time, as long as they were work related. These changes meant that claims could be made for conditions such as occupational cancer, chronic stress, and post-traumatic stress disorder (PTSD).

Workers' compensation legislation typically outlines the roles and responsibilities of workers, employers, and the WCB when a workplace injury or illness occurs. These roles and responsibilities are described in Table 3.1.

Table 3.1

Workers' Compensation: Roles and Responsibilities

Workers	Employers	Workers' Compensation Board
• Report the illness or injury to the employer • Mitigate further loss • Cooperate with the employer if or when suitable modified workplace duties are offered	• Provide first aid and arrange and pay for transportation for medical treatment, as needed • Pay full wages and benefits for the period during which the injury occurred • Investigate the workplace incident and keep a record of corrective steps taken • Report the injury or illness to the respective workers' compensation board • Provide accurate payroll information • Offer suitable, modified work to the employee to allow for an early and safe return to work	• Review the reported incidents and determine benefits entitlement • Issue medical benefits and/or loss of earnings/wages benefits as applicable • Arrange specialist appointments and independent medical examinations, as appropriate • Interpret and enforce workers' compensation legislation • Review the evidence and make decisions on any appeals that may be initiated by the worker, the employer, or a third-party adjuster

Principles of Workers' Compensation in Canada

Meredith's principles continue to underlie workers' compensation systems in Canada. The principles are as follows:

- **No-Fault Compensation.** Workers are compensated for injuries, no matter who is at fault.
- **Collective Liability.** All employers share the cost of workers' compensation by contributing to a common fund.
- **Security of Benefits.** An independent fund is established for the payment of benefits to workers to guarantee that compensation is always available.
- **Exclusive Jurisdiction.** The WCB is the only authority on claims.
- **Independent Administration.** The WCB is an independent agency not under the influence of government or employers and is focused only on the needs of workers and employers.

Workers' Compensation: System Basics

Each jurisdiction regulates workers' compensation differently, including which businesses must register with its WCB. Generally, unincorporated businesses without employees do not have to register.

The funds for WCB benefits and services are collected from registered employers in the form of premiums. The premium is a particular rate per $100 of payroll. It differs by industry and jurisdiction. It also differs based on a business's experience rating, which is determined by the number of accidents and claims reported by the business. The safer the business, the lower the premium; and the more workers' compensation claims a business reports, the higher the premium.

The benefits employees receive from the WCB can be complicated and vary from one jurisdiction to another. However, these are the most common benefits:

- Health care payments
- Wages lost until full recovery
- Permanent disability benefits if the employee is never able to return to work
- Survivor benefits, including a lump sum and sometimes annuity benefits
- Rehabilitation, both physical and mental

In theory, both workers and employers benefited from the historic compromise established by Meredith's principles. However, many labour advocates say that, in their current form, "workers' compensation boards function more like private insurance companies than public utilities" (Bedard, 2014a, para. 22). As well, similar issues are appearing in compensation systems across the country: "an increase in the number of claims denied, a decrease in the amount of benefits received, and an increasingly adversarial compensation system" (para. 19).

Today, workers' compensation programs must also address injuries and illnesses that did not exist or were not recognized a century ago—ergonomic injuries, workplace harassment, and work-related stress disorders.

Older Displaced Workers

Because of their long job tenure and sector-specific skills, older workers (45 to 64) often cannot transfer easily to another job after they have been laid off. Some individuals may resort to early retirement. However, this is not a real option for those younger than age 60, since they are not eligible for Canada Pension Plan benefits (Finnie & Gray, 2011)

Older laid-off workers who manage to find new jobs experience about a 40% loss of earnings relative to their previous job (Finnie & Gray, 2011). By comparison, those under 45 are more likely to find re-employment at or above their previous levels.

For older workers, the ability to find comparable work after being laid off seems to be associated with difficulty transferring skills to other firms, industries, and occupations as well as age-related job discrimination. In addition, the shorter length of their remaining career might discourage some older workers from retraining or relocating to find comparable work.

Policy options to support older workers who seek to remain in the labour force include the following:

- Education and training upgrades until new and equivalent work is found
- Wage insurance (subsidy of a proportion of the wage losses for a fixed period until re-employment)
- Intensive job search assistance that encourages workers to look further afield than their previous industry and occupation (Finnie & Gray, 2011)

Social Welfare in Perspective

Health and Well-Being in the Workplace

Safety in the Health and Social Service Sector

Workplace health and safety has traditionally focused on industrial accidents. However, increasing attention is being paid to the levels of stress and violence in the health and social service sector.

Workplace health and safety concerns emerged during the Industrial Revolution in the nineteenth century when workers began to form unions and demand better working conditions. Employers and governments responded by regulating the workplace and forcing safer work practices. Most safety regulations were industry specific, and industries developed safety regulations independent of one another (SafetyLine, 2019).

Workplace health and safety has become an area of growing concern in the health and social service sector.

As one example, in 2018 in British Columbia, workplace injury claim costs for this sector were reported to be $107 million, a 10% increase over the previous year (British Columbia, 2019). In December 2019, in response to the rise in workplace injuries, British Columbia committed $8.5 million over three years to a new organization to address workplace safety in this sector.

Workplace Stress

Workplace stress is on the rise and is associated with harmful physical and emotional effects. Typically, workplace stress arises when an employee has conflicting job demands and limited control over meeting them.

The nature of health and social service work exposes people to stressful work situations, such as unwieldy case loads, court appearances, overwhelming paperwork, and negative media attention (Regehr, 2018). If not managed, they can lead to burnout that can affect a person's ability to make competent and consistent judgments and be flexible in their decision making.

Workplace Violence

The health and social service sector has some of the highest rates of workplace violence, according to Sarah Ryan (2016), a researcher for the Canadian Union of Public Employees. Moreover, Ontario's Workplace Safety and Insurance Board reported that "violence accounted for 13% of all lost-time injuries in the health care sector in 2018" (Government of Ontario, 2019).

Although no national data are collected on violence in the health and social service sector, Ryan (2016) points out:

- 90% of Canadian front-line residential care workers experienced physical violence from residents (or their relatives)
- 74% of surveyed community social service workers in British Columbia said they had experienced at least one type of violence in the past year
- 75% of child welfare staff in Ontario reported experiencing violence during their careers
- 73% of respondents to a survey in Ontario's developmental services sector reported that they had experienced an incident of violence at work

In a recent study, workers in long-term care homes reported unprecedented levels of assault and harassment against staff (Brophy et al., 2019). The study's author noted: "We heard very disturbing stories about the almost daily occurrence of physical violence, verbal abuse, sexual and racial harassment and even sexual assault that is so pervasive that it's become normalized — as if it's part of the job" (Flanagan, 2019).

Health care workers also find themselves dealing with client-on-client violence. In a survey of Ontario's developmental services sector, 64% of respondents reported that they had witnessed violence by one supported individual against another supported individual (Ryan, 2016).

Workplace Health and Safety Programs

Today, most medium- and large-sized workplaces have a health and safety program. According to the Canadian Centre for Occupational Health and Safety (2019), a comprehensive workplace health and safety program should have four main components:

- **Occupational Health and Safety.** This component focuses on promoting and maintaining the physical, mental, and social well-being of employees. It involves reducing work-related injuries, illness, and disability by addressing the hazards and risks of the physical environment. Reducing physical job hazards can also reduce the stress employees may feel in the workplace.
- **Psychosocial Work Environment.** This component focuses on identifying real and potential hazards and risks in the psychosocial environment in the workplace. It includes reviewing the attitudes, values, and beliefs that guide workplace behaviours and the factors that influence the interaction between employees and the organization.
- **Workplace Health and Wellness Promotion.** This component focuses on programs that take a proactive approach to healthy living for all employees at the workplace. Workplace health programs support a broad range of health and wellness initiatives, such as active living, healthy eating, smoking cessation, and personal fitness.
- **Organizational Community Involvement.** This component focuses on voluntary involvement in the community. It includes activities that are often called "corporate social responsibility" or "community engagement" activities. For example, a business may support a local charity, sponsor an employee team engaged in a cause, or encourage employees to volunteer in the community.

Policy Implications

A systemic policy approach is needed to further reduce workplace stress and violence in the heath and social service sector. This approach would involve the following:

- Ensuring adequate funding models and better staffing levels
- Promoting, establishing, and maintaining an organizational culture of safety and security (National Association of Social Workers, 2013)
- Ensuring that violence prevention is included in collective bargaining and health and safety committees (Ryan, 2016)
- Developing proactive preventive approaches to violence management and risk (NASW, 2013)
- Providing annual safety training, including universal safety measures, use of mobile phones and panic buttons, safety risk assessments, and personal Internet safety/privacy
- Encouraging all workers to report all incidents of violence and harassment (Ryan, 2016)
- Ensuring post-incident reports and forms are completed

3.5 Proactive Approaches to Labour Force Participation

A social investment approach to social welfare is about enhancing human capital. This approach is more in line with the policies of several Nordic countries that have used social programs successfully to reduce poverty and increase employment (Palme & Cronert, 2015).

The central idea behind social investment is to use employment and social programs proactively to encourage all people to gain the knowledge, experience, and skills necessary to participate in the labour market. It means investing in supports for workers affected by sickness and caregiving, working parents, people with disabilities, Indigenous people, older displaced workers, people who want to upgrade their education or training, and the working poor.

A Social Investment Approach to the Labour Market

- **Workers Affected by Sickness and Caregiving**

Each year, about 6% of the Canadian workforce adjusts their work status to deal with a health issue (Institute for Research on Public Policy, 2015). They may leave a job, take a leave of absence, or work part-time to reduce their work hours (Meredith & Chia, 2015). At a personal and household level, the impact can be significant.

Meredith and Chia (2015) recommend coordinated policy action on this issue that uses the following principles as a starting point:

- All workers have access to a minimum standard of disability insurance that provides high-quality support and income replacement.
- Employers have access to the resources they need to promote a healthy and productive workforce.
- There is broad harmonization between benefit programs in terms of the length and sequencing, and the duration and timing of job-protected leave.
- Eligibility for benefits and employment supports are flexible, broadly defined, and reflect the diverse needs of those living with episodic, chronic, and intermittent illnesses.
- All actors have a common language for understanding what constitutes a major health condition and this is reflected in program design and practice.
- Case management and program transitions are well coordinated to minimize the disruption of benefits for recipients.
- There is a more standardized approach to the extent of active employment supports that are provided and the way in which employment income is treated while on claim.
- Caregiving is broadly supported by both employers and governments, and access to benefits is not limited solely to the risk of death.
- There is a household-level approach to the needs of those giving as well as receiving care. (pp. 25–26)

- **Working Parents**

The EI system provides benefits for parents who take a temporary leave from paid work to care for a newborn or newly adopted child. In 2017, the federal government changed the period for maternity and parental benefits from 12 months to 18 months. Even with this policy change, there are significant gaps in the system, especially for low-income families and parents in non-standard employment (Robson, 2017). For this policy change to work for low-income families, Robson (2017) recommends the following additional reforms:

- A more responsive and inclusive eligibility test so that more parents who work and already pay EI premiums are able to collect benefits
- Targeted help for low- and modest-income families through the Family Supplement
- Changes aimed at better coordinating EI benefits with income-tested child benefits
- Improved incentives for employers who top up leave benefits for their employees and increase the coverage of lower-wage workers (p. 1)

Robson (2017) also questions whether parental benefits should stay within the EI system, since maternity benefits was a niche program added to the income security system about 50 years ago. She recommends taking a broader view of parental benefits to ensure that they better respond to the needs of today's working families.

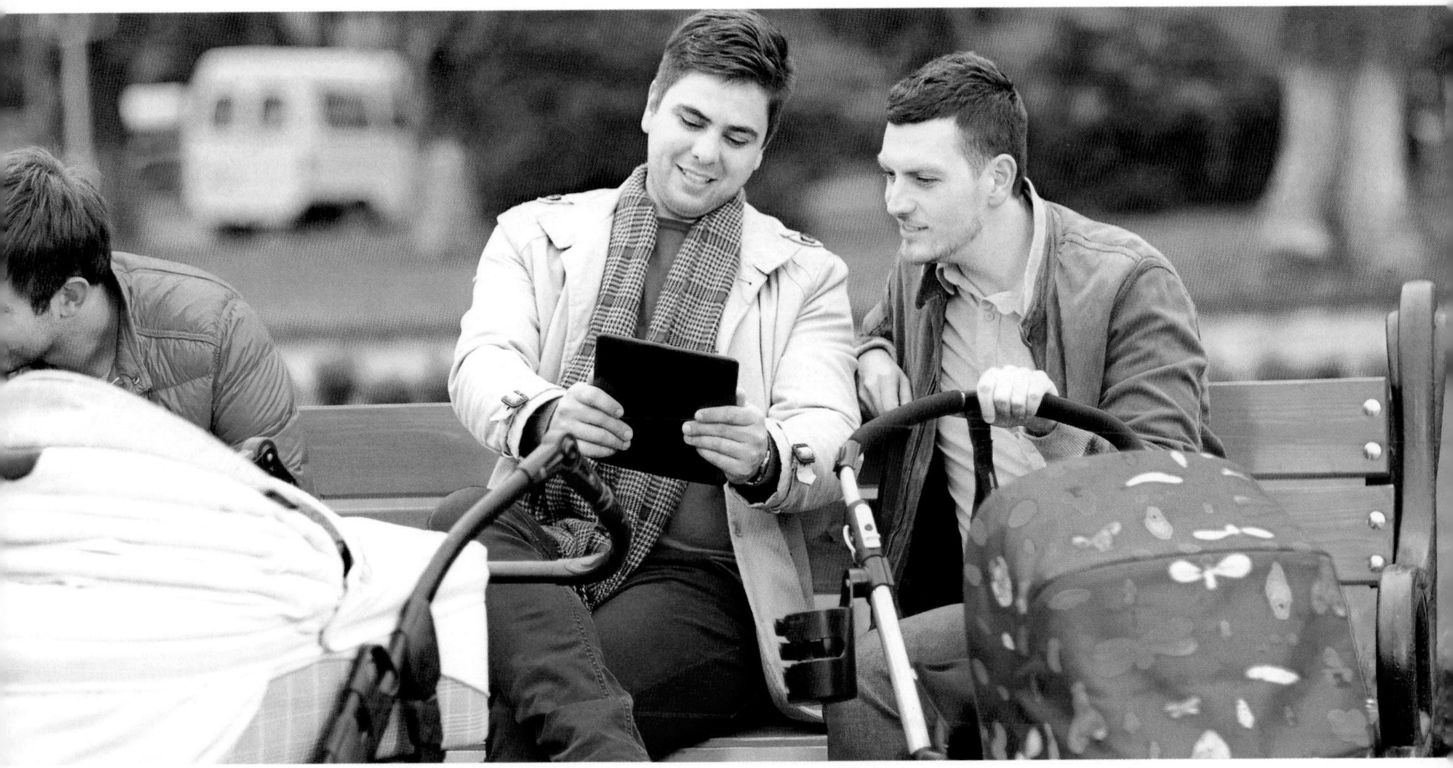

- **People with Disabilities**

Canadians with disabilities consistently experience low levels of employment and barriers to participating in the education, economic, and social spheres. Many need accommodations and supports, especially those with severe challenges or low educational attainment. Of those who are employed, many work for less than minimum wage and are not protected by labour legislation.

While all governments have developed measures to increase participation of people with disabilities in the labour force, the current situation is "a disjointed patchwork of widely varying practices and uneven accessibility, affordability and responsiveness" (Prince, 2016, p. 1). Prince recommends a six-point strategy for a new policy framework to improve labour force participation by people with disabilities:

- Renew the Canadian vision on disability and citizenship
- Improve transition planning for youth with disabilities
- Expand post-secondary education
- Foster improvement in workplace practices
- Enhance employment services and supports
- Modernize labour market agreements (p. 14)

- **Indigenous People**

In 2016 and 2017, a participatory engagement process with key Indigenous partners and organizations and the federal government was conducted to review the Aboriginal Skills and Employment Training Strategy (ASETS), which had been in place since 2010. The following challenges were identified as barriers to the participation of Indigenous people in the labour market:

- Lack of child care spaces
- Lack of flexibility to support post-secondary education (for example, university) through ASETS
- Inability to support youth through earlier interventions
- The need for many clients to upgrade essential skills before beginning training
- The many barriers encountered by ASETS agreement holders in remote locations
- High costs related to remoteness
- Lack of necessary infrastructure for economic development
- Lack of training opportunities
- Lack of job opportunities (in some areas) (Employment and Social Development Canada, 2016, para. 12).

In 2019, the co-developed Indigenous Skills and Employment Training (ISET) program replaced ASETS and is designed to help Indigenous people improve their skills and find employment.

COVID–19: The "She-cession" in Canada

***"Simply put: there will be no recovery without a she-covery, and no she-covery without childcare."* –Armine Yalnizyan**

The world's first recession that hit women (and low-paid, racialized, and young) workers first continues to hit women hardest.

In February, before the pandemic hit, women made up half of payroll, but — except for the levels of part-time employment — women's metrics were lower than men's on virtually all paid-work parameters (average actual hours worked, employment rates, full-time employment, participation rates). By December, working women had fallen even further behind on every front except average weekly hours worked (a sign of how many part-time jobs had been lost by women), notwithstanding a labour market that had recovered 98% of total hours worked (mostly by both part-timers and over-timers putting in longer hours). The last Labour Force Survey results for 2020 showed that employment growth was slowing, as contagion rates accelerate. We are flattening the wrong curves.

The most troubling trend is that, between February and December, 28,000 more men joined the labour force despite the pandemic's economic impact, while 45,000 women left it. The ranks of those who are no longer in the labour force grew almost twice as fast for women as men (159,000 more women were added to the "not in the labour force category" from February to November, compared to 87,000 more men). This includes retirees, and women who cannot get back into the job market or have thrown in the towel because of lack of childcare.

This is not just a woman's problem; it's a macroeconomic problem. Household spending accounted for 57% of GDP before the pandemic hit; the biggest block of spenders are households with young children; and women make up 40% of the incomes of such households. The longer women don't recover paid work, the slower will be recovery, for all.

Armine Yalnizyan is an economist, Atkinson Fellow on the Future of Workers, and the person who coined the term "she-cession," in March of 2020. Reproduced by permission of the author.

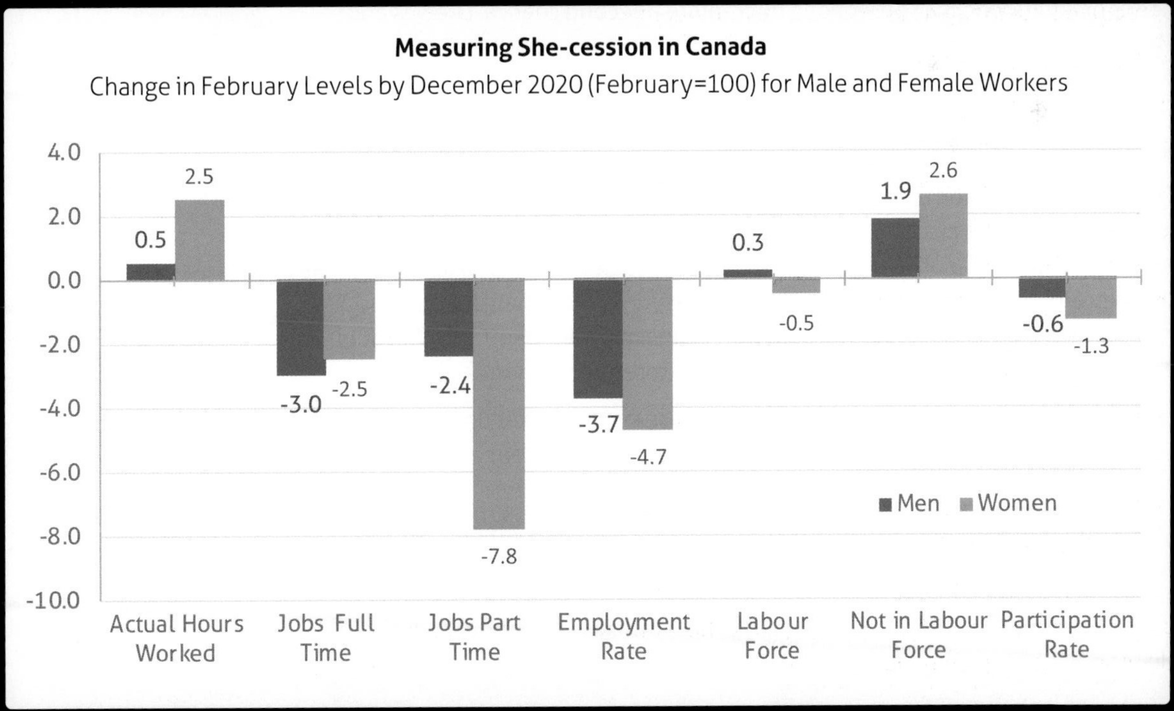

Armine Yalnizyan, based on seasonally adjusted date from Statistics Canada Tables 14-10-0287-01 and 14-10-0036-01.

The Working Poor: The Need for a Basic Income

In a just society, people working full-time should not find themselves living in poverty. Setting a higher minimum wage would raise the floor for low-income earners and reduce the costs of many income security programs. People would then be getting their income from the labour market rather than having to turn to government transfers for help.

A universal basic income (UBI), sometimes referred to as a "guaranteed livable income," is meant to reduce poverty and improve lives by making sure that no one's income falls below a certain level. Supporters on the ideological left see it as a way to raise incomes, improve health and quality of life, and remove the stigma of collecting social assistance. Conversely, opponents see it as a dangerous approach that drives up wages and allows some workers to drop out of the workforce because they no longer need to work (Ontario Public Service Employees Union, 2017).

The idea of a universal minimum level of income security has been debated in Canada since the 1930s and was first recommended in 1971 by the Croll committee. Today, both the Liberal Party and the Green Party continue to advocate for a basic income in Canada. Hugh Segal, a Progressive Conservative and a former chief of staff to both Ontario Premier Bill Davis and Prime Minister Brian Mulroney, is one of the strongest advocates. However, the debate over the need for a basic income continues.

People Who Want to Upgrade Their Education or Training

Canada's education and training system does a fairly good job of producing highly educated workers, but it does not provide sufficient support to meet the learning needs of adults who may be working but require a second chance. Drewes and Meredith (2015) found that "a considerable portion of Canada's labour force might benefit from improved access to learning later in life, including the 1 in 7 working-age adults who report having insufficient qualifications for their current job, and the 1 in 5 who lack basic literacy and numeracy skills" (p. 1).

The costs of education and training for older adults is often a barrier. As well, lower-skilled adults are less likely to participate in job-related learning compared with higher-skilled adults. Another concern for adult education and training is that the apprenticeship training system, the largest source of learning for older adults, is broken. Drewes and Meredith (2015) call for an ambitious pan-Canadian adult education and training strategy centred around three key reforms:

- Improving labour market information and research to better understand the unique needs of adults, including the development of a permanent adult education and training survey
- Developing a comprehensive, income-contingent loans system targeting older adults
- Overhauling provincial apprenticeship systems to make the learning process and the capacity of training institutions more similar to those in the post-secondary education system (p. 1)

Universal Basic Income: "An Investment, Not a Cost"

There was renewed interest in basic income programs during the COVID–19 pandemic due to the unprecedented shock to the Canadian economy.

According to a report by the Canadian Centre for Economic Analysis, a universal basic income (UBI) would not only lift more than 3.2 million Canadians out of poverty, it would also create hundreds of thousands of new jobs, grow the economy by tens of billions of dollars, and eventually pay for itself.

As the report pointed out, "It can be thought of as an investment as opposed to a cost."

Canadian Centre for Economic Analysis (2020). *Potential Economic Impacts and Reach of Basic Income Programs in Canada*. Research Report.

Making Strategic Investments for the Future

For too many people in Canada, especially those who are systematically marginalized and excluded from full labour market participation, the ideal of a full-time job with good pay and benefits is still a pipe dream. Many are faced with having to cobble together multiple part-time and precarious jobs. Some have dropped out of the labour force altogether.

Labour market analysts and policymakers are beginning, albeit slowly, to take a more proactive, social investment approach to reducing the underemployment, poor wages, and unemployment associated with people who are vulnerable due to their identity.

Federal and provincial public sector employment equity legislation is beginning to make a difference in the percentage of women in leadership roles in business. Education policies are helping to increase the number of Indigenous people completing their secondary and post-secondary qualifications. Increases in minimum wage laws are assisting the working poor in some provinces. The federal government is also addressing the gender wage gap through pay equity legislation (equal pay for work of equal value) in the federal sector. Other initiatives include more workplace flexibility to allow time for child rearing and elder care. In addition, multi-pronged approaches are being used to address the disadvantages faced by people with disabilities.

However, there is a long way to go. Traditional labour market policies have not always worked well enough or quickly enough. In particular, there has not been enough of a focus on the integration of all people in the Canadian labour market. There are also serious concerns about the way the Employment Insurance and workers' compensation systems have been systematically weakened over the past 30 years. At this point, they are struggling to meet their original goals of providing adequate social protections for employees against the risk of unemployment and injury, not too mention the new risks of workplace violence and stress.

What is required, as this chapter has argued, is a more consistent and coherent approach to the labour market and human resource development. That approach should be based firmly on the principles of inclusion, equity, and social justice to promote social and economic well-being for all.

Minimum Wages

These are the minimum hourly wage rates set by the provinces and territories in Canada at the end of 2020.

- Alberta, $15.00
- BC, $14.60
- Manitoba, $11.90
- New Brunswick, $11.70
- NL & Labrador, $12.15
- NWT, $13.46
- Nova Scotia, $12.55
- Nunavut, $16.00
- Ontario, $14.25
- PEI, $12.85
- Québec, $13.10
- Saskatchewan. $11.45
- Yukon, $13.71

Retail Council of Canada (2020). *Minimum Hourly Wage Rates*. www.retailcouncil.org.

Social Welfare Policy in Action

Canada's Pay Equity Act

Federal Legislation Advances Gender Equality

In October 2018, the Government of Canada passed historic legislation that fundamentally transformed how the right to pay equity is protected.

In 2016, following a pay equity report entitled *It's Time to Act*, the Government of Canada committed to designing new federal pay equity legislation. In 2017, roundtable discussions took place with 40 employer, employee, and advocacy stakeholders. The result was An Act to Establish a Proactive Pay Equity Regime within the Federal Public and Private Sectors (Pay Equity Act), which was passed in 2018.

Under the new Pay Equity Act, men and women in federally regulated workplaces are to receive equal pay for equal work. The Act protects pay equity in federally regulated workplaces with 10 or more employees. It also sets out clear steps for employers to follow to achieve pay equity. Employers were given three years to develop a plan before the Act would become enforceable in 2020.

The Honourable Maryam Monsef, Minister for Women and Gender Equality, said the following when the Act passed: "Today is an historic day, because when Canadian women in federally regulated industries can count on equal pay for work of equal value, our economy becomes stronger, families prosper, and communities thrive" (Employment and Social Development Canada [ESDC], 2018c).

The Act also established the role of Pay Equity Commissioner to administer and enforce the Act.

Sections 10 and 11 (1) of the Act state that the governments of Yukon, the Northwest Territories, and Nunavut, and Indigenous governing bodies that are employers are currently exempt. However, the Act may apply to these groups at a later date by order of the Governor in Council.

Background

Since 1977, the Canadian Human Rights Act has recognized pay equity as a right for employees in the federal jurisdiction. However, the onus was placed on employees to bring complaints forward to redress instances of pay discrimination (ESDC, 2018b).

In 2017 in Canada, for every dollar a man earned, a woman earned 88.5 cents (on an hourly basis) (ESDC, 2018b). When overall earnings were compared, women earned just 69 cents for every dollar earned by men.

An employment standards act exists in Ontario, Manitoba, Saskatchewan, Yukon, Newfoundland and Labrador, and the Northwest Territories, covering equal pay for the same or similar work (Pay Equity Commission, 2018). "Equal pay" (covered under provincial/territorial employment standards acts) is not the same as "pay equity." Pay equity compares jobs done by women with jobs done by men to determine whether women are being compensated equitably.

The gender wage gap is a complex issue with multiple underlying causes. In addition to the undervaluation of work traditionally performed by women, causes include:

- Over-representation of women in part-time work
- Labour market segmentation of women in low-paying sectors
- Lack of representation in senior positions
- Bias and discrimination in the workplace
- Women's greater share of unpaid work

The Purpose of the Pay Equity Act

"The purpose of [the] Act is to achieve pay equity through proactive means by redressing the systemic gender-based discrimination in the compensation practices and systems of employers that is experienced by employees who occupy positions in predominantly female job classes" (section 2).

Employers' Pay Equity Plan

Employers must establish a pay equity plan (to be reviewed every five years) that does the following:

- Identifies job classes within their workplace. Positions are in the same job class if they have similar jobs and responsibilities, require similar qualifications, and are part of the same compensation plan
- Identifies the gender predominance of the identified job classless. A job class is gender predominant if at least 60% of the positions are occupied by one gender, and that the job class is commonly associated with that gender
- Evaluates the value of work performed by each job class
- Identifies the compensation associated with each job class
- Identifies when compensation increases are due
- Provides information on the dispute resolution procedures available to employees (ESDC, 2018a)

Pay Equity Wage Adjustments

The Act states that an increase in compensation is required the day after the third anniversary of the passing of the Act, when employers become subject to the Act.

If the total amount of the increase is more than 1% of the previous year's payroll, the employer can phase in the increases (Pay Equity Commission, 2018).

Pay Equity Commissioner

On September 10, 2019, Karen Jensen was appointed as the first Federal Pay Equity Commissioner. She is responsible for administering and enforcing the new Pay Equity Act.

The commissioner has funding and a range of compliance and enforcement tools, including the power to initiate audits, conduct investigations, and issue orders and monetary penalties (ESDC, 2019a). She is supported by subject-matter experts and is responsible for assisting individuals in understanding their rights and obligations under the Act and facilitating the resolution of disputes.

Questions for Reflection

The Pay Equity Act is available here: https://laws-lois.justice.gc.ca/eng/acts/P-4.2/index.html. Once you have reviewed the Act, answer the following questions:

1. What social indicators pointed to the need for federal pay equity legislation?
2. How is gender pay equity understood in this Act?
3. What are the social welfare approaches that underpin this Act?
4. How might this Act affect women's professional "caring" work, which is often invisible and undervalued?
5. How might this Act affect early childhood education policies and the pay early childhood educators receive?
6. How are the principles of inclusion, equity, and social justice framed in this Act?
7. What is your perspective on the exclusions in the Act?
8. What are the mechanisms of accountability in the Act?

A Moment in Time: May 9, 1992

The Westray Mine Disaster

Nova Scotia Tragedy Leads to Criminal Code Amendments

Too often, it seems that it takes a major disaster to spur governments into putting policies, laws, and regulations in place that could have prevented the tragedy in the first place.

Such was the case with the Westray Mine explosion on May 9, 1992, when all 26 coal miners working there at the time lost their lives. The large coal mine in Plymouth, Nova Scotia, had received both federal and provincial money to open the mine and supply the local electric power utility with coal.

Mismanagement, inadequate safety precautions, and poor oversight by government regulators were the principal causes of the underground methane explosion, according to the public inquiry launched immediately after the disaster. The inquiry, headed by NS Supreme Court Justice K. Peter Richard, produced a final report that did not mince words. The final report asserted that Westray "is a story of incompetence, of mismanagement, of bureaucratic bungling, of deceit, of ruthlessness, of cover-up, of apathy, of expediency, and of cynical indifference" (Richard 1997, Executive Summary).

Important safety legislation did ensue from the disaster. After lobbying by unions and families, the federal government introduced Bill C-45 in 2002, establishing a duty for all persons who "direct the work of others" to take reasonable steps to ensure safety. It also added sections to the Criminal Code, allowing corporations and their representatives to be charged criminally. Since becoming law in 2004, few charges have been laid, and no one has been handed a jail sentence (Dubreuil, 2014).

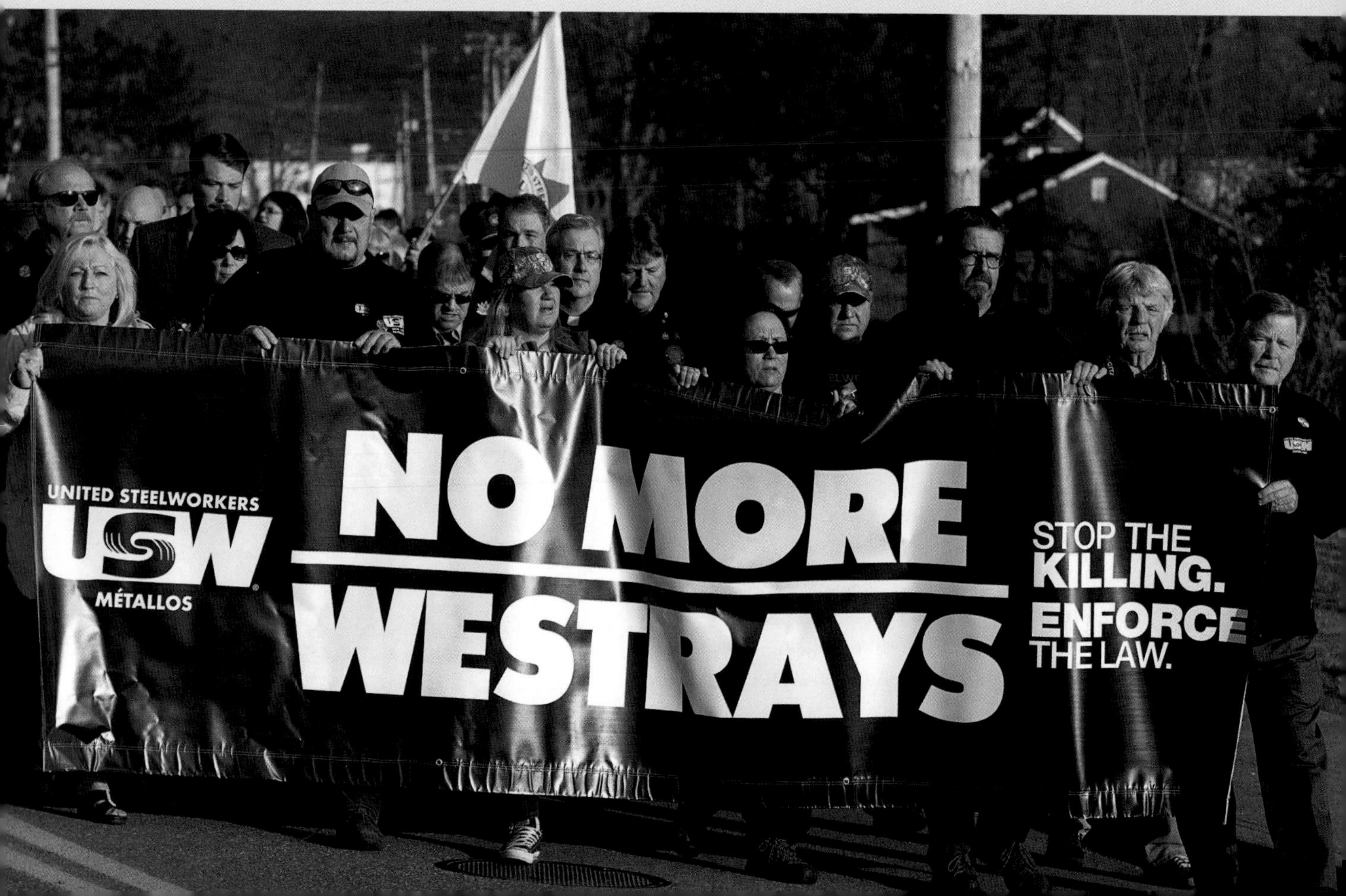

Tracy Smith-Carrier

4 Dignity for All: A Human Rights Framework

Racialized and marginalized persons are even more vulnerable in a crisis – that's the lesson of COVID–19.

In 2018, after two years of consultation, the government released its much anticipated national poverty strategy, called "Opportunity for All — Canada's First Poverty Reduction Strategy." For the first time, the federal government established an official poverty measure, set clear targets, and put in place mechanisms to monitor the strategy's success. Many anti-poverty activists felt the government set the bar too low, pledging to reduce poverty only by half and not until 2030. Moreover, there was no "new money."

Certainly, poverty in Canada was bad before the COVID–19 pandemic of 2020; experts are now concerned that the economic and health crisis will push many more people into poverty, if it hasn't already. "There's no doubt that the huge decline in employment is going to push people under the poverty line," said David Macdonald, a senior economist at the Canadian Centre for Policy Alternatives. "The real question is — how much can government programs push back?"

Key Concepts

- Dignity for All
- Human rights
- Market Basket Measure (MBM)
- Low Income Measure (LIM)
- Social determinants of health
- Campaign for a Living Wage
- Opportunity for All — Canada's First Poverty Reduction Strategy
- Poverty headcount
- Poverty gap
- Poverty duration
- Quintile distributions
- Gini coefficient
- Universal basic income
- Working poor
- Campaign 2000
- Homelessness
- Housing First
- At Home/Chez Soi
- Food banks and feeding programs
- Social assistance
- Workfare
- Social and economic costs of poverty

Dignity for All: A Human Rights Framework

This chapter explores different aspects of poverty: how it is defined, its extent, diverging explanations for its continued existence, its devastating effects, and, most importantly, what to do about it.

After completing this chapter, you should be able to:

- Explain the need for a national anti-poverty strategy based on principles rooted in human rights and personal dignity;
- Describe the core elements of an effective, national anti-poverty plan;
- Interpret quintile distributions and Gini coefficients, which are indicators of income inequality;
- Describe the extent and depth of child and family poverty in Canada;
- Describe the extent of the "working poor" in Canada today;
- Describe the extent to which food banks are relied upon;
- Explain how social assistance works and how eligibility criteria are applied; and
- Describe the social and economic costs of poverty.

4.1 Dignity for All

In 1989, the House of Commons vowed to end child poverty by the year 2000. Over 30 years later, little has changed. Based on the Low Income Measure (LIM), 12.1% of Canadian children (about one in eight) still live in poverty (Statistics Canada, 2017a). However, statistics are only part of the story. Poor nutrition, poor health, poor education outcomes, a lack of shelter, and a host of other social problems are all root causes and consequences of poverty and primary contributors to decreased social well-being.

According to a 2018 Agnus Reid survey, two-thirds of Canadians said that both the federal and provincial governments are not doing enough to address poverty and assist the people living in it (Angus Reid Institute, 2018). Undoubtedly, this widespread public concern was the impetus behind the federal government's 2018 announcement of a new, national anti-poverty strategy.

Why Focus on Human Rights?

Dignity for All is an anti-poverty campaign launched in 2009 by Canada Without Poverty and Citizens for Public Justice. Its approach to the problem of poverty is unique: it is built on the principles of social justice, inclusion, and human rights. Dignity for All seeks concrete and sustained action by the federal government so that everyone can pursue opportunities for achievement and fulfillment, embrace the rights and responsibilities of citizenship, and live with a sense of dignity.

The focus on human rights is especially relevant — human rights are inviolable — that is, they are never to be broken, infringed, or dishonoured. This means that whenever and wherever people are denied adequate housing, adequate income, and adequate food, their human rights are being violated. "To put poverty behind us," observes Elizabeth McIsaac, president of Maytree, an anti-poverty advocacy group that also emphasizes human rights, "we must support the best instincts of Canadians, harness our values of equality of opportunity and human dignity, and turn these values into actions" (McIsaac, 2017).

Traditional residualist policy responses to poverty often result in an erosion of benefits and protections: reduced access to Employment Insurance (EI), frozen or reduced social benefits, barriers to affordable housing, a lack of affordable child care, and reliance on food banks. The reasoning behind this way of thinking is that the "poor" are poor of their own volition and simply need a little shock treatment to get back on track.

An anti-poverty plan based on a human rights approach is committed to non-discrimination and equality; meaningful consultation and engagement with all stakeholders; measurable goals, targets, and timelines; monitoring mechanisms to remain transparent and accountable; and meaningful rights protection (Canada Without Poverty, 2018).

"Langar is a very pivotal aspect of our religion. Nobody should go hungry."

The Dashmesh Culture Centre in Calgary runs a community kitchen (a "langar") that provides a free vegetarian meal to anybody who needs one, regardless of race, religion. or creed, 24/7.

The serving of a free meal is a religious practice that is part of the Sikh tradition. The langar took on special importance during the COVID–19 pandemic.

As Canadians dealt with the anguish of losing their jobs and income and as food banks struggled to keep up, Sikh temples across the country, as well as other religious organizations, found ways to support their communities.

During the COVID–19 pandemic, the Dashmesh temple provided tens of thousands of meals to people of all backgrounds — including elderly people, students, and single mothers.

A Role for the Federal Government

The Dignity for All campaign has held that the federal government has a fundamental role to play in poverty reduction.

For one thing, the federal government has the fiscal ability to resolve poverty because of its jurisdiction over national taxes. Taxation is a way the federal government can generate the revenues needed to support national anti-poverty programs in consultation with the provinces and territories. Unfortunately, the federal government's tax revenues have decreased substantially over the past 20 years due to a string of tax cuts.

In addition, as a signatory of international treaties, Canada has committed to uphold human rights around the world, as well as in Canada, including the right to an adequate standard of living. Such agreements require the federal government to meet its obligations and demonstrate national leadership in doing so.

The Dignity for All campaign has aimed to achieve three federal policy goals:

- Creation of a federal plan for poverty eradication that complements the work of other partners, notably the provinces/territories and communities
- Introduction and implementation of a federal Anti-Poverty Act to eradicate poverty, promote social inclusion, and strengthen social security
- Collection and allocation of sufficient federal revenue to provide for social and economic security for all (Canada Without Poverty & Citizens for Public Justice, 2015, p. 7)

Relative Poverty in the Canadian Provinces

"Absolute poverty" refers to whether individuals are able to meet a basic threshold for survival. "Relative poverty," on the other hand, refers to whether people fall below the prevailing standards of living in a given societal context.

- >14
- 13–13.9
- 12–12.9
- 11–11.9
- <10
- No data

Conference Board of Canada (2018, July 30). *Poverty.*

Human Rights Aspects of the Poverty Crisis That Must Be Addressed

The Dignity for All campaign stresses that poverty reduction is, first and foremost, a human rights issue. Whereas traditional responses to poverty involve piecemeal, short-term solutions, a human rights approach "provides more solid ground upon which laws, policies, and programs aimed at ending poverty must be based" (Canada Without Poverty & Citizens for Public Justice, 2015, p. 12).

According to the Dignity for All campaign, the following six areas must be addressed in a comprehensive anti-poverty plan:

1. Income security
2. Housing and homelessness
3. Health care
4. Food security
5. Early childhood education and care
6. Jobs and employment

1. Income Security

In 2017, 3.4 million Canadians, or 9.5% of the population, lived below the newly established poverty line, the Market Basket Measure (MBM) (Statistics Canada, 2017a). Based on the Low Income Measure (LIM), 4.8 million Canadians, or 13.9% of the population (one in six people), lived below the poverty threshold that same year. It is often a good idea to take into account both measures — which calculate low income differently — for a more complete picture of low-income trends.

The rising cost of living, soaring accommodation prices, unaffordable child care costs, weakened labour laws, persistent low wages, and an increasingly precarious labour market make it exceedingly difficult for people to get ahead. Governments' unwillingness to address these issues through robust policy decisions has had adverse impacts on Canadians' health, economic well-being, and social well-being.

Canada uses a system of income taxes and income transfer programs to attend to the growing gap between rich and poor. Although it is not as effective as it once was, this system is vital in cultivating the higher standard of living many people enjoy today. The federal government is responsible for a number of income security programs that Canadians have come to rely on:

- **Employment Insurance (EI).** EI was once available to the vast majority of people who lost their jobs. The program was set up at a time when standard 9-to-5 employment was the norm, and people could access its benefits regardless of the reason for job loss (whether they were dismissed or laid off, or voluntarily left their place of work). In 2017, only 42.1% of unemployed Canadians had access to EI regular benefits (Employment and Social Development Canada, 2019), despite the fact that they and their employers pay into the EI system. This low percentage is largely due to the substantial work hours needed to qualify for benefits. The current precarious work environment (contract, seasonal, and casual/temporary jobs) makes it difficult for many to meet the eligibility criteria.

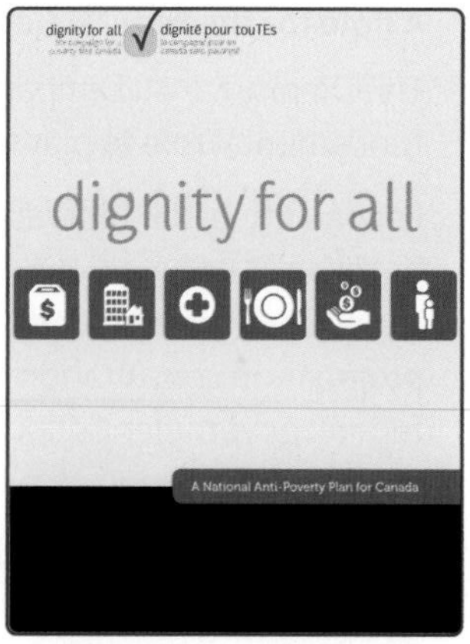

Over the past five years, Dignity for All has garnered support from 15,000 people in Canada who believe it is time for the federal government to step up and take responsibility for this country's impoverished populations.

With the input of people living in poverty, faith groups, organizations, academics, and others, Dignity for All has created a model national anti-poverty plan with six areas of focus.

- Income security
- Housing and homelessness
- Health care
- Food security
- Early childhood education and care
- Jobs and employment

This collaborative document is a model for what Canada's national anti-poverty plan could look like.

- **Old Age Security (OAS) and Guaranteed Income Supplement (GIS).** The OAS and GIS programs have played an instrumental role in reducing poverty among older adults. In the 1970s, Canada's older adult poverty rate soared to about 30% (using Low-Income Cut-Off [LICO] measures). However, because of these programs, along with the introduction of the Canada Pension Plan in 1965 and the Québec Pension Plan in 1966, poverty among older adults plummeted, dropping to 3.9% in 1995 (Conference Board of Canada, 2013). Although poverty among older adults is steadily increasing, these programs continue to create a buffer for many.

  Based on the LIM, the poverty rate for people age 65 and older has increased in recent years, rising from 12.2% in 2012 to 15.4% in 2017 (Statistics Canada, 2017a). By contrast, based on the MBM, there has been a decrease. In 2016, the poverty rate for older adults using the MBM was 11%, and it declined to 8.4% in 2017. The LIM and MBM rates calculate low income differently, which is why they are sometimes at odds.

  OAS was once a demogrant program (universal in scope — anyone eligible for the program would receive it) that was offered to all citizens and permanent residents over age 65. In 1989, the government introduced a clawback on high-income earners, taking the view that people making a significant amount of money should not be entitled to receive public money after they have turned 65. GIS acts as a means-tested benefit (allocated only to people with a low income) for adults over age 65 who are also eligible for OAS. The monthly (non-taxable) benefit is calculated based on an older adult's income as indicated on their income tax application.

"Annual income twenty pounds, annual expenditure nineteen [pounds] nineteen [shillings] and six [pence], result happiness. Annual income twenty pounds, annual expenditure twenty pounds ought and six, result misery."

— Charles Dickens (1812–1870), *David Copperfield*, 1850.

- **Canada Child Benefit (CCB).** Before it was changed, the federal child tax benefit system included the Canada Child Tax Benefit, the National Child Care Supplement, and the Universal Child Care Benefit. In 2016, Canada did away with its universal system and replaced it with a means-tested program under the single CCB program. The program is based on income (the more a person makes, the lower the benefit), is tax-free, and was, in 2018, indexed to inflation. In 2019, the CCB was increased to maximums of about $6,600 a year per child under age 6 and roughly $5,600 a year per child aged 6 to 17.
- **Canada Workers Benefit (CWB).** Prior to 2019, the Working Income Tax Benefit (WITB) was available for individuals engaged in paid work but whose income was insufficient. In the federal budget of 2019, the program was renamed the "Canada Workers Benefit" and was enhanced, offering a refundable tax rebate intended to supplement the earnings of low-income Canadians.
- **Social Assistance.** Social assistance systems (including financial and employment support for people in need, and a benefit program for people with disabilities) are a responsibility of the provinces/territories, although they receive block grants to fund them from the federal government (i.e., through the Canada Social Transfer). Many are calling for increases to enhance the Canada Social Transfer to better support people and to help sustain local poverty reduction efforts.

• **2. Housing and Homelessness**

Access to safe, affordable, and adequate housing is fundamental for our health and survival. Due to the rising cost of accommodation, inadequate wages, low vacancy rates, a meagre stock of affordable rental units, discrimination, and family/intimate partner violence, more people are at serious risk of becoming homeless. There is substantial literature documenting the negative outcomes associated with homelessness, including the deterioration of physical health, mental illness, stress, family breakdown, and increased mortality.

Due in large part to the legacy of colonialism and exploitation experienced by Indigenous people, First Nations, Inuit, and Métis people are most at risk of living on the streets, in shelters, or in inadequate and/or unsafe accommodations. In addition, housing on-reserve is often in deplorable condition, characterized by dilapidated buildings, poor heating, contaminated water, and overcrowding.

In 2018, the federal government introduced its first ever National Housing Strategy (NHS), "A Place to Call Home" (Government of Canada, 2018a). The strategy, a $40 billion plan, committed to removing 530,000 families from housing need and cutting chronic homelessness by 50% over the next decade. New initiatives would be introduced to create new housing supply, modernize existing housing, create resources for community housing providers, and support research and innovation in the housing sector. For the first time, the federal government referred to adequate housing as a human right — a declaration that was legislated in the National Housing Strategy Act of 2019. In so doing, the government has committed to realizing the right to housing across Canada, using Housing First principles.

Housing First is a recovery-oriented approach to ending homelessness that focuses on quickly moving people out of homelessness and into permanent housing, with additional supports as needed. Whereas in the past, individuals were required to be sober or in addiction recovery to qualify for housing support, a Housing First approach is based on the idea that people are best able to move ahead with their lives if they are first housed.

While there may be reasons to applaud policymakers for taking this important step, the strategy does not go far enough. Some argue that the exorbitant-sounding funding infusion promised by the strategy was built on previous funding programs that have yet to materialize.

David Hulchanski, a housing researcher and advocate, notes that the "federal government spent more on housing Canadians almost a decade ago than it has since the introduction of the new national housing strategy — the first federal housing program in 25 years" (Gold, 2019). Hulchanski and his team examined data from the Public Accounts of Canada to determine the actual grants and expenditures of the federal government. They found that in 2018, the federal government had spent only 0.8% of the federal budget on housing (less than the 1.1% it had spent in the 2010–2011 budget!). Sadly, this percentage is only marginally better than in 2016, the lowest year on record since the 1970s, when housing accounted for only 0.7% of the budget.

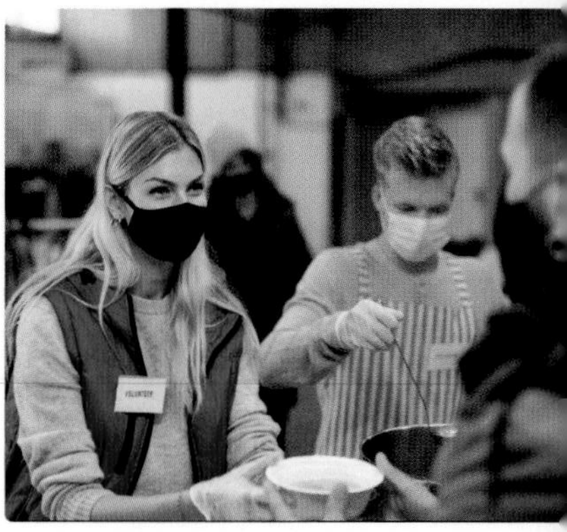

COVID–19 Homelessness

The COVID–19 pandemic exposed long-standing failures to protect the health and well-being of people experiencing homelessness in Canada.

"We've known about the perils of homelessness and not having housing, not being able to attain health without housing, for decades," Dr. Andrew Boozary, executive director of health and social policy at Toronto's University Health Network, told *The Current's* Matt Galloway on April 15, 2020.

"And what COVID–19 is doing is blowing the top off our ability to ignore this anymore."

"Whether it's in long-term care homes, whether it's in shelters, whether it's individuals who are racialized and working in low-paid jobs and underpaid jobs — these are the decisions that ... have exposed people to risk chronically."

• 3. Health

A person's health and well-being are highly dependent on economic and social factors. These factors are referred to as the **social determinants of health**. According to the Canadian Public Health Association (n.d.), the social determinants of health are as follows:

- Income and income distribution
- Education
- Unemployment and job security
- Employment and working conditions
- Early childhood development
- Food insecurity
- Housing
- Social exclusion
- Social safety network
- Health services
- Indigenous status
- Gender
- Race
- Disability

The social determinants of health encompass factors that extend far beyond those traditionally assumed to predict health outcomes: that is, adequate nutrition, limited alcohol consumption, smoking cessation/abstinence, and vigorous exercise. Many of the social determinants of health outlined are considered in various ways in other parts of this text, so we will consider only income and health services here.

Income has a significant influence on health status. One study in Hamilton, Ontario, found a massive 21-year difference in life expectancy across the highest and lowest income neighbourhoods in the city (Buist, 2015). People in poverty live significantly shorter lives. Moreover, poverty increases the risk of acquiring innumerable health problems; it has thus been deemed by the World Health Organization (n.d.) as the single most important determinant of health.

The national health care system is a hallmark of Canadian society. Canadians pride themselves on having access to quality health care services, free of charge to the individual, for all Canadians and resident newcomers alike. Yet, Canada is the only developed country with a universal health care system that excludes prescription drug coverage. Many people have to pay out of pocket for important drugs because they do not work for an employer that offers prescription benefits. In fact, a 2015 report by the Wellesley Institute found that only one-third of working Canadians had access to employer-provided health benefits, an amount that dropped to only one-quarter for workers age 25 and under (Barnes et al., 2015).

Pharmacare 2020, a group of experts in health and public policy, medical professionals, and health care researchers, has called upon the federal government to include a national pharmacare program in the Canadian universal health care system. Prior to the fall 2019 election, the Liberal Party, under Justin Trudeau, indicated that it would run on a platform that included a full national pharmacare program. However, in the end, the topic became more of a background promise and did not feature prominently in the Liberals' election campaign.

Intersectionality

While Canada has achieved high rankings internationally for its high quality of life, not all groups have equitable access to the resources that would engender better health and well-being.

Intersectionality, a theory first proposed by Kimberlé Crenshaw in 1989, recognizes that disadvantage is compounded when people occupy multiple marginalized axes of identity (based in gender, race/ethnicity, disability, sexual orientation, socio-economic status, and age, among others).

It is important to capture these intersections in our data collection measures to identify if there are differences in health processes and outcomes. Without good data, one is not able to argue that there are problems that must addressed. This is the first step in ensuring equity for everyone.

• 4. Food Security

Food security emerged as a new concept in the 1970s in the midst of a global food crisis. However, defining "food insecurity" is challenging, and there are many definitions in the research and policy literature.

The most recent definition emphasizes issues of access and entitlements: "Food security [is] a situation that exists when all people, at all times, have physical, social and economic access to sufficient, safe and nutritious food that meets their dietary needs and food preferences for an active and healthy life" (Food and Agriculture Organization of the United Nations, 2003, para. 13).

Therefore, it is important not only that people have enough food but also that the food they have actually meets their dietary needs and personal and cultural preferences. Also, they should be able to access such food in "socially acceptable ways," meaning that there should be no stigma attached to how they obtain it (Food and Agriculture Organization of the United Nations, 2003).

Food banks are a recent invention. Canada's first food bank opened in 1981 in Edmonton, Alberta, to contend with the financial crisis at the time (Edmonton Gleaners Association, 2020). Although food banks were meant to be a temporary solution, they became entrenched and institutionalized as *the* public solution to the problem of food insecurity.

Since the 1980s, financial vulnerability and food insecurity have grown across Canada. Rather than strengthening the social safety net, the federal and provincial governments, by imposing a series of austerity measures, have looked to the charitable sector for solutions to poverty and food insecurity. Yet, the vast majority of households (about 80%) rendered food insecure do not actually use a food bank (Tarasuk et al., 2019).

The stigma and shame attached to asking for food assistance can be devastating, and some would rather go hungry than seek help. Research has identified many barriers with charitable food access that make it challenging for individuals and families to obtain the food they need: limited food selection, excessive eligibility rules, food shortages, narrow facility operating hours, and difficulties with transportation (Smith-Carrier et al., 2017).

While many people, politicians included, continue to point to the charitable sector for answers to food insecurity, the solution lies not in access to food per se (e.g., through community soup kitchens, food banks, and breakfast programs), but rather in access to an adequate income. People need to be able to purchase the food they require and prefer and to do so in "socially acceptable ways" — in grocery stores — to avoid being demeaned in the process.

The Dignity for All campaign called on the federal government to create a National Right to Food Policy as part of a broader anti-poverty plan (Canada Without Poverty & Citizens for Public Justice, 2015). Moreover, it called on the federal government to increase investment in the high levels of Indigenous household food insecurity in ways that respect cultural considerations and Indigenous land sovereignty, and preserve traditional ways of knowing.

The Global Food Chain

The global food chain is a complex network so delicately balanced that the shocks of COVID-19 threatened to throw it off course at almost every turn. And that's what happened.

Food security, as defined by the United Nations' Committee on World Food Security, means that all people, at all times, have physical, social, and economic access to sufficient, safe, and nutritious food that meets their food preferences and dietary needs for an active and healthy life.

Yet, for many the food crisis during COVID-19 was particularly acute. Within just a few weeks of the lockdown, the demand at food banks shot up by 20% and as much as 40% in some Canadian cities.

• 5. Early Childhood Education and Care

In 1970, the Report of the Royal Commission on the Status of Women in Canada made 167 recommendations, including establishing a National Daycare Act (Bird, 1970). Since that time, calls for a federally funded, affordable, accessible, and high-quality system have resounded time and again, yet to no avail. Despite the fact that a nationwide early childhood education system is likely the smartest investment Canada could make, it has not happened yet.

In 1999, the Honourable Margaret McCain and Dr. Fraser Mustard released the first of a series of early years reports emphasizing the importance of early childhood education and child care. In this work, they highlighted the economic argument for early childhood education: every $1 invested in universal childhood education has a return of $6 in economic benefits. Québec's low-fee child care system confirms this statement (Early Years Study, 2020).

In 2012, Fortin, Godbout, and St-Cerny found that Québec's government-subsidized low-fee child care system increased female labour force participation and increased Québec's gross domestic product (GDP) (total earnings in the province) by billions of dollars (e.g., $5 billion in 2008). The original program was offered at a mere $5 per day, which was later increased to $7 per day. In 2014, a sliding scale was introduced to provide greater support for low-income families, while keeping rates still relatively low for middle- and higher-income earners (under $200 per month). Québec's child care program is widely regarded as a resounding success.

Meanwhile, in cities in the Greater Toronto Area and Metro Vancouver, child care rates continue to soar, with fees that are unaffordable for many. A family in Toronto can expect to pay about $1,685 per month for infant care (about $20,220 annually), according to calculations by the Canadian Centre for Policy Alternatives (Macdonald & Friendly, 2019). Wait lists remain common in urban cities, making regulated child care not only unaffordable but also often inaccessible.

Taking lessons from Québec, Canada could benefit from a universal affordable and accessible child care system; such a system would yield a host of positive economic, social, and health outcomes. As McCain and Mustard point out, early childhood education is not simply babysitting or daycare, it provides a nurturing environment fostered by seasoned educators (Early Years Study, 2020). Early childhood education also includes a focus on literacy, numeracy, problem-solving skills, language development, and emotional regulation and confidence.

The importance of the early years cannot be overstated. Research shows that they are a time when children can make positive gains in reading, writing, and number sense, as well as the ability to effectively respond to stress and self-regulate. Yet, today, only six provinces and territories have full-day kindergarten for five-year-olds (and only Ontario has it for four-year-olds) (Early Years Study, 2020).

"Canadians need more accessible, affordable, inclusive, and high quality childcare... Recognizing the urgency of this challenge, the Government will make a significant, long-term, sustained investment to create a Canada-wide early learning and childcare system. The Government will build on previous investments, learn from the model that already exists in Québec, and work with all provinces and territories to ensure that high-quality care is accessible to all. There is broad consensus from all parts of society, including business and labour leaders, that the time is now."

Governor General of Canada (2020). A stronger and more resilient Canada. Speech from the Throne to Open the Second Session of the Forty-third Parliament of Canada, September 23, 2020.

- **6. Jobs and Employment**

About 50 years ago, paid employment was considered the responsibility of the male breadwinner. Women were expected to stay at home to care for the home and children (their labour, although still work, was unpaid). At this time, the labour market largely reflected standard wage employment: 9-to-5 standard work hours, stable wages, and usually workplace benefits (e.g., vacation days, sick days, an occupational health plan, and a pension plan).

Today, the vast majority of families require two (fairly well-paying) jobs to be included in the middle class. Moreover, many jobs today are precarious: they are seasonal, contract, part-time, or "flexible" (to the employer, but not necessarily the employee). While wages have either remained the same or stagnated, the cost of living has skyrocketed, leaving many individuals and families feeling the crunch.

It would take a commitment to strengthening labour laws, and focusing on job creation (including significant investments in infrastructure, housing, and transportation) to break this trend. The federal government has not made labour laws more robust, and it has been reluctant to impose labour regulations on the private (and public) sector. This reluctance may be due to government philosophy: that is, the idea that it is not the government's responsibility to interfere in the workplace. It may also be due to a fear that industries and businesses may relocate, moving jobs elsewhere, if labour laws are stronger. Under little pressure to change, many companies have not had to focus on adequate wages or benefits or commit to stable employment.

Social Exclusion

A person living in poverty not only lacks basic resources—food, shelter, clothing—but also has limited opportunities to participate in the social, economic, and cultural activities of her or his society, thereby experiencing social exclusion.

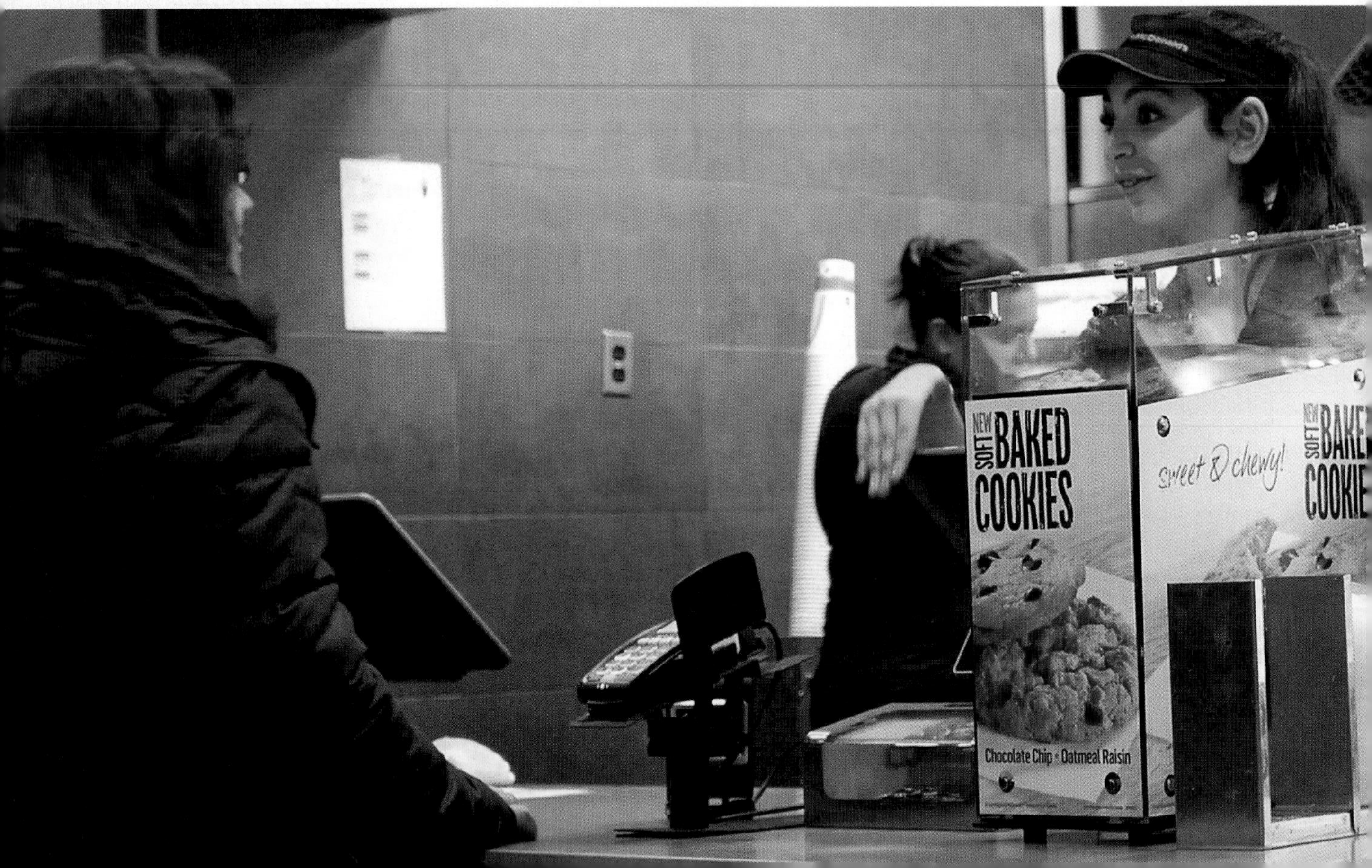

Campaign for a Living Wage

The Campaign for a Living Wage originated in the United States in the 1990s. Advocates in some US cities put pressure on local businesses to adopt a living wage — a minimum income floor that people living in a particular area should be able to live on adequately.

A living wage is different from a minimum wage. The minimum wage is the legislated minimum set by the provincial government, while a living wage is a community-led initiative. Ideally, the minimum wage should be set at a rate high enough to lift an individual worker out of poverty. An adequate minimum wage is a strategy for governments to address working poverty, while a living wage is a demand for employers to do better.

The living wage campaign seeks to convince employers to offer wages above prescribed thresholds (using a cost-of-living calculation in each given region). It calls on employers to meet a higher standard for their staff and contractors to ensure that wages reflect the actual costs of living in that community so that individuals and parents can earn what they need to support themselves and their families.

Critics of the living wage point out that it is typically focused exclusively on the responsibility of the employers (thereby, they would argue, effectively letting governments off the hook). They also point out that often efforts are focused on full-time employees alone and not necessarily on the precariously employed workers who are in most need of a living wage.

Social Welfare in Perspective

Canada's Poverty Reduction Strategy

Opportunity for All

On August 21, 2018, the federal government announced details of the first Canadian poverty reduction strategy. The strategy was welcomed, but some feel that it falls short.

Opportunity for All—Canada's First Poverty Reduction Strategy, the new anti-poverty strategy released by the federal government, is something that social welfare advocates, the United Nations, and people who have lived experience of poverty have long called for.

It establishes official poverty targets and a way for the government to closely monitor them (Government of Canada, 2018b). Notably, it also references Canada's international obligations on human rights and the United Nations' Sustainable Development Goals.

According to government estimates, existing and planned spending will lift 650,000 more people out of poverty by 2019. Moreover, by 2020, poverty would be 20% lower than 2015 levels (a decrease from 12% to 10%), with 900,000 fewer people existing below the income threshold (Government of Canada, 2018b). If these reductions are achieved, that would be significant.

The federal strategy promises a further reduction over the next decade, so that by 2030 poverty would be 50% lower than in 2015 (a decrease from 12% to 6%), which equates with lifting 2.1 million people out of poverty (Government of Canada, 2018b).

Market Basket Measure (MBM)

One problem has been that Canada has never had an official measure of poverty. Going forward, Canada's official measure will be the Market Basket Measure (MBM; also referred to as "Canada's Official Poverty Line"), a measure first created in the 1990s.

The MBM calculates the amount of income needed by a household to meet its daily needs. A family or person is considered to be living in poverty if they cannot afford a basic basket of goods and services. The measure is adjusted for 50 different communities across Canada to account for cost-of-living differences. The MBM currently is not calculated for Canada's three territories, an issue the government intends to rectify in the future.

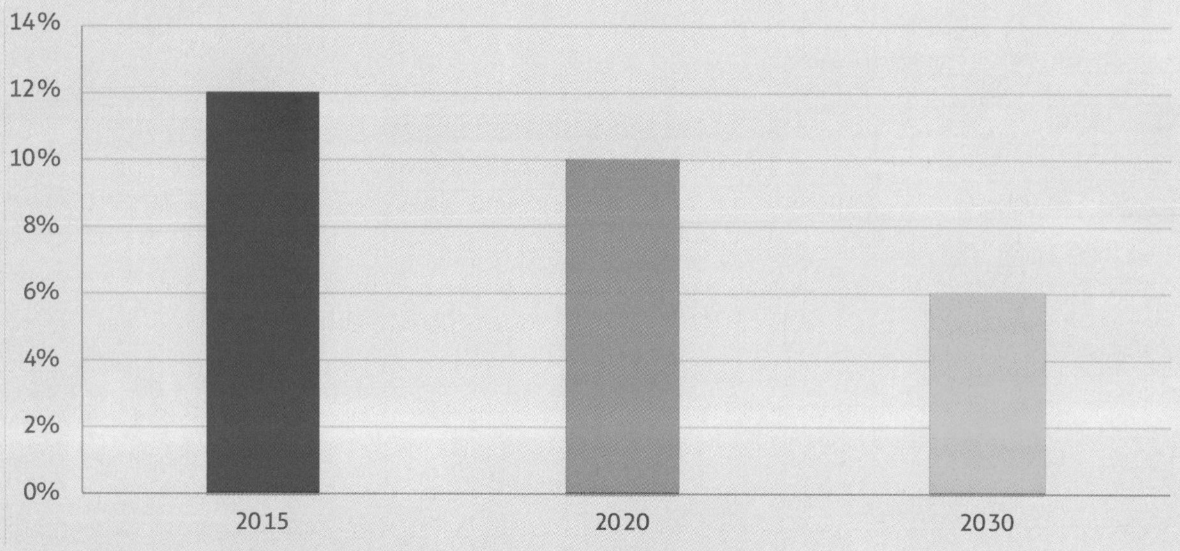

Employment and Social Development Canada (2018). Opportunity for All — Canada's First Poverty Reduction Strategy. Ottawa, ON.

No New Funding and No New Programs

Now that the scourge of poverty is acknowledged at the highest levels of the Canadian government, anti-poverty activists are optimistic that more will be done. They are prepared to hold the government accountable for its promises.

To be sure, programs such as the new Canada Child Benefit, the National Housing Strategy, and the increase to Old Age Security are having a meaningful impact on those working hard to make ends meet. However, poverty is deep, and anti-poverty activists feel that much more effort is needed if it is to be eradicated. The United Church of Canada, a faith-based organization working to eradicate poverty, noted the following:

> The federal poverty reduction strategy sets a target to reduce poverty rates in Canada by 50% of 2015 rates by 2030. We are pleased that this target and timeline, along with a National Advisory Council, will all be enshrined in legislation.
>
> At the same time, the United Church is concerned that the plan does not contain new funding commitments or programs to enable it to reach this target. Substantial and ongoing funding is needed to reduce poverty rates. It is our expectation that the National Advisory Council will serve as an accountability mechanism centred on the voices of people living in poverty.
>
> The plan also falls short in failing to recognize the centrality of working directly with Indigenous governments, respecting their right to self-determination as found in the United Nations Declaration on the Rights of Indigenous Peoples as a way of eliminating poverty among Indigenous peoples in Canada, including the loss of language, land, and so on. (United Church of Canada, 2018, paras. 2–4)

Even if the federal targets are achieved, this would still leave 2.1 million people in poverty by the end of the planned time period, including just over 534,000 children under age 18 (Scott, 2018). Anti-poverty coalitions, including Campaign 2000 (which advocates for an end to child poverty in Canada), responded that they intend to press for more ambitious targets.

PROVINCIAL INITIATIVES

Poverty reduction is another policy area that has largely been left to provincial and territorial governments. These programs have not eliminated the scourge of poverty.

Newfoundland and Labrador
Reducing Poverty: An Action Plan for Newfoundland and Labrador

Prince Edward Island
Social Action Plan to Reduce Poverty

Nova Scotia
Preventing Poverty. Promoting Prosperity: Nova Scotia's Poverty Reduction Strategy

New Brunswick
Overcoming Poverty Together: The New Brunswick Economic and Social Inclusion Plan

Québec
The Will to Act. The Strength to Succeed: National Strategy to Combat Poverty and Social Exclusion

Ontario
Realizing Our Potential: Ontario's Poverty Reduction Strategy

Manitoba
All Aboard: Manitoba's Poverty Reduction Strategy

Saskatchewan
Taking Action on Poverty: The Saskatchewan Poverty Reduction Strategy

Alberta
Together We Raise Tomorrow: An Alberta Approach to Early Childhood Development

British Columbia
TogetherBC: British Columbia's Poverty Reduction Strategy

4.2 How Much Poverty Is There?

When examining poverty, three dimensions need to be considered: (1) How many people are poor (poverty headcount)? (2) How far do people's incomes fall below the poverty line (poverty gap)? and (3) How long are people living in poverty (poverty duration)? One of the challenges is to ensure that, whichever measure is used, it allows for reliable estimates, consistent monitoring, and complete accuracy.

Poverty Headcount

The poverty headcount measures the number and proportion of persons living in poverty. There are at least three ways it has been measured:

- In the past, the measure used was Low-Income Cut-Offs — the level at which a family has to spend a greater proportion of its income on necessities than the average family of a similar size and community. (LICOs are now discontinued.)
- In 2018, the federal government announced that the Market Basket Measure (MBM) would be Canada's new poverty line. (It is also referred to as "Canada's Official Poverty Line.") The MBM calculates low income based on the cost of a specific basket of goods and services in a given community.
- The Low Income Measure (LIM) is the internationally preferred measure. It calculates poverty at a rate of 50% of the median household income.

Figure 4.1 tracks poverty rate trends using the MBM and LIM measures.

Figure 4.1

Poverty Rate Comparison: Market Basket Measure (MBM) vs. Low Income Measure — After Tax (LIM-AT)

Statistics Canada, Table 11-10-0135-01. Low income statistics by age, sex and economic family type, 2016.

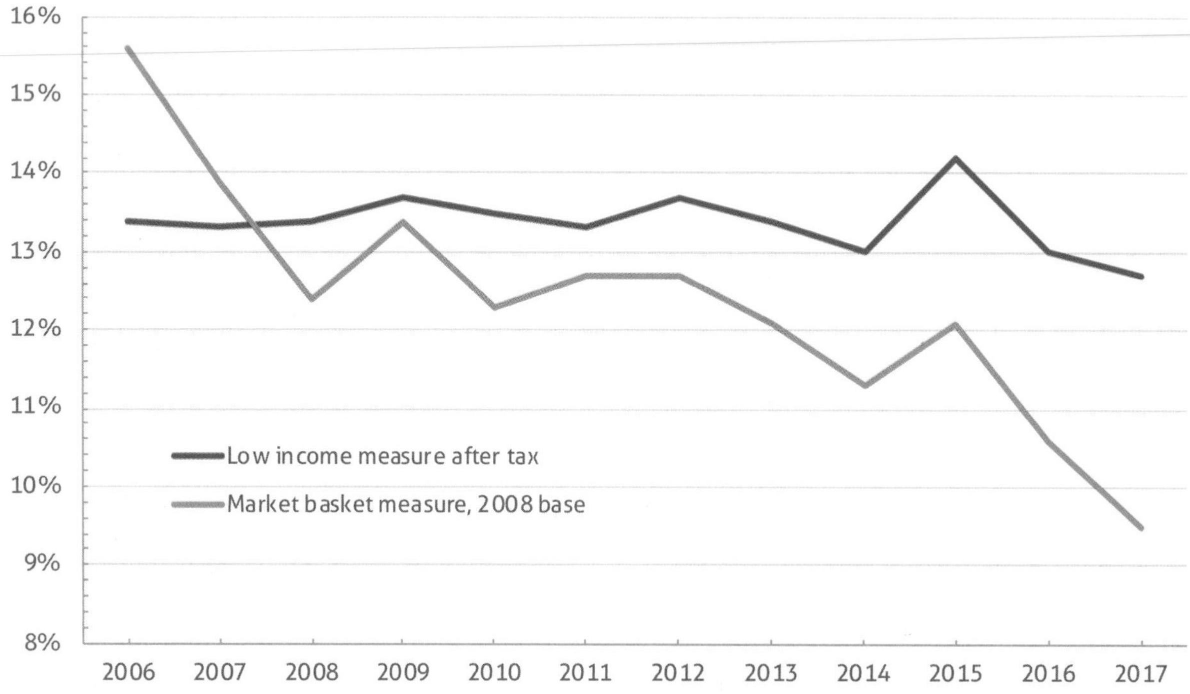

Poverty Gap

Poverty rates do not always show whether people are living in abject poverty or a few dollars below the poverty line. To determine the depth of poverty, we need to measure the poverty gap. The **poverty gap** is "a ratio showing the average shortfall of the total population from the poverty line" (Liberto, 2019). The poverty gap can also refer to the amount of income a family living in poverty would need to lift them to the poverty line. Statistics Canada refers to this measure of the depth of poverty, euphemistically, as the "average income deficiency."

The OECD (2019) reported that in 2019, Canada had a poverty gap of roughly 0.305. To compare, Finland had a poverty gap of 0.210 (the lowest in OECD countries), while South Africa had a poverty gap of 0.485 (the highest in OECD countries). The lower the value, the smaller the poverty gap.

The poverty gap statistic can be used to calculate the poverty gap index, which is the mean shortfall from the poverty line divided by the value of the poverty line (Liberto, 2019). The higher the poverty gap index, the greater the severity of poverty. If the poverty gap index is multiplied by the poverty line and the number of individuals in a population, the result is the amount of money people living in poverty would need to reach the poverty line (Liberto, 2019). (See Figure 4.2.) Although the poverty gap is a useful measurement, it does not capture qualitative information, such as personal capabilities and community resources that may contribute to or help eradicate poverty.

Figure 4.2

The Depth of Poverty in Canada

Statistics Canada Table F-20. After-tax, low-income status of Census families by family type and family composition, 2016.

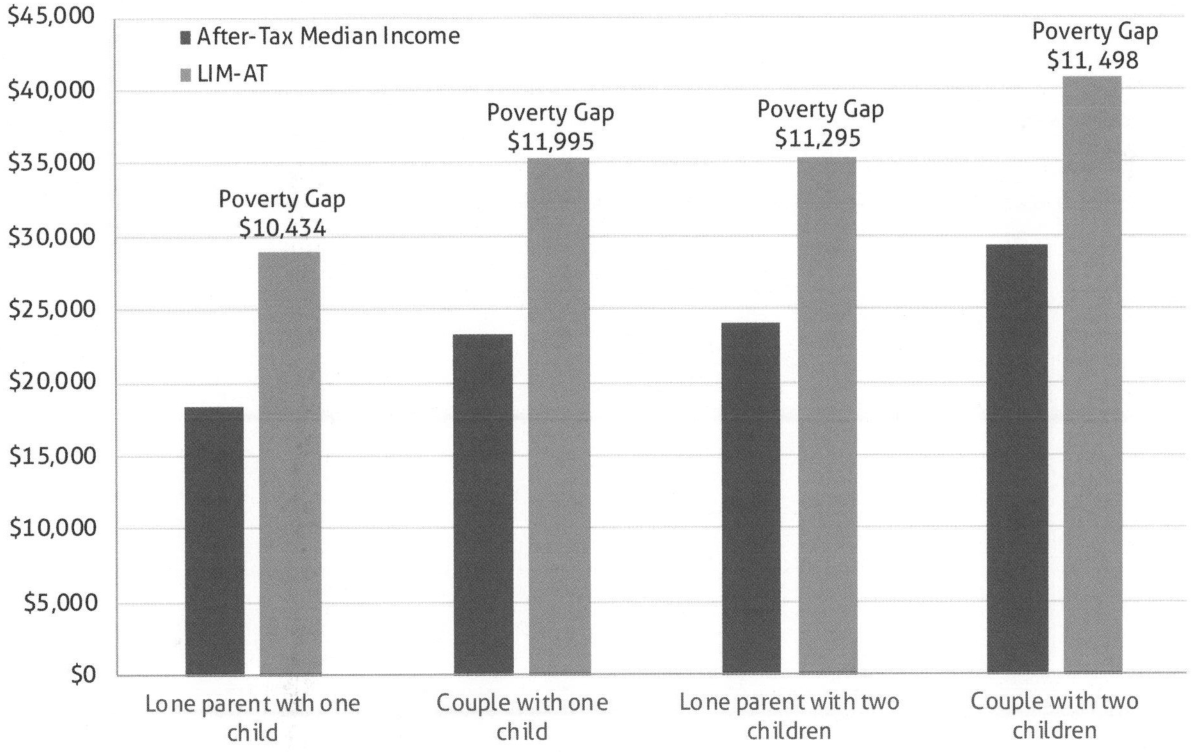

Poverty Duration

Finally, it is important to consider poverty duration, or how long people experience low income. Statistics Canada's Survey of Labour and Income Dynamics (SLID) followed the same set of people for six consecutive years and was designed to capture changes over time. Unfortunately, it was abandoned in 2012 and replaced with the Canadian Income Survey (a cross-sectional survey that only captures data for a single point in time rather than at multiple times).

Data from the SLID showed that, over the long term, poverty affects a greater number of Canadians than yearly poverty rates might suggest. Clearly, vulnerable groups, such as people with disabilities, people with lower levels of education, racialized communities, lone parents, recent immigrants, and Indigenous people all face a risk of longer-term poverty.

How long do people stay in poverty? Most low-income Canadians experience poverty for a short period of time, exiting low income within a year (see Figure 4.3). From 2005 to 2010, only 1.5% of low-income Canadians lived in low income for up to six years, based on the LICOs (after-tax) (Statistics Canada, 2011). People have experienced greater difficulty exiting low income since the "Great Recession" of 2008–2009. The economic downturn triggered a system-wide upheaval, including increased unemployment rates and social assistance caseloads, and substantially higher rates of poverty. Rates of poverty among the vulnerable groups mentioned above would have been substantially higher during and following this downturn (Pasma & Citizens for Public Justice, 2010).

Figure 4.3

Duration of Low-Income Status, 2005–2010, Low-Income Cut-Offs — After Tax (Base Year 1992)

Statistics Canada, Survey of Labour and Income Dynamics, CANSIM Table 202–0807.

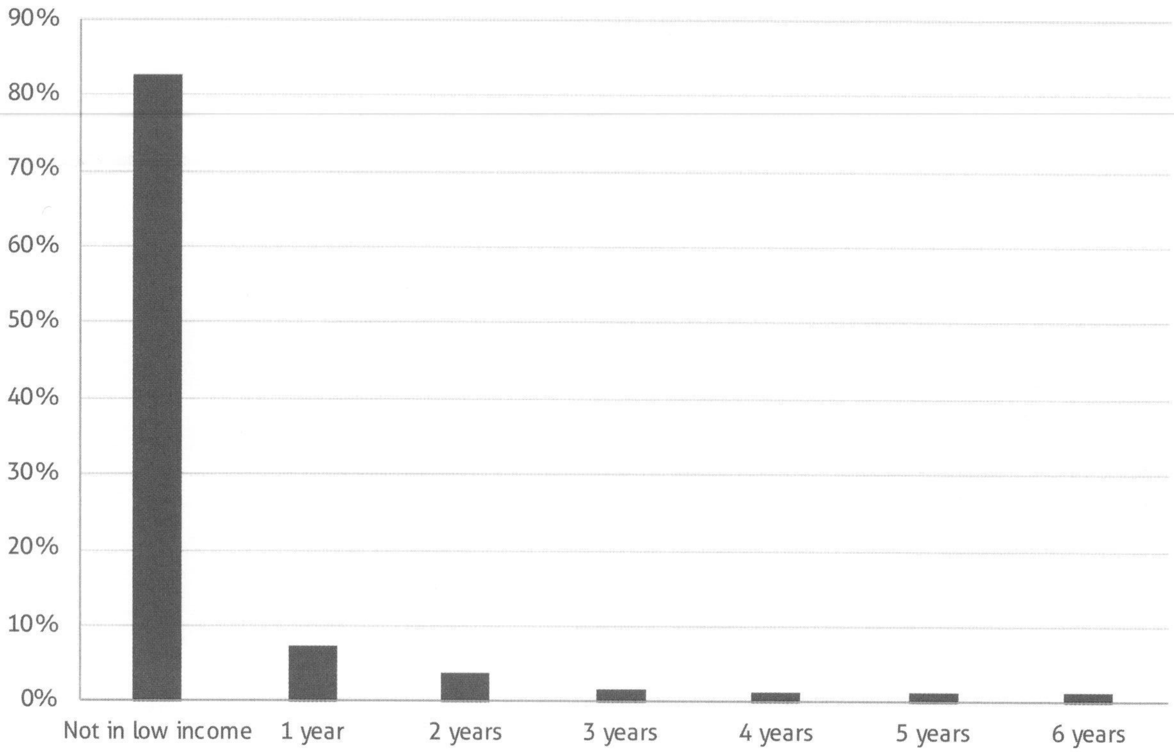

Poverty versus Inequality

Generally speaking, poverty and inequality align — one tends to be associated with high levels of the other. "Poverty" refers to how many people live under a low-income benchmark, whereas "inequality" refers to the differences between income groups. Common measures of income inequality include the quintile distribution and the Gini coefficient:

- Quintile Distribution. In a quintile distribution, the highest quintile represents one-fifth (20%) of the population with the highest incomes, while the lowest quintile represents one-fifth (20%) of the population with the lowest incomes. In 2018, households in the highest quintile had an income that was 2.4 times higher than the overall average (Statistics Canada, 2019a). According to Statistics Canada, between 1999 and 2012, the average net worth of Canadian families increased by 80% among households in the highest quintile (from $721,900 to $1.3 million) (Uppal & LaRochelle-Côté, 2015).
- Gini Coefficient. The Gini coefficient measures the degree of inequality in the overall income distribution, with values ranging from 0 to 1. A value of 0 indicates that income is equally distributed within the population. A Gini coefficient of 1 represents a perfectly unequal income distribution. Based on the Gini coefficient, inequality in Canada went down during the 1980s, when it reached a low of 0.281 (in 1989). However, it rose steadily in the 1990s and hovered around 0.32 in the 2000s (Conference Board of Canada, 2011). The Gini coefficient also varies depending on the income measure used (see Table 4.1).

Table 4.1

Measuring Inequality: Gini Coefficients

	2013	2014	2015	2016	2017
Market income (income before taxes and transfers)	0.437	0.427	0.436	0.432	0.439
Total income (gross income from all sources less certain deductions, such as expenses, allowances and reliefs	0.358	0.352	0.354	0.347	0.352
After-tax income	0.318	0.311	0.314	0.306	0.309

Statistics Canada, Table 11-10-0134-01. Gini coefficients of adjusted market, total and after-tax income. DOI: https://doi.org/10.25318/1110013401-eng

What the COVID–19 pandemic has revealed ...

Social Injustice Shapes COVID–19 Outcomes

Identifying Health Disparities and Promoting Equity

Diversity matters. There have been calls for race and ethnicity data collection to identify health disparities and promote heath equity in Canada for decades. They have not been heeded.

Canada is a multi-cultural country which claims diversity as a strength. There is social and cultural heterogeneity rarely seen in high-income countries. And this has been used to develop a high standard of living. Canada consistently ranks as one of the best places to live in the world.

But this is not the case for all. There are significant socio-economic disparities and these lead to health disparities. Indigenous and racialized groups, particularly Canada's Black populations, have an increased risk of a number of illnesses, poorer access to care, and worse health outcomes. A one-size-fits-all strategy is unlikely to work in a population with diverse needs.

Behind the Numbers

Numbers have been vital in the fight against COVID–19. Countries have relied on the number of cases and the R- number to monitor the effectiveness of pandemic interventions and to decide when to move through lockdown phases. And the same numbers can be used to identify whether our interventions are working for everyone. To do this we need to collect socio-demographic data which can be disaggregated during analysis. If you are part of an aggregated sum you can be invisible in the numbers, your story will not be told, your needs will not drive policy action, and your needs will not be met. Disaggregated data are particularly vital in pandemics because of the need for collective action.

Good sociodemographic data and race-based data are important tools for health equity but data collection is not an end in itself; it has to be linked to action. There are valid concerns about governance, accountability, and protections against misuse of data. These issues need to be addressed because data are vital to the proper functioning of public health.

Saving Lives

We have already seen in Ontario that disaggregated data can save lives. Once Cancer Care Ontario was able to show that Black women were not being screened for cancers, they were able to deploy one of the legion of evidence-based strategies available to decrease disparities.

Collecting race and ethnicity data is now considered standard practice in health worldwide. But Canada has lagged behind in the collection of these data. Race and ethnicity data are rarely routinely collected or reported at the federal, provincial, or local level. This is despite evidence that it is feasible, there are Canadian evidence-based tools to aid collection, and there is a wealth of evidence that these data are useful in improving the quality of health systems in general and that they can be important specifically in pandemics.

A study by Public Health Ontario during the H1N1 influenza pandemic reported that those who identified as South-East Asian were 3 times more likely to be infected, those who identified as South-Asian were 6 times more likely to be infected, and Ontario's Black population was 10 times more likely to be infected. And, because Indigenous populations were at such high risk, the Ontario government culturally adapted its public health response to try to improve outcomes.

Federal bodies such as Statistics Canada and health providers, planners, and funders at all levels have resisted developing good race and ethnicity data streams. Because of this, Canada went into the COVID–19 pandemic unable to identify or monitor crucial factors for the effectiveness and equity of our pandemic response.

Flattening the Curve

Later decisions to analyze existing data and collect race and ethnicity data during the COVID–19 response followed reports of clear race and ethnicity differences in illness rates from the USA and the UK.

Manitoba was the first province to start collecting race and ethnicity data. Three public health units in Ontario — Peel, Middlesex-London and Toronto — started collecting data between April and May 2020 and then the province of Ontario followed suit. Québec initially said it would consider collecting race and ethnicity data for its COVID–19 response and then did not. Local Black entrepreneurs and community groups eventually launched their own website and app in August 2020 to try to get data collected. They hoped this would spur their government to action.

By the end of the first wave, the collection of race and ethnicity data in COVID–19 was not widespread. Most federal COVID–19 linked programs were not collecting these data, and only two provinces were routinely collecting race and ethnicity data. There were no adaptations of the public health or social pandemic response.

Focusing on Who Is under the Curve

Canada's COVID–19 response has been good. In fact, our death rate of 23 per 100,000 is better than many other high-income countries. But it is worse than many others such as Germany. One reason for this is that our initial response was focused on flattening the curve, not who was under the curve.

Long-term care is the best example. Countries that had central control of long-term care or developed clear early guidance did a better job at protecting this at-risk group and had much lower death rates.

Focusing on who is under the curve as well as flattening the curve produces better outcomes. Public health interventions can then be improved to ensure they decrease risk. Subsequent data collection can monitor the effectiveness of interventions.

McKenzie, K. (2020, November 12). "Race and ethnicity data collection during COVID–19 in Canada." Reproduced by permission of the Royal Society of Canada. It has been reduced for reasons of space. The original is available at: www.rsc-src.ca.

Dr. Kwame McKenzie is CEO of the Wellesley Institute. He is an international expert on the social causes of mental illness, suicide. and the development of effective, equitable health systems.

4.3 Children and Families Living in Poverty

The income security of children's families in the early years of life is especially important for the health, education, and personal well-being of children as they grow into adulthood. In 2018, Canada had the highest rates of child poverty among the OECD countries and the 16th highest newborn death rate of 50 high-income countries (Campaign 2000, 2018). The number of Canadian children living in poverty has declined over the past few years. In 2017, 9% of children in Canada experienced poverty, down from 14.5% in 2012 (Statistics Canada, 2017a). Still, 34.1% of those relying on food banks in Canada are children (Food Banks Canada, 2019).

Without access to child care, some women who may otherwise be able to work are forced to go on social assistance.

Indigenous children continue to be the most marginalized and economically disadvantaged (Beedie et al., 2019). In 2016, an average of 47% of status First Nations children on- and off-reserve lived in poverty. This average is based on the 53% of status First Nations children on-reserve and the 41% of status First Nations children off-reserve who are living in poverty.

Working Poor Families

Not all children who live in families with a low income are on social assistance. Many parents struggling to survive on low income are employed, often in multiple jobs. Being poor today does not mean being without a job. The problem is that the marketplace is not providing enough income for many Canadian families to live poverty-free. Members of the working poor work similar hours to the average Canadian worker, but earn less money. Moreover, their hours are more likely to rise and fall unpredictably, making it hard to balance work and family responsibilities.

Market poverty refers to a situation in which a household remains below some measure of poverty (e.g., the MBM) even though one or more household members earn a market income or are employed. People who have paid employment but do not earn enough income to lift them above the poverty line are commonly referred to as the working poor. About 746,000 Canadians live in a household where the main income earner is considered "working poor" (Statistics Canada, 2017a). There are two obvious causes of market poverty: low wages and limited access to the labour market. Low wages contribute to market poverty when wages do not provide an adequate income to support families. Individuals have limited access to the labour market when they are afforded fewer work hours than what would be required to meet their basic needs. Inadequate access to gainful employment can be due to a lack of skills and training or to barriers such as racial discrimination, a lack of recognition of education (as is the case with some immigrants), or a lack of workplace accommodations for a disability.

Changes in Canada's labour market are putting more workers at risk for poverty. Today, more jobs are precarious. Temporary and part-time jobs have grown at a fast rate. Often, these jobs are associated with fewer benefits, such as paid vacation and sick leave, prescription drug and dental benefits, and workplace pensions. Limited benefits can have serious repercussions for a family's well-being.

Policies Are Needed That Support Children and Families

Traditionally, the thrust of poverty reduction policy has been that families should become more "self-reliant" through labour market participation, whether they are lone-parent or two-parent families. However, this approach gives little consideration to how realistic this solution is in terms of the quality of the jobs available, the minimum wage, or the cost of child care for these families. Shaming individuals who live in poverty is not helpful.

For example, a single mother with a young child who is not in school needs full-time child care if she has a full-time job. If her income is minimum wage, the cost of child care takes up a large percentage of her earnings. Even when her child is in school and she works full-time during school hours, her income may be so low that her family still falls below the poverty line. Two-parent families are not much better off, especially if both parents earn wages at a low hourly rate and have to pay for child care. Even if their combined income places the family above the poverty line, the cost of child care can be enough to plunge them into poverty.

Government poverty reduction policies tend to be based on the idea that if people can get a job, they will not live in poverty. However, the quality of the job is important — it has to be meaningful and well paid. According to the Broadbent Institute, one in three families with children living in poverty had one or more parents working full-time all year round (Jackson, 2014). Having a job is not enough — many hard-working parents are not earning enough in their jobs to support themselves and their families adequately.

Campaign 2000: Child Poverty 30 Years On

Good health and development during childhood are among the most important factors in ensuring that individuals grow up healthy enough to learn, find work, raise families, and participate fully in society throughout their lives. Yet, children in low-income families have a higher risk for poorer health and poorer developmental outcomes. Indeed, parents' socio-economic status is the strongest predictor of children's health outcomes (Raphael, 2014; von Rueden et al., 2006).

Campaign 2000 is a nationwide coalition of 120 partners that focused on building awareness and support for the 1989 all-party House of Commons resolution to end child poverty (Campaign 2000, 2020b). It reports yearly on the progress made toward the goal of eliminating child poverty. Its 2018 national report card noted that over 1.4 million children (nearly one in five) continue to live in poverty and that "children are more likely than adults to live in poverty in every province and territory — except for Québec" (Campaign 2000, 2018, p. 6).

High rates of child poverty continue across Canada, despite the recent changes to tax and income security policies (e.g., increases to the Canada Child Benefit) that were aimed at ameliorating them. Differences in child poverty arise when employing different measurements of poverty (i.e., the LIM or the MBM). For example, Campaign 2000 (2020a), using Statistics Canada data, showed that the after-tax LIM rate for child poverty was 18.6% in 2017. This is significantly higher than the MBM rate for 2017, which was 9.0%. Figure 4.4 shows child poverty levels across Canada in 1917.

Figure 4.4

Child Poverty in Canada, Children under 6 Years of Age (Low Income Measure—After-Tax)

Statistics Canada (2016). T1 Family Files, Income Statistics Division; Campaign 2000 (2018).

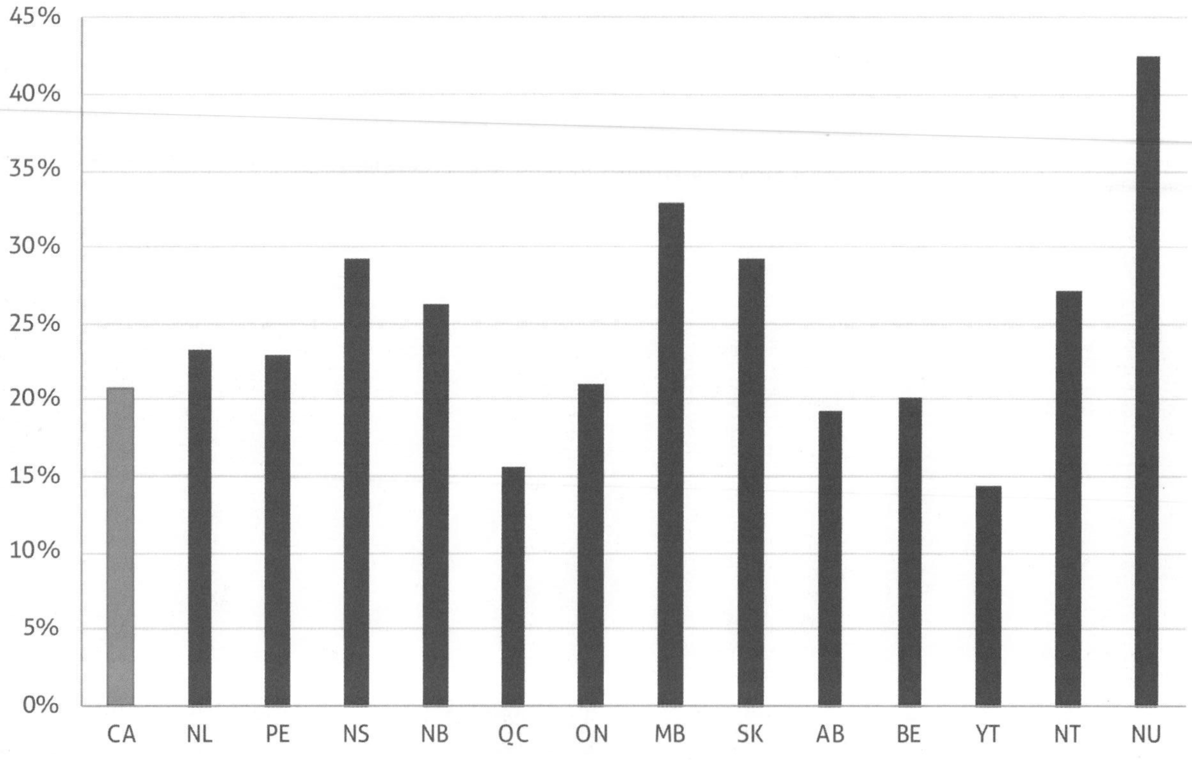

Poverty in Indigenous Communities

The poverty rates for Indigenous children in Canada are particularly dire. Comparing data from the 2006 census and 2016 census, researchers at the Canadian Centre for Policy Alternatives found that poverty rates barely budged for most Indigenous communities (Macdonald & Wilson, 2016).

Overall, 47% of First Nations children live in poverty, more than two-and-a-half times the national rate. That percentage rises to 53% when looking at First Nations children living on-reserve (or four times the rate of non-racialized, non-Indigenous children).

There is a clear need for an immediate public policy response to resolve the crisis affecting Indigenous people across the country. That response should include reporting poverty rates on-reserve and in the territories, substantially improving direct income supports, boosting employment prospects on-reserve, and working closely with Indigenous leaders to implement locally developed solutions that address the concerns of their communities.

Social Welfare in Perspective

Tackling Indigenous Child Poverty

An Urgent Crisis That Demands Immediate Attention

Child poverty on-reserve has remained almost unchanged for a decade. Little improvement has been registered for Inuit or non-status First Nations children either.

In August 2018, the federal government introduced the first Canadian poverty reduction strategy, with goals to decrease poverty by 20% (using 2015 income estimates) by 2020 and by 50% in 2030. While these goals are laudable, there was no specific mention in the strategy of efforts being made to alleviate poverty among Indigenous people. Moreover, the Market Basket Measure (MBM), Canada's newly announced poverty line, falls short in helping us understand poverty among Indigenous people. Currently, there are no MBM calculations for Canada's territories or First Nations reserves, although there has been a commitment to develop a northern basket in the future.

The most economically disadvantaged group in Canada is by far First Nations children. Looking at trends from the 2006 census to the 2016 census, Natasha Beedie, David Macdonald, and Daniel Wilson (2019) found that child poverty rates among First Nations children have not significantly changed over this 10-year time period.

Child poverty on First Nations reserves has particularly stagnated over the past decade, with little improvement for non-status First Nations children or children registered for Inuit status. Some minor increases may have occurred for Métis children, although these improvements may in fact be due to changes in self-reporting, and thus require further investigation.

While there have been relatively modest improvements in child poverty among status First Nations from the 2006 census (a rate of 52%) to the 2016 census (a rate of 47%), this improvement is in large part due to the decreased number of children living off-reserve. Status First Nations children living on-reserve witnessed minimal decline.

Three Disturbing Trends

Beedie et al. (2019) note three disturbing trends in child poverty:

- **Tier 1.** At the highest rung of poverty, almost half (47%) of status First Nations children live in poverty; specifically, 53% of those living on-reserve and 41% of those living off-reserve.
- **Tier 2.** In the second highest rung, a quarter (25%) of Inuit children, 32% of non-status First Nations children, and 22% of Métis children live in poverty. This tier also includes racialized and recent immigrant children, whose poverty rates are estimated at 22% and 35%, respectively.
- **Tier 3.** The lowest rung encompasses non-racialized, non-recent immigrants, and non-Indigenous children, who experience the lowest rate of child poverty at 12% (only one-quarter of the rate for First Nations' child poverty).

Improvements in child poverty among Inuit children were mixed. Métis children experienced a persistent decline in child poverty, dropping 5% over the 2006–2016 period (from 27% in 2006 to 22% in 2016). At the same time, there was a significant increase in the number of children self-identifying as Métis (rising by 30%).

To tackle Indigenous child poverty, structural and legislative remedies are necessary. The inadequate housing, unclean water supply, poorer health care service delivery, and inferior education funding point to a crisis that demands immediate policy attention.

Adapted from Natasha Beedie, David Macdonald, and Daniel Wilson. (2019). *Towards Justice: Tackling Indigenous Child Poverty in Canada*. Upstream Institute, the Canadian Centre for Policy Alternatives, and the Assembly of First Nations. Reproduced by permission.

In Canada in 2015, 17.6% of children lived in poverty. That's one in five. But different groups experience poverty differently.

Tier 1: Deepest level of poverty

The highest results of poverty are found among status First Nations children: close to half of these children live in poverty.

53%	41%	47%
Status First Nations children living **on reserve**	Status First Nations children living **off reserve**	The **average** of on- and off-reserve status First Nations child poverty

Tier 2: Next level of poverty

The second tier of child poverty is worse than the national average of 17%. Non-status Indigenous children have poverty rates of 35%, twice the national average.

35%	32%	25%	22%
Recent immigrant children	Non-status First Nations children	Inuit children	Métis children
			Racialized children

Tier 3: Least level of poverty

12%
Non-racialized, non-Indigenous children

Non-racialized, non-recent immigrant, non-Indigenous children, register the lowest rate of child poverty: 12%, below the national average and one quarter the rate for First Nations child poverty.

Beedie et al., 2019. Census of Canada, 2016, Custom Tabulations.

4.4 Homelessness

Symptomatic of the troubling problem of poverty, homelessness is on the rise in Canada. Simply defined, **homelessness** is the absence of a place to live. A person who is homeless has no regular place to live and may stay in an emergency shelter, an abandoned building, an all-night shopping area, a laundromat, outdoors, or any place where there is protection from the elements.

Types of Homelessness

Homelessness is often categorized as absolute homelessness or relative homelessness, but however it is characterized, it places an unacceptable burden on the individuals and families involved.

Absolute homelessness is a situation in which an individual or family has no housing at all or is staying in a temporary form of shelter. Relative homelessness is a situation in which a person's home does not meet the United Nations' basic housing criteria:

- Security of tenure (e.g., legal protection against forced evictions)
- Availability of services, materials, facilities, and infrastructure (e.g., safe drinking water)
- Affordability
- Habitability (e.g., sufficient space, protection from the elements)
- Accessibility (e.g., able to meet the needs of marginalized or disadvantaged groups)
- Location (e.g., close to employment, child care)
- Cultural adequacy (e.g., housing that takes into account cultural needs) (Office of the United Nations High Commissioner for Human Rights, 2014)

Dej and Ecker (2018) outline several other categories of homelessness. These include unsheltered, emergency sheltered, provisionally accommodated (temporarily housed or short-term housing arrangements), and at risk of homelessness. Their definition of "homelessness" includes forms of precarious housing; for example, people who are "couch surfing" or in overcrowded housing situations.

People in precarious or inadequate housing are typically described as being in "core housing need." According to Statistics Canada, a household is in core housing need if its housing falls below one or more of the following criteria:

- Adequacy (housing that does not require major repairs)
- Suitability (housing that has sufficient bedrooms for residents in the household)
- Affordability (housing that costs equal to or less than 30% of before-tax household income) (Statistics Canada, 2017b).

Access to safe and affordable housing is an important aspect of well-being. Unfortunately, some Canadians are unable to secure stable housing and, for various reasons, may stay in a shelter or other form of precarious accommodation.

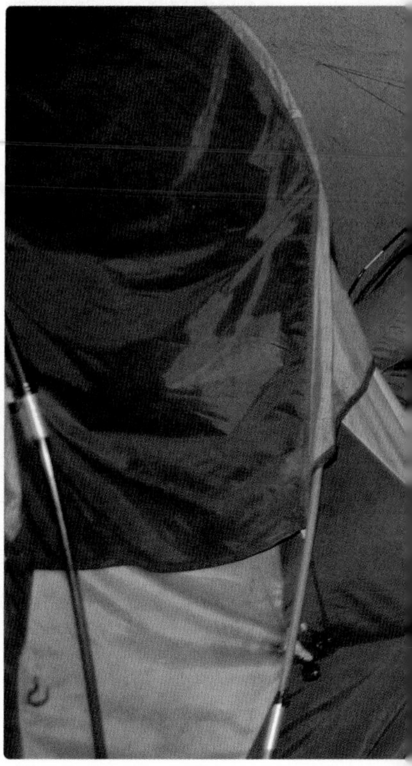

Reasons for Homelessness

People become homeless for a variety of reasons. The major reasons are unemployment or low income, mental health problems, other severe health problems, violence or abuse in the home, eviction, mental health and substance use issues, and a lack of support from family and friends. Changes to government policy, such as the Tenant Protection Act in Ontario, have removed rent controls and made it easier to evict tenants. When combined with a decrease in affordable housing, homelessness becomes a growing problem.

For those with low incomes, only 24.5% of households in the lowest quintile own their own homes, compared with 88.2% for the highest quintile (Uppal, 2019). In large urban centres such as Vancouver and Toronto, housing ownership has become possible only for those who are wealthy, with many young people and newcomers shut out of the housing market altogether.

However, the raw numbers on homelessness do not capture the full desperation experienced by those living on the streets. People seen living on the streets typically experience long-term or chronic homelessness and represent less than 15% of the overall homeless population (Culhane, 2018). The rest are families and individuals who find themselves without a place to live for a period of time. They include people (men and women) in supervised or publicly operated emergency shelters (episodic homelessness), people living in substandard or overcrowded situations such as a relative or friend's basement or couch (hidden homelessness), and people who are briefly homeless (transitional homelessness).

Homeless Shelters

Homeless shelters across Canada provide emergency accommodation for a large segment of the homeless population.

The 2016 census counted 995 shelters with 22,190 residents. Almost 7 in 10 of these residents had no fixed address and one-quarter (5,365) were at shelters for women and children escaping abuse (Statistics Canada, 2019b).

The Need for a "Housing First" Strategy

Homelessness has increased over the past few decades, in large part due to government cutbacks in affordable housing. In many cases, people simply cannot afford the housing available in their community. What is called for is a Housing First strategy — a program of investment in low-cost affordable housing and related supports to the community (Hughes, 2012).

Before the 1990s, when Housing First became popularized by Sam Tsemberis and Pathways to Housing in New York and the Beyond Shelter program in Los Angeles (where the term originated), individuals experiencing chronic homelessness were typically not placed into permanent housing arrangements until they were deemed to be "housing ready" (i.e., mentally healthy, sober, and/or in addiction recovery).

Rather than a paternalistic approach that suggests an outside "expert" (e.g., a housing worker) should determine when someone is ready to be housed, Housing First emphasizes that everyone has a right to housing, and this right should not be conditional on one's lifestyle, actions, or behaviours. Housing First starts with where the person is at, recognizing that people first need to be housed before they can effectively move forward with their lives. It abandons the traditional "treatment first" model, in which individuals must address their mental health or substance abuse issues before housing is made available. Moreover, it seeks to place individuals into housing arrangements that meet their needs and preferences, giving them the choice of location and type of housing.

Housing First has been proven to be a humane and effective way of responding to homelessness. The At Home/Chez Soi initiative that took place from 2009 to 2013, funded by the Mental Health Commission of Canada, demonstrated the effectiveness of the Housing First approach. The project funded housing units in Montréal, Toronto, Winnipeg, and Vancouver for specific populations, including Indigenous people, newcomers, and youth.

Key findings of the At Home/Chez Soi initiative were as follows:

- Housing First can be implemented in cities of different sizes and with different ethno-racial and cultural composition.
- Housing First can rapidly end homelessness.
- Housing First is a solid investment as it leads to significant cost savings (every $10 invested in Housing First services resulted in $21.72 in avoided costs).
- Housing First is not simply housing but must include relevant supports and services.

The At Home/Chez Soi project demonstrated and evaluated the effectiveness of the "housing first" approach, where people are provided with a place to live and then receive recovery-oriented services and supports that best meet their individual needs. It underlined the fundamental point that having a home with supports leads to positive outcomes in many areas of a person's life, including improved health and quality of life (Goering et al., 2014).

Housing First

Housing First is both a philosophy and a programmatic approach. According to the homeless hub (n.d.), it is governed by the following principles:

- (1) Immediate access to permanent housing with no readiness requirements
- (2) Consumer choice and self-determination
- (3) Recovery orientation
- (4) Individualized and client-driven supports
- (5) Social and community integration

Photo: A person experiencing homelessness living under a bridge at the centre of the city, Victoria, B.C.

4.5 Food Insecurity

With the cutbacks in many income security programs, many more Canadians rely on food banks and feeding programs in order to survive.

In March 2019 alone, Canadians visited food banks 1.1 million times (Food Banks Canada, 2020). According to Food Banks Canada (2019), over 34.1% of those who accessed food banks nationally were children, although they represent only 19.4% of the Canadian population.

Feeding programs provide cooked meals at specified times during the day. They often operate out of shelters or church basements and provide one to two meals per day. Typically, such programs are operated by volunteers and by those who use the service. Many feeding programs are run in conjunction with emergency shelters.

Feeding programs often provide additional services, such as free laundry facilities, telephone access, free newspapers, and free clothing. In certain instances, access to computers and the Internet is also available. Sometimes, social workers are available and may even work directly within the program.

Of those Canadians using food banks, the majority also rely on income security programs as their main income source. As social assistance rates decline and eligibility requirements for EI tighten, food bank usage by Canadians will likely continue to increase.

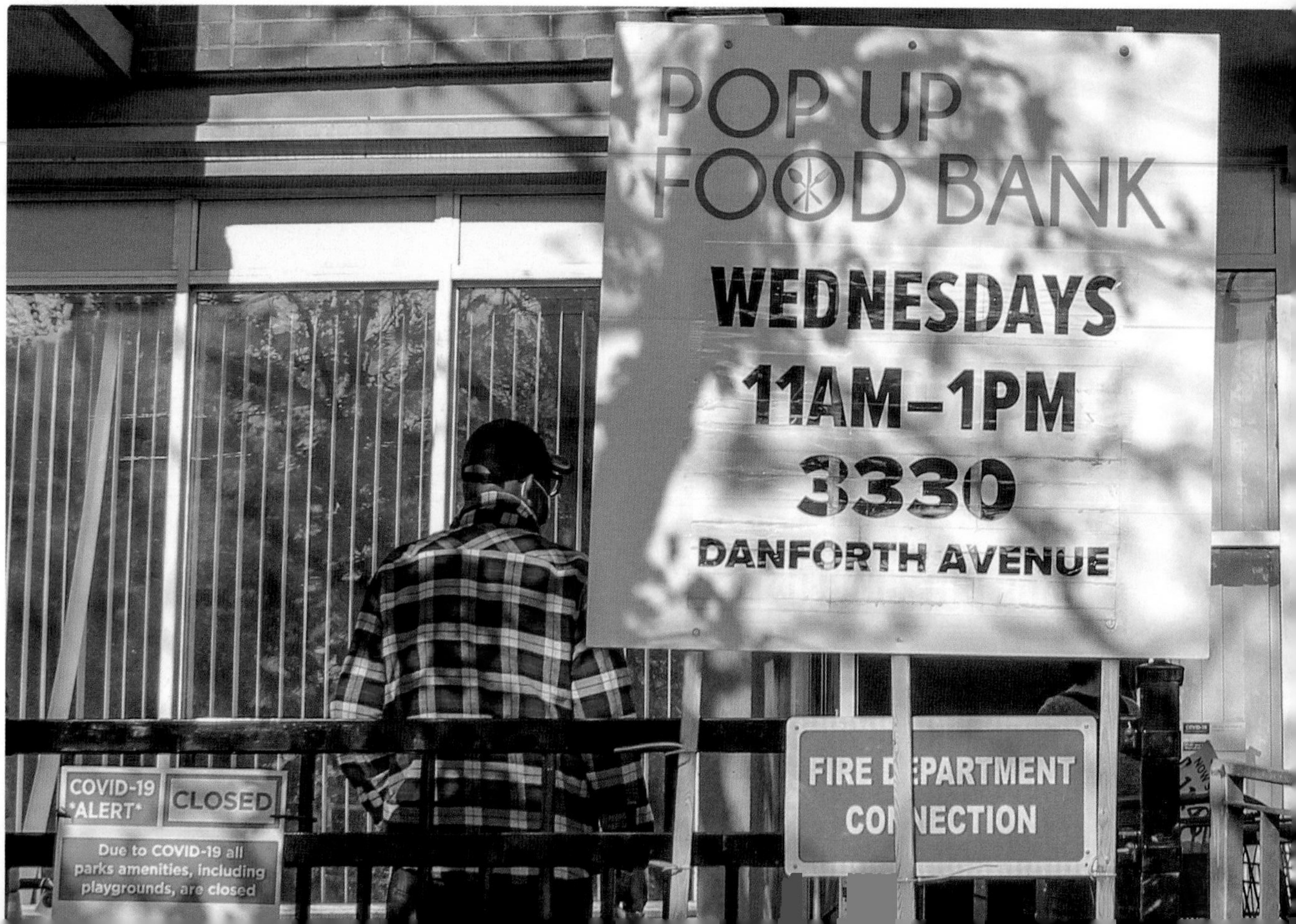

Inability to Keep Up with Demand

Many food banks have to cut back on the amount of food provided to each household, as they rely on donations that are unpredictable and in limited supply (Dachner & Tarasuk, 2017). Many believe that the unravelling of the social safety net means that access to basic food is in jeopardy.

At the release of the HungerCount 2018 Report, Chris Hatch, CEO of Food Banks Canada, stated, "The fact that 1.1 million Canadians still need to access food banks in one month alone is unacceptable and just not Canadian. ... People in our most vulnerable communities are struggling to provide for themselves and their families" (Montgomery, 2019). Hatch went on to say, "At Food Banks Canada, our vision is a Canada where no one goes hungry. ... We understand the enormity of this task, but we strongly believe that we can collectively help drive our country toward that goal with government policies that support vulnerable Canadian communities and groups" (Montgomery, 2019).

What people who experience food insecurity lack is not so much food, but an adequate income. Poverty is at the core of food insecurity. For people to be food secure, they must have access to an adequate income to buy the food they both need and prefer. Food Banks Canada, along with a number of other organizations interested in alleviating hunger nationwide, are calling for the federal government to introduce a national basic income program to ensure that all Canadians have access to good, nutritious food.

Photo: People waiting to get food from the Daily Bread Food Bank on the Danforth in Toronto in 2020 during the coronavirus pandemic.

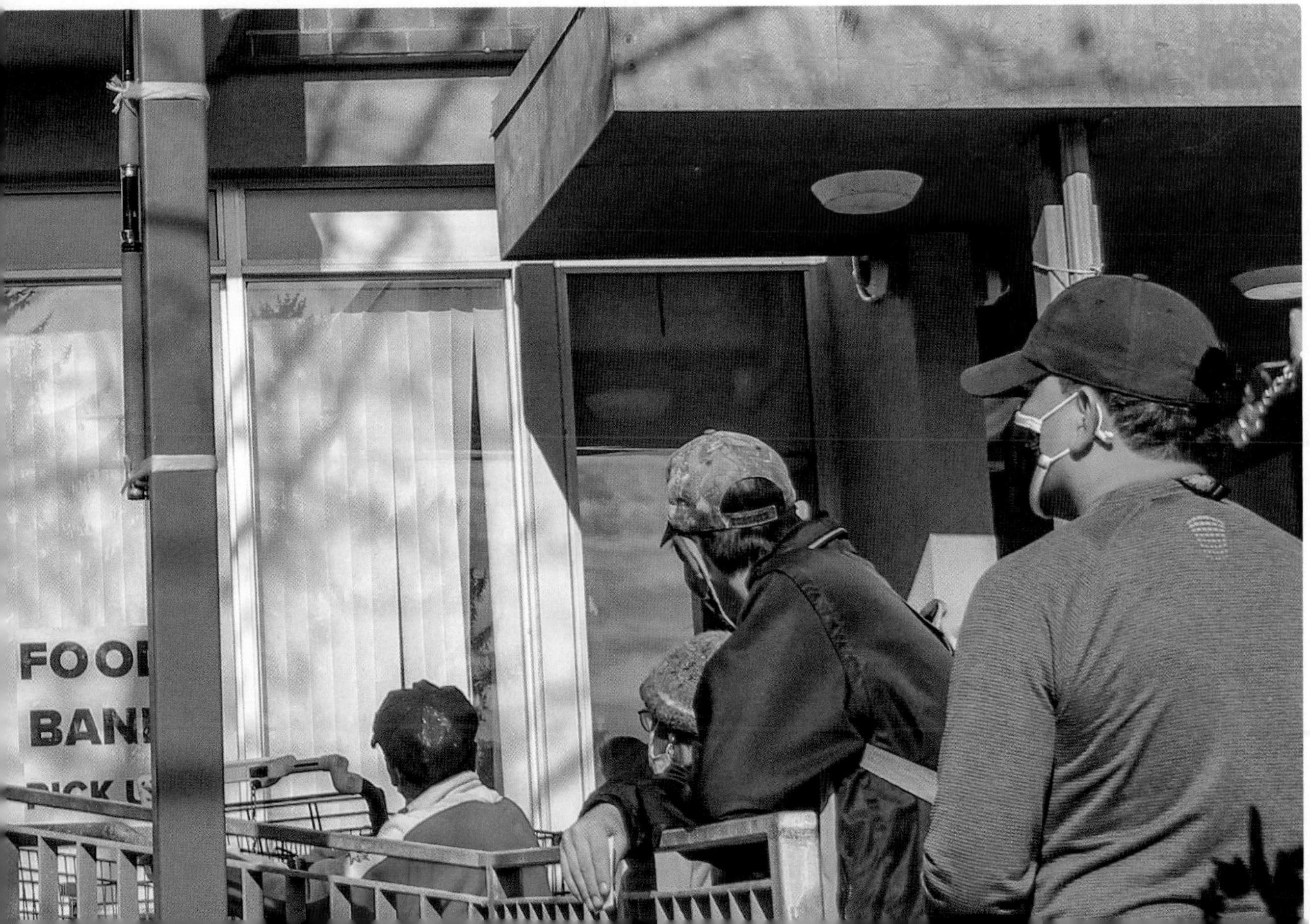

Social Welfare in Perspective

HungerCount

Policy Recommendations

Food Banks Canada is a national organization dedicated to helping Canadians living with food insecurity. Its latest HungerCount report emphasizes that short-term solutions are not enough.

The data are clear: food bank use in Canada remains at unacceptably high levels. While food banks are finding new and innovative ways to provide healthy, nutritious food and a wide variety of services to support those they serve, only long-term policy solutions can address the root causes of hunger in Canada (Riches & Tarasuk, 2014).

Poverty and Low Income

The root cause of food bank use is, and always has been, related to poverty and low income — and this core issue can only be addressed through government policies.

With a newly elected Liberal minority government in Ottawa, and with many new progressive voices representing communities right across the country, there is an opportunity to build on the foundational pieces that were put into place over the last few years.

The introduction of the Canada Child Benefit, the national poverty reduction strategy, and the National Housing Strategy, as well as the expansion of the Canada Workers Benefit (just to name a few) are positive and important steps. However, it is clear that much more still needs to be done if we are to reach the intended goals of significantly reducing poverty and food bank use in Canada.

Good intentions and well-laid-out strategies alone will not be enough to meet Food Banks Canada's vision of a Canada where no one goes hungry.

To that end, implementing the following policy recommendations is essential if the federal government wants to meet the targets set forth in its poverty reduction strategy and ultimately reduce the need for food banks in the long term.

Policy Recommendations

1. **Support the creation of affordable early learning and child care across the country.**

   Affordable early learning and child care will allow parents to remain in the workforce or upgrade their education and skills.

2. **Increase supports for single adults living with low incomes.**

   The percentage of single people using food banks has increased over the last decade, having grown from 38% of households in 2010 to almost half of all households (48%) in 2019.

3. **Implement the Canada Housing Benefit.**

   The high cost of housing is one of the main reasons why people seek the support of food banks. People across the country spend so much of their monthly incomes on their housing costs that very little, if any, is left over for food.

4. **Advocate for federal leadership for a basic income for all Canadians.**

   Under our current system of social assistance, one must be virtually penniless before being able to apply for support. A basic income will provide a new path forward for Canada's most vulnerable citizens.

5. **Reduce northern food insecurity.**

   Household food insecurity levels remain unacceptably high in the territories and the cost of food has barely changed since 2011. It is time for the government to review its food security strategy in the North (Food Banks Canada, 2019).

CANADA - KEY HUNGERCOUNT FINDINGS

Canada	ALL	RURAL
Total Visits	1,084,386	150,732
Total Visits (Child)	374,474	49,620
% Change in Total Visits 2018-2019	-1.1%	-1.0%
Total meals and snacks	5,570,329	332,131
Food Banks Reporting	2,326	672
% of food banks reporting an increase, 2018-2019	47.0	45.3

Age categories served as % of total, by age group

	ALL	RURAL
% 0 - 2 years	5.2	4.6
% 3 - 5 years	6.1	6.7
% 6 - 11 years	12.9	12.3
% 12 - 17 years	9.9	10.4
% 18 - 30 years	16.3	15.1
% 31 - 44 years	20.0	18.6
% 45 - 64 years	22.8	25.0
% 65 + years	6.8	7.0

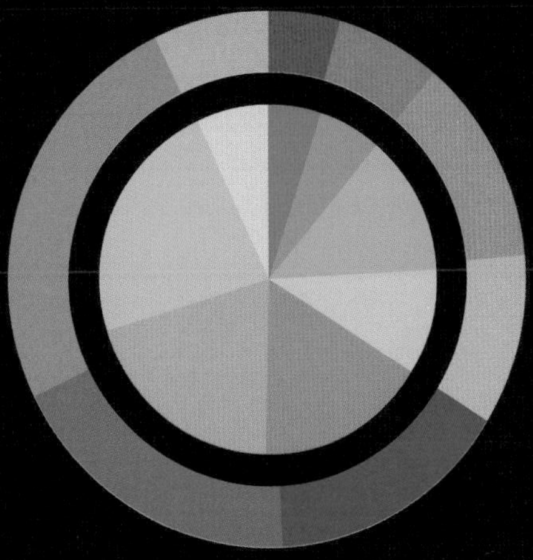

	ALL	RURAL
% children	34.1	34.0
% seniors	6.8	7.0
Food Banks Reporting	1,513	517

Food Banks Canada, 2019. *HungerCount 2019*. Reproduced by permission

4.6 When All Else Fails: Social Assistance

Many families and individuals experience difficult situations, challenges, or changes that may affect their health and/or employment status. Stressful life events can happen to anyone. When individuals have no source of income, they are entitled to social assistance.

In Canada, provinces and territories have primary jurisdiction over the provision of social services. As a result, social assistance and supports are different from one province/territory to another. Each jurisdiction has its own official name for social assistance; that is, social assistance may be called "income support," "income assistance," or "welfare."

Social assistance is a province- or territory-based minimum income system for people "in need." It is a program of last resort with roots in early charity relief and the English Poor Laws. Strict eligibility criteria, with means and assets tests, are typically applied to determine whether people qualify for social assistance.

Without social assistance, the lack of employment in Canada would leave many people completely destitute. Nonetheless, the current level of social assistance provided in Canadian jurisdictions is not enough to combat food insecurity, poor health outcomes, and the risk of homelessness.

Thirteen Provincial/Territorial Social Assistance Systems

Canadians usually seek social assistance only when all other public and private means of support have been exhausted. Entitlement is based on the assets and income of the applicant's household and the household's basic needs (food, clothing, shelter and utilities, household necessities, and personal needs) as defined in the jurisdiction's legislation.

There are 13 different social assistance systems across the country. Each province and territory has its own social assistance legislation. Moreover, each social assistance system has different eligibility criteria and benefit levels. The result is a patchwork of social assistance systems across the country.

First Nations with self-government agreements have their own "income assistance" programs. For First Nations without self-government agreements, income assistance is funded by Indigenous and Northern Affairs Canada but aligned with the rates and eligibility criteria for off-reserve residents of the reference province or territory. Such programs are delivered by First Nations communities, organizations, or other service providers (depending on the province) in accordance with the prevailing social assistance rules and regulations of that province or territory. The Department of Indigenous Services Canada reimburses the province for costs (Government of Canada, 2019; Flavo, 2017).

Social assistance is referred to as a "minimum income" program: it transfers income to people who have little or no employment or other income, but it supplies only a bare minimum of funds for survival. The transfer is also conditional insofar as it is based on means and assets tests. Social assistance systems may also include a distinct program or increased benefits for people with disabilities. For example, Ontario has the Ontario Disability Support Program, British Columbia has Disability Assistance, and Saskatchewan has the Assured Income for Disability.

How Effective Is Social Assistance?

One way to evaluate the effectiveness of social assistance benefits is to compare social assistance benefit amounts to the poverty line (currently, the MBM). The difference between the two is a fair indicator of the effectiveness of social assistance. A significant gap between the incomes of those relying on social assistance and what is necessary to meet their basic needs puts the health and well-being of these Canadian families and children at risk.

Tweddle and Aldridge (2019) examined social assistance incomes in 2018 and compared them to the poverty line (the MBM) for various household types. For a single person considered employable, the lowest welfare income was in Halifax, at 39% of the MBM threshold (representing a poverty gap of $11,687); and the highest was in St. John's, at 58% of the MBM threshold (representing a poverty gap of $8,119). For a single person with a disability, the lowest welfare income was in Calgary, at 50% of the MBM threshold (representing a poverty gap of $10,284); and the highest was in Montréal, at 76% of the MBM threshold (representing a poverty gap of $4,375). In all cases, welfare income was below the poverty line — in some cases, significantly below.

Social assistance programs intend to provide a minimum income as a last resort, but the levels are not enough to allow people and families to find their way out of poverty. Indeed, according to Tweddle and Aldridge (2019), the rates in some provinces and territories, especially rates for "single employable adults," do not reach even half of the MBM threshold.

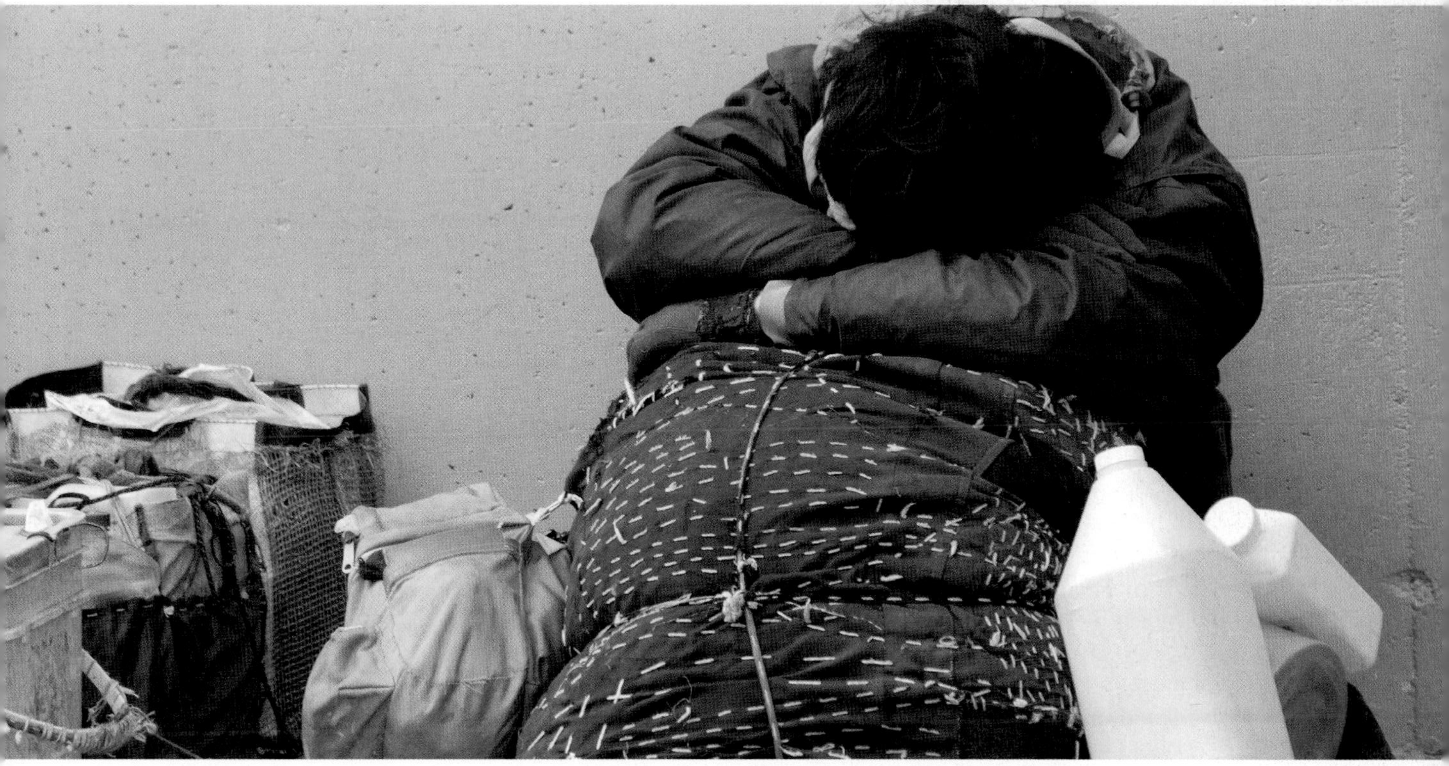

Workfare

With the replacement of the Canada Assistance Plan in 1996 by the Canada Health and Social Transfer, followed by the Canada Health Transfer/Canada Social Transfer split in 2004, the federal government effectively cut much of the fiscal transfers to the provinces. In so doing, the provinces and territories were given greater say about how to administer these programs, but they were also given less funding to do so. These changes have weakened standards nationwide, leading social assistance to become more uneven across the country. To attempt to deal with budget shortfalls, some provinces have opened the door to more coercive programs, such as "workfare" or one of its variants.

Workfare requires unemployed people to work as a term of eligibility for social assistance. This approach has drawn sharp criticism from social welfare advocacy groups. Refusal to participate in a workfare program results in some sort of penalty. For example, workfare could require people to accept specific jobs or it could provide a smaller cheque to those who refuse to accept work through a government program. It might involve community participation in a wide range of approved volunteering activities. Workfare might also require applicants to retrain or participate in a self-employment program.

Reinforcing Myths about the Poor

Critics of workfare equate it with a return to the "work test" of the Elizabethan Poor Laws (see Chapter 2). Some cite research to show its failure in other countries, particularly in the United States (Handler & Babcock, 2006). Workfare has also been criticized for being expensive to administer (Krueger et al., 1997) and for pressuring people into low-wage work that keeps them in poverty (Peck & Theodore, 2000). Some see workfare as a "blame-oriented" approach that ignores job creation, arguing that people want to work but do not have access to enough good jobs (Herd et al., 2005).

A variety of terms are used to describe workfare, such as "formal workfare," "de facto workfare," "welfare-to-work," and "trainfare." Terminology aside, across the country, a more coercive and disciplinary approach is being used toward social assistance recipients. The programs are redefining people as "employable" without adequate attention to the barriers that keep people out of full-time work. Most workfare schemes rely on the same myths that have always plagued social assistance: that the average recipient will stay on social assistance indefinitely if not forced to do useful work, even though the main reason for the increased welfare rolls are that many households are finding it impossible to meet their basic needs while working in low-wage jobs.

Peck (2001) has argued that "workfare is not about creating jobs for people who don't have them; it is about creating workers for jobs that nobody wants" (p. 6). He maintains that these jobs fuel the "flexible" labour market, with increasing expectations that respond to corporate demands, rather than workers' needs. For example, some jobs require employees to be willing to work on-call or on rotating evening/weekend shifts.

"Spouse-in-the-House"

Welfare advocacy groups have long been critical of the so-called "spouse-in-the-house" rule. In some cities, social assistance case workers were trained to determine whether a person of the opposite sex had stayed overnight at a welfare recipient's home (they looked for things such as an extra toothbrush or shoes).

If so, that person could be deemed to be financially responsible for the person receiving welfare support. The rule is still applied in a modified way.

The Women's Legal Education and Action Fund (LEAF), a national, non-profit organization working to promote equality for women and girls, maintains that the rule directly affects single mothers who may want to form relationships.

The Charter Committee on Poverty Issues, an anti-poverty organization, also argues that Canada falls short in a number of areas stipulated in international human rights law, and the "spouse-in-the-house" rule is just one example.

The Goals of Social Assistance Systems

A central goal of social assistance is "to provide basic protection against loss of income or employment" (Gardner et al., 2011, p. 10). However, social assistance systems should do more.

Social assistance should create the conditions for people to build the capacity to participate actively in their communities, provide training and support to expand employment and educational opportunities, and be flexible and centred on the needs and situations of participants (Smith-Carrier & Lawlor, 2016). In other words, social assistance systems should seek to "enhance the opportunities for well-being and good health for all people on Social Assistance" (p. 11).

Some of the principles capturing this way of thinking are set out by Gardner et al. (2011). As a minimum, a progressive social assistance system should do the following:

- Provide a basket of essential supports to enable good health (e.g., income, housing, and nutrition supports)
- Enhance the development of human capital, conditions that support early child development, transportation accessibility, and the flexibility and portability of benefits
- Provide a person-centred model of social assistance service delivery that is aligned with and adjusted to the particular circumstances of the individual involved with the system

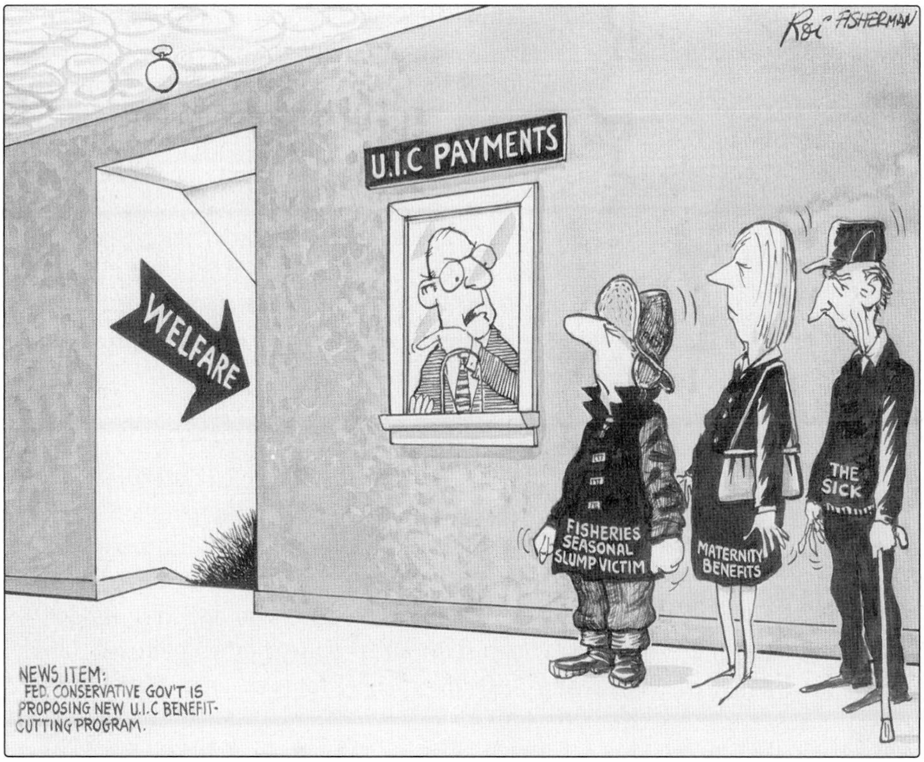

Library and Archives Canada

"You're all on the wrong floor, try the basement"

Social Welfare in Perspective

A Universal Basic Income

A Strategy for Lifting All Canadians Out of Poverty

A universal basic income guarantees that every individual receives a minimum income. The concept has regained popularity in Canada as a way to combat poverty.

To provide a secure income floor for all Canadians, some people call for a national basic income program. Basic income is a benefit program that has been experimented with in many countries around the globe. It can be offered in a number of different ways (e.g., as a demogrant or as a means-tested program), but the overarching goal is to ensure everyone can have their basic income needs met.

The values underlying a **universal basic income** program, according to the Ontario Basic Income Network (OBIN), are as follows:

- Adequacy. It must provide enough money to live on.
- Autonomy. It must offer people more choices.
- Dignity. There must be no stigma attached to receiving it.
- Equality of opportunity. It must offer opportunities for everyone.
- Non-conditionality. It must not be subject to the rules and monitoring of social assistance.
- Universality. It must be universal in access (anyone who needs it would receive it).

Based on research conducted around the globe, there is strong evidence that a basic income guarantee can improve the quality of life, health, and well-being of those receiving it (Smith-Carrier & Green, 2017).

"Mincome" in Manitoba

Between 1974 and 1979, the town of Dauphin, Manitoba, entered into an experiment called "Mincome." Everyone was entitled to participate. The Mincome experiment provides evidence that basic income can be an effective strategy to address poverty.

The data were collected and archived, but the program itself was closed down in 1979 under the Progressive Conservative government of Manitoba and the federal Conservative government without much further study by government officials.

Decades later, Evelyn Forget (2011), a health economist at the University of Manitoba, undertook to analyze some 1,800 cubic feet of data from the old experiment. She found evidence of improved health and high school completion, and even an overall improved sense of community.

Forget's research also determined the following:

Mincome did not discourage work. Two main groups, however, had increased unemployment rates during this time: school-aged males and new mothers. But high school graduation rates increased with this group of males not needing to work to support their families and new mothers were given the chance to stay home with their children without the pressure of having insufficient income to survive (Gunaseelan, 2018, para. 12).

Forget (2011) also found that providing a basic income led to an 8.5% reduction in hospitalizations, improvements in mental health, and reductions in the number of accidents, injuries, and intimate partner violence reports.

Ontario's Basic Income Pilot Program

In 2017, the Ontario Basic Income Pilot Project was set up to study the effects of providing a basic income to 4,000 people in Ontario. The project aimed to test whether "Basic Income [would] reduce poverty more effectively, encourage work, reduce stigmatization, and produce better health outcomes and better life chances for recipients" (Segal, 2016, p. 5).

The program was put into effect by the Liberal government. Later, however, the newly elected Progressive Conservative government terminated it. One writer went so far as to say that the program was ended early due to fears that the results would show that the program works (Aivalis, 2018). Québec has also brought in a form of basic income for those who have a limited capacity to work.

Ontario and Québec's steps are a starting point, but the idea of a basic income may have enough merit as an anti-poverty strategy that it needs to be discussed by politicians and policymakers from coast to coast. Vinusha Gunaseelan (2018) of the Wellesley Institute argues that "having a basic income would give individuals access to basic necessities, preventing chronic stress. It may also result in decreased use of the health system" (para. 10).

At the federal level, in 2017, a motion was put forward in the Senate that encouraged further investigation of the cost and impact of a national basic income program. The motion passed with cross-party support.

COVID–19 and the Case for a Universal Basic Income

Public interest in the idea of a universal basic income grew significantly during the COVID–19 pandemic, which had exposed major flaws in the Canadian social safety net.

In April 2021, the Parliamentary Budget Office (PBO), the government's spending oversight body, outlined the case for a guaranteed income. According to the PBO, a no-strings-attached government benefit to Canadians could quickly cut poverty levels by half.

The PBO analysis was based on the Ontario pilot program in 2017. A single person would get up to $16,989 a year and a couple would get $24,027. Canadians with disabilities would receive a $6,000 top-up. The more someone earns, the less they would receive, at a rate of $0.50 for every dollar earned. The guaranteed basic income's effect on labour supply would be "small," the PBO wrote.

The PBO also explained that, if a guaranteed income were implemented, a wide array of federal and provincial tax credits would no longer be needed and these savings could fund much of the project.

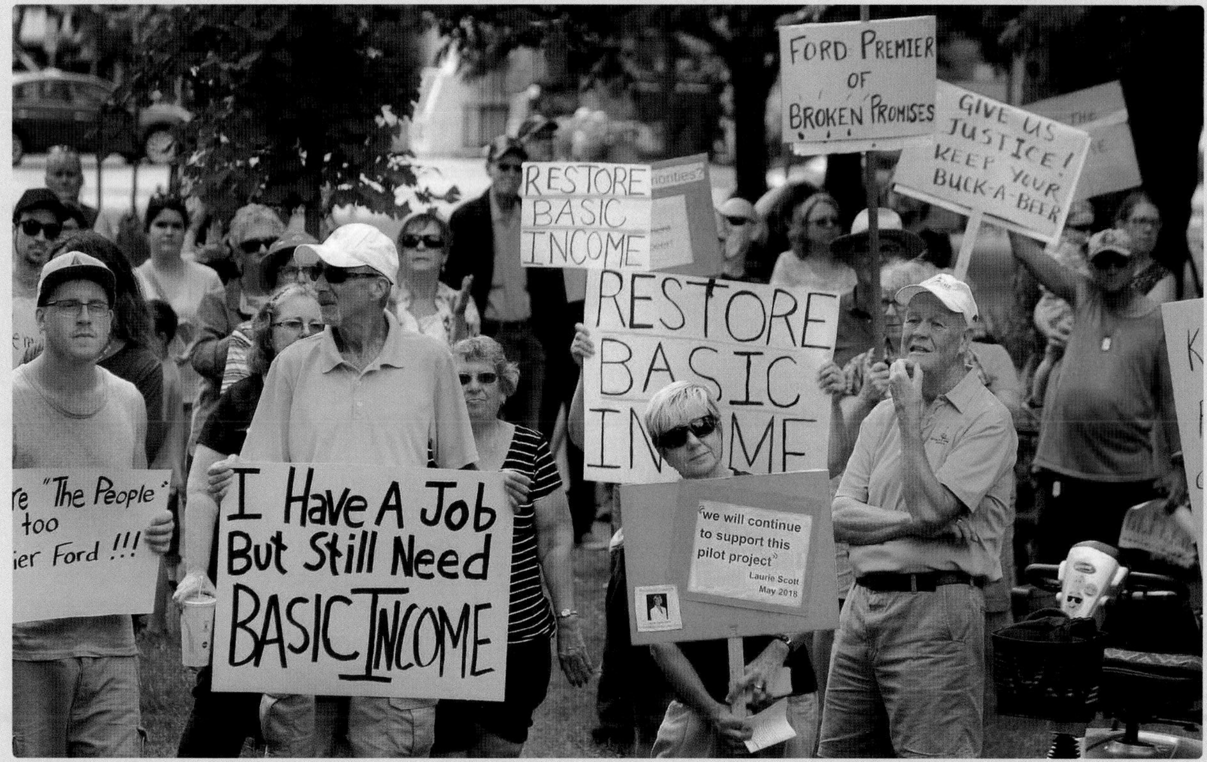

4.7 A Sense of Urgency

Canadian governments have long recognized that Canada's children need protection — not only is it the ethical thing to do, but our economic and social well-being depends on it. In 1944, a universal benefit called the Family Allowance was instituted, and this benefit went to all families with children regardless of income; it was a "demogrant" program. Over time, this benefit became geared to middle- and low-income families. In 1993, it was eliminated entirely.

Nowadays, most income security benefits available to families with children have been, and continue to be, delivered through the tax system in the form of tax credits and exemptions. Others are distributed through direct cash transfers. The Canada Child Benefit is now the principal child-related benefit for families with children. It is applied through the tax system, with eligibility determined by family income.

The reality is that many families living in poverty have one or both parents working — the household income is just not enough to bring them above the poverty line. Questions remain about why so many working families are still left with inadequate incomes. Are there other policy solutions that can be adopted that might eliminate poverty among the working poor altogether?

The Social and Economic Costs of Poverty

Poverty takes its first toll on the people living in poverty themselves, and then on society at large. The true social and economic costs of poverty may be difficult to compute precisely, but they must be large.

A recent report by Feed Ontario (2019) concluded that poverty costs the province of Ontario between $27.1 billion and $33 billion per year. The report points to the relationship of poverty to poor health, the justice system, and lost productivity. As well, it underscores that investing in people is not just the socially responsible thing to do but is financially smart. Vast sums are spent dealing with the consequences of poverty and in servicing the welfare system. Michael Maidment, the chair of Feed Ontario, says that anti-poverty initiatives can benefit individuals and families and lead to significant cost savings and revenue generation for provincial governments as well (Brown, 2019).

In a country as wealthy as Canada, 4.8 million Canadians struggle to make ends meet — that is, to pay rent, feed their families, and address their basic needs (based on the LIM; Statistics Canada, 2017a). Poverty not only causes individual hardship and lost opportunities but also weakens the country's economic performance. Poverty reduction results in better management of health care costs, reduced crime, a more productive labour force, improved well-being, and greater social cohesion and public confidence.

At the individual and family levels, income security can literally be a matter of life and death.

Social Assistance Rates Fail to Address the Problem of Poverty in Canada

No Canadian province or territory offers social assistance rates that are sufficient to bring people even close to the poverty line, according to recent numbers from Maytree Foundation.

Even where welfare incomes were the highest, they still fell well short of the poverty threshold. The closest was in Québec where the welfare income of a single parent reached 85 percent of the poverty threshold and in PEI where welfare incomes for a couple with two children also reached 85 percent of the threshold.

Anti-poverty advocates have long maintained that income security systems are inadequate in addressing poverty and should be replaced with a universal basic income system.

Laidley, J. & Aldridge, H. (2020). *Welfare in Canada 2019*. Maytree Foundation.

Essential Workers during COVID–19

Low-wage, immigrant, racialized, and migrant workers have been disproportionately impacted by the COVID–19 pandemic. Many work in temporary, part-time, contract, or precarious jobs, and often in more than one workplace.

Even before the pandemic, many workers were living in poverty due to low wages, inadequate hours, and high costs of living. Many also faced racism and other systemic barriers that affected their lives and well-being. During the COVID–19 crisis, these are the workers who were hardest hit by job loss and hours reductions.

They are also often workers with precarious immigration status who have been unable to access income supports like the Canada Emergency Response Benefit (CERB), Employment Insurance, or the Canada Recovery Benefit (CRB). They are migrant workers and frontline workers who have continued to work throughout the COVID–19 pandemic for low wages and without adequate protections. They work in grocery stores, caregiving, health care, cleaning, warehouses, agriculture, food delivery, and all the other sectors that keep our economy (and lives) running.

Brynne Sinclair-Waters. (2020). *Protecting the rights of workers hardest hit by the COVID–19 pandemic.* Maytree.

Photo: A Montréal construction worker during the COVID–19 shutdown, April 2020.

The Essential Elements of a Meaningful Anti-Poverty Plan

Much is still needed in order to achieve the goal of serious poverty reduction. The Dignity for All plan lays out the next steps, based on the principles of human rights and a sense of urgency.

Based on consultation with people who have lived in poverty and anti-poverty activists, the Dignity for All campaign proposed that an effective anti-poverty strategy must be the following:

- **Comprehensive.** The strategy must involve integrated policy in a minimum of six areas, including income security, housing and homelessness, health care, food security, early childhood education and care, and employment. This must include a whole-of-government approach for departmental coordination, as well as coordination with provincial/territorial and municipal strategies.
- **Rights-Based.** People with lived experience of poverty, anti-poverty groups, and community organizations must be engaged in an ongoing way in the further development, implementation, and evaluation of the Canadian Poverty Reduction Strategy. The plan must address the most urgent needs immediately, particularly for those highly marginalized, including Indigenous communities, new immigrants and refugees, single-parent families, children, people living with disabilities, and seniors. It must also set strong targets and timelines with a goal of not just reducing but ending poverty in Canada.
- **Legislated.** The strategy requires federal anti-poverty legislation, based in human rights, that includes accountability mechanisms for review and evaluation. The Federal Poverty Reduction Act (2018) legislated in 2018 "aspires" to reduce the 2015 level of poverty by 20% by 2020 and reduce the 2015 level of poverty by 50% by 2030. Noah Zon (2018) argues that the problem of legislating a strategy with "aspirational" targets is that future governments have the ability to ignore or repeal them — they are not binding.
- **Fully Funded.** Adequate funding commitments must be made to support a robust and responsive strategy. This includes a plan for tax reform to support income equity, along with increased and targeted funding through the Canada Social Transfer to support provincial/territorial poverty reduction strategies.

The Dignity for All campaign's "Essential Elements of a Meaningful Plan" appear on the next page.

Essential Elements of a Meaningful Plan

Successful anti-poverty strategies must include the following elements:

Consistency with International Human Rights Obligations

An effective anti-poverty plan must be informed by Canada's international human rights obligations. This includes the obligation to take reasonable steps to effectively address poverty, using the maximum of available resources. It also includes many of the elements described below.

A Comprehensive Approach

An effective anti-poverty plan must deal with the multiple dimensions and causes of poverty, incorporating a range of strategies and investments targeting family income, the high cost of essentials such as housing and education, and needed community supports and services.

A Focus on Those Most in Need

An effective plan must address the unique and particular needs and circumstances of groups most vulnerable to poverty (such as youth, single mothers, Inuit, First Nations and Métis peoples, people with disabilities, as well as newcomers and immigrants) and their particular experiences of poverty (such as homelessness or inadequate housing, low-wage precarious employment, and lack of affordable child care).

Measurable Goals, Targets, and Timelines

An effective anti-poverty plan must have clear and realistic goals, as well as realistic timelines to achieve these goals, using widely accepted measures of progress. The benchmarks for the timelines must be concrete enough, and frequent enough, that a government can be held accountable within it's mandate. While the goals are an important part of the plan, other and emerging factors should always be taken into account. Goals and timelines should be legislated.

Review and Accountability

Accountability mechanisms are key to an effective and credible anti-poverty plan. Transparent and timely mechanisms and indicators are needed to track progress. A detailed implementation plan must be established for the government and individual departments to follow, which is coordinated and monitored by a lead minister or department. The lead minister, in turn, should be required to report annually to Parliament. And individuals must have opportunities to hold their government accountable to a national anti-poverty plan – be it through existing or newly established mechanisms.

Community Involvement

Meaningful and ongoing country-wide consultations and engagement is essential to producing, implementing, and monitoring an effective anti-poverty plan that speaks to the diverse experiences of people living in poverty in Canada. In particular, it will be critical to meaningfully engage First Nations, Métis, and Inuit communities, as well as other groups at high risk of poverty, including: recent immigrants, single mothers, single senior women, people with disabilities, and people with chronic illness and addictions.

Integration

Provinces and territories have led the way in introducing poverty reduction plans in Canada over the past decade. A new federal plan should link with existing efforts at the provincial/territorial and community levels, recognizing in particular the unique position of Québec and its approach to social policy within the Canadian context.

Dignity for All (2015). Dignity for All: A National Anti-Poverty Plan for Canada. Ottawa, Ontario.

Social Welfare Policy in Action

Indigenous Women's Poverty Reduction

Holistic Cultural and Spiritual Approaches Are Essential

Indigenous women face multiple layers of marginalization. Cultural identity and social inclusion are essential elements of any effective strategy for poverty reduction.

Indigenous women experience poverty based not only on race and gender but also on class and culture.

Poverty reduction must start by acknowledging and protecting Indigenous culture and cultural practices, in addition to providing increased employment and access to education and health care (Native Women's Association of Canada [NWAC], 2017).

For Indigenous women, improvement in social and economic well-being requires the following: better access to cultural activities, recognition of Indigenous cultural identity, appropriate employment opportunities, and the provision of quality social services that are Indigenous centred.

THE NWAC Survey on Poverty Reduction

In September 2017, NWAC undertook three engagement processes to develop recommendations for a poverty reduction plan for Indigenous women:

- A grassroots survey from 128 Indigenous women administered over social media
- A full-day roundtable with NWAC's board of directors, which includes 23 Indigenous women who are leaders of grassroots organization across the country
- A full-day discussion with 40 Indigenous women who participate in the Communities at Risk (CAR) program, a five-month course for Indigenous women with multiple barriers

The recommendations from the three consultations are contained in final report issued by NWAC (2017), entitled Poverty Reduction Strategy: The Native Women's Association of Canada Engagement Results.

An overview is provided here.

1. The Social Media Grassroots Survey

The survey was distributed on social media websites such as Twitter and Facebook. The participants were women, mainly between the ages of 30 and 49 years of age. Of those who identified as women, two individuals identified as transgender and two others as Two Spirit individuals. The majority identified as status-holding First Nations, with only one identifying as Inuk. Half resided in cities and a quarter on-reserve. Almost 20% lived in unstable housing and, on average, there were two generations under the same roof.

The two main recommendations were as follows:

- **Access to Culture.** Participating in cultural activities is essential to reducing social exclusion. Land is an important cornerstone for many cultural practices, which was described as a "source of identity and spirituality." The majority stated a need for increased access (including reliable and affordable transportation) to land for ceremony. A large proportion of the respondents wanted access to land for food sources.
- **Access to Services.** Indigenous women experience more barriers to accessing social services than non-Indigenous women. Participants noted that many of the services they require are unavailable to them when they need them. For urban Indigenous women, access to Elders and traditional teachers was reported as urgently needed, and culturally appropriate health care and child care was lacking coast to coast. Participants reflected on their access to basic needs (food, shelter, clothing, water, health care, education, and sanitation). The majority had challenges meeting their basic needs, and all had struggled with this at some point.

2. Roundtable of NWAC's Board of Directors

In a one-day roundtable of 23 Indigenous women's leaders, the following areas were identified as being essential in a poverty reduction plan:

- **Accurate Data.** Quantitative and qualitative data is needed about the prevalence and impact of poverty on First Nations, Inuit, and Métis women.
- **Cultural Supports.** Following cultural teachings would improve access to quality housing and food, and wellness.
- **Women in the Workforce.** The difficulty of securing safe and rewarding employment in their home communities was highlighted.
- **A Holistic Approach.** An approach that looks at layers of marginalization and intersectionality is required (including reintegration for Indigenous women within and after release from prisons).
- **Violence.** Indigenous women recount staying in abusive relationships because of economic dependency created by poverty.
- **Housing First.** Indigenous women are overrepresented among the homeless, and emergency beds and domestic abuse shelters are in short supply.

3. Communities at Risk (CAR) Roundtable

All of the women in this roundtable have experienced or currently experience poverty. Their best practices for poverty reduction included the following:

- **Elimination of Arbitrary Barriers to Services.** This would mean that Indigenous women living just above the standardized poverty line are not denied access to necessary programs, such as daycare or mental health counselling.
- **A Collective, Holistic Approach to Services.** A holistic approach would create a connection between cultural knowledge and the administration of social services and should include cultural resources and funding to access sacred land, water, and ceremonies.
- **Increased Access to Services.** Many services remain inaccessible or unaffordable due to a lack of transportation or due to systemic racism.

Questions for Reflection

All poverty reduction plans should respond to diverse experiences. However, the core needs of Indigenous women, who are overrepresented in all dimensions of poverty, are frequently ignored.

In this NWAC report, the need to access land, water, cultural supports, and social services (such as mental health services and housing) were highlighted as a necessary part of building resiliency and reducing poverty.

The NWAC's Poverty Reduction Strategy report is available here: www.nwac.ca/wp-content/uploads/2018/08/Poverty-Reduction-Strategy-Revised-Aug23.pdf. Once you have reviewed the report, answer the following questions:

- What indicators were used to determine the need for a specific poverty reduction plan for Indigenous women?
- What social welfare principles underpin such a need?
- What social welfare principles should be incorporated into a poverty reduction plan for Indigenous women?
- How were the principles of inclusion, social equity, and social justice addressed in the recommendations from the three groups of women consulted?
- Identify the key themes that you would want to include in an Indigenous women's poverty reduction plan. Compare them to Canada's national poverty reduction strategy and other poverty reduction plans that exist in your province.

A Moment in Time: January 16, 1981

Canada's First Food Bank

The Edmonton Gleaners Association

The food bank idea was first successfully developed on a large scale in Canada by the Edmonton Gleaners Association in 1981.

On January 16, 1981, the Edmonton Gleaners Association received its official charter of incorporation, and Canada's first food bank was born. Since 1981, it has been the mission of the Edmonton Gleaners Association (Edmonton's Food Bank) to collect food in order to feed those in need within the city.

Conferences held in Edmonton in 1985 and Toronto in 1986 led to the establishment of a national organization, the Canadian Association of Food Banks (now Food Banks Canada). Forty-three food banks across the country made up the membership of the association in 1989. Its membership has since risen to some 450 food banks.

Each year since 1989, Food Banks Canada has released HungerCount, a national survey of food bank use in Canada. The three largest groups using food banks are people receiving social assistance, people with disabilities, and the working poor.

Hunger is not just an issue for people in Canadian cities. About half of the food banks that participate in HungerCount are in rural areas (Bechtel, 2013). In 2019, 34% of food bank users in rural areas were children (Food Banks Canada, 2019).

Photo: People at work in a Jewish Food Bank in Toronto in November 2020, preparing food for families in need of help during the COVID-19 pandemic.

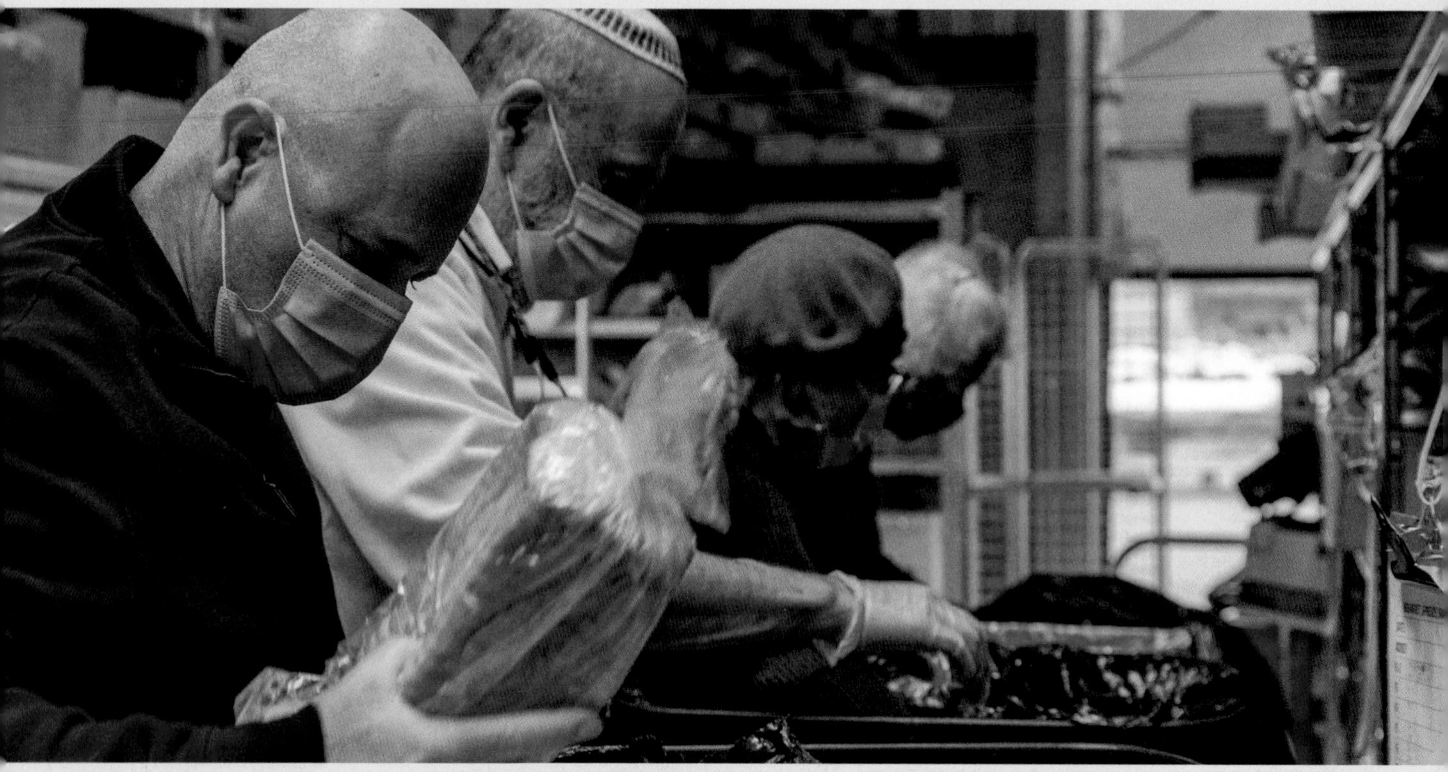

Chapter Review

Questions

1. In 2018, the federal government introduced Canada's first national poverty reduction strategy (Opportunity for All). What are its strengths and weaknesses?
2. What is the extent of food insecurity and homelessness in Canada today? What are some of the myths surrounding food bank usage?
3. What is meant by the term "workfare"? Research how workfare programs have been applied in provincial jurisdictions across the country.
4. Make the case for and against the idea of implementing a universal basic income as an effective/ineffective anti-poverty strategy.
5. Describe the essential components of the anti-poverty strategy advanced by the Dignity for All campaign. Do you think the strategy has merit?

Exploring Social Welfare

1. Engage your friends and family in a discussion about poverty and people living in low income. Assess whether their views in any way might be influenced by prevailing myths about "the poor."
2. What are some anti-poverty initiatives that have been successful in your city or community?
3. The two reports listed below can be easily accessed over the Internet. Read the two reports and describe what each report proposes for how Indigenous poverty should be addressed Identify any similarities and differences between the two reports.
   - Beedie, Macdonald, and Wilson's *Towards Justice: Tackling Indigenous Child Poverty in Canada* (www.policyalternatives.ca).
   - Native Women's Association of Canada's *Poverty Reduction Strategy: The Native Women's Association of Canada Engagement Results* (http://www.nwac.ca).

Websites

Canada Without Poverty
www.cwp-csp.ca
Canada Without Poverty is a federally incorporated, non-partisan, non-profit, and charitable organization dedicated to the elimination of poverty in Canada. Its work includes raising awareness about poverty, participating in research to generate new knowledge about poverty, and striving to demonstrate the connection between poverty and human rights.

Food Banks Canada
www.foodbankscanada.ca
Food Banks Canada is the national charitable organization representing and supporting the food bank community across Canada. Food Banks Canada strives to meet the short-term need for food and find long-term solutions to hunger in order to reduce the need for food banks and emergency food services in Canada.

Maytree
https://maytree.com
Maytree is committed to advancing systemic solutions to poverty and strengthening civic communities. Maytree believes that the most enduring way to fix the systems that create poverty is to have economic and social rights safeguarded for all people living in Canada. The Maytree website includes the Caledon Institute of Social Policy's collection of social policy research. (The Caledon Institute was active from 1992 to 2017.)

The Welfare and Well-Being of Women and Families

"Family law and policy in Canada are now characterized by a flexible pluralism that reflects the acceptance of multiple traditions and changing family forms ... few of us imagine that there is a single model of family that is 'traditional,' any more than we imagine that Canada is a nation with a singular identity."

— Eric W. Sager, "Family and Social Memory: Why History Matters," in *Families Count: Profiling Canadian Families IV*, The Vanier Institute of the Family, 2010

Katherine Scott and David Macdonald

Family Policies for the Way We Live Now

5

The lives of Canadian families have evolved – it is time our family policies caught up.

Family life in Canada is not the same today as it was years ago, and public policy is struggling to catch up. There are over 3.6 million more women in the workforce today than there were 40 years ago (Statistics Canada, n.d.m.). In households where there is a working male parent, the mother of young children is more likely to work, and more than three-quarters of these mothers work full-time (Statistics Canada, n.d.l.).

This seismic change has proven to be an economic boon to the economy and a critical financial contribution to families. At the same time, the benefit to Canadian women has been uneven. Paid work comes on top of an unequal division of labour at home as women continue to perform many more hours of unpaid work than men do.

Child care, parental leave, support for caregivers, and economic policies that level the playing field between families of different means can all make a substantial difference to advancing gender equality and the quality of family life in Canada.

Family Policies for the Way We Live Now

Important gains have been made in family policies over the years. However, newer policies are now needed that take into account the changing context of women and families today. This chapter looks at many of these important new policy questions and debates.

After completing this chapter, you should be able to:

- Describe the main changes that have taken place in family arrangements and some of the factors underlying these changes;
- Explain why it is important for families to have access to affordable, quality child care and elder care;
- Identify the gaps in Canada's current parental leave system;
- Explain why a comprehensive strategy to support caregivers is needed;
- Describe the different phases in the history of benefits programs designed to support families in Canada and the degree to which these programs have advanced gender equality; and
- Identify the barriers that women face in the labour market and how these challenges impact their economic security and the security of their families.

Key Concepts

- Women's labour force participation
- Québec's child care program
- Maternity and parental leave
- Elder care
- Canada Caregiver Credit
- Family Allowance Act, 1944
- Child Tax Benefit (CTB) and Working Income Supplement (WIS)
- Canada Child Tax Benefit (CCTB) and National Child Benefit Supplement (NCBS)
- Universal Child Care Benefit (UCCB)
- Income splitting
- Canada Child Benefit (CCB)
- Tax supports for families
- Industry and job gender segregation
- Wage-setting policies

5.1 What Has Changed for Work and Family Life

One of the most significant changes in the lives of Canadians over the past several decades has been the increase in women's labour force participation in paid work. In 1978, 2.3 million women (ages 25 to 54 years) were employed. By 2018, that number had risen to 5.9 million. Almost all of that increase has come from women taking full-time jobs. In 1978, less than half of all women worked full-time (39.8%). Today, two-thirds of women (64.7%) hold down full-time jobs (Statistics Canada, n.d.m.).

Women entering the workforce are not replacing men. Today, 86.3% of core working age men are employed — roughly the same share that were employed 30 years ago. The most significant shift in male employment rates has been a 3.9 percentage point decline in men's participation in full-time work following each of the major recessions in the last four decades and a parallel increase in their participation in part-time work (Statistics Canada, n.d.m.).

Economic growth is not a "zero-sum game." Rather, there can be positive feedback loops where, for example, as more women make and spend money, opportunities for new businesses expand and they, in turn, hire more women who make and spend more money, and so on. The substantial growth in women's paid work in Canada has created an economy that is much larger today than in the past. That economy generates higher family incomes and higher government revenues that, in turn, support key public programs such as health care.

Figure 5.1

Employment Rates of Women Aged 25–54 Years, 1978–2018

Statistics Canada. Table 14–10–0327–01. *Labour force characteristics by sex and detailed age group, annual.*

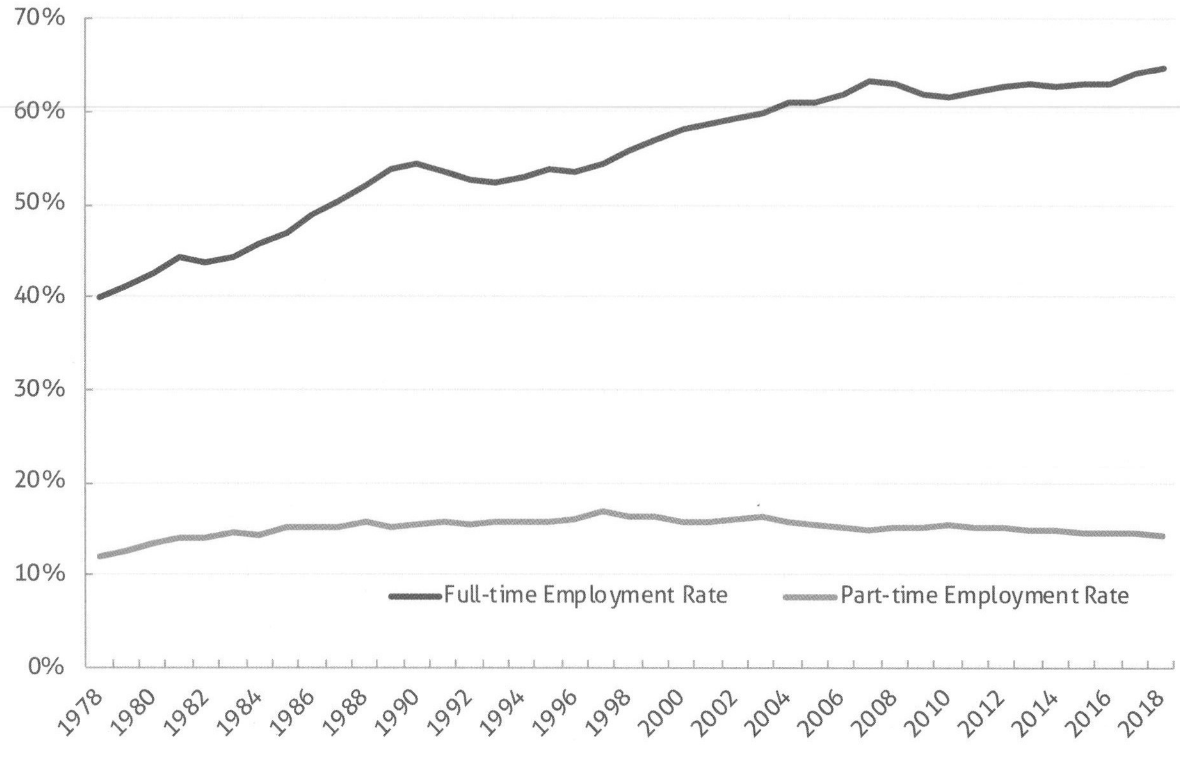

Dual-Earning Families Now the Norm

The movement of women into the workforce has fundamentally changed the working and family lives of Canadians:

- It has helped families compensate for the lack of growth in men's earnings (Statistics Canada, n.d.d., n.d.e.).
- It has increased the financial security of working women and their children and reduced the risk of family poverty, notably in Québec (Fortin et al., 2012).
- It has also created a time deficit for many working parents and left families with young children struggling to meet the demands of their employers and the needs of their children.

Women's hours of household and care work have not fallen as their hours of paid work have increased. Today, women are putting in 4.1 hours of household and care work per day, roughly the same number of hours as 20 years ago (Statistics Canada, n.d.s.). However, for the majority of women, these 4.1 hours are in addition to a full day of paid work (Statistics Canada, n.d.l.).

Indeed, taking paid and unpaid work into account, Canadian women have the highest total work burden of women in all the G7 countries (Moyser & Burlock, 2018).

With the increase in the aging population, the demands of household and care work will only grow.

Figure 5.2

Median Employment Incomes (1978–2017)

Statistics Canada. Tables 11-10-0239-01 and 11-10-0191-01. *Income of individuals by age group, sex and income source, (constant 1917 dollars).*

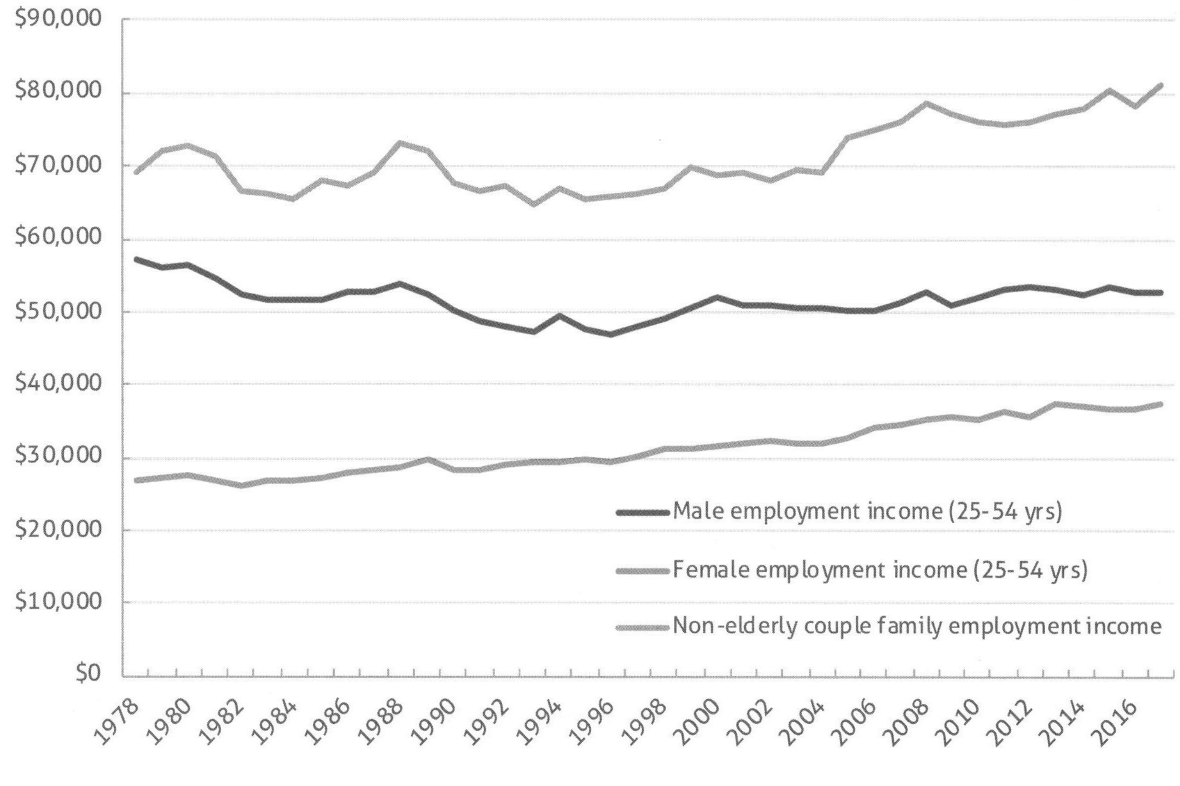

New Challenges and New Priorities

The share of Canadians who live as married or common-law partners today stands at 57%, effectively unchanged over the past two decades (Statistics Canada, n.d.n.). While the fertility rate has dropped from a high in 1959 of 3.9 children per woman to 1.5 children per woman in 2017, the fertility rate today is roughly where it was 20 years ago (Milan, 2015; Statistics Canada, n.d.g.). What has changed is that most of those children now have two working parents. Between 1976 and 2015, the percentage of dual-income families with at least one child went from 36% to 69%. In 1976, 24% of couples with children had two full-time working parents (two-thirds of dual-earner couples with children). By 2014, this figure had risen to more than 50% (three-quarters of all dual-earner couples with children) (Uppal, 2015).

The employment rate of mothers of children under age six has risen steadily over the past three decades. In households where there is a working male parent, the mother of young children is more likely to work than in the past, and a majority of these mothers (77%) work full-time (Statistics Canada, n.d.l.). This is also true among caregivers who provide support to older family members or to those with disabilities. Among caregivers aged 19 to 70 years old, 82% were employed and over 70% in this group were employed full-time (Fast et al., 2014).

These changes add up to priorities for families. Families need policies and programs that respond to the way that they live now — not outdated patriarchal models about women's presumed availability to provide care in the home.

Figure 5.3

Total Fertility Rate (Average Number of Children per Woman), 1977–2017)

Statistics Canada. Table 13-10-0418-01. *Crude birth rate, age-specific fertility rates and total fertility rate (live births);* Milan (2015).

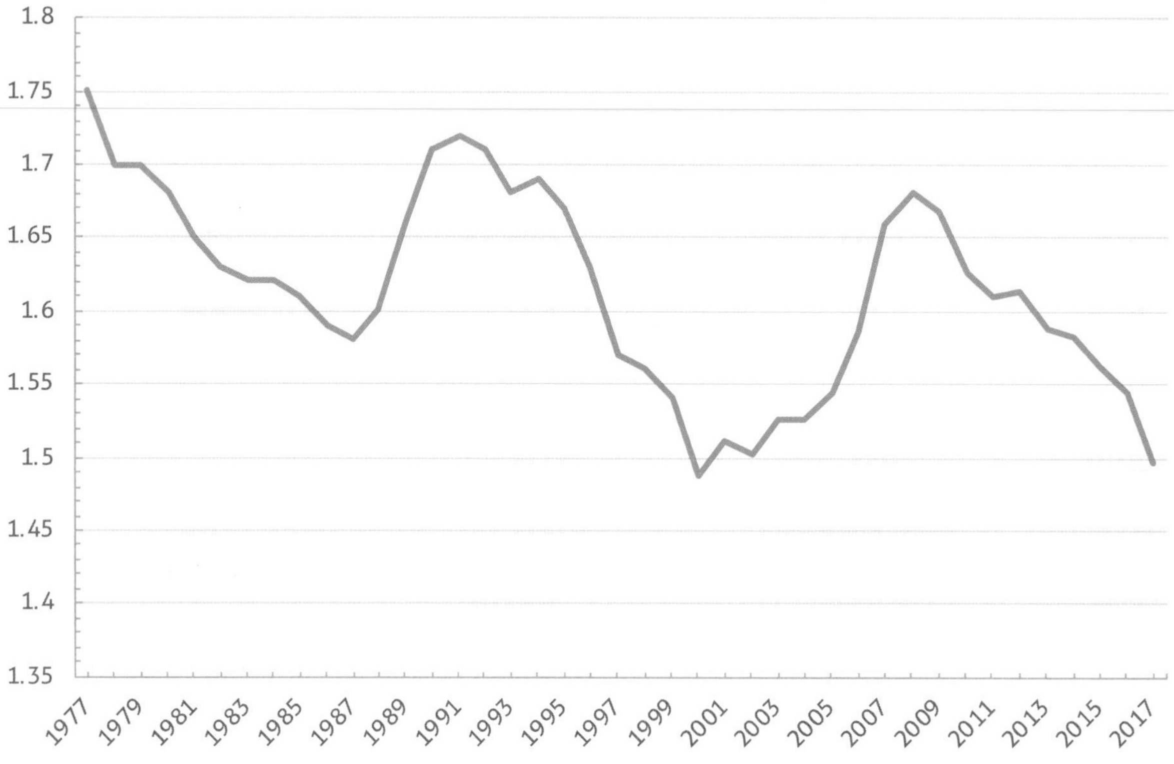

Supports for Families Today

Today, new parents want to spend time with their children. Both parents need parental leave policies that meet the pressures of work and family life. Families with two working parents need to know that their children will be looked after in safe and supportive environments while they work.

Parents need economic policies that allow them both to contribute to their family's economic security. Families supporting older adults or family members with disabilities need to be able to rely on high-quality services and supports — for both care receivers and care providers.

Governments and employers have an important role to play in helping families meet these needs — underwriting some of the costs involved in having and caring for family members as well as providing common goods and services such as health care and home care support. Governments also create the conditions under which families' caring work takes place. For example, they regulate labour markets and set employment standards, establish and enforce family law, offer job-protected caregiving leave and income replacement programs (e.g., maternity and parental leaves), and uphold human rights. Progressive policies such as these can go a long way to helping parents and caregivers meet their own needs as well as those of their children and other dependents.

For their part, employers can help families reconcile work and family life by allowing flexible work arrangements as well as access to leave for caregiving (beyond what is mandated) and information and support services.

Figure 5.4

Employment Rates, Women (Aged 25–54 Years) and Mothers (Children under Age 16 and Age 6), 1978–2018

Statistics Canada. Table: 14-10-0120-01. *Labour force characteristics by family age composition, annual.*

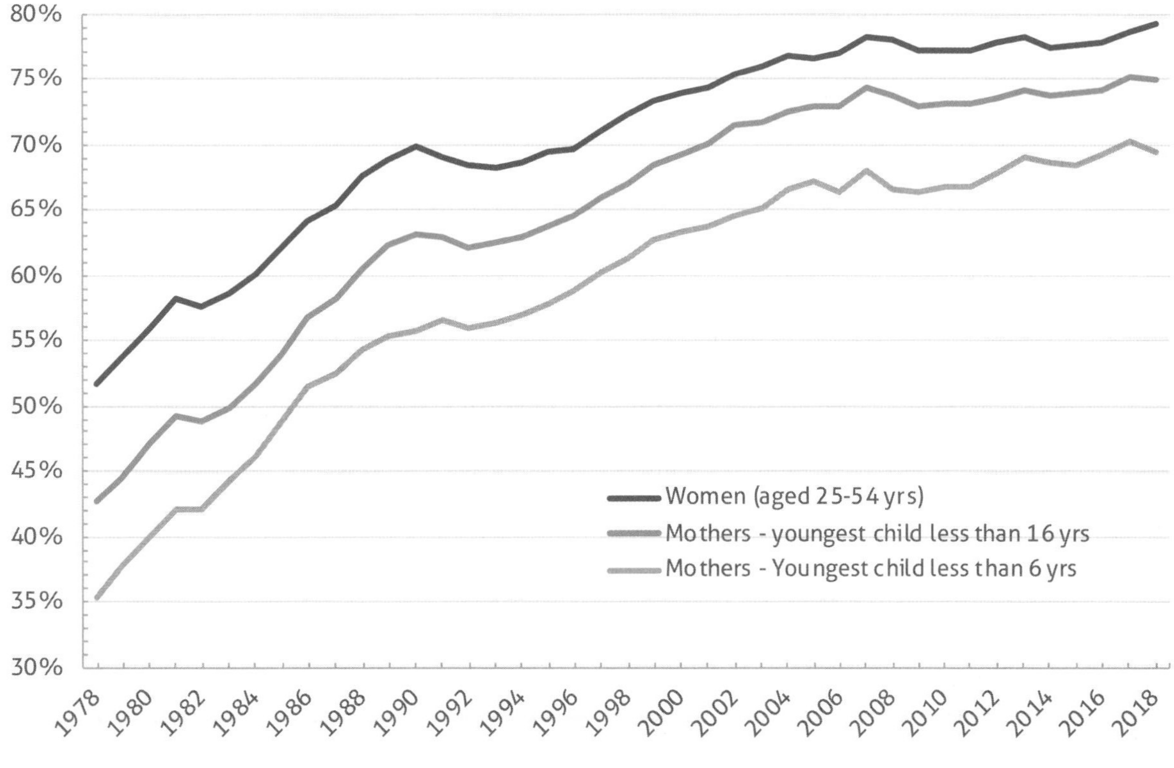

Families Count

Modern Families Are Diverse

Policies aimed at supporting Canadian families are largely based on outdated ideas as to what modern families are and how they function. It is time that these policies were brought up to date.

Statistics Canada defines a "census family" as follows:

> A married couple and the children, if any, of either and/or both spouses; a couple living common law and the children, if any, of either and/or both partners; or a lone parent of any marital status with at least one child living in the same dwelling and that child or those children. All members of a particular census family live in the same dwelling. A couple may be of opposite or same sex. (Statistics Canada, 2015a)

This definition focuses on what can be measured — who lives with whom and under what circumstances.

A family can also be defined, as The Vanier Institute of the Family does, in terms of what the members of the family do for each other and for the larger society. The Vanier Institute defines family as "any combination of two or more persons who are bound over time by ties of mutual consent, birth and/or adoption or placement, and who together assume responsibilities for combinations of the following:

- physical maintenance and care of group members;
- addition of new members through procreation, adoption, or placement;
- socialization of children;
- social control of members;
- production, consumption, and distribution of goods and services; and
- affective nurturance (i.e., love)." (Mirabelli, 2018)

The Vanier Institute's definition of family emphasizes the work and accomplishments of people who commit themselves to one another over time. It acknowledges heterosexual and same-sex couples, lone-parent families, extended patterns of kinship, blended families (step-families), couples with children and those without, the commitments of siblings to one another, and the obligations and affection that unite the young and the old in their lives together.

Changing Families

The results of the 2016 census show a growing number of census families characterized by increasing diversity. Here are some insights:

- There were 9.8 million census families, up 4.8% from 9.4 million families five years earlier (Statistics Canada, 2016a).
- Married couples were the predominant family structure (65.8%), although they continue to decrease as a share of all families (Statistics Canada, 2016a).
- The percentage of common-law couples grew rapidly between 2011 and 2016, increasing 11.9% compared with 2.9% for married couples and 5.6% for lone-parent families. In 2016, over one-fifth of all couples (21.3%) were living common law, more than three times the percentage in 1981 (6.3%) (Statistics Canada, 2016a).
- The share of lone-parent families continued to edge up, reaching 16.4% of all census families in 2016. About eight in 10 lone-parent families were female lone-parent families (accounting for 12.8% of all families) (Statistics Canada, 2016a).
- Among couple families, the share of families living without children has been rising, largely due to population aging. In 2016, the share of couples living with at least one child at home fell to 51.1% — the lowest level on record (Statistics Canada, 2016a).
- This trend has been partly offset by an increasing share of young adults living with their parents over the last four decades (Statistics Canada, 2017b).
- In the 2016 census, 72,880 couples identified themselves as same-sex couples, one-third

(33.4%) were married and about one in eight (12.0%) had children living with them (Statistics Canada, 2017a).

Changing Expectations, Changing Realities

Despite all the changes over the past 60 or 70 years, in many ways, our ideas about families and the roles of women within families have not kept pace. The "traditional" notion of a family, consisting of two parents — a working father and a supportive non-working wife — and a couple of children persists.

Families have never fit neatly into one mould. Examine our history, and we find diversity and change among families and households. Today's families are smaller. Adults wait longer to marry and to have children, if they do so at all. Common-law unions are no longer just a preliminary stage before marriage but an alternative to marriage for a growing number.

The dual-earner family has gone from an exception to the norm, and a growing number of women are primary income earners within their families. In contrast to the past when most children growing up with only one parent were living with a widow or widower, children growing up today with a lone parent (most often their mother) are likely to have another parent who lives elsewhere.

In considering older adults, the long-term decline in fertility rate is creating enormous challenges in the caring capacity of families as parents age and fewer children, often separated by distance, are available for support. The two basic resources all families require are time and money, and for a growing number of families, these basics are in short supply.

How we choose to respond to these and other challenges, not just as individuals, but as a society, is vitally important.

Figure 5.5

Distribution (%) of Private Households by Number of People, 1941–2016

Statistics Canada. (2015b). The shift to smaller households over the past century. *Canadian Megatrends*. Statistics Canada Catalogue no. 11–630-X.

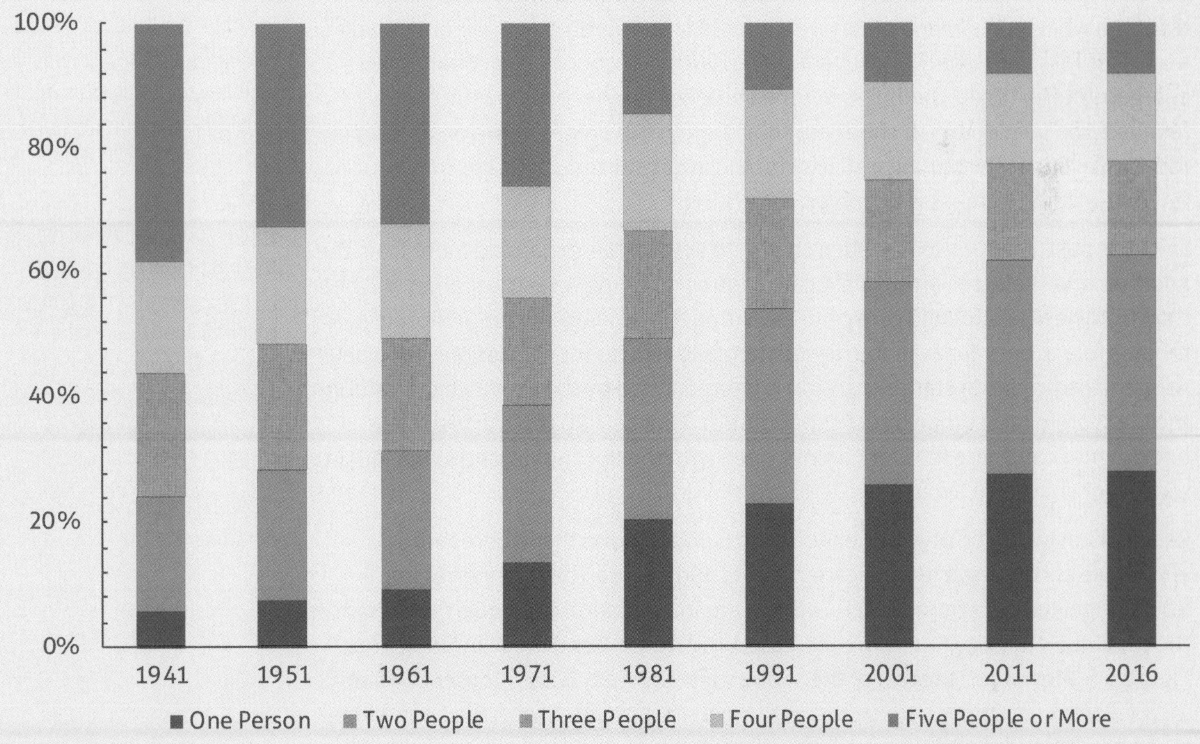

5.2 Child Care

The cost and availability of child care and other key supports have a significant and demonstrable impact on the choices families are able to make. These choices include when and how many children to have, the distribution of unpaid and paid work between parents (in two-parent households), and the financial security of families (particularly in lone-parent households). A review of the experiences of other high-income countries indicates that when child care is affordable and readily available, more women take up paid work and are more likely to have children (Hegewischa & Gornick, 2011; Samman & Lombardi, 2019; Thévenon, 2011). On this score, Canada continues to lag behind other Organisation for Economic Co-operation and Development (OECD) countries, ranking at the bottom of the list in terms of the scope and quality of available services (Adamson, 2008).

A Prize Worth Pursuing

Stephen Poloz, the head of the Bank of Canada, has pointed to Québec's childcare program as a way to boost the Canadian economy. In a prepared speech at Queen's University in 2018, Poloz credited the Québec's child-care program for raising prime-age female workforce participation from 74% 20 years ago to about 87% today.

"If we could simply bring the participation rate of prime-age women in the rest of Canada up to the level in Québec, we could add almost 300,000 people to our country's workforce," said Poloz.

"Clearly, that is a prize worth pursuing."

Child Care in Québec

In Canada, the delivery of child care and other early education programs is the responsibility of provincial and territorial governments. As such, the affordability, availability, and quality of child care varies considerably in different provinces and territories.

Québec has been a leader in child care policy in Canada. Québec's child care program, introduced in 1997, is the most heavily subsidized child care program in Canada and offers the lowest fees in the country, at $8.25 per day per child in provincially subsidized centres. In 2019, the typical family paid just under $200 per child, per month (Macdonald & Friendly, 2020). That amount is seven times less than what Vancouver families with infants or toddlers had to pay, and nearly five times less than what Vancouver families with preschool-aged children were charged. Interestingly, Québec is not the cheapest province for low-income families who gain access to child care subsidies. In this area, Ontario comes out on top. However, given the long wait lists for those subsidized spots, it is only a lucky few low-income families who end up benefiting.

Over the past 10 years, the Québec child care system has expanded more from the addition of private (for-profit) child care centres charging what the market will bear than from new public child care centres. Within that private system, generous tax rebates for parents are available to substantially reduce the market fees they pay. As such, the private system expansion is being funded by the province but through the tax system rather than direct expenditures (Hurteau, 2018). The result has been higher child care fees for parents, even with the tax credits, and lower-quality spaces for children (Lavoie et al., 2015).

Research on family policy in Québec and in Europe shows that where there is affordable and accessible child care, parents and children benefit (Ferragina, 2017; Hegewischa & Gornick, 2011). Since the introduction of Québec's program, the province's fertility rates have increased and now exceed those in Ontario (as Figure 5.5 shows) and the rest of the country (Fortin et al., 2012; Moyser & Milan, 2018). Parents in Québec are choosing to have more children with the knowledge that affordable care and support are available.

The Impact of Affordable Child Care

Women's labour force participation in Québec has also increased at a faster rate than in the rest of Canada. Several economic studies have found that a significant portion of this increase in employment levels is directly attributable to the affordability and accessibility of child care (Baker et al., 2008; Fortin et al., 2012; Lefebvre & Merrigan, 2008). These rates even held steady during and after the 2008 recession, in contrast to the experience in Ontario.

Québec's child care program has also had a demonstrable impact on employment levels for the families most likely to live in low income — lone-parent households. Single mothers of young children have seen their employment rates increase from 37.6% in 1996, the year prior to the introduction of Québec's program, to 69.1% in 2018 (Statistics Canada, n.d.m.). Single female parent households have also seen their poverty rates decline from 52.3% in 1996 to 30.2% by 2017 — moving more than 100,000 single mothers and their children out of poverty (Statistics Canada, n.d.b.).

The affordability of child care, however, is not the sole factor behind Québec's positive results. Availability is also a key factor. Across Canada, there is a huge gap between the number of young children in households with working parents and the number of regulated child care spaces available. In 2018 in Canada, there were 2.3 million children under the age of six, and only 630,000 regulated, centre-based child care spaces for this age group (Friendly et al., 2018; Statistics Canada, n.d.o.).

Figure 5.6

Total Fertility Rates and Labour Force Participation of Women Aged 15–44 Years, Québec and Ontario, 1996–2016

Moyser, M., & Milan, A. (2018). Fertility rates and labour force participation among women in Québec and Ontario. *Insights on Canadian Society*, Catalogue no. 75-006-X. Statistics Canada.

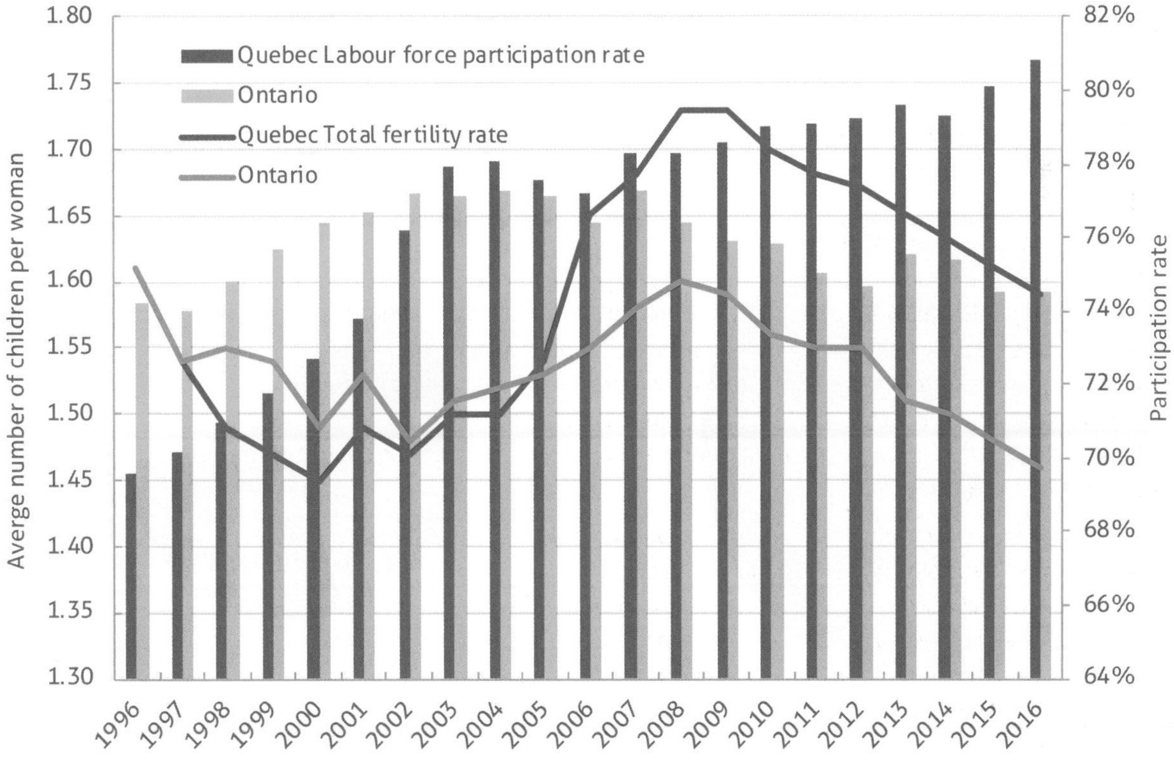

Broader Societal Benefits

The size of the shortfall of regulated, centre-based child care spaces reveals a significant unmet need among families where both parents work and those who would work, or increase their hours of employment, if child care were affordable and available. Survey data confirm that affordability, availability, and quality are critical concerns for families seeking child care (Statistics Canada, 2019).

Child care is also important for parents who do not work or who work part-time. Under Québec's child care program, parents who do not work can and do access child care (Baker et al., 2008). Many parents, whether they are in paid work or not, see child care as an important social and educational benefit for their children — a perception that is supported by the evidence on childhood development and educational outcomes. Further, access to child care can help stay-at-home parents by providing important time for training and job seeking (Evans, 2002).

The benefits of early childhood education and care programs are consistently found to exceed costs, particularly for disadvantaged groups (Fairholm, 2009). The presence of affordable and available child care stimulates economic growth by increasing employment and, therefore, spending and tax revenues. For example, estimates suggest that Québec's child care program has contributed as much as 1.7% in increased economic growth annually to its economy (Fortin et al., 2012). Additional benefits to government revenues come from cost savings that result from lower rates of social assistance and other benefits provided to low-income families who are able to move out of poverty as a result of access to child care.

Figure 5.7

Use of Child Care Arrangements, Children Aged 0–5, 2019

Statistics Canada. Table 42-10-0005-01. *Type of child care arrangement, household population aged 0 to 5 years.*

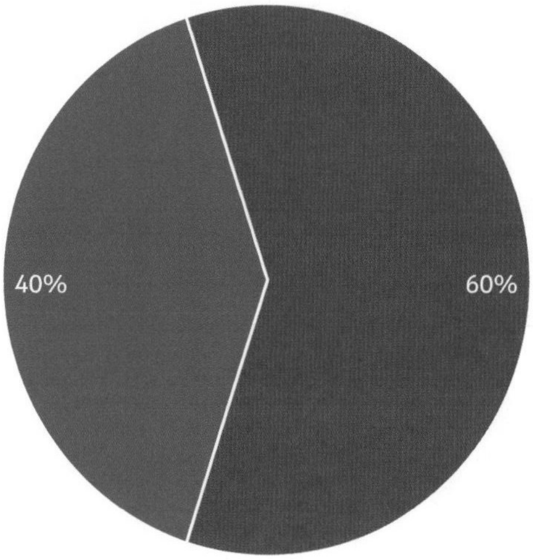

40% of children do not use regular non-parental child care.

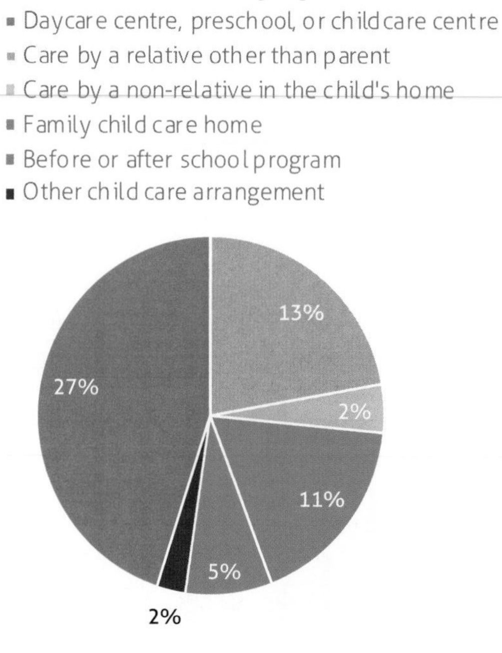

Type of child care utilized by the 60% of children using regular non-parental child care (60%)

A Program That Pays for Itself

The result is that Québec's child care program now contributes more in increased revenues than the program costs — providing an estimated annual net gain of over $200 million to the province (Fortin et al., 2013). Increased employment also provides increased tax revenues to the federal government — providing the federal government with an estimated net gain of $650 million annually (Fortin et al., 2013). Paradoxically, this asymmetrical gain may act to impede further expansion, since provincial expenditures result in federal revenue gains.

In 2017, the federal government increased financial support for child care after a decade of stagnation, allocating $7.5 billion over an 11-year period and negotiating a Multilateral Early Learning and Child Care Framework (Employment and Skills Development Canada [ESDC], 2017) and related bilateral agreements with the provinces, territories, and Indigenous communities (Pasolli, 2019). In 2018, the federal government released an Indigenous Early Learning and Child Care Framework, co-developed with Indigenous organizations (Canada, 2018). New federal funding is helping to lower child care fees in Alberta, British Columbia, Ontario, New Brunswick, and Newfoundland and Labrador.

However, the multilateral framework fails to provide the tools or sufficient funding to tackle the patchwork of services and create a universal and inclusive system of high-quality child care. Promising fee reduction pilots, for example, were cancelled when new governments came to power in Ontario and Alberta.

5.3 Maternity and Parental Leave

Maternity and parental leave is another key support for parents struggling to balance paid employment and care. Like a child care program, the impact of a parental leave program is highly dependent on its design. Many governments offer a mixture of leave available only to mothers (maternity leave) and leave that can be taken by either parent (parental leave). A few offer an additional period of leave for second caregivers (fathers or non-birthing parents). Depending on the design, parental leave programs can work to encourage mothers' labour market participation and protect women's earnings, reduce work–life stress and financial strain on families, and promote gender equity in both paid employment and unpaid caregiving (Robson, 2017).

Canada has two parental leave benefit programs for the care of newborn or adopted children: a federal program offering support to families outside of Québec and the Québec Parental Insurance Plan (QPIP) for Québec residents. The federal plan was launched almost 50 years ago as part of the Unemployment Insurance program, now called Employment Insurance (EI). It currently provides 15 weeks of maternity leave and up to 35 weeks of standard parental leave for those parents who qualify under the EI program. This means that only those parents who have worked at least 600 hours in the year prior to a child's birth are eligible. Those who do qualify receive a standard 55% of their average insurable weekly earnings up to a maximum of $562 per week. Parents can also choose (as of 2017) to take up to 61 weeks of extended parental leave at 33% of their average weekly earnings up to maximum of $337 per week. For low-income families with total family earnings below $25,921 in 2019, incomes can be replaced at a rate of up to 80%. Parental benefits are subject to taxation. The average benefit received under special benefits (including maternity, parental, sickness, and caregiver benefits) is approximately $430 per week (Statistics Canada, n.d.h.).

A new "use it or lose it" EI parental sharing benefit for second caregivers was introduced in 2018. An additional five weeks of leave are available to a second caregiver if the five weeks are taken over the standard 12-month period. Alternatively, an additional eight weeks of extended parental leave are available to a second caregiver if the eight weeks are taken using extended parental benefits over 18 months (Department of Finance Canada, 2018a). These options reflect the same amount of income replacement over different periods of time.

In Québec, parents are covered by QPIP, which provides 18 weeks of leave to mothers, 32 weeks of leave that can be shared between parents, and 5 weeks of leave for a father or second caregiver (Gouvernement du Québec, 2020). QPIP also offers parents leaves of shorter duration with higher income replacement rates. QPIP replaces between 70 and 75% of a parent's earnings (depending on the length of leave taken) up to a maximum of $1,030 to $1,100 per week. Québec's plan also differs from the federal program in offering benefits to the self-employed and requiring only $2,000 of insurable earnings during the qualifying period. As well, it offers flexibility: parents can take fewer weeks of leave at a higher rate of earnings replacement, and parents can take leave at the same time.

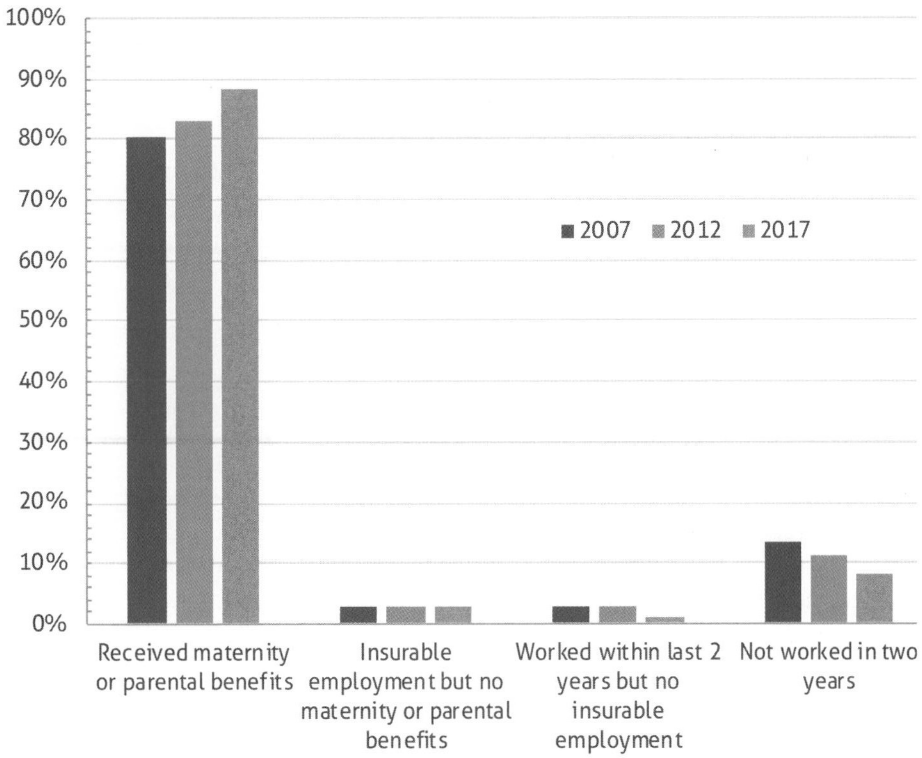

Figure 5.8 (a)

EI Maternity/Parental Benefit Status of New Mothers, Québec, Selected Years (% of Total)

Statistics Canada. (2018c). *Employment Insurance coverage survey — Public use microdata file*, 2007–2017 *[and author's calculations]*.

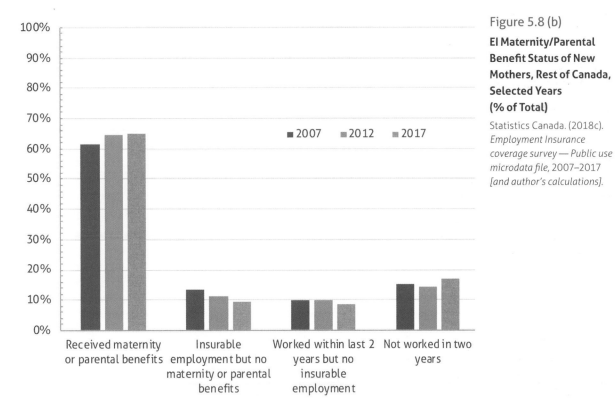

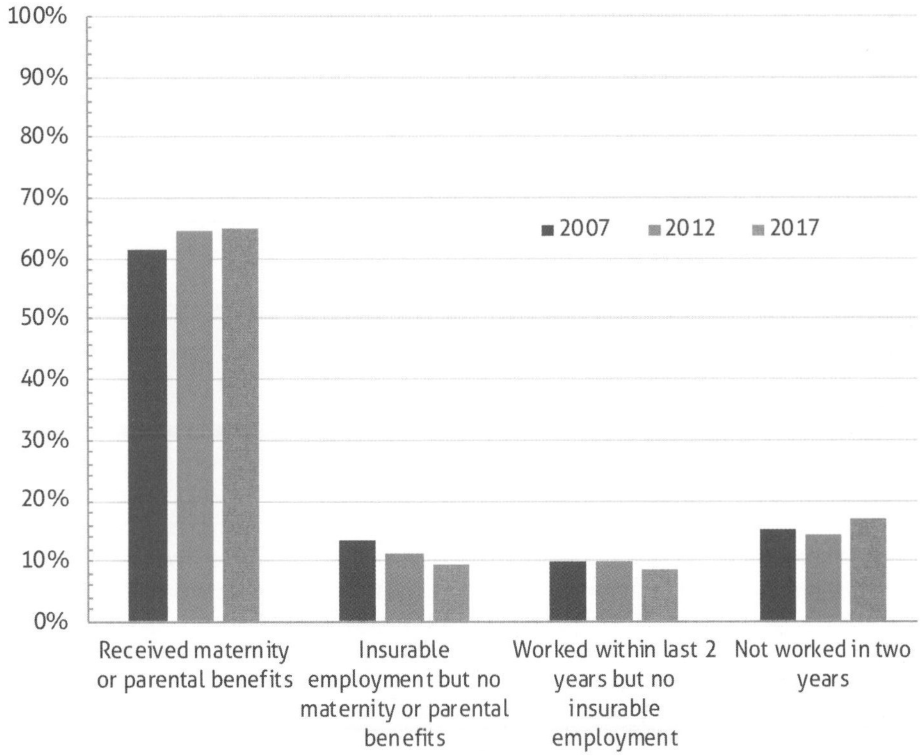

Figure 5.8 (b)

EI Maternity/Parental Benefit Status of New Mothers, Rest of Canada, Selected Years (% of Total)

Statistics Canada. (2018c). *Employment Insurance coverage survey — Public use microdata file*, 2007–2017 *[and author's calculations]*.

Gaps in Canada's Parental Leave System

In 2017, seven in 10 (70.6%) recent mothers received maternity and/or parental benefits, up four percentage points over the last decade. This figure, however, is misleading as the bulk of the increase were concentrated in Québec: in 2017, 88.5% of new mothers in Québec received maternity or parental benefits as compared with only 65.0% of mothers living in the rest of Canada (Statistics Canada, 2018b, 2018c [custom calculations]).

Québec's plan has successfully broadened access to maternity and parental leave benefits, strengthened women's labour market participation, and increased family incomes. It has also worked to reduce the disparities characteristic of Canada's federal maternity and parental leave program, providing improved access to the roughly 30% of mothers nationally who are not eligible for support because they do not meet the 600-hour test to qualify for benefits; do not have EI coverage (e.g., are self-employed [Robson, 2017]); or did not have sufficient paid employment in the past two years (Statistics Canada, 2018b). Québec mothers living in low-income families, for instance, are twice as likely to receive maternity and/or parental benefits compared with those in the rest of country (85.4% versus 43.6%), a proportion that has increased since 2007 (McKay et al., 2016).

The current federal system is working well for some families — especially those with higher incomes and access to employer-paid top-ups (Margolis, et al., 2019). However, other families struggle with EI's rigid rules and limited options for balancing caregiving and work. Income replacement levels are low by international standards, creating challenges for many trying to make ends meet. Low income-replacement rates also work to reinforce the economic vulnerability of the lower-income partner (most often the mother) and deter the second higher-income parent (most often the father) from sharing in parental leave.

Flexible and adequate maternity and parental leave programs are critical for families — and a key tool in promoting gender equality. Women across the economic and educational spectrum face a long-term lag in their earnings after having children as a result of missed opportunities, a reduction in hours of employment, and gender discrimination. In Canada, mothers experience an estimated 8% decrease in their lifetime earnings upon having a child, even after taking into account differences in age, employment level, and education (Budig et al., 2012). Well-designed parental leave policies can help minimize the unintended negative economic consequences of having children (Organisation for Economic Co-operation and Development [OEDC], 2018).

Recent federal reforms to increase the duration of parental benefits and broaden the category of caregivers and receivers eligible for EI benefits are welcome. However, these reforms have done little to improve access by or tackle the needs of low- and modest-income families. Indeed, there are concerns that offering the option of taking the same total benefits over an 18-month period — instead of a 12-month period — effectively targets this benefit to higher-income families (who can afford to take the leave) and reinforces a gendered division of labour in the home (as lower-income spouses drop out of work to provide care) (Bezanson, 2019).

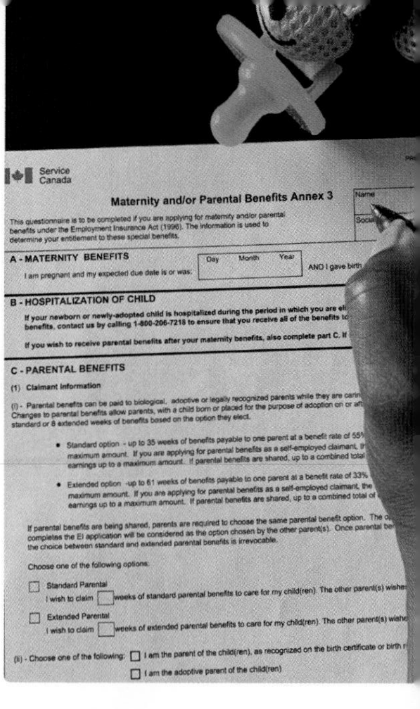

Parental Leave

A new parental leave program, launched by the federal government in March 2019, includes five to eight weeks of extra paid leave for the second parent. The length of time depends on whether a family chooses standard or extended EI benefits.

Designed to mostly target fathers, the program was modelled after the successful program adopted in Québec over a decade earlier. The difference lies in the income-replacement rate — Québec's is about 70%, while EI is 55% (up to a limit).

Québec's program is also more accessible and offers greater flexibility for families than EI. Low-income mothers in Québec, for instance, are twice as likely receive benefits than mothers living elsewhere in Canada.

Encouraging the Sharing of Benefits among Parents

One of the hopes for the new extended parental leave was to encourage the sharing of benefits among parents. Early evidence suggests that roughly one-quarter of all beneficiaries opt for extended parental leave, but that women continue to make up the largest share of this group. Nine out of 10 (90.3%) "standard" parental leave beneficiaries are women, while women's share of "extended" parental leave beneficiaries is even higher, at 93%. In June 2019, three-quarters of all beneficiaries (75.4%) opted for standard benefits (35 weeks at 55% of earnings), and one-quarter (24.6%) chose extended benefits (61 weeks at 33% of earnings) (Statistics Canada, n.d.i.).

It is too early to say whether the "use it or lose it" EI parental sharing benefit for second caregivers will spur greater take-up of benefits among second caregivers. Comparative research demonstrates that targeted leave for second caregivers can be very successful. When Sweden introduced paternity leave in 1995, the percentage of fathers taking leave rose from 9 to 47% (Ekberg et al., 2013). Our own experience in Canada, in the province of Québec, also demonstrates the potential impact of targeted paternity leaves. By 2017, 81% of fathers in Québec were taking leave, compared with 12% of fathers in the rest of the country (Statistics Canada, 2018b [custom calculations]).

The difference that targeted paternity leave makes, as opposed to parental leave, suggests that the "use it or lose it" nature of paternity leave may lessen the social and economic pressure on fathers to stay at work following the birth of a child and encourage the uptake of leave — but the evidence on this point is mixed (Robson, 2017). In 2014, when Norway reduced the number weeks of leave reserved for fathers from 14 to 10, men quickly reduced their leave (Lindahl, 2018). (In 2019, Norway had 15 weeks of parental leave reserved for each parent, and 16 weeks that could be distributed freely.)

Men are more likely to take parental leave when it comes with a substantial level of income replacement (van Belle, 2016). In Sweden, Norway, and Iceland, which all offer high wage replacement rates, the majority of fathers take parental leave (Marshall, 2008). When Germany shifted to a parental leave program that replaced earnings at a higher level (67% of earnings), the percentage of fathers participating tripled (De Henau et al., 2011).

The design of the broader set of family policies is also important insofar as it affects the family circumstances that allow a second caregiver to take up leave (van Belle, 2016). Flexibility in the timing of uptake (e.g., when the leave is taken; how it is organized; and whether it can be full-time or part-time), the availability of affordable child care, and the design of the tax system are all important factors (Blum et al., 2018). In addition, gendered expectations and the perceived expectations of employers can influence the use or non-use of second caregiver leave.

Lessons from Québec

Québec's maternity and parental leave program provides several important lessons for policymakers:

Men and women will choose to take parental leave under the right conditions.

- Men and women have distinct needs with respect to parental leave. For women, a lower threshold for qualification is important; for men, income replacement and targeted paternity leave is important.
- Parental leave by itself can have a negative impact if it is not accompanied by other policies and programs, particularly affordable and accessible child care.
- Where policies are offered in unison, parents are able to take longer periods of leave after their children are born and are more likely to return to work at the end of that leave.

Social Welfare in Perspective

The Well-Being of Women and Families

Different Models of the Family in Social Policy

It is important to unpack the ideas about gender, family, and the role of government that are embedded in different family policies and programs.

Women are an integral part of the labour force, and most families could not survive economically without the income they provide. At the same time, many government policies and programs continue to be based on the outdated assumption that women are at home, ready and able to care for family members and undertake domestic chores 24/7.

The Patriarchal Model

Historically, a "patriarchal model" of the family influenced the development of income security policy, social programs, and family law (Eichler, 1997). Under this paradigm, the wife/mother was seen as responsible for providing care and services to family members in the home, while the husband/father was responsible for earning income outside of the home.

These assumptions were built into policy and programs. For example, women were not eligible to receive public income assistance if their husbands were alive. In the federal government, formal restrictions on the employment of married women were introduced in 1921. Women who held permanent positions and then married had to resign. These restrictions were in place until 1955.

This model has fallen out of favour, but the idea of the independent family — responsible for its own economic and social well-being — is still a powerful influence. We see this in policies that offer "cash for care," such as the old Universal Child Care Benefit or the Children's Arts Tax Credit, which reflected a "hands-off" approach to social policy. This approach — directly rewarding the (usually traditional) family unit with income to spend as they please — is populist in appeal and, as usually designed, offers the greatest value to families at the top of the income scale who are best positioned to take full advantage of these tax-funded opportunities.

The Individual Responsibility Model

The "individual responsibility" model of the family marked a break from the past in recognizing formal gender equality, shared caregiving, and gender-neutral language. Labour market policies, for example, promote the participation of both women and men in the labour market, including mothers.

Yet, by ignoring the differences in life experiences and caring responsibilities between men and women, gender neutrality in this limited sense can work to hide and reproduce existing social inequalities. For example, lack of recognition that one parent cannot care for dependent children and work full-time has led to an erosion of entitlements for lone-parent families — the majority of which are headed by mothers.

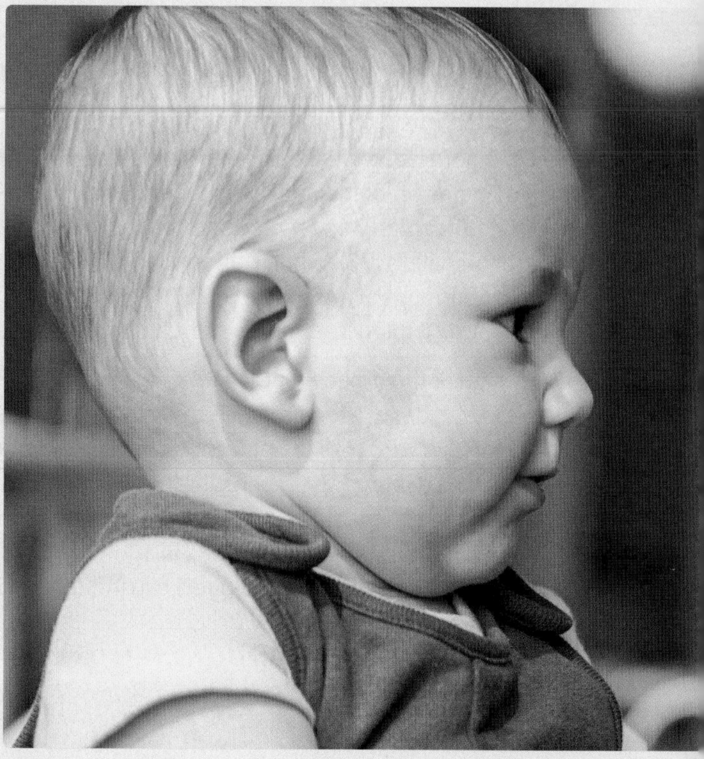

The Social Responsibility Model

As an alternative to the above approaches, the "social responsibility model" of the family regards the well-being of the individual, rather than the family unit, as the societal unit of administration — in the same sense that our health care system treats every person as an individual.

Within this model of the family, familial caring and housework are viewed as socially useful services (rather than privately useful services). In this regard, the public at large shares the responsibility with families for the care of dependent children and other family members with caring needs — and it derives broadly shared benefits.

Universal, high-quality child care, for example, supports the health and well-being of individual children (especially children that face barriers such as low income or the presence of disabilities). Such programs also generate collective, societal benefits in the form of higher family incomes; stronger economic growth through increased employment, household spending, and tax revenues; as well as greater gender equality.

Advancing the Well-Being of All Families

Family policies are not inherently progressive or regressive. However, they are informed by a particular vision and set of values.

To address the needs and concerns of families today, we need policies and programs based on the principles of inclusion, equity, and social justice — policies that support the equitable division of caring labour and facilitate access to shared supports and resources.

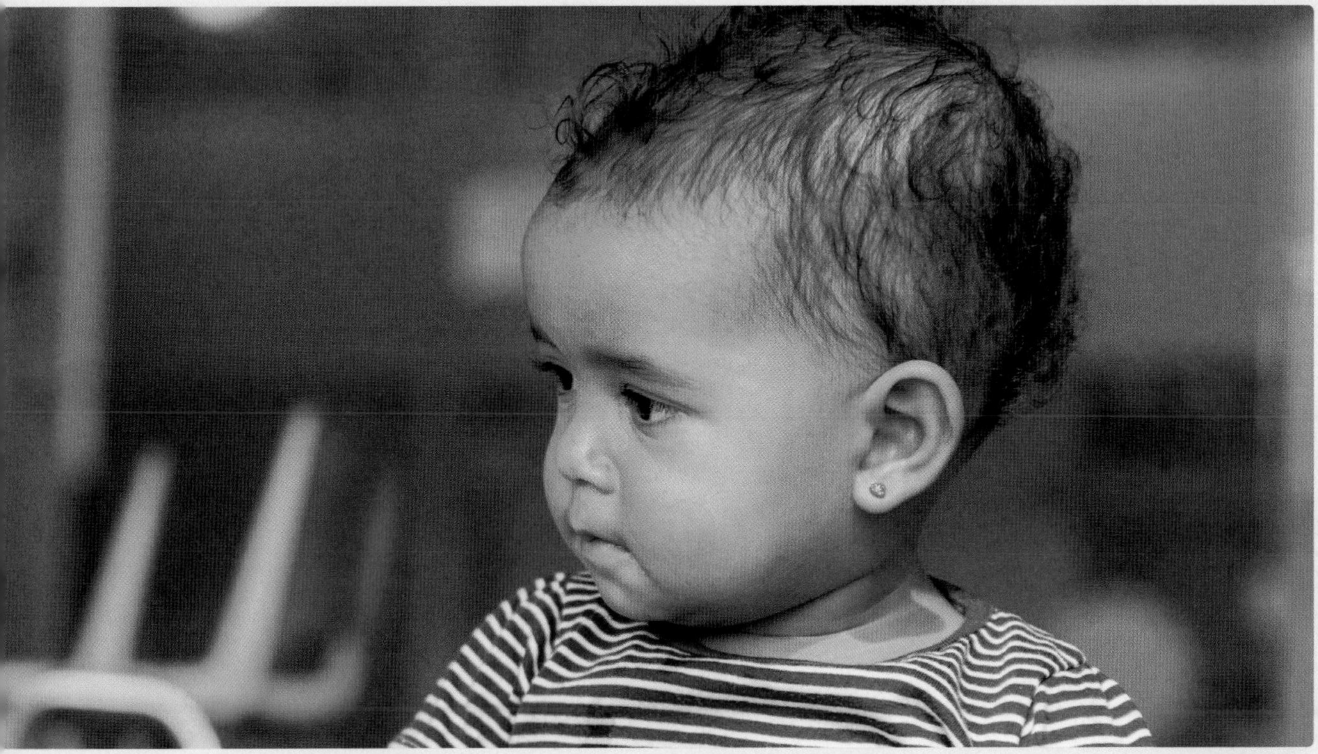

5.4 Support for Caregivers

Child care and parental leave are two of the most significant levers available to governments seeking to help families balance work and family life, and to advance gender equality. Yet, increasingly, caregiver support is also gaining attention in light of Canada's aging population and the significant gaps in public supports.

Caring for Older Canadians

Lack of affordable, quality care for older parents and relatives is a major source of stress in family lives. The time and financial cost associated with providing such care has a direct bearing on the income security of families, men and women, and especially the income security of women. For these reasons, care for older Canadians figures prominently in current discussions of family policy reform.

Several factors are contributing to demand for major change in this area of family and public life:

- Canada has an aging population with a growing number of older adults with need for support and care. The demands on caregivers increase as their family members age (Sinha, 2013). Most of the responsibility currently falls on families and friends, and, again, most of the responsibility within families falls on women (Sinha, 2013; see also Turner & Findlay, 2008).
- According to the 2018 General Social Survey, 7.8 million people aged 15 and older were involved in care and assistance to a family member or friend with a long-term health condition, a physical or mental disability, or problems related to aging (Statistics Canada, 2020).
- Almost half of all caregivers (47%) reported caring primarily for their parents or parents-in-law. Caring for parents was the most common form of caregiving reported, and was particularly common among caregivers aged 45 to 64 (61%). Almost 13% provided support for a spouse or partner (Statistics Canada, 2020).
- Caregivers perform a range of tasks in caring for older adults: personal care and help with tasks inside and outside the older adult's house (transportation, medical care, and care management). Older adults living in care facilities also count on family and friends for care: more than one in five caregivers provided care to older adults living in care facilities (Cranswick & Dosman, 2008).
- While roughly equal numbers of men and women are involved in caregiving for older adults, women are more likely to provide more hours (a higher intensity) of care, more personal care, and assume a disproportionate amount of responsibility for managing care (Cranswick & Dosman, 2008).
- In 2018, the median number of hours family caregivers (aged 15 and older) spent caring for their parents or parents-in law was four hours per week. For those caring for a spouse with long-term health problems, the median number of hours was 14 (Statistics Canada, 2020).

The Crisis in Long-Term Care Homes

With more than 80% of deaths coming from within their ranks, Canadians living in long-term care paid the highest price during the COVID–19 pandemic. But many of the problems with long-term care were already apparent before the pandemic.

COVID–19 underlined the urgency of these challenges: a reliance in the sector on a subcontracted labour force whose members work multiple low-wage jobs to make ends meet, and conditions of employment that work against quality care.

The long-term care system was built for a Canada as it existed 50 years ago, not the 2020s. The pandemic has painfully highlighted the need for national standards of care and increased investment.

A Comprehensive Strategy to Support Caregivers Is Needed

Disproportionate responsibilities for elder care, as with child care, have consequences for women's status in the labour force. In a comprehensive review of the research literature, Lero and Joseph (2017) found that women are more likely to take on part-time or casual labour as a way to balance work and family responsibilities. They are also more likely to require time off from work to respond to pressing family needs: on average, women lose 6.9 work days per year to family responsibilities as compared with 0.9 days for men.

In short, women incur greater non-financial and financial costs as a result of caregiving. The financial costs include reduced wages, savings, and pensions, with implications for caregivers' long-term financial security. Caregivers are also at greater risk of experiencing poor social, economic, physical, and mental health outcomes. Elderly spousal caregivers who report high levels of caring-related stress, for example, have been found to have a 63% higher mortality rate than non-caregivers in the same age group (Family Caregiver Alliance, 2006).

For the economy, Canada effectively loses the equivalent of 558,000 full-time employees from the workforce due to the conflicting demands of paid work and care (Fast, 2015). For governments, the most time-consuming care situations result in lost income tax revenues and additional social assistance payments when caregivers can no longer maintain their employment alongside of care work (Jacobs et al., 2013).

Federal and provincial/territorial governments have introduced new policies to help families manage competing demands on their time and offset at least some of the costs related to caregiving, but there is still no comprehensive public policy strategy to support caregivers (Keefe, 2011). As in most policy domains, caregiver support policies are characterized by split jurisdiction among different levels of government. This, in turn, means that there is a complex, variable, and uneven network of public caregiver support policies and programs.

Federal and provincial labour laws include a range of provisions that allow caregivers to provide care to family members without the fear of losing their jobs. Family responsibility leave is available in all jurisdictions, providing short-term leave to fulfill a range of responsibilities, including caregiving. Longer-term leaves are also available. The Canada Labour Code, for example, provides for compassionate care leave and critical illness leave for workers in federally regulated industries, protecting workers whose employment is disrupted by caregiving. The compassionate care leave program guarantees 28 weeks of job-protected leave over a period of 52 weeks to provide care or support to gravely ill family members at risk of dying within six months. Critical illness leave provides up to 37 weeks for the care of a critically ill child or 17 weeks for the care of a critically ill adult.

Caregiving and COVID–19

Almost one-quarter of Canadian seniors aged 65 years and older are caregivers themselves. The pandemic has created tremendous challenges and stress for this critical group.

Not only are seniors more at risk of severe illness, they are also more affected by isolation measures. As a result, many senior caregivers who help people living outside of their household may not have been able to provide the same level of care that they usually do. And those living in the home no longer have access to needed supports and services.

While the data were collected prior to the COVID–19 pandemic, a new study underscores the many challenges that senior caregivers face and the urgent need to support these caregivers during the post-pandemic recovery period.

Arriagada, P. (2020). The Experiences and Needs of Older Caregivers in Canada. Statistics Canada, Catalogue Number 75-006-X.

Income Benefits for Caregivers

The federal government and a few provincial governments also provide some income tax relief for caregivers. The Canada Caregiver Credit, introduced in 2017, is a non-refundable tax credit that provides support to individuals providing care for a spouse or partner, child, grandchild, or other family member with a physical or mental impairment. This tax credit is an improvement over previous benefits, recognizing a larger range of caring relationships among family members. Two other federal non-refundable credits provide 15% back for either medical expenses (via the Medical Expense Tax Credit) or home accessibility construction (via the Home Accessibility Tax Credit). Someone who claims the Disability Tax Credit can also transfer a portion of this credit to a caregiver. As these credits are non-refundable, only taxpayers with sufficient taxable income (against which to apply the benefit) derive any benefit. Low-income caregivers who might need assistance are not eligible.

Compassionate care benefits (offered through EI) are also available to caregivers. They provide partial income replacement for up to 26 weeks to those providing end-of-life care (maximum benefit of $547 per week in 2018). Caregiver benefits for critically ill children (for up to 35 weeks) and family caregiver benefits for critically ill adults (for up to 15 weeks) are also available. As these benefits are offered through EI (like maternity and parental leave), only workers employed in "insurable employment" and with sufficient hours of employment within the qualifying period are eligible. Among those who qualify, women make up the largest group of beneficiaries, at 70.8% (Statistics Canada, n.d.i.).

Figure 5.9

Taxonomy of the Hidden Costs of Elder Care

Fast, J., Williamson, D. L., & Keating, N. C. (1999). The hidden costs of informal elder care. *Journal of Family and Economic Issues, 20* (3), 301–326.

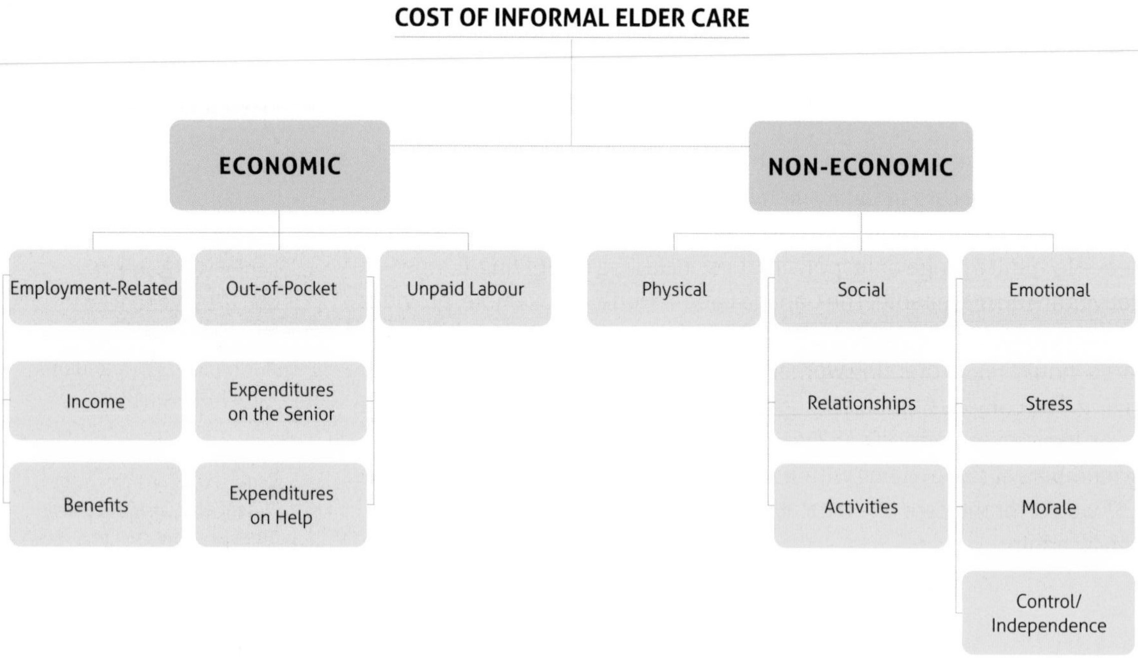

Critical Gaps in Services and Supports

In addition to income security measures and caregiving leave, adequate, accessible, and affordable services for care receivers and caregivers are critical. In Canada, only Nova Scotia provides direct compensation for caregiving labour. It is a cash benefit of $400 per month (in 2020) if providing care to low-income adults with a high level of disability or impairment (Government of Nova Scotia, 2020). Québec provides a refundable caregiver credit, although at a much lower rate of only $1,205 per year (in 2020) (Revenu Québec, 2020). Canada lags behind other countries — Australia, the UK, France, Germany, Sweden, and Finland offer some form of caregiver allowance or wage (Kröger et al., 2013; OECD, 2011).

Federal transfer payments also help to support provincial and territorial long-term and continuing care programs. However, because such programs are not covered by basic public health insurance plans, their availability varies across jurisdictions (Canadian Health Coalition, 2018). Caregiving pressures are acute and, increasingly, community-based service supports such as home care are being rationed. Federal funding increases for health care have been fixed until 2027 at 3% or growth in nominal GDP, whichever is higher — far from enough to maintain existing programs and services or keep pace with population growth. Targeted funds for home and mental health care ($3 billion over four years), announced in 2017, will not be enough to provide services on equitable terms (Canadian Health Coalition & Ontario Health Coalition, 2017). As a result, we can expect increased pressure on caregivers and higher out-of-pocket costs for care.

Figure 5.10

Distribution of Caregivers by Time Spent Providing Care to Family Member or Friend with a Long-Term Illness, Disability, or Aging Needs, 2012

Statistics Canada. Table 44-10-0005-01. *Population providing care to a family member or friend with a long-term illness, disability or aging needs by sex and relationship between respondent and primary care receiver.*

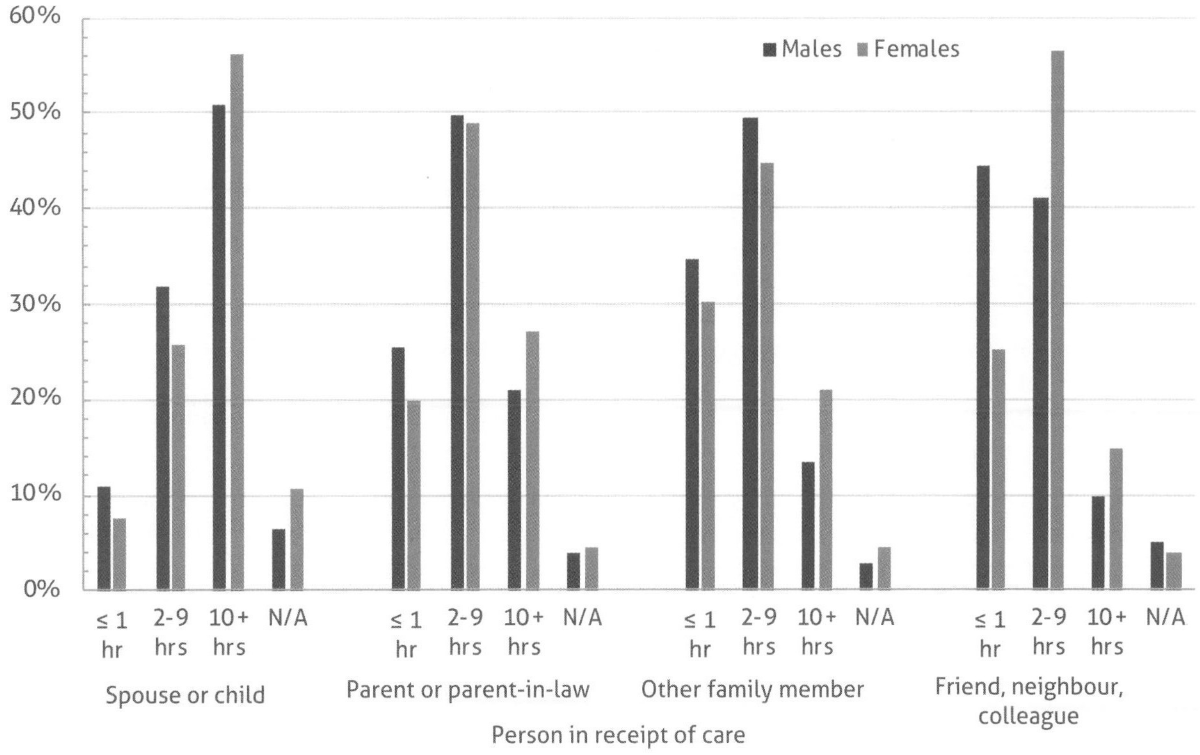

What the COVID–19 pandemic has revealed ...

A Recovery Plan for a Gender-Just Future

Making Gender Equality a Top Priority Going Forward

Whether through willful negligence or through callous disdain, we risk setting back women's equality by a generation. The road back won't be easy or quick.

From health to the economy, physical security to income security, the COVID–19 crisis has magnified and exacerbated existing gender disparities, especially among people facing intersecting forms of discrimination (e.g., gender plus class, class plus race, race plus disability, etc.). As primary caregivers and care workers in the public and private sectors, women are at the forefront of the crisis, containing the pandemic and providing needed care and support.

Women also represent the majority of workers in sectors hardest hit by the economic shutdown and slowdown, such as accommodation and food services, child care and educational services, business administration, and retail trade. Large numbers of racialized women and immigrants work in these sectors, which include some of the lowest-paying and most precarious jobs in Canada. These people have scant access to paid sick leave, health benefits, or other workplace protections. Those with precarious immigration status or in criminalized work have no protection at all.

Growth in the number of women outside the labour market points to the huge barriers that women (mothers in particular) are facing right now. Women with children between the age of six and 12 had recovered only 36% of their lost hours by mid-June, while mothers of young adults (18–24) were 78% of the way back. Lone-parent mothers had only recovered 23% of their pre-pandemic hours by June.

Indigenous women, women with disabilities, those with precarious immigration status, racialized women, and members of the trans and non-binary community face the greatest challenges. They are most likely to live in poverty, with the least access to affordable food, quality housing, needed health services, and social supports.

Government austerity has left us unprepared for this moment. Decades of public-service cuts and increased privatization shifted more of the costs and labour involved in caring work onto women and their families. Community services won't be able to meet demand as revenues dry up and the cost of operating safely increases.

In a recent survey, one-third of child care centres and homes reported they either weren't sure they would be re-opening or had already decided not to. The remaining child care operations will be offering fewer spaces in order to comply with new physical distancing measures.

A Feminist Recovery Plan

The COVID–19 pandemic has revealed the ways our economy and care work are fundamentally intertwined. It has also shown the critical role that our social safety net plays, or fails to play, in times of crisis.

A just recovery requires that our governments seriously tackle entrenched barriers to gender equality. A return to normal won't cut it. But to create the new programs that will meet the immediate and future needs of women, it is essential to collect and integrate gender disaggregated data, broken down by racialized group, disability, immigration status, etc., to reflect how different people experience daily realities and challenges differently.

A feminist recovery plan must also continue to financially support people with continuing caring obligations, or facing the ongoing loss of employment or reduced earnings, as the economy recovers. Without child care, many mothers won't be able to return to work at all. And if that happens there can be no recovery.

Now is the moment to create a system of comprehensive, high-quality, publicly managed caring services across the country. Investments in the care economy pay for themselves over time through increased employment and earnings, reduced reliance on income security benefits and emergency services, and healthier communities.

This is also the moment to take decisive action to end violence against women, girls, and gender-diverse peoples, a situation made much worse by the current crisis, whose requirement to shelter in place closes down routes to safety. These pressures are acute among Indigenous women, women with significant mental health concerns, LGBTQ+2S people, women with disabilities, rural residents, and immigrant and refugee women, all of whom are at higher risk of violence than others.

Next steps must finally include a comprehensive, appropriately resourced national action plan on violence against women and gender-based violence, and the implementation of the Calls for Justice of the National Inquiry into Missing and Murdered Indigenous Women and Girls.

Looking Forward

It will take strong voices to advance a feminist recovery plan. One week, the federal government issues an "Economic and Fiscal Snapshot" that acknowledges the gendered impact of the crisis. The next, it gives $19 billion to the provinces and territories to restart their economies, but only 3% of that money is set aside for child care, 2.5% for people experiencing challenges related to mental health and homelessness, and perhaps 4% for long-term care.

These missteps and missed opportunities by government are setting back women's equality by decades. A gender-just recovery must instead centre the needs and perspectives of women, girls, and gender-diverse people. It will take all of our voices to bend this curve.

Scott, K. (2020). A feminist recovery plan for a gender-just future. *Monitor, 27* (3) (September/October). Canadian Centre for Policy Alternatives. Reduced for reasons of space and a different graph added.

Women's and Racialized Women's Share of the Canadian Workforce in the Caring Occupations at the Frontlines of COVID–19

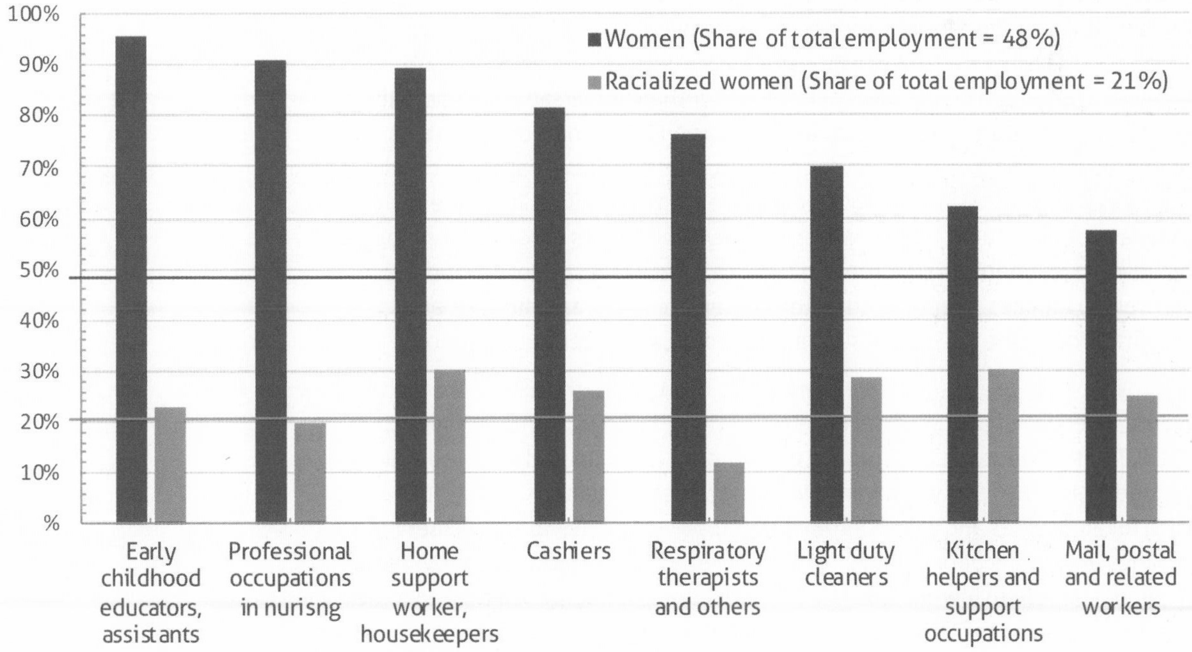

Statistics Canada (2016). Census. Catalogue Number 98-400-X2016356.

5.5 Child and Family Tax Policies

Canada has a long history of income security programs supporting children and families dating back more than 100 years. These include direct income transfers to individuals and families as well as benefits and credits delivered through the tax system. All have distinct impacts on how families spend their time (in work and at home) and, more generally, on the organization of caregiving between the public sector, private market, and households.

History of Child Benefits

Concern about widowed mothers with small children after World War I led to Mothers' Allowances, first in Manitoba in 1916, in Saskatchewan in 1917, and in Ontario and British Columbia in 1920. All provinces followed suit within the next decade. This program provided a needs-tested monthly income benefit to selected families. Eligibility requirements varied between provinces, but one element remained steadfast — any mother deemed to be of "bad character" was not eligible, a throwback to the British Poor Laws and the practice of distinguishing between the deserving and undeserving poor that is still evident in Canada today.

The Family Allowance Act, 1944 was the first "universal" income security program and part of a larger plan to build up Canada's welfare state and boost the purchasing power of families (and the electoral fortunes of the federal government). The tax-free benefit was directed to all families, rich and poor alike, and varied according to age of the child. Children under age five received $5 per month; those six to nine years old received $6; those 10 to 12 years old received $7; and those 13 to 15 years old received $8.

The modest support then available under the Family Allowance program was (and is) characteristic of Canada's "residual" approach to social policy. That is, the responsibility for the care work needed to ensure our collective survival is largely understood as a private family responsibility. Social supports are usually (but not always) provided on the basis of need rather than universally. Traditionally, residual welfare states such as Canada's have been less generous than other industrialized countries, offering less public funding and fewer supports and programs (Jenson, 2013). The most recent data from the OECD (2019a) reveal that Canada continues to lag behind most other OECD countries in social spending, including investments in children and families. These investments include cash transfers to families, spending on children's services such as child care, and support through the tax system such as the Child Care Expense Deduction.

The push to reduce government expenditures throughout the 1980s led to the eventual demise of the universal Family Allowance in 1993 (Burton & Phipps, 2017). The then federal Conservative government consolidated selected child tax credits and the Family Allowance into a new income-tested Child Tax Benefit (CTB) for all families and a Working Income Supplement (WIS) to supplement the earnings of working poor families. Unlike universal benefits, the CTB provided a maximum benefit to low-income families, a declining amount to middle-income families, and no benefit to those at the very top of the income ladder.

However, CTB benefit levels were still comparatively modest (Milligan, 2016) and, as a result, were largely ineffective in stopping the rise in child poverty in the aftermath of the 1990–1991 recession. Child poverty grew to a record high of 17.4% in the mid-1990s (Statistics Canada, n.d.a.). Broad-based government spending cuts made at this time in the name of deficit reduction severely weakened the ability of federal and provincial income benefits to protect family incomes (Heisz et al., 2002).

In 1998, the federal Liberal government revamped the children's benefit system again "to prevent and reduce the depth of child poverty" and "to promote attachment to the labour market" (Ministers Responsible for Social Services, 1997). The federal government, working in collaboration with the provinces and territories, introduced a new and enhanced Canada Child Tax Benefit (CCTB), a non-taxable, income-tested child benefit paid monthly to eligible families, and a National Child Benefit Supplement (NCBS) for low-income families.

The NCBS agreement involved an understanding that provinces and territories could claw back the additional funds from poor families receiving provincially/territorially delivered social assistance benefits to ensure that welfare recipients would not be better off as a result of the NCBS and that parents would not be discouraged from pursuing paid employment. The proviso was that if a province or territory did so, it would have to use those funds for anti-poverty initiatives, such as child care or extended health care benefits. Certainly, the rule to reinvest provincial/territorial savings into ne w anti-poverty programs was not evenly applied across the country.

Figure 5.11

Public Spending on Family Benefits as % of GDP among OECD Countries (2015)

Organisation for Economic Co-operation and Development. (2019a). *Family benefits public spending (indicator).*

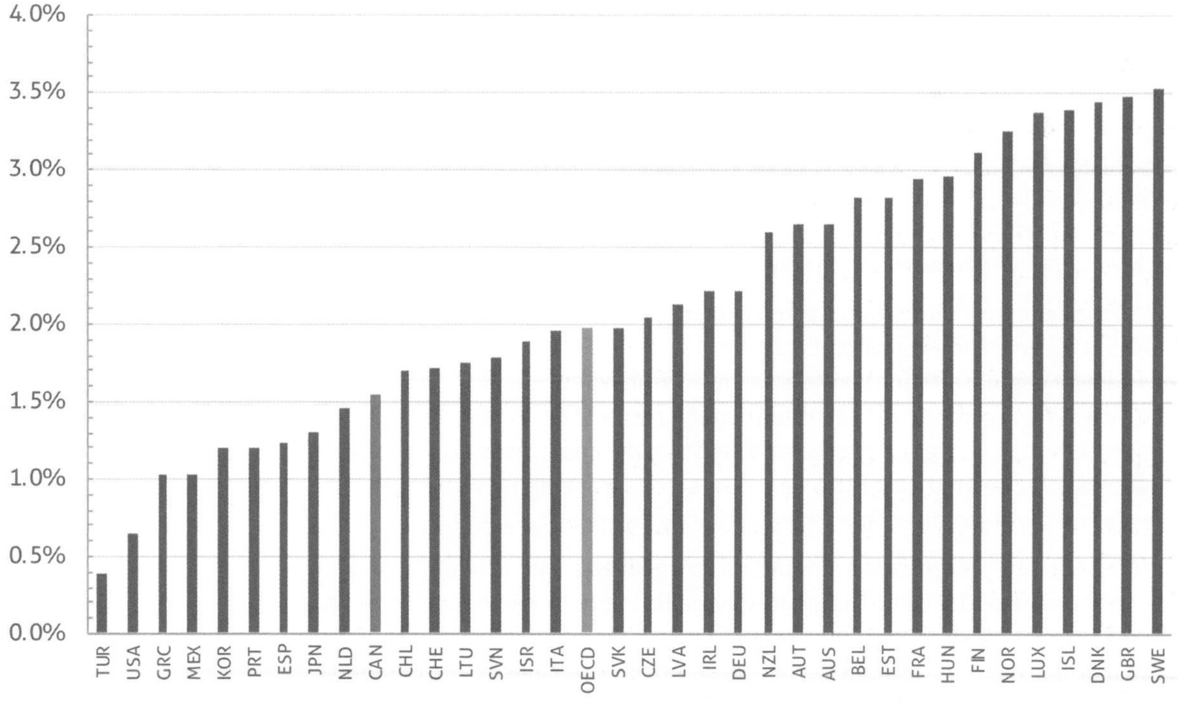

Higher child benefits — both federal and provincial — have had a positive impact on the educational, social, and health outcomes of low-income children (Milligan & Stabile, 2008) and on the economic standing of low-income parents, especially lone parents. Research has shown a 3 to 4% increase in the employment levels of single mothers following the introduction of enhanced child benefits (Milligan & Stabile, 2007). We have seen a boost in the employment of single mothers in Québec in particular, where governments have pursued a more comprehensive approach to family policy that combines higher children's benefits with sizable investments in child care and maternity and parental leave. Elsewhere in Canada, a lack of child care, affordable housing, employment supports, and other key public services continues to undermine the economic security of low-income families — as described earlier in this chapter (Campaign 2000, 2018). These gaps reflect an individual responsibility view of the family — governments step in only when a family's ability to provide fails.

The Harper Government on Child Care

In the 2007 federal budget, $1 billion of previously committed early learning and child care funding was cut and replaced with tax credits to businesses for the creation of workplace child care spaces. The budget also included a new flat child tax credit — the Universal Child Care Benefit (UCCB) — paid to parents for each child.

The Code Blue for Child Care Campaign argued that this money, combined with the UCCB, would have been enough to federally fund universal child care for three- to five-year olds.

Conservative Government Family Policy

The income security landscape for families changed again in 2006 with the introduction of the Universal Child Care Benefit (UCCB). This new program was introduced by the Harper Conservative government after it cancelled then Liberal Prime Minister Paul Martin's promised plan to make federal funds available to the provinces to create new child care spaces. The Conservatives created a taxable $100 per month benefit for each child under the age of six. The UCCB was enhanced in 2015 to boost benefits and extend support to children between six and 18 years of age. Unlike the CCTB, the UCCB provided relatively similar levels of benefits across income groups (although higher-income families saw the benefit taxed back at higher rates than low-income families). The UCCB was put in place on top of the pre-existing CCTB and NCBS income transfers.

The Conservative government argued that the UCCB would help families juggle work and family life by supporting their child care choices through direct financial support (e.g., to stay home to care for children, to purchase needed care, or to access public programs). However, the transformation of money for child care spaces into "cash for care" did nothing to expand the supply of needed spaces, and the level of benefits was modest in comparison to average child care bills.

The new government also introduced a Children's Arts Tax Credit and a Children's Fitness Tax Credit, allowing partents to claim a 15% non-refundable tax credit for fees paid for eligible arts and sports activities. The maximum benefit per child per credit was $75. In order to realize the tax benefit, parents had to spend $1,000 on eligible activities. Subsequent research found that the impact was minimal, as the families eligible and most likely to use the tax credits were higher earners who already had the means to support those activities (Spence et al., 2010).

The Conservative government's new programs signalled a shift in family policy. Favoured programs delivered the greatest benefits to single-earner families with a stay-at-home caregiver over lone-parent families and two-earner couples (as the UCCB did), and high-income families over lower-income families (as the Children's Arts Tax Credit and Children's Fitness Tax Credit did).

Income Splitting

The Conservative government's plan to introduce an income splitting tax break for couples with children was another example of this shift in family policy. Income splitting was originally promised in the Conservatives' 2011 election platform, and it was rolled out in time for the 2014 tax year (Canada, 2014). The policy allowed married and common-law couples with children under the age of 18 to transfer up to $50,000 in earned income from one spouse to the other, for a maximum tax benefit of $2,000 per year, at an initial cost to the government of $3 billion per year.

Unlike the CCTB and NCBS, income splitting is highly regressive. First, income splitting is only possible if there is a second parent present, and so lone-parent families — almost always poorer than two-parent families — do not benefit. Second, income splitting favours families where there is a large difference in incomes between spouses (e.g., families with stay-at-home caregivers). As a result, there is no benefit to the many couples where spouses earn roughly the same income (and are in the same tax bracket) or to lower-income families who have already benefited from other tax credits and deductions (Macdonald, 2014).

Research confirms these concerns. In 2015, only 12% of families with children received the maximum value of income splitting at tax time, while half (48%) got nothing. The biggest benefits were for families with income over $233,000. Families at the bottom of the ladder had virtually no chance of benefiting at all (Macdonald, 2014). Families whose choices were most constrained did not see a benefit sufficient to allow them to forgo further hours of earned income in order to spend more time with their children (Laurin & Kesselman, 2011).

Recent Liberal Government Reforms

One of the first steps of Justin Trudeau's Liberal government in the fall of 2015 was to collapse existing child benefit programs into a new enhanced income transfer called the Canada Child Benefit (CCB). The government also cancelled the Children's Arts Tax Credit and the Children's Fitness Tax Credit and rescinded the family income-splitting policy (but retained gender-regressive pension income-splitting among older adults). With the creation of the CCB, federal spending on child benefits immediately increased from $14.3 billion to $18.2 billion (Department of Finance Canada, 2015). The design of the new program made it more generous for low- and middle-income households, and less generous for higher-income households, with the richest households receiving nothing.

With the CCB, Canadian households can receive up to $6,640 per year for each child under the age of six and $5,600 per year for each child between the ages of six and 17 (maximum benefit levels apply to households earning less than $31,120 annually). The levels decrease with rising income. A supplement for children with disabilities provides up to $2,800 per year for each child and is reduced for families with net incomes over $67,400. (These figures are for 2019 and rounded to the nearest $100.) Roughly 90% of all families with children receive the benefit. The federal government estimates that the CCB helped almost 300,000 children exit poverty between 2015 and 2017 (Employment and Skills Development Canada, 2019). During the 2019 election campaign, the Liberals pledged to boost benefits again by up to $1,000 for children under the age of one (Liberal Party, 2019).

The CCB is touted as being simpler and much more generous for those who need it most, and generally it is. However, to receive it, one must file income taxes. Canadians who face barriers to filing a tax return, such as those living in shelters and Indigenous people living in remote communities, can miss out. Recent steps to improve the uptake of the CCB — and other tax-delivered income benefits — are important. Further action by the federal government is also needed to ensure that all families, regardless of immigration status, have access to children's benefits (Campaign 2000, 2020).

Tax Support for Families

Income transfers such as Family Allowances or the Canada Child Benefit are highly visible supports to families. Governments also deliver another group of important measures in the form of tax supports for families, such as tax exemptions, allowances, and deductions (called "tax expenditures") that often fly under the radar. Federal programs — such as the eligible dependent credit ($1.025 billion), the spouse or common-law partner credit ($1.895 billion), and the Canada Caregiver Credit ($245 million) — transfer sizable benefits to families through the reduction of personal income taxes, offsetting what individuals would typically pay under standard income tax brackets (Department of Finance Canada, 2019b; all figures are projected costs for 2020). The child care expenses deduction is another important tax program for families. Introduced in 1971, it is designed to assist with the costs of child care for parents in the labour market. It is currently worth $1.4 billion and was claimed by 1.4 million individuals in 2016 (Department of Finance Canada, 2019b).

These tax programs have their problems, however. The first and key consideration is that many low-income families do not pay income taxes because their incomes are too low. Programs designed to deliver tax relief as a means to support families engaged in paid employment or providing care, by definition, exclude this group. The other related challenge is that again, depending on design, the value of tax deductions are worth more to families in high income brackets.

It is also true that many programs targeting the needs of families (both income transfer and tax programs) also work to disincentivize women's paid work and keep women focused on unpaid work and care. "Canadian tax law is riddled with well over a hundred different tax provisions that treat spouses or common law couples as presumptively interdependent and financially integrated tax units" (Lahey, 2015). This special set of joint tax and benefit laws increases the after-tax incomes of individuals (usually men) who get special tax benefits for supporting family members who perform unpaid work, while creating tax incentives for other family members (usually women) to reduce their own earnings. As such, these programs "disincentivize" women's paid work, resulting in lower after-tax incomes and increased financial vulnerability among women (Lahey, 2016). The scale of these barriers is significant, yet largely invisible.

Gender Bias in the Tax System

This is an example of how public policy can work at cross purposes. Programs such as the Canada Child Benefit or GST/HST credit are subject to a household income test. This test creates an incentive for women (typically the lower-income spouse) to reduce earnings so as to increase the benefit's value, thereby increasing their own long-term financial vulnerability. The unequal division of caring labour already puts women at high risk of poverty. The inadequate supply of quality child care, home care, and other supports — in addition to tax penalties for second earners — compounds these risks exponentially.

A key reason that governments impose household income tests is to reduce program costs, and these tests have significant consequences for women. More generally, the drive to lower taxes through tax loopholes or broad-based tax cuts is not gender-neutral either. Women lose out from the cumulative impact of "de-taxation" twice: first, when they lose access to essential public services like child care due to insufficient or reduced revenues and funding, and second, when they are forced the fill the gaps in services with many hours of unpaid caring work.

To truly address gender disparities and level the playing field between families of different means, we need the right mix of policies and programs and the resourcing to make them happen. We also need to unpack the ideas about gender, family, and the role of government that inform each policy and program. When social and economic policies are made based on gender-informed analysis, we have the opportunity to advance gender equality and family well-being.

Impacts of COVID-19 on Parenting

The unequal division of unpaid family work has long been recognized as having direct impacts on women's labour force participation, time spent at work, wages and job quality, and physical and mental health stressors. The COVID-19 pandemic has intensified parental tasks and added new responsibilities, such as homeschooling.

A recent study by Statistics Canada indicates that women continue to perform the lion's share of the work even among couples working from home. In families with children, women reported that they were largely responsible for parenting tasks. 64% of women said they were primarily responsible for home schooling and helping with homework versus 19% of men.

Zossou, C. (2021). Sharing household tasks: Teaming up during the COVID-19 pandemic. Statistics Canada.

Social Welfare in Perspective

The Gender Gap

The Unequal Earnings of Men and Women

The average wage earned by women has risen slightly in comparison to that of men. However, it remains substantially lower and fairly consistently so.

By virtue of the primary role they are expected to play in caregiving and their disadvantaged position in the labour market, more women than men still live in poverty. In the case of lone-parent families, the burden is even greater. Despite all the legislative changes in the area of pay equity and employment equity, there is a continuing need for social policymakers and social work practitioners to be aware of the economic problems women continue to face.

Equal Pay and Employment Equity

Since the 1950s, increasing numbers of women have entered the labour force. As a result, there has been a shift in the policy representation of women from "stay-at-home mothers" to "worker-mothers." This shift has helped to reverse the economic dependency of women. However, it has by no means completely altered the disadvantages that women face in the workplace or in the home.

In the economic sphere, many legislative changes took place in the post-World War II period (especially in the 1970s and beyond) aimed at fostering greater gender equality at work (Armstrong & Armstrong, 2010; Gunderson, 1998). Among these policy initiatives were the following:

- Equal pay policies (including pay equity or equal pay for work of equal value) designed to improve women's pay
- Equal employment policies (including employment equity) to help women's employment and promotion opportunities
- Other facilitating policies (e.g., child care, parental leave) to put women on an equal footing with men in the labour market

Male Jobs and Female Jobs

Nevertheless, although more and more Canadian women entered the labour force in this period, they seldom did so on equal terms with men. The industries and occupations initially open to women were less prestigious that those open to men. Women's incomes were far inferior to those of men in the same occupations, and all sorts of sexist justifications for this fundamental inequality were readily available.

In addition, many women ended up doing double duty — working and taking on primary responsibility for child care and elder care at home.

Much of the gender wage gap can be explained by differences in the typical workplaces of women and men. Research consistently indicates that "women are concentrated in low-paying occupations, industries, establishments, and occupations ... and that gender segregation accounts for a sizable portion of the overall gender wage gap" (Drolet, 2002, p. S42). For example, men have higher levels of representation in manufacturing industries as well as in construction, transportation, wholesale, and trade. On the other hand, women are more concentrated in retail services, education, and health.

Paradoxically, gender inequality in employment is increasingly out of step with changes in household incomes. For many families today, the income of women is much more than just "pin money." In fact, a majority of families rely on the income of both working parents. Indeed, among female workers aged 25 to 54 years, over 40% contributed more than 50% of their family's income in 2015, up from 17% in 1976 (Fox & Moyser, 2018).

Recent Policy

One of the fundamental issues facing women in the labour force is pay inequality: paying women less than men for work of the same value.

Pay equity is now policy in most of Canada's provinces and territories, as well as in several countries of the European Union, Australia, New Zealand, and many American states. The goal of pay equity standards is to prevent discrimination related to the undervaluation of work traditionally performed by women.

However, in most of these jurisdictions, the burden to file complaints about pay discrimination rests on employees. This system is patently unjust. Individual cases have taken decades to adjudicate while significant disparities in earnings persist (Pedwell, 2018). Canada's pay gap remains one of the largest among OECD countries, ranking 30th out of 36 countries (Organisation for Economic Co-operation and Development, 2018, 2019b).

In 2018, the federal government introduced the Pay Equity Act, a proactive pay equity regime for federally regulated industries, following in footsteps of Québec and Ontario (ESDC, 2018). Federal employers are now required to proactively develop pay equity plans for their workplaces and take action to address any systemic disparities. This system is overseen by a Pay Equity Commissioner at the Canadian Human Rights Tribunal.

The adoption of proactive pay equity legislation is an important milestone for the federal government. However, experts have raised several concerns that the legislation provides opportunities for employers to avoid their obligations and drag out the process. Moreover, without significant investment in the Pay Equity division to pursue outreach and support, and enforcement, positive momentum to close damaging pay gaps will end (Scott, 2019a).

Percentage Difference between Men's and Women's (25–54 Years) Annual Full-Time Employment Income, 2016

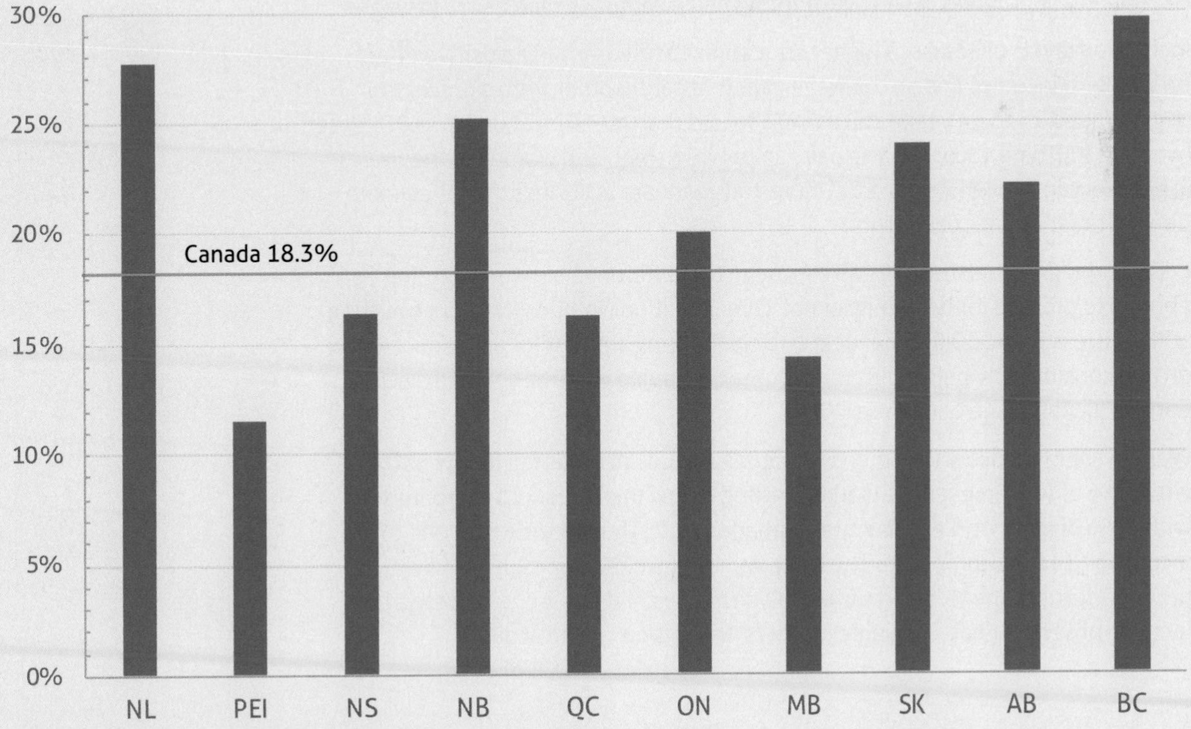

Statistics Canada (2016). Canadian Income Study. Custom tabulations.

5.6 Jobs and Income

A wide variety of factors contribute to the decisions families make about care, about who takes time away from paid work, for how long, and when (or if) they return to work. Many of these factors are personal and social. As argued earlier, these decisions are also shaped by a constellation of government policies, including those that set out the availability and affordability of child care and elder care, the type of parental leave available, and tax incentives.

However, economic conditions also shape the choices available to families, such as gender segregation in employment. Women and men tend to work in different sectors and for different rates of pay. As a result, sectoral development strategies, wage-setting policies, and education and training programs all impact the incomes and employment levels of men and women differently.

Gender Disparities in Pay

In almost every industry, at every educational level, working part-time or full-time, women in Canada — and especially women from marginalized groups — are paid less than men.

Despite the steep increase in women's participation in paid work and their increasing levels of post-secondary education, the gap in what men and women earn has yet to close. Forty years ago, women working full-time, full year made 38% less than their male peers. Today, they make 22% less, while those in the key 25- to 54-year age group make 18% less (Statistics Canada, n.d.c.). These figures are based on the annual median employment income of full-time workers. At the current rate of progress, it will take another half a century to see parity in wages.

Increasing levels of access to higher education has clearly had a positive effect on women's incomes and on the wage gap. That said, women with a university degree (aged 25 to 64 years) still earn 15% less than men with a university degree (working full-time, full year). The pay gap between men and women in the trades is even larger: women working full-time, full year earn 40% less than their male peers (Statistics Canada, 2016b).

For a working mother, the pay gap can mean the difference between earning enough to provide for her family or not. Over 2 million women who work full-time still earn less than $30,000 per year — a challenging amount for any family to live on and considerably below different community living wage benchmarks across Canada (Living Wage Canada, 2020).

Women are more likely than men to see their annual incomes fall below $30,000, with 33% of full-time female workers falling below this threshold compared with 26% of male workers (Statistics Canada, n.d.f.). Thus, at the lower end of the income and educational scale, the wage gap can turn the decision about which parent returns to the workforce after the birth of a child into a choice between living in poverty or not. For single mothers, there is no choice at all.

The Effects of Wage-Setting Policies

Wage-setting policies are particularly important policy instruments in expanding the choices available to low-income mothers. Higher minimum wages and collective bargaining will help to narrow the wage gap between men and women where it makes the biggest difference — for mothers with lower educational levels and lower earning potential (Blau & Kahn, 2003).

A comparison of public- and private-sector wages demonstrates the impact of public-sector wage-setting policies on narrowing the gender wage gap in Canada (McInturff & Tulloch, 2014). The wage gap narrows for women at every educational level in the public sector. For the least educated women, that additional $5,688 per year represents a 20% increase in their salaries (compared with their average private-sector earnings). It also pushes women's earnings closer to the amount required to pay for the needs of their family. This finding is consistent across industrialized countries, where the presence of unions and a larger public sector makes one of the biggest differences in the incomes of the most vulnerable parents (Blau & Kahn, 2003; Dirk et al., 2010; Mandel, 2012).

The Gender Gap within and between Industries

One of the main reasons for the persistence of the pay gap at all income and educational levels is that men and women tend to work in different industries, and male-dominated industries tend to pay more than female-dominated industries. The segregation into different job sectors has changed little over the past few decades, despite an increase in the numbers of women with a post-secondary education.

Figure 5.12

Gender Employment Gap (Full-Time Workers, Aged 25–54 Years), 2017

Statistics Canada. Table 14-10-0018-01. *Labour force characteristics by sex and detailed age group, annual, inactive (x 1,000).*

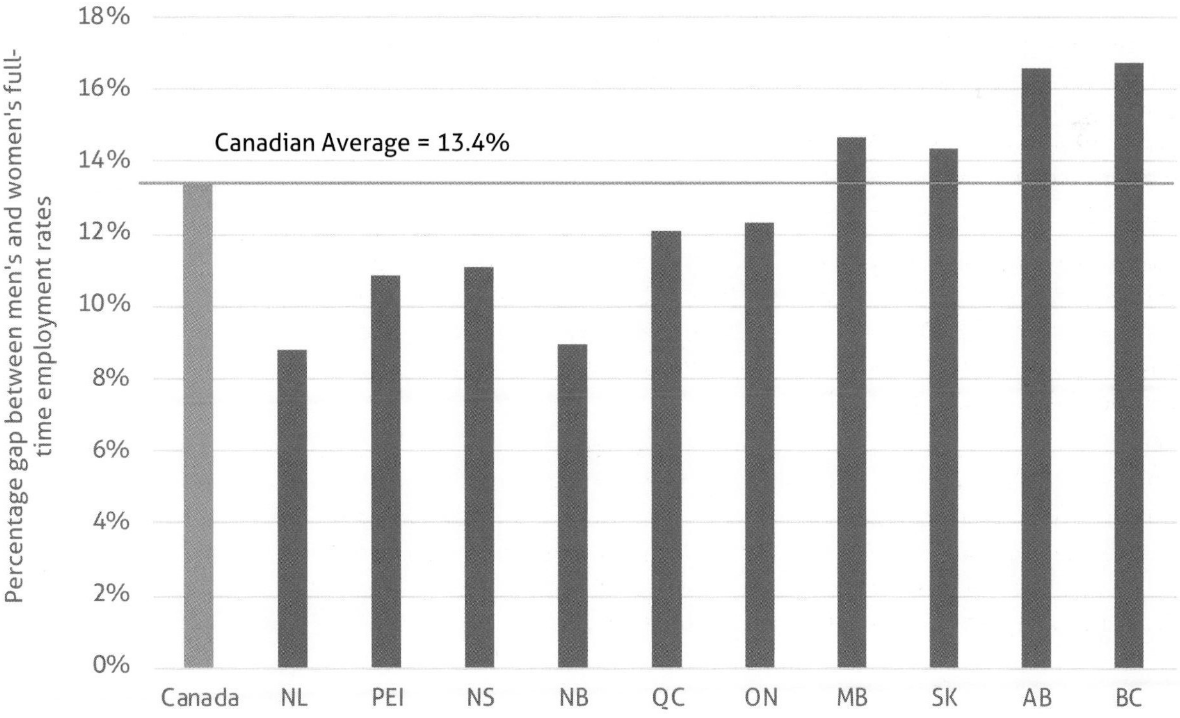

In 2016, of the students who graduated with a BA in education, 78% were female, an increase of 2% over 2011. Of those who graduated with an architecture or engineering degree, 78% were male (Statistics Canada, n.d.p.). Education graduates who pursue careers as teachers can expect to earn an average of $73,000 per year, working full-time. Engineering graduates who work as engineers can expect to earn at least $87,000 per year (Statistics Canada, 2016a).

Post-secondary education is clearly having a positive impact on the size of women's earnings and narrowing the gap in pay within different sectors. However, the fields in which the majority of women study and work come with smaller paycheques than the fields in which the majority of men study and work. A female dentist, physician, or veterinarian working full-time and full year still earns only 74 cents for every dollar her male colleague earns. Indeed, women earn less than men (working full-time, full year) in 471 out of the 500 occupations tracked by Canada's census (Statistics Canada, 2016c). The pay gap is even larger for women who experience discrimination and other barriers to employment (Block & Galabuzi, 2019).

Attempts to increase women's participation in male-dominated sectors face significant challenges — many of them related to the need for better family policies. Efforts to increase the presence of women in Canada's generally highly paid extractive industries are a good example. Today, women make up only 18% of workers in mining, oil, and gas (Statistics Canada, n.d.k.). Research indicates that child care and the lack of flexible work hours are key impediments to women's increased participation in this sector (Catalyst, 2019; Hill et al., 2017; Women in Mining Canada, 2010). This example demonstrates the dynamic relationship between family leave policies and broader economic policies.

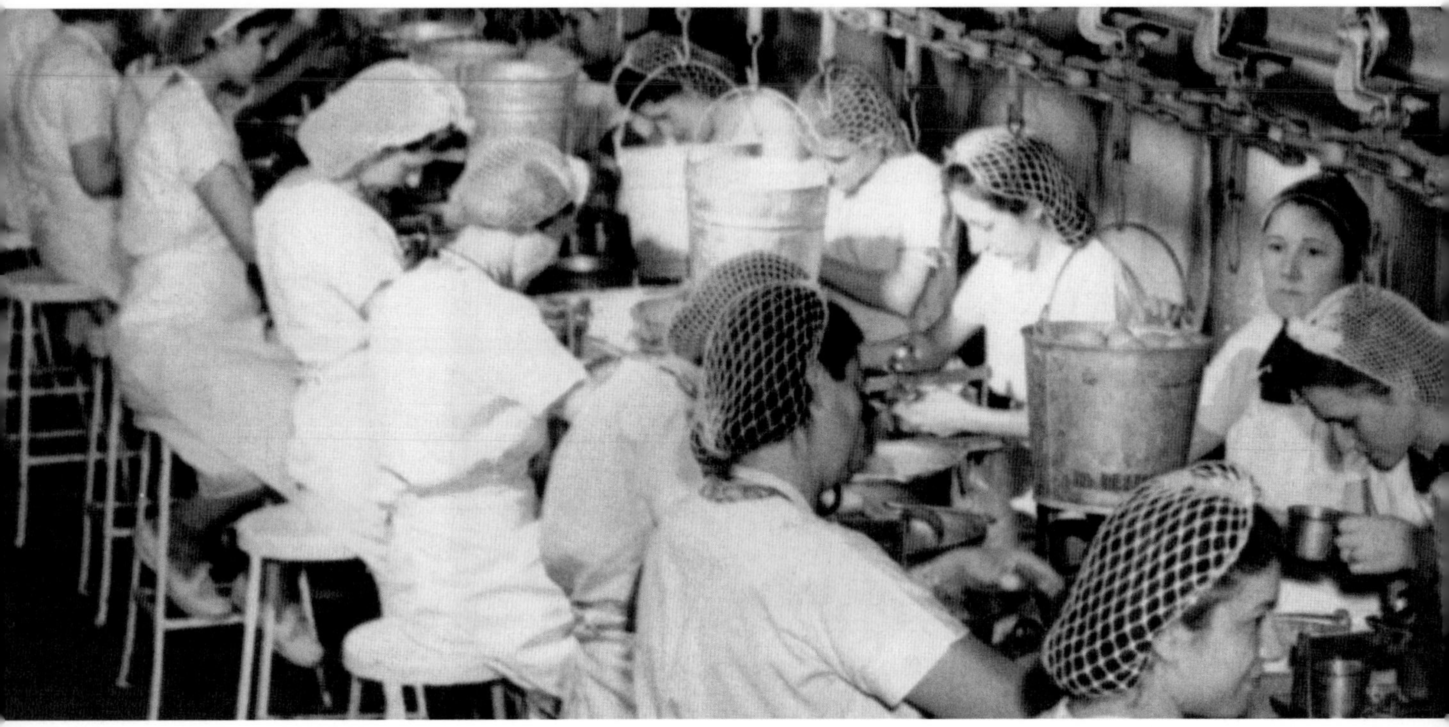

Investing in Sectors Where Women Work

Given the persistence of the segregation of male and female workers into different industries and the slow rate of change, governments also need to respond to the fact that, today, men and women are as likely as in the past to hold jobs in different economic sectors.

As a consequence, economic development policies that focus narrowly on male-dominated sectors — without parallel investment in female-dominated sectors — tend to widen the economic gap between men and women. They also create greater inequality within families and constrain the ability of women to contribute to their own financial security and that of their families. Consider Alberta, where a strong focus is placed on the development of the extractive sector. This province has the largest gap in men's and women's full-time wages and the greatest gap in men's and women's access to full-time work compared with the rest of Canada (Hussey & Jackson, 2017).

In order to expand and support the choices available to Canadian families, government policies need to address both the economic differences between families and the difference in the economic constraints on men and women within families. The gender wage gap tilts the floor heavily in favour of women forgoing more hours of paid work, rather than men, after the birth of a child (regardless of the preferences of either parent). Lopsided labour force development policies — compounded by a lack of access to affordable, high-quality care services and flexible work hours — further limit the ability of mothers to contribute to their own and their family's financial security.

5.7 Family Policies Need to Catch Up

Today's families are not living in a world of limitless choices. Parents must make difficult decisions in constrained circumstances about how to do best by their children, their employers, and each other. Small, complicated tax benefits that go largely to the most well-off families do nothing to make these decisions easier for the majority of families. Yawning gaps in community-based supports compound the challenges associated with earning a sufficient living while providing care and support to family members.

Governments have an important role to play supporting families that are working hard to meet the challenges of a changing socio-economic landscape. However, many social programs still assume the existence of the traditional "male-breadwinner" model of the family.

This outdated approach not only fails to keep up with the times but also places great strain on those (increasing in number) who do not fit in this mould: for example, single mothers, the working poor, and women with child care and elder care responsibilities. For many women and families, caregiving limits women's full engagement in the labour market, a key reason behind women's overrepresentation in vulnerable, low-wage, precarious employment. Gender inequality exacerbates economic inequality between men and women and between families at different ends of the income spectrum.

Governments have the means to lessen the constraints on families and to better support the decisions they are making about the way they live now. Access to affordable child care and elder care, parental leave that fits the parent, and economic policies that level the playing field between families and between women and men within families have all been demonstrated to provide increased support for families and the decisions they want and need to make.

The work and family lives of Canadians have evolved over the past four decades. It is time our family policies caught up too.

Social Welfare Policy in Action

Canada's New Gender Budgeting Legislation

Closing the Gap for Women in Canada

In December 2018, Canada's first-ever gender budgeting legislation was approved. The new legislation requires reporting on gender and diversity in taxation and resource-allocation decisions.

Government budgets do not impact men and women in the same way, since men and women generally occupy different social and economic positions. Asking how an economic policy will impact men and women is important. It strips away the idea of budget neutrality. It also recognizes that budgets are fundamentally about people: they reflect a set of values and choices about how to generate and redistribute a country's resources.

Gender budgeting highlights the differential impact of budget choices. It also generates the evidence needed to inform policy and program development that successfully delivers on its stated goals while, at the same time, provides a vehicle for strengthening public accountability and transparency.

As Scott (2019b) notes, "When economic policies are made based on gender-informed analysis, we have the opportunity to reduce the number of women experiencing violence and poverty. We have the chance to clear the way for women to have equal access to decent work and decent pay."

New Gender Budgeting Legislation

On this score, the Canadian Gender Budgeting Act, passed in 2018, represents an important milestone, requiring present and future governments to apply a gender and diversity lens to existing and proposed policy and program decisions.

The government has carried out "gender-based analysis" (GBA) — and now "gender-based analysis plus" (GBA+) — since the mid-1990s (Status of Women Canada, n.d.). Also, it has expanded the scope of this analysis in recent years to apply to all Memoranda to Cabinet, Treasury Board Submissions, departmental plans and results reports, and now all budgetary and financial management policies.

Budget 2017 and budget 2018 both included separate chapters on gender equality, summarizing key challenges facing women, girls, and gender diverse people, as well as related budgetary measures. A Gender Results Framework was introduced in budget 2018, setting goals and selected indicators to track progress in meeting gender-equality objectives (Department of Finance Canada, 2018b).

Budget 2019 presented the most detailed budgetary analysis to date, including updates on Canada's progress indicators and a Gender Report that applied GBA+ to every budget measure (Department of Finance Canada, 2019a). As a result, federal departments developed mitigation strategies to compensate for and/or offset the negative impacts of 15% of the measures announced in the budget. In another 8% of cases, departments proactively took steps to reduce barriers to participation.

A Work in Progress

That said, gender-based budgeting — and GBA+ more broadly — remains a work in progress. Canada has struggled to implement GBA+ across all levels of government.

A 2015 report from Canada's Auditor General mirrored the findings of an earlier 2009 audit that found GBA/GBA+ has been applied "incompletely" and "inconsistently" across federal government agencies (Office of the Auditor General of Canada, 2009, 2015). A 2016 study by the Standing Committee on the Status of Women corroborated these same findings (Standing Committee on the Status of Women, 2016).

More recently, results from a 2018 survey of public servants found that fewer than half of departments and agencies have a GBA+ plan in place, with most departments saying they lack the internal mechanisms to apply one (Wright, 2019). Many more are familiar with the concept of GBA+, but they continue to struggle with implementation despite the rollout of new tools, training, and support for individuals tasked with conducting GBA+ analysis (Status of Women Canada et al., 2016).

Action Needed to Strengthen Gender Budgeting Processes

The federal government has introduced some of the infrastructure needed to pursue gender equality. The question is whether these efforts will produce results.

On this score, as Helaina Gaspard and Emily Woolner of the Institute for Fiscal Studies and Democracy write, "the current parameters for GBA+ analysis are compelling at first glance but may be insufficient to have a real policy impact beyond a change in rhetoric" (Gaspard & Woolner, 2019).

The government's Gender Results Framework remains "quite vague," they note. Key objectives are identified alongside recent government initiatives, but there are no explicit connections between the two and no global plan for achieving desired outcomes.

Action is needed to strengthen Canada's gender budgeting process — to ensure that the purpose and goals of GBA+ are defined in concrete terms, with clear metrics against which to evaluate progress, and that resources are in place to support the process, and, as important, to eliminate the gender disparities that are identified (International Monetary Fund, 2017, p. 7).

The Promise and Reality of Gender Budgeting

In a world of concentrating wealth and privilege, refundable child care credits or even universal care strategies cannot on their own reduce deeply rooted structural barriers to economic gender equality or the narrow formalistic approaches being taken to gender equality in taxation.

The very composition of tax systems and their detailed distributional gender and intersectional impacts need to be identified and taken into account in devising a tax system that can advance — rather than stymie — gender equality. This is why getting gender budgeting right is so important. To truly close the gap for women living in Canada, we need fiscal policies and budgetary processes that can advance gender equality — and the political will to make it happen.

Questions for Reflection

1. Why did the federal government introduce gender budgeting legislation?
2. How might gender budgeting legislation affect public policy making? Consider different areas such as health, training, or the environment.
3. What do you think of the government's gender statements in budget 2018 and budget 2019?

A Moment in Time: March 22, 1945

The "Baby Bonus"

Canada's First Universal Social Welfare Program

The Family Allowance Act was passed unanimously by the Canadian Parliament in 1944. It was the first universal welfare program in Canada.

Family benefit payments started in 1945 and were given tax-free to all women with children under the age of 16 who attended school. The payments were made regardless of family income or means. All costs were incurred by the federal government (Moscovitch & Falvo, 2017).

The preceding 15 years had been difficult. Canadians had just gone through the Great Depression of the 1930s and then the tragedy of World War II. As the war was drawing to a close, avoiding another economic calamity and finding a way forward to postwar reconstruction were top of mind.

At the time, the "baby bonus" was seen as a radical and also expensive program, but political and economic factors prompted William Lyon Mackenzie King, the Liberal prime minister at the time, to seize on it as a welfare program that could attract voters and undercut the rising fortunes of the political left.

While the Family Allowance Act passed unanimously in Parliament on second reading, Conservatives nevertheless regarded it as giveaway to the poor and criticized its universal character. For their part, the Act's supporters saw universalism as a way to ensure the benefit would not be progressively eroded by future governments.

A Not-So-Sacred Trust

During the 1984 federal election, Brian Mulroney, then leader of the Progressive Conservative Party, described social programs as a "sacred trust." However, once in power, these programs became targets of the new government. As Guest (2006) observes:

> The Conservative government ended the universal nature of family allowances by requiring upper-income parents to repay all of their benefit at tax-filing time as part of its program to target social benefits to low-or-moderate-income recipients. Paradoxically, it maintained and increased a tax deduction for child-care expenses, which provided the greatest benefit to high-income families.

In 1992, the federal Conservative government replaced the Family Allowance with a new Child Tax Benefit. Between 1992 and today, almost as a first order of business, successive federal governments have introduced their own variation on the family benefit, changing the form the benefit takes and the amounts families receive.

Chapter Review

Questions

1. The increased labour force participation of women since the 1950s is remarkable. What factors contributed to this shift, and what have been some of its major implications?
2. What factors have contributed to the continuing disadvantaged economic status of women in Canadian society? What are some of the solutions being proposed?
3. Describe how families have changed over the past few decades. What factors have led to these changes?
4. Responsibility for child care and elder care falls disproportionately on women. Why is this the case, and what can be done about it?
5. The COVID–19 pandemic affected men and women in different ways, and therefore the measures to address it must take gender into account. Discuss.

Exploring Social Welfare

1. Identify and discuss the key factors contributing to women's lower pay situation.
2. Québec's child care program is widely regarded as one of Canada's success stories. Draw up your own list of "pros and cons" and "strengths and weaknesses" of the Québec model.
3. Pick one of the key issues facing Canadian families today, and locate empirical research that addresses this issue. Write a short report, complete with data portraying the issue and proposed solutions.
4. Gender-based analysis plus (GBA+) can be used to assess "how diverse groups of women, men and non-binary people may experience policies, programs and initiatives" (Status of Women, n.d.). Pick one social policy area and describe how and why women and men are affected differently by it using GBA+ analysis.

Websites

Canadian Centre for Policy Alternatives (CCPA)
www.policyalternatives.ca
The Canadian Centre for Policy Alternatives (CCPA) is an independent, non-partisan research institute concerned with issues of social, economic, and environmental justice. Founded in 1980, the CCPA produces the research and analysis necessary for policymakers, activists, and everyday Canadians to make informed decisions and press for social change. The CCPA has a National Office in Ottawa and has provincial offices in British Columbia, Saskatchewan, Manitoba, Ontario, and Nova Scotia.

The Vanier Institute of the Family
www.vanierinstitute.ca
The Vanier Institute of the Family is a national, charitable organization dedicated to providing leadership on issues affecting the well-being of Canadian families. Its work includes collecting and analyzing information on changing patterns of family formation and function; advocating social change to create more supportive environments for families; and advising government, corporations, and religious organizations on matters of family policy.

Women and Gender Equality Canada (WAGE)
www.swc-cfc.gc.ca
After 42 years of serving Canadian women, the small but mighty agency known as Status of Women Canada has become a full department under the law. The new department is called Women and Gender Equality Canada (WAGE). It continues the work of advancing more equitable economic, political, and social outcomes for Canadian women. It also has an expanded mandate for gender equality that includes sexual orientation, and gender identity and expression.

The Welfare and Well-Being of Canadian Children

"Safety and security don't just happen, they are the result of collective consensus and public investment. We owe our children, the most vulnerable citizens in our society, a life free of violence and fear."

— Nelson Mandela, South African anti-apartheid political leader who served as president of South Africa from 1994 to 1999

Child welfare policy in Canada is a complex web of international guidelines, national policy, and provincial legislation that seeks to contribute to the well-being of all children. Of particular interest to social workers are policies focused on protecting vulnerable children from maltreatment.

In Canada, child protection occurs within a context of jurisdictional tensions and complex ideological philosophies. Although frequently considered an individual family problem, child maltreatment, particularly child neglect, is intertwined with broader structural socio-economic and cultural inequities. For example, Indigenous, Black, and poor families are much more likely to be investigated for child maltreatment, and children from these families are much more likely to be removed from the family home and placed into care.

This chapter describes children's rights in Canada; examines the characteristics of children and families in the child welfare system; identifies the principles on which Canadian child protection legislation and policy are based; and reviews the themes that underlie modern child protection systems.

Protecting Children from Maltreatment

Social policy and legislation in Canada protecting children from maltreatment has traditionally followed a predominantly residual approach. More universal approaches to children's rights, health, and well-being require a system in which families are provided income and social supports, and a child's agency and voice are respected. After completing this chapter, you should be able to:

- Describe child protection within a child rights perspective;
- Recognize the multiple and overlapping jurisdictional responsibilities for child protection;
- Describe key child, family, and socio-economic characteristics associated with child abuse and neglect investigations;
- Recognize the importance of an evidence-based approach to child protection legislation and policy
- Describe the outcomes for children who have been in care; and
- Explain the difference between a universal child welfare model and a residual approach to child welfare.

Key Concepts

- Child maltreatment
- United Nations Convention on the Rights of the Child
- Provincial/Territorial Protocol on Children, Youth and Families Moving between Provinces and Territories
- Canadian Incidence Study of Reported Child Abuse and Neglect (CIS)
- Bill C-92
- Evidence-based policy
- Best interests of the child (BIC) principle
- Least intrusive intervention model
- Child-centred approaches
- Risk assessment
- "Good enough" parenting
- Kinship care
- Signs of Safety (SoS)
- Aging out of care
- Universal child welfare model

6.1 The Rights of the Child

Child maltreatment has existed since ancient times, although exactly what constitutes harm to a child has changed over time and place. Developing policies to prevent and respond to child maltreatment is challenging in part because of the varying terminology and definitions associated with child abuse and neglect. The most recent World Health Organization (WHO) definition of child maltreatment is as follows:

> All forms of physical and/or emotional ill-treatment, sexual abuse, neglect or negligent treatment or commercial or other exploitation, resulting in actual or potential harm to the child's health, survival, development or dignity in the context of a relationship of responsibility, trust or power. (World Health Organization, 2016)

Social workers have a long history of being practice and policy leaders in efforts to prevent and address child maltreatment through identifying, assessing, and supporting the needs of children and their families.

The Early History of Child Protection in Canada

Early child welfare practices in Canada developed in response to the growing number of homeless families during and following the period of rapid industrialization (1870s–1930s). During this time, up to 100,000 poor and orphaned children arrived in Canada from Britain through the Barnardo's homes program. These children were to be farm labourers and domestic servants. Some of them were treated well, but others were abused.

The first Children's Aid Society was established in 1853 by a group of social reformers in New York. John Joseph Kelso brought the Children's Aid Society to Toronto in 1891 in order to create a social safety net to protect the number of homeless, impoverished, and abandoned children in the city.

In 1893, the Act for the Prevention of Cruelty to and Better Protection of Children (commonly called the "Children's Protection Act") came into force. This Act laid the foundation for Canada's child welfare program (Until the Last Child, 2014). This period of the late nineteenth century and early twentieth century, commonly referred to as the "child-saving" era, saw a variety of organizations operate orphanages, training schools, and housing for the poor to ensure that all children were reared as disciplined, industrious, and literate citizens.

During the early twentieth century, a rapid expansion of children's services took place in most provinces. These services became increasingly bureaucratized and professionalized, greatly influencing the subsequent development of child welfare services. "Changes in child welfare were also affected by changing attitudes toward the participation of children in the labour market, by the increasing support for the importance of formal education, and through a gradual recognition that children had a right to be free from a variety of harms" (Albert & Herbert, 2013, para. 11).

The United Nations Convention on the Rights of the Child, 1989

Children's rights occur within the larger context of human rights, with children being afforded special protections due to the recognition that they are "developing beings who have ensuing needs related to their development, education, and relations with their family on whom they generally depend" (Paré, 2017, p. 28).

The United Nations set a universal standard for human rights with the adoption of the Universal Declaration of Human Rights in 1948. Since then, a number of treaties have been developed to recognize the basic rights of all persons.

The 1989 United Nations Convention on the Rights of the Child recognizes the specific rights of children. Children have rights to the following:

- Protection (e.g., from abuse, exploitation, and harmful substances)
- Provision (e.g., for education, health care, and an adequate standard of living)
- Participation (e.g., listening to children's views and respecting their evolving capacities)
- Specific protections and provisions for vulnerable populations such as Indigenous children and children with disabilities (UNICEF Canada, n.d., para. 5)

The convention has inspired change in all regions of the world. The convention makes clear the idea that a basic quality of life should be the right of all children, rather than a privilege enjoyed by a few. Children's human rights apply to all children at all times, without exception.

Children's Rights in Canada

Canada ratified the United Nations Convention on the Rights of the Child on December 13, 1991. Since then, a number of laws, policies, and practices affecting Canadian children have advanced children's welfare in this country.

Canada has legislation recognizing human rights: the Canadian Charter of Rights and Freedoms and provincial human rights acts that prohibit discrimination. Canada does not have any specific legislation at the federal or provincial levels recognizing children's rights as distinct from human rights, although there are legal concepts that apply to children specifically (Paré, 2017).

The principle of the "best interests of the child" (BIC) is present in Canadian family law, education law, immigration law, the Youth Criminal Justice Act, and, of course, child welfare law. The BIC doctrine is used to decide what would best protect children's safety, security, and well-being.

Paré (2017) observes that in order to recognize children's rights separately from human rights, institutions such as child advocate and ombudsman's offices would need to be routinely in place. Such institutions would be "beneficial to children, fostering a more comprehensive protection of their rights, and would ensure that Canada complies with its own legal obligations" (Paré, 2017, p. 41).

Provincial/Territorial Child Welfare Legislation

In Canada, provincial and territorial governments are primarily responsible for child welfare legislation. Federal legislation that affects child welfare includes the Indian Act and Bill C-92, the Youth Criminal Justice Act, and the Criminal Code of Canada. The provinces and territories are the primary provider of child protection services and the primary collector of data on child maltreatment.

Provincial and territorial legislation may differ in certain areas, for example, in relation to the age of protection, the grounds of intervention, the standards of verification, the duty to report and false reporting, and the nature of interagency protocols. However, all include provisions for delegated authority to Indigenous child welfare agencies and place an emphasis on culture, heritage, and the best interests of the child.

Protocol among Statutory Child Welfare Organizations

Since there are times when children and families need to move to another province or territory, the provinces and territories have agreed to work together to provide child welfare services to children and families no matter where they move to in Canada. These guidelines are outlined in the Provincial/Territorial Protocol on Children, Youth and Families Moving between Provinces and Territories.

The protocol covers child protection, children and youth in care, children and youth in out-of-home placements, supports to families, services to alternative care providers (e.g., foster parents and kin), and adoption services (Government of British Columbia et al., 2016). Twelve provinces and territories are signatories to the provincial/territorial protocol, with only Québec not participating. The principles underlying the protocol are as follows:

- The safety, best interests, and well-being of children and youth is the paramount consideration in all decisions
- This Protocol shall be administered so that the rights of children and youth as defined in the United Nations Convention on the Rights of the Child (1990) are respected
- The originating PT [province or territory] always maintains the legal responsibility for children and youth in their care, custody, or guardianship and this legal responsibility ends in accordance with that jurisdiction's legislation
- In unique situations, exceptions to the Protocol can be made where necessary to promote the best interests of a child or youth
- In unforeseen circumstances where the Protocol does not provide sufficient direction, the PTs will work collaboratively to promote the child or youth's best interests consistent with both PTs' legislation
- Services are not delayed due to budgetary, administrative, or jurisdictional issues or disputes and, where these do arise, a timely and effective resolution is promoted (Government of British Columbia et al., 2016, p. 2)

Provincial and Territorial Legislation

Each jurisdiction has its own legislation in relation to child and family welfare:

- **Alberta**
  Child, Youth and Family Enhancement Act (2004)
- **British Columbia**
  Child, Family and Community Service Act (2000)
- **Manitoba**
  Child and Family Services Act (1985)
- **New Brunswick**
  Family Services Act (1980)
- **Newfoundland and Labrador**
  Children and Youth Care and Protection Act (2011)
- **Northwest Territories**
  Child and Family Services Act (1998)
- **Nova Scotia**
  Children and Family Services Act (1990)
- **Nunavut**
  Child and Family Services Act (1998)
- **Ontario**
  Child, Youth and Family Services Act (2018)
- **Prince Edward Island**
  Child Protection Act (1988)
- **Québec**
  Youth Protection Act (1984)
- **Saskatchewan**
  Child and Family Services Act (1990)
- **Yukon**
  The Child and Family Services Act (2010)

Federal and Provincial Responsibility for Indigenous Children

The federal government has jurisdiction over and provides funding for First Nations children living on-reserve. Provincial/territorial child protection legislation also applies. Moreover, according to the Supreme Court of Canada's Daniels decision in 2016, non-status Indians and Métis are "Indians" under the Constitution Act.

As a result:

> like First Nations Peoples with status, non-status First Nations and Métis Peoples may be able to access services from existing First Nations agencies, or be eligible for Department of Indigenous and Northern Affairs Canada funding to create or support their own agencies. (National Collaborating Centre for Aboriginal Health, 2017, p. 3)

Nevertheless, the organization of child welfare services for Indigenous children differs across the country. Some provinces and territories provide culturally relevant services within the mainstream model. Others have a dedicated model for Indigenous child welfare services in which Indigenous child and family service agencies provide either full or partial child welfare services.

Notably, Yukon has no reserves and no First Nations child and family service agencies. Funding for its child welfare services is provided by the federal government and delivered by the Yukon government (National Collaborating Centre for Aboriginal Health, 2017).

Photo: Two children from the Lake Manitoba First Nation sit on a bus outside a hotel in Winnipeg in October of 2019, following a severe winter snowstorm that forced a lockdown and evacuation of their entire community.

The Assembly of Manitoba Chiefs said Indigenous Services Canada and the province didn't do enough to help the evacuees. Grand Chief Arlen Dumas stated that while the governments' policies may work in an urban setting where alternative resources are available, they fail in remote Indigenous communities.

Social Welfare in Perspective

Children and the Opioid Crisis

A Public Health and Child Welfare Policy Issue

While Canada has no formal child welfare policies associated with the opioid crisis, the data and research are providing some ideas for consideration.

The opioid crisis is not only a public health crisis but also a child welfare policy issue. When parents become addicted to opioids or die from an overdose, the child welfare system is required to respond.

How Canadian Children Are Being Affected

According to the Public Health Agency of Canada (PHAC), between January 2016 and March 2019 an estimated 12,800 Canadians died from an apparent opioid-related overdose. In the first three months of 2019, there were more than 1,000 opioid-related deaths (Public Health Agency of Canada, 2019).

The growing number of opioid-related overdoses and deaths represents a public health crisis. Although the focus of this issue is often adults, Canadian children are also being affected in numerous ways:

- Child or adolescent poisoning and overdose
- Opioid misuse during pregnancy
- Impaired parenting and attachment
- Material deprivation
- Extended separation from parents (Feder et al., 2019)

US Research: A Growing Number of Children in Foster Care

Although the data from Canada have not yet provided a full understanding of the intersection of the opioid crisis and child welfare, analyses of the linkage are emerging from US research.

In the United States, Collier (2018) has linked the opioid crisis to an increase in the number of children in foster care. Between 2013 and 2015, the number of children in foster care across the United States jumped by almost 7%, and parental substance use was cited as a factor in about 32% of all foster placements (Collier, 2018).

Since more children are being placed in foster care due to a parent's opioid use, social workers are required to respond to unique needs of these children.

The increasing demand for foster care comes at a time when opioid deaths have surged, and many children are the indirect victims of the crisis as they are not getting the care and services they need (Collier, 2018). John Kelly, a PhD in psychiatry and addiction medicine at Harvard Medical School, states, "Because we're trying to put out the fire in terms of stopping overdose deaths, we haven't really been attending to other casualties, including kids most importantly" (Collier, 2018).

The Canadian Context

In Canada, men are more likely to die of an opioid overdose than women, but it is not known how many of those men are fathers (Bimman, 2018).

Canada's response to the opioid crisis has focused primarily on harm reduction (such as supervised consumption sites and the Good Samaritan Drug Overdose Act), a public awareness campaign, and an emphasis on supply restriction. The federal government's response to treatment initiatives includes the Emergency Treatment Fund, which is one-time emergency funding of $150 million for provinces and territories to improve access to evidence-based treatment services.

Although the opioid crisis is an emerging issue in Canada, little to no policy research has focused on its effects on children's well-being. However, in the United States, Waite et al. (2018) are making important contributions and policy recommendations for children and families affected by the opioid crisis.

Finding Policy Solutions

Any policy solutions in this area must involve input from many voices. Above all, opioid users and family members (including children and youth) of those who have overdosed or died must be among those involved in policymaking. An interprofessional approach would include the following:

- Social workers involved with children and family services
- Medical professional involved in pain management and prescription use
- Nurses in neo-natal units
- Substance use counsellors

Substance use occurs within a personal, family, and societal context. "Despite the even distribution of substance use across demographic categories, poor women and women of color are far more likely to be reported to health and child welfare authorities for use of substances when pregnant compared to other women" (Waite et al., 2018). Child protection workers face a difficult task in balancing the risks to child safety with the benefits of family preservation and treatment.

An especially vulnerable group is women of reproductive age who use opioids. In the United States, "from 1992 to 2012, hospital admissions of pregnant women reporting prescription opioid abuse increased from 2 percent to 28 percent" (Waite et al., 2018, p. 3). This increased rate is likely associated with better reporting data along with an increase in actual use.

Child Welfare Policy Considerations

Waite et al. (2018) identified a number of policy considerations for serving children and families affected by parental substance use disorders. They include:

- **Supporting Attachment and Child Development.** Children who have parents with substance-use disorders need healthy attachment bonds in order to grow, develop, and thrive. The identification of parental substance use disorders offers the opportunity for policies to address unmet parental needs that may threaten a parent's ability to attach and care for their child or children.
- **Supporting the Resilience of Families.** By equipping parents with the skills to successfully parent children, policy can ensure children who have experienced parental substance exposure or use have the safe, stable, nurturing relationships they need to thrive.
- **Providing Resources to Treat Parental Substance Use and Trauma History.** Policies that support healthy parent–child attachment within the family of origin as one component of substance use services reduces any additional trauma of family disruption and alternative care.
- **Better Serving Maternal and Child Health.** Policies and programs can support the health and safety of infants prenatally exposed to substances; ensure access to appropriate diagnosis and treatment of developmental and behavioural needs; ensure that parents have access to outpatient treatment and services that can allow families to stay together when safe and appropriate; provide access to effective treatments for pregnant women, including medication-assisted treatment; and ensure stronger parent–child attachment and family resilience.
- **Embracing a "Family First" Approach.** Policies can provide access to inpatient treatment and at-home support options (when safe and appropriate) that serve parents and children together.

6.2 The Incidence of Child Abuse and Neglect

The provincial and territorial governments collect data on the contexts, risk factors, and types of child maltreatment in their jurisdiction. They use this evidence to inform their child welfare policies, programs, services, and interventions. In addition, the Public Health Agency of Canada (PHAC) has, for more than two decades, collaborated with provincial and territorial partners in national data collection, analysis, and interpretation (PHAC, 2018).

The Canadian Incidence Study of Reported Child Abuse and Neglect (CIS) of 1998 was the country's first national child maltreatment study. The CIS is a survey of reported cases of child maltreatment from a sample of child welfare agencies in all provinces and territories, including those on-reserve. Research cycles took place in 1998, 2003, and 2008. At the time of writing, the 2019 cycle and the 2019 First Nations/Canadian Incidence Study of Reported Child Abuse and Neglect (FN/CIS-2019) were in their initial stages.

Canadian Incidence Study of Reported Child Abuse and Neglect (CIS)

The CIS is a national initiative to collect data on children who come to the attention of a child welfare authority due to alleged or suspected abuse and/or neglect. The CIS examines the incidence of reported child maltreatment and the characteristics of the children and families investigated by child-welfare authorities.

Major Findings from the CIS-2008

In 2008, an estimated 235,842 child maltreatment–related investigations were conducted in Canada (PHAC, 2010). Based on the CIS-2008, 36% of the investigations (85,440 investigations) were substantiated. In 92% of the investigations (215,878 investigations), there were no placements. Of the approximately 8% (19,599 investigations) that resulted in a change of residence for the child, 4% were moved to an informal arrangement with a relative, 4% were moved to foster care or kinship care, and fewer than 1% were moved to a group home or residential/secure treatment.

The two most frequently occurring categories of substantiated maltreatment were exposure to intimate partner violence (IPV) and neglect (PHAC, 2010). IPV was the primary category of substantiated maltreatment in 34% of the investigations (an estimated 29,259 investigations). In another 34% of substantiated investigations (an estimated 28,939 investigations), neglect was identified as the overriding concern.

In 20% of the substantiated investigations (an estimated 17,212 investigations), the primary form of maltreatment was physical abuse (PHAC, 2010).

Emotional maltreatment was identified as the primary maltreatment category in 9% of substantiated investigations (an estimated 7,423 investigations) (PHAC, 2010). Sexual abuse was identified as the primary maltreatment category in 3% of substantiated investigations (an estimated 2,607 investigations).

In 18% of substantiated investigations, more than one category of maltreatment was involved, with the most frequently identified combination being neglect and exposure to IPV (PHAC, 2010).

Characteristics of Children and Families Documented in the CIS-2008

The CIS-2008 data documents information in a number of areas. These include children's characteristics (e.g., age and sex); child functioning (i.e., 18 items across physical, emotional, cognitive, and behavioural domains); primary caregiver risk factors (i.e., potential stressors); household risk factors (including social assistance, household moves in the past 12 months, and household hazards); and previous child maltreatment investigations (PHAC, 2010). CIS-2008 findings were as follows:

- **Children's Characteristics.** The incidence of all maltreatment-related investigations was nearly identical for males and females. In terms of age, the highest rate of investigation was for infants (104 investigations per 2,000). The incidence of substantiated maltreatment was also nearly identical for males and females. The highest substantiation rate was for infants (34 per 2,000 infants).
- **Child Functioning.** In 46% of substantiated investigations, at least one child functioning issue was indicated. The most frequent was academic difficulties (23%), followed by depression/anxiety/withdrawal (19%). Fifteen percent involved aggression, while 14% involved attachment issues. Eleven percent of substantiated investigations involved children experiencing ADD/ADHD, and 11% involved children with intellectual/developmental disabilities (PHAC, 2010, p. 38).
- **Primary Caregiver Risk Factors.** For each investigated child, the social worker identified the person who was the primary caregiver. In 91% of substantiated investigations, the primary caregiver was female, and nearly half (45%) of substantiated investigations involved caregivers between the ages of 31 and 40. In 94% of substantiated investigations, the primary caregiver was a biological parent. In cases of substantiated maltreatment, rarely was the caregiver under the age of 20 or over 50. In 78% of substantiated child maltreatment investigations, at least one primary caregiver risk factor was reported. The most frequently noted concerns for primary caregivers were being a victim of domestic violence (46%), having few social supports (39%), and having mental health issues (27%) (PHAC, 2010, pp. 39–40).
- **Household Risk Factors.** One-third of the children in substantiated investigations were living in purchased homes, compared with 44% in rental accommodation and 11% in public housing. Thirty-three percent of substantiated investigations involved families receiving social assistance or other benefits as their source of income. Twenty percent of investigations involved families that had moved once in the previous year. In 12% of substantiated investigations, at least one household hazard was noted (PHAC, 2010, p. 5).
- **Previous Child Maltreatment Investigations.** In 2008, the number of children who had been previously investigated for child maltreatment was roughly the same as those who had not. In approximately 48% of the investigations carried out in 2008, social workers indicated that the child had been referred previously for suspected maltreatment (PHAC, 2010, p. 28).

Indigenous Overrepresentation

"We suffer infant mortality rates that are three times the Canadian average, an education gap that will take over two decades to close, and the realization that our children are more likely to end up in jail than to graduate from high school."

National Chief Shawn Atleo, CBC News.

The Socio-Economic Context

In Canada, child protection systems tend to be dominated by a forensic and individualistic approach to maltreatment and neglect. These approaches place the burden of the blame on parents for not meeting their children's safety and well-being needs. The underlying residual model, frequently associated with a neoliberal approach, holds the family responsible for the welfare of their children (Schumaker, 2012, p. 17). However, research clearly indicates that socio-economic status and structural factors play a significant role in maltreatment, reporting, substantiation, and entry into care. For example, the CIS-2008 data noted that 33% of substantiated investigations involved families receiving social assistance or other benefits as their source of income (PHAC, 2010).

The association between socio-economic status and child maltreatment is particularly visible in situations of child neglect. As the CIS-2008 found, neglect is the second most common form of child maltreatment (PHAC, 2010). It can be challenging for social workers and other service providers to address neglect because situations can be chronic, complex, and overwhelming. Moreover, there are few meaningful interventions available to address the issues properly. Poverty is correlated with all forms of abuse and neglect, but it is most strongly associated with neglect (Schumaker, 2012).

Socio-economic disparities are further confounded with racial factors. The overrepresentation of Indigenous children in child welfare is well established. The primary driver for this overrepresentation is child neglect: six First Nations children are investigated for neglect for every one non-Indigenous child investigated for neglect (Sinha et al., 2013). Moreover, cases involving neglect for an Indigenous child are more likely to be substantiated. Poverty, inadequate housing, and limited access to services have consistently been shown to be the driving factors in the overrepresentation of cases of child neglect involving Indigenous children (Trocmé et al., 2013). It is important to bear in mind that in Canada, Indigenous families experience extreme levels of poverty and poor housing relative to non-Indigenous families.

Racial factors also affect Aboriginal and Torres Strait islander children in Australia, Maori and Pacific Islander children in New Zealand (van Miert, 2015), and Black children in the United States (Fluke et al., 2010; Jonson-Reid et al., 2013). Research indicates that both community poverty factors and family poverty factors contribute to racial disparity and disproportionality in the child welfare system in the United States (Jonson-Reid et al., 2013).

Clearly, the broader socio-economic context is relevant in child welfare. Taylor et al. (2008) argue that while seeking effective and non-stigmatizing individual approaches is important in child neglect situations, it is crucial for social workers to tackle the underlying structural causes at the same time. In contrast to the residual approach, an institutional approach to child welfare advances universal systems that provide socio-economic resources to children and families finding themselves in need.

Systemic Risks

The persistent over-representation of First Nations families in investigations of child maltreatment cannot be adequately understood through the dominant individual and forensic perspectives. It can be tied to the low incomes and poor housing conditions of many First Nations families (Sinha et al., 2011) and is exacerbated by social issues of substance use and domestic violence.

These issues are structural factors that "place children and families at risk [and] that are largely beyond their ability to control" (First Nations Child and Family Caring Society of Canada, 2013).

Indigenous Children in the Child Welfare System

According to the CIS-2008 data, 22% of substantiated investigations (an estimated 18,510 investigations) involved children of Indigenous heritage as follows: 15% First Nations status, 3% First Nations non-status, 2% Métis, 1% Inuit, and 1% with other Indigenous heritage (PHAC, 2010, p. 4). This rate of substantiated child maltreatment is four times higher than the rate for non-Indigenous child investigations: 49.69 per 1,000 Indigenous children versus 11.85 per 1,000 non-Indigenous children (PHAC, 2010, p. 39).

Sinha et al. (2013) examined this overrepresentation further through an exploration of the findings in the First Nations Incidence Study (FNCIS-2008). Here too they found that First Nations children were overrepresented. The disproportionate representation of First Nations children that existed at the investigation stage was similar to that of the substantiation rate.

In 2008, an estimated 140.6 child maltreatment–related investigations took place for every 1,000 First Nations children (Sinha et al., 2013, p. 826). By contrast, an estimated 33.5 child maltreatment–related investigations took place for every 1,000 non-Indigenous children. That means the rate for First Nations children was 4.2 times higher than for non-Indigenous children.

This disproportionality was most profound in neglect investigations. The rate for First Nations children was 6.0 times higher than for non-Indigenous children (Sinha et al., 2013). There was no significant difference between First Nations and non-Indigenous investigations in relation to child functioning. However, a higher proportion of First Nations investigations had multiple primary caregiver risk factors (57.2% versus 34.8%) and household risk factors (44.6% versus 27.2%). As Sinha et al. (2013) noted:

> The most commonly identified risk factor concerns for caregivers of First Nations children were substance abuse (55.7% of investigations involving First Nations children vs. 25.3% of non-Aboriginal investigations), domestic violence (43.7% vs. 31.6%) and having few social supports (40.3% vs. 31.5%). The most commonly identified household risk factor concerns were low income (53.6% of investigations involving First Nations children vs. 31.8% of non-Aboriginal investigations) and caregiving resource strain (56.3% vs. 46.4%). (p. 828)

The authors concluded that "it would be extremely difficult to reduce First Nations overrepresentation at later decision points (e.g., alternative care) without addressing overrepresentation at the investigation stage. Despite the serious needs of investigated First Nations families, alternatives to traditional child protection responses may be more appropriate. If First Nations overrepresentation is to be reduced, child welfare agencies must be equipped to provide supports needed to help families address factors such as poverty, substance abuse, domestic violence, and lack of social supports" (Sinha et al., 2013, p. 821).

Housing Risks

Almost half of First Nations adults and children live on-reserve. The average number of family members living in a house is 3.7, compared with the Canadian average of 2.5.

More than a quarter of on-reserve First Nations live in crowded homes, a rate 7 times greater than that of non-Indigenous people. Furthermore, 43% of houses on reserve are in need of major repairs, compared to 7% of Canadian houses.

Poor housing conditions contribute to many health and social problems. This includes increased prevalence of infectious diseases; increased social challenges associated with having less success at school; as well as increased vulnerability to injury or death resulting from an unsafe home environment, such as fires.

Canadian Institute of Child Health (2020). *The Health of Canada's Children and Youth.*

Black Children in the Child Welfare System

Based on the 2016 Canadian census, close to 1.2 million people reported being Black, representing 3.5% of the country's population (Statistics Canada, 2019). In all, 52.4% of all Black Canadians (627,710) live in Ontario, representing 4.7% of the provincial population. Toronto has the largest Black population in the country (36.9%).

"For decades, African Canadians, advocates, service users, community partners, and most recently the media have raised concerns that African Canadian children and youth are overrepresented in Ontario's child welfare system" (Turner, 2016, p. i). Data released by the Children's Aid Society of Toronto show a disproportionality rate of 4.8, with Black Canadian children representing 40.8% of children in care (Turner, 2016, p. i).

Further, the overrepresentation of Black youth in child welfare and youth justice, particularly in large urban areas, has been noted, with youths "often placed in residential group home programs, programs ... characterized as the most intrusive and constraining type of service" (Mosher & Hewitt, 2018, p. 2).

In 2015, the Ontario Ministry of Children and Youth Services funded the development of a practice framework to support child welfare agencies in providing better services to children, youth, and families in the Black community (Turner, 2016). During consultations with Black communities across Ontario, "participants raised concerns that anti-Black racism operates throughout child welfare agencies" (Turner, 2016, p.iv). Among the recommendations of the final report, the steering committee raised the need to acknowledge the long history of anti-Black racism and to develop a protocol that requires and supports child welfare agencies to engage Black Canadian child and family services agencies once a Black child or family is brought to the attention of the agency.

The child welfare system in Ontario is beginning to grapple with the issue of Black–white disparities in reporting, service involvement, and placement in out-of-home care (Ontario Human Rights Commission, 2017). In 2018, provincial guidelines were identified for the collection and reporting of race-based information.

In a study of child protection decision-making in Ontario, King et al. (2017) found the following:

> Black children were more likely to be investigated than White children, but there was little evidence to suggest that workers in Ontario child welfare agencies made the decision to substantiate, transfer to ongoing services, or place the child in out-of-home care based on race alone. Black and White children differed significantly with respect to child characteristics, characteristics of the investigation, caregiver risk factors, and socio-economic circumstances. When adjusting for these characteristics, Black families had 33% greater odds of being transferred to ongoing services compared to White families. Among Black families, the assessed quality of the parent-child relationship and severe economic hardship were the most significant and substantial contributors to the decision to provide child welfare services. (p.89)

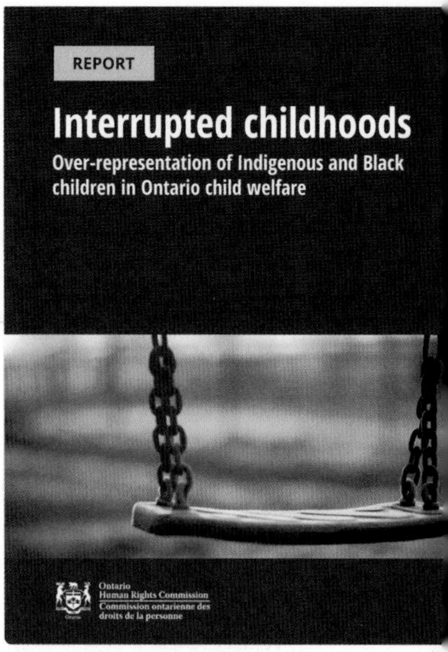

Interrupted Childhoods

"The issues that give rise to the over-representation of Indigenous and Black children in the child welfare system are multi-faceted. For example, low income, which is one of the inter-generational effects of colonialism, slavery and racism in society, is strongly associated with caregiver and household risk factors for children.

"In Ontario, children who are the subject of a child welfare investigation whose families run out of money for food, housing or utilities face approximately double the odds of being placed into care. Poverty and race intersect."

Ontario Human Rights Commission (2018). Interrupted childhoods: Over-representation of Indigenous and Black children in Ontario child welfare.

Asian Canadian Children in the Child Welfare System

The South Asian community represents the fastest growing and largest visible minority group in Canada (Statistics Canada, 2007). It is projected that South Asian people could represent 28% of the visible minority population by 2031 (Statistics Canada, 2011). In Canada, Asian children are underrepresented in child welfare services, compared to white children (13.9 per 1,000 Asian children vs. 36.1 per 1,000 white children) (Lee et al., 2016)

Lee et al. (2017) undertook a secondary analysis of the CIS-2008 data to understand the similarities and differences in child welfare involvement for Asian Canadian (East and Southeast Asian children and families) versus white Canadian children and families. Asian Canadian households had a higher proportion of child maltreatment investigations compared with white Canadian households (84.8% versus 74.3%) and a lower rate of risk investigations (15.2% versus 25.7%) (Lee et al., 2017). The investigations of Asian Canadian households for physical abuse were almost twice that of white Canadian households involved in the child welfare system (35.5% versus 18.9%). The proportion of neglect, emotional maltreatment, and exposure to IPV was similar for child maltreatment investigations involving Asian Canadian and white Canadian households. Of these investigations, a slightly higher proportion of child maltreatment investigations involving Asian Canadian households was substantiated (55.6% versus 46.5%).

Cross-cultural training for child welfare workers with particular attention to the cultural values and practices of Asian families and the level of acculturation are also warranted.

Child maltreatment investigations involving Asian Canadians were more likely to consist of two caregivers as compared with white Canadian households (81.3% versus 59.2%). Moreover, as compared with white Canadian households, both caregivers were more likely to be biological (93.8% versus 63.5%) and employed full-time (73.4% versus 56.3%) (p. 347). Gender of the investigated child, age of the child, and number of children in the family were comparable.

Following the data analysis, a series of focus groups were held in southern Ontario with child welfare workers, community service providers, and multicultural family services agencies. The focus group discussion suggested that the "maltreatment-related investigations involving Asian children and families were typically due to physical discipline, but were likely low severity and single incidences of involvement with the child welfare system" (Lee et al., 2017, p. 349). One child welfare worker suggested that the closed and rigid family boundaries among Asian Canadian families contribute to the type of child maltreatment investigations. Participants believed that the use of physical discipline is considered a "cultural norm" in the Asian Canadian families, framing the disproportionality of physical abuse as physical discipline rather than abuse.

Based on their findings, the authors recommended further research with a focus on how to guide preventive intervention before child welfare involvement. As many Asian Canadian families and communities lacked awareness and understanding of the child welfare system, working collaboratively and forging positive relationships are key.

Social Welfare in Perspective

Indigenous Children in Care

Discriminatory Policies and Principles

The systemic injustices against Indigenous children and families in the child welfare system has been referred to as a humanitarian crisis. In 2019, there were a few glimmers of hope.

The Indian residential school system resulted in about 150,000 First Nations, Inuit, and Métis children being forcibly removed from their homes.

Then, a second wave of removals was initiated by the addition of section 88 to the Indian Act, which resulted in a large number of Indigenous children being apprehended from their homes beginning in the 1950s and continuing through the 1960s and 1970s. This period is commonly referred to as the "Sixties Scoop."

In January 2018, then Indigenous Services minister Jane Philpott referred to the overrepresentation of First Nations, Inuit, and Métis children in foster care today as a humanitarian crisis (Edwards, 2018).

Truth and Reconciliation

The first five calls to action of the 2015 Truth and Reconciliation Commission of Canada (TRC) final report relate to child welfare.

Call to Action #4 states, "We call upon the federal government to enact Aboriginal child-welfare legislation that establishes national standards for Aboriginal child apprehension and custody cases and includes principles that:

1. Affirm the right of Aboriginal governments to establish and maintain their own child-welfare agencies
2. Require all child-welfare agencies and courts to take the residential school legacy into account in their decision-making
3. Establish, as an important priority, a requirement that placements of Aboriginal children into temporary and permanent care be culturally appropriate (Truth and Reconciliation Commission of Canada, 2015, p. 144)

Bill C-92

In June 2019, the federal government's changes to the First Nations, Métis, and Inuit child welfare system passed its third reading in the Canadian Senate.

Bill C-92 (An Act Respecting First Nations, Inuit and Métis Children, Youth and Families) recognizes Indigenous peoples' jurisdiction over child and family services as part of an inherent and Indigenous right to self-governance and that there is an urgent need to establish national standards in this area in response to the Truth and Reconciliation Commission's Call to Action #4.

The new legislation also committed Canada to implementing the United Nations Convention on the Rights of the Child (UNCRC) and United Nations Declaration on the Rights of Indigenous Peoples (UNDRIP). Section 8 states that the primary purpose of the legislation is to (a) affirm the rights and jurisdiction of Indigenous peoples in relation to child and family services; and "set out principles applicable, on a national level, to the provision of child and family services in relation to Indigenous children."

The legislation was not without its shortcomings, but it was an unprecedented step forward (King & Pasternak, 2018). The new legislation marked the first time that the federal government has exercised its jurisdiction in the area of Indigenous child welfare, and this legislation is consistent with a priority to reduce the number of Indigenous children in care. It recognizes the importance of Indigenous communities and groups developing policies and laws based on their particular histories, cultures, and circumstances. It also establishes national principles such as the best interests of the child, cultural continuity, and equality (Canada, 2019).

Human Rights Tribunal Ruling

In September 2019, a long-awaited ruling by the Canadian Human Rights Tribunal (CHRT) ordered Ottawa to compensate First Nations children impacted by the on-reserve child welfare system. The human rights case was originally initiated by the Family and Child Caring Society and the Assembly of First Nations in 2007 and was fought by the federal government at every stage.

The CHRT ordered Ottawa to pay $40,000 to each First Nations child — along with their parents or grandparents — forced to leave their homes to access services, or who were denied services covered by the policy known as "Jordan's Principle." Estimates place the number of potentially affected First Nations children at about 50,000, with the largest proportion in the Prairies and British Columbia.

In October 2019, the Liberal government challenged the CHRT ruling, stating that it was not questioning compensation but rather the best way of providing it. Indigenous leaders interpreted this as the government seeking to quash the order.

Jordan's Principle

The Jordan's Principle portion of the CHRT order begins December 12, 2007, when the House of Commons adopted Jordan's Principle. Jordan's Principle makes sure that all First Nations children can access the services and supports they need, when they need them. It can apply to a wide range of health, social, and educational needs.

Jordan's Principle is named in memory of Jordan River Anderson. He was a young boy from Norway House Cree Nation in Manitoba who languished in hospital for two years and died while federal and provincial child welfare agencies haggled over who was to pay for the boy's home care.

Following the CHRT Interim Motion Ruling in February 2019, First Nations children without Indian Act status, or not eligible for Indian Act status but recognized as members by their Nation, would be provided with the services required to meet urgent or life-threatening needs, pursuant to Jordan's Principle.

Indigenous children in care

In Canada, 52.2% of children in foster care are Indigenous, but account for only 7.7% of the child population according to Census 2016. This graphic indicates the disproportionate percentage of children under 14 who are in foster care and are Indigenous.

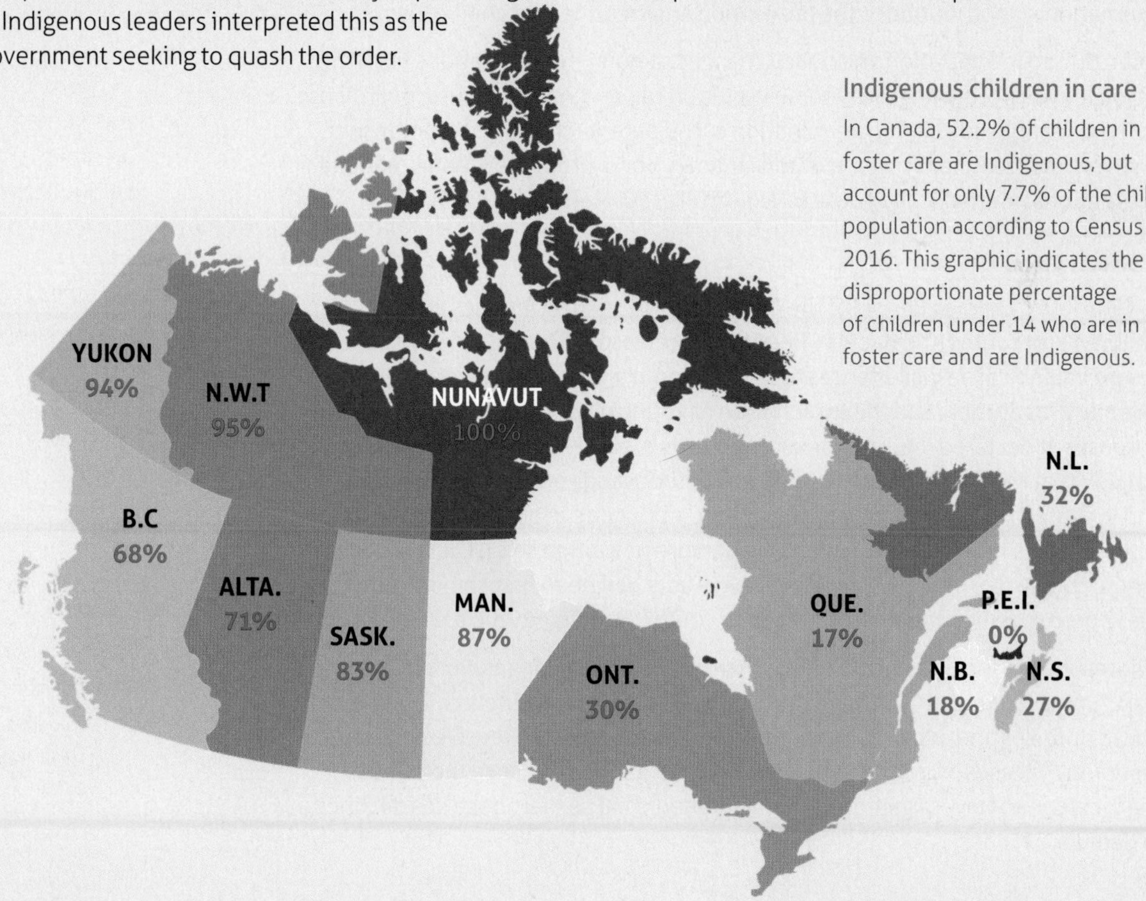

Statistics Canada (2016). Census of Canada.

6.3 The Case for Evidence-Based Policymaking

Evidence-based policy refers to policy that is informed by evidence, rather than political ideology or pressure from special-interest groups. Evidence-based policy typically uses the best available surveillance data, practitioner experiences, media reports, formal research, and government inquiries to inform policy development and implementation. The goal of an evidence-based approach is to produce well-informed policies that successfully address the social problems identified.

The Effects of an Evidence-Based Approach on Child Protection Laws and Policy

Below is a review of how an evidence-based approach has informed child protection legislation and policy in the areas of physical abuse, sexual abuse, and intimate partner violence.

- **Physical Abuse**

In 1962, Dr. C. Henry Kempe, a pediatrician and researcher based in Colorado, was the first to recognize and identify child abuse and neglect. In a defining paper, "The Battered Child Syndrome," Kempe and his colleagues provided irrefutable evidence that physical abuse could occur in the child's own home. Kempe advocated for practices and programs that would address the problem of child abuse, and he received two nominations for the Nobel Prize, one recognizing his international contribution to the prevention and treatment of child abuse.

This resulted in legislation and policy changes. Among the innovations from this advocacy were reporting laws, home visitation to prevent child abuse, guardians ad litem for abused children, termination of the parent–child legal relationship in severe maltreatment cases, multidisciplinary child-protection teams, and the international journal, *Child Abuse & Neglect* (Bross & Matthews, 2013).

- **Sexual Abuse**

In 1984, the Canadian Report of the Committee on Sexual Offences against Children and Youths (the Badgley Report) was released (Badgley, 1984). It revealed the prevalence of sexual offences against children and youths, the problems of juvenile prostitution, and the exploitation of young persons for pornographic purposes. It declared that child sexual abuse "is a largely hidden yet pervasive tragedy that has damaged the lives of tens of thousands of Canadian children and youths" (p. 1). The committee found that "about one in two females and one in three males have been victims of one or more unwanted sexual acts" and that "about four in five of these unwanted sexual acts had been first committed against these persons when they were children or youth" (Badgley, 1984, p. 2).

This resulted in legislation and policy changes. In 1988, changes were made to the Criminal Code and the Canada Evidence Act that "created new child sexual abuse offences and expanded the opportunities for courts to receive children's testimony in cases of child sexual abuse" (Wells, 1989, p. 3). Since the 1990s, the incidence of investigated and substantiated child sexual abuse has declined in Canada.

- **Intimate Partner Violence**

Intimate partner violence (IPV) (historically called "domestic violence" or "domestic abuse") and child maltreatment have traditionally been addressed in isolation by researchers and policymakers (Guedes & Mikton, 2013). Indeed, the link between family violence and child abuse was slow to emerge (Humphreys & Stanley, 2006). The women's movement played a pivotal role in highlighting this issue, and studies subsequent to Kempe's 1962 report have identified the effects of IPV on children (Black, 2009). Extensive empirical findings now indicate that the exposure of children to angry or violent outbursts between intimate partners can have negative effects on child development and well-being.

In 1982, following a "policy directive from the solicitor general, all provinces and territories moved to more active law enforcement in reports involving IPV by implementing mandatory charging (or per-charge) policies" (Black, 2009, p. 36). A 1997 report released by the Ontario Child Mortality Task Force made recommendations to include family violence in child protection legislation as a separate ground for protection.

In the 1990s, Saskatchewan was the first province in Canada to add exposure to IPV to the definition of child maltreatment (Black, 2009, p. 39). Many provinces (currently, Alberta, Manitoba, Newfoundland and Labrador, Northwest Territories, Nova Scotia, Nunavut, Prince Edward Island, Saskatchewan, and Yukon) have made laws in the area of family violence legislation. Other jurisdictions, such as British Columbia, have made family violence protection orders under the Family Law Act. In 2021, changes to Canada's Divorce Act included the impact of family violence when weighing the best interest of the child when deciding parenting orders.

Table 1.1: **Intimate Partner Violence (IPV) in Canada**

Prevalence • Number of people in Canada report experiencing intimate partner violence in the previous five years	• 750,000+
High-Risk Groups • Those groups in Canada who are at a higher risk for intimate partner violence	• Women • Gender and sexual minorities • Indigenous peoples • People with disabilities
Health Impacts • Impairments to health and well-being	• Mental health (e.g., depression, PTSD) • Physical health (e.g., chronic brain injury)
Economic Burden • Health and social services costs • Lost productivity and educational costs • Criminal and civil justice costs	• $7 billion

Taylor, G. (2016). *A Focus on Family Violence in Canada : the Chief Public Health Officer's Report on the State of Public Health in Canada.* Public Health Agency of Canada.

Guiding Principles in Child Protection Legislation and Policies

Using the best available evidence clearly helps policy decisions. However, the values and ideology of the decision makers also has a significant impact on policies and legislation (Brehaut & Juzwishin, 2005). Typical guiding principles in legislation and polices associated with child welfare include the "best interests of the child," "least intrusive measures," a "child-centred approach," and "risk reduction." These guiding principles are reviewed below.

- **The Best Interests of the Child**

The best interests of the child (BIC) principle is a child rights principle that derives from Article 3 of the United Nations Convention on the Rights of the Child. Today, the best interests of the child doctrine (as it is sometimes called) is seen throughout child welfare laws and is a paramount consideration when making decisions.

Anna Freud (the daughter of Sigmund Freud) was instrumental in developing a best-interests standard applicable to child protection. Favouring family autonomy against state intervention, Anna Freud and her colleagues highlighted the importance of child–parent attachment and continuity with parent(s), except in extreme cases that could be detrimental to the child's psychological well-being (Freud et al., 1979).

The best-interests principle is also apparent in Canadian family law and policy. Consider, for example, Bill C-78, a bill to amend the Divorce Act and other acts, which was given royal assent in 2019. Among other things, this bill amended the Divorce Act to maintain the best interests of the child as the only consideration for parenting decisions. In 2021, amendments to the Canada's Divorce Act set out the factors to consider when weighing the best interests of the child.

- **Least Intrusive Measures**

The least intrusive intervention model of child protection intervention provides for a testing of the need for state intervention into the family to ensure that the state is not unduly intruding on the private sphere of the family and violating family autonomy and integrity.

Ontario and Alberta were the first provinces to introduce this model of child protection in 1984. Nova Scotia followed in 1991, with the introduction of the Children and Family Services Act, which replaced the Children's Services Act (Luther, 2015). As Luther notes,

> the introduction of the least intrusive intervention standard marked a shift by the child welfare system to a more exacting, legalistic and rights-based approach to "child protection." (p. 317)

Less intrusive options in child welfare might include recommending such things as voluntary, preventive, and community child and family services or mandating services to the intact family prior to moving to more intrusive court proceedings and alternative care processes.

Individual vs. Structural Solutions

In addition to addressing individual needs, many child welfare advocates and practitioners argue for policies that address poverty and discrimination, since these are "structural" factors that can seriously jeopardize the well-being of individual families and children.

Inequalities based on gender, race, and length of time in the country can result in disproportionately high rates of child and family poverty. Along with putting stronger child protection measures in place, social policies are needed that address deep-rooted systemic barriers to the well-being of Canadian children and families.

- **A Child-Centred Approach**

During the 1980s and 1990s, there were a number of highly publicized scandals in the United States, the United Kingdom, and Canada in which social workers had left children in dangerous situations (Callahan & Swift, 2007, p. 160). This led to a legislative and policy shift to child-centred approaches to child protection.

Based on a children's rights perspective and the best-interests principle, placing the child at the centre of policy and service delivery is an axiom of good child protection practice. A child-centred approach involves respecting and seeking to understand the individuality and circumstances of the child and the family and ensuring that the child has a voice (Winkworth & Mcarthur, 2006).

In their review of the literature on child-centred practice, Winkworth & Mcarthur (2006) found four themes relevant to child-centred practice:

- Recognizing critical time frames in childhood and adolescence
- Taking into account the developmental needs of children and young people in all interventions
- Providing children and young people with appropriate opportunities to participate in decisions that affect them
- Promoting a collaborative approach to the care and protection of children, including the strengthening of networks that support their well-being

- **Risk Reduction**

Following the scandals of the 1980s and 1990s, comprehensive reviews of the child welfare system occurred (see, for example, "The Gove Inquiry in British Columbia" feature at the end of this chapter). Practice shifted from family service orientations to an emphasis on predicting "risk" of child harm in order to control that risk and avoid system culpability (Houston & Griffiths, 2000).

This context provided an impetus for the wide-ranging implementation of risk assessment tools in child welfare across Canadian jurisdictions. These tools were "supposed to predict difficulties and dangers in advance so that administrative steps could be taken to manage problems and reduce, deflect, or obviate the need for actual services" (Callahan & Swift, 2007, p. 160). Risk-oriented systems were based on a high threshold in which interventions only occur when a serious risk of harm to a child exists as compared to family-oriented services in which services to families are provided at a lower threshold in order to assist families improve their capacity (Skivenes & Sørsdal, 2018).

Risk assessment has always been used to identify whether a child is safe and, where maltreatment has occurred, the likelihood of recurrence. In the late 1990s, subjective judgments in child-protection decision making were replaced with more formal risk-assessment tools and measures. It was hoped that these measures would promote more reliable, more accurate, and less biased decision making (Hughes & Rycus, 2006). However, no gold standard tool has emerged, and today risk assessment is one component of, rather than the central focus of, an area of decision making that requires expertise and training.

Social Welfare in Perspective

Permanency and Family Preservation

Maintaining Family and Cultural Ties

Since the 1980s, child welfare policy has prioritized achieving "permanence" for children and youth involved with the child welfare system.

Permanency is a concept that suggests stability and is defined as "an enduring family relationship that is safe and meant to last a lifetime; offers the legal rights and social status of full family membership; the child or youth has a sense of belonging and affiliation to a family/extended family with significant community connections and provides for physical, emotional, social, cognitive, and spiritual well-being" (Ontario Association of Children's Aid Societies, n.d.).

Beginning in the 1970s, preserving the family and preventing an out-of-home placement for a child has become a favoured orientation. Two performance indicators to ensure accountability around the principle of permanency are the number of days a child spends in care and the amount of time before permanency is developed.

Preserving the Unit: "Good Enough" Parenting

A core decision for child protection workers is whether to leave a child with the parent or, if the child is removed, when to return the child safely. Ultimately, workers have to try and determine whether a parent is or is not good enough (Choate & Engstrom, 2014).

Good enough parenting is a child-centred approach. It recognizes that parenting does not fall into a neat binary of "good" or "bad." Social workers play a central role as a gatekeeper in deciding whether the parenting behaviours are not "good enough" and require substitute care (Taylor et al., 2009). While there is no clear line over which a parent is considered good enough, "good enough" parenting implies that parenting can be good enough to raise children who will become functional adults through a variety of parenting routes (Choate & Engstrom, 2014).

Kinship Care

Kinship care refers to a living arrangement in which a relative, community member, or another person who has a connection to a child or the parent takes primary responsibility for caring for and raising the child.

In most cases, kin is a family member with a biological connection. However, kin may be somebody who is considered to be family by the child, such as a godparent, friend, teacher, or neighbour.

Few evidence-based studies compare kinship care to other forms of foster care (Gough, 2006). However, this research suggests that kinship placements, when adequately resourced, are more stable and give children a stronger sense of belonging than regular foster care.

Sibling Relationships

The majority of children entering out-of-home care have siblings. Recent international research indicates that between 87% and 92% of children in out-of-home care have at least one biological sibling (Jones et al., 2019).

Placing siblings together has been found to aid resilience when children face adversity. Although there is some evidence that a child in care may present a risk to a sibling under some circumstances, this occurs in a very small number of cases and, typically, children in care emphasize the importance of maintain a sibling relationship (Jones et al., 2019).

The Signs of Safety (SoS) Approach

Initially developed by Andrew Turnell and Steve Edwards in Australia, the **Signs of Safety (SoS)** approach has been widely accepted as a strength-based, collaborative, and culturally safe child protection intervention strategy. SoS is a constructive approach to increasing safety and reducing risk by focusing on the family's strengths, resources, and support networks.

The SoS approach focuses on this question: "How can the worker build partnerships with parents and children in situations of suspected or substantiated child abuse and still deal rigorously with the maltreatment issues?" (Signs of Safety, 2019). It integrates professional knowledge with local family and cultural knowledge, and the focus is on ensuring success for all in the future (Signs of Safety, 2019).

SoS Risk Assessment

SoS risk assessment involves a conversation with the family about the safety of children using four domains of inquiry:

1. What are we worried about? (i.e., past harm statements, future danger statements, and complicating factors)
2. What is working well? (i.e., existing safety and strengths)
3. What needs to happen? (i.e., future safety goals)
4. Who will do what to build safety? (i.e., actions, tasks, and rules)

The case is assessed on a scale of 1 to 10, indicated at the bottom of the form. 10 means there is enough safety to close the case, and 0 means it is certain the child will be abused (Resolutions Consultancy, 2012), The conversation is recorded in a four-column form like the one below.

Signs of Safety Assessment and Planning Form

What are we worried about?	What's working well?	What needs to happen?	Who will do what to build safety?
• Harm statements • Danger statements • Complicating factors	• Existing safety • Strengths	• Agency safety goals • Family safety goals • Next steps	• Safety actions, tasks, rules

How worried are we?

A judgement about risk using the safety scale

0 ← — — — — — — — — — — — — — — — — — → **100%**

6.4 Measuring the Well-Being of Children in Care

In some cases, in order to provide care and protection to a child, the more intrusive decision of alternative care may occur — either temporarily or permanently. Alternative care may include kinship care, foster care, group care, legal custody, or adoption. Responsibility for the child's well-being while in out-of-home care rests with the child welfare authorities.

In Canada, national data on the number of children and youth placed in out-of-home care by child welfare authorities are not routinely collected. In 1992, the rate of children in out-of-home care was estimated at 5.5 per 1,000. In 2007, the rate increased and was estimated at 9.2 per 1,000 (or about 67,000 children in care on any given day). In 2013, the rate decreased slightly to an estimated 8.5 per 1,000 (Jones et al., 2015; Mulcahy & Trocmé, 2010).

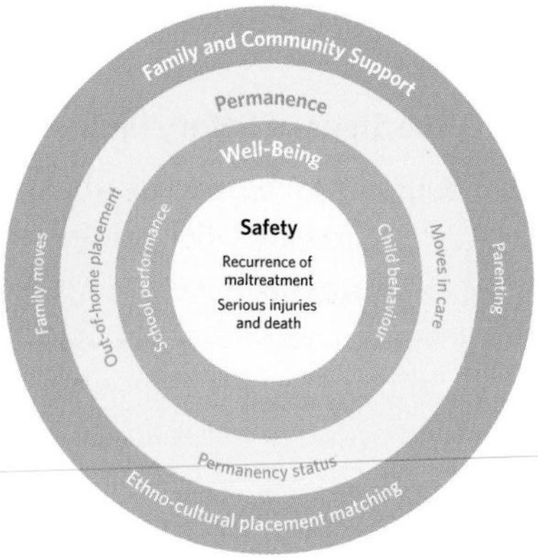

National Outcomes Matrix

Over 200,000 children and youth come into contact with child welfare authorities every year, and on any given day of the year, over 67,000 children and youth are living in out-of-home care. Nico Trocmé and his colleagues put forward an "outcomes matrix" that can be used by child welfare managers and policymakers to track trends and evaluate programs and policies (Trocmé et al., 2009).

The NOM framework consists of four nested domains that are key indicators: the child's safety, the child's well-being, permanence, and family and community support. The permanence indicator tracks a child's out-of-home placement(s) and the number of moves made by a child who is in out-of-home care.

Indicators of Well-Being

The goal of child protection policy is to promote the well-being of children and youth by providing health, safety, stability, and permanence. Many children in care have resilience to overcome the obstacles they face to live happy and healthy lives. However, children in care are known to have generally poorer outcomes than children who have never been in care (Kendall & Turpel-Lafond, 2007). Governments have a responsibility to assess their progress in improving the outcomes of children in care, and increasingly work is being conducted to establish baselines to measure this progress.

Three important social indicators (or performance indicators) of well-being are (1) health and mortality, (2) mental health, and (3) education.

- **Health and Mortality**

In a BC provincial study of the health of children in care between 1997 and 2005, it was found that children in continuing care were diagnosed with common health conditions at a rate of 1.2 to 1.4 times more often than children in the general population (Kendall & Turpel-Lafond, 2007). They were also prescribed medications much more often and for longer periods of time than children who had never been in care (1.3 to 1.9 times more often). Children in care were admitted to hospital mostly for the same reasons as children in the general population, but they were hospitalized 2 to 3.5 times more often, and generally for longer periods (p. 11). Young women in continuing care saw medical practitioners for pregnancy or birth-related issues more than four times as often as women who had never been in care.

The most extreme and adverse health indicator is mortality. Between 1986 and 2005, children in care died of natural causes at a rate more than four times the rate of children in the general population. As well, they died of external causes at more than three times the rate of children in the general population. "Between the ages of 19 and 25, young people who had been in care died at a rate 6.5 times higher than children in the general population" (Ministry of Health, 2006, p. 53)

- **Mental Health**

While mental health disorders are not a common diagnosis for children in the general population, approximately 65% of children in care in British Columbia are diagnosed with a mental health disorder. This is about four times the rate for children who have never been in care (Kendall & Turpel-Lafond, 2007, p. 11).

Children with a history of child abuse and neglect have a higher risk for suicidal ideation, self-harming behaviours, and suicide (Baiden & Fallon, 2018). Hadland et al. (2015) found that children with a history of abuse and neglect were three to four times more likely to have attempted suicide than children without this history. Moreover, in a Canadian study, Martin et al. (2016) found that as many as 80% of individuals who attempted suicide had a history of child abuse.

Although children who come into contact with the child welfare system often have serious mental health problems and are in need of mental health services, many do not receive these services when they need them (Baiden & Fallon, 2018). In their review of the Ontario Incidence Study of Reported Child Abuse and Neglect, Baiden and Fallon (2018) found that of the maltreated children who identified engaging in self-harming behaviour and suicidal thoughts, only 10% were referred to mental health services.

The data indicate that more research is needed to understand the lower rates of referral to mental health services for children in care. In the meantime, child welfare social workers should receive training to identify children in care who need mental health services, to recognize early mental health symptoms, and to know when children should be referred to mental health services. Attention should be placed on specialized training for practitioners and on improvements to income support measures, particularly for low-income families, to assist with accessing mental health services (Baiden & Fallon, 2018).

- **Education**

A study by the BC Representative for Children and Youth on educational outcomes found that "children and youth in continuing care have realized significantly lower academic achievement in the provincial K to 12 education system than their contemporaries, generally trailing well behind other students on most measures" (Representative for Children and Youth, 2017, p. 3).

For example, in the 2014–2015 year, only 34% of BC grade 7 students in continuing care met or exceeded expectations in numeracy, compared with 73% of children not in care (Representative for Children and Youth, 2017, p. 3). These results continued into grade 10, where 71% of children not in care received a C+ or better in science compared with 39.5% of students in care. Most glaring were the high school completion and graduation rates. "Of B.C. students in continuing care who began Grade 8 in 2009/10, only 51 percent graduated within six years. This compares to a nearly 89 percent graduation rate for all other students in the province" (Representative for Children and Youth, 2017, p. 3). These disparities were exacerbated when the student in continuing care was Indigenous or had special needs.

Youth Who Age Out of Care

Many young people simply "age out" of the children's care system. Aging out of care involves youth reaching a certain age and being expected to fend for themselves, often without a family support network and with limited or no financial resources. Lacking life skills, often having not completed high school, and suffering from emotional scars due to the trauma of childhood neglect or abuse, the life outcomes of adults who were children in care tend to be significantly worse compared with adults who grew up in forever families. In Ontario, an estimated 800 to 1,000 youth age out of care annually (Kovarikova, 2017). While this figure represents a high-risk group, only limited research exists about what happens to these young people and their well-being as adults.

In a research review, the Ontario Provincial Advocate for Children synthesized the data from selected academic and "grey literature" and conducted informal interviews with stakeholder organizations serving youth in care (Kovarikova, 2017). The typical outcomes for youth who age out of care are as follows:

- Low academic achievement
- Unemployment or underemployment
- Homelessness and housing insecurity
- Criminal justice system involvement
- Early parenthood
- Poor physical and mental health
- Loneliness

A systematic literature review of 32 original quantitative studies on youth who aged out of care found similar consistent but troubling results: "children who leave care continue to struggle in all areas (education, employment, income, housing, health, substance abuse and criminal involvement) compared to their peers from the general population" (Gypen et al., 2017, p. 74).

• Policy Implications

Much of the focus of programs for youth who age out of care has been on supporting independent living in relation to education, training, and financial needs. However, increasingly jurisdictions are extending the maximum age for government responsibility and providing greater mandatory supports for youth.

Ontario now has continuing care programs for youth leaving care, including financial supports as well as prescription drugs, dental, vision, and extended health for eligible youth. In some situations, youth may be eligible to receive counselling and life skills support up to the age of 29. Youths who need additional time to complete high school may be eligible to remain with their caregivers.

Post-secondary education support varies across the country. In Ontario, full tuition coverage for youth leaving care (if eligible) is provided, with additional support through student assistance. In British Columbia, all public post-secondary institutions waive tuition fees for former youth in care who are between 19 and 27.

• **Measuring the Well-Being of Adults Who Have Been Children in Care**

According to the Conference Board of Canada, youth who age out of foster care today will earn about $326,000 less income over their lifespan as compared with the average Canadian (Bounajm et al., 2014). Consequently, they will likely require a greater level of social assistance and pay less taxes over their lifespan as compared with their Canadian peers.

The Conference Board of Canada further estimates that "each former foster child, over his or her lifetime, will cost all levels of Canadian government more than $126,000 in the form of higher social assistance payments and lower tax revenues" (Bounajm et al., 2014, p. 2). Over a 10-year period, this represents about $7.5 billion, as a new cohort ages out of care each year.

Afifi et al. (2018) conducted a retrospective on the 2012 Canadian Community Health Survey — Mental Health data to determine whether adults who report exposure to child abuse had differing current mental health status based on their child protection services (CPS) contact. After controlling for demographic factors, the findings were that CPS contact was not associated with a statistically significant improvement for any mental disorder, any self-reported mental disorder, lifetime or past year suicidal ideation, lifetime or past year suicide plans, past year suicide attempts, positive functioning, emotional well-being, or current distress. However, those with CPS contact were more likely to report lifetime suicide attempts.

Figure 6.1

High School Graduations: Youth in Care Compared with General Population, Ontario

Kovarikova, J. (2017). Exploring youth outcomes after aging out of care. Office of the Provincial Advocate for Children and Youth.

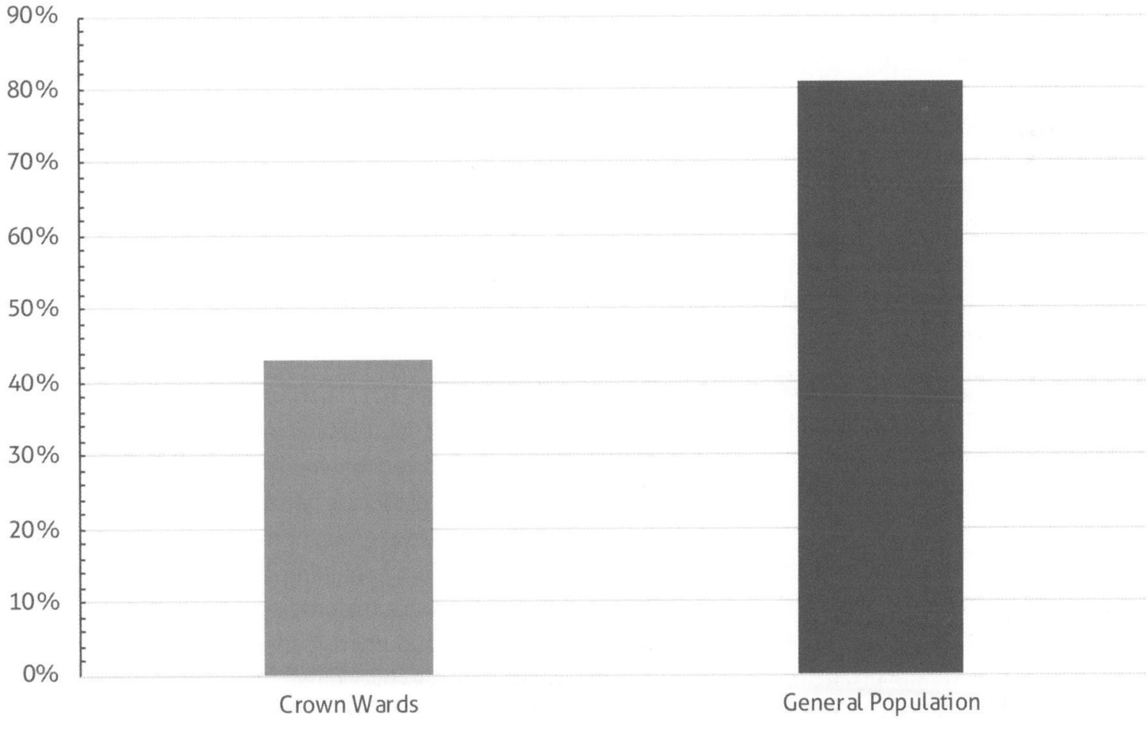

What the COVID–19 pandemic has revealed ...

Child Welfare during COVID–19

Children's Well-Being Is at Risk of Being Compromised

In order to protect Canadian children and families who are most at risk, child advocacy and child protection–specific programming are the keys to an effective child-centred response to COVID–19.

For more than a decade, Canada has had an increasingly dismal record for protecting its children. Based on UNICEF data on 38 affluent nations, Canada has dropped from twelfth place in 2007 to thirtieth in 2019 (Children First Canada, 2020). Poverty remains a persistent threat to the well-being of 20% of children, and one-third of Canadians report experiencing abuse before the age of 15.

Children who are Black or Indigenous face systemic racism that affects their lives even more starkly due to their disproportionate likelihood of experiencing poverty and exclusion.

COVID–19 — Heightened Risks to Childhood

Worldwide, policies associated with the controlling the pandemic, particularly lockdown policies, have raised concerns about children's well-being and the increasing levels of child maltreatment.

In addition to the health risks of COVID–19, young children are affected by the public health restrictions in response to the pandemic. School closures interrupt learning and decrease human interaction for all children, and the elimination of school nutrition programs and psycho-social and behavioural programs disadvantage children who are vulnerable.

The full effects of COVID–19 will become clearer over time, but early indicators suggest that young people are also experiencing a decline in their mental health. In addition to the anxiety caused by the virus itself, the pandemic has had a major financial impact on families, with almost one in seven experiencing food insecurity during the early phases of the pandemic. In addition, half of Canadian adults of Chinese ethnicity have reported discrimination and unpleasant encounters (Children First Canada, 2020).

Child Maltreatment Risks

The public health measures needed to control the coronavirus exacerbated risks of child maltreatment. For example, educators play an important role in reporting alleged child abuse and neglect (about 24% according to CIS-2008), but during COVID–19 times, reports were less frequent because daycares and schools were closed (De Cao & Sandner, 2020).

Likewise, the economic hardship related to COVID–19 is likely a contributing risk factor to maltreatment (De Cao & Sandner, 2020; Frioux et al, 2014). In a non–COVID-19 study of unemployment on child maltreatment, it was found that "a one percentage point increase in the unemployment rate leads to a 20% increase in neglect" (Lindo et al. as cited in DeCao and Sandner, 2020).

In addition, the social distancing measures that were introduced to control the virus compelled children to spend most of their time at home with their parents, who themselves are often the main perpetrators (94% of child maltreatment substantiation, according to CIS-2008, is by the biological mother or father).

Residential Treatment Facilities and Group Homes

It is also important to remember that many children live in group homes, residential facilities, and foster care. Based on 2017/18 data, there were also 792 incarcerated youth (Malakieh, 2019). In May 2020, Ontario reported that four children living in group homes and foster care had tested positive, as had eight staff members at group homes and youth detention facilities. A former children and youth advocate for Ontario said that the province should be testing all children and youth residential facilities: "We need to know how the children are doing. And we need to know that they're safe" (Browne, 2020).

Vulnerability Due to Socio-Economic Exclusion

Pandemics like COVID–19 change the context in which children and families live. The stressors associated with quarantines and school closures are felt by all children, but especially by families who are vulnerable due to their Indigeneity, race, gender identity, and socio-economic exclusion.

Using a socio-ecological framework, the Alliance for Child Protection in Humanitarian Action has grouped the risk and protective factors associated with COVID–19 (see chart below). These factors include limited access to basic services, reduced access to community supports, family breakdown and caregiver distress, disrupted family connections, fear of the disease itself, and stigma toward certain ethnic groups.

Child Welfare System Response

Going forward, Sistovaris et al. (2020) recommend child-specific interventions and strategies that

> allow for and encourage increased coordination across all sectors that involve children in care; build on the strengths and positive coping mechanisms of communities, families, caregivers and children; address the challenges of highly vulnerable populations such as youth in residential care; and provide for the required resources and supports to function not only during an epidemic but also in pre- and post-pandemic environments. (p. viii)

Child welfare programs and initiatives along these lines will be critical to protecting children and families at this time, especially children who are most at risk.

The Ecological Impact of COVID–19 on Children and Families

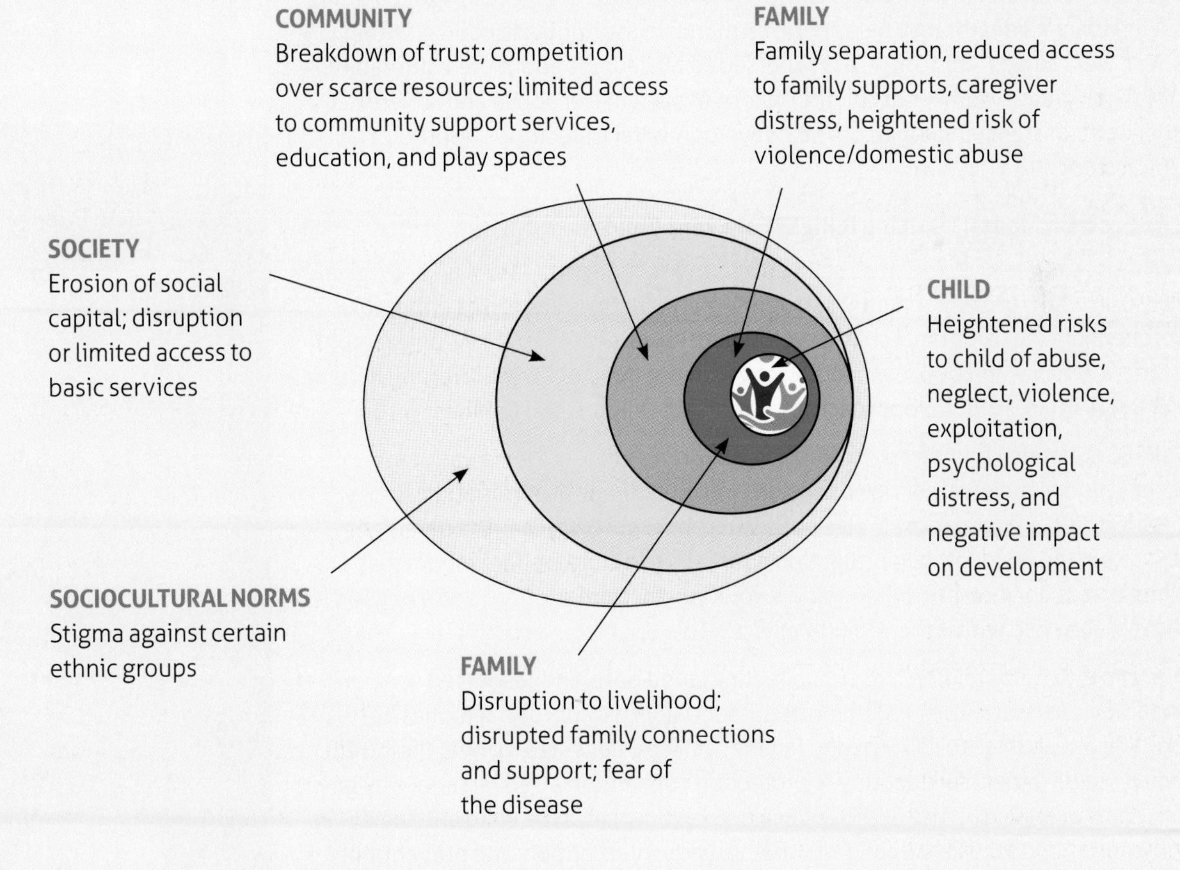

Alliance for Child Protection in Humanitarian Action (2019).

6.5 Modernizing Child Welfare Policy

According to Hyslop (2017), since the 1970s, the child welfare mandate has become synonymous with a residual approach centred on a child protection brief. This approach makes invisible the inequalities that are frequently "inscribed within the lives of those who come to the attention of child protection systems" (p. 1802). This is particularly evident in the interrelationship between poverty and child neglect — the proverbial elephant in the child-protection room (Gupta, 2017).

Neoliberal Influences

At the same time, social work has increasingly become subject to managerial oversight and to demands for evidence that it is effective at reducing client pathology in a cost-effective way. Increasingly, child protection is required to be dispassionate, clinical, and risk averse rather than engaged with the socio-economic struggles of impoverished families (Hyslop, 2017). This is in contrast with a social investment approach that seeks to develop children's capacity.

Child protection has become, arguably, a public issue of our time. For example, the public intolerance for the deaths of children in which professionals are involved has led to the development of forensic techniques and defensively oriented bureaucratic systems to manage risks to children (Spratt et al.,2015). While finding blame for child deaths may be a recurring theme in the public discourse, within social work circles "this concern is superseded by debates about the vulnerability of a much greater number of children whose experience of abuse and adverse social circumstances impinge on their developmental trajectories" (Spratt et al., 2015, p. 1509).

The Scottish Model: "Getting It Right For Every Child"

From a social work perspective, child protection is understood from an ecological sense, in which the environment surrounding childhood is viewed as either toxic to, or enhancing of, optimal child development (Spratt et al., 2015). As an example of this approach, in 2006, the Scottish government developed the "Getting It Right For Every Child" (GIRFEC) approach to supporting children and families.

GIRFEC is a policy framework "to improve children's well-being via early intervention, universal service provision, and multiagency coordination across organizational boundaries" (Coles et al., 2016, p. 334). It represents a paradigm shift from the residual child protection approach to a child welfare model that emphasizes universality, collaboration, solution-focused support, and a holistic view of the child within the wider family.

The aim is to help children to grow up feeling loved, safe, and respected so that they can realize their full potential. Essentially, this approach emphasizes providing resources to children and families at an earlier stage to meet their well-being needs rather than reacting to protection concerns in an adversarial way later on (Coles et al., 2016). The GIRFEC policy framework places the child and family "at the centre" and focuses on child well-being, early intervention, and prevention.

Moving from a Residual Approach to a Universal Model

Over the years, child welfare policy has tended to swing from being highly interventionist and focused on risk protection to less intrusive and focused on preserving and strengthening families. These shifts in policy orientation have resulted in different spending levels, variations in the number of children and families in the child welfare system, and diverse opinions on where the optimal balance lies in protecting children and supporting families (Commission to Promote Sustainable Child Welfare, 2012).

Today, child welfare is once again increasingly moving away from a residual approach to an early intervention approach focused on improving the well-being of all children through universal public services (Coles et al., 2016). In contrast to the adversarial and investigatory response to child protection, a **universal child welfare model** emphasizes child and family service provision and support-based principles. The aim is to support families by making sure children and young people receive the right help, at the right time, from the right people.

This reorientation represents a "child-focused" view that sees "children as active agents, individuals with intrinsic rights, whose lives should be considered holistically, thus requiring broader, more comprehensive policy responses to address the wider social context that affects their lives" (Coles et al., 2016, p. 341). It acknowledges the high rates of child poverty and fragmented, uncoordinated services. It also acknowledges the need to support children's and parents' rights and the overall well-being of children (Coles et al., 2016).

Emerging Policy Themes: Investing in Children's Well-Being

Shifting from a residual, reactive, parent-blaming child protection system to a universal child welfare model focused on children's short- and long-term well-being is not simple. However, Canada can draw on research evidence, particularly from European models that have adopted social investment models of child welfare for quite some time.

- **Commonalities across Child Protection Systems**

Spratt et al. (2015) undertook a comparison of child protection practices across five countries (Finland, the United Kingdom, Sweden, Germany, and Australia) in order to recommend improvements to the Swiss child protection system. They found that the "lessons to be learnt from these comparator countries, both positive and negative, are remarkably consistent and coherent" (p. 1523).

Based on their comparative research, the authors identified three common drivers in the development of child protection systems:

- **Epidemiological Evidence on the Prevalence and Effects of Child Abuse.** Evidence as to the prevalence, distribution, and lifelong effects of child abuse leads to a better understanding of child abuse and more effective ways to deal with it.
- **The Need for Early Investment in Children.** In line with a social investment approach, children are considered primary targets for strategies to improve the global competitiveness of countries. Children who have experienced child abuse are more likely to experience poor economic outcomes. Therefore, early intervention and investment in children are viewed as helping prevent such outcomes.
- **International Performance in Relation to Child Well-Being.** It is important to have international data that compare the performance of countries in relation to child protection. International bodies that chart the progress of countries in relation to child well-being include the United Nations (in relation to the UN Convention on the Rights of the Child), UNICEF, and the WHO. As Spratt et al. (2015) note: "international league tables make governments sensitive to possible criticism as their policies and practices may be interpreted negatively. In turn, this creates a moral imperative to demonstrably improve child protection policies and practices for children" (p. 1513).

Spratt et al. (2015) found that the aims of the countries studied converged:

> The five countries essentially share an ideology predicated on the central idea that early interventions to help children before problems become too acute should be promoted. There is also, however, a requirement for a system to protect children from serious abuse in situations where their parents are unable or unwilling to provide such protection.

An optimal child protection system therefore is one that includes support for families designed to prevent poor outcomes for children at risk alongside legally mandated interventions for those children with immediate need for protection (Spratt et al., p. 1520).

Engaging with Individuals and Families

A strengths-based approach to working with families and children is a powerful practice model.

Strengths-based practice involves a shift from a "deficit" approach, which emphasizes problems and pathology, to a positive partnership with the family.

This approach to working with families and children acknowledges each child and family has a unique set of strengths and challenges. It engages the family as a partner in developing and implementing a service plan that works for them.

Themes That Underlie Modern Child Protection Systems

In their research, Spratt et al. (2015) identified six themes, summarized here, that shape modern child protection systems:

- **Theme 1.** Children require protection because of societal changes that make their needs visible and the requirement for services necessary. The causes of child maltreatment "are primarily located in societal or global changes and not generally, within the family" (p. 1518).
- **Theme 2.** Children require protection from parents who abuse their children. Physical abuse is the most visible form of child abuse and as such frequently drives the procedural infrastructure of child protection systems. Recognizing that physical abuse is an act of commission, systems default to assessment of risk, policing of parents, and individualistic interventions with victims and perpetrators as a response.
- **Theme 3.** Children who require protection frequently live within families that need resources. Child maltreatment and neglect are associated with structural inequalities, particularly poverty. From this perspective, interventions must address the cause (through poverty-reduction strategies) and the effect (through the amelioration of stressors) and involve a wide range of policies and professional interventions.
- **Theme 4.** The protection of children can be conceptualized within an ecological model wherein a wider range of harms and protective factors are located across the concentric and interlocking influences of family, community, and society. An ecological approach promotes a nuanced and universal set of protective interventions for children, as risks are located across a wider range of dimensions, not just within the family.
- **Theme 5.** The UNCRC legislation represents the rights of children as separate and sometimes different from the rights of their parents. This has led to the promotion of children's active agency in decisions involving them. Focusing on the rights of the child shifts the perspective from looking at children as primarily objects in need of protection to competent subjects entitled to such protection.
- **Theme 6.** The protection of children is best effected early, rather than late. Using a public health model, children who are most at risk of suffering child abuse are identified at the earliest stages for evidence-informed interventions.

Social Welfare Policy in Action

Child Welfare in the Twenty-First Century

Ontario's Child, Youth and Family Services Act

Ontario's most recent legislation aims to provide more prevention services, be more inclusive to children's and youth's voices, and be more equitable to uniqueness.

Ontario's Child, Youth and Family Services Act

In 2017, Ontario modernized the legislation for child and youth services with a new law called the Child, Youth and Family Services Act (CYFSA). The CYSFA came into force on April 30, 2018.

Highlights of the CYSFA include:

- The rights of youth to participate in decision about them
- A rise in the age of protection from 16 to 18
- Recognition that race, culture, heritage, religion, sexual orientation, and gender identity should be reflected in decisions, services, and supports for the child and family
- Recognition of culture and connections for First Nations, Inuit, and Métis in social services
- Strengthening of the focus on early intervention, helping prevent children and families from reaching crisis situations at home
- Improving oversight of service providers so that children and youth receive consistent, high-quality services across Ontario (Ontario Ministry of Children, Community and Social Services, n.d.).

The guiding principles of the CYSFA are youth-centred protection; least-disruptive approach; permanency; connection to kin, community, and culture; culturally appropriate services for Indigenous youth; and diversity (Ontario Ministry of Children, Community and Social Services, 2018).

Ontario Association of Children's Aid Societies Strategic Plan: 2018–2023

In Ontario, child protection services are governed by the Child, Youth and Family Services Act and provided by Children's Aid Societies. There are 49 independent, non-profit Children's Aid Societies across Ontario, including 11 Indigenous societies (Ontario Ministry of Children, Community and Social Services, 2019). The Ontario Association of Children's Aid Societies (OACAS) is a collective member agency that works closely with government and provides advocacy to provide optimal services to Ontario's children and families (OACAS, 2018b).

In 2018, a strategic plan was developed that set the direction for the child welfare sector in Ontario until 2023. This plan was developed after "an extensive stakeholder engagement process of 1,800 participants through numerous provincial meetings, key informant interview, focus groups, and online survey" (para. 1).

- **Provincial Goals of the OACAS Operational Plan**

Each year, the OACAS develops an operational plan to guide the work toward the larger strategic plan. The provincial goals of the OACAS 2018–2019 operational plan were as follows:

1. A child welfare system that is transparent, responsive and accountable to service users and community partners
2. A child welfare system that effectively advocates for strengthened social supports and resources for families facing challenges
3. A child welfare system with the capacity to use legislative, regulatory, and standards requirements and child welfare tools and technology to improve services to children, youth, and families
4. A child welfare system that addresses disproportionality and disparity and achieves equitable outcomes by providing culturally appropriate services

5. A highly skilled child welfare workforce, leadership, and governance representing the diversity of people in Ontario that provides the highest quality of service, decision making, and oversight of the child welfare system
6. A provincial awareness campaign to strengthen awareness of the child welfare sector's work
7. A child welfare system that returns the child protection mandate to Indigenous communities to address the historical injustices perpetrated by the federal and provincial government and provincial child welfare system
8. Child welfare practices that are evidence-informed, responsive, and culturally appropriate to increase safety, well-being, and permanence for children and youth (OACAS, 2018a, p. 9)

Culturally Responsive Service Delivery

Ultimately, legislation and policy that include long-term strategic plans and short-term operational plans guide the child welfare service delivery system. Based on a commitment to continuous improvement, the operational plan outlines processes to support the path to reconciliation between child welfare and Indigenous communities in Ontario. For example, it will continue to support the Association of Native Child and Family Service Agencies of Ontario (ANCFSAO) as it develops its capacity as the voice for Indigenous child welfare.

In addition, the OACAS has committed to support agencies to implement the 11 race equity practices outlined in the One Vision One Voice Practice Framework to support better outcomes for Black children and youth.

The OACAS is also committed to ongoing education and training known as the Ontario Practice Model. Registration with the Ontario College of Social Workers, a key element of public accountability, is required for local directors of Children's Aid Societies as of January 2019. However, the College has expressed concerns that the new legislation does not require the registration of child protection workers, which ignores the public protection mandate of the Social Work and Social Service Act, 1998.

Questions for Reflection

The Child, Youth and Family Services Act (CYFSA) and the regulations under this Act are available here: https://www.ontario.ca/laws/statute/17c14. Once you have reviewed the legislation and regulations, and the OACAS strategic plan consider the following questions:

1. The CYFSA has increased the age of protection to 18 years. Is that inclusive? Why or why not?
2. The CYFSA highlights culturally appropriate services for Indigenous children and youth. Black Canadian children are also overrepresented in Ontario's child welfare system. What aspects of the legislation respond to this known social indicator?
3. The CYFSA aims to strengthen the focus on early intervention. Is this the same as having a universal well-being focus?
4. Children who have been in government care have notoriously low outcomes in health, mental health, and educational attainment. As you look at the legislation and policies, what responsibilities are embedded in it to ensure better outcomes for children in care?
5. What accountability processes are identified in the Act or regulations to ensure the CYFSA meets its goals?
6. How does the OACAS strategic plan incorporate principles of inclusion, equity, and social justice?
7. Does the OACAS strategic plan address the racial inequities present in Ontario?
8. How does the OACAS strategic plan consider underlying structural issues such as unemployment, housing, and food insecurity?

A Moment in Time: July 5, 1992

The Gove Inquiry in British Columbia

A Child's Tragic Death Leads to a Provincial Inquiry

Child services were involved in Matthew Vaudreuil's life from birth to his death before age six. However, the system failed him dramatically.

Child Welfare System Failure

During Matthew's short life, there had been 21 social workers responsible for providing him services and at least 60 reports about his safety and well-being. He had been taken to the doctor 75 times and seen by 24 different physicians (Gove, 1995). In 1992, Matthew died of asphyxia when he was five years and nine months old. His mother was convicted of manslaughter and sentenced to 10 years, later reduced to four years on appeal.

In 1994, following Matthew's death, the Government of British Columbia appointed Judge Thomas Gove to conduct an inquiry into and make recommendations about the services, policy, and practices of the BC Ministry of Social Services (Armitage & Murray, 2007). The Gove Inquiry's report was released in November 1995.

The Inquiry's 118 Recommendations

Judge Gove made 118 recommendations in his report. Some were implemented, while others were not (or at least not in the way Gove envisioned). One recommendation that was implemented was to amend the legislation to clarify that "the safety and well-being of the child was paramount in the administration and interpretation of the act" (Armitage & Murray, 2007, p. 144).

In 1996, a new Ministry for Children and Families was established in response to the Gove Inquiry (recommendations 95 to 108). It brought together the following areas of child and family services that had been previously spread among five ministries:

- Child protection, child and family support services, services to children with developmental delays (from the former Ministry of Social Services)
- Youth corrections (from the Ministry of the Attorney General)
- Child mental health and substance use programs, services for children with disabilities, and financial responsibility for child-related public health services (from the Ministry of Health)
- School for the deaf and school-based social programs (from the Ministry of Education)
- Child care (from the Ministry of Women's Equality) (Armitage & Murray, 2007, p. 146).

Risk assessment became the focus of the new ministry, which led to an increase in the number of children in care.

Chapter Review

Questions

1. What are the relative merits and drawbacks of having children's rights as the underlying principle of Canadian child protection systems?
2. Review the child protection legislation in your province or territory. What aspects are consistent with social work values? Which areas could be modified? What would your recommendations for change be?
3. What is being done in your region, province, or territory to ensure that the needs of children affected by the opioid crisis are being met?
4. Review the most recent Canadian Incidence Study of Reported Child Abuse and Neglect (CIS). What changes are occurring to reporting over time?
5. Some socio-economic and racialized populations are overrepresented in child welfare investigations. What approaches could be taken to reduce this disproportionality?
6. How is your region, province, or territory responding to the Truth and Reconciliation of Canada Calls to Action and to Bill C-92 pertaining to child welfare?
7. In Canada, child protection systems follow a predominantly residual approach that focuses on child protection rather than child well-being. Some European countries have adopted a universal child welfare model. How could this model be adapted to your province or territory?

Exploring Social Welfare

1. Read a recent news item concerning child maltreatment. Describe the social discourse that frames the discussion.
2. The Scottish model of child welfare (Getting It Right For Every Child) was introduced in this chapter. Research this model and compare its focus to the focus of child protection legislation and policy in your province or territory.

Websites

Canadian Child Welfare Research Portal (CWRP)
www.cwrp.ca
The Canadian Child Welfare Research Portal provides single-point access to up-to-date research on child welfare programs and policies. The portal includes a searchable database of Canadian research publications.

First Nations Child and Family Caring Society
www.fncaringsociety.com
The First Nations Child and Family Caring Society works to ensure the safety and well-being of First Nations youth and their families through education initiatives, public policy campaigns, and the provision of quality resources to support communities.

Inuit Tapiriit Kanatami (ITK)
www.itk.ca
Inuit Tapiriit Kanatami (ITK) is the national representational organization protecting and advancing the rights and interests of Inuit in Canada. Through engagement sessions and research, ITK has developed a series of priorities for child protection and has taken part in the dialogue on Bill C-92.

Métis National Council
www.metisnation.ca
The Métis National Council represents the Métis Nation nationally and internationally. In spring 2018, work began on an action plan to respond to the social and economic situation of Métis children and youth in the child welfare systems of the five western-most provinces. As of publication, this action plan had not been published.

Ontario Black History Society (OBHS)
www.blackhistorysociety.ca
The Ontario Black History Society (OBHS) was created to study, preserve and promote Black history to address the absence of Black Canadian educational/historical material.

Social Welfare and Mental Well-Being in Canada

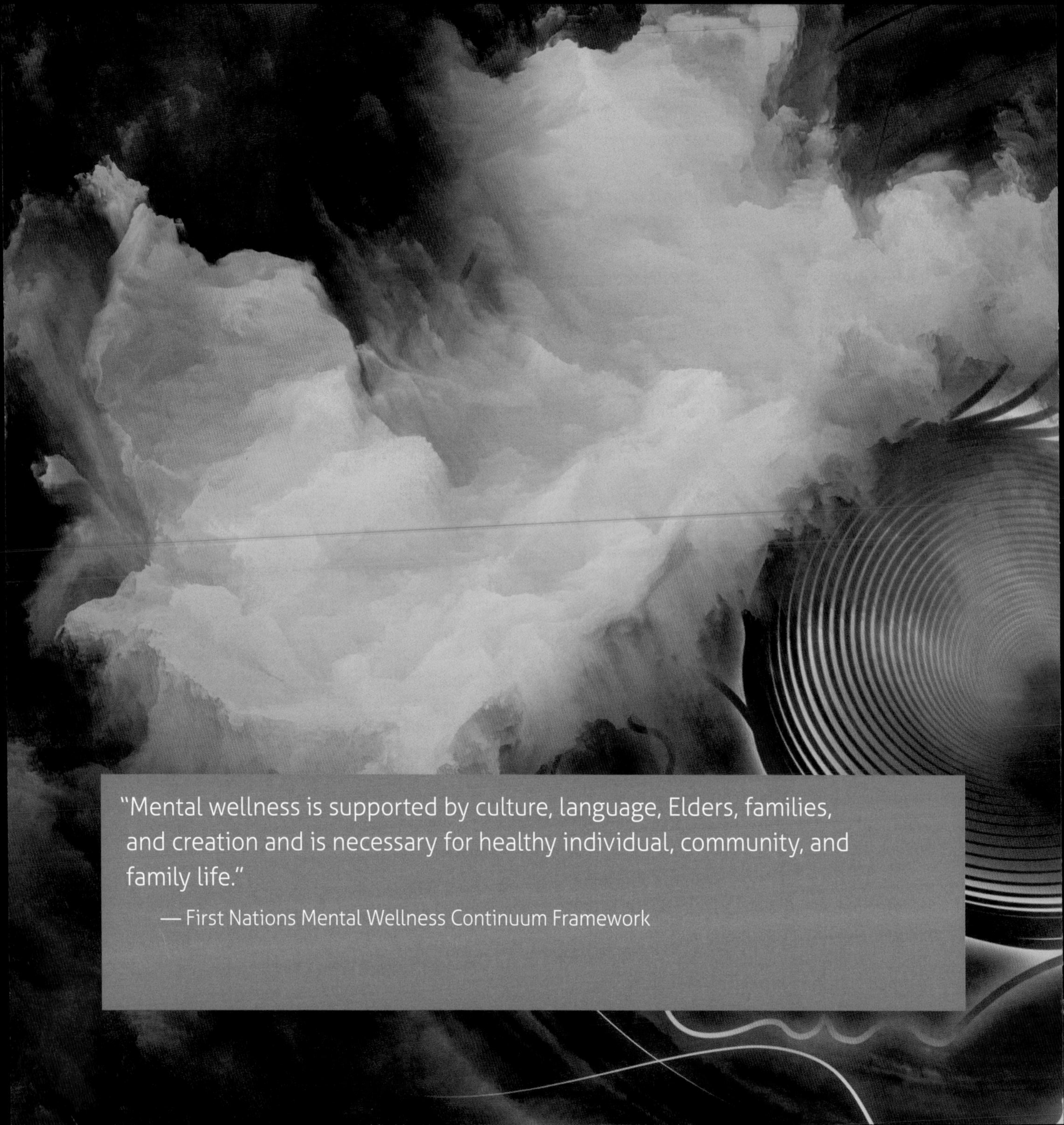

"Mental wellness is supported by culture, language, Elders, families, and creation and is necessary for healthy individual, community, and family life."

— First Nations Mental Wellness Continuum Framework

Mary Holliday Bartram

No More "Us" and "Them"

7

The COVID–19 pandemic has led to a perfect storm for mental health and substance use concerns.

Mental health and substance use have emerged as top policy priorities for Canadian governments at all levels over the past decade. Youth advocates in particular have pressed for more initiatives directed against stigma and for improved access to services in schools and the community. After 2020, the uncertainties resulting from the COVID–19 pandemic, especially for vulnerable individuals and communities, underscored the urgent need to expand health funding and include improved mental health services.

In 2012, the Mental Health Commission of Canada released the first Mental Health Strategy for Canada. Unlike most other industrialized countries, Canada had never previously developed a national mental health strategy. This was due to many factors that also confront the substance use sector, including a highly diverse group of stakeholders and a federalist system where primary responsibility for health care resides with the provinces and territories. Then, in 2017–2018, the federal budget confirmed that $5 billion would be transferred to provincial and territorial governments over the next 10 years to improve access to mental health and substance use services.

No More "Us" and "Them"

Canada's mental health strategy and the $5 billion in funding are historic. Still, an estimated additional $3.1 billion in mental health and substance use funding is needed. This chapter looks at mental health and substance use policy formation in the Canadian context.

After completing this chapter, you should be able to:

- Assess the importance of mental well-being for individual citizens and Canadian society at large;
- Apply core concepts such as mental health, mental illness, substance use, recovery, and harm reduction to the analysis of policy issues;
- Understand the evolution of Canadian mental health and substance use policy and the major issues that continue to face policymakers;
- Explain the ideas underlying the recovery and harm reduction models and the kinds of policy initiatives that derive from this approach;
- Understand the existing funding gaps and the inequalities in accessing mental health and substance use services; and
- Evaluate and communicate options for addressing mental health and substance use policy problems.

Key Concepts

- Mental health / illness
- Substance use
- Asylums
- Disease model
- Deinstitutionalization
- Alcoholics Anonymous
- Holistic care
- National Inuit Suicide Prevention Strategy
- Paradigm shift toward recovery and well-being
- Shared Indigenous understandings of wellness
- Stigma and discrimination
- Mental Health Strategy for Canada
- Integrated conceptual model
- Harm reduction
- Supervised consumption sites
- Housing First
- Opioid crisis
- Performance indicators for mental health and substance use and for home care

7.1 The Impact of Mental Health, Mental Illness, and Substance Use

Mental health has a positive impact on social well-being. Mental health in this positive sense may also be called positive mental health or flourishing and is not the same thing as the absence of mental illness. As defined by the Public Health Agency of Canada (PHAC) (2015), **mental health** is "the capacity of each and all of us to feel, think, act in ways that enhance our ability to enjoy life and deal with the challenges we face. It is a positive sense of emotional and spiritual well-being that respects the importance of culture, equity, social justice, interconnections and personal dignity." In moderation, substance use is not a problem in and of itself but rather part of a mentally healthy lifestyle for many Canadian adults.

Mental health and mental illness are not mutually exclusive. People living with a mental illness or substance use disorder can have excellent mental health, and people can languish even without a mental illness or substance use disorder.

Mental illnesses are characterized by changes in how we think, feel, and behave that are associated with significant distress and interfere with our ability to function at school, work, and home (PHAC, 2015). Examples of mental illnesses include mood disorders such as depression, anxiety and bipolar disorder; schizophrenia; and substance use disorders. Sometimes mental illness and substance use disorders can bring about profound feelings of hopelessness and worthlessness that can lead to thoughts of suicide.

Most social policies have a strong relationship to mental health, mental illness, and substance use disorders. For example, policies regarding income, housing, employment, child welfare, health services, and the criminalization of drug use have a strong influence on our ability to flourish, as well as on our risk of developing a mental illness or substance use disorder.

Prevalence of Mental Health, Mental Illness, and Substance Use

According to Statistics Canada, four out of every five Canadians report that they are flourishing, with high levels of emotional well-being and positive functioning in their everyday lives and excellent mental health (Gilmour, 2014). **Substance use** is also very common, with 78% of Canadians over the age of 15 reporting drinking alcohol and 15% reporting use of cannabis (Statistics Canada, 2018).

Despite this overall well-being and commonplace substance use, mental illnesses and substance use disorders are widespread. One in five Canadians report a mental illness or substance use disorder in any given year, with mood and anxiety disorders being the most common, followed by substance use disorders, dementia, and schizophrenia (Mental Health Commission of Canada, 2017). Mental illness and substance use disorders are often concurrent, with up to a third of people who have one also having the other, and also comorbid with chronic physical illnesses (Khan, 2017). Suicide is closely linked, with nine out of ten Canadians who die by suicide having a diagnosed mental illness or substance use disorder (Arsenault-Lapierre et al., 2004).

The Costs to Society

As communicable diseases have declined over recent decades, mental illness and substance disorders have taken on a larger share of the global burden of disease. The 2017 Global Burden of Disease found that mental disorders and substance use disorders made up 23% of years lived with disability compared with 18% in 1990. Depression on its own makes up 5% of years lived with disability globally compared with 4.5% for diabetes and 4.2% for cardiovascular disease (Institute for Health Metrics and Evaluation, 2018).

Given such high prevalence, it is not surprising that the economic impact of mental illness and substance use disorders is estimated to be well over $50 billion per year (Mental Health Commission of Canada, 2017). Direct health and social service provision makes up a large part of these costs. However, so do costs arising from people not being able to work to the best of their ability.

People living with mental health and substance use problems are contributing and productive members of society. Nevertheless, the impact of mental health and substance use problems on employment and productivity is significant.

According to the OECD, employment rates are 10–15 percentage points lower for people with moderate mental disorders and 30 percentage points lower for people with severe mental disorders (OECD, 2012). Mental illness is also associated with higher rates of days off work (absenteeism) and being less productive at work (presenteeism). For example, 69% of people with moderate mental illnesses report reduced productivity at work because of emotional or physical health problems, compared to 26% of people with no mental illness.

In Canada, mental illnesses account for approximately 30% of disability claims and are rated one of the top three drivers of such claims by more than 80% of Canadian employers (Mental Health Commission of Canada, 2013). These productivity impacts result in lost revenue for employers, loss of tax revenue for governments, and direct costs for income support programs and disability claims.

There are also significant costs to society when family members take time away from work to care for loved ones who are living with mental health and substance use problems, particularly as such problems can be both chronic and unpredictable. In 2006, caregiver costs were estimated to be $3.9 billion per year in Canada (Lim et al., 2010).

The impact of mental health and substance use problems are also felt across other sectors such as education and corrections. The costs to the criminal justice system from substance use more broadly has been estimated at more than $9 billion per year (Canadian Institute for Substance Use Research, 2018).

It is also important to recognize the costs to society not just of having a mental illness or substance use disorder, but of experiencing anything less than optimal mental health. Even when compared to people with moderate mental health, people who are flourishing have been found to have the less absenteeism and lower rates of chronic disease (Keyes, 2007).

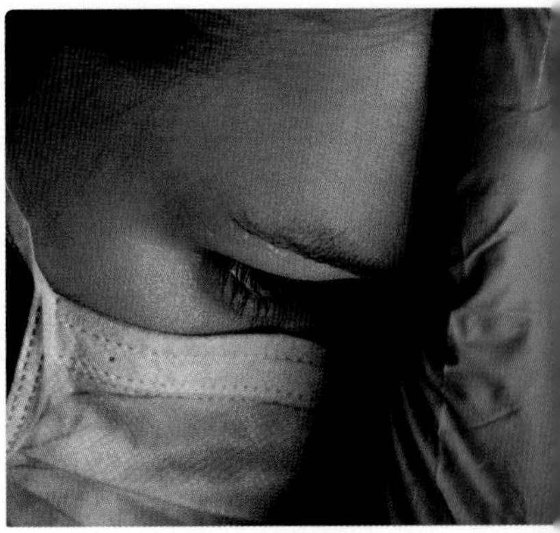

COVID–19 and the Mental Health of Canadians

Social isolation. Financial uncertainty. Health anxiety. Living through a pandemic has increased mental health challenges for many and exacerbated the conditions of those already struggling with their mental health.

Many Canadians have seen their stress levels double since the onset of the pandemic. A Nanos survey of 1,003 Canadians, commissioned by *CTV News* in the early fall of 2020, found that two in five Canadians said that their mental health was worse than before the pandemic. The survey also found that Canadians reported a 20% increase in alcohol consumption compared to before the pandemic.

Who Is Affected

There is considerable variation in mental illness and substance use disorders across the population. The highest rate is among young adults aged 20 to 29, a time when young people are beginning post-secondary education and careers. Women have higher rates of depression, anxiety, and suicide attempts, and men have higher rates of substance use disorders and death by suicide (Mental Health Commission of Canada, 2017). There is also variation by ethnicity, such as higher rates of mood and anxiety disorders among Chinese, South Asian, and Black Canadians than white Canadians (Chiu et al., 2018). Rates of mental illnesses other than substance use disorders follow a clear income gradient, from the highest rates at the lowest income levels to the lowest rates at the highest income levels.

Such differences are best viewed through an intersectional lens, which is a framework for understanding how multiple social identities such as race, gender, sexual orientation, socio-economic status, and disability intersect at the micro level of individual experience to reflect interlocking systems of privilege and oppression at the macro social-structural level (Bowleg, 2012).

For example, higher rates of mental illnesses among lesbian, gay, bisexual, and trans populations have been linked to discrimination, but also vary according to individual intersecting identities. Intergenerational trauma from colonial policies such as residential schools and forced relocation is considered a root cause of mental illness, suicide, and substance use disorder among First Nations, Inuit, and Métis peoples. At the same time, suicide rates have been found to vary across communities depending on factors such as self-governance and culture (Chandler & Lalonde, 1998).

Lack of Access to Services

Access to mental health and substance use services in Canada is characterized by long-standing gaps and inequities. Just under half of Canadians who have mental health or substance use disorders report that they have not accessed professional help, with the largest gap for people with substance use disorders (Statistics Canada, 2013). Much of this treatment gap can be explained by public policy that provides full coverage for mental health and substance use services when they are provided by physicians or hospitals, but limited or no coverage of services provided by psychologists or social workers or in privately run treatment centres.

These policies mean that access to services varies according to income. For example, the least wealthy Canadians are the least likely to use the services of psychologists, even after taking into account the higher concentration of mental health problems at lower income levels (Bartram, 2019).

In addition to policy barriers, people sometimes do not seek help due to stigma or concerns about the cultural appropriateness and language of services offered. Other people may prefer to manage on their own or to rely on family and friends for support. Rates of help-seeking also vary by gender and ethnicity, with lower rates for men and for ethnic groups such as Chinese Canadians (Chiu et al., 2018).

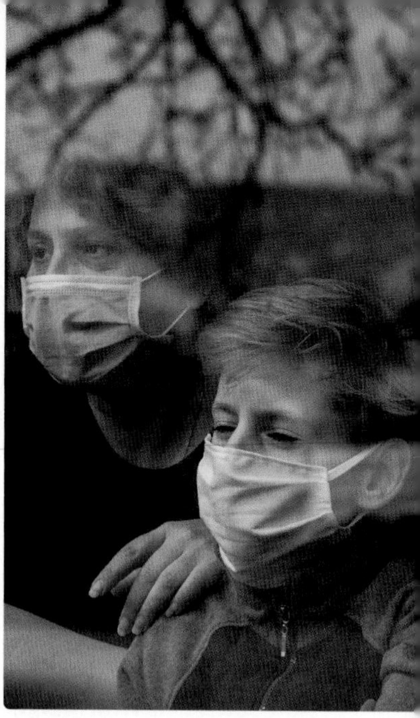

Accessing Care during COVID–19

In a "normal" crisis, one is likely to feel stress, fear, and worry. In a pandemic, the pressures can be overwhelming — job and/or income loss, social isolation, health anxiety, worry for loved ones, and — for many families— the concurrent strain of financial and family responsibilities.

For Canadians living with a pre-existing mental illness or substance use disorder, the pressures are likely even more serious. Social and physical isolation can cause the return or increase of symptoms and there will be disruptions in services owing to additional pressures on the health care system.

Statistics Canada. (2017). Canadian survey on disability, 2017.

MENTAL HEALTH-RELATED DISABILITIES IN CANADA, 2017

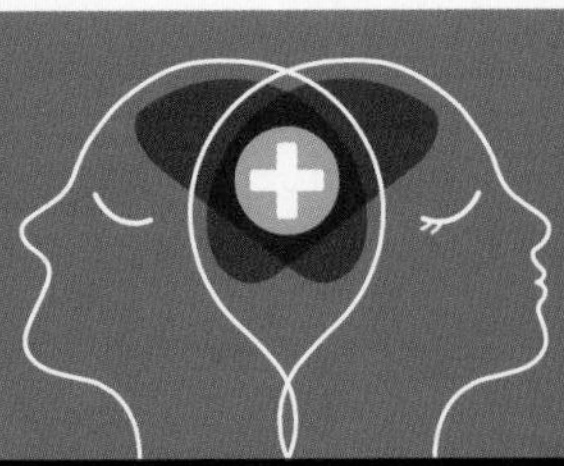

The Canadian Survey on Disability covers Canadians **aged 15 years and over who experience limitations in their everyday activities** because of a **long-term condition** or **health-related problem**.

OVER 2 MILLION

Canadians aged 15 years and over have a mental health-related disability. This represents **7%** of Canadian adults and youth.

Four of the most frequently reported mental health-related conditions are:

ANXIETY | DEPRESSION | BIPOLAR DISORDER
SEVERE STRESS DISORDERS

Among youth, **women** are twice as likely as **men** to have a mental health-related disability.

Youth aged 15 to 24 years

4 IN 5

Canadians with a mental health-related disability **also** have **at least one other type of disability**.

63 PERCENT

of those with a mental health-related disability also have a pain-related disability.

Nearly half of employed Canadians with a mental health-related disability feel that one or more of their conditions makes it difficult to change or advance in their job.

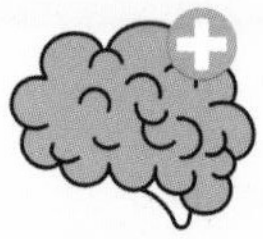

Of these, **1 in 4** believe it is due to **discrimination** or **stigma**.

OVER 1 MILLION

Canadians with a mental health-related disability say they require counselling services from a **psychologist**, **psychiatrist**, **psychotherapist**, or **social worker**.

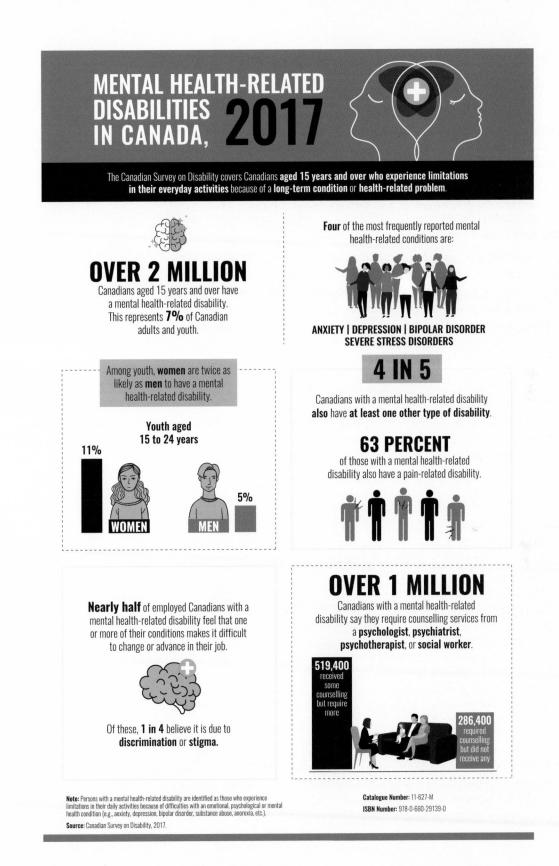

Note: Persons with a mental health-related disability are identified as those who experience limitations in their daily activities because of difficulties with an emotional, psychological or mental health condition (e.g., anxiety, depression, bipolar disorder, substance abuse, anorexia, etc.).

Source: Canadian Survey on Disability, 2017.

Catalogue Number: 11-627-M
ISBN Number: 978-0-660-29139-0

Statistics Canada. (2017). *Canadian survey on disability, 2017.*

7.2 A History of Mental Health and Substance Use Policy

The history of mental health and substance use policy in Canada has been marked by separations, both between the two sectors and with health policy overall. For the most part, separate service systems have evolved for people who are living with mental illnesses, substance use problems, or physical illnesses.

Each of these systems is run by different organizations, funded by different parts of government and the private sector, and delivered by different workforces.

The Early Years

Before Confederation, asylum and prohibition policies were driven by concerns regarding morality and social control. By 1867, asylums were so widespread that they were specifically named as an area of provincial jurisdiction in the Canadian constitution. Asylums were intended to provide moral treatment away from the corrupting influences of society and as an alternative to warehousing people with mental illness in jails and poorhouses. By investing in asylums, colonial governments were also exercising social control by getting unmanageable numbers of people with mental illness off the streets.

The first asylum was established in Saint John in 1837, where higher rates of immigration made "the plight of the insane more evident and more urgent" (Francis, 1977).

With a similar focus on moral protection and social control, the temperance movement gained strength over this same period. From Confederation to the late 1920s, local and provincial prohibition laws banned the sale of alcohol in most of the country (except Québec). Unlike asylum policies, the prohibition era did not see a similar investment in treatment infrastructure. While some people with substance use problems received treatment in asylums, jail time for public drunkenness was the dominant policy response during this era (Rush & Osborne, 1992).

After the Second World War, policies shifted to the disease model, which considered mental health and substance use problems to be diseases rather than moral failings. In response to the urgent mental health and substance use problems of returning soldiers, governments began to increase investments in services. Nevertheless, these investments fell short of meeting the needs of the population and left lasting gaps and inequities in both mental health and substance use policy.

In 1948, the federal government introduced a $7 million annual mental health grant, the largest of a suite of grants for priority health issues under the new national health program. However, this program was only a first installment on universal health insurance coverage. When the far more significant investment was made in universal hospital insurance with the Hospital Insurance and Diagnostic Services Act in 1957, mental hospitals were excluded.

The Exclusion of Mental Health Coverage

As can be seen from the debates in the House of Commons, jurisdiction, stigma, and balking at the cost all played a role. The federal minister of health at the time, Paul Martin (Senior), used the long-standing provincial role in funding asylums as well as the pre-existing federal mental health grant as a rationale: "It would be wrong by any principle ... for us to include as part of the hospital insurance scheme ... mentally ill people who receive treatment in provincial institutions" (Canada, House of Commons, 1957, p. 2677). Federal opposition parties criticized the efforts to exclude mental health in overall health coverage. For example, Saskatchewan MP Andrew Nicholson argued that:

> "[I]t is most unfortunate that half of the people who are sick every day in the year are barred from the benefits of this so-called national health insurance plan... The cost per day for the patients in the mental hospitals of Canada [was] $2.70 per patient per day in the mental hospitals ... and $10.77 per day in the public hospitals. It now becomes clear why the minister is trying to get [out] from under the responsibility of the federal government for this very large group" (Canada, House of Commons 1957, p. 3382).

The leader of the opposition, John Diefenbaker, put it thus: "Why are these [mental] hospitals ... discriminated against? ...This load of responsibility cannot be discharged properly by the provinces" (Canada, House of Commons 1957, p. 3386). The debate continued right up until moments before the hospital insurance legislation was passed excluding mental hospitals from public health insurance.

Deinstitutionalization

The move to close mental hospitals (known as **deinstitutionalization**) that started in the 1970s was driven as much by the cost pressures on provincial health systems as by the imperative to provide higher quality care for people living with mental health problems and illnesses. By the mid-20th century, new pharmacological and psychotherapeutic treatments had opened up opportunities for people living with mental illnesses to do well in the community (Canadian Mental Health Association, 1964). In combination with a new wave of advocacy to address deplorable conditions in mental hospitals, these treatment advances built public support for deinstitutionalization (Mulvale et al., 2007).

However, the re-allocation of funding from mental hospitals to community-based services was never fully realized. According to Orlikow:

> With the development of the tranquilizer drugs, many people who earlier spent years, if not their whole lives, in mental hospitals have been and are being released. The idea was that they would be serviced outside in the community which would help them in the transition years. ... [E]ven in a city like Toronto there are very few services for these people, so they are going back to the hospitals again (Canada, House of Commons 1982, p. 15869)

The 1984 Canada Health Act upheld the exclusion of mental health services by not requiring provincial and territorial insurance plans to cover services provided outside of hospital settings or by professionals such as psychologists and social workers.

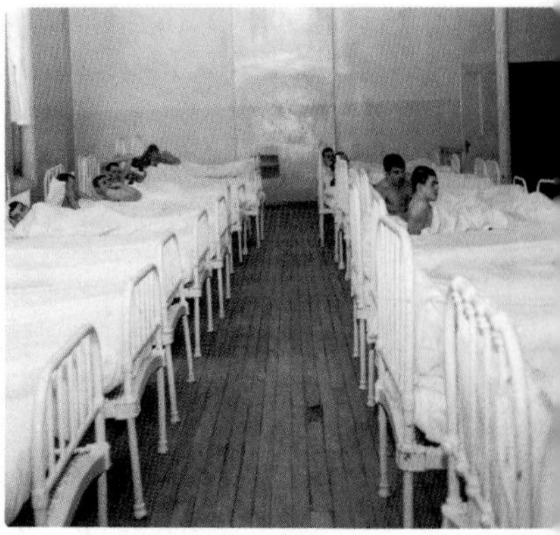

The Cuckoo's Nest

From 1960 to 1976, about two-thirds of Canada's 47,633 beds for the mentally ill were closed. The noble idea behind the policy was to free those with mental-health problems from the inhumane asylums made famous in the 1975 movie *One Flew Over the Cuckoo's Nest* (like the dormitory shown above at the Huronia Regional Centre in 1960).

Yet, the resources saved by deinstitutionalization were not re-invested as promised in community services and supports to help people once they were released.

All too often, lacking essential supports, people ended up living in inadequate housing, on the streets, or in prison.

The Introduction of Substance Use Treatment

Although the quality of care provided in asylums was questionable, the establishment of asylums meant that extensive infrastructure for mental health treatment was at least in place early on. By contrast, substance use treatment capacity only started to be built up in the post-war period.

Pressure for new investments came from the emerging Alcoholics Anonymous movement and its view of alcoholism as a disease that both warranted and could respond to treatment. Provincial governments began to invest, with the most growth happening in the 1960s and 1970s under the direction of provincial alcoholism foundations and commissions.

> Of about 340 specialized agencies operating in 1976, fully two-thirds had been established since 1970, and their costs had increased from $140,000 to $700,000 over this six-year period. (Rush & Ogborne, 1992)

The federal government also contributed to this expansion through the cost-shared Vocational Rehabilitation Disability Services program, insofar as employment was identified as a goal of treatment. This alcohol-focused service system began to address a broader range of problems as the use of drugs increased over this same time period. Deinstitutionalization policies were not applied to the substance use treatment centres, which had been built far more recently than most mental hospitals.

Nevertheless, the 1980s saw a tailing off of the growth of residential centres and, as with mental health policies, a new emphasis on community-based health care. Ultimately, despite the overall growth of substance use treatment infrastructure in the decades following the Second World War, substance use policy was not able to fully catch up to the needs of the population.

In 1983, to more accurately reflect the services offered, the AFM's name was changed from the Alcoholism Foundation of Manitoba to the Addictions Foundation of Manitoba.

The AFM's mandate was also expanded to include problem gambling in addition to alcohol and drugs and the AFM expanded its operations to more rural Manitoba communities.

the history of mental health and substance use policy.

Despite many shared risk and protective factors for mental health, substance use, and physical health, little collaboration has taken place between promotion and prevention efforts. It is also common for people with mental health problems to have substance use problems and vice versa, and for physical health problems and social problems to also be part of the mix. Nevertheless, the separation of mental health, substance use, and physical health policies and services makes it difficult for to obtain holistic care. These separations both stem from and reinforce stigma.

Despite the shift to the disease model, the idea that mental illness and substance use problems are moral failings continues to influence attitudes and policies. What mental health, substance use, and physical health systems have had in common is an overreliance on funding inpatient and residential care as opposed to services in the community. The exclusive focus of public health insurance on general hospital and physician services has contributed to this overreliance and has left serious gaps and inequities in funding for both the mental health and substance use systems.

Wait times are very long for the limited services that do exist in publicly funded community mental health clinics and substance use treatment centres. People with money and jobs can afford to pay out-of-pocket for private treatment services or have access to employment-based benefits, which means that access depends on the ability to pay rather than on need.

In a 2016 survey of people living with substance use problems, 25% of respondents identified long delays and 21% identified high costs as barriers to recovery (Canadian Centre on Substance Use and Addiction, 2017b).

Holistic Care

A holistic approach to mental health and substance use acknowledges that their impacts will not be reduced through treatment alone. Attention needs to be paid to the promotion of well-being and to facilitating open conversations surrounding mental health and substance use.

Mental health and substance use are not the problem of the health sector alone but require collaboration among multiple government departments, nongovernmental actors, and members of the community.

Social Welfare in Perspective

National Inuit Suicide Prevention Strategy

Identifying Risk Factors and Protective Factors

The high rates of suicide in Inuit Nunangat are a symptom of the social and economic inequities that have existed between Inuit Nunangat and most other regions of Canada since Inuit began to be impacted by colonization and transition off the land into permanent settlements.

The elevated rate of suicide among Inuit in Canada is the most urgent challenge facing our people and it demands a national response. The four Inuit regions in Canada (Inuvialuit Settlement Region in the Northwest Territories, Nunavut, Nunavik in Northern Québec, and Nunatsiavut in Northern Labrador), collectively known as Inuit Nunangat, have rates of suicide that range from five to 25 times the rate of suicide for Canada as a whole.

Inuit did not suffer from disproportionately high rates of suicide, historically. Globally, the World Health Organization characterizes suicide as an immense but preventable public health problem. It is a public health crisis in Inuit Nunangat that can and must be prevented.

High rates of suicide among Inuit are a shared challenge across Inuit Nunangat, yet suicide prevention in each of our jurisdictions is not based on a shared understanding of the factors that create risk for suicide. Similarly, we have not had a shared, evidence-based, Inuit-specific approach to suicide prevention across Inuit Nunangat that informs a united response.

The **National Inuit Suicide Prevention Strategy (NISPS)** envisions suicide prevention as a shared national, regional, and community-wide effort that engages individuals, families, and communities. It provides a unified approach to suicide prevention in Inuit Nunangat that transforms our collective knowledge, experience, and research on suicide into action.

It does so by promoting a shared understanding of the context and underlying risk factors for suicide among Inuit, by providing policy guidance at the regional and national levels on evidence-based approaches to suicide prevention, and by identifying stakeholders and their specific roles in preventing suicide. The NISPS outlines how different stakeholders can effectively coordinate with each other to implement a more holistic approach to suicide prevention.

The NISPS will promote the dissemination of best practices in suicide prevention, provide tools for the evaluation of approaches, contribute to ongoing Inuit-led research, provide leadership and collaboration in the development of policy that supports suicide prevention, and focus on the healthy development of children and youth as the basis for a healthy society.

The specific objectives and actions Inuit Tapiriit Kanatami (ITK) will take to prevent suicide among Inuit fall within six priority areas: (1) creating social equity, (2) creating cultural continuity, (3) nurturing healthy Inuit children from birth, (4) ensuring access to a continuum of mental wellness services for Inuit, (5) healing unresolved trauma and grief, and (6) mobilizing Inuit knowledge for resilience and suicide prevention.

Although making progress within each priority area is critical to achieving success in preventing suicide among Inuit, our strategy envisions holistic, concurrent actions across all six priority areas as the only way to effectively lower our rates of suicide. ITK will advance each of the objectives in the priority areas through actions within its own scope and mandate and will partner with governments and Inuit regional organizations to advocate and support existing Inuit regional strategies and suicide prevention initiatives.

Reproduced by permission of Inuit Tapiriit Kanatami from The National Inuit Suicide Prevention Strategy (NISPS), 2016. Executive Summary: www.itk.ca

RISK AND PROTECTIVE FACTORS ASSOCIATED WITH SUICIDE FOR INUIT IN CANADA

RISK FACTORS	PROTECTIVE FACTORS
HISTORICAL TRAUMA Impacts of colonialism, residential schools, relocations, dog slaughter	**CULTURAL CONTINUITY** Strongly grounded in Inuit language, culture and history
COMMUNITY DISTRESS Social inequities including crowded housing, food insecurity, lack of access to services	**SOCIAL EQUITY** Adequate economic, educational, health and other resources support and foster resilience
WOUNDED FAMILY Intergenerational trauma, family violence, family history of suicide	**FAMILY STRENGTH** Safe, supportive and nurturing homes
TRAUMATIC STRESS AND EARLY ADVERSITY Experiencing acute or toxic stress in the womb, witnessing or experiencing physical or sexual abuse	**HEALTHY DEVELOPMENT** Providing children with safe environments that nurture social and emotional development
MENTAL DISTRESS Depression, substance misuse, mental health disorder, self-harm	**MENTAL WELLNESS** Access to Inuit-specific mental health services and supports
ACUTE STRESS OR LOSS Recent loss, intoxication, access to means, hopelessness, isolation	**COPING WITH ACUTE STRESS** Ability to cope with distress, access to social supports and resources

ᐃᓄᐃᑦ ᑕᐱᕇᑦ ᑲᓇᑕᒥ
INUIT TAPIRIIT KANATAMI

7.3 Paradigm Shift: Toward Recovery and Well-Being

A paradigm shift toward recovery and well-being is underway in mental health and substance use policy. This shift builds on earlier efforts to reorient service systems from institutional to community-based settings, and from acute care to promotion and prevention further upstream.

Shared Recovery Principles

There are conceptual differences and shared principles between recovery in the mental health and substance use sectors. While abstinence has played a central role in substance use recovery, mental health recovery is believed to be possible even with limitations caused by illness.

Nevertheless, recovery is driving system transformation in both the substance use and mental health sectors, with shared roots in advocacy and a shared focus on hope in the face of stigma, self-determination, and meaningful lives (Canadian Centre on Substance Use and Addiction, 2017a; Mental Health Commission of Canada, 2015).

Shared recovery principles are as follows:

- **Recovery is possible.** Whether people are experiencing a substance use or mental health problem, hope is the foundation of the recovery journey. For too long people have been told by friends, family members, and service providers that there is no hope for recovery of a meaningful life. Such attitudes are being challenged more and more by first-hand accounts of people with lived experience of recovery.
- **Recovery is personal.** With strong roots in advocacy and lived experience, both the substance use and mental health sectors view each person's recovery journey as personal, unique, and typically non-linear. Each unique path is best determined by each individual, with support from families, friends, peers, professionals, and the wider community.
- **Recovery is multi-dimensional.** Recovery places a high value on the many dimensions of life in the community. These may include improvement in symptoms, but also adequate housing, meaningful activities and connections, and freedom from discrimination of all forms.
- **Recovery respects diversity.** Recovery is grounded in principles that encourage and enable respect for diversity and are consistent with culturally responsive, safe, and competent policies and practices.
- **Recovery is transformational.** The substance use field has emphasized changes to one's social identity through acceptance into a new recovery community. Mental health recovery has similarly focused on developing a new positive identity that is not associated with mental illness. Both the substance use and mental health sectors also identify recovery as a key driver of system transformation and changes in societal attitudes.

Indigenous Understandings of Wellness

There is common ground between these shared recovery principles and shared Indigenous understandings of wellness that provides a rich opportunity for learning and for strengthening mental health and substance use policy (Mental Health Commission of Canada, 2015). Many principles that are grounded in Indigenous knowledge and cultures — such as promoting self-determination and dignity, adopting a holistic and strengths-based approach, fostering hope and purpose, and sustaining meaningful relationships — also form the foundation of a recovery orientation. At the same time, recovery-oriented policy must recognize the distinct cultures, rights, and circumstances of First Nations, Inuit, and Métis across the country, and understand how recovery for Indigenous peoples is uniquely shaped by Canada's ongoing history of colonization, discrimination, and racism.

Cultural safety is a core principle of recovery in the Indigenous context. Originally developed by Maori nurses in New Zealand, according to the Thunderbird Partnership Foundation,

> cultural safety extends beyond cultural awareness and sensitivity within services and includes reflecting on cultural, historical and structural differences and power relationships within the care that is provided. It involves a process of ongoing self-reflection and organizational growth for service providers and the system as a whole to respond effectively to First Nations. (National Native Addiction Partnership Foundation, 2011, p. 8; National Aboriginal Health Organization, 2008)

Meaningful Reconciliation

The Truth and Reconciliation Commission of Canada has described attempts to assimilate Indigenous peoples as tantamount to cultural genocide.

Draconian policies aimed at complete assimilation have resulted in high rates of mental health and substance use problems and suicide among First Nations, Inuit, and Métis. Respectful relationships need to be at the centre of any meaningful reconciliation with Indigenous peoples.

Stigma and Discrimination

Stigma and discrimination are major challenges for people living with mental health and substance use problems. More than a third of Canadians agree that most employers would not consider an application from someone with depression, and 28% of Canadians who have been treated for a mental illness in the past year say that they have been treated unfairly at school or work because of their illness (Stuart et al., 2104).

According to a Bell Let's Talk survey, Canadians believe that stigma about mental health issues is declining (Bell Canada, 2016). However, anti-stigma work regarding substance use disorders is just starting to gain momentum. Nearly half of people with active substance use disorders report experiences of stigma and discrimination. This includes such things as being judged, being shunned, or facing difficulties at work (McQuaid et al., 2017).

Hearing directly from people who are in recovery is known as contact-based education and is one of the most effective ways to change people's stigmatizing attitudes and behaviours. It is also essential to strengthen and uphold people's right to access housing, employment, and education without being discriminated against as a result of having a mental health or substance use problem.

No More "Us and Them" — The Mental Health Strategy for Canada

With the release of Changing Directions, Changing Lives: The Mental Health Strategy for Canada in 2012, the Mental Health Commission of Canada laid out a road map for mental health systems transformation (Mental Health Commission of Canada, 2012).

The Mental Health Strategy for Canada was developed through consultations with thousands of Canadians and hundreds of stakeholder groups, and through careful review of the latest research and the experiences of other countries in developing national mental health strategies. In order to respond to the needs of people living with mental illness but to also be meaningful for all people in Canada, the Strategy rests upon a paradigm shift in mental health policy toward not just recovery but also well-being.

The concept of well-being draws from the fields of population health, mental health promotion, and mental illness prevention, where efforts to improve the overall mental health of the population are shifted "upstream" to include the social determinants of health (Health and Welfare Canada, 1986; World Health Organization, 2008). Whether or not we are living with a mental illness, the Strategy highlighted how we all need a home, a job, and friends; freedom from discrimination; and access to services and supports when problems arise in order to achieve the best possible mental health and well-being.

By arguing that at the core we are all the same, that there is no us and them, the Strategy aimed to ensure that people are no longer treated as two separate groups. This is critical for reducing the stigma that keeps people with mental health problems and illnesses from seeking care and being able to flourish in society, and for promoting optimal mental health for the population as a whole.

Mental Health Commission of Canada

Mental Health Commission of Canada (MHCC)

The Mental Health Commission of Canada/Commission de la santé mentale du Canada leads the development and dissemination of innovative programs and tools to support the mental health and wellness of Canadians.

Through its unique mandate from the Government of Canada, the MHCC supports federal, provincial, and territorial governments as well as organizations in the implementation of sound public policy.

Mental Health Commission of Canada. Who we are. www.mentalhealthcommission.ca

Table 7.1

Integrating Recovery and Well-Being into Mental Health Policy

Policy Domain	Opportunity
Social determinants of health	Action to improve access to housing, education, income, and employment can simultaneously promote well-being, prevent mental illness, and foster recovery.
Raising awareness	Equal emphasis on positive mental health and mental illness can be designed into public information campaigns, mental health literacy training, and education modules in schools, colleges, universities, and workplaces.
Professional development and training	Competency development programs/continuing medical education credits for existing health professionals and professional training programs in colleges and universities emphasize the common foundation for recovery and well-being.
Cross-departmental exchanges and learning programs	Joint workshops that include representatives of agencies and departments of government focus on health promotion, prevention, early intervention, and treatment to identify potential areas of intersection and develop associated programming.
Re-orienting funding	In addition to increasing overall funding, re-orient existing resources across the full range of promotion, prevention, intervention, and supports.
Health and social service delivery	Assessment, primary health care, and treatment can integrate evidence-based interventions to improve well-being on a par with reducing symptoms.
Adopting an integrated approach across the lifespan	Integrate approaches to prenatal care, early childhood care, school-based programs, workplace mental health programs, inclusive communities, and the promotion and care for seniors.

Integrating Recovery and Well-Being into Mental Health Policy

An integrated framework was developed to support the implementation of the Strategy. The **integrated conceptual model** rests upon the two-continuum model of mental health and mental illness, which reflects the fact that a person may have poor mental health but no diagnosable mental illness. Similarly, a person with a mental illness can experience a high level of mental health in the sense of having a positive outlook and feeling engaged and satisfied in life.

The integrated model takes the two-continuum model as its starting point and rotates it by 45° to position optimal recovery and well-being at the top (Figure 7.1). The model highlights that recovery can be as much about improving one's mental health as it is about reducing symptoms of mental illness, and that movement toward well-being includes both improving mental health and preventing the onset of mental illness. The inner circular arrows indicate the dynamic movement of people between quadrants of the model at different times in their lives.

Each person's placement in the model reflects his or her particular mix of individual, social, and structural risk and protective factors. These are shown at the centre of the sides of the integrated model, because they can either support (an upward movement) or hamper (a downward movement) people's experiences of recovery and well-being.

Individual factors include biology and genetics, personality traits, outlook on life, and level of resilience. Social factors include cultural practices and relationships among family members, friends, neighbours, and in the school or workplace. Structural factors relate to the social determinants that affect health, such as income, education, employment, housing, access to health and social services, and freedom from discrimination (including discrimination against people living with mental health problems and illnesses, as well as racism, sexism, and homophobia).

At the base of the model are situated resources for promotion, prevention, intervention, and support that can influence people's recovery and well-being. These resources serve as a foundation that people can draw on as they improve their recovery and well-being. These are an integrated part of improving people's recovery and well-being and as enveloping the whole population (represented by the inner circle) to denote that they must be accessible to everyone when required.

While concepts and models may seem a long way from making a real difference in the lives of real people, ideas have an important role to play in policy. This model is designed to guide the development of mental health policy across the population.

To be effective, mental health policy must offer an integrated mix of promotion, prevention, and recovery-oriented intervention and support in a way that advances recovery and well-being depending on the starting point for each person. This means that opportunities to integrate policy exist at many levels (see Table 7.1). These include actions to address the social determinants of health, efforts to raise awareness about mental health and mental illness, training and competency development for health and social service providers, and revisiting the design of service delivery.

The Recovery Model

In the past, individuals experiencing mental health issues and their families were often told to lower their expectations in light of the fact that the individual's symptoms would probably worsen over time. Today, the idea of recovery is at foundation for how social workers and other health professionals engage with individuals living with mental health issues and with their families.

Recovery encompasses a holistic approach toward treatment. This approach focuses on the person as a whole rather than on symptoms alone, and it avoids making assumptions based on an individual's diagnosis (Mental Health Commission of Canada, 2011).

Substance Use Policy and the New Recovery Movement

The recovery movement in the substance use field is closely associated with the Alcoholics Anonymous (AA) program that originated in the United States in 1935 (Bartram, 2019). While AA views alcoholism as a disease rather than a moral failing, it shares a commitment to abstinence with the earlier temperance movement. Day-by-day abstinence is marked by sobriety tokens or chips edged with the words "unity, "'service," and "recovery." Today, AA is a movement with meetings held in most communities and a global reach. As such, AA has had a powerful influence over how recovery is conceptualized in substance use policy.

In the 1990s, a new recovery movement emerged that shifted AA's disease-based model of recovery toward one based around hope and resilience, while still maintaining AA's focus on support from people with lived experience. People who once defined themselves around Alcoholics Anonymous (AA) increasingly define themselves as "people in long-term recovery" and embrace recovery's message of hope in the face of stigma.

In a 2017 survey, nine out of ten people in recovery reported having a good quality of life and half said that stigma — being worried about what other people would think — had been a barrier to initiating recovery (Canadian Centre on Substance Use and Addiction, 2017c). In response, the Canadian Centre on Substance Use and Addiction has built a public awareness campaign around messages such as "recovery is attainable and sustainable" and "words matter" (Canadian Centre on Substance Use and Addiction, 2017b).

Figure 7.1

Integrating Recovery and Well-Being into a Common Conceptual Model for Mental Health Policy

Mulvale, G., & Bartram, M. (2015). No more "Us" and "Them:" Integrating recovery and well-being into a conceptual model for mental health policy. *Canadian Journal of Community Mental Health*, 34(4): 31–67

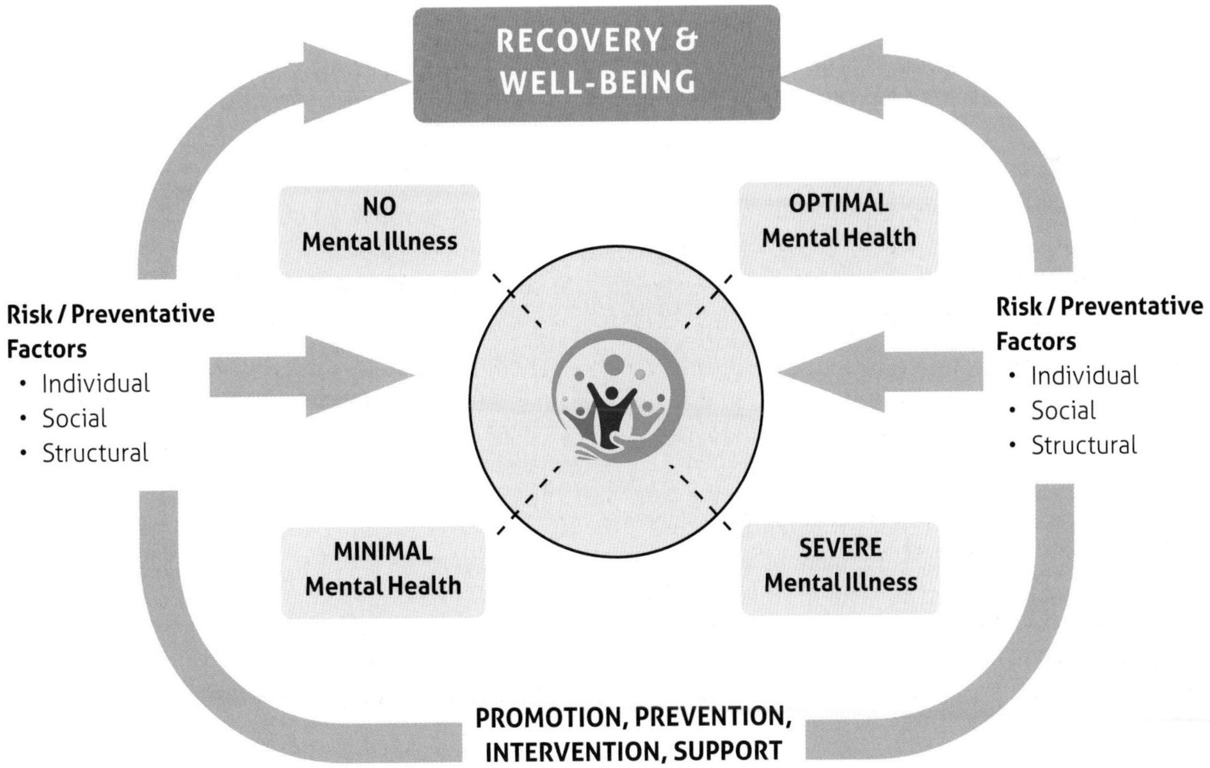

Social Welfare in Perspective

Expanding Access to Psychotherapy

Lessons from Australia and the United Kingdom

With a $5 billion federal transfer and lessons from Australia and the UK, Canada is well positioned to address gaps and inequalities in access to psychotherapy.

Australia and the United Kingdom have significantly expanded access to psychotherapy over the past decade. With this international experience, the many Canadian innovations that are underway, and a new $5 billion federal transfer to draw upon, Canada is well positioned to address long-standing gaps and inequities in access to psychotherapy.

"Better Access" in Australia

In 2006, the Australian Commonwealth government introduced the Better Access to Psychiatrists, Psychologists, and General Practitioners through the MBS Initiative (Better Access). This was in response to 1997 population health survey data showing that only one of every three Australians with common mental disorders was utilizing mental health services.

Better Access is an insurance-based approach that expanded universal public insurance (through Medicare) to cover psychotherapy provided by psychologists, social workers, and occupational therapists. Better Access providers work in private practice and are regulated by their respective professional associations. Providers can either provide services free at the point of delivery, or they can choose to charge copayments over and above the Medicare rate.

Better Access is complemented by smaller amounts of federal funding for two other kinds of mental health care services: Access to Allied Psychological Services, which is a grant-based program targeting low-income and vulnerable populations, and various Internet-based cognitive-behavioural therapy (CBT) initiatives coordinated through a digital mental health gateway.

IAPT in the United Kingdom

Improving Access to Psychological Therapies (IAPT) was introduced in the United Kingdom in 2008 in response to new evidence and a strong business case. In 2004, the National Institute for Health and Care Excellence identified CBT and interpersonal therapy as effective alternatives to antidepressants.

Policymakers were further convinced by a cost-benefit analysis showing that the costs of expanded psychotherapy services would be fully recouped within two years through increased productivity in the workplace and a reduction in disability benefit payments.

This approach to expanding access to psychotherapy differs from Better Access in just about every way.

- Improving Access to Psychological Therapy is a grants-based program with distinct staff and standards, centrally administered by the National Health Services (England) and offered in every district.
- The program is free at the point of delivery and provided by a workforce with either IAPT-specific or IAPT-approved training
- Improving Access to Psychological Therapy follows a stepped-care model, with the majority of services offered through lower-intensity interventions (such as online CBT-based self-help and psychoeducation groups) and a smaller number of face-to-face therapies offered as required. Pre- and post-measures of symptoms are collected at every session and reported monthly through NHS Digital on a district-by-district basis.
- Clear targets for access, wait times, and recovery were set at the outset and have since been met.

Results and Challenges

Although both the "grants-based" approach (by IAPT) and the "insurance-based" approach (by Better Access) have achieved impressive results, both models have also confronted challenges.

In the UK, IAPT targets have been met on average but there is considerable variation by districts and population groups. For example, completion rates drop off with increased socio-economic deprivation, and recovery rates are only 35% in the most deprived group compared with 55% in the least deprived group. In Australia, utilization of Better Access services has been found to be much higher in urban than in rural areas, and much lower in areas with greater socio-economic disadvantage.

Although such disparities existed prior to 2006, they were likely compounded by the ability of mental health professionals to charge copayments under the Better Access scheme. Such copayments not only pose financial barriers for service users, they also provide disincentives for providers to practise in more disadvantaged (often rural) areas.

Lessons for Canada

In Canada's more decentralized context, a concerted effort from health leaders at all levels and across multiple sectors and professions is needed to expand access to psychotherapy, and to ensure that this expansion address inequities in access. Key priorities include:

- Using the full range of policy levers for either a grants-based or insurance-based approach
- Implementing a strong approach to performance monitoring, with built-in equity targets
- Addressing gaps in workforce planning integrating substance use and lived experience
- Forming a pan-Canadian coalition for expanding access to psychotherapy

Reforms in this area will not only generate health and economic benefits but will also help to turn the corner on more inequitable features of Canadian Medicare. Additional efforts to address financial and cultural barriers are also needed in collaboration with communities facing disproportionate risks.

Bartram M. (2019). Expanding access to psychotherapy in Canada: Building on achievements in Australia and the United Kingdom. *Healthcare Management Forum*. 2019, 32(2), 63–67.

7.4 Harm Reduction as Policy

As defined by Health Canada, harm reduction policies generally refer to efforts to reduce the negative impacts from the use of illegal drugs and other substances without requiring abstinence (Health Canada, 2018).

Harm reduction is most often associated with illegal drugs. Services that aim to reduce harms from illegal drug use include needle exchanges that provide clean needles to reduce the risk of infection from hepatitis and HIV/AIDs, supervised consumption sites where people can use illegal drugs in a safe setting, and Opioid Agonist Therapies that substitute safer drugs such as methadone for more dangerous drugs such as heroin.

Roots in Activism and Public Health

Harm reduction as a policy concept first emerged in the 1980s, when needle-sharing programs were endorsed in response to the AIDS crisis. Harm reduction has roots in both public health and activism.

Public health stresses the pragmatic benefits of harm reduction. Since people are going to keep using risky substances, it is better to provide them with access to safe supplies in order to reduce the risk of death and other harms to individuals and the broader community.

For activists, harm reduction is a movement for social justice built on a belief in the rights of people who use substances, including the right to self-determination and the right to use substances without censure. Activists, often people with lived experience of illegal drug use, have been the driving force behind harm reduction innovations from needle exchanges to supervised consumption sites, whether officially sanctioned or not.

Social workers are at the forefront of developing innovative and evidence-based practices to reduce substance-related harm. Harm reduction principles are congruent with social work values, which promote a non-judgmental approach to substance use, recognize self-determination, perceive that outcomes are in the hands of people who are living substance use problems, and provide options in a non-coercive way.

Harm reduction approaches can also be targeted to legal substance use in the broader population. For example, Canada's Low-Risk Alcohol Drinking Guidelines recommends that Canadian women limit their drinks to ten per week and no more than three in one sitting on special occasions. Safer partying guidelines and dry froshes are examples of harm reduction initiatives aimed at university and college students.

Harm reduction is sometimes set up in opposition to abstinence-oriented recovery. However, harm reduction can also be looked at as another way that people can move toward greater recovery and well-being, even when they continue to use substances.

Figure 7.2

Canadian Drugs and Substances Strategy (2016)

A Comprehensive, Collaborative, Compassionate, and Evidence-Based Approached to Drug Policy

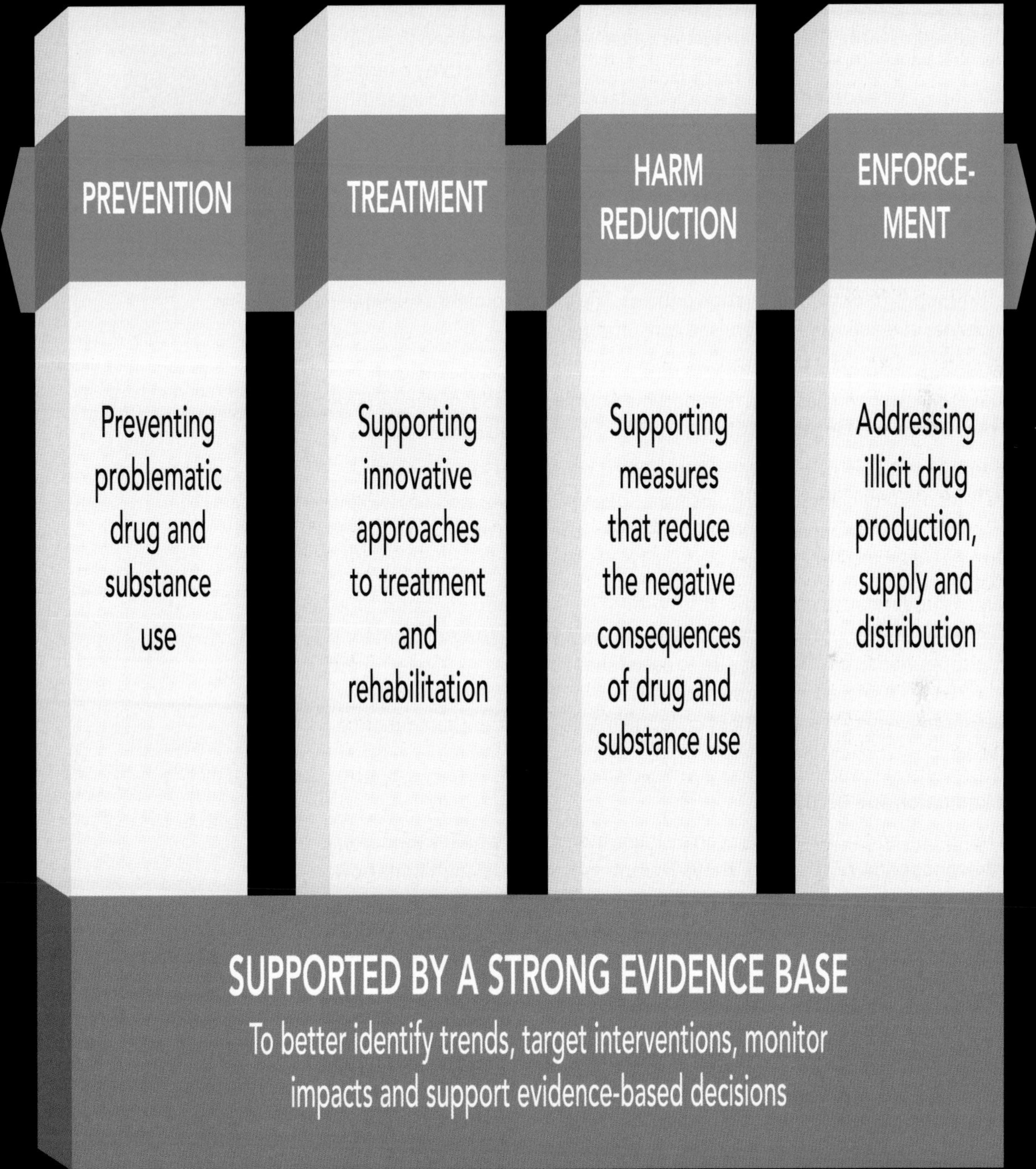

Supervised Consumption and the Importance of Evidence

Harm reduction policy has been highly polarized along ideological lines and has come in and out of favour in Canadian substance use policy in close step with changes of government.

At the federal level, harm reduction was one of four pillars in Canada's Drug Strategy starting in 2003, along with prevention, treatment, and enforcement (Health Canada, 2004). The harm reduction pillar was removed when the National Anti-Drug Strategy was launched by Stephen Harper's Conservative government in 2007 and was then reintroduced as a key pillar of the Canadian Drug and Substances Strategy by Justin Trudeau's Liberal government in 2016.

Similar shifts are ongoing at the provincial level, as government responses to the opioid crisis emphasize access to treatment or harm reduction approaches depending on where they sit on the ideological spectrum.

In this highly charged political context, evidence has been particularly important for getting support for harm reduction policies. The most prominent example has been the role of evidence in supervised consumption sites.

In overturning the federal government's decision in 2006 to close Insite in Vancouver's Downtown Eastside, the Supreme Court of Canada invoked a large body of research showing the positive benefits of supervised consumption sites:

> The Minister's failure to grant [an exemption] to Insite...contravened the principles of fundamental justice...Insite has been proven to save lives with no discernible negative impact on the public safety and health objective (Canada (Attorney General) v. PHS Community Services Society, 2011).

Research is underway to strengthen the evidence for assisted injection, an even more controversial approach where drug users are allowed to bring someone into the supervised consumption site to assist them in injecting (Government of Canada, 2019a). Assisted injection is particularly important for female drug users who are more likely to rely on others to do the injection rather than injecting themselves.

Harm Reduction and Recovery

Harm reduction and substance use can be integrated into the policy framework described in section 7.3 (Bartram, 2019). This integrated model highlights how people can move upward toward recovery and well-being along any of the four distinct but related continua: by improving mental health, by reducing symptoms of mental illness, by reducing symptoms of substance disorder, or by reducing the harms associated with ongoing substance use (see Figure 7.3).

Just like the other continua, harm reduction can be either helped or hindered by individual, social, and structural factors such as our genetic makeup, coping skills, social support, the impact of childhood experiences, discrimination, and poverty. The integration of harm reduction into the model also underscores the role of criminalization as key structural factor.

InSite

Vancouver's InSite clinic has been operating since 2003. Research into the community impact of InSite, and similar programs around the world, shows that they have a positive effect on community safety: reducing the rates of public drug use and discarded supplies without increasing substance use, violence, or property crime.

Harm reduction principles are congruent with social work values, which promote a non-judgmental approach to substance user and provide options in a non-coercive way.

Figure 7.3

Toward a Shared Vision for Mental Health and Addiction Recovery and Well-Being

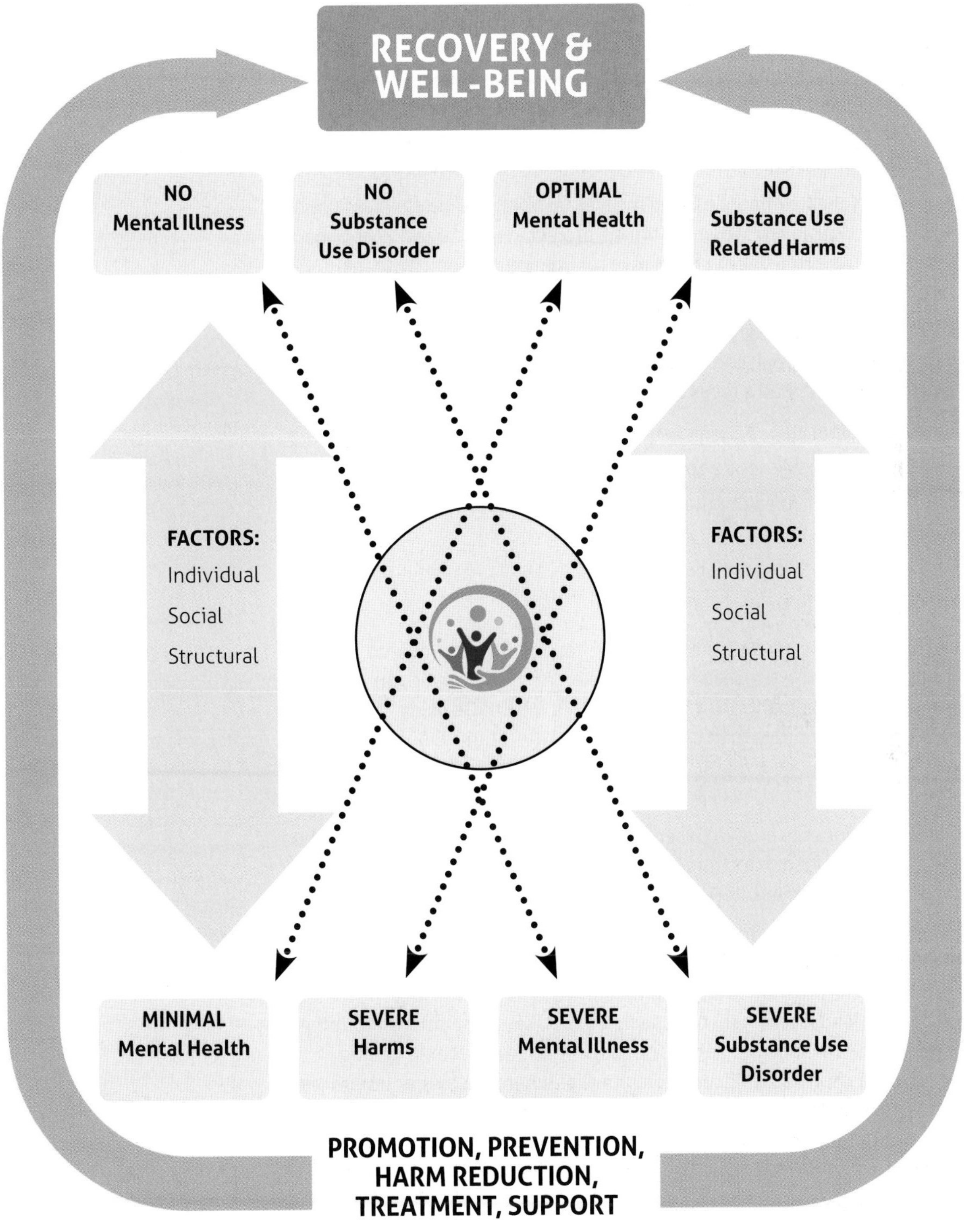

Bartram, M. (2019). Toward a shared vision for mental health and addiction recovery and well-being: An integrated two-continuum model. *Journal of Recovery in Mental Health, 2*(2–3), 55–72.

At Home/Chez Soi

One key structural factor that can both help and hinder recovery and well-being is access to safe and affordable housing, particularly as people living with substance use and mental health problems are overrepresented among the homeless population in Canada.

Housing First is a harm reduction policy that provides rapid access to housing without requiring people to first stop using drugs or other substances or to first have their symptoms of mental illness under control. Housing First is not only housing. Wrap-around services and supports are also offered alongside housing.

In 2008, the federal government funded the Mental Health Commission of Canada to run a five-year Housing First demonstration project in five cities across Canada. At Home/Chez Soi is a Housing First initiative for homeless people with mental health problems.

Using a $110 million federal grant, this was a four-year, five-city (Vancouver, Winnipeg, Toronto, Montréal, and Moncton) research demonstration project. Each of the five test sites also had a focus on a specific sub-population:

- Vancouver (people also experiencing problematic substance use)
- Winnipeg (urban Indigenous population)
- Toronto (ethno-racialized populations, including new immigrants who do not speak English)
- Montréal (includes a vocational study)
- Moncton (services in smaller communities)

With over 1,000 people housed, the At Home/Chez Soi project provided opportunities for extensive research into homelessness. In comparison with the control group, participants in At Home/Chez Soi were more likely to get and keep housing and to improve their overall quality of life (Stergiopoulos, 2014). Significant cost savings were found from fewer hospital admissions, fewer shelter visits, and less time spent in jail or prison.

Housing First continues to evolve. Based on the experiences of the At Home/Chez Soi project, tools and resources were created that are practical and user-friendly for groups and communities interested in the Housing First approach.

On the strength of the evidence from At Home/Chez Soi, and in response to feedback received through national consultations, the federal government has since broadened the program to allow communities to adapt Housing First to local needs and priorities (Government of Canada, 2019b). Key populations requiring flexible approaches include Indigenous peoples, youth, and women fleeing violence as well as Northern and rural communities where housing and services are in shorter supply.

COVID–19 and the Opioid Crisis

COVID–19 has adversely affected Canadians' mental health, but it has also exacerbated an existing opioid crisis across the country.

"The opioid crisis, which governments have struggled to manage for years, significantly worsened during COVID–19," observes Lori Spadorcia, the vice-president of communications and partnerships at the Centre for Addiction and Mental Health.

Writing in *Policy Options*, Spadorcia points out that "Due to a more toxic drug supply and service reductions at supervised consumptions sites, opioid-related deaths have soared and have outpaced the daily death rates due to COVID–19 on a regular basis.

"These record overdoses reflect a crisis that was in existence before the pandemic but were exposed and enhanced by it" (Spadorcia, 2020).

Getting Ahead of the Mental Health and Substance Impacts of COVID–19

A third wave of response focused on the needs of people living with severe and persistent mental health and substance use problems. With so many services and supports moving online, can more be done to support people and caregivers who are having to fall back even more than normal on their own resources?

Are acute care and first responder systems ready for people who go into crisis during the pandemic? Are plans in place for people who have both severe psychosis and acute COVID–19, and do these plans protect human rights? Hard lessons being learned in other countries suggest that these plans are urgently needed. We are now also just starting to see a collective focus on grief as the number of deaths steadily increases.

If we act now, we have an opportunity to get ahead of the mental health and substance impacts of COVID–19. This effort will require collaboration across the public and private sectors. Now is not the time to forget that up to two-thirds of Canadians have access to private mental health and substance use services through employment-based benefits, or that the one-third with more precarious or no employment rely on more limited public services or go without.

To assess surge capacity, we urgently need to do something we should have done a long time ago: take full stock of the mental health and substance use workforce across the public system, but also employee assistance programs, private practitioners, private residential treatment centres, and informal peer support. The Canadian Institute for Health Information collects information on the number of different types of providers across the country. However, addiction counsellors are not included, and many critical pieces of data are collected for physicians and nurses but not for other providers such as psychologists and social workers.

Looking ahead, we should expand the number of providers if we want to see a true increase in the availability of services. We will also need to consider bigger reforms such as decriminalization of all substances, broader access to housing first programs, and addressing gaps in public health insurance for long-term care and psychotherapy, so that our society is more mentally well in the first place.

Bartram, M. (2020). Mental health, substance use and COVID–19: Getting ahead of a perfect storm. *Behind the Numbers*. Canadian Centre for Policy Alternatives.

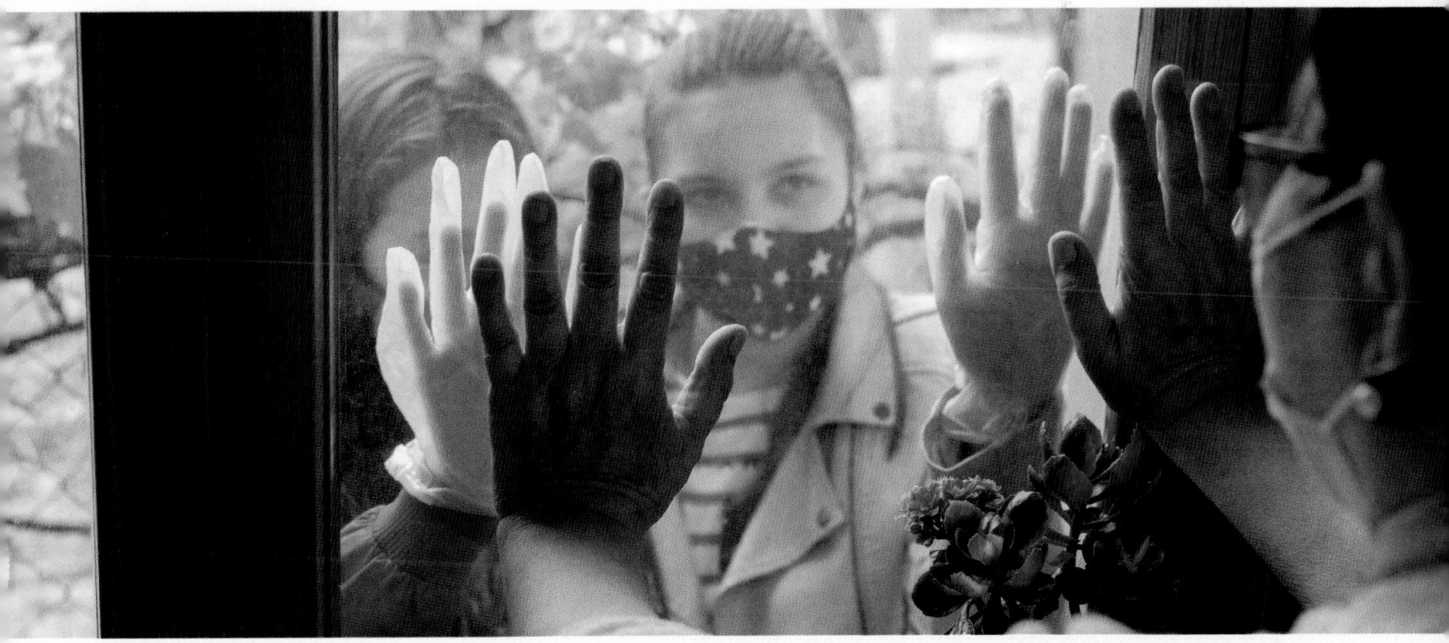

7.5 Mental Health and Substance Use Policy Renewal

The twenty-first century ushered in a renewal of mental health and substance use policy in Canada. In 2005 the Canadian Centre for Substance Use and Addiction released the National Framework for Action to Reduce the Harms Associated with Alcohol and Other Drugs and Substances in Canada. Since the Senate's release in 2006 of its report on the federal role in mental health and addiction, *Out of the Shadows at Last*, there has been no turning back from increased public awareness and demand for policy reform. Strategies and action plans have been developed at the pan-Canadian level and in every province and territory, and grassroots initiatives have taken off across the country.

After dramatic negotiations in 2016, federal, provincial, and territorial governments reached an historic agreement that will see $5 billion transferred over ten years from federal to provincial and territorial governments with a focus on improving access to mental health and substance use services, as well as $6 billion for home care. How far does this new transfer go toward addressing long-standing gaps and inequities in mental health and substance use policy?

"Canada was already in the midst of a mental health crisis prior to COVID–19. The pandemic has both magnified and added to this crisis and highlighted how crucial mental health promotion and care are to our overall well-being.

"It is time for governments and decision-makers to continue to step up and make mental health a priority by investing in a long-term, system wide response. It is time to recognize that mental health is health."

Centre for Mental Health and Addictions (2020, July). *Mental Health in Canada: COVID–19 and Beyond*. CAMH Policy Advice.

Closing the Gap in Health Funding

The OECD (2014) has found that some countries devote as much as 18% of their health spending to mental health, with the UK sitting at 13%. In Canada, estimates of public spending on mental health and substance use range from 5% to 7%. What would it take to bring this share to 9% over 10 years, as recommended in the Mental Health Strategy for Canada? How far does the new federal $5 billion over 10 years go toward reaching this target?

According to the Canadian Institute for Health Information, Canada's health spending by both federal and provincial governments in 2015 totalled $219 billion (Bartram & Lurie, 2017). Spending by the private sector accounts for 29%, with public sector spending accounting for 71%. At 71%, the public share of total health spending in 2015 was $155.4 billion, and the mental health and substance use share at 7% was $10.9 billion. Increasing the amount spent on mental health and substance use from 7% to 9% would require an investment of $3.1 billion annually, or $85.43 per person.

While falling short of $3.1 billion annually, the new federal mental health and substance use transfer of $5 billion over 10 years stands to make a significant contribution to narrowing the spending gap (see Figure 7.5). Over 10 years, $5 billion averages to $500 million annually or 16% of the $3.1 billion annual gap. To close the gap fully, provincial and territorial governments will need to come up with an additional $2.6 billion per year over and above the new federal transfer.

Of course, more money is not the only answer. Making the best possible use of resources that are already invested is just as important. New funding can be leveraged to reallocate resources from acute to community-based care, to foster recovery and well-being across the lifespan, and to achieve a better balance of investments so that people get support before problems become entrenched.

What about Social Spending?

The Mental Health Strategy for Canada also called for a two-percentage point increase in social spending, in light of the key role that social spending plays in improving mental health and substance use outcomes across the population.

Breaking down the numbers for social spending is more complex. Canada's GDP was estimated to be $1.78 trillion in 2016. Canada spends 17.0% of GDP on social spending, less than the OECD average. Accordingly, the social spending figure can be calculated to be $303 billion. A 2% increase in social spending would be $6 billion. Spread over 10 years, this would provide scope for activities such as scaling up Housing First and supportive employment initiatives across the country.

Taken together, the $3.1 billion increase in health spending and the $6 billion increase in social spending would total $9.1 billion per year.

Just on the health spending side, based on Ontario's population, it will receive $1.9 billion of the $5 billion federal transfer. Ontario's share of the $3.1 billion annual gap for the country as a whole is $1.2 billion, or $12 billion over ten years. As of 2019, the Ontario government has committed $3.8 billion of additional funding for mental health and substance use services over ten years.

In other words, the federal transfer will close 16% of the gap in funding required to improve mental health and substance use outcomes across the population, new provincial funding will close 32% of the gap, and just over half of the gap will remain.

Figure 7.5

Closing the Mental Health Gap (Annual Amounts)

Bartram, M., & Lurie, S. (2017). Closing the mental health gap: The long and winding road? *Canadian Journal of Community Mental Health*, 36, 1–14.

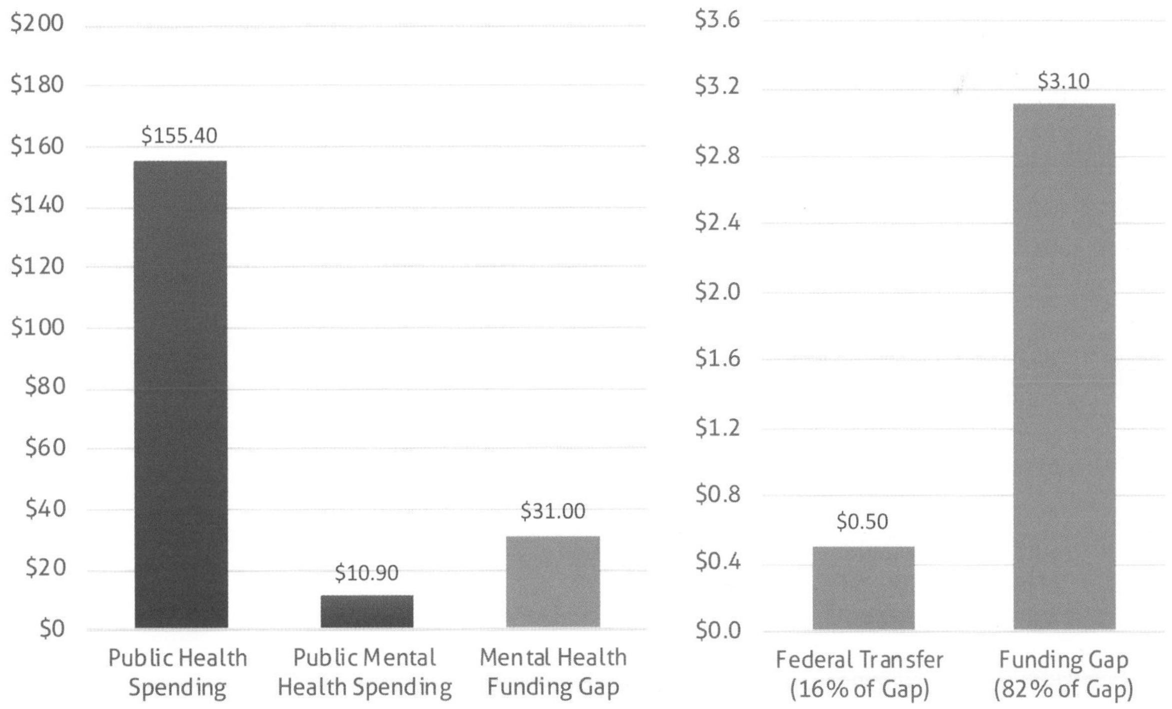

Making the Most of the New Transfer

Given the lessons from Canadian history, it will take vigilance to make the most of the new federal transfer (Bartram, 2017). There is a risk that policy gains may be derailed yet again by jurisdictional dynamics, stigma, and fiscal pressures. Vigilance from all levels of government, the stakeholder community, and the voting public will be required to ensure that governments are held to account for how new funds are spent.

Bilateral funding agreements are now in place between the federal government and twelve provinces and territories. These agreements spell out the priorities for spending and commit to collaboration on a high-level framework of performance indicators. In collaboration with federal provincial and territorial governments, the Canadian Institute for Health Information (CIHI) has developed performance indicators for mental health and substance use and for home care (see Table 7.2). An asymmetrical agreement is in place with Québec that recognizes its ability to set its own priorities and its accountability.

This set of common indicators will measure pan-Canadian progress on the shared priorities, with a commitment to report back to Canadians every year. The first indicator reports were released in 2019, with the rest scheduled for release over the coming years. Where possible, CIHI will use an equity lens to report on the how these outcomes are distributed amongst different population groups. For example, to what extent are people who have lower incomes, are racialized, or live in rural areas overrepresented among people who are hospitalized for harms caused by substance use, or who have long waits for community services?

Table 7.2

Pan-Canadian Progress on Shared Health Priorities: Performance Report Schedule, 2019–2022

Canadian Institute for Health Information (2019). *Common Challenges, Shared Priorities: Measuring Access to Home and Community Care and to Mental Health and Addictions Services in Canada.*

Year	Indicator Rollout			
2019	Hospital stays for harm caused by substance use*	Frequent emergency room visits for help with mental health and/or addictions*	Hospital stay extended until home care services or supports ready+	
2020	Self-harm, including suicide*	Caregiver distress+	Long-term care provided at the appropriate time+	Plus 2019 indicators
2021	Wait times for community mental health services, referral/self-referral to services*	Wait times for home care services, referral to services+	Home care services helped the recipient stay at home+	Plus 2019 and 2020 indicators
2022	Awareness and/or successful navigation of mental health and addiction services*	Early identification for early intervention in youth age 10 to 25*	Death at home/not in hospital+	Plus 2019, 2020, and 2021 indicators

* Mental Health and Addictions + Home and Community Care

The Future of Policy Renewal

With funding agreements and performance indicators in place and open to the watchful eyes of stakeholders, the stage is set for a spirit of learning. Here, Canada can take advantage of the benefits of its decentralized system. Jurisdictions have flexibility under each funding agreement to implement a range of approaches, depending on their unique priorities and opportunities, and to learn from each other by sharing information and best practices.

Also, a window of opportunity is open to work together with people with lived experience of both mental health and substance use problems to develop a shared, transformative vision for policy that is oriented to recovery and well-being.

There are several key roles that social work principles can play in this period of mental health and substance use policy renewal. The federal transfer's focus on access to mental health and substance use services can be viewed as a social justice issue in and of itself. Longstanding gaps in funding and inequities in what is and isn't covered by public health insurance have created financial and other barriers to access. In their service delivery role, social workers can champion mental health parity along with practices that are based on strengths, oriented to recovery and harm reduction, and culturally safe.

Last but not least, social work principles recognize that access to services is only one part of what contributes to an equitable distribution of health and social outcomes across the population. Safe and affordable housing, child care, income support, meaningful occupations, healthy environments, and freedom from discrimination are just a few of the factors that play essential roles in promoting well-being.

Social Welfare Policy in Action

Mental Health Parity in Canada

Mental Health as a Fundamental Human Right

In September 2019, the Canadian Association of Social Workers released a statement calling for a new Mental Health Parity Act and a federal Minister for Mental Health and Well-being.

The Canadian Association of Social Workers (CASW) is calling for a Mental Health Parity Act, enhanced and facilitated by measures such as a new federal Minister for Mental Health and Well-being. The proposed Act is a concrete way forward to more holistic well-being for all those who live in Canada.

Mental health parity or parity of esteem means "valuing mental health as much as physical health in order to close inequalities in mortality, morbidity or delivery of care" (Mitchell et al., 2017). Although the new $5 billion targeted federal transfer is dedicated to address disparities in access to mental health care, we are behind in terms of recognizing the importance of parity through legislation as has been done through the 2008 Mental Health Parity and Addiction Equity Act in the United States and the 2010 Equality Act in the United Kingdom.

The current approach to the opioid crisis and mental health more generally is lacking when it comes to recognizing health and well-being as a human right. Specifically, CASW proposes a re-visioning of mental health which recognizes the inseparable relationship with substance use and takes into consideration the structural dimensions limiting access and care.

A Mental Health Parity Act for Canada

Recommendation 1: Recognize mental health as a human right through the legislation of a Mental Health Parity Act.

Without parity legislation, the discussion falls short and action appears to be restricted to raising awareness rather than creating change to move toward mental health equity. Legislation that results in a more holistic, collaborative health care system would recognize the importance of secondary care for mental health and substance use issues, which is often offered by registered social workers and counsellors.

Complementary Measures

To support the success of such an Act, CASW recommends four complementary measures:

1.1 Ensure equitable access to mental health care and services to address problematic substance use, and ensure accountability through the creation of a Minister for Mental Health and Well-being

A new federal Minister for Mental Health and Well-being would cement mental health as a fiduciary, social, and philosophical priority in our country. There needs to be a shift from addressing mental health and problematic substance use in isolation to a joint approach toward overall mental wellness. The federal government has a responsibility to provide a coordinated vision and leadership in this area, not lag behind the provinces and territories.

CASW encourages the government to move beyond project-based approaches toward a comprehensive and integrated system of care. In one survey, 56% of Canadian adults strongly agreed that mental health care should be covered by provincial or territorial health insurance plans to the same extent as a visit to a family physician or community medical clinic (Abacus Data, 2019). Whatever reforms are made, it is imperative to track whether changes lead to improved access to mental health and substance use services, especially among marginalized populations.

1.2 Work towards health equity through the implementation of a universal Basic Income Guarantee

CASW encourages the federal government to work toward health equity by addressing the social determinants of health, including by creating a universal Basic Income Guarantee to provide consistent income support for all Canadians.

Poverty is known as a leading factor influencing health. Universal, unconditional programs are more effective in combatting adverse health conditions than conditional programs with extensive eligibility criteria.

1.3 Decriminalize the personal use of psychoactive substances through an expanded public health approach

The use of illegal psychoactive substances in Canada persists despite ongoing efforts to limit their consumption. Criminalization of those who use these substances leads to stigmatization and causes most harm to those at the lower end of the social gradient, which results in greater health inequity.

1.4 Adopt a Social Care Act that sets principles for the delivery of social services

Health care in relation to mental wellness cannot be separated from other social influences. CASW has proposed a Social Care Act to set principles for the delivery of social services, much as the Canada Health Act does for health care.

From Advocacy to Policy

While it remains to be seen how the federal government will respond, CASW and other professional associations and advocacy groups play a key role in the policy process.

They seek to inject new ideas, mobilize their membership and the broader public, and advocate for reform.

Questions

1. Do you think a Mental Health Parity Act would close the equity gap between mental health care and physical health care in Canada? Why? Why not?
2. Provincial and territorial governments have jurisdiction of health and social service delivery. How would a new federal Minister of Mental Health and Well-being improve accountability for equitable access to mental health and substance use services?
3. Why are a universal Basic Income Guarantee, decriminalization, and a Social Care Act important for advancing mental health parity? What other policy reforms would be helpful?
4. What are the chances of the federal government implementing these proposals? Why?
5. What role can social workers play in advocating for mental health parity?

For Further Information

For further information on mental health parity, consult the following sources:

Schibli, K. (2019). *Mental health parity in Canada: Legislation and complementary measures.* 2019 Position Statement. Ottawa, ON: Canadian Association of Social Workers.

Canadian Mental Health Association (2018). *Mental health in the balance: Ending the health care disparity in Canada.* Toronto, ON.

Mental Health Foundation. (2019). *Parity of esteem.* London, UK.

Frank, R. G. (2018). Reflections on the Mental Health Parity and Addiction Equity Act after 10 years. *The Milbank Quarterly,* 96 (4), 615–618.

A Moment in Time, 1850

CAMH

From Lunatic Asylum to Modern Health Facility

The changing view of mental health over the years is reflected in the institution's name changes over the past century.

In many ways, the history of the Queen Street West site and its physical evolution are the history of mental health care in Canada. The address has been home to a mental health facility for over 160 years, since the opening of the Provincial Lunatic Asylum in 1850 to house patients in often difficult conditions.

Originally Provincial Lunatic Asylum, it was renamed Asylum for the Insane in 1871, Hospital for the Insane in 1905, and simply Ontario Hospital, Toronto as of 1919. In 1996, it became Queen Street Mental Health Centre and finally, Centre for Addiction and Mental Health (CAMH) in 1998.

Today's CAMH was formed from the merger of the Queen Street Mental Health Centre, the Clarke Institute of Psychiatry, the Addiction Research Foundation, and the Donwood Institute. As Canada's largest mental health teaching hospital, CAMH sets the standards for care, research, and education.

The Health Services Restructuring Committee, an agency appointed by the provincial government to redesign the Ontario health system, tasked CAMH to address four key challenges: quality of care, access to care, fragmentation of services, and stigma — a mandate CAMH continues to grow to this day.

Chapter Review

Questions

1. What factors should be taken into account when weighing the individual and social costs of mental health and substance use problems?
2. Describe the major risk factors and protective factors associated with mental well-being.
3. "The history of mental health policy in Canada has been largely one of exclusion, evasion, and neglect." Discuss.
4. How large is the mental health spending gap in Canada and what should be the role of the federal government in this closing this gap?
5. Explain what is meant by "concurrent disorders" and give some examples.
6. Make the case either "for" or "against" harm reduction (e.g., supervised consumption sites) as effective social policy.
7. Describe the key similarities and differences in the application of the model of recovery and well-being in the mental health and substance use sectors.

Exploring Social Welfare

1. Develop a timeline with respect to mental health and substance use policy in Canada, including major policy initiatives and influential policy documents.
2. Access to mental health and substance use services is not evenly distributed throughout Canadian society. Describe ways to help overcome these inequities for various population groups.
3. Develop a slide presentation that clearly explains the model of recovery and well-being its implications for policymaking.
4. Describe some local initiatives that can be developed in your community to help counteract the stigma often associated with mental illness and substance use.

Websites

Mental Health Commission of Canada (MHCC)
www.mentalhealthcommission.ca
The Mental Health Commission of Canada leads the development and dissemination of innovative programs and tools to support the mental health and wellness of Canadians. The MHCC's current mandate aims to deliver on priority areas identified in the Mental Health Strategy for Canada in alignment with the delivery of its strategic plan.

Canadian Centre on Substance Use and Addiction (CCSA)
www.ccsa.ca
The Canadian Centre on Substance Use and Addiction was created by Parliament to provide national leadership to address substance use in Canada. The CCSA seeks to help decision makers by synthesizing research and data into a coherent, objective body of evidence, and thereby providing national guidance to inform policy and practice.

Centre for Addiction and Mental Health (CAMH)
www.camh.ca
The Centre for Addiction and Mental Health is Canada's largest mental health teaching hospital and a leading research centre. The organization conducts ground-breaking research, provides expert training to health care professionals and scientists, develops innovative health promotion and prevention strategies, and advocates on public policy issues at all levels of government.

Canadian Association for Suicide Prevention (CASP)
www.suicideprevention.ca
The Canadian Association for Suicide Prevention was launched in 1985 by a group who saw the need to provide information and resources to communities to reduce the suicide rate and minimize the harmful consequences of suicidal behaviour. CASP's goal is to reduce the suicide rate and minimize the harmful consequences of suicidal behaviour.

The Welfare and Well-Being of Indigenous Peoples

"Words don't change children's lives. Real action by the government and equality would."

— Cindy Blackstock, Executive Director of the First Nations Child and Family Caring Society of Canada.

Shiri Pasternak and Damien Lee

Creating a Post-Colonial Canada

8

© The C… (Photo ID: …)

Addressing land claims on a nation-to-nation basis is the key to reconciliation with Indigenous peoples.

The wealth of Indigenous peoples, their lands and resources, has effectively been stolen for generations. As a result of what is referred to as "colonialism" (or, more specifically, "settler colonialism"), Indigenous peoples have been targeted by a history of oppressive policies. They have also had their children targeted and their movement restricted. Such policies have resulted in a gap between Indigenous people and Canadians on every socio-economic indicator. The impact of the COVID–19 pandemic has presented serious additional risks to the health and well-being of Indigenous communities.

All efforts to improve the situation are commendable., but Canada seems continually to be getting it wrong. The changes underlying the 2018 Indigenous Rights Framework, for instance, which focus on reconstituting Indigenous communities and improving service delivery, do not address underlying issues of treaty rights and land claims.

Creating a Post-Colonial Canada

Successive governments have attempted to address this state of affairs; however, the strategies are simply not working. This chapter provides an overview of the relationships between Canadians and Indigenous peoples and the underlying policy issues.

After completing this chapter, you should be able to:

- Discuss the importance of governance and gender-based issues surrounding the Indian Act of 1876;
- Explain the origins and impact of the reserve system and the residential schools and the deep harm they caused;
- Describe the historical significance of the Royal Commission on Aboriginal Peoples (1996) and the events leading up to it;
- Understand the scope and impact of the Truth and Reconciliation Commission (2015) and its 94 Calls to Action;
- Understand the importance of the UN Declaration on the Rights of Indigenous Peoples (2007);
- Gain a better insight into recent policy shifts on the part of the federal government; and
- Appreciate why Indigenous peoples demand a nation-to-nation relationship with the Government of Canada, respecting treaty rights and the right to self-determination.

Key Concepts

- Idle No More
- Numbered Treaties
- Indian Act, 1876
- Reserve system
- Residential schools
- Indigenous self-determination
- National Inquiry into Missing and Murdered Indigenous Women and Girls (MMIWG)
- Sixties Scoop Settlement
- United Nations Declaration on the Rights of Indigenous Peoples (UNDRIP), 2007
- Jordan's Principle
- Citizens Plus (Red Paper)
- Royal Commission on Aboriginal Peoples, 1996
- Indian Residential Schools Settlement Agreement, 2007
- Truth and Reconciliation Commission (TRC), 2015
- Principles Respecting the Government of Canada's Relationship with Indigenous Peoples, 2017
- Recognition and Implementation of Indigenous Rights Framework, 2018 (RIIRF)

Photo: A construction site at the centre of an Indigenous land dispute in Caledonia, Ontario, in 2020

8.1 The Indigenous Peoples of North America

The Indigenous peoples of what is currently Canada are the original nations of North America. Sometimes referred to as "Aboriginal" peoples, Indigenous nations existed in organized political societies both before and after the arrival of settlers in their territories. Today, Canada's Constitution Act, 1982, recognizes three groups of Aboriginal peoples: Indians, Métis, and Inuit. However, it is important to note that these demarcations are legal categories created by non-Indigenous politicians for the purposes of governing. They reflect geographic and historic differences among Indigenous peoples, but they also obscure a tremendous amount of diversity.

The term "Indian," for example, is defined in the Indian Act legislation and determines who has Status and is a Registered Indian under the Act. This definition does not reflect the citizenship and membership processes that define belonging according to Indigenous practices. Today the term "First Nations" has replaced the term "Indian" in an everyday sense, and, more broadly, "Indigenous" is generally preferred to the term "Aboriginal." While the latter is a pan-national term unilaterally applied by the Canadian federal government, "Indigenous" is a political category that unites struggles across the world of people colonized by European and other imperial forces.

The reality is that Indigenous people in Canada include 60 distinct nations with distinct histories, languages, cultures, economies, legal and political orders, and spiritual beliefs. Many Indigenous peoples prefer to be called "Indigenous" rather than "Aboriginal," but many would also prefer to be called by their own names for themselves, such as Anishinaabeg, Nehiyaw, Kanien'kehá:ka, etc.

Idle No More

Indigenous communities have worked in good faith with successive governments to improve their overall well-being and social welfare, yet many continue to live in what George Manuel described as Fourth World conditions (1974). For Manuel, the term referred to people living in third-world conditions within a first-world country.

It is important to note that Indigenous people have never been prepared to sit and wait for governments to act. The broad-based Idle No More movement, for example, which began at the end of 2012, is part of an historical struggle by Indigenous people for distinct rights and lasting solutions. This specific push was re-sparked that year in response to further intrusions by the federal government on Indigenous rights.

Idle No More quickly became one of the largest Indigenous mass movements in modern Canadian history — sparking hundreds of teach-ins, rallies, and protests across North America and beyond. What began as a series of discussions in Saskatchewan to protest impending parliamentary bills that would erode Indigenous governance and environmental protections eventually changed the social and political landscape of Canada.

The Impact of Colonialism on Indigenous Peoples

The impetus for the Idle No More movement lies in centuries-old resistance of Indigenous nations to the impacts of exploration, invasion, and colonization. The demands of Idle No More are varied and diverse, like Indigenous peoples, but there is a clear thread of unity around asserting inherent rights to exercise jurisdiction on their territories and social, political, and economic control over their lives.

For treaty nations (because not all nations have treaties), agreements with the British Crown and Canadian government are understood as land-sharing arrangements, rather than surrenders or contracts as commonly depicted by the courts, politicians, and academics. Sharing meant that newcomers could have access to some land and resources, and could live in peace and friendship with First Nations. In exchange, those newcomers would provide health and education resources, among others, and share the wealth generated from Indigenous lands. This was the spirit and intent of the treaty relationship. Instead, First Nations have experienced a history of broken promises, which has resulted in outstanding land claims, lack of resources, and unequal funding for services such as housing and child welfare.

For First Nations that did not sign treaties, there is no agreement on how to share the land. The Supreme Court of Canada has designated these territories as "Aboriginal title" lands. While a different set of rights applies to them, and Canada has sought to make new treaties in these areas, many First Nations have learned from experience and reject the idea of treaty altogether.

Each day that Indigenous rights are not honoured or fulfilled, inequality between Indigenous peoples and the settler society grows.

Inequalities in Income and Unemployment

Colonialism has left Indigenous peoples among the poorest in Canada. The median income for Indigenous peoples is 30% lower than for that of non-Indigenous Canadians, and it shows very little improvement over time. What is more, the gap in earnings and employment persists regardless of community (First Nations, Métis, and Inuit), where they live (rural/urban), or increases in educational attainment over the past 10 years (Wilson & Macdonald, 2010).

There is one exception — Indigenous peoples with university degrees seem to have overcome much of the income differential. However, there continues to be a significant gap in the number of Indigenous peoples obtaining a Bachelor's level degree — 8% compared to 22% of the non-Indigenous population in Canada. Indigenous people who have less than a Bachelor's degree consistently earn far less than other Canadians with the same level of education.

As Wilson and Macdonald argue, income and other disparities have historical roots that are deep-seated and require policy intervention. They will not solve themselves. It starts by acknowledging that the legacy of colonialism lies at the heart of the problem. What is needed are new approaches and solutions that come from Indigenous peoples themselves based the right of Indigenous people to self-determination and control over their own lands and communities.

Social Welfare in Perspective

The Indigenous Population of Canada

A Demographic Profile

The Indigenous peoples of Canada are the original nations of North America. Three groups are recognized by the Constitution Act, 1982: Indians, Métis, and Inuit.

While the word "Indian" is still a legal term in Canadian law, many Indians now refer to themselves as either First Nations, Indigenous, or by the name of their specific nation (for example, Anishinaabe). First Nations communities are located in every province throughout Canada. The highest population numbers for First Nations are within the western provinces — British Columbia, Alberta, Saskatchewan, and Manitoba — which contain two-thirds of total First Nations communities.

Almost three-quarters of Inuit in Canada live in Inuit Nunangat. Inuit Nunangat stretches from Labrador to the Northwest Territories and comprises four regions: Nunatsiavut, Nunavik, Nunavut, and the Inuvialuit region.

The Métis represent 8% of the total population of the Northwest Territories, 6.7% of Manitoba's population, and 5.2% of Saskatchewan's population.

The Indigenous population is increasing at a much faster rate than the non-Indigenous population. The Indigenous population increased by 232,385 people, or 20.1%, between 2006 and 2011, compared with 5.2% for the non-Indigenous population. The Indigenous share of the total Canadian population was projected to increase to 4.1% by 2017, up from 3.4% in 2001.

The Indigenous population is also considerably younger on average than the non-Indigenous population. In 2011, the median age of the Indigenous population was 28 years, 13 years younger than the median of 41 years for the non-Indigenous population.

The Aboriginal population in Canada

The Aboriginal population in Canada is young and growing

Total population in 2016:
1,673,785
(4.9% of Canada's total population)

Growth (2006 to 2016):
+42.5%

Average age:
32.1 years
(almost a **decade** younger than the non-Aboriginal population)

	First Nations people	Métis	Inuit
Population count	977,230	587,545	65,025
10-year growth	39.3%	51.2%	29.1%
Average age	30.6	34.7	27.7

Three-quarters of the First Nations population had registered Indian status

44% of the First Nations population with registered Indian status lived on reserve

Eight CMAs[1] had a Métis population of more than 10,000 people...

Vancouver
Calgary
Edmonton
Saskatoon
Winnipeg
Toronto
Ottawa-Gatineau
Montréal

...which made up one-third (34%) of the Métis population

1. CMA = Census Metropolitan Area

The majority of the Inuit population lived in Inuit Nunangat, the homeland of Inuit in Canada

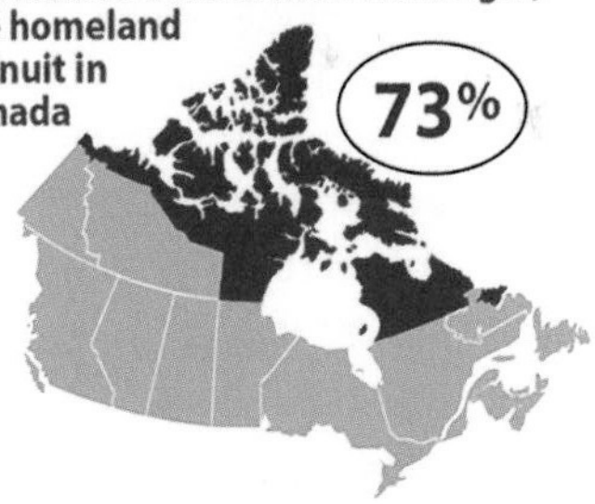

More than 70 Aboriginal languages were reported on the 2016 Census.

36 of those had at least 500 speakers.

Woods Cree, Gitxsan (Gitksan), North Slavey (Hare), Slavey, Montagnais (Innu), Dogrib (Tlicho), Michif, Dakota, Stoney, Malecite, Oji-Cree, Okanagan, Cree, Inuvialuktun, Naskapi, Nisga'a, Atikamekw, Halkomelem, Blackfoot, South Slavey, Mohawk, Lillooet, Inuktitut, Kwakiutl (Kwak'wala), Northern East Cree, Ojibway, Algonquin, Plains Cree, Mi'kmaq, Chilcotin, Dene, Carrier, Nuu-chah-nulth (Nootka), Swampy Cree, Shuswap (Secwepemctsin), Inuinnaqtun

Statistics Canada (2016. *Census of Population.*

8.2 First Nations Peoples

The weight of Canadian history on First Nations peoples is truly overwhelming. This legacy can be captured in six key issues or themes: (1) the struggle for land and treaty rights; (2) the Indian Act; (3) the effects of the reserve system; (4) the experience of the residential schools; (5) the ongoing call by Indigenous peoples for full governance over their lives and communities; and (6) missing and murdered Indigenous women and girls.

(1) Treaty and Land Rights

The British government signed various treaties with Indigenous groups before Confederation (when Canada was formally created), such as the Peace and Friendship Treaty (1752) and the Robinson Treaties (1850). After Confederation, the area called Rupert's Land (which included much of what is currently the prairies and territories) was transferred by sale from the Hudson's Bay Company to the Canadian government. However, because Canadian law recognized that Indigenous people held title on that land, the government had to form agreements with Indigenous leaders.

The treaties signed by the Canadian government are known as the **Numbered Treaties**, beginning with Treaty No. 1 in 1871 with the Ojibway and Swampy Cree of Manitoba. By signing these treaties, the Indigenous peoples agreed to share large tracts of land with the Canadian government in exchange for certain benefits in perpetuity. Between 1760 and 1923, the British Crown signed 56 land treaties with First Nations peoples. Many if not all treaties were written in such a way that it appears that First Nations surrendered all of their rights to the land in exchange for small reserves and meagre compensation. In many cases, the written versions differ from what was promised verbally.

The land treaties generally stipulated the relinquishment of Indian rights and title to specific land and provided for annual payments called "annuities." This amount never changed and was not generally indexed to inflation. Descendants of the Robinson-Huron treaty recently challenged this in court, with the judge ruling that Canada had failed to increase treaty annuities in step with the amount of wealth extracted from their lands. This is why many treaty annuities today amount to what might seem like an insignificant sum, such as $4 per year. Symbolically, however, an annuity payment is important because it represents the nation-to-nation relationship embodied in the treaties themselves.

Almost half of the land in Canada is not under a treaty, which means that no agreement exists between the Canadian government and First Nations peoples for use of the land. For example, no treaties were signed between the Indigenous peoples of Québec, the Maritimes, and most of British Columbia; other pockets throughout the country were left out of treaty as well. Only since the mid-1970s, when the "modern treaty" process was introduced, could nations and communities left out of the historical treaty process enter into negotiations for their lands.

Land Treaties

While land treaties differed in their terms and complexity, they generally aimed to force Indigenous peoples to surrender land to the Canadian government. The major treaties were signed in the West. These treaties allowed the vast territories of the West to be settled and the Canadian Pacific Railway to be constructed.

No treaties were signed between the First Nations of Québec, the Maritimes, and most of British Columbia. In fact, almost half of the population of Registered Indians did not sign land treaties. Treaties and other land claims are now disputed across the country.

- **Acknowledging Indigenous Land Rights**

These historical land treaties (or, in many cases, the lack of them) are currently in dispute across the country. First Nations leaders believe the very idea of surrendering land was not a right they held. Indigenous territorial authority tends to extend from the land to the people, rather than from the people to the land — the lands were and are seen as part of Creation and the people are merely the stewards of it. The "surrender" of land rights is based on the concept of private property — and this is a rejected concept in many First Nations political philosophies. Though their separate territories are bounded by borders and protocols, mutual hospitality is respected.

For those nations that did not sign treaties, dispossession was often treated as a de facto power of the state, despite foundational agreements like the Royal Proclamation of 1763 and treaties such as the Treaty of Niagara. The Royal Proclamation was issued by King George III during the transfer of European imperial claims from the French to the British over the colony. It contained a provision to ensure that the Indigenous peoples of these lands would not be "molested" on their territories and could only relinquish land through a voluntary cession to the Crown. The Treaty of Niagara the following year affirmed in mutual agreement the terms of these conditions through Indigenous protocols of political alliance. Those nations that did not treaty, therefore, should have been protected under these agreements, but instead they were, and are, forced continually to fight to have their jurisdiction over their land respected.

Figure 8.1

The Numbered Treaties

Eleven Treaties were signed between 1871 and 1921. Numbers 1–7 (1871–1877) were key in advancing European settlement. For numbers 9–11 (1899–1921), resource extraction was the government's main motive.

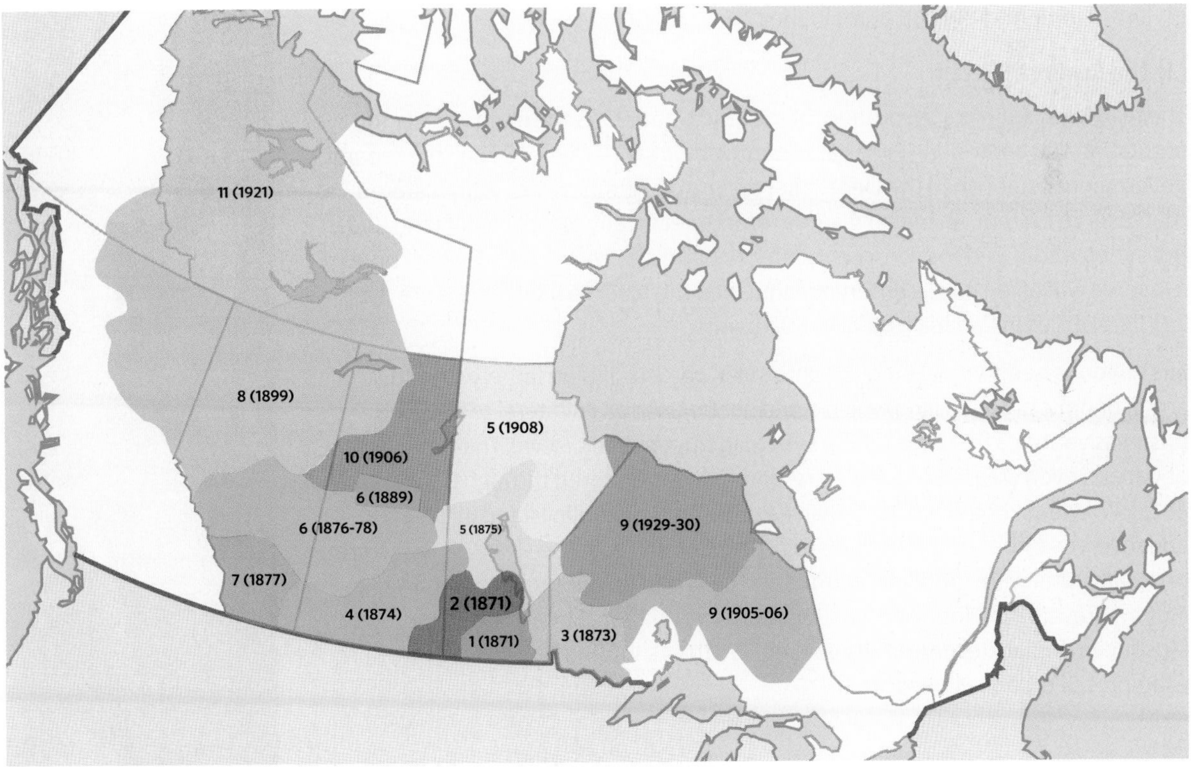

Map of Numbered Treaties of Canada. Borders are approximated. Wikimedia Commons. Canada location map.svg. Modifications made by Themightyquill.

(2) The Indian Act of 1876

The Indian Act of 1876 was, and still is, a piece of legislation that regulates virtually every aspect of First Nation life. The Indian Act ("An Act respecting Indians") was enacted under the provisions of Section 91 (24) of the Constitution Act, 1867, which delegates Canada's federal government exclusive authority to legislate in relation to "Indians and the Lands Reserved for the Indians." The Indian Act was administered in First Nation communities by government officials known as Indian Agents. In 1983, a Special Parliamentary Committee on Indian Self-Government (the Penner Report) aptly called it a "mechanism of social control and assimilation."

The Indian Act remains largely intact today, though an increasing amount of issue-specific legislation supplements it. The Indian Act is a paradigmatic symbol of Canada's oppressive social control over First Nation lives. It has undergone substantive amendments from 1876 to today, creating a record of state attempts to both segregate and assimilate First Nations. The Act determined who could call themselves "Indian," creating two classes of Indians — Status and Non-Status — based on racialized and gendered stereotypes.

Attacking the role of First Nation women in governance, Status was further weaponized, for example, when Indian women lost it when marrying non–First Nation men, rendering their children white in law and deprived of the special rights of their people or formal access to their homelands. The Indian Act mandated the attendance of children in residential schools, prohibited First Nations from hiring lawyers to advocate for their land rights, and encouraged enfranchisement (the right to vote and claim Canadian citizenship) in exchange for giving up their identity and place in their communities.

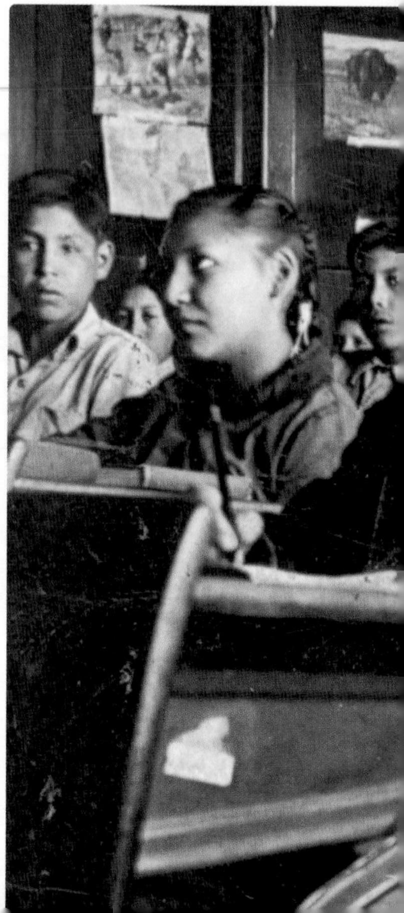

(3) The Reserve System

The reserve system is a by-product of the land treaties. As the main vehicle for regulating and controlling First Nations movement and ways of living, the federal government established the Department of Indian Affairs, which administered that reserve system. An Indian reserve refers specifically to a parcel of land and is not synonymous with nation, community, or band; the community that occupies a reserve will often have a different name than the reserve itself. There are over 2,000 reserves in Canada with over 600 bands.

First Nations peoples were moved onto small parcels of land largely devoid of any economic potential and which could not be used as collateral to develop business ventures (because land was held in trust by the Crown). The Government of Canada even created reserves in regions not surrendered through treaty, such as the Wikwemikong Unceded Indian Reserve on Manitoulin Island in Ontario and reserves throughout Québec and British Columbia. Some reserves that were originally rural were gradually surrounded by urban development. Kahnawá:ke Mohawk reserve in Montréal; Tsleil-waututh First Nation, Squamish Nation, and Musqueam Indian Reserve in Vancouver; and the Tsuu T'ina Nation in Calgary are examples of urban reserves.

(4) The Residential Schools System

The residential schools were a range of institutions, including industrial schools, boarding schools, student residences, hostels, billets, and day schools tasked with "educating" First Nations children.

The residential schools prohibited the use of First Nations languages, culture, and customs, and were ultimately predatory environments for young, defenceless children. Children also suffered from hunger and lack of nutritious food and died at a rate higher than soldiers who perished in World War II. One school even used an electric chair to punish children. Later, many people resorted to litigation to obtain compensation, forcing the federal government ultimately to announce the Residential Schools Settlement Agreement in 2006. The Settlement involved five components: the Common Experience Payment, Independent Assessment Process, the Truth and Reconciliation Commission, Commemoration, and Health and Healing Services.

On June 11, 2008, Prime Minister Stephen Harper offered a public apology on behalf of the Government of Canada in the House of Commons. Nine days prior, the Truth and Reconciliation Commission (TRC) was established to uncover the truth about the schools. In 2015, the TRC concluded with the establishment of the National Centre for Truth and Reconciliation and the publication of a multi-volume report detailing the testimonies of survivors and historical documents from the time and issuing 94 Calls to Action to right the underlying wrongs of the system. The TRC report found that the school system amounted to cultural genocide.

Residential Schools

A hundred or so schools were operated by various religious organizations in partnership with the Government of Canada.

Dating back to the passage of the Indian Act in 1876, most schools were closed by the mid-1970s, but seven were left open, with the last school closing only in 1996.

Photo: Students from Fort Albany Residential School reading in a class overseen by a nun, c. 1945.

Photo: Truth and Reconciliation Commission

(5) The Call for Indigenous Self-Determination

The call for Indigenous self-determination is the natural response to hundreds of years of colonial oppression. In fact, First Nation communities have maintained wherever and however possible their political orders of government, despite attempts by Canada to replace them with the Indian Band Council system, introduced in the Indian Act and forced onto First Nations communities. But efforts to restore recognition for First Nations' political orders was revived in the Penner Report of 1983. The Special Parliamentary Committee report, chaired by Liberal MP Keith Penner, stated that First Nation communities would prefer self-government and recommended that the Indian Act and the Department of Indian Affairs be phased out and replaced by local governments established by First Nation peoples themselves. With the election of a Conservative government under Brian Mulroney the following year, that process did not unfold. Instead, federal governments have since focused on "devolution" programs that offer increased control to First Nations over programs and services, however without providing sufficient funds to run them and while maintaining excessive oversight.

In 1995, Canada introduced the Inherent Right Policy. This policy emerged from the rights affirmed in Section 35 of the Constitution Act, 1982, and set out a framework for negotiated agreement with First Nation, Métis, and Inuit governments to devolve governance powers to Indigenous communities. Twenty-two self-government agreements are currently in place, and more are being negotiated, but there is also criticism of the policy. The policy was passed unilaterally by Canada and is adjudicated by non-Indigenous courts. It is not a nation-to-nation agreement. As the policy itself states, "The Government takes the position that negotiated rules of priority may provide for the paramountcy of Aboriginal laws, but may not deviate from the basic principle that those federal and provincial laws of overriding national or provincial importance will prevail over conflicting Aboriginal laws."

The First Nations in Canada recognize that they are not alone in their decolonial struggle. The challenges Indigenous people face in Canada are intertwined with the struggles of colonized peoples all around the world.

In this context, it is important to note that "self-determination" is different than "self-government." Self-government is something "given" by Canada to Indigenous peoples, whereas "self-determination" comes from within Indigenous governments regardless of Canadian law. Canada is a party to the International Covenant on Civil and Political Rights and the International Covenant on Economic, Social and Cultural Rights, also known as the "decolonization covenants," which it is bound to implement. These decolonization covenants share the same overarching provision on self-determination. Article 1, paragraph 1, of both covenants states, "All peoples have the right of self-determination. By virtue of that right they freely determine their political status and freely pursue their economic, social and cultural development." The same wording is replicated in Article 3 of the UN Declaration on the Rights of Indigenous Peoples, confirming that the right applies to Indigenous peoples.

Inuit Disc List System

in 1941, the federal government chose to register each Inuk with a unique numeric identifier, which was stamped on a disc or printed on a card.

The stated reason was to facilitate federal payments and insurance, but records from the Department of Indian and Northern Affairs show that white administrators in the North were just frustrated at their inability to pronounce Inuit names. According to some accounts, children were asked to call out their disk number at school rather than a name.

These numbers were used until 1972 except in Québec where the practice continued for a few more years.

(6) Missing and Murdered Indigenous Women and Girls (MMIWG)

For years, the families of missing and murdered Indigenous women, girls, trans, and Two-Spirit people could only turn to one another to express their outrage, sadness, and fear at what felt like an epidemic of violence against their relatives and friends. But their advocacy fell on deaf ears. In 2002, serial killer Robert Pickton was finally arrested after years of police non-action. Women in the Downtown Eastside of Vancouver had watched friends disappear for years but were ignored when they raised alarm about the pattern of loss. The Pickton Inquiry affirmed in 2012 what Missing Women Commissioner Wally Oppal called "blatant" police failure. Nearly all of these women — as many as 49, according to Pickton — were Indigenous.

Many Indigenous women, trans, and Two-Spirit advocates pushed for a national inquiry into the issue as well, in the hope that these systemic issues would be revealed and addressed. Former Prime Minister Stephen Harper responded to requests for an inquiry in 2014 by saying, "Um it, it isn't really high on our radar, to be honest ... Our ministers will continue to dialogue with those who are concerned about this."

Soon after Prime Minister Justin Trudeau came to power, he formally launched the National Inquiry into Missing and Murdered Indigenous Women and Girls (MMIWG) in 2015. The final report came out on June 3, 2019. It concluded:

> The violence the National Inquiry heard about amounts to a race-based genocide of Indigenous Peoples, including First Nations, Inuit and Métis, which especially targets women, girls, and 2SLGBTQ+IA people. This genocide has been empowered by colonial structures, evidenced notably by the Indian Act, the Sixties Scoop, residential schools and breaches of human and Indigenous rights, leading directly to the current increased rates of violence, death, and suicide in Indigenous populations. (National Inquiry into Missing and Murdered Indigenous Women and Girls, 2019)

The findings of the MMIWG report point to hard truths about the impacts of colonization, racism, and sexism — aspects of Canadian society that many are reluctant to accept. The Inquiry names their impacts as genocidal.

On the day that the report came out, it was the term "genocide," in particular, that rattled the media establishment — not the underlying conditions of gendered, racialized, and heterosexist violence that led to the charge. Findings showed that Indigenous women and girls are 12 times more likely to be murdered or to go missing and 16 times more likely to disappear or be killed than white women.

The Inquiry was neither the beginning nor the end of the fight for justice for murdered and missing loved ones. Communities have taken prevention and protection into their own hands. For example, the Bear Clan was formed in 1992 in Winnipeg's North End and later spread to other Canadian cities, such as Thunder Bay. Indigenous community members patrol the street to protect the vulnerable, including women and children. As well, grassroots organizations like No More Silence work with Indigenous families to create resources and support to stop the murders and disappearance of Indigenous women.

National Inquiry: Reclaiming Power & Place

The National Inquiry's Final Report revealed that persistent and deliberate human and Indigenous rights violations and abuses are the root cause behind Canada's staggering rates of violence against Indigenous women, girls and 2SLGBTQ+IA people.

The two-volume report calls for transformative legal and social changes to resolve the crisis that has devastated Indigenous communities across the country.

8.3 First Nations Children in Care

The over-representation of First Nations, Inuit, and Métis Nation children in the child welfare system is a humanitarian crisis of the first order. First Nations, Inuit, and Métis Nation children make up 7.7% of the population under 15 but represent 52.2% of children in foster care in private homes.

Every day, Indigenous children are separated from their parents, families, and communities, often due to poverty as a result of loss of land — for example, poor housing conditions and lack of proper clothing and food. Children may also be apprehended due to a lack of resources to heal inter-generational trauma, leading to addiction, mental health crises, and feelings of rootlessness.

Critical, as well, is the fact that Indigenous families are the most closely surveilled group in the country and most likely to be subject to intervention compared to non-Indigenous families. Systemic racism and cultural bias play a major role in child apprehension.

Bill C-92: An Act Respecting First Nations, Inuit and Métis Children, Youth and Families

First Nations, Inuit, and Métis Nation groups agree that this situation is unacceptable. Urgent action must be taken by all orders of government — federal, provincial, and territorial — to support Indigenous families to raise their children within their families, homelands, and nations; to increase efforts to address the root causes of child apprehension; and to reunite children with their parents, extended families, and communities and nations.

The Government of Canada, together with the provinces and territories, has stepped back to allow some of this work to happen, but they have also acted as a hindrance to the cause. On November 30, 2018, the Minister of Indigenous Services, together with Assembly of First Nations National Chief Perry Bellegarde, Inuit Tapiriit Kanatami President Natan Obed, and Métis National Council President Clément Chartier, announced that the federal government would move forward with co-developed legislation. This legislation was introduced on February 28, 2019 and on June 21, 2019, Bill C-92 An Act Respecting First Nations, Inuit and Métis Children, Youth and Families became law, legislating in the area of Indigenous child welfare by the federal government for the first time.

During the Bill's readings, Indigenous child advocates suggested multiple amendments to ensure systemic issues were addressed in five areas in particular: national standards, jurisdiction, funding, accountability, and data collection (Metallic et al., 2019b).

The majority of these suggested amendments were rejected in the House of Common's final vote on the bill. For example, advocates challenged harmful legal precedents that "timed-out" opportunities for children to return to their original family's care. While the Senate recommended this amendment be adopted, it was not accepted by the House of Commons in the final version of the Act (Metallic et al., 2019a).

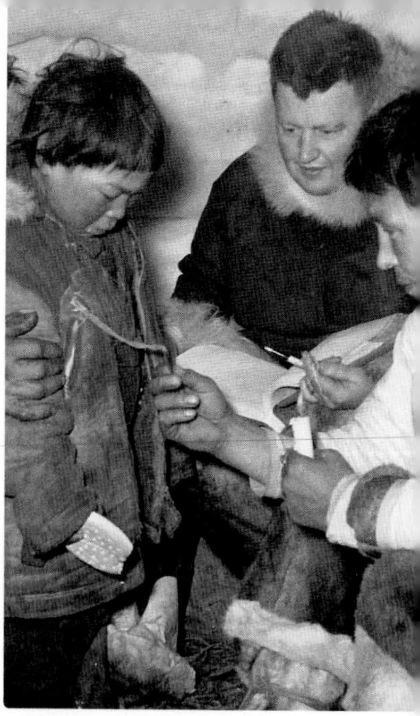

Project Surname

Today, Inuit use a mixture of Euro-Canadian and traditional Inuit names. But this was not always the case.

From 1968 to 1971, the federal government with the Northwest Territories Council undertook to change the identification system from disc numbers to the use of last names under "Project Surname."

The surnames were intended to replace the personal disk numbers that Inuit had been given by the Canadian government in the 1940s. While some Inuit and non-Inuit peoples viewed Project Surname as a more effective and politically correct system of identification, others saw it as yet another instrument of paternalism and control on the part of the federal government.

The Sixties and Millennial Scoops

According to Raven Sinclair (2016), the rise of the child welfare system emerged in response to the deterioration of the residential school programs in the 1950s. As provincial child welfare programs grew, Indigenous families were subjected to intense scrutiny and intervention as they struggled to address the traumatic aftermath of abuse, neglect, and cultural degradation of the residential school system.

During the 1960s, thousands of Indigenous children were removed from their families and communities and adopted out to non-Indigenous families in a period of Canadian history that has come to be known as the Sixties Scoop. This experience had devastating impacts on the health and well-being of Indigenous families and communities. Recently, as a result of numerous class-action lawsuits, a national Sixties Scoop Settlement was negotiated, offering individual financial compensation to those affected by apprehension, as well as funds to establish a foundation to memorialize stories of Sixties Scoop survivors. In his ruling on the Ontario class-action lawsuit by Sixties Scoop survivors, Justice Belobaba stated that the Sixties Scoop might have been worse by measures of cultural genocide than the Indian residential school system, since the residential boarding schools at least allowed children to remain within an Indigenous peer group and eventually return to their families and communities. By contrast, children taken in the Scoop often lived their lives as the only Indigenous person in their families and communities.

Moving forward, Indigenous community leaders insist that emphasis needs to be given to kinship care and customary adoption to ensure that Indigenous children grow up in a familiar environment, connected to their culture, language, and members of their family and clan. Such an approach is consistent with Indigenous peoples' culturally rooted approaches to caregiving, where child-rearing was and is seen as a communal responsibility. Such approaches might differ from those in mainstream Canadian society, but they are no less valid. There is strong evidence that when Indigenous peoples have sovereignty over their children and adequate resources, outcomes for children are better (Blackstock, 2010).

Yet, after decades of wrestling with the impact of the residential school system — and then with the Sixties Scoop that placed so many Indigenous children in non-Indigenous homes — First Nations are now facing another tragedy in the new millennium. There are more First Nations children in care right now than at the height of the residential school system.

Former Minister of Indigenous Services, Jane Philpott, explained in 2018 that this humanitarian crisis is driven by the "perverse incentive" by child welfare agencies to receive funding proportionate to child apprehension. She stated that the agencies should be rewarded for keeping children within "kinship care," rather than for the number of removals. She also argued that much more preventative work must be undertaken, such as substantial investments in housing and health services for parents.

Birth of a Family

Three Dene sisters and a brother, adopted as infants into separate families across North America, meet together for the first time in a deeply moving documentary film by director Tasha Hubbard.

Removed from their young Dene mother's care as part of Canada's infamous Sixties Scoop, Betty Ann, Esther, Rosalie and Ben were four of the 20,000 Indigenous children taken from their families between 1955 and 1985, to be either adopted into white families or to live in foster care. Now all in middle age, each has grown up in different circumstances, with different family cultures, different values and no shared memories.

The film, *Birth of a Family*, follows the siblings through pain, trepidation and laughter as they work together to re-build their family.

Recognizing and Protecting the Cultural Identity of Indigenous Children

The United Nations Declaration on the Rights of Indigenous Peoples sets out the minimum standards, norms, and rights applicable to Indigenous peoples and children. These standards, norms, and rights are interconnected, inter-related, and interdependent and serve as a framework for reconciliation in child, youth and family services.

The first five Calls to Action by the Truth and Reconciliation Commission (TRC) relate to child welfare, recognizing a continuity with the Indian residential school system and child apprehension today. Call to Action #4 calls "upon the federal government to enact Aboriginal child-welfare legislation that establishes national standards for Aboriginal child apprehension and custody cases and includes principles that:

- Affirm the right of Aboriginal governments to establish and maintain their own child-welfare agencies.
- Require all child-welfare agencies and courts to take the residential school legacy into account in their decision-making.
- Establish, as an important priority, a requirement that placements of Aboriginal children into temporary and permanent care be culturally appropriate."

"At its foundation, Indigenous public health must be self-determined: adapted for the needs of specific nations and grounded in local Indigenous language, culture and ways of knowing; developed, implemented and led by Indigenous Peoples; and informed by ongoing monitoring of data as governed by appropriate data sovereignty agreements."

Richardson, L., & Crawford, A (2020, September). COVID–19 and the decolonization of Indigenous public health. *Canadian Medical Association Journal (CMAJ).*

The number of Indigenous children in care has not changed significantly, however, since 2015 when the Calls to Action were issued.

Very similar recommendations were made in 1985 in the *No Quiet Place* report produced about the child welfare system in Manitoba. Taking stock of the "systematic, routine manner" in which Indigenous children were removed from their homes, the lead author of the report, Justice Kimelman, named this process as "cultural genocide" (51). As Raven Sinclair (2016) describes, Indigenous leaders rallied around the report, affirming this conclusion, and calling Canada to account under the Convention on the Prevention of the Crime of Genocide, to which Canada is a signatory.

The courts could also prove a barrier to attempts to end the practice of mass adoption. The leading case on inter-racial adoption of Indigenous children, *Racine v. Woods* (1983), erroneously concluded that attachment bonding superseded the importance of cultural belonging. In other words, the judge declared that children could form secure bonds with white parents, thereby negating a need to be raised in their communities.

However, as Sinclair describes, research studies show that the best interests of the child are in fact ensured when Indigenous children stay in their communities, since emotional bonding can change over time while the feelings of social dislocation tend to grow. Nearly all of the Sixties Scoop survivors that Sinclair has interviewed over the years eventually sought out and returned to their biological families.

Jordan's Principle

Jordan's Principle is a child-first principle intended to ensure that First Nations children do not experience denials, delays, or disruptions of services ordinarily available to other children due to jurisdictional disputes. It is named in honour of Jordan River Anderson, a young boy from Norway House Cree Nation in Manitoba. Jordan encountered tragic delays in services due to jurisdictional disputes that denied him an opportunity to live outside of a hospital setting before his death in 2005. Jordan died in hospital—rather than at home in his community—while the service disputes were being negotiated. Jordan's Principle states that in cases involving jurisdictional disputes, the government or government department first approached should pay for services that would ordinarily be available to other children in Canada; the dispute over payment for services can be settled afterwards.

In 2007, a motion endorsing Jordan's Principle was unanimously adopted by the House of Commons. However, there is growing recognition that the governmental response does not reflect the vision advanced by First Nations and endorsed by the House of Commons. Reviews by the First Nations Child and Family Caring Society, Canadian Paediatric Society, and UNICEF Canada have highlighted shortcomings in the governmental response, including a lack of clarity on the ground about funding, implementation, and whether systemic change will be introduced to address gaps in service delivery.

In September 2018, the federal government announced that Inuit children are eligible under the federal Child First Initiative (CFI) program for Jordan's Principle funding. This followed a commitment made in June 2018, during a meeting of the Inuit–Crown Partnership Committee in Inuvik, Northwest Territories, to work with Inuit, as well as provinces and territories, to develop a long-term Inuit-specific CFI framework consistent with Inuit rights and self-determination.

Figure 8.1

Indigenous Children in Foster Care

Statistics Canada, Census, 2016.

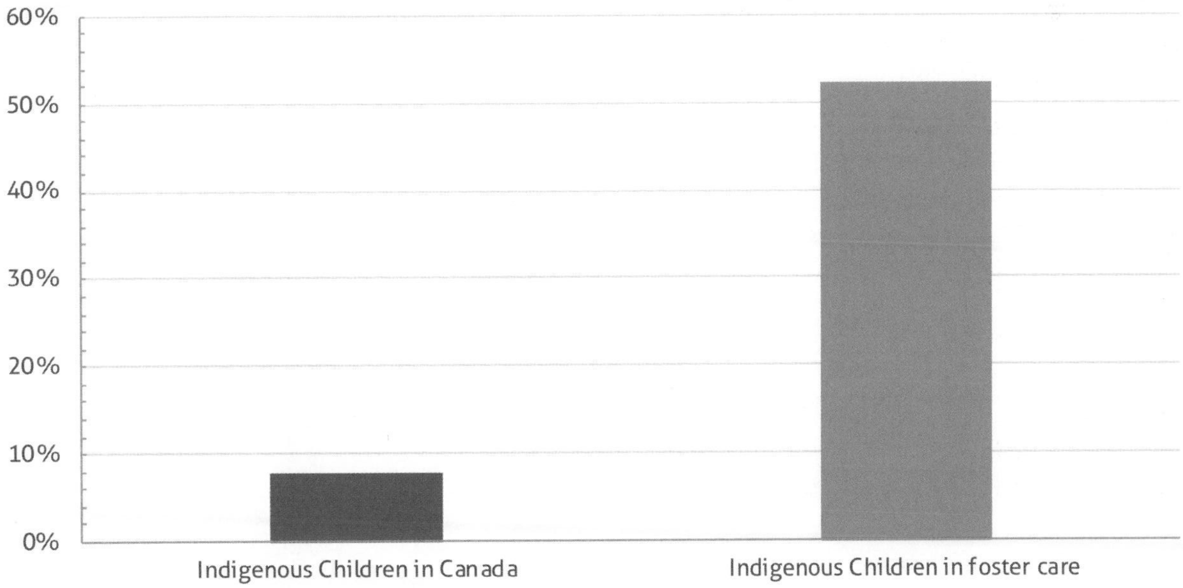

Cindy Blackstock

Executive Director, First Nations Child and Family Caring Society of Canada

"Cumulatively, First Nations children have spent over 66 million nights away from their families. That's 187,000 years of childhood. And in too many cases those children are being placed in non-Aboriginal homes where they're not learning their culture, they're not learning their connections to their families, they're not learning their languages.

"So I would argue that we're going to see many of those same harmful effects in this generation of First Nations children that we saw in residential schools if we don't stop what we're doing right now and make sure these kids have a proper chance to grow up with their families because that's where they learn their cultures."

Blackstock, C. (2014). Reconciliation means not having to say sorry a second time: Conversation with Cindy Blackstock, First Nations Child and Family Caring Society. Amnesty International Canada.

The Human Rights Tribunal Ruling

In a landmark legal decision, the Canadian Human Rights Tribunal (CHRT) ruled on January 26, 2016 that the federal government's underfunding of child and family services on First Nations reserves and its failure to ensure that First Nations children can access government services on the same terms as other children discriminates against 163,000 First Nations children on the grounds of race and national and ethnic origin. The Canadian government was subsequently issued with 10 non-compliance orders for failing to follow the Tribunal's order to make up the discrepancy in funding.

In a new ruling on September 6, 2019, the Tribunal instructed the government to pay compensation to children (and affected families) apprehended by the child welfare system. The Tribunal ordered the federal government to pay $40,000 to each child — the maximum allowed under the Canadian Human Rights Act — who was apprehended or taken from their home on reserve, no matter what the reason.

In October 2019, the federal government appealed the decision and requested a full quashing of the Human Rights Tribunal's order. "I think that is another sign that they are not accepting responsibility for their own behaviour," said Cindy Blackstock, the Executive Director of the First Nations Child and Family Caring Society. The First Nations Child and Family Caring Society, along with the Assembly of First Nations, first launched the complaint more than a decade ago.

"I've given up putting a lot of faith into what they say. I measure them by what they do and what it means for kids on the ground.

"I want to see those youth formerly in care get their tuition money. That's where I measure success."

Cindy Blackstock, social worker and longtime children's advocate who is also the executive director of the First Nations Caring Society, a non-profit that supports and advocates for child and family service agencies.

Indigenous Resistance to Child Removal from Homes and Communities

There has never been a period of state child removal where Indigenous people have not done everything in their power to reunite families. For example, the Saskatchewan Native Women's Association launched the "Native Home for Native Children" initiative in Saskatoon and the Métis Foster Home committee, led by Howard Adams, Phyllis Trochie, Nora Thibodeau, and Vicki Racette, fought the Adopt Indian and Métis (AIM) program in the 1960s.

In more recent years, Indigenous nations have obtained legislative authority to regain jurisdiction over families and children in care. For example, since 1980, Splatsin resumed power over the welfare of their children through the Splatsin Stsmamlt Services, which strives to return the care of the nation's children to the community, to implement preventative care, and to support families and individuals so that children can remain in their care.

Similarly, the Anishinabek Nation passed the Anishinabek Child Well-Being Law, which is designed to restore the nation's inherent rights and jurisdiction over child welfare and care. In June 2019, the Anishinabek Nation announced the creation of Koganaawsawin, a central body supporting the law that will manage the law's implementation.

Social Welfare in Perspective

Broken System

Why Is a Quarter of Canada's Prison Population Indigenous?

Even though Indigenous people make up only 4% of Canada's population, 26.4% of those incarcerated in Canadian prisons are Indigenous.

In the wake of the acquittal of Gerald Stanley in the death of Colten Boushie, there have been loud calls for reform to address Canada's blatant systemic racism in the criminal justice system.

Boushie, 22, died after being shot by Stanley in the back of the head as he sat in an SUV on a farm near Biggar, Saskatchewan.

The Canadian justice system works against Indigenous people at every level, from police checks and arrests to bail denial and detention, sentencing miscarriages and disparities, and high incarceration rates.

These trends are also well-documented in countries like the United States, Australia, and New Zealand. It is clear that the problem lies in our justice systems.

Around the time that Canada started receding its formal "Indian assimilation" policies in the 1950s, including the end of the residential school requirement, penitentiary and child welfare systems started to quietly assume a new role in the lives of Indigenous people.

In fact, prior to the 1960s, Indigenous people only represented one to two percent of the federal prison population. The rates have consistently increased every year since.

The Office of the Correctional Investigator reports the incarceration rate of Indigenous people is now at 26.4% of the federal prison population, while they comprise only 4% of the Canadian population. This is in spite of the fact that the Canadian crime rate has fallen in the last 20 years.

Placed in Segregation

Not only are Indigenous people more likely to be imprisoned, but they are also more often subjected to some of the most restrictive levels of punishment, including segregation, forced interventions, higher security classifications, involuntary transfers, and physical restraints. These punishments sometimes result in self-harm.

- Kinew James died of a heart attack after the emergency call button in her cell was routinely ignored at the Saskatoon Regional Psychiatric Centre.
- Eddie Snowshoe committed suicide after 162 days in solitary confinement at the Edmonton maximum security institution.
- Renee Acoby accumulated an additional 21 years of charges in prison, spent more than half of her time in segregation, and was eventually given a dangerous offender designation for a series of prison hostage-takings. She is now effectively behind bars for life.

Addressing these deeply problematic prison realities is currently at the forefront of the Government of Canada's criminal justice review, including two House of Commons studies and one by a Senate committee.

Imprisoned More Often

In considering remedies, two important issues are at play. First, Indigenous people are more often criminalized and imprisoned for acts that are linked to poverty; lack of educational and employment opportunities; lifestyles of substance use; and mental health concerns and histories of sexual abuse, violence, and trauma — in other words, colonialism.

Second, prisons are characterized by authoritarianism, power imbalances, restriction of movement and activities, isolation, lack of freedom of association, and enforcement of sometimes arbitrary and trivial demands. Prison environments often reflect and even perpetuate the very trauma and violence experienced by Indigenous people.

The Royal Commission on Aboriginal Peoples, 1996

The Royal Commission on Aboriginal Peoples (RCAP) was established to examine the relationship between Canadians and Indigenous peoples in the wake of the Oka Crisis (1990) and the failed Meech Lake Accord (1990).

The RCAP's Final Report was released in 1996. The central conclusion was that "the main policy direction, pursued for over 150 years, first by colonial then by Canadian governments, has been wrong." Its 440 recommendations called for a rebalancing of political and economic power between Indigenous nations and Canadian governments. As the Report noted: "Indigenous peoples must have room to exercise their autonomy and structure their solutions." It had six key themes:

1. Indigenous nations have to be reconstituted.
2. A process must be established for the assumption of powers by Indigenous nations.
3. There must be a fundamental reallocation of lands and resources.
4. Indigenous people need education and crucial skills for governance and economic self-reliance.
5. Economic development must be addressed if poverty, unemployment, and welfare are to change.
6. There must be an acknowledgement of injustices of the past.

The Oka Crisis, 1990

The Oka Crisis, also known as the Mohawk Resistance at Kanesatake, was a tense land dispute in the town of Oka, Québec. It lasted 78 days, with two fatalities. The crisis was sparked by the proposed expansion of a golf course and townhouses on Indigenous land that included a Mohawk burial ground.

Photo: Canadian soldier Patrick Cloutier and Anishinaabe warrior Brad Larocque come face to face in a tense standoff at the Kahnesatake reserve in Oka on September 1, 1990.

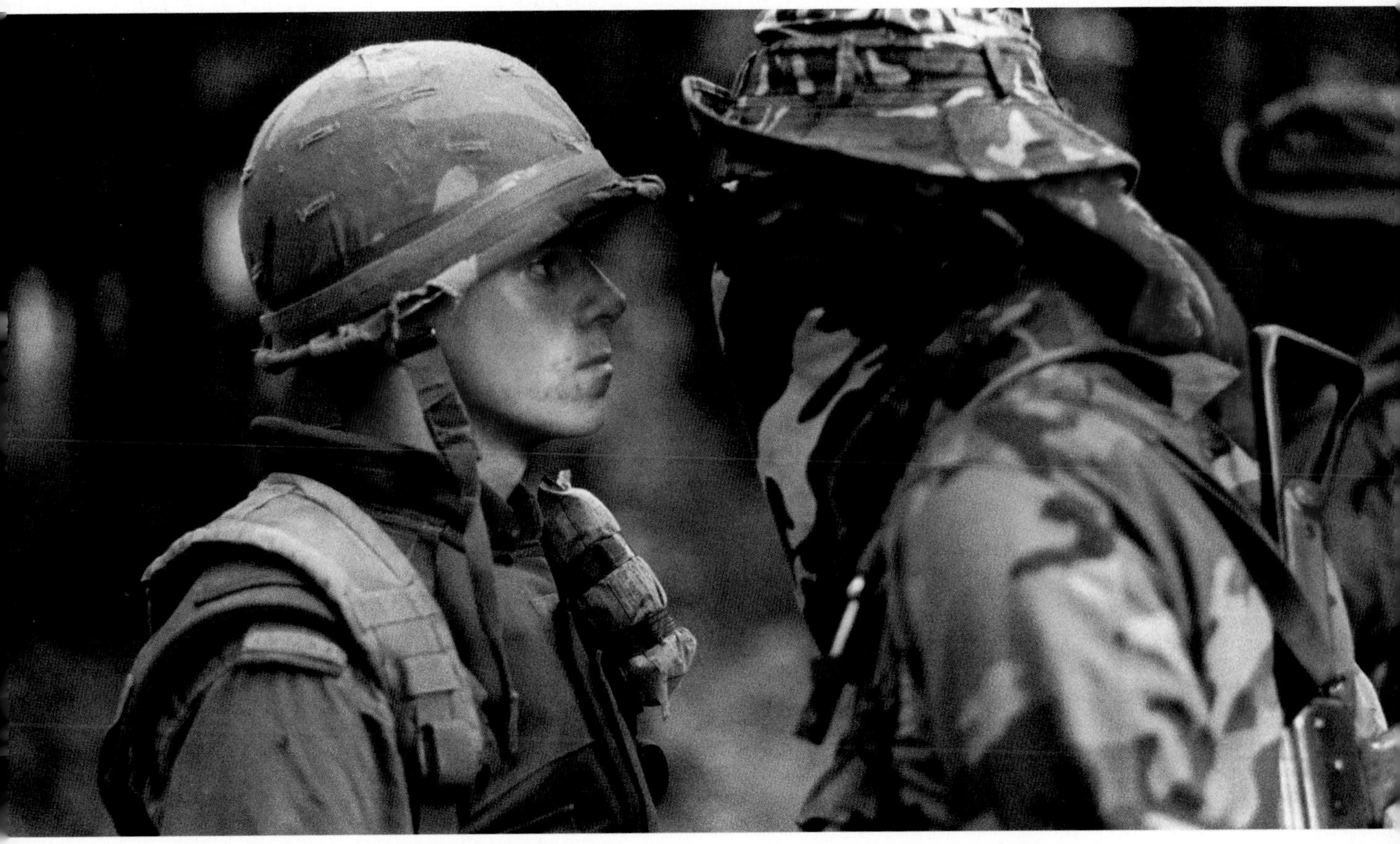

The Indian Residential Schools Settlement Agreement, 2007

The Indian Residential Schools Settlement Agreement (IRSSA) between the Government of Canada, various churches, and the Indigenous peoples of Canada was the largest class-action settlement in Canadian history. The IRSSA, which came into effect in September 2007, has five main components:

- **Common Experience Payment (CEP).** Under the IRSSA, $1.9 billion was set aside for former residents of the schools. Every former student would receive $10,000 for the first year of schooling, and $3,000 for each subsequent year. According to Indigenous and Northern Affairs Canada (INAC), 98% of the estimated 80,000 eligible former students had received payment by the end of December 2012, with over $1.6 billion in total approved for payment.
- **Independent Assessment Process (IAP).** In addition to the CEP, funds were allocated for the Independent Assessment Process, an out-of-court process for resolving claims of sexual abuse and serious physical and psychological abuse. As of December 31, 2012, over $1.7 billion had been issued through the IAP. According to Dan Ish, chief adjudicator of the Indian Residential School Adjudication Secretariat, around three times more applications were received than expected. The IAP hearings continued until around 2017.
- **Truth and Reconciliation Commission (TRC).** The Settlement Agreement also set aside $60 million for a five-year Truth and Reconciliation Commission that would provide opportunities for individuals, families, and communities to share their experiences. The Commission, established in 2008, was directed to raise public awareness through national events and its support of regional and local activities. It would also create a "comprehensive historical record" on the residential schools (and, budget permitting, a research centre).
- **Commemoration.** An important aspect of the IRSSA was the emphasis on acknowledging the impact of the residential schools and honouring the experiences of former students and their families and communities. To this end, the Settlement Agreement established a fund of $20 million for commemorative projects. This process involved the TRC, which would review and recommend proposals, and Aboriginal Affairs and Northern Development Canada (AANDC), which would allocate the funds.
- **Health and Healing Services.** The Settlement Agreement also included $125 million for the Aboriginal Healing Foundation (AHF) and established the Indian Residential Schools Resolution Health Support Program. This program would provide support for former students, with services provided by elders and Aboriginal community health workers as well as psychologists and social workers.

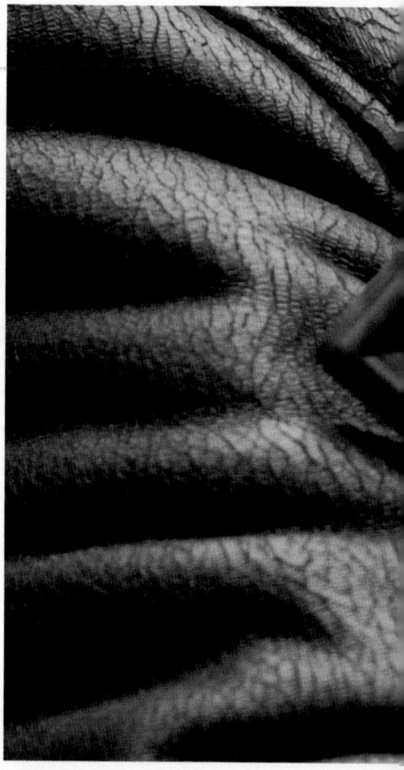

A decade later, with more than $3 billion paid out to survivors, it could still take several years before the process to compensate students who suffered the worst abuses is finally wrapped up. The initial budget for was $960 million. To date, more than 38,000 people have applied for compensation and $3.1 billion has been paid out. Combined with another payment to former residential school students as part of the settlement, more than $4.7 billion has been paid to survivors.

The Truth and Reconciliation Commission, 2015

Following the announcement of the IRSSA, the newly established Truth and Reconciliation Commission (TRC) spent six years travelling across Canada hearing from Indigenous persons who had been taken from their families and placed in residential schools. The TRC's mandate was to create an historic record about residential schools and their impact, and then share this record with the public.

Under its chair, Chief Justice Murray Sinclair, the TRC's final report was released in December 2015 and included 94 Calls to Action. The Calls were for sweeping changes to child welfare, education, and health care; recognition of Indigenous language and cultural rights; an inquiry into missing and murdered Indigenous women; and recognition and visibility of Indigenous sovereignty and histories. One of the main messages is that too many Canadians know little or nothing about how Canada has treated Indigenous peoples. In government circles, this makes for poor public policy decisions; in the public realm, it reinforces racist attitudes and fuels civic distrust (TRC, 2015, p. 8).

In 2015, Prime Minister Justin Trudeau promised to implement all 94 of the TRC's recommendations. The TRC presented an opportunity to address the historic trauma caused by residential schools and to work toward meaningful change. Seventy-six of the Calls to Action fall under federal jurisdiction. The CBC has kept track of implementation progress on its "Beyond 94" webpage, reporting that 10 of the Calls have been "completed" and 26 have "not started." In between, most are in the proposal stage and a smaller number are currently underway.

Photo: Joyce Carpenter holds a photo of her daughter during the 9th Annual Strawberry Ceremony on February 14, 2014 in Toronto. The annual ceremony honours the women and girls in Indigenous communities who have been murdered or who have gone missing.

What the COVID–19 pandemic has revealed ...

Indigenous Communities and COVID–19

Strengthening the Resilience of Local Communities

Pandemics and diseases loom large in the history of Indigenous populations in Canada. Past outbreaks have had devastating outcomes, fuelled by historical colonial policies and persistent inequalities.

Today, Indigenous communities are both receiving and giving support to counter COVID–19. But it is important that the public health response acknowledges Indigenous histories. By examining past pandemics, we can better understand how Indigenous communities are experiencing the current crisis.

Diseases and European Contact

During the periods of early contact, European settlers spread novel pathogens such as smallpox throughout the Americas. Indigenous groups had no immunity to these diseases. Estimates show that Indigenous populations in North America may have declined by over 50% in Arctic regions due to European contact. Declines along the Northwest Coast may have been as high as 90%. Estimates vary and identifying the role of disease in these figures is difficult, but there is no question that the impact was significant.

Colonial oppression of Indigenous groups worsened the effects of these new diseases. Communities were forced out of their traditional social and family structures. Settler lawmakers banned many traditional healing practices. And by the end of the 19th century, Indigenous peoples endured starvation, forced relocations, the loss of community and family, imposed religions, and violence.

The Spanish Flu of 1918–1920

No one had natural immunity when the Spanish flu spread across the globe after the First World War. But for Indigenous peoples, the systemic challenges they faced once again worsened the impacts. Higher rates of tuberculosis in Indigenous communities, for example, made the flu more deadly.

Canada's public health system lacked the capacity it has today, but the government's response — even by early 20th century standards — was prejudicial. Year over year, the Department of Indian Affairs reported the exact same number of deaths from the flu in Indigenous peoples in British Columbia between 1917 and 1919 — an impossible statistical claim. Even with the limited data available, it is evident from the National Archives of Canada that in 1919 Indigenous peoples in British Columbia died from the flu at a rate of over seven times the non-Indigenous rate. In addition, public health resources were often prioritized for non-Indigenous populations.

The Heavy Health Burden of H1N1

In 2009–2010, the H1N1 influenza spread to 214 countries, including Canada. As reported to the Public Health Agency of Canada, Indigenous peoples accounted for 28% of all hospital admissions and 18% of deaths in the first wave. With Indigenous peoples making up 4% of Canada's population at the time, this was a stark over-representation.

As in previous pandemics, the socio-economic inequalities facing Indigenous peoples increased the impacts of H1N1. These inequalities remain part of the current context in many Indigenous communities — as do their risks. Household crowding makes it easier for viruses to spread from one person to another. Limited access to health services in small or remote communities prolongs the time it takes to get appropriate care. And high rates of pre-existing health conditions increase the risk of a severe infection.

The federal government made several missteps in its public health response to H1N1. It delayed sending alcohol-based hand sanitizers to First Nations' communities, believing residents might consume it. It also sent body bags to several Manitoba First Nation reserve communities when those communities asked for medical supplies.

For many Indigenous communities, this botched public health response signalled a need for change. It was time to develop pandemic plans that would work for their communities. It was time for location-specific and culturally appropriate responses.

COVID–19: Moving Forward

Today, Indigenous communities continue to cope with many of the socio-economic disadvantages that made them vulnerable to previous pandemics. But many communities are successfully drawing on their strengths and resilience to respond to COVID–19.

The chief of Pasqua First Nation in Saskatchewan made international headlines when he prepared his community for a lockdown. He did this weeks before the Canadian government recognized the novel coronavirus as a serious threat. At least 18 First Nations in Northeastern Ontario proactively closed their borders to outsiders. They felt they did not have the necessary resources to fight COVID–19.

Indigenous leaders across the country are stepping up to support their people. Communities have supplied food hampers to residents. They have also provided financial support to residents who chose to go out on the land as a social distancing measure. And coronavirus hotlines have been set up to deliver medical and social support throughout communities.

Even as some regions start to reopen, there has been a recent rise in infection rates in some Indigenous communities. Governments must ensure that communities have the broader resources and funding they need. But they must also stay committed to developing public health responses in partnership with Indigenous communities — and they must not ignore history. They must remember the past experiences, both historical and recent, that Indigenous communities have with pandemics, and the social injustices that surrounded them. It will help support the resilience of Indigenous communities as they confront health crises now and in the future.

The Conference Board of Canada (2020, June 5). Health emergencies in Indigenous communities in Canada: Then and now. Ottawa, ON.

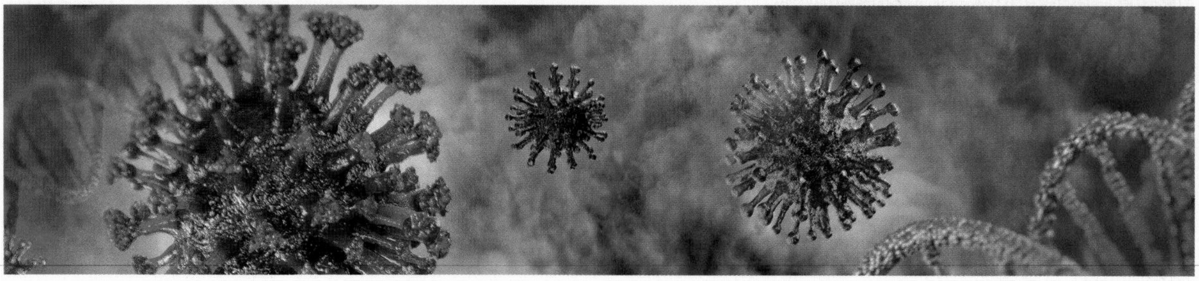

Risk factors identified in First Nations, Inuit, and Métis communities and examples of strategies to begin addressing them

	COVID–19 risk factors identified	Examples of temporary solutions	Examples of permanent solutions
Health Inequities	• **Overcrowding** on-reserve and in Northern regions that prevents self-isolation	• Create temporary housing supports or the repurposing of public spaces to permit self-isolation (Joannou, 2020; Nassif-Pires et al., 2020)	• Adequate government funding for housing construction on-reserve • Explicit and adequate government action to address poor housing conditions
	• **Lack of access to clean water** in some remote First Nations and Inuit communities and for homeless urban Indigenous populations	• Increase production and distribution of hand sanitizers (Ngabo, 2020) • Install handwashing stations in public spaces (Bui, 2020)	• Adequate government funding to construct and/or repair water distribution and decontamination facilities • Explicit government policy that guarantees access to clean and safe water and proper sanitation systems for all
	• **Increased presence of underlying health conditions** in certain First Nations, Inuit, and Métis communities	• Prioritize health resources to those identified as being most at risk (DeBruin et al., 2012)	• Adequate government funding across public services to address factors such as overcrowded or inadequate housing and food insecurity that contribute to the development of health issues • Systematically record ethnicity in health registries to track overrepresentation and identify populations most at risk
	• **Difficulties in accessing medical supplies and treatment** in remote First Nations and Inuit communities	• Create resource stockpiles that are easily accessible locally (DeBruin et al., 2012) • Promote the use of local traditional medicines that help alleviate symptoms of COVID–19 (PAHO, 2020; Wood, 2020)	• Adequate government funding to improve transportation infrastructure to remote communities and address higher costs related to remoteness • Substantively equitable allocations of medical supplies and equipment and pharmaceuticals for remote communities

• **Distrust in health structures** experienced by First Nations, Inuit, and Métis populations	• Outreach and educational activities (DeBruin et al., 2012) • Train available practitioners in the provision of culturally competent care and equitable practice (PAHO, 2020) • Protect the right of Indigenous communities to hold traditional healing ceremonies, such as sun dances, during COVID–19 (Shield & Martell, 2020)	• Explicit government policy to increase the number of Indigenous health practitioners and to integrate Indigenous worldviews into health practice (Lafontaine, 2018) • Implement reforms to eliminate systemic racism in health care provision (e.g., see recommendations in Preston, 2014) • Adequate measures from the government to assist Indigenous communities in preserving and enriching the cultural and linguistic experiences of community members
• **Lack of public health information** available to communities for whom English is not their first language	• Translate and disseminate clear and culturally appropriate information on COVID–19 into local Indigenous languages (PAHO, 2020)	• Explicit government policy that requires all public health information to be translated into each Indigenous language (as is already the case for English and French) • Support for Indigenous communities to design and implement public health education programs
Health Inequities • **Limited access to food** in remote Inuit and First Nations communities	• Rely on networks of traditional harvesting (Krishna, 2020; Wood, 2020) • Provide school lunches to low-income families (Nassif-Pires et al., 2020)	• Explicit government policy to reinstate access to traditional foods and allow for traditional hunting and fishing practices • Government subsidies for healthy food options and other necessities in communities
• **Limited availability of computers and Internet** to access education during confinement for remote Indigenous communities	• Service providers supplying additional Internet or hot spots to low-income families or remote areas (Castelo, 2020; Truong, 2020) • Schools' provision of computers/tablets to students (Truong, 2020) or physical take-home materials that do not require Internet or computers (Castelo, 2020; Noonoo, 2020)	• Adequate government funding to develop reliable digital communications infrastructure in remote communities (Stollery, 2018) • Funding to ensure IT platforms are responsive to Indigenous languages and cultures

Saint-Girons, M., Joh-Carnella, N., Lefebvre, R., Blackstock, C., & Fallon, B. (2020). *Equity concerns in the context of COVID–19 — A focus on First Nations, Inuit, and Métis communities in Canada.* Toronto, ON: Canadian Child Welfare Research Portal.

8.5 Principles Respecting Canada's Relationship with Indigenous Peoples, 2017

In the federal election in 2016, the Liberals ran on a platform of changing the relationship between the Crown and Indigenous peoples in Canada. They promised a new nation-to-nation relationship based on respect, cooperation, partnership, and the recognition of Indigenous rights. In February 2018, Prime Minister Justin Trudeau announced the development of a new and transformational Indigenous Rights, Recognition and Implementation Framework.

The Ten Principles

The Rights Framework was preceded by the Department of Justice's Principles Respecting the Government of Canada's Relationship with Indigenous Peoples, made public in July 2017 by then Minister of Justice Jody Wilson-Raybould. Some Indigenous leaders have criticized the government for failing to consult on the development of the Principles, but the ten Principles became the basis of subsequent government policy.

According to the Government, these Principles were rooted in Section 35 of the Charter of Rights, guided by the UN Declaration, and informed by the Report of the Royal Commission on Aboriginal Peoples (RCAP) and the Truth and Reconciliation Commission's Calls to Action. In addition, they are meant to reflect a commitment to good faith, the rule of law, democracy, equality, non-discrimination, and respect for human rights. Subsequently, the Principles have appeared in government literature in reference to their role guiding the Cabinet Committee review of Canada's laws and policies, and the Nation-to-Nation Memorandums of Understanding with the Assembly of First Nations (AFN). Indigenous leaders have approached things more cautiously.

Much of the Principles document attempts to grapple with how best to incorporate Indigenous peoples into pre-existing Canadian legal orders (largely neglecting Indigenous pre-existence). For example, Principle 3 asserts that governments should "ensure that Indigenous peoples are treated with respect and as full partners in Confederation," while Principle 4 motions toward "cooperative federalism" and supports "developing mechanisms and designing processes which recognize that Indigenous peoples are foundational to Canada's constitutional framework."

Similarly, Principle 7 states that, "any infringement of Aboriginal or treaty rights requires justification in accordance with the highest standards established by the Canadian courts and must be attained in a manner consistent with the honour of the Crown and the objective of reconciliation." Muskrat Falls, Site C, and the Kinder Morgan Trans-Mountain pipeline expansion — projects Indigenous peoples have vigorously contested — are all examples of so-called justifiable infringement.

Principle 6 states that the Crown will "consult and cooperate in good faith with the aim of securing their *free, prior and informed consent*" (emphasis added). This principle commits Canada only to *attempting* to honour free, prior and informed consent — even though it is a principle of international law.

Free, Prior and Informed Consent

"Free, prior and informed consent" is a specific right that pertains to Indigenous peoples and is recognized in the United Nations Declaration on the Rights of Indigenous Peoples (UNDRIP).

This principle allows Indigenous peoples to give or withhold consent to a project that may affect them or their territories. Once they have given their consent, they can also withdraw it at any stage. Furthermore, the principle enables Indigenous people to negotiate the conditions under which the project will be designed, implemented, monitored, and evaluated.

This principle is also embedded within the universal right to self-determination.

IN SUMMARY

THE GOVERNMENT OF CANADA RECOGNIZES THAT

01 All relations with Indigenous peoples need to be based on the recognition and implementation of their right to self-determination, including the inherent right of self-government.

02 Reconciliation is a fundamental purpose of section 35 of the *Constitution Act, 1982.*

03 The honour of the Crown guides the conduct of the Crown in all of its dealings with Indigenous peoples.

04 Indigenous self-government is part of Canada's evolving system of cooperative federalism and distinct orders of government.

05 Treaties, agreements, and other constructive arrangements between Indigenous peoples and the Crown have been and are intended to be acts of reconciliation based on mutual recognition and respect.

06 Meaningful engagement with Indigenous peoples aims to secure their free, prior, and informed consent when Canada proposes to take actions which impact them and their rights, including their lands, territories and resources.

07 Respecting and implementing rights is essential and that any infringement of section 35 rights must by law meet a high threshold of justification which includes Indigenous perspectives and satisfies the Crown's fiduciary obligations.

08 Reconciliation and self-government require renewed fiscal relationship, developed in collaboration with Indigenous nations, that promotes a mutually supportive climate for economic partnership and resource development.

09 Reconciliation is an ongoing process that occurs in the context of evolving Indigenous-Crown relationships.

10 Distinctions-based approach is needed to ensure that the unique rights, interests and circumstances of the First Nations, the Métis Nation and Inuit are acknowledged, affirmed, and implemented.

Principles Respecting the Government of Canada's Relationship with Indigenous Peoples. Department of Justice. Ottawa, ON.

Social Welfare in Perspective

The True Test of Reconciliation

The Right to Say "No"

Canada will only truly give effect to reconciliation when Indigenous peoples have the right to say "no," argues Pam Palmater, Chair in Indigenous Governance at Ryerson.

Conflict is coming. There is no getting around that fact. Anyone who believes that reconciliation will be about blanket exercises, cultural awareness training, visiting a native exhibit at a museum. or hanging native artwork in public office buildings doesn't understand how we got here.

Reconciliation between Canada and Indigenous peoples has never been about multiculturalism, diversity, or inclusion. Reconciliation is not an affirmative-action program, nor is it about adding token Indigenous peoples to committees, advisory groups, or boardrooms. We cannot tokenize our way out of this mess that Canada created

Real reconciliation requires truth be exposed, justice be done to make amends, and then Canada's discriminatory laws, policies, practices, and societal norms be reconciled with Indigenous rights, title, treaties, laws, and jurisdiction. That process of truth, justice, and reconciliation will be painful. It requires a radical change. Nothing less than the transfer of land, wealth, and power to Indigenous peoples will set things right.

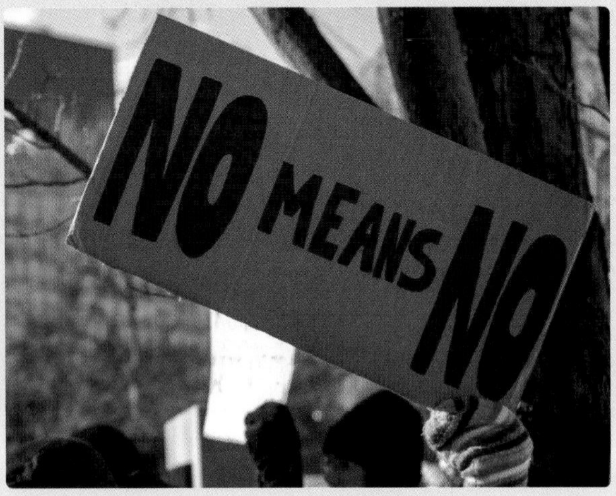

A protest supporting Wet'suwet'en First Nation opposition to the Costal GasLink Pipeline in BC, February 17, 2019.

UN Declaration on the Rights of Indigenous Peoples

The true test of reconciliation will be whether Canada respects the Indigenous right to say no.

Canadian courts have been issuing decisions about Aboriginal rights and title and treaty rights, sending the strong message to governments that they must obtain the consent of Indigenous peoples before taking actions or making decisions that will impact our lives. Governments have not listened. Canada's failure to listen is one of the reasons why Indigenous peoples spent more than 25 years negotiating the United Nations Declaration on the Rights of Indigenous Peoples which guarantees the right of Indigenous peoples to free, prior and informed consent. Article 19 of UNDRIP provides:

> States shall consult and cooperate in good faith with the Indigenous peoples concerned through their own representative institutions in order to obtain their free, prior and informed consent before adopting and implementing legislative or administrative measures that may affect them.

Consent is a legal concept that can be defined as the voluntary acquiescence of one person to the proposal of another. In general, it is the right to say yes or no to something and/or put conditions on an agreement. Consent must be free from misrepresentations, deceptions, fraud, or duress. This is a very basic right, but one which has been denied to Indigenous peoples since contact.

Take, for example, the actions of Indian agents and police, who used food rations to extort sex from Indigenous women and girls. In the context of being forced to live on reserves, not being allowed to leave the reserve, and being dependent on food rations, what real choice would a young girl have? Similarly, when police officers or judges detain Indigenous women and girls, drive them to secluded locations, and force them to perform sexual acts — there is no real consent when the threat of lethal force or arrest on false charges is ever-present.

This is especially so given our knowledge of the number of assaults and deaths of our people in police custody. There was no consent when they stole our children and put them into residential schools, nor was there any consent when priests, nuns, and others raped those children. There was no consent when doctors forcibly sterilized Indigenous women and girls — sometimes without their knowledge.

Free, Prior and Informed Consent

Today, the right of Indigenous peoples to free, prior and informed consent has become the central issue in Canada's reconciliation agenda. Justin Trudeau campaigned on the promise of implementing UNDRIP into law and respecting the right of Indigenous peoples to say no. When asked by APTN host Cheryl McKenzie whether no would mean no under his government, he responded "absolutely." Another way of putting this is that Indigenous peoples could exercise their legal right to refuse to approve or authorize a project.

This veto right stems from various sources, but primarily our inherent rights as Indigenous governments with our own laws and rules which govern our traditional territories.

They may also come from specific Aboriginal rights, treaty rights, and Aboriginal title. These rights are not only protected within our own Indigenous laws, but also section 35 of Canada's Constitution Act, 1982 and various international human rights laws, including UNDRIP. Yet, after Trudeau announced his latest idea to create a legislative framework to recognize Indigenous rights and avoid litigation, Justice Minister Raybould stated clearly that "consent doesn't mean a veto" for Indigenous peoples.

So, we are now back where we started. Canada has not yet reconciled its laws, policies, or political positions to the fact that Indigenous peoples have the right to say no to development projects on our lands. This means that conflict will continue to grow over mining, forestry, hydraulic fracking, and pipelines on Indigenous lands.

The true test of reconciliation will inevitably play out on the ground, like it did in Oka, Ipperwash, Gustafsen Lake, Esgenoopetitj (Burnt Church), and Elsipogtog. Will Canada force pipelines to go ahead against the will of British Columbia and First Nations? Will Canada isolate and exclude First Nations who do not subscribe to the extinguishment requirements of Canada's land-claims process? What will happen to First Nations who stop provincial social workers and police officers from entering their reserves to steal more children into foster care? This will be the real test of our inherent right to say no.

The True Test of Reconciliation

Canada will only truly give effect to reconciliation when Indigenous peoples have the right to say no — no to discriminatory government laws and policies; no to federal and provincial control over our Nations; no to racism from society, industry and government; no to sexualized violence, abuse, and trafficking; no to theft of our children into foster care and the imprisonment of our peoples; no to the ongoing theft of our lands and resources; and no to the contamination and destruction of our lands, waters, plants, animals, birds, and fish.

The right to say no is the core of any future relationship with the Canadian state and its citizens. It's a basic right — one which is grounded in our sovereignty as individuals and Nations to decide for ourselves the life we wish to live. Canada has made it clear we have no right to say no, only an obligation to say yes.

First Nations leaders and citizens should not wait to see how this plays out in court — they should assert and defend their right to say no now.

Palmater, Pam (2018). True test of reconciliation: Respect the Indigenous right to say No. *Canadian Dimension*, 52(1).

Pam Palmater is a Mi'kmaw citizen and member of the Eel River Bar First Nation in northern New Brunswick. She has been a practising lawyer for 18 years and is Associate Professor and the Chair in Indigenous Governance at Ryerson University.

8.6 The Indigenous Rights Framework, 2018

On February 14, 2018, on the heels of the acquittal of Gerald Stanley for the shooting death of Colten Boushie, a Nehiyaw man from the Red Pheasant First Nation of Saskatchewan, Prime Minister Trudeau outlined a new Recognition and Implementation of Indigenous Rights Framework (RIIRF) that would include new ways to recognize and implement Indigenous rights.

Though it was not ratified as law, a suite of related legislation and policy has been rapidly deployed. It includes fiscal policy, omnibus legislation, changes in negotiations for land and self-government, and splitting Indigenous and Northern Affairs Canada (INAC) into two ministries. There is the establishment of the National Reconciliation Council, a Working Group of Ministers to Review Laws and Policies Related to Indigenous Peoples (also known as the Cabinet Committee to "Decolonize" Canada's Laws), and the Principles Respecting the Government of Canada's Relationship with Indigenous Peoples.

The Indigenous Rights Framework

Certainly, progress has been made on a number of fronts. After 150 years of anti-Indigenous governments, Indigenous activists and leaders are making gains. The Idle No More movement has forever changed the discourse in this country, Indigenous women and Two-Spirit organizers intervened to demand justice. The Truth and Reconciliation Commission brought focus to our collective challenges.

There now are formal commitments to ensure the right of Indigenous peoples to say no to development in Indigenous territories, full implementation of the United Nation's Declaration on the Rights of Indigenous Peoples (UNDRIP), a federal inquiry into missing and murdered Indigenous women and girls, repealing laws that infringe on Indigenous rights, honouring the Truth and Reconciliation (TRC) Calls to Action, keeping land disputes out of the courts, funding for water infrastructure on reserve, resources slowly trickling into communities for education, and a settlement for the victims of the Sixties Scoop.

All this is progress. But rather than move toward a recognition of First Nation territorial authority, which would mean a return of land to Indigenous peoples, the new Recognition and Implementation of Indigenous Rights Framework appeared to move the federal government toward a resource-specific approach that avoids the issue of Aboriginal title in any fulsome way. "Aboriginal title" is the legal right recognized for underlying proprietary interest in the land.

Government literature encourages more comprehensive land claims, while government action moves away from them toward simply fishing or forestry agreements. Moreover, the federal government insists that the Aboriginal title aspects of the Rights Framework legislation will be "co-developed." Meanwhile, communities participating in the rights and recognition tables report frustration, little space for substantive dialogue, and apparent status quo federal mandates, rather than self-determination, when it comes to Aboriginal title and self-government.

"For Indigenous people in Canada, matters of disease, sickness, and famine are not unprecedented and the historical record tells us that we cannot simply sit by and trust that either the feds or provinces will provide adequate levels of support and aid.

"Indigenous people are particularly vulnerable to communicable diseases due to long-standing and ongoing structural asymmetries that pertain to the administration of health services, environmental racism, and the inaccessibility of healthy food sources.

"And while all human beings are susceptible to the coronavirus, it has particularly injurious, and sometimes fatal, implications for those with pre-existing medical conditions, which Indigenous people experience at disproportionately high rates."

Starblanket G. & Hunt, D. (2020). *COVID–19, The Numbered Treaties & the Politics of Life: A Special Report.* Yellowhead Institute.

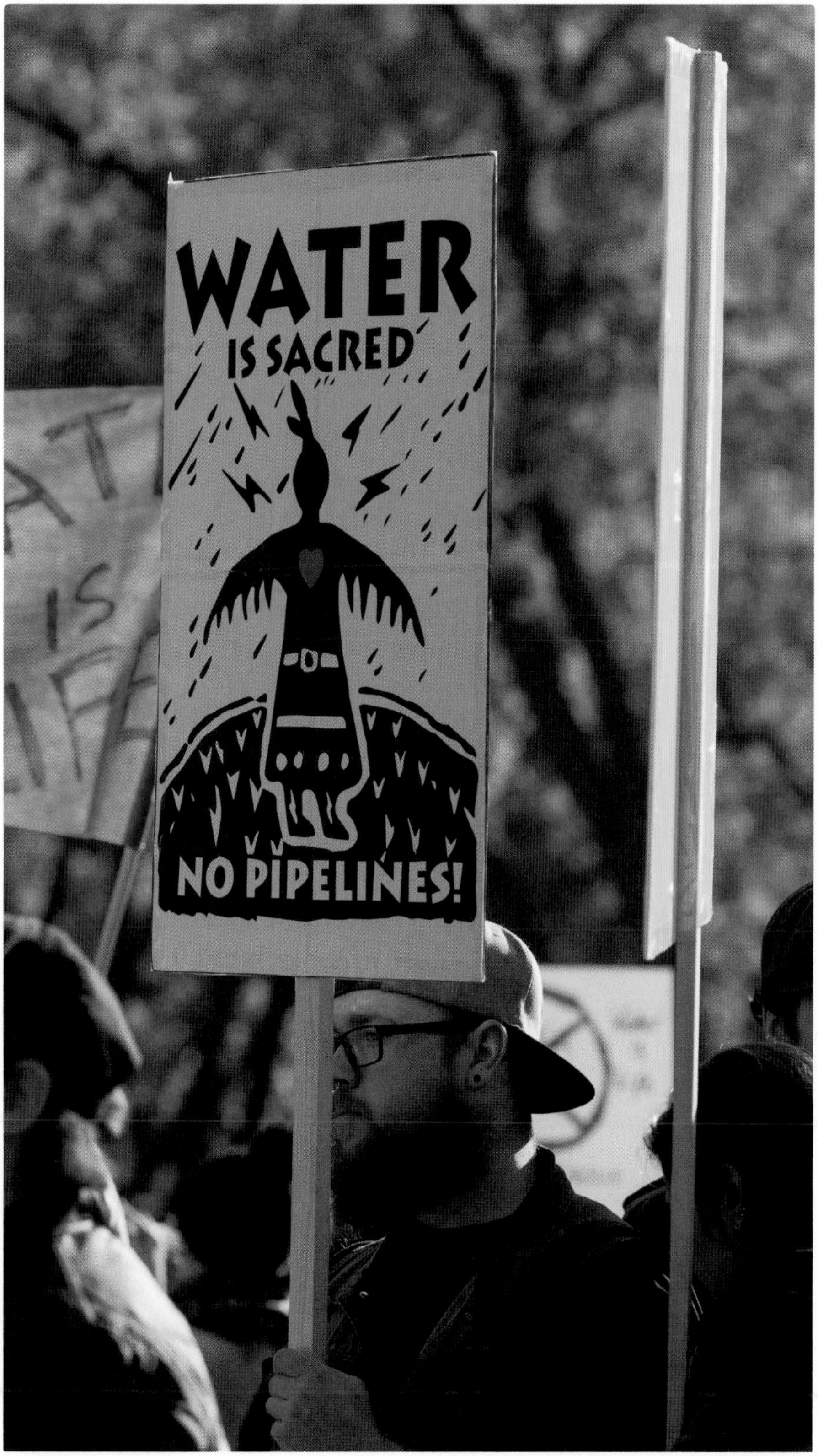

Drinking Water Advisories

Thousands of people in First Nations communities across Canada live without access to clean drinking water. Some communities have gone without clean water for decades.

Drinking water advisories have been a persistent injustice in First Nations communities. There are still more than 100 communities without clean drinking water.

After years of pressure from Indigenous and social justice organizations nationwide, the federal government has finally committed to ending all long-term drinking water advisories by 2021.

The New/Old Self-Government Model

In statements and government literature prior to and since the announcement of the Rights Framework, it became clear that central to the new legislation will be a process to recognize self-determining First Nation governing collectivities and offer alternatives to the Indian Act once and for all. The federal government insists this will be open-ended and that it will be up to First Nations to determine the shape of their re-constituted nation.

While the federal government is pointing to UNDRIP, the TRC, and RCAP for inspiration, precedents for its vision for self-government may be found in Bill S-212 First Nations Self-Government Recognition Act. Though that Bill never became law in British Columbia, the ideas were repackaged in the 2014 BC AFN Governance Toolkit, A Guide to Nation Building. Both emphasized constitution development with authority to legislate reserve-based affairs and established a process for amalgamating bands.

This appears to be the mechanism through which the federal government will prepare First Nations for post-Indian Act, reserve-based self-government. Opting in will likely be required to qualify for further steps along the self-government path. When federal officials speak of "removing barriers" to the expression of First Nation self-determination, they seem to mean the need for more capacity and transparency. First Nations themselves have identified the barriers rather differently — government paternalism, treaty violations, and dispossession of lands and resources.

Reconstituting Nations

When the federal government decides First Nations are ready to take on more administrative responsibility, a likely solution to service delivery will be via an aggregation model. "Reconstituted nations" will mean scaling up along regional, treaty, or national lines and then creating new institutions to deliver programs and services. The choice would remain with First Nations as to how they decide to organize as aggregates.

With the Rights Framework legislation, we can expect to see all of the above formalized in legislation and framed as a movement away from the Indian Act. But this vision of self-government is limited and focused on entrenching a reserve-based administrative governance model with improvements in service delivery, transparency, and accountability. It includes nothing of the "transformational" policy the government has promised.

First Nations will not be forced into this process, only encouraged to participate. But what kind of choice is voluntary if alternative models — ones that might focus on traditional territories, title lands, or expanded governing authority — are not an option? For those who object to this process, the Indian Act will likely remain in place but with pressure to conform or be labelled "dissidents" or criminalized. (In the past, a federal strategy has been to withhold or reduce federal transfers as leverage to obtain consent from those who object to policies.)

Incrementalism as Federal Policy

Sectoral and incremental approaches to Aboriginal title were devised almost two decades ago within the BC Treaty Process as a solution to the lack of interim measures for bands during lengthy, decades-long processes. (They are also called "slim AIPs" [Agreements in Principle] or "pre-treaty" agreements.) Within the context of the BC Treaty Process, "incrementalism" is demonstrated by the BC Treaty Commission recommendation that First Nations, Canada, and BC shift the emphasis from final agreements to building treaties gradually over time, setting in place all the pieces, to ensure the success of the broader agreement once ready to be signed.

The movement away from the comprehensive claims and modern treaty model is already underway. In June 2016, INAC revealed 20 "exploratory tables" on land claims and governance matters but refused to reveal the list of communities with whom it was negotiating. A year later, the number of tables had jumped to 50, and the "exploratory tables" were renamed as "Recognition of Indigenous Rights and Self-Determination Discussion Tables."

In 2020, there were 60 discussion tables involving 320 communities affecting 700,000 Indigenous people in Canada. This is a tremendous number, nearly half the total population. It includes approximately 265,000 Métis represented by five provincially organized groups. There is one Inuit group. And nearly half of the First Nations groups at the table are advocacy organizations, such as Political Territorial Organizational (PTOs) and tribal councils.

Treaty Rights

Mi'kmaq fishers in Nova Scotia won at the Supreme Court, but they are still fighting for their livelihoods.

Facing cut traps and threats of violence 21 years after a landmark Supreme Court ruling, the fight over treaty rights in Nova Scotia still rages on.

Photo: Sipekne'katik First Nation members stand as non-Indigenous boats protest the fishery launch on September 17, 2020.

The Future of Aboriginal Title

This movement away from land claims settlements toward more sectoral, incremental agreements over particular issues and resources was also emphasized by former Conservative Prime Minister Stephen Harper, whose last government commissioned a special report, "A New Direction: Advancing Aboriginal and Treaty Rights."

The Harper government's report reviewed the comprehensive land claims policy in Canada and recommended that Canada should "develop an alternative approach for modern treaty negotiations, one informed by the recognition of existing Aboriginal rights, including title, in areas where Aboriginal title can be conclusively demonstrated."

Sectoral agreements allow the federal government to insist it is no longer extinguishing or modifying title, yet there are still "certainty" clauses that prevent First Nations from exercising jurisdiction over their lands and resources. First Nations temporarily suspend claims in exchange for financial compensation and/or a co-management regime. These agreements may then be re-visited and re-negotiated on a regular basis, offering some flexibility for First Nations, but none of these agreements have recognized a substantive form of First Nation jurisdiction.

"Nothing about Us without Us"

Key questions arose in response to this strategy that can now also be posed to Prime Minister Justin Trudeau's government, such as:

- What guidance does the Rights Framework give as to the legal criteria for making a claim acceptable or unacceptable?
- Will these tables "test positions" for the Crown that they wish to advance in litigation?
- Is the Crown pushing positions that have failed in litigation or through the comprehensive land claims policy?
- Do sectoral agreements erode broader claims for Aboriginal title and rights of Indigenous nations?

Nearly all of Canada's proposed changes to its relationship with First Nation peoples neglect issues of land restitution and treaty obligations. Whether relational, policy, or legislative reform, they focus on the creation of self-governing First Nations with administrative responsibility for service delivery on limited land bases. Provincial, territorial, and federal governments will continue to patronize and intervene in the lives and lands of First Nation peoples.

While there are some welcome changes, including resources for program and service delivery, there is also a clear attempt to maintain a modified version of the status quo. Such efforts only serve to mislead First Nations and the Canadians on the transformational nature of these changes.

Much More Work To Do

Since well before the time of the Indian Act in 1876, Indigenous peoples in Canada have been subjected to colonial government policies concerned mainly with seizing their land and keeping it, first for the settlers and more recently for the economic gains of resource extraction. Government policies were aimed at "assimilating" Indigenous peoples by breaking their cultural and language ties. Through such policies, Indigenous families and communities suffered immeasurable harm, such that even today many communities experience poverty and housing conditions resembling those of Third World countries.

Positive developments are to be welcomed, but many Indigenous leaders and scholars question the government's commitment to acknowledging Indigenous rights, saying that the high expectations stated in public are not matched by actions that would guarantee them in practice. The process has proceeded without adequate Indigenous consultation, and the core issue of treaties and land rights is not being addressed.

Social justice initiatives such as the Residential Schools Settlement Agreement and the Truth and Reconciliation Commission are steps in the right direction. Such measures provide opportunities for both compensation and healing. Underlying all this is the need for Indigenous self-determination — Indigenous control of Indigenous affairs in ways that go beyond circumscribed "self-government" agreements. Indigenous peoples have a nation-to-nation relationship with the Crown, and this must be respected.

Photo: One of the signs displayed as protesters shut down the Burrard Street Bridge in Vancouver for a day of action on climate change, part of co-ordinated events across the country (Margarita Young, October 7, 2019).

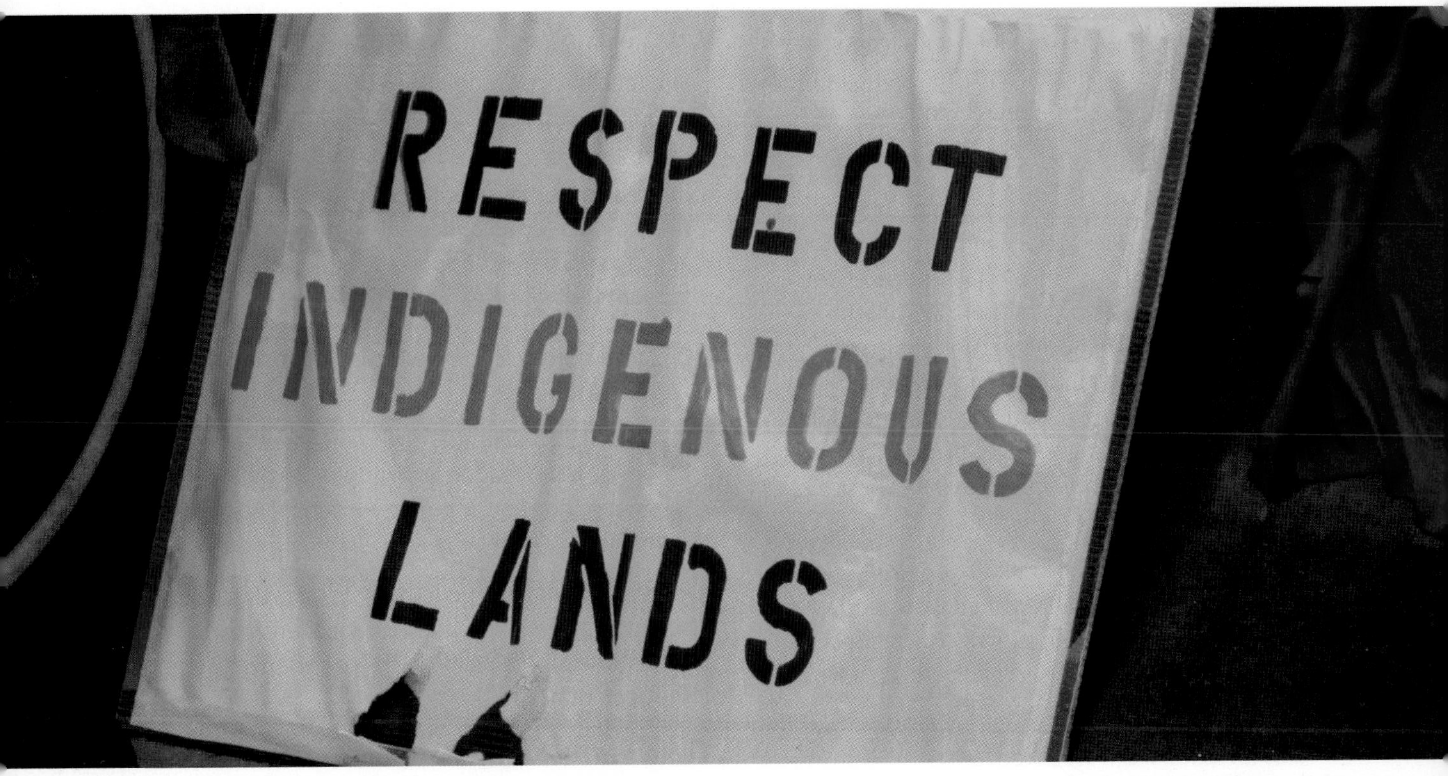

Social Welfare Policy in Action

The TRC's 94 Calls to Action

A Preliminary Progress Report

In 2015, the government committed to implement the Truth and Reconciliation 94 Calls to Action. Five years on, only 10% had been completed and almost 25% had not been started.

In 2015, the Truth and Reconciliation Commission identified 94 Calls to Action, all of which Prime Minister Justin Trudeau promised his government would implement.

As of December 2019, according to the CBC's "Beyond 94" website, only 10 of the Calls to Action had been completed, 26 hadn't been started, and the remaining were in the early development stage.

Accountability and transparency are cornerstones of any public policy. Below, we look at the progress to date on some specific Calls to Action. Social workers in particular will need to monitor the progress being made in these areas.

Child Welfare

The first five Calls are related to child welfare, the first being to reduce the number of Indigenous children in care and the second to account for the number of Indigenous children in care.

Call #2 states:

> "We call upon the federal government, in collaboration with the provinces and territories, to prepare and publish annual reports on the number of Aboriginal children (First Nations, Inuit, and Métis) who are in care, compared with non-Aboriginal children, as well as the reasons for apprehension, the total spending on preventive and care services by child-welfare agencies, and the effectiveness of various interventions."

Progress to date: As of the fall of 2018, the Government of Canada identified that meetings had occurred to discuss how collectively to collect and publish data on Indigenous children in care. However, no annual report has been published.

Call to Action #2: Not started.

Education

The next seven Calls to Action (#6–12) are related to education. Similar to the funding for child welfare on reserve, Call #8 calls for equity in funding for education on-reserve.

Call #8 states:

> "We call upon the federal government to eliminate the discrepancy in federal education funding for First Nations children being educated on reserves and those First Nation children being educated off reserves."

In 2016, the federal government claimed to have made "significant investments, totalling $2.6 billion over 5 years, for primary and secondary education on reserve." However, the CBC claims that this "commitment falls short of a 2015 campaign promise, and much of that funding — $801 million — has been backloaded to 2020–21, one year after the ... federal election."

In April 2019, the federal government released a new co-developed policy and improved funding approach to better support the needs of First Nations students on-reserve.

Call #10 is a call for new education legislation. Call #10 states in part:

> "We call on the federal government to draft new Aboriginal education legislation with the full participation and informed consent of Aboriginal peoples."

Progress to date: The government states that a new policy framework has been established; however, as of the time of writing, no such education legislation has been drafted.

Calls to Action #8 and #10: In progress.

Health Care

Seven Calls to Action (#18–24) are on health. Call #21 and Call #22 are associated with ensuring funding for Indigenous healing centres and that the broader Canadian health care system recognize and respect Indigenous health practices.

Call #21 states:

> "We call upon the federal government to provide sustainable funding for existing and new Aboriginal healing centres to address the physical, mental, emotional, and spiritual harms caused by residential schools, and to ensure that the funding of healing centres in Nunavut and the Northwest Territories is a priority."

The federal government provided $350 million in the 2016 and 2017 budgets for various mental wellness, substance use, and suicide prevention programs. In August 2019, the government announced a partnership with the Government of Nunavut and Nunavut Tunnagavik for a new Nunavut Recovery Centre.

Call to Action #22 requires health and social care professionals to value Indigenous healing practices.

> "We call upon those who can effect change within the Canadian health-care system to recognize the value of Aboriginal healing practices and use them in the treatment of Aboriginal patients in collaboration with Aboriginal leaders and Elders, where requested by Aboriginal patients."

Progress to date: The government highlights a number of additions to the 2017 and 2018 budgets, but it is unclear if this is new money.

Other initiatives include an investment of $6 million over 5 years in midwifery investment with the National Aboriginal Council of Midwives.

In addition, the Canadian Medical Association, the Royal College of Physicians and Surgeons, and the Canadian Nurses Association are all working on ways to incorporate Indigenous knowledge and practices in health care.

Call to Action #21 and #22: Underway.

Justice

There are 18 Calls to Action (25–42) in the area of (Criminal) Justice. Call #42 states:

> "We call upon the federal, provincial and territorial governments to commit to the recognition and implementation of Aboriginal justice systems in a manner consistent with the Treaty and Aboriginal Rights of Aboriginal peoples, the Constitutional Act, 1982 and the United Nations Declaration on the Rights of Indigenous Peoples, endorsed by Canada in November 2012."

Progress to date: Meetings have been held with Indigenous partners to recognize and implement Indigenous justice systems. In February 2018, the federal government committed to create a legal framework to recognize Indigenous rights, to review laws and policies related to Indigenous peoples, and to build mechanisms for supporting Indigenous systems of justice consistent with self-determination and the inherent right of self-government (CBC, 2019). However, as of December 2019, no such justice systems had been fully implemented either federally, provincially, or in the territories.

Call to Action #42: Not started.

Questions for Reflection

Look at the CBC's "Beyond 94: Delivering on Truth and Reconciliation Commission Calls to Action" and then give some thought to the following questions:

1. How much more progress has been made on the 94 Calls to Action?
2. An essential component of policy development is knowing the prevalence of an issue. How much progress has been made in accounting for the number of Indigenous children in care, their experiences in care, and their outcomes?
3. Review a Call of Action that is of particular interest to you. Brainstorm how you would move forward with this obligation.
4. In what ways can you and your colleagues commit to implementing some of the Calls to Action in your own area of work or study?

A Moment in Time: 1996

The Last Residential School

Cultural Genocide

It wasn't until 1996 that the last residential school was closed. The TRC report found that the residential school system amounted to nothing less than cultural genocide.

In Canada, the Indian residential school system was a network of boarding schools that targeted Indigenous children for assimilation. The network was funded by the Canadian government's Department of Indian Affairs and administered by Christian churches.

The school system was created for the purpose of removing children from the influence of their own culture and assimilating them into the dominant Canadian culture. Over the course of more than 100 years, about 30%, or roughly 150,000, of Indigenous children were placed in residential schools nationally. At least 6,000 of these students are estimated to have died while residents.

As a means of destabilizing Indigenous nations, the residential school system severely harmed Indigenous children by removing them from their families, by depriving them of their ancestral languages, and by exposing many of them to physical and sexual abuse. This effectively undermined Indigenous nationhood across Canada, since it robbed First Nations communities of the next generation of leaders who knew their languages and their peoples' political systems.

The legacy of the residential school system has been linked to an emerging syndrome — the Indian Residential School Syndrome — which manifests with increased prevalence of post-traumatic stress, alcoholism, substance abuse, rootless identity, cultural shame, and suicide, which persist within Indigenous communities intergenerationally (that is, it is passed down from one generation to the next).

Disconnected from their families and culture and forced to speak English or French, students who attended the residential school system often graduated unable to fit into either their communities or Canadian society. The system was successful in disrupting the transmission of Indigenous practices and beliefs across generations. It was also, for the most part, a dismal education, often forcing girls to learn domestic housework skills and boys to learn about farming and other skills deemed appropriate to their sex.

On June 11, 2008, Prime Minister Stephen Harper offered a public apology on behalf of the Government of Canada and the leaders of the other federal parties in the House of Commons of Canada. Nine days earlier, the Truth and Reconciliation Commission (TRC) was established to uncover the truth about the schools.

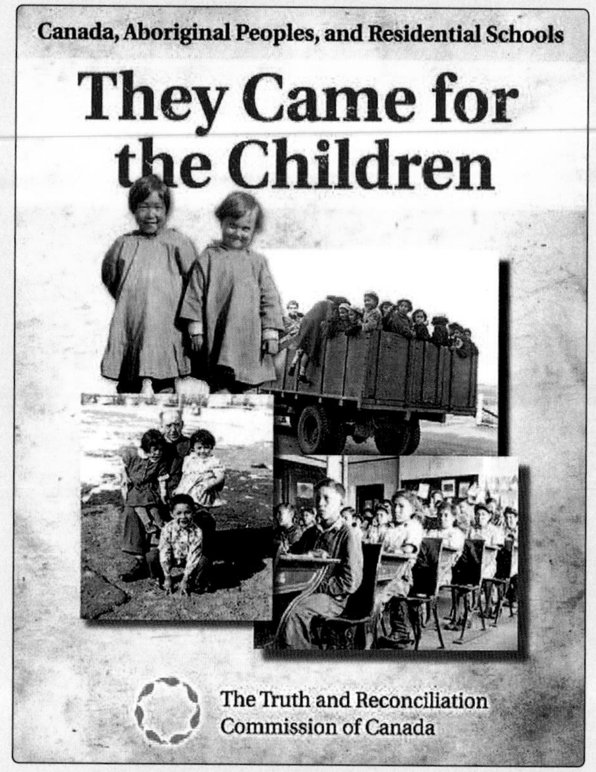

Chapter Review

Questions

1. How do the social and economic conditions of Indigenous people differ from those of non-Indigenous persons in Canada?
2. What was the residential school system, and why did it have such a devastating effect on First Nations families and communities?
3. Why is Indigenous self-determination such an important idea for promoting the social welfare of Indigenous peoples?
4. The ten Principles Respecting the Government of Canada's Relationship with Indigenous Peoples contain seemingly contradictory claims. What are they?
5. The Indigenous Rights, Recognition and Implementation Framework of 2018 opts for reconstructing First Nations and reaching sectoral agreements and avoiding treaty disputes and land claims. Is this a good thing?
6. Indian and Northern Affairs Canada has now been split into two separate ministries. What is the rationale for the split and what is the responsibility of each new ministry?

Exploring Social Welfare

1. The Oka Crisis of 1990 was one of the defining events that led to the creation of the Royal Commission on Aboriginal Peoples (1996). Research the background to the crisis and the outcome. Using the Library and Archives Canada website, you can browse all the RCAP reports and transcripts by keyword, unlocking a deep vault of research.
2. Review the 94 Calls to Action resulting from the Truth and Reconciliation Commission report. Prime Minster Justin Trudeau has committed his government to fulfilling all 94 recommendations. Do you think this is feasible? Why or why not?

Websites

National Centre for Truth and Reconciliation (NCTR)

www.nctr.ca

The National Centre for Truth and Reconciliation, housed at the University of Manitoba in Winnipeg, was created as part of the 2007 Indian Residential Schools Settlement Agreement. The NCTR is a repository for the complete history and legacy of the residential school system, with the goal of teaching Canadians about this history.

Assembly of First Nations (AFN)

www.afn.ca

The Assembly of First Nations (AFN), formerly known as the National Indian Brotherhood, is a body of First Nations leaders across Canada. The aims of the organization are to protect the rights, treaty obligations, ceremonies, and claims of citizens of the First Nations in Canada.

The Congress of Aboriginal Peoples (CAP)

www.abo-peoples.org

The Congress of Aboriginal Peoples (CAP) is an organization that represents off-reserve and Métis people. Founded in the 1970s, the organization's mission is to represent the interests of Indigenous people who are not legally recognized under the Indian Act, including non-Status Indians and Métis peoples.

The Yellowhead Institute

www.yellowheadinstitute.org

The Yellowhead Institute is a First Nation-led research centre based at Ryerson University in Toronto and focused on policies related to land and governance. It seeks to shape new governance models and support governance work in First Nations communities and urban communities, influence policy development, contribute to public education, facilitate opportunities for research, and build solidarity with non-Indigenous students and researchers.

The Welfare of Immigrants and Temporary Residents

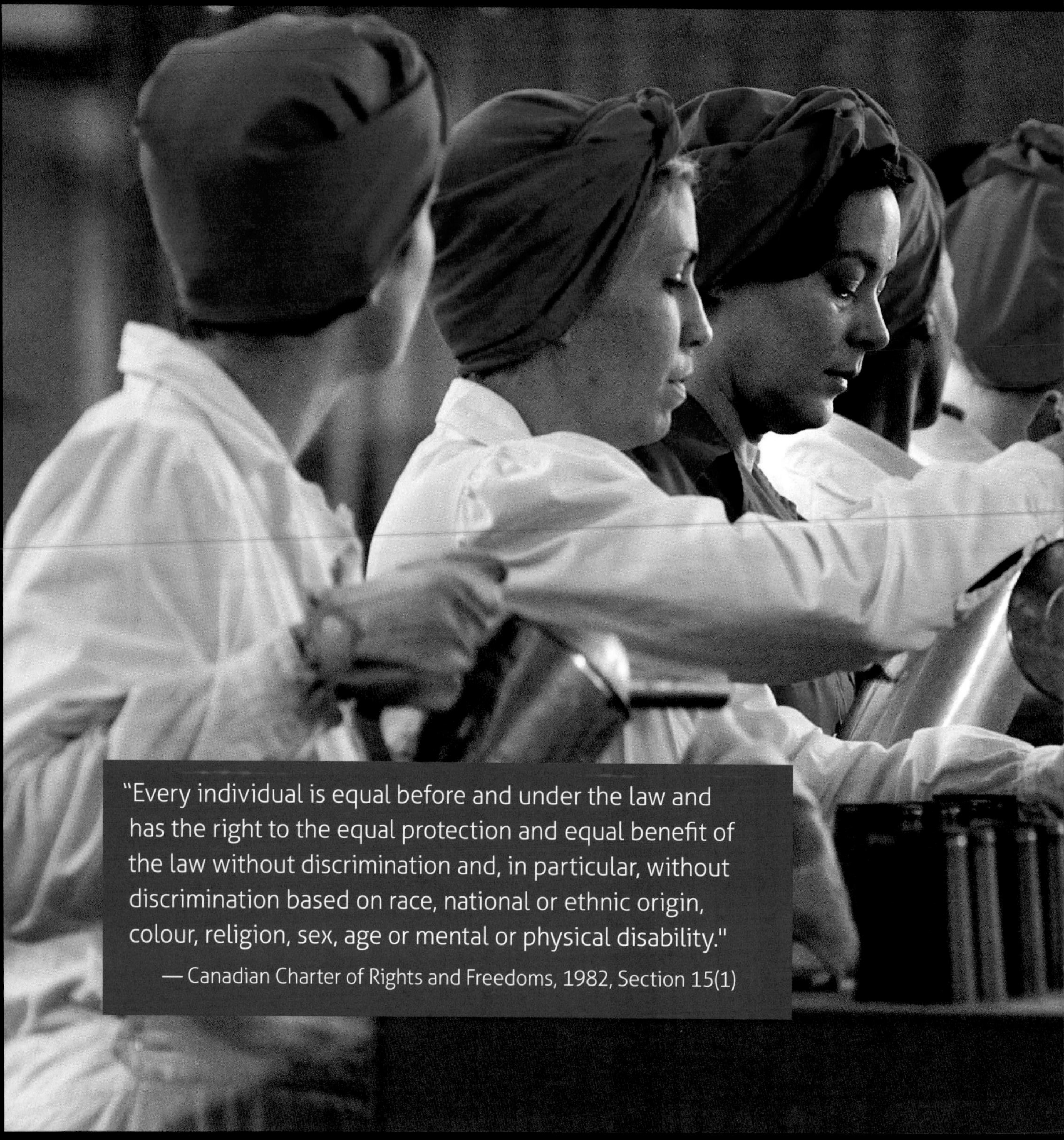

"Every individual is equal before and under the law and has the right to the equal protection and equal benefit of the law without discrimination and, in particular, without discrimination based on race, national or ethnic origin, colour, religion, sex, age or mental or physical disability."

— Canadian Charter of Rights and Freedoms, 1982, Section 15(1)

Fostering Multiculturalism and Social Inclusion

Settlement is difficult and many new immigrants face barriers to full participation in Canadian society.

Canada has seen successive waves of immigrants settling on land that had already been home to Indigenous Peoples for millennia and is a very ethnically and racially diverse nation. It has an official policy of multiculturalism that protects and promotes diversity and allows immigrants to retain cultural traditions. Many also regard Canada as a safe haven for refugees. Yet there are also many critiques of Canadian immigration and settlement policies: Only certain people are welcome, settlement can be difficult, and immigrants face many barriers to full participation in Canadian society. The health and income insecurities resulting from the COVID–19 pandemic significantly compounded the obstacles faced by this vulnerable population.

Recurring themes reaching as far back as the 1600s continue to be reflected in contemporary immigration policy. These policies have always been, and continue to be, determined by economic and political considerations, while deprioritizing family and humanitarian migration. A Liberal government elected in 2015 promised more openness to humanitarian migration, yet retained many of the restrictive policies. Settlement policies designed to support immigrants after arrival in Canada — and shared between the federal and provincial levels of government — have been slightly more stable over time.

Fostering Multiculturalism and Social Inclusion

What are the impacts of immigration and settlement policies on the well-being of immigrants and their families and on the communities in which they live? What do Canadians, and others who live in Canada, want in relation to immigration? Have we had time to think about what recent changes really mean? This chapter explores these issues.

After completing this chapter, you should be able to:

- Describe the relationship between migration and well-being;
- Describe historical instances of discrimination, especially on the basis of race and gender, that prevented immigrants from coming to Canada;
- Critique the current immigration system, including the three streams through which permanent residence is granted, provisions and policies that relate to temporary and undocumented migration, and the implications for the well-being of migrants;
- Discuss the pros and cons of Canada's multicultural policy; and
- Describe the settlement challenges faced by new immigrants to Canada.

Key Concepts

- Chinese head tax
- Continuous journey requirement
- Points system
- Immigration and Refugee Protection Act, 2001 (IRPA)
- Economic stream
- Family class
- Refugee and humanitarian stream
- United Nations High Commission for Refugees (UNHCR)
- Canada–US Safe Third Country Agreement
- International Mobility Program
- Temporary Foreign Worker Program
- Undocumented migrants
- Multiculturalism
- Settlement services
- Naturalization
- Deportation

9.1 Migration and Well-Being

As of 2017, 258 million people, or 3.4% of the global population, lived in a different country than the one in which they were born (United Nations, 2017). Theories of why people migrate draw on a wide range of disciplines and address a range of questions.

Theories of Migration

While some try to explain why migration occurs in the first place, others explain what causes migration to continue. What is common through most theories is an emphasis on migrants moving, whether forced or voluntarily, for reasons related to well-being.

Economists, for example, explain migration from macro and micro perspectives. From a macroeconomic perspective, immigration is viewed as an exchange of labour and capital between labour-rich, capital-poor areas and capital-rich, labour-poor areas. From a microeconomic perspective, migrants are viewed as individuals working to maximize their individual economic potential (Todaro & Maruszko, 1987).

Others focus on the family as a decision-making unit that works together to minimize risk by spreading out across locations in order to compensate for deteriorating conditions in the country of origin (Stark, 1991). Migrant network theory argues that globalization has led to the unprecedented development of migrant networks that encourage further migration (Samers, 2010). These theories, and the economic theories, are all criticized, however, for ignoring differences in migration patterns from similar countries, and the fact that most people do not migrate across borders (Arango, 2004; Massey et al., 1998).

Another connected body of theories, including world systems theory (Wallerstein, 1974) and dependency theory (Frank, 1967), see international migration as an inevitable consequence of global inequality that leads to migration to the Global North. These theories fail to consider the amount of migration that happens between countries in the Global South.

Gender-sensitive approaches to migration have emerged in recent decades to counteract the traditional male bias in theories of migration (Samers, 2010). These theories argue that state policy and societal expectations in both source and destination countries have influenced the migration of women, for example by treating women only as dependents or, alternatively, by encouraging women to immigrate into caregiving jobs (Cheng, 1999).

Finally, transnational theory cannot be overlooked. This moves away from the idea of source and destination countries, and instead acknowledges cross-border connections among individuals, institutions, and communities (Samers, 2010). This gives more agency to the individual in the context of globalization than traditional theories of settlement and recognizes that citizenship includes connections (for individuals and communities) with the destination country and the country of origin.

Pier 21

From 1928 to 1971, more than one million people entered Canada via Pier 21, a humble-looking building on the waterfront of Halifax, Nova Scotia.

Pier 21 is now an immigration museum and no longer a holding depot, but one in five Canadians alive today has a direct link to Pier 21, according to Ruth Goldbloom, chair of the Pier 21 Foundation.

Decades ago, most immigrants came from Britain, Ireland, Ukraine, Italy, Hungary, Netherlands, and other European countries. Today, they come from all corners of the world.

Immigration Policy: Economic Interests and Ongoing Discrimination

With their own diverse systems of governance and rich cultural practices, Indigenous peoples had been living on the land that is now labelled "Canada" for many thousands of years before the Europeans arrived. However, the first Europeans considered the land to be available for the taking (on behalf of their monarchs) and proceeded with a program of settlement and colonization that bore no regard to, and had devastating consequences for, Indigenous peoples. The settlement of the land is an essential factor in colonialism and thus immigration to Canada cannot be looked at in isolation from the subjugation of Indigenous populations.

Historically, immigration policies demonstrated clear political considerations about the "ideal" source countries from which the Canadian "nation" should be built, and economic considerations about who would best be able to contribute to the economy. Patriarchy limited women to the role of dependents. In the 1660s, for example, 800 women, known as *les filles du roi*, were sent from France to marry male colonizers and balance gender disparity, and to discourage men from marrying and reproducing with Indigenous women (Knowles, 2007). The British later mirrored this policy until they decided the "wrong" kind of women were immigrating (Kelley & Trebilcock, 2000). Other forms of discrimination were also rampant, including exclusion on the basis of disability and of sexual orientation.

Canadian immigration policy has always been full of racial discrimination too, though the targets of this discrimination have changed over time. In the 1700s, the British and French majorities forced Indigenous and Black slaves to migrate to Canada (Dirks, 1977; Stasiulus & Jhappan, 1995), for example during the migration boom of loyalists from the United States. In the 1800s, after US independence, British fears about maintaining Canada as a colony led to a migration policy based on fear and discrimination, and a desire to develop a loyal population from their home country (Knowles, 2007).

Post-Confederation, Canada encouraged the immigration of Europeans considered to be assimilable and beneficial to the economy, particularly (European and white American) male farmers and female domestic workers (Stasiulus & Jhappan, 1995). Those perceived to be agriculturally competent, such as Mennonites and Doukhobors, were granted special concessions upon immigration (Dirks, 1977; Taylor, 1991). Meanwhile, policy excluded those considered to have "unsuitable" ethnic or racial backgrounds, such as Italians and Black Americans.

Non-European immigration was encouraged on a temporary basis when it was beneficial to the Canadian economy. For example, Chinese immigrant labour built much of the Canadian Pacific Railway in the late 1800s. However, Canada developed a series of immigration policies aimed at discouraging permanent Chinese immigration, including a ban on migration of female family members. The Chinese Immigration Act (1885) established a **Chinese head tax** of $50 on all immigrants of Chinese origin, which increased to $500 in 1903, followed by an effective ban on Chinese immigration from 1923 until the 1940s. In 2006, the Government of Canada officially apologized for the tax and issued compensation to the few survivors of this measure and their spouses.

Racism

1. a belief that race is a fundamental determinant of human traits and capacities and that racial differences produce an inherent superiority of a particular race, also behaviour or attitudes that reflect and foster this belief; racial discrimination or prejudice. **2. a:** the systemic oppression of a racial group to the social, economic, and political advantage of another **b:** a political or social system founded on racism and designed to execute its principles.

The Merriam-Webster Dictionary. https: //www.merriam-webster.com/dictionary/racism

Continuous Journey Requirement

In the late 1800s and early 1900s, over 2,000 individual members of the Commonwealth from the Indian subcontinent arrived to work in Canada with the hope of creating a better economic situation for themselves and their families. Fear and racism among mainstream Canadians, however, led to strict policies that discouraged South Asian immigration.

Canada circumvented Commonwealth obligations by imposing a continuous journey requirement that permitted immigrants entry only if they arrived directly from their country of birth or citizenship (Kelley & Trebilcock, 2000). The government simultaneously encouraged commercial shipping agents to refuse to sell direct passage to Indians. The privately chartered Komagata Maru challenged this requirement by sailing directly from India. This led to a months-long stand-off in Vancouver harbour, during which Canada refused to allow the passengers to disembark. The ship ultimately was forced to return to India with its passengers. While the government formally apologized for the incident in 2016, refugee claimants who arrive by boat continue to be treated with similar suspicion.

The Immigration Act of 1910 allowed for the right to exclude "immigrants belonging to any race deemed unsuited to the climate or requirements of Canada" (Knowles, 2007). During World War I, the government constructed certain immigrants and their descendants, such as east and central Europeans, as "enemy aliens" and imposed a host of racist policies.

During the Second World War, Canada grudgingly accepted Roman Catholics from Sudetenland but refused Jewish refugees; this included forcing another boat — the SS St. Louis, which was full of refugees fleeing the Holocaust — to turn around and return to Europe. Canada also detained and forced the repatriation of many Japanese Canadians, while not meting out such extreme treatment to white European German and Italian Canadians (Dirks, 1977; Whitaker, 1987).

In the decades that followed World War II (1939–45), an increased demand for labour necessitated a complete overhaul of immigration policies. Immigration policy clearly prioritized the United States, anglophone Commonwealth countries, and France, followed by Western Europe, then Eastern Europe, the Middle East, and the rest of the Americas, and finally Asia (Corbett, 1957; Hawkins, 1988; Stasiulus & Jhappan, 1995). Potential Jewish and Black immigrants were frequently rejected for their "undesirabilty" and "unsuitability" (Kelley & Trebilcock, 2000).

Legislative policy was clearly discriminatory in this era, and public administrators often took this discrimination further during implementation by rejecting French immigrants at much higher rates than Americans and British (Whitaker, 1987).

Canada eliminated explicit racial discrimination from most official immigration policy in 1962, though family reunification rights still depended on country of origin (Chow, 2000; Daniel, 2005; Hawkins, 1988) and policy implementation practices continued to benefit applicants from traditionally favoured countries (Knowles, 2007; Whitaker, 1987).

Remembering Africville

Today, Canada prides itself on its multiculturalism and ethnic diversity. But, in the 1960s, a different approach was evidenced in a small village on the edge of Halifax, named Africville.

Its residents were descendents of freed and escaped slaves, and Black refugees from the War of 1812. In the name of urban renewal, between 1964 and 1969 Africville was plowed under to make way for a new bridge to Dartmouth.

In 1969, residents formed the Africville Action Committee in order to seek redress and to keep the community alive. The site was eventually declared a National Historic Site in 1996, calling it "a site of pilgrimage for people honouring the struggle against racism."

In 2014, Canada Post issued a commemorative stamp depicting seven young girls — all community members — against an illustrated background of the village.

From Explicit to Implicit Discrimination

In 1967, a new approach to economic immigration called the points system was introduced. The goal of the points system was to meet the economic and labour needs of Canada while ensuring that greater justice and fairness characterized the immigration process. The points system did away with official discrimination against applicants from certain countries of origin and allowed for the possibility of economic migration to Canada from all corners of the globe by focusing on the potential to contribute economically in Canada. Family reunification continued to be an important stream of immigration policy (Kelley & Trebilcock, 2000).

Following these changes in the late 1960s, increasing numbers of newcomers arrived in Canada from countries in Asia, Africa, the Middle East, South and Central America, and the Caribbean. The resulting change in the ethno-racial makeup of Canada brought a new dimension to the multicultural experience, and Canadian multicultural policy (discussed below) was introduced in 1971. However, the changing face of the big cities brought racism to the surface with negative media and public responses (Hawkins, 1988; Knowles, 2007). In response, governments after the late 1980s moved to tighten restrictions on family reunification and refugee migration while retaining the overall emphasis on economic migration, which continues today (Kelley & Trebilcock, 2000).

While legislation no longer explicitly excludes on the basis of race, gender, and other aspects of identity, the implementation of immigration policy continues to discriminate, with important outcomes for the well-being of migrants and Canadian society.

Figure 9.1

Distribution of the Foreign-Born Population in Canada by Region of Birth, 1871 to 2036

- British Isles
- Europe (excluding the British Isles)
- United States
- Caribbean, Bermuda, Central and South America
- Africa (including the Middle East
- Asia (including the Middle East)
- Oceania and others

Statistics Canada, Census of Population, 1871 to 2006, 2016; National Household Survey, 2011; Immigration and Diversity: Population Projections, 2011 to 2036.

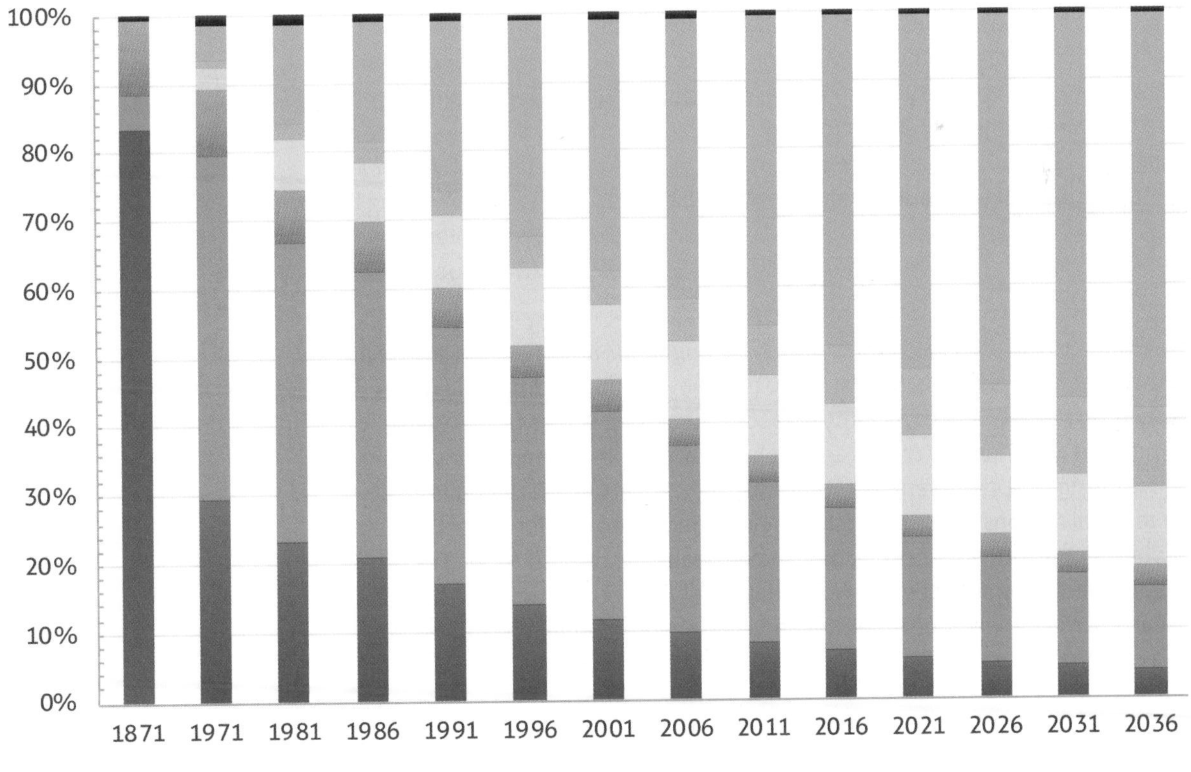

9.2 The Route to Permanent Residency

The Immigration and Refugee Protection Act (IRPA) — the cornerstone of current immigration policy — came into force in 2002. It is regularly amended, for example in recent years through the 2008 Action Plan for Faster Immigration, the Budget Implementation Act of 2008, and the Protecting Canada's Immigration System Act of 2012. The Liberal government that came to power in 2015 made several changes, in particular to family class policy, while retaining many of the changes brought in by the previous Conservative government. The minister responsible for immigration exercises considerable power over policy decisions by issuing Ministerial Instructions, for example on processing priorities (Budget Implementation Act, 2008 s.118).

While the federal level of government is primarily responsible for immigration policy, Québec has a degree of independence in creating and implementing policies for immigration to that province, and other provinces also have specific programs to attract immigrants to meet their own needs.

Three Immigration Streams, Multiple Programs

Current immigration policy includes provisions for both permanent and temporary immigration. The three streams that account for the vast majority of permanent immigration are the economic stream, family class, and refugee and humanitarian stream, each of which consists of multiple programs.

In all programs, a principal applicant must prove that they qualify for permanent residency according to the eligibility criteria for that program. Principal applicants can include dependent family members (spouse or partner and dependent children) on their application; those family members do not have to meet the eligibility criteria for the program independently. Depending on the program, applicants may apply from outside Canada, or they may already be in Canada, for example as an international student or refugee claimant. Applicants in the economic stream and family class must pay an application processing fee (e.g., for Express Entry this was $550 per adult in 2019). Once approved, they must also pay a Right of Permanent Residency fee, which in 2019 stood at $490 per adult.

In addition to the principal applicant proving eligibility, all applicants, including dependent family members, must prove that they are not inadmissible for medical or security reasons. Inadmissibility for security reasons ranges from having committed war crimes or crimes against humanity, to past criminal convictions with a maximum prison sentence of at least 10 years in Canada. Inadmissibility for medical reasons is based on either being a perceived danger to public health or placing a perceived excessive demand on health or social services. The latter includes requiring services that would negatively affect wait times or that would likely cost more than three times the Canadian average (Immigration, Refugees and Citizenship Canada, 2018).

Immigrants with Disabilities

Disability advocates have long protested the discriminatory implications of the "medical inadmissibility" criteria, which have excluded applicants due to ongoing needs related to disability, such as special education for deaf children.

Critics of the legislation have long called for a full repeal of section 38(1)(c) of the Immigration and Refugee Protection Act of 2001. Advocacy efforts on behalf of immigrants led to the government reducing, though not eliminating, the criteria for medical inadmissibility in 2018.

Setting Immigration Levels in Advance

The Government of Canada sets annual immigration target levels in advance. These immigration targets lay out the annual number of new permanent residents for most programs within the three immigration streams. In response to calls from industry, and following the 2015 election, the new Liberal government set immigration levels to increase each year, from 272,000 in 2015 to 421,000 people in 2023.

The economic stream will continue to account for the largest proportion of new permanent residents to Canada, though the government did also increase the family class levels. Refugee targets were significantly increased temporarily in response to the Syrian refugee crisis, though the numbers have since been restricted once more. Given Canada's international obligations under the Refugee Convention, there is no target for the number of refugee claims that will be processed within Canada. In 2017, for example, the latest year for which figures have been released, there were 286,000 new permanent residents, of which 159,000 arrived through the economic stream, 82,000 through the family class, and 44,000 through the refugee and humanitarian stream. This latter number was unusually high in 2016 due to the Syrian refugee resettlement.

Faced with an aging population and declining fertility rates, as well as labour and economic challenges, the Canadian labour force and population growth will depend even more on immigration. Immigrants are projected to make up to 30% of Canada's population by 2036, compared with 20.7% in 2011.

Figure 9.2

Immigration to Canada by Category (2015–2017), Principal Applicants and Immediate Family Members

Government of Canada, *Annual Report to Parliament on Immigration*, 2018.

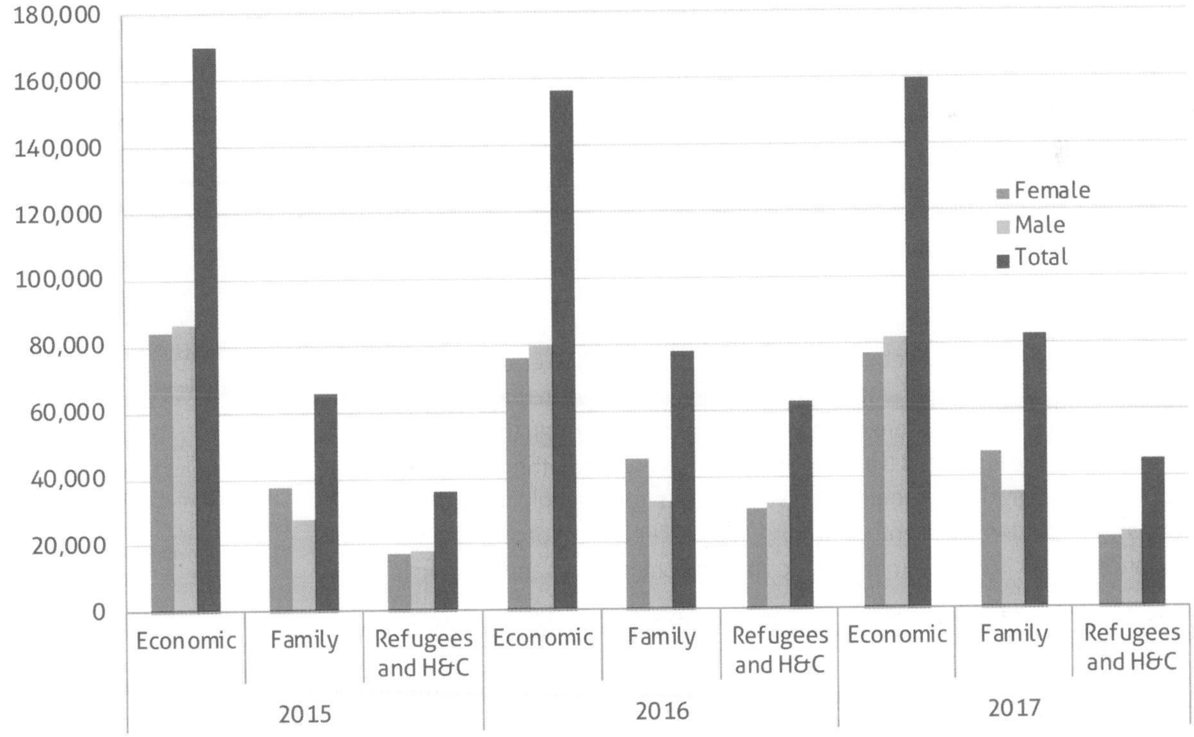

Economic Immigration

The immigration programs that fall under the economic stream are designed to respond to the economic needs of Canada. The largest programs within the economic stream use the points system.

The Federal Skilled Worker Program, Federal Skilled Trades Program, and Canada Experience Class are all implemented through the Express Entry process. Though each has a different emphasis, all three programs grant the principal applicant points for certain criteria: most importantly education, proficiency in at least one of the official languages, employment experience, and age. Further points are given for "adaptability criteria" such as having a relative in Canada, being proficient in the second official language, and having pre-arranged employment.

Before Express Entry was introduced in 2012, applications were processed on a first-come, first-served basis. In 2012, the government decided to cancel 280,000 unprocessed applications that had been submitted prior to 2008 and told applicants who had been waiting that they would need to reapply under the new rules. Applications that had been submitted between 2008 and 2012 continued to be processed through the old first-come, first-served system. In the Express Entry system, applicants submit an Expression of Interest, and the system ranks applicants against each other. At certain intervals, invitations are sent to the highest ranked applicants to submit full applications for permanent residency (Immigration, Refugees and Citizenship Canada, 2019).

The government promoted the system as a "fast, flexible, just-in-time immigration system" (Citizenship and Immigration Canada, 2012). For applicants, however, the new system can increase uncertainty and precarity, particularly for those, such as international students, who are already in Canada on temporary status with the hope of transitioning to permanent residency (Dam et al., 2018). It also fails to address policy gaps, for example by awarding points for professional education, in full knowledge that it may be very difficult for immigrants to have those credentials recognized once in Canada.

• Province-Specific Programs

Another component of the economic stream is the group of programs that are specific to provinces. Québec has long exercised control over immigration to that province and has its own Québec Skilled Worker Program (the equivalent to the Federal Skilled Worker Program); applicants who wish to live in that province must be approved by Québec before completing the process through the federal level. More recently, the Provincial Nominee Program has enabled other provinces to encourage immigration to meet their distinct needs, for example by targeting international students and entrepreneurs. More recently, a pilot program was also announced to encourage immigration to smaller communities and the north.

There are also several smaller programs within the economic stream. These too change regularly, but over time have included programs for entrepreneurs (currently the Start- Up Program) and self-employed people (currently either in the arts or sports). The most recent program for investors was cancelled in 2014.

Behind Closed Doors

A new report by the Migrant Rights Network has documented the challenges faced by Canada's foreign careworkers, a crisis the COVID–19 pandemic has made worse.

The report compiles hundreds of surveys from careworkers during COVID–19. It tells a story of entrapment, long hours, stolen wages, and workers being barred from leaving the home for fear of bringing in the coronavirus.

Behind Closed Doors, the Migrant Rights Network report advocates for creating clear pathways to permanent residence for Canada's careworkers.

"There is a clear demand for caregivers in Canada,." observes Lou Janssen Dangzalan, an immigration lawyer, "and the vocation deserves its own permanent place in the immigration system."

Migrant Rights Network (2020). *Behind Closed Doors: Exposing Migrant Care Worker Exploitation during COVID–19.*

- **The Caregiver Program**

The economic immigration program for caregivers has changed a great deal in recent years, in part in response to community advocacy efforts. This highly gendered and racialized program has traditionally granted permanent residency (which gives the right to bring family members to Canada) to temporary foreign workers who have worked as caregivers for a set number of years. Immigration for caregiving has been a feature of Canadian history since the early days of colonization; most recently women, especially from the Philippines, arrive in Canada as live-in caregivers for children and other family members.

Advocates and researchers had documented multiple abuses due to the design of the live-in caregiving program (Bhuyan et al., 2018). Demand for caregivers, which has always been higher than the number of caregivers to be processed for permanent residency according to immigration levels, also led to extremely long wait times and extended family separation of the caregiver mothers from their children.

The program has been revised repeatedly, both to remove the live-in requirement and, more recently, to allow caregivers (in line with temporary workers who arrive through the International Mobility Program discussed later in this chapter) to be accompanied by family members, thus avoiding the issues associated with family separation.

Anti-Black Racism

Deep-seated barriers exist that prevent many people from fully participating in all aspects of Canadian society. This is especially true for Black Canadians, whether they are recent immigrants or descendants of people who were enslaved.

The Black Lives Matter (BLM) movement in Canada is part of a worldwide movement to end white supremacy and systemic discrimination against Black people.

Photo: A Montréal woman wears a BLM face mask during a 2020 protest march calling for justice following the death of George Floyd in the United States.

Family Immigration

Family class is based on the internationally recognized human right to family life. It allows Canadian citizens or permanent residents who are at least 18 years old to sponsor certain family members for permanent residency in Canada. Different programs within the class deal with different types of family members. In each case, the family members must prove their relationship, the sponsor (the Canadian citizen or permanent resident) must meet certain eligibility criteria, and the sponsored family member must prove they are not inadmissible due to any of the conditions described earlier. If the relationship existed prior to the sponsor immigrating to Canada, they must have declared the family members in their own immigration documentation. If they did not, they are usually not permitted to subsequently sponsor the family member; this has led to permanent separation and devastating consequences that have been well-documented by advocacy organizations and the media (Canadian Council for Refugees, 2016).

By far the most commonly used family class program is sponsorship of spouses or (common-law or conjugal) partners and dependent children under the age of 22. The sponsor may have immigrated themselves and later sponsor their family members, or they may be Canadian-born and sponsor a partner and/or child who has a different nationality. Another widely discussed program, which has changed frequently in recent years, is the program for sponsorship of parents and grandparents; this has much more stringent criteria for eligibility. A final, much smaller program is for other relatives (usually orphaned minors) and adopted children, with extremely strict criteria.

Proof of relationship for spouses and common-law partners requires much more than, for example, a simple marriage certificate. Common-law couples must prove co-habitation for at least one year. Conjugal couples must successfully argue that they were prevented from cohabiting or marrying (for example, same-sex couples who lived in situations where it was dangerous to live openly as a couple). All couples must submit enough documentation to convince the visa officer that the relationship is genuine and has not been entered into for the purposes of immigration. Multiple critiques have been made of inconsistent processing of such applications and the expectation that couples meet Eurocentric expectations of a relationship (Martin, 2017). Between 2012 and 2017, spouses and partners who had been with their partner for less than two years at the time of sponsorship became "conditional permanent residents," and had to cohabit for two years following immigration, before being granted full permanent residency. The implications of this for domestic abuse were clear and advocates successfully lobbied to have the status removed.

Biological parent-child relationships are proven through birth certificates and, increasingly, DNA tests. Literature has highlighted the disproportionate demands for DNA tests for applicants from certain parts of the world, for example for parents and children from African countries (Joly et al., 2016). Adoptive parent-child relationships that take place across borders must conform to the Hague Convention on Intercountry Adoption and be approved by provincial adoption

COVID-19 and Family Reunification

The projected 2020–2022 immigration levels were announced in March 2020, just before the coronavirus outbreak. Family immigration was targeted at 91,000 per year. The levels for the economic and the humanitarian and refugee streams were each scheduled to increase over subsequent years.

The COVID-19 pandemic resulted in significantly reduced numbers. The family-class sponsorships were down 78% in the second quarter. Refugee and humanitarian-stream levels were the hardest hit, down 85%. Economic-stream immigration was down 52%.

authorities. This has grave implications for immigrants who adopt domestically in their home countries before realizing the adoption authorities do not recognize adoptions from those countries; for them, it will be extremely difficult and expensive to bring their child to Canada (Redmond & Martin, n.d.).

Those wishing to sponsor their parents or grandparents must prove a minimum income of the Low-Income Cut-Off (LICO) plus 30% for the three years prior to the application. For a couple with two children who wished to apply in 2019 for one set of parents (two people) to join them, they would have required a joint income of at least $75,000 in 2016 to $77,000 in 2018. This discriminates against, for example, women who have taken breaks from the workforce for maternity reasons, and recently graduated students who wish for their parents to join them in Canada (Martin, 2017). There are no explicit minimum income requirements to sponsor other family members, though sponsors need to prove that they are not on social assistance (other than for reasons of disability) and that they are able to provide for the basic needs of the family members they are sponsoring. Sponsors may also be ineligible if they are in default on certain payments, such as immigration loans or family support payments.

In a requirement that is explicitly designed to download responsibility for social welfare to the family, sponsors sign an official sponsorship undertaking that they will assume financial responsibility for their family members for a certain period of time. This ranges from 3 years for spouses and 10 years for dependent children (or their 25th birthday, whichever is first), to 20 years for parents and grandparents. By signing the undertaking, the sponsor guarantees to provide for the basic needs of the sponsored family members. The undertaking remains valid regardless of any change such as marriage breakdown or loss of employment.

The number of sponsorship applications accepted each year for spouses, partners, and dependent children is unlimited, though the government does announce the levels they expect to process. The strict limits on applications processed for parent and grandparent sponsorship, however, are far lower than the demand for the program. The notorious application process has alternated between first-come, first-served and a lottery system. When it has been first-come, first-served, the annual quota for applications has filled within hours or minutes of opening; this has led to complaints of discrimination based on accessibility. However, the lottery system was critiqued for its randomness and failure to guarantee a spot to those who had been working on applications over many years (Harris, 2018).

Processing priorities and levels of demand at different visa offices in recent years led to long wait times for certain types of family members and for applicants from certain regions. The extended separation that results from these backlogs, and uncertainty over when cases will be resolved, has huge implications for the well-being of family members, as discussed below (Martin, 2017). The refusal of authorities to grant visitor visas for family members from certain countries only exacerbates the impacts of separation. While wait times have recently been reduced, in some cases significantly, there remains a lot of work to be done to ensure families can be together.

Canadian Attitudes toward Immigration

Canadians generally agree that immigration is necessary and important to long-term economic growth, but they would like to see family members given more priority for immigration in the future.

In a 2020 survey by Leger Marketing on behalf of the Association of Canadian Studies, 36% of the respondents. said that the family members of people already in Canada should be given priority. Four years earlier, in a 2016 survey, that figure was only 30%.

Support for increasing economic-stream immigration remained about the same (at 27%) between 2016 and 2020. The refugee and humanitarian stream saw a significant drop in support from 29% in 2016 to 16% in 2020.

Jedwab, J. (2020). *Canadian Views on Immigration Levels and Immigration Categories in the Covid Era.* Association for Canadian Studies.

Refugee and Humanitarian Immigration

While the media and public perhaps discuss the refugee and humanitarian stream more than any other, this stream is the smallest in terms of numbers of arrivals. A refugee, according to the United Nations Convention on the Status of Refugees, is someone who (a) "has a well-founded fear of persecution for reasons of race, religion, nationality, political opinion or membership in a particular social group," (b) is outside their country of nationality and (c) cannot return home or is afraid to do so (UNHCR, 2011).

• The Worldwide Refugee Crisis

The United Nations High Commission for Refugees (UNHCR) reports that, as of 2018, it considered more than 70 million people worldwide to be "people of concern" (UNHCR, 2019). This includes 41 million people who are internally displaced within their countries of origin and more than 25 million officially recognized refugees. Contrary to popular discourse in many immigrant-receiving countries, the majority of refugees live in countries that neighbour those from which they have fled. At the time of writing, the top three refugee-producing countries were Syria, Afghanistan, and South Sudan. Correspondingly, the top refugee-hosting countries in terms of numbers were Turkey, Pakistan, Uganda, and Sudan. As a proportion of population, Lebanon hosts by far the largest number of refugees at over 15% of its population, followed by Jordan at 7%.

Canada signed the Refugee Convention in 1969 and has two completely separate (though often confused) programs for refugees. The In-land Refugee Program is carried out as part of Canada's commitment under the Refugee Convention to allow refugee claimants (sometimes referred to as asylum seekers) already on Canadian soil to make a claim for protection. Within this program, refugee claimants are given the opportunity to argue that they meet the definition of a refugee. Under Canada's Refugee Resettlement Program, the country accepts a very small proportion of the refugees that the UNHCR deems in need of resettlement each year.

The relatively low number of refugee claimants arriving in Canada is a result of both simple geography and interdiction measures that deliberately prevent potential claimants from reaching the country. Since Canada is surrounded by oceans on three sides and is a long distance from most refugee-producing countries, this naturally restricts the number of refugee claimants who arrive. When boat arrivals do happen, this continues to provoke both disproportionate public outrage and discriminatory policy responses, as seen throughout history. Interdiction measures include imposing visitor visa requirements for countries that are known to violate human rights and/or produce significant numbers of refugee claimants. Canada also carries out its own inspections, for example for fraudulent documents, on foreign soil to prevent potential refugee claimants from boarding flights to Canada. It expects air carriers to do the same, charging fees to those who transport passengers with fraudulent documents (Canada Border Services Agency, 2019b). This means potential refugee claimants, as well as those who simply want to visit, are prevented from travelling to Canada.

COVID–19 and Refugee Protection

"The pandemic has thrown up a number of challenges and led to setbacks for refugee protection. At the height of the crisis, 168 countries fully or partially closed their borders, with around 90 making no exception for those seeking asylum. Some have pushed asylum seekers, including children, back to their countries of origin.

"Aside from the threats to health and access to asylum, the pandemic has also undermined the social and economic rights of refugees and the displaced. With the most vulnerable populations often depending on the informal economy, they were among the first to suffer the economic impacts of lockdown, losing their jobs and being evicted from their homes."

Gillian Triggs, Assistant High Commissioner for Protection, UNHCR, the UN Refugee Agency, October 7, 2020.

The Global Refugee Crisis

WHO IS A REFUGEE? —A refugee is someone who has been forced to leave their country in order to escape war, persecution, violence or natural disaster. These reasons can be caused by race, religion, ethnicity, nationality, political affiliation.

REFUGEE AGE DISTRIBUTION

51% —UNDER 18 YEARS OLD

49 % —ADULTS

DISPLACED PEOPLE BREAKDOWN (2016)

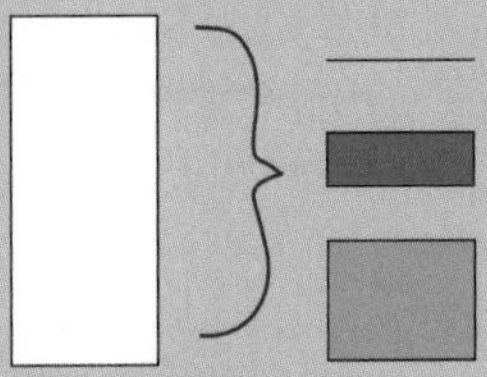

189,300 RESETTLED REFUGEES

10 MILLION STATELESS PEOPLE

22.5 MILLION REFUGEES

65.6 MILLION
FORCIBLY DISPLACED PEOPLE

REFUGEE HOST REGIONS

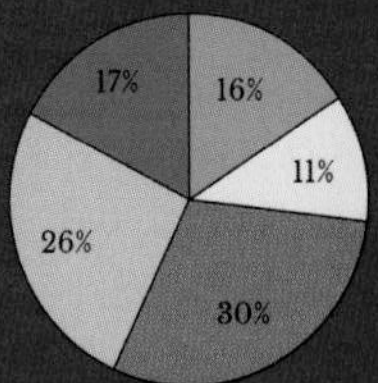

Europe
Middle East and North Africa
Africa
Asia and Pacific
Americas

Turkey, Pakistan and Lebanon currently hosts the most refugees.

RESETTLEMENT SUBMISSIONS TO UNHCR

January - April 2018

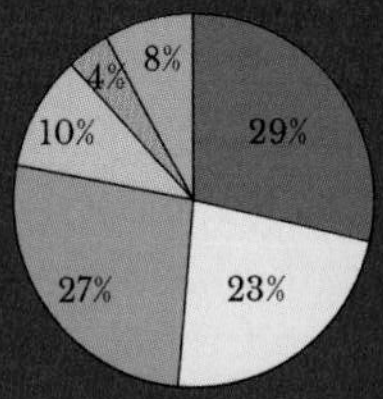

Children and Adolescents at Risk
Medical Needs
Women and Girls-at-Risk
Survivor of Violence and/or Torture
Lack of Forseeable Alternative Durable Solutions
Legal and/or Physical Protection Needs

ISSUES THAT REFUGEES FACE

POVERTY
UNEMPLOYMENT
HOUSING
MENTAL ILLNESS
HEALTH
EDUCATION
ASSIMILATION
DISCRIMINATION

CURRENT HIGH RISK AREAS

AFGHANISTAN
SYRIA
SOUTH SUDAN
SOMALIA
SUDAN
MYANMAR
YEMEN
DEMOCRATIC REPUBLIC OF CONGO

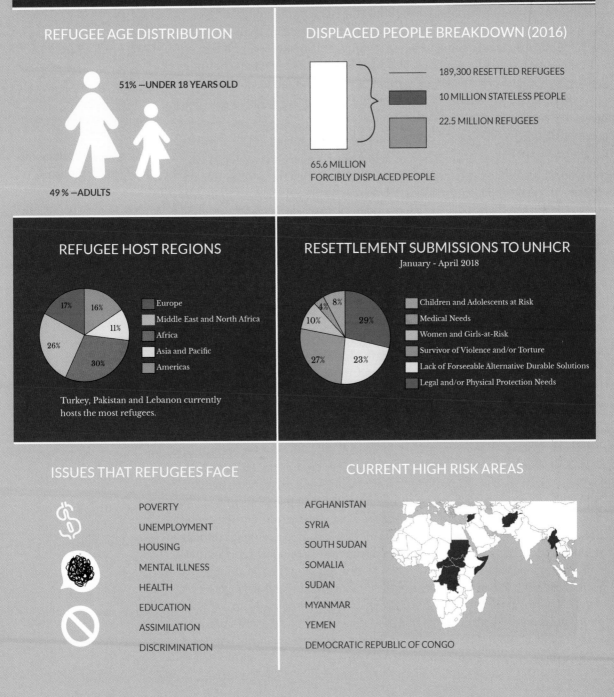

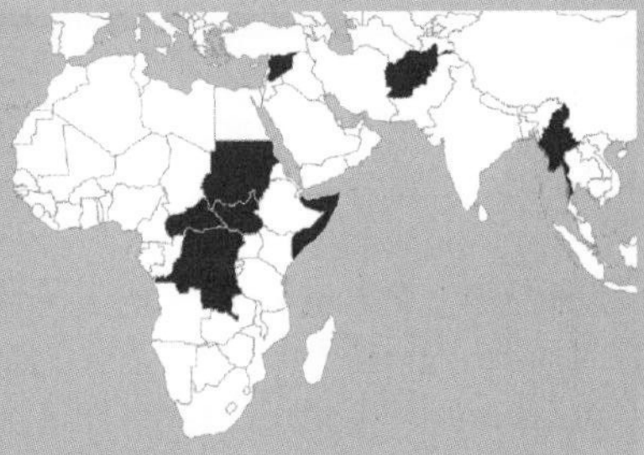

United Nations and the United Nations High Commissioner for Refugees (UNHCR) (2018, June).

- **Canada–US Safe Third Country Agreement**

Finally, perhaps the most effective policy in denying refugee claimants access to the In-land Refugee Program is the **Canada–US Safe Third Country Agreement**, which has been in force since 2004. Under this agreement, Canada can turn away refugee claimants who present themselves at a Canada–US border crossing on the premise that the United States already provides safe haven to those who are fleeing persecution. The agreement does not apply, however, to those who have already entered Canada and then submit the claim. International refugee law allows for irregular border crossing for the purpose of claiming asylum, so the Safe Third Country Agreement has led to refugee claimants finding alternate routes to enter Canada, for example at Roxham Road in Québec, where they are intercepted by the RCMP immediately after entering for refugee-claim processing. The Safe Third Country Agreement has come under increasing scrutiny, with many advocates arguing that the US is no longer a safe country.

Refugee claimants who arrive in Canada are ineligible to submit a claim if they have a previous rejected, abandoned, or withdrawn claim in Canada, if they have received refugee status in another country, or because they are inadmissible on security or certain criminality grounds. More recently the Liberal government, as part of an omnibus budget bill, included a provision to make claimants ineligible if they have even submitted a claim in certain other countries, including the United States, Britain, or Australia.

Refugee claimants who do reach Canada, including men, women, and children, are increasingly detained either in immigration detention facilities or in provincial jails; a total of 8,781 claimants were detained in 2017–2018 (Canada Border Services Agency, 2019a). Those who are classed as "designated foreign nationals" — which is commonly applied to those arriving on boats — are automatically detained. Detention, particularly when lengthy, has serious consequences for the physical and mental health of the immigrant (Koopowitz & Abhary, 2004). Oversight is extremely limited and detention has been challenged in the courts on multiple grounds (Atak et al., 2017).

To make a claim for refugee status, claimants must submit paperwork and attend a hearing in front of an Immigration and Refugee Board (IRB) member, according to timelines laid out in the legislation. The system has been critiqued for having timelines that make it very difficult for the most vulnerable of claimants to tell their stories and gather the appropriate evidence (for example, those who may have experienced the trauma of gender-based violence or torture and may need to obtain psychological reports). Access to Legal Aid to support refugees through the process depends on the province, with six provinces providing services that are partly funded federally (Department of Justice, 2019). In Ontario, refugee lawyers criticized the recent decision of the province not to fund any legal aid for refugee claimants. With a shortfall that was only partly made up by the federal government, and on a temporary basis, lawyers are now only able to provide minimal support through the difficult process, with significant negative consequences for claimants (Balakrishnan, 2019).

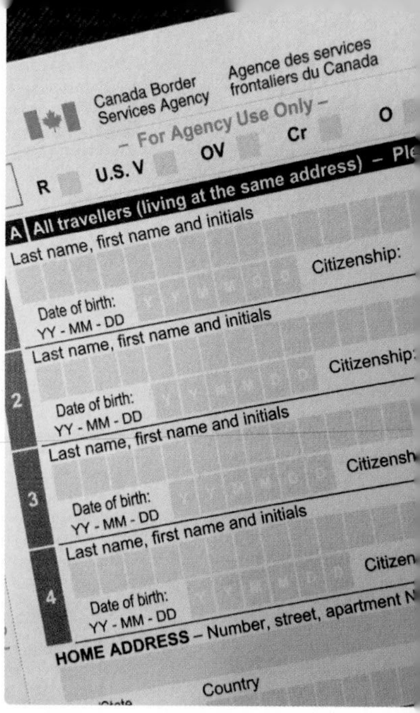

Federal Court Declares the STCA Unconstitutional

In July 2020, the Federal Court declared the Canada–US Safe Third Country Agreement unconstitutional on the grounds that it violated "the right to life, liberty and security of the person" as guaranteed in the Canadian Charter of Rights and Freedoms.

The case had been filed by Amnesty International, the Canadian Council for Refugees, and the Canadian Council of Churches. The Trudeau government nonetheless is appealing the court decision, and thereby clinging onto a dangerous agreement when racist policies of the US administration continue to make it all the more deadly.

- **Refugee Resettlement**

The second main component of the refugee and humanitarian stream is refugee resettlement. Refugees may be resettled in one of three ways; as Government Assisted Refugees (GARs), Privately Sponsored Refugees (PSRs), or Blended, Visa-Office Referred Refugees (BVORs). Traditionally, the PSR program was based on the principle of additionality (i.e., PSRs were over and above stable levels of GARs). Private sponsorship was responsible for many of the Syrian refugees recently resettled in (relatively) large numbers. Resettled refugees are identified by UNHCR, private sponsors, or other organizations and are only resettled if they are recognized as refugees by UNHCR or a foreign state.

Resettled refugees go through the application process outside of Canada and receive permanent residency immediately upon arrival in Canada. Refugees who are assisted by the government are expected to repay the costs of their flights and medical checks and most do so despite the financial implications this has as they settle. Organizations and groups of individuals are all eligible to privately sponsor refugees, which involves taking responsibility for supporting the settlement of the refugee(s) for at least 12 months following arrival.

In 2018, 55,695 refugee claims were made, of which fewer than 20,000 resulted from RCMP interceptions. That year, 70% of refugee claims were approved (not the same cases, as it usually takes longer than a year). Resettlement saw a spike in 2015–2017 but has since gone down. Finally, a very small number are granted residency based on very specific humanitarian and compassionate grounds.

Figure 9.3

Highlights of Protected Person, Refugee, and Humanitarian Admissions in 2017

Government of Canada, *Annual Report to Parliament on Immigration*, 2018.

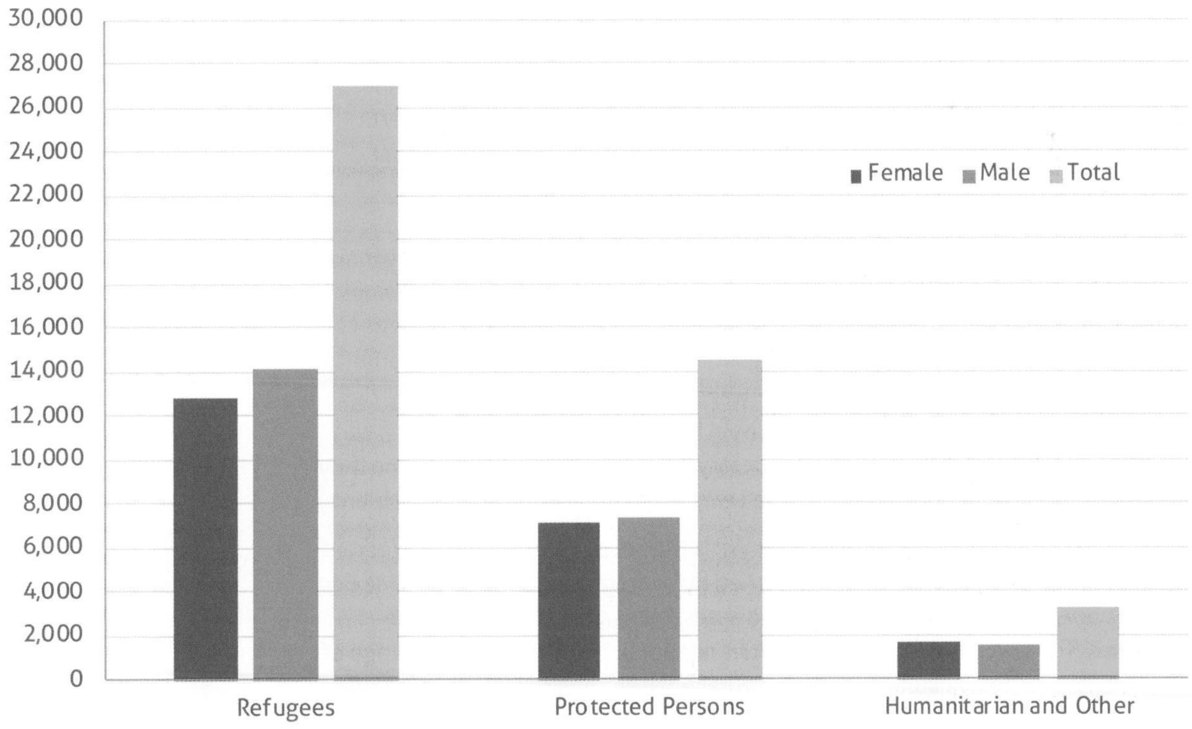

9.3 The Growth of Temporary Migration

In recent decades, temporary migration to Canada has been growing. Temporary migration streams under IRPA include two programs for temporary workers and one program for international students. The move toward increased temporary migration has important implications for social welfare, because temporary residents have fewer rights and access to fewer services than immigrants with permanent residency, though this varies considerably among different types of temporary workers.

The Temporary Foreign Worker and International Mobility Programs

Programs for temporary workers at the federal level fall into two categories: the Temporary Foreign Worker Program and the International Mobility Program, each of which is sub-divided into further programs.

The International Mobility Program implements often reciprocal, temporary work provisions found in multilateral and bilateral agreements such as CUSMA (Immigration, Refugees and Citizenship Canada, 2019), with the goal of "advancing Canada's broad economic and cultural interest" (Employment and Social Development Canada, 2014). Employers who hire foreign workers through this program need not complete a Labour Market Impact Assessment to show that there are no Canadians to fill the position. Participants have open work permits, allowing them flexibility to move between employers, and are usually highly skilled and highly paid. Sub-programs include international students who have graduated from a Canadian school and have a temporary work permit in their field, workers who fall under free trade agreements, participants in the International Experience Program for young people (e.g., those on "gap years"), and spouses of highly skilled foreign workers.

Conversely, the Temporary Foreign Worker Program is framed as a "last resort" to fill gaps where employers cannot find qualified Canadians. Employers must complete a Labour Market Impact Assessment and there is a limit on what percentage of their workforce can be temporary foreign workers. Workers' permits are usually employer specific. Most positions are low-skilled and the main source countries, with whom there is no reciprocity, are often, though not always, developing countries. Programs that fall under the Temporary Foreign Worker Program include the Seasonal Agricultural Workers Program, a program for other low-wage positions, and another for high-wage positions. Caregivers, whose right to transition to permanent residency (unusual for temporary foreign workers) was discussed above, also fall under the Temporary Foreign Worker Program while they are working as caregivers to complete the years to qualify for permanent residency.

One of the largest programs within the TFWP is the Seasonal Agricultural Workers Program, which is highly critiqued. Governed by bilateral agreements with Mexico and Caribbean countries, recruitment and assessment are done in the home countries. The TFWP cap for employers does not apply here, given the shortage of Canadians who are available to fill agricultural jobs. Permits require a minimum of 240 hours of work, but a maximum stay in Canada of 8 months each year.

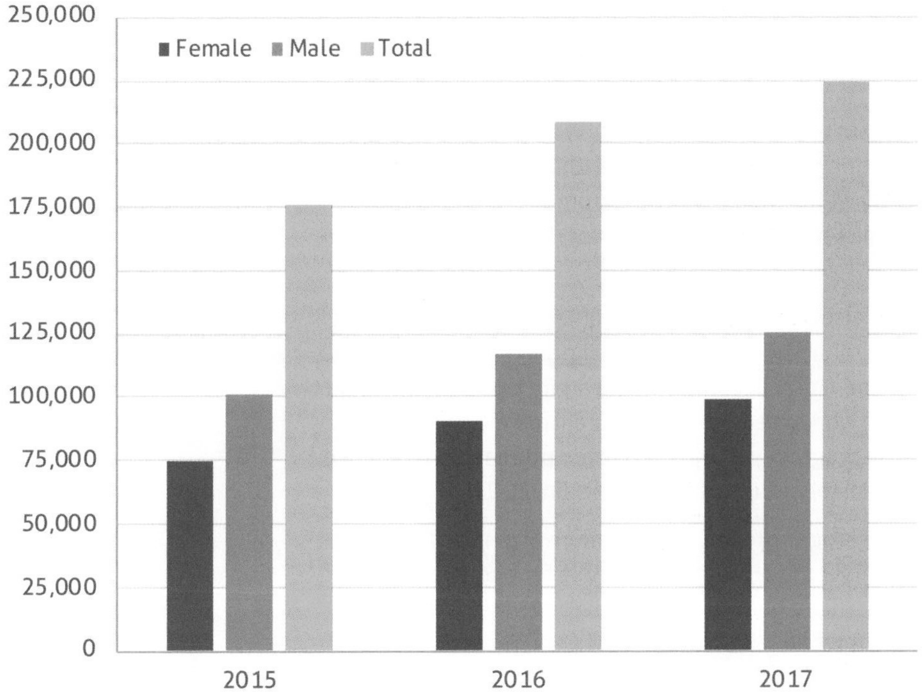

Figure 9.4

International Mobility Program (2015–2017)

Government of Canada, *Annual Report to Parliament on Immigration*, 2018.

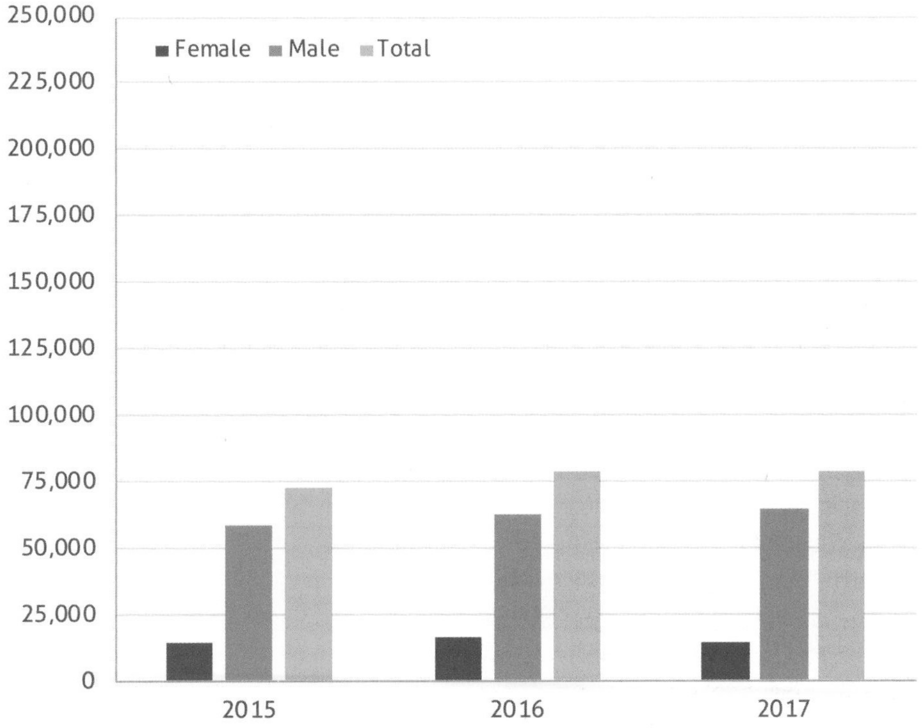

Figure 9.5

Temporary Foreign Worker Program (2015–2017)

Government of Canada, *Annual Report to Parliament on Immigration*, 2018.

- **Criticisms of the Temporary Foreign Worker Program**

Advocates have repeatedly critiqued the Temporary Foreign Worker Program. They point to the potential for abuse that results from indebtedness to recruiters, employer-specific permits, and employer-provided housing. Working and living conditions are often substandard with limited oversight. Workers experience isolation and a lack of information and may have limited (though growing) access to support services. Temporary workers are prevented from unionizing, may not be paid overtime, and pay Employment Insurance but experience problems when they try to make claims.

Their lack of permanent status also serves to increase vulnerability: fear of losing their job and being required to return home can leave temporary workers afraid to speak out about poor employment practices. Advocates argue that programs that see large numbers of returning workers each year are surely not filling temporary gaps; instead, workers in these programs should be granted permanent residence (Bauder, 2008; Canadian Council for Refugees, 2014; Macklin, 2003).

The Temporary Foreign Worker Program receives much more attention than the International Mobility Program, yet the TFWP is responsible for a smaller and decreasing number of workers since a peak of almost 200,000 workers with TFW permits in 2009. By 2017 this had gone down to 114,000. The International Mobility Program, by contrast, has continued to steadily climb from less than 100,000 in the 1990s to 474,000 in 2017.

Undocumented Migrants

The term undocumented migrants, or non-status migrants, refers to migrants who are living in Canada without permission from the government. They may have arrived irregularly, or they may have arrived with regularized status (e.g., student permit, visitor visa waiver) that has since expired. They also include migrants who cross into Canada outside of the regular border crossings but do not subsequently apply for any type of regular status.

The number of undocumented migrants in Canada is not clear; a study in 2010 reported estimates of between 20,000 to 200,000 undocumented workers (Magalhaes et al., 2010). What is clear is that their status as undocumented creates significant barriers to accessing services, with important implications for well-being, as described below.

Undocumented migrants in Canada also include those who have been trafficked. Trafficking involves the recruitment, transportation, and control of individuals for the purposes of (usually sexual or labour) exploitation. It is separate from smuggling, as the latter does not imply exploitation upon arrival, when smuggled migrants are left to themselves. While there are many trafficked people in Canada who are not migrants (e.g., Indigenous women and girls) there have been regular exposures of migrant trafficking, for example, of Mexicans working as cleaners in Barrie, Ontario in 2019 (Draaisma, 2019).

International Students

Consistent with other countries in the Global North, Canada has seen a large increase in the number of international students, from 145,000 in 1998 to 614,000 in 2017. This trend is attributed to several factors. Decreased public spending on universities has led universities to rely on international student fees, which are much higher than domestic fees, as an increasing source of revenue. Both countries and universities perceive international students to be a way of increasing international competitiveness; in Canada, for example, this has led to more open policies and clearer routes for international students to post-graduation permanent residency. International students can be accompanied by spouses and partners, and both they and their partners have access to temporary work permits during their studies.

Contrary to their temporary worker counterparts, international students are often portrayed as "ideal immigrants" who have spent time in Canada before applying for permanent residency and have therefore already started the settlement process. International students who are juggling work and studies in an unfamiliar environment have diverse needs. They do not have access to federally funded settlement programs during their studies, though universities usually provide some level of support (Sá & Sabzalieva, 2018). Their settlement support is, for at least part of their transition, effectively downloaded to individual students and their universities, who may or may not have expertise in the area of immigration.

Photo: As of late 2020, Alia Youssef had not seen her fiancee since the border between Canada and the United States closed in March 2020. They hoped to meet up over Christmas. Couples like Youssef and El-Sawah were in a grey area after pandemic-related travel restrictions came into effect, unable to reunite due to their unmarried status. Translation on her shirt reads, "You're beautiful as you are." (The Canadian Press/ Rob Gurdebeke)

Social Welfare in Perspective

Guest Workers or Citizens-in-the-Making

Which Way for Canada's Immigration Policy?

No one has answered the core question: "Why are temporary foreign workers good enough to work, but not good enough to stay?"

There was an outpouring of criticism at one time when Disney, that most iconic of American companies, moved to replace a number of its homegrown techies with low-cost temporary foreign workers. The company was forced to beat a hasty retreat following an outpouring of criticism.

Around the same time, amid all the commentary about where America is headed, blogger and finance professor Noah Smith turned his eyes north and gave Canada a mighty shout-out in a column for Bloomberg titled "Canada, Tomorrow's Superpower."

Prof. Smith rightly pointed out that immigration policy is one of the fundamental Canadian strengths that bode well for our future. But in his haste to explain what's right about our policies, he skipped over the part of the story where we've begun to ape something that's wrong about the American way: a growing reliance by business on temporary "guest" workers.

Canada's immigration reforms have pivoted from family reunification to economic immigration, with a focus on new permanent residents who have high educational skills and/or high net worth. Most people don't realize that our intake of foreign workers has almost doubled since 2006 — right through the recession, amid rising unemployment rates and with no recovery for young workers.

Almost all of our net new immigration growth is driven by the escalating use of temporary foreign workers, rather than permanent economic migrants.

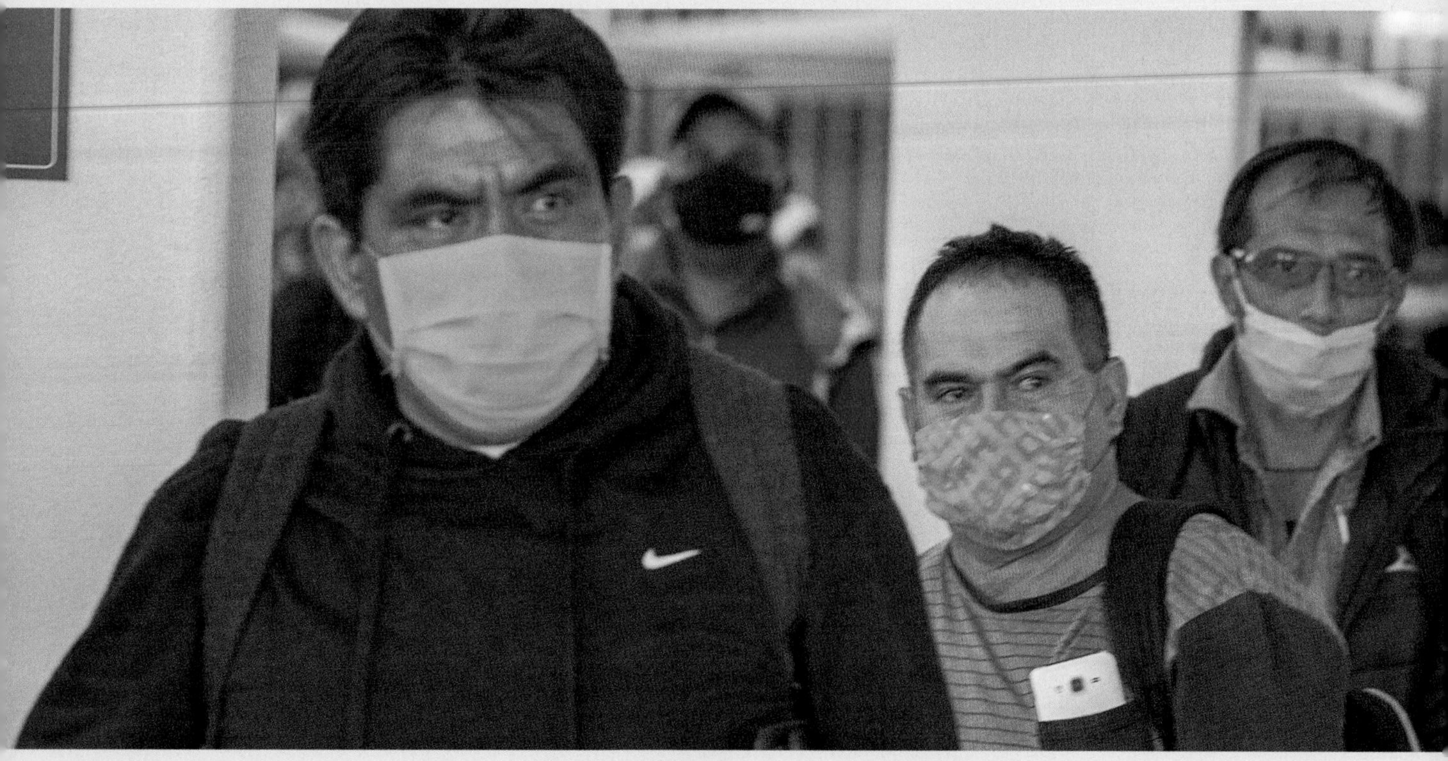

Canadian businesses have turned to these workers for a variety of reasons, including legitimate shortages in certain pockets of the labour market, inadequate workplace training, and a desire to cut costs.

The Disney story that so riled Americans is almost a perfect mirror image of a 2013 story that alarmed Canadians about practices at the Royal Bank of Canada and other big banks. We've since learned that the hiring of temporary foreign workers is routine in the finance sector and beyond.

The distinction between policies that encourage permanent or temporary newcomers is critical to Canada's future and the future of a world dogged by aging populations. All the advanced industrialized nations are aging. Japan is first, but South Korea, China, and virtually all of Europe are close behind. Canada is among the most rapidly aging societies because of our postwar baby boom.

Our labour shortages are currently limited to booming pockets of the economy, but they will become endemic as boomers begin to retire in droves, which will happen long before the robots take over. In the meantime, economic migrants are becoming the tail that wags the dog of economic development and the evolution of nations.

Recently, the United Nations Refugee Agency noted that 59 million people were displaced in 2014 by violence and persecution, the highest number on record, and the fastest increase in a single year. These numbers do not include the displacement of peoples because of climate change, which is a growing phenomenon as well. Nor do they include rising numbers of international students and professionals who go abroad to seek greater opportunity.

Pushed or pulled, human beings are on the move as never before. So is capital. For the past three decades, nations have tried to become magnets for money, in the hopes of drawing investments that create growth and jobs. For the next three decades, nations with aging populations will need to be magnets for both capital and labour, just to maintain standards of living.

The stakes are high. We are establishing the terms of the game for decades to come, for migrant workers and citizens alike. There is perhaps no more fundamental test of policy success or failure than how labour-force needs will be met in the coming years. Will newcomers be invited in as guest workers or as citizens in the making? This is a new issue for Canada, and an increasingly contentious one. Numerous policy announcements meant to quell concerns have done little to change the trends. No one has answered the core question: Why are temporary foreign workers good enough to work, but not good enough to stay?

Professor Smith is right — Canada has the potential to become a superpower, a country the world regards with respect and envy for its economic, social, and political strength. But it won't get there by relying on the permanently temporary.

Yalnizyan, A. (2018, May 15). Immigration policy should foster new Canadians, not temporary workers. *The Globe and Mail* (originally published July 6, 2015). Reproduced by permission.

Armine Yalnizyan is senior economist at the Canadian Centre for Policy Alternatives, and business columnist for CBC Radio's Metro Morning in Toronto.

9.4 Canada and Multiculturalism

Settlement is the process after arrival in a country, as the migrant "settles in" to their new place of residence. Settlement theories (also known as acculturation theories) argue that the position of immigrants in relation to the society in which they live depends on a number of factors, including attitudes and behaviours of individuals in the host society, host society culture, attitudes and behaviours by individual migrants, and migrant culture (Berry, 2003; Potocky, 2008). Societies that expect newcomers to assimilate and adopt the dominant culture are sometimes referred to as "melting pots" (Berry, 2003).

Multiculturalism Act, 1988

Canada's official policy is of multiculturalism within a bilingual framework. Multiculturalism is repeatedly cited as a defining feature of the country and one that sets it apart from the USA (and other destination countries) (Guo & Wong, 2015). Emerging from work done in response to the Quiet Revolution in Québec, the overall goal of multiculturalism was to reframe ethnic or racial differences as a national agenda of "unity within diversity," rather than forced assimilation.

Prime Minister Pierre Trudeau adopted multiculturalism as official policy in 1971. Its chief purposes, as described by Mahtani (2004), were:

1. To assist all cultural groups that demonstrate a desire and effort to develop a capacity to grow and contribute to Canada
2. To assist members of all cultural groups to overcome cultural barriers to full participation in Canadian society
3. To promote creative encounters and interchange among all Canadian cultural groups in the interest of national unity
4. To assist immigrants to acquire at least one of Canada's official languages

Multiculturalism was integrated into the constitution in 1982 and the federal Multiculturalism Act was passed in 1988 (Guo & Wong, 2015). Equivalent legislation at the provincial level was implemented between 1977 and 2008.

There are debates about the benefits of multiculturalism, including whether it is divisive or whether it unites; whether it serves to marginalize or whether it includes; whether it essentializes or whether it hybridizes; whether it fails to address the root causes of inequality or whether it acts as a catalyst to do so and whether it is hegemonic and manipulative, or whether it counters hegemony (Guo & Wong, 2015). Multiculturalism policy also fails to adequately address the relationship between Indigenous peoples and the state (St. Denis, 2011).

In Québec, many greeted multiculturalism with hostility and suspicion, and viewed it as diminishing the position of French Canadians as one of the two founding linguistic communities. In his book *Multicultural Citizenship*, Will Kymlicka (1994) argues that it is important to distinguish national minorities from immigrant groups, while Charles Taylor (1994) notes that "the supposedly fair and difference-blind society is ... in a subtle and unconscious way, itself highly discriminatory."

Multiculturalism Act, Section 3 (1)

It is hereby declared to be the policy of the Government of Canada to

(a) recognize and promote the understanding that multiculturalism reflects the cultural and racial diversity of Canadian society and acknowledges the freedom of all members of Canadian society to preserve, enhance and share their cultural heritage

(b) to recognize and promote the understanding that multiculturalism is a fundamental characteristic of the Canadian heritage and identity and that it provides an invaluable resource in the shaping of Canada's future.

An excerpt from the Canadian Multiculturalism Act, R.S.C., 1985, c. 24 (4th Supp.). [1988, c. 31, assented to 21st July, 1988].

Other Critiques of Multiculturalism

Recent populist political discourse — for example by Maxime Bernier of the People's Party of Canada — critiqued multiculturalism for the emphasis on preserving traditions and customs from immigrants' home countries. The argument is that multiculturalism encourages a lack of commitment to the "Canadian" way of life. This line of thinking has a parallel in the populist and anti-immigrant sentiments gaining ground in several major European countries and in the United States under former President Donald Trump. In the 2019 Canadian federal election, although securing the votes of a small minority, proponents of this anti-immigrant discourse were soundly defeated — not even one MP was elected from the People's Party, and Bernier himself lost his "safe" seat in Québec.

Other Canadian scholars have argued that multiculturalism has failed to reach its intended goals and that certain aspects of multiculturalism may be detrimental to Canadian society. For example, George Dei, a professor at the Ontario Institute for Studies in Education, has suggested that by displaying superficial aspects of a culture (such as ethnic foods and dance) to mainstream audiences at ethnic and cultural fairs and festivals, multiculturalism diverts our attention away from the disturbing effects of racial inequality in society.

Such critiques of multiculturalism policy challenge policymakers to reshape and improve the programs offered. Policies should address the real concerns of immigrants and be responsive to the needs of all residents of Canada, including newcomers facing the multiple barriers in settlement, to which we now turn.

Figure 9.6

Admissions of Permanent Residents by Top 10 Countries in 2017

Government of Canada, *Annual Report to Parliament on Immigration*, 2018.

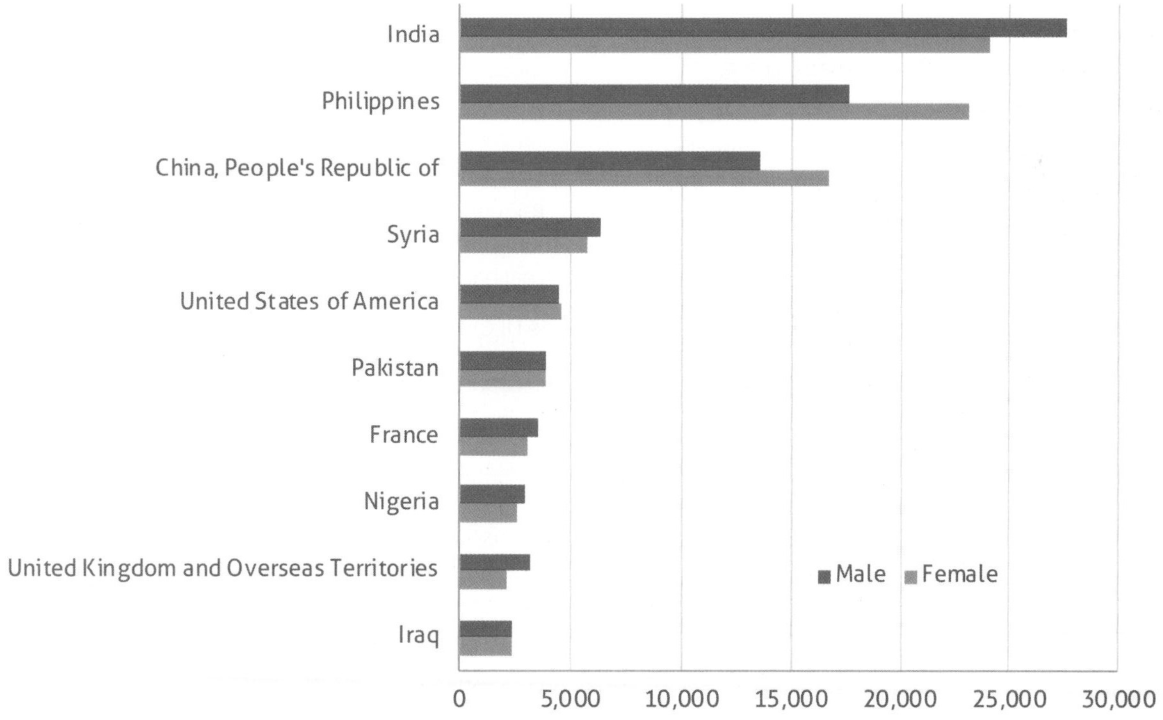

What the COVID–19 pandemic has revealed ...

Migrant Farm Workers and COVID–19

Time for a Meaningful Reform to Protect Migrant Workers

Canada's immigration system doesn't protect or provide citizenship paths to so-called "unskilled" foreign workers. It fails to recognize their worth and, as a result, often fails to protect them.

In the mid-1960s, in an attempt to meet the seasonal labour needs of Canadian agricultural producers, the federal government created the Seasonal Agricultural Workers Program (SAWP), turning to the Caribbean for a temporary stream of foreign workers. The SAWP now falls within the primary agricultural stream of the Temporary Foreign Worker program (TFWP), which is administered by Employment and Services Development Canada (ESDC).

Initially, this program was intended to be a last resort and only a temporary solution. Over 50 years later, this program has become a central component of Canada's primary agricultural industry (UFCW, 2020).

An Exploitative System

The SAWP program has continuously expanded. Seasonal workers arrive from Mexico or participating Caribbean countries such as Barbados and Grenada. They now account for half of Canada's paid agricultural workforce.

In 2019, the *Toronto Star* detailed 3,100 complaints made to Mexico's Ministry of Labour since 2009. About 40% of the complaints pointed to living conditions — rat infestations, no running water, open latrines, and sleeping on tables and chairs (Mojtehedzadeh, 2019).

Recently, the COVID–19 pandemic has shone a spotlight on these deplorable conditions as contributing to COVID–19 deaths and more than a thousand positive tests for the virus.

A June 2020 report from the United Food and Commercial Workers Union (UFCW) compiled complaints from more than 1,100 workers. It found that 316 workers weren't paid in part or in full for their quarantine period and 539 reported they didn't have enough food to eat (UFCW, 2020).

A More Protective Immigration System

The COVID–19 crisis underlined the urgency for systemic change. During the pandemic, it became clear that the fair treatment of Canada's agricultural workers required significant reforms at both the federal and provincial levels.

Federal regulations during the pandemic stipulated that workers must be quarantined for 14 days after arriving in Canada. If a worker became sick after their quarantine they might have been eligible for CERB under the same requirements as other Canadians but for many, these requirements were not attainable.

Paid sick leave is not guaranteed, as it depends on provincial regulations, observes author and journalist Sadiya Ansari, writing in *Macleans* magazine:

> Like most provinces, there is no requirement for employers to pay sick leave in Ontario, where most migrant workers are located. In Québec, which brings in the second-highest number of farm workers (over 14,000 in 2018), two days of sick leave are legally mandated but access isn't guaranteed — lack of access to information, language barriers and fear of employer reprisal are real barriers. (Ansari, 2020)

The UFCW/AWA report — *The Status of Migrant Farm Workers in Canada, 2020* — calls for urgent changes to protect the health, safety, and rights of tens of thousands of migrant agricultural workers who are essential to Canada's food supply. The report concludes with 14 legislative and regulatory reforms to an unjust immigrant system that currently leaves migrant agricultural workers vulnerable to exploitation, health risks, and employer reprisal.

The UFCW/AWA recommendations are provided in full on the following page. The full report is available on the UFCW's website at http://www.ufcw.ca.

REQUIRED REFORMS

Federal reforms urgently needed:

1. Make union representation a necessary condition of the Temporary Foreign Worker Program, as the best practical measure in providing proper representation and protection to Canada's most precarious and vulnerable worker population

2. End employer-specific work permits and replace them with open work permits, or at least, occupation-specific work permits

3. Expand the Agri-food Pilot Program to allow for an additional 5,000 permanent residency opportunities, per year, dedicated to the primary agricultural stream

4. Establish a tripartite sector council dedicated to reducing Canada's over-reliance on temporary foreign workers by collaborating on innovative active labour market policy options

5. Establish a federal tribunal to properly allow for the review and appeal of repatriation decisions in advance of TFWs being sent home by employers

6. Provide SAWP and TFWP workers with access to Canada's Employment Insurance Program, into which they have paid since 1966

7. Sign the International Convention on the Protection of the Rights of All Migrant Workers and Members of Their Families, which was adopted by the United Nations General Assembly in December 1990

Provincial reforms urgently needed:

1. Repeal Ontario's Agricultural Employees Protection Act. The Ontario Labour Relations Act must be amended to include agricultural workers, or the Agricultural Labour Relations Act should be revived to respect the bargaining rights of agricultural workers

2. Bill 26 must be repealed in Alberta; all agricultural workers should be fully included in Alberta's Labour Code without exception

3. Bill 8 must be repealed in Québec; all agricultural workers should be fully included in Québec's Labour Code without exception

4. Institute and properly enforce the Manitoba model in all provinces with respect to regulating and penalizing offshore recruiters of foreign workers

5. Establish significant fines and/or jail sentences for domestic recruiters and temporary work agencies who are found to exploit migrant workers

6. Eliminate piece rate and set quotas as they facilitate labour exploitation and create physical and mental issues that impact the well-being of migrant workers

7. Ban the practice of housing workers above or adjacent to greenhouses in recognition of the apparent dangers associated with living in buildings housing chemicals, fertilizers, boilers, industrial fans, and/or heaters

Temporary Foreign Workers, 2012–2019

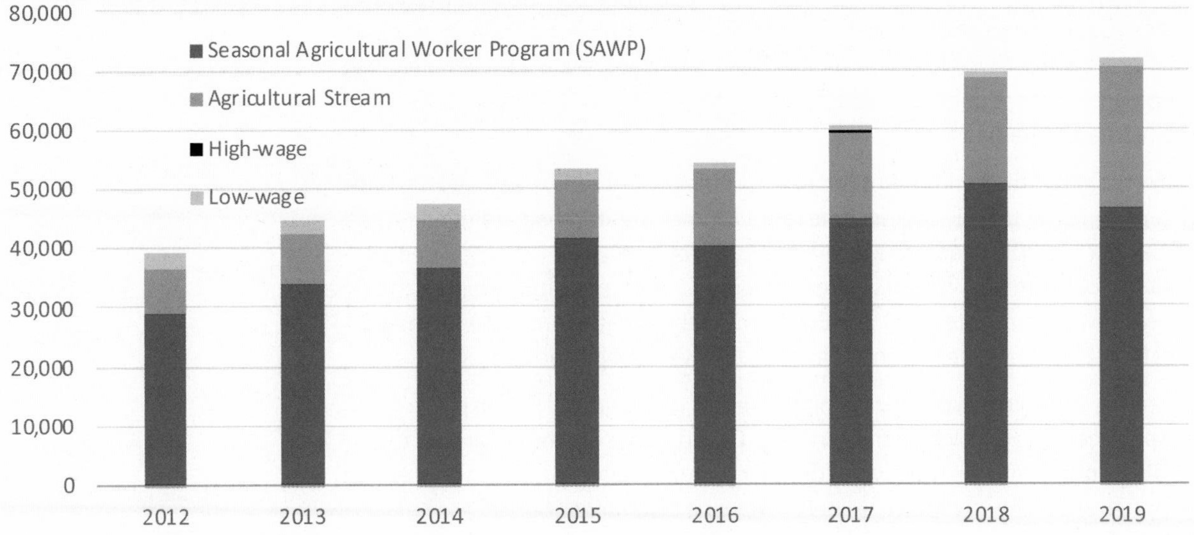

Employment and Social Development Canada (2020, March). *Temporary Foreign Worker Program 2012–2019.*

9.5 Settlement Challenges

Settlement is an extremely complex process that is influenced by a number of factors, not least whether a migrant has permanent status on arrival in Canada, has temporary status (with or without the intention to transition to permanency), or is undocumented. Migrants arrive in Canada with a range of strengths and skills, yet they often face considerable barriers to economic, social, and political integration that are well-documented in the Canadian literature.

Multiculturalism notwithstanding, the challenges related to immigration and settlement, now and in the past, can include any or all of the following:

- Poverty and barriers to employment
- Struggling with language and accessing educational programs
- Difficulties finding suitable and affordable housing
- Having to deal with racism, exclusion, and discrimination
- Learning to navigate complex health and social service systems
- Family separation and social isolation

Responsibility for settlement services to address these barriers is shared between federal and provincial levels of government; multiple organizations work to provide different services. However, many services are only available to permanent residents — there are far fewer services for temporary migrants, though they have many of the same needs.

Refugee claimants can access most services only when they are granted refugee status, which for some can take many years. Temporary residents and international students must rely on themselves, their community, and any locally or provincially funded services that are available.

Core Housing Need

An important recent report has highlighted how immigration category and racialized status intersect to produce deep inequities with respect to rental housing in Toronto.

Among other things, the researchers found that:

- New and long-term immigrants have higher rates of core housing need and deep affordable housing need.
- Refugees have the highest rates of core housing need and unsuitable housing compared to individuals from other immigrant admission categories.

The research team goes on to outline measures that would help to address these urgent housing needs and foster a just recovery from the COVID–19 pandemic.

Wilson, B., Lightman, N., & Gingrich, L-G. (2020). *Spaces and Places of Exclusion: Mapping Rental Housing Disparities for Toronto's Racialized and Immigrant Communities*. Social Planning Toronto.

Employment Barriers

One of the most pressing challenges experienced by newcomers today is related to employment barriers and ensuing income insecurity. Far too many recent immigrants (those who have been in Canada for five years or less) are searching for employment or are underemployed and are more likely to face low income than mainstream Canadians.

Unfortunately, this trend seems to be worsening over time. For example, in 1980, recent immigrants had a low-income rate 1.4 times greater than individuals born in Canada. In 2009, nearly one-quarter (23.8%) of immigrants who had been in Ontario for less than five years were considered low income, much higher than the overall low-income rate of 13.1%. Even among those in the province for longer — less than 10 years — nearly one in five (19.1%) was living in poverty.

There are multiple reasons for the high levels of immigrants living in poverty, despite the skills with which they arrive in Canada. These include barriers to finding work, exclusion from work for which they are qualified, and racism experienced in the workplace — including wage discrimination.

- **Barriers to Finding Work**

Many immigrants are more highly skilled than Canadian-born individuals, but they experience disproportionate levels of poverty, unemployment, and underemployment, especially in the short term.

One of the main reasons for this is a lack of recognition of international credentials. Remember that, in the points system, the federal government grants significant points for professional qualifications and experience. In theory, this is intended to safeguard people from experiencing unemployment or underemployment by ensuring that newcomers arrive with skills and experiences that are needed in Canada. However, professional accreditation in Canada is usually managed by professional bodies, which often do not recognize that same education and experience for which the immigrant was granted permanent residency.

These immigrants (referred to by those who work in this area as "foreign-trained professionals") are then required to go back to school or take intensive exams in order to become "recredentialized," a costly and time-consuming process.

Worse, the Canadian job market favours Canadian experience. This puts immigrants in a classic conundrum; unable to gain employment without Canadian experience, but unable to get experience without employment. As a result, many highly skilled immigrants spend years trying to break into the labour market, and the longer it takes, the more difficult it is.

Figure 9.7

Unemployment Rate in Canada in 2018, 15 Years and Older, by Immigrant Status

Statistics Canada, Table 14-10-0083-01. Labour force characteristics by immigrant status, annual.

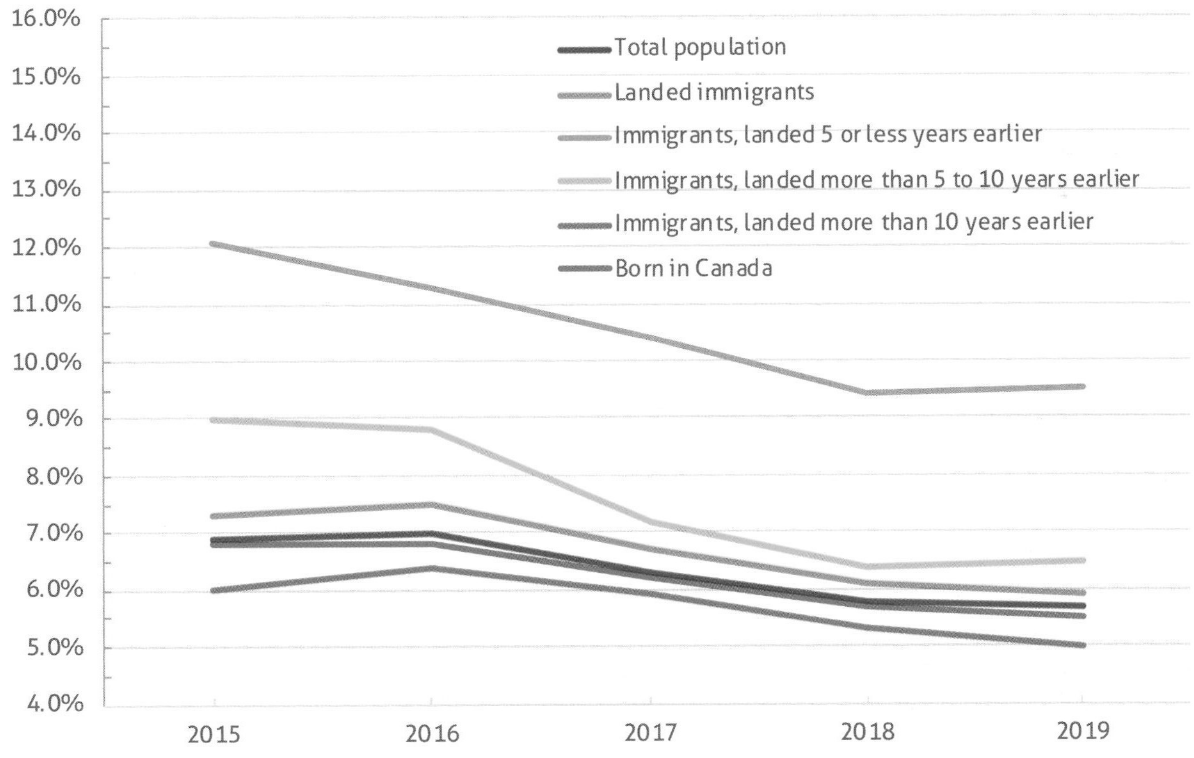

- **Racism and Discrimination in the Workplace**

Further discrimination in the job market, especially due to race, affects both immigrants and Canadian-born people of colour. Multiple studies have documented discrimination based solely on an applicant's name; these studies detail the much higher levels of callbacks for applicants with European-sounding names but otherwise identical resumés than for those whose names sound non-European (Banerjee et al., 2018). Moreover, culturally biased hiring practices that favour certain skills and behaviours can also make it difficult for newcomers during the hiring process. For example, in North America, "selling oneself" and one's skills is necessary when searching for most jobs, behaviour that some immigrants might find rude and uncomfortable to emulate.

A person's gender is also an important factor in determining how successful they will be in gaining suitable employment. While immigrant women deal with many of the same work-related barriers that immigrant men face, they also confront certain stressors that are unique to their gender. For example, many women must manage the added complexities of child care and family responsibilities, which can make it difficult to gain Canadian work experience. As well, women, transgender, and non-binary immigrants face unique forms of discrimination from the combined effects of their ethno-racial backgrounds and gender identities.

The ability to secure suitable employment can sometimes be counteracted by the presence of certain skills that immigrant-supporting agencies can help job-seekers to develop. Knowledge of where to look for work, how to write a resumé, how to prepare for an interview, and so on help to increase success in finding the right job. However, removing barriers to finding work also requires substantial changes within Canadian society. Measures include reconsidering the credential recognition practices, challenging employer racism, and addressing immigrants' lack of knowledge about education systems and work experience in countries other than Canada.

Even when immigrants are hired in suitable positions in their field, they can experience difficulties. Problems with language, for example, can interfere with how work is performed and can make communicating with coworkers and managers difficult. Not understanding norms and conventions can introduce challenges that make a workplace unaccepting of newcomers.

Racism within the workplace can be overt, taking the form of discriminatory remarks or behaviours meant to set BIPOC (Black, Indigenous. and people of colour) employees apart from white Canadians. The expression of such personal prejudices not only creates a toxic work environment but has serious negative psychological consequences for the victims of racism. On a more subtle level, racism might be reflected in the gross earning differentials between immigrants and their Canadian-born, white counterparts. If hired, newcomers often make less money than non-immigrant Canadians. This is especially true for people from visible minority groups (Reitz, 2001). The argument that skills and education acquired in European countries fit better with Canadian employment needs fails to reflect current global realities. Race is a factor that is clearly at play.

Systemic Racism

A recent data compilation demonstrates the depth and pervasiveness of anti-Black racism in Canada across the lifecycle:

- Black students are four times more likely to be expelled from a Toronto high school than white students.
- Black workers are twice as likely as Asian workers and four times as likely as white workers to report experiencing racial discrimination at workplaces in Canada.
- Black university graduates earn only 80 cents for every dollar earned by white university graduates despite having the same credentials.
- Black women are three times less likely to have a family doctor than non-racialized women in Ontario.
- Black residents are 20 times more likely than a white resident to be shot dead by police in Toronto.

DasGupta, N., Shandal, V., Shadd, D., & Segal, A. (2020). *The Pervasive Reality of Anti-Black Racism in Canada: The current state, and what to do about it.*

- **Blocked Upward Mobility**

Another example of subtle racism is the "glass ceiling effect." This involves preventing newcomers, especially people of colour (along with Indigenous people, women, and others) from advancing to the highest organizational ranks. Top-level management positions are reserved for those who are usually white, cis-gendered, heterosexual men. This phenomenon is referred to as the glass ceiling effect, since the racial barrier is not apparent — and therefore, not seen as a formal obstacle.

Whether obvious or somewhat hidden, acts of racism and discrimination within the work environment threaten an immigrant's emotional and psychological well-being and can result in her or him leaving the workplace.

Struggling with Official Language and Barriers to Education

While many immigrants speak multiple languages, if this does not include English or French, they can experience multiple additional barriers. Ability in English or French varies significantly according to country of origin and immigration stream and can have a substantial impact on an immigrant's settlement trajectory (Ravanera et al., 2014). Along with employment potential, language proficiency affects the immigrants' awareness of their rights, as well as their ability to access settlement services and other social welfare programs (Drolet & Teixeira, 2019). Language difficulties have typically been connected to difficulties navigating health care and therefore lead to worsening health outcomes (Ng et al., 2011).

Figure 9.8

Linguistic Profile of Immigrants, Self-Identified (2017, by Percentage of Category)

Government of Canada, *Annual Report to Parliament on Immigration*, 2018.

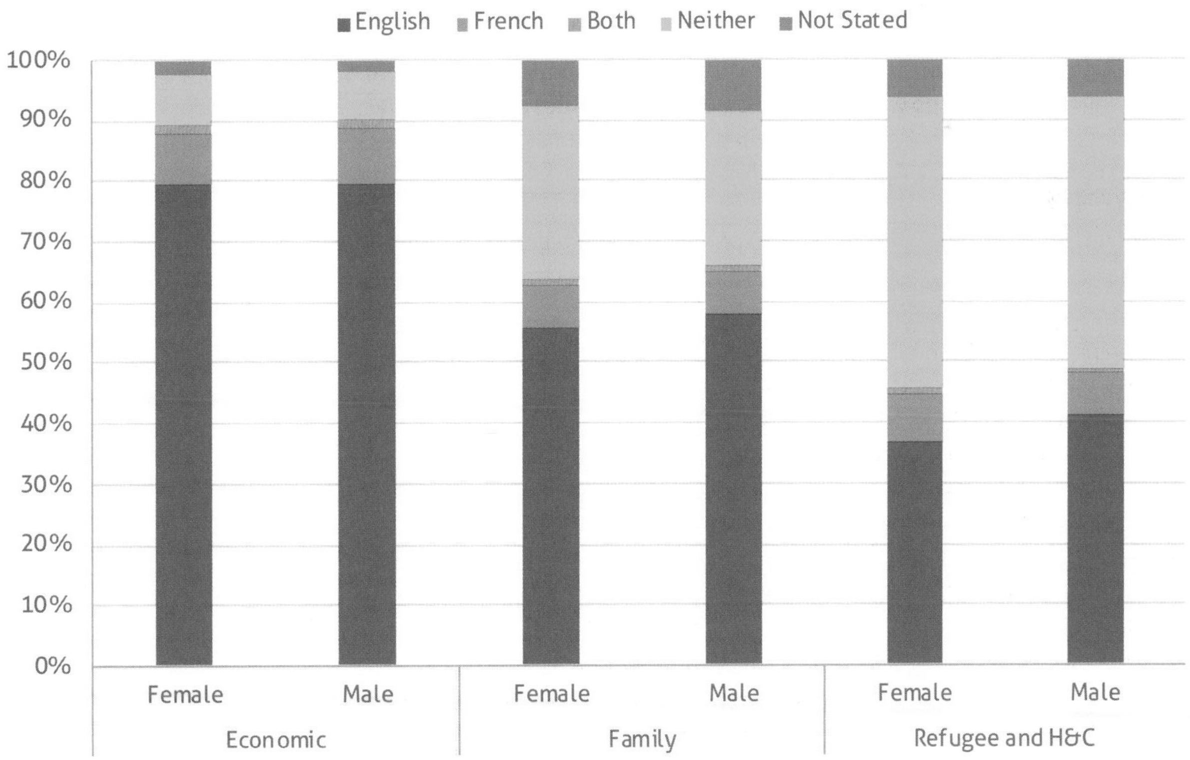

Provinces often provide support through official language classes but access can be limited by a lack of child care, by location (classes are more readily available in larger population centres), by available time (some immigrants work multiple jobs to stay afloat financially), and by a lack of permanent status.

Educational outcomes of those who migrate as children and second-generation immigrants (the children of immigrants) are well-documented. Those who migrate as older children are much more likely than their younger counterparts to experience difficulties in school. This has been linked both to language acquisition and structural racism in the schooling system (Corak, 2011). The children of immigrants, on the other hand, have higher education outcomes than their contemporaries who are at least third generation (Aydemir et al., 2013).

Access to Suitable Housing

Studies have also shown that racism is rampant in the housing marketplace. Immigrants, particularly racialized immigrants, face difficulties with gaining access to housing, with the cost of housing, and with the quality of housing. These barriers intersect closely with issues of official language ability and socio-economic status. For example, the media has documented numerous cases of landlords over-charging and demanding illegal extra payments from potential immigrant renters who were unaware of their rights in the Canadian system (Keung, 2012). Landlords may also simply refuse to rent to racialized immigrants, claiming that the unit is "already rented."

The cost of housing in the large cities, which is precisely where most recent immigrants settle, is prohibitive particularly to refugees and other low-income immigrants who may be forced into sub-standard housing. Studies have shown that a sizeable proportion of the homeless population is immigrants (Britneff, 2018). Immigrants who do wish to buy a home face difficulties getting credit, regardless of how good their history was in their home country.

Family Separation

One of the factors that most affects the experiences of immigrants as they settle in Canada has consistently been shown in the literature to be family relationships.

Presence of positive relationships can act as a buffer against migration stressors. Conversely, separation from family members, especially children, and especially when their family members are in dangerous situations, is consistently cited as an ongoing source of worry and stress that creates an inability to focus on other aspects of settlement. This gets worse over time, particularly when there is uncertainty over the process or possibility of reunification. There can be a huge impact on relationships both during the separation and upon reunification. Social isolation and separation from family and community are also associated with lost feelings of identity and belonging (Mansouri & Cauchi, 2007; Rousseau et al., 2001; Silove, 1999).

Child Protection and Migrant Children

Separating children from parents is allowed under the Immigration and Refugee Protection Act as a "last resort." But a 2017 report titled "Invisible Citizens: Canadian Children in Immigration Detention" points out that parents who are detained often face a difficult decision of surrendering their child to foster care or bringing them into detention.

"Children are surely the most innocent and defenceless among us," observes Audrey Macklin, Director, Centre for Criminology and Sociolegal Studies at the University of Toronto. "Yet Canada Border Services Agency (CBSA) detains both citizen and non-citizen children, without acknowledging detention of the former or adequately justifying detention of the latter."

Gros, H. & Muscati, S. (2017). *Invisible Citizens: Canadian Children in Immigration Detention*. International Human Rights Program, University of Toronto Faculty of Law.

Health

Finally, the physical and mental well-being of immigrants and temporary workers in Canada is intimately connected to their immigration process, status, and service provision upon arrival and is also very well studied. The "healthy immigrant effect" describes how, upon arrival, immigrants are generally healthier than their Canadian-born counterparts, regardless of socio-economic status; this is likely due to the immigration system excluding those in poor health. However, over time, the health of immigrants and their Canadian-born counterparts converges (Khan et al., 2017), meaning that the health of immigrants deteriorates to levels that are on par or below those of other Canadians despite their initial health-related advantage.

However, there is heterogeneity within immigrant populations. Level of exposure to pre-migration trauma is significant as shown by levels and persistence of mental illness. The recurrent nature of many refugees' traumatic experiences, for example, has effects that can be interrelated and cumulative (Beiser, 2005). Then there is the migration process itself, which for most immigrants, regardless of stream, is exhausting. Many immigrants experience a gap between expectations and reality, leading to feelings of uncertainty and powerlessness. For those going through the asylum process, possible detention, the pressure of "proving" their case, and fear of denial and deportation can all contribute to negative mental and physical health outcomes. Refugees who are sponsored by private groups may feel pressure, whether explicit or imagined, to conform to the expectations of their sponsors (Beiser, 2005; Hyman, 2011; Koopowitz & Abhary, 2004; Mansouri & Cauchi, 2007; Silove et al., 2000; Spitzer, 2011).

There is also heterogeneity in health outcomes by ethnicity. Unfamiliarity with Canadian food and the environment can lead to illness. Racism and discrimination directly increase stress and lower self-esteem. They also interact with other factors, for example by increasing barriers to accessing health care, and lead to lower socio-economic outcomes, which are significantly connected to poorer health outcomes (Beiser, 2005; Hyman, 2011).

Gender also plays a role in predicting health outcomes, including through exposure to gender-based violence, interaction with other social determinants of health (such as poverty and official language ability) that predict poorer health outcomes, and the extra burden of responsibility for caregiving that is usually borne by women (Beiser, 2005; Hyman, 2011; Spitzer, 2011). Immigrant seniors are associated with higher levels of depression, often due to linguistic and social isolation (Hyman, 2011).

Temporary and undocumented workers are in particularly precarious positions that add to health stressors. They are often employed in industries and positions with dubious working conditions (Magalhaes et al., 2010). They have the stress of "temporariness" associated with their status, as described above. Moreover, they often have limited access to support and health services.

Health Care Coverage during COVID-19

Lack of access to health care is a problem for those with precarious immigration status, including migrant workers, refugee claimants, and those without documentation.

As COVID-19 among migrant farm workers continued to escalate, in 2020 more than 200 organizations, including the Canadian Medical Association, College of Family Physicians of Canada, and the Canadian Paediatric Society warned that the federal government was placing the entire society at risk by failing to guarantee health care to all people.

Naturalization

Naturalization refers to the process of applying for and being granted Canadian citizenship. Until recently, Canada placed a great emphasis on the rates at which immigrants to Canada naturalized. For example, the government and media frequently pointed out how much higher the rate of naturalization was in Canada when compared to the United States. This was seen to demonstrate Canada's commitment to welcoming newcomers and to a perception of immigrants as "new Canadians" who already belong. Unfortunately, this approach has been changing.

To qualify for citizenship, immigrants must be permanent residents who have lived in Canada for three of the previous five years, have filed taxes if they need to, demonstrate a knowledge of Canada, and have the ability to communicate in one of the official languages. They must also pay the application and citizenship fees, which in 2019 were raised to $530 per adult and $100 per child. (In 2014 the adult application fee was $100.)

The recent increase in fees represents a significant barrier, especially for families on low incomes who are working against other barriers, as already discussed, to establish themselves financially. Perhaps not surprisingly, naturalization rates decreased significantly following the fee increases (Griffith, 2018). This disenfranchises those permanent residents who do not naturalize and limits their ability to access certain employment positions, for example with the federal government. It also maintains them in a more precarious status, particularly in relation to deportation, as described next.

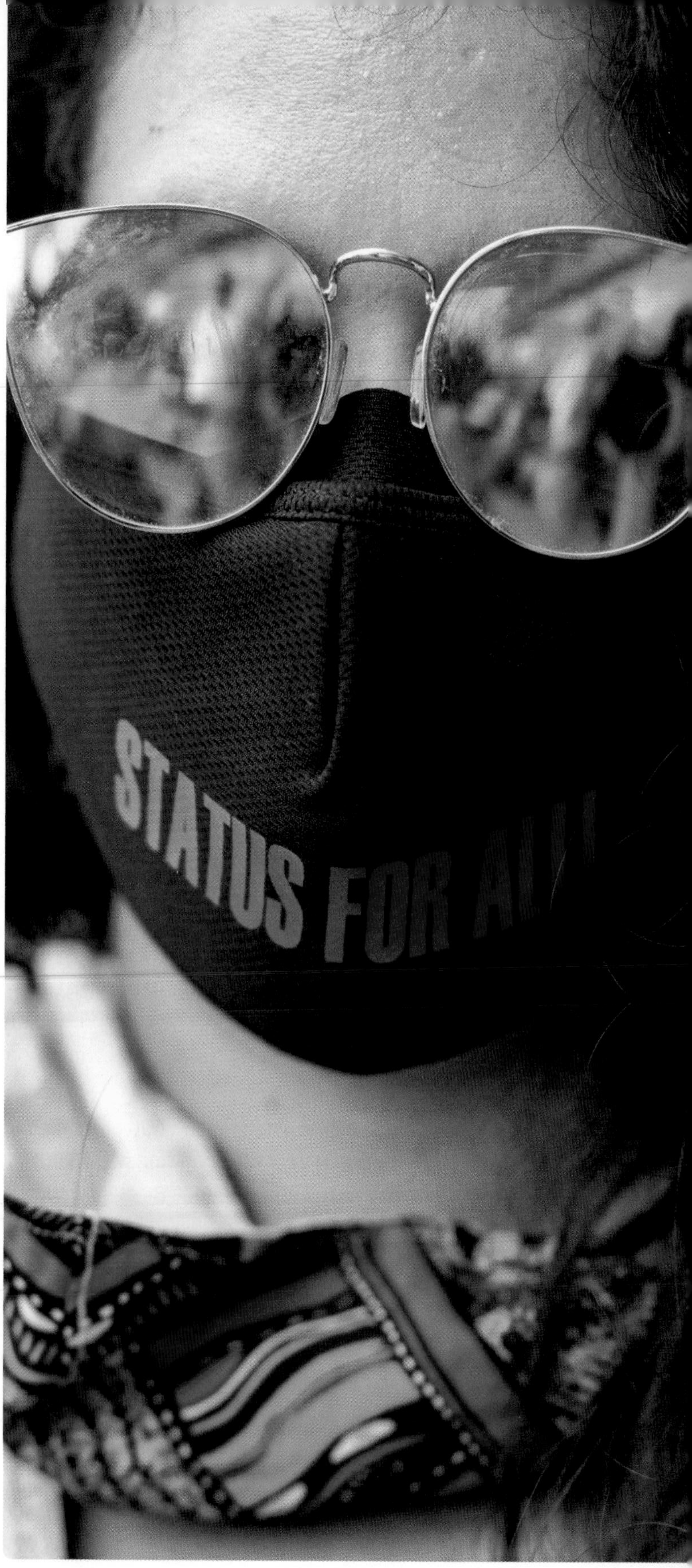

Photo: A protestors in front of the federal Immigration Minister's office in Toronto after the deaths of three migrant workers who contracted COVID–19. The protestors demanded full immigration status for all non-permanent residents in order to extend the benefits of health care, emergency income support, and labour protections (July 4, 2020).

Deportation

Deportation is a topic that Canada does not like to talk about in great detail, yet it happens on a very regular basis. Canada deports not only temporary and undocumented migrants but, under certain circumstances, permanent residents and, to a much smaller extent, individuals who have been stripped of their citizenship. This has important implications for the well-being of immigrants, for the meaning of Canadian citizenship, and for those who work with immigrants.

Temporary and undocumented migrants who are deported include those without status who are refused entry by border guards, those whose refugee claim has been refused, those who have overstayed temporary visas, and those who have entered, and remained, undocumented. Permanent residents who can be deported include refugees who have their refugee status revoked; since 2014 Canada has been revoking permanent residency (known as cessation) for some refugees who have returned to their home country, even if for a short visit (Canadian Council for Refugees, 2014). Permanent residents who commit crimes with a maximum possible jail sentence of more than 10 years, or an actual jail sentence of more than 6 months, can face deportation, as can those who are deemed to be "a threat to Canada." This includes those who immigrated as children and do not remember anything about their home country.

When permanent residents and citizens are found to have misrepresented themselves on their permanent residency application, their status is revoked, leading to deportation. Finally, citizens (Canadian-born or naturalized) who have access to dual nationality and who are convicted of terrorism, treason, or spying abroad or who are involved in an organized "armed conflict" within Canada face a loss of citizenship and deportation to their other country of nationality.

Temporary Suspension and Administrative Deferral of Removals defer deportation to unsafe countries. However, those who have been issued a deportation order have limited right to appeal and will face considerable difficulties returning to Canada in the future.

The implications of deportation for the well-being of the migrant are many. On a personal level they face lost agency and a threatened sense of self. They may face not only danger in the country to which they are returned, but also invisibility, stigmatization, poverty, and the consequences of having failed to conform to family and societal expectations (Peutz, 2006). For migrants who are deported after living in Canada for many years, they may be separated from Canadian family and children, which is clearly contrary to the best interests of the child.

Child protection and migrant children

In a recent case, child protection services in Nova Scotia were found to have failed in their duty toward a refugee child in their care, as they had failed to apply for citizenship on his behalf.

In 2019, Abdoul Abdi (who had arrived from Somalia as a young child) received a reprieve from deportation for criminality only at the last minute.

The Nova Scotia Department of Community Services has since changed its policy to ensure that the citizenship status of migrant children in care is reviewed on a regular basis (Luck, 2019).

9.6 Issues to Consider in Canadian Immigration

The seeming shift from permanent residency as a nation-building project toward more temporary and just-in-time migration is happening with very little public debate. To be sure, international competition to attract immigrants is more intense than ever before. Other countries in addition to Canada are more actively courting immigrants.

For Canada to prosper and remain competitive internationally, it still needs more immigrants, both skilled and unskilled. To attract them, it also must ensure that programs and services are in place to facilitate settlement and integration, and that equivalent foreign experience and credentials are recognized.

Canada needs to do this while facilitating an immigration system that is consistent with principles of reconciliation and respect for the Indigenous peoples upon whose land we have settled. Indeed, increasingly there are discussions about the relationships between those who have been on this land the longest and those who have most recently arrived. The final two Calls to Action of the Truth and Reconciliation Commission in 2015 pertain to newcomers: (1) to add observation of Treaty relationships into the Oath of Citizenship; and, (2) to improve the information on Indigenous peoples provided to newcomers and future citizens.

What Kind of Country Do We Want Canada To Be?

Multiple changes continue to be made to immigration policy and there also has been a substantial increase in ministerial powers. Recent years have seen restrictions on "permanent" immigrants (economic, family reunification, and humanitarian), tightened rules for obtaining citizenship (though these were somewhat rescinded by the Justin Trudeau government), and larger numbers of "temporary" workers. Many policy shifts have favoured short-term fixes over long-term solutions and provinces, employers, and educational institutions are increasingly involved in immigrant selection. This all has important consequences for the well-being of immigrants. Yet the burden for provision of support in settlement has been downloaded to provinces, universities, employers, and the migrants and their communities.

The Canadian public needs to be engaged in a national conversation on what kind of country we want, how immigration can help us get there, and what this means for all racialized people, whether immigrants or not. Four principles can guide that discussion and lead to good choices for Canada and all Canadians:

1. Immigration policy should be based mainly on long-term social and economic objectives and a commitment to citizenship.
2. Immigration policy should be evidence-based, comprehensive, fair, and respectful of human rights.
3. Immigration policy should be developed through public engagement, federal–provincial consultation, and democratic processes.
4. Policies that frame the settlement process should work to eliminate discrimination on the basis of race, immigration status, and all other factors.

Immigration after COVID–19

Canada depends on new waves of immigrants each year. Beginning with the Conservative government of Brian Mulroney, Canada has maintained immigration levels of more than 225,000 new arrivals and prioritized the economic stream in order to help grow the economy.

Due to travel restrictions, reduced capacity for processing applications, and flight cancellations, only 60% of projected levels were expected to make it to Canada by the end of 2020.

Many immigration policy experts now warn if Canada doesn't stay the course of pre–COVID-19 levels, the Canada's population growth and economy will be in trouble.

Policy Debates and Objectives

Canada obviously continues to need a strong immigration program to help meet its population and labour market needs. It also needs to ensure good welfare services for immigrants when they arrive and while they fully integrate into Canadian society, and to eliminate racism against immigrants and non-immigrants alike. However, policy shifts are altering the landscape for economic immigration to Canada, and this has happened without a great deal of public debate (Alboim & Cohl, 2012).

There are important questions about immigration policy that must be discussed and debated at both the political and social levels. Among the important questions that must be seriously considered by policymakers, and by all Canadians, are the following:

1. What is the impact on Canadian society when a considerable proportion of net migration is temporary?
2. What is the impact of increasingly exclusionary refugee and humanitarian policies for refugees, and for Canadian society?
3. What is the impact of a significant portion of the labour force having limited access to services, little chance of obtaining permanent residency or citizenship, and limited access to labour rights?
4. Is a "two-step" immigration process, from temporary to permanent migration, the best strategy in dealing with the declining labour market outcomes of economic immigrants? How can we support better social and political outcomes for migrants using this process?
5. What is the impact of downloading the settlement process onto individuals, employers, educational institutions, and community and settlement agencies?
6. What can we do to address discrimination against migrants and racialized minorities in employment and housing and other areas to improve settlement outcomes?
7. How can we work toward reconciliation, recognizing the ongoing impacts of immigration and settler colonialism on Indigenous lands?

Social Welfare Policy in Action

The Resettlement Assistance Program

Greater Investments Will Reduce Costs over Time

In addition to needs related to housing, employment, and education, Government Assisted Refugees (GARs) may have experienced high levels of trauma or have higher medical needs.

The number of Government Assisted Refugees (GARs) resettled to Canada has generally ranged between 5,425 (2012) and 9,488 (2017), with the exception of a huge increase in 2016 to 23,624. Since the Blended Visa Office Referred Refugees (BVOR) program started in 2013, its numbers have been relatively small — from 155 (2013) to 1,284 (2017), again with a much higher number of 4,500 in 2016.

Settlement support for GARs and, to a lesser extent, BVORs (who also receive support from private organizations and citizens), is provided through the Resettlement Assistance Program (RAP). The RAP includes both services and income support specifically for refugees. It is provided by the federal government, although services are often delivered by "service provider organizations" such as immigrant settlement agencies in major population centres.

Upon Arrival

Supporting agencies are notified shortly before Government Assisted Refugees are to arrive in their town or city. Refugees, after going through customs, are either met at the airport or at airport welcome centres to ensure they are safely transported to temporary accommodation.

All refugees are provided with basic information about, for example, their rights and responsibilities, and are given access to health care. For Government Assisted Refugees, the Resettlement Assistance Program provides accommodation and meals for the first weeks, often in residential facilities run by settlement agencies.

RAP also provides immediate assistance to these individuals in finding more permanent housing and help with registration for the income support component of the program.

Ongoing Support

Under the Resettlement Assistance Program, agencies provide ongoing case management to ensure that refugees are connected to services in the community in which they live. They will support the refugees, for example, in accessing language classes and enrolling their children in schools (and connecting with school settlement workers). They may help them to connect with employment services or medical services. They may also refer the refugees to community-building activities and programs run by many local community organizations.

The income support component of the RAP includes one-off start-up allowances and monthly income support. The start-up allowance is designed to cover the basic needs for someone arriving in Canada for the first time with very little; everything from clothing (including for the winters) to furniture, kitchen equipment, and utility installation.

In 2019, the start-up allowance was $3,065 for a single person and $6,660 for a couple with two children (Refugee Sponsorship Training Program, 2017). For BVOR clients, the start-up costs are covered by the private sponsoring group.

The monthly income support, which is tied to provincial social assistance rates and therefore varies by province, is supposed to cover ongoing basic needs such as shelter, food, and communications. In November 2019, for a single person this was $763/month in Ontario (Refugee Sponsorship Training Program, 2019a), and $896/month in Alberta (Refugee Sponsorship Training Program, 2019b), while for a couple with two children this was $1,280 per month for Ontario and $1,789 for Alberta. Some support with transportation costs is also provided.

After One Year

The Resettlement Assistance Program lasts for one year. After that, refugees are expected to be self-sufficient or to transition to provincial social assistance.

After one year and one month, refugees are generally expected to start making monthly installments to repay the immigration loan that they owe to the government for the costs of transportation to Canada.

Following recent changes, they now have three years to pay back the first $1,200, with another year for each additional $1,200 (Government of Canada, 2019).

Misrepresentations in the Media

There have been major misrepresentations of the RAP program in the media over the years. Viral memes have frequently been shared on social media claiming that refugees are provided more than is true.

This mis- or disinformation may obscure the difference between resettled refugees and refugee claimants (who are not eligible for RAP). It may portray the one-off start-up expenses as recurring payments. Or it may claim that an individual is receiving an amount that, in fact, is intended for a whole family.

These claims have been addressed in detail by the Canadian Council for Refugees at https://ccrweb.ca/en/refugees-social-assistance.

Program Evaluation

The government's own study in 2016 found RAP financial assistance rates to be insufficient "to meet GARs' immediate and essential needs" (Immigration, Refugees and Citizenship Canada, 2016, p.31), despite it matching provincial social assistance in most places. It also found that more support needs to be provided for GARs with greater needs.

The evaluation report recommended that RAP financial assistance be provided at "a sufficient level of support" to "support their successful integration" (Immigration, Refugees and Citizenship Canada, 2016, p. v).

Questions

1. Do you think that the Resettlement Assistance Program would provide sufficient support for someone relocating from another country to your community? Why? Why not?
2. According to one representative of the community, quoted at the time of the changes to the transportation loans, "There is somewhat of a running joke in the sponsorship community, which is: 'How do we welcome refugees to Canada? With debt'" (Levitz, 2017). What do you think about refugees to Canada arriving already with debt? How do you think this might affect their settlement process?
3. Why do you think there is persistent misrepresentation of the support provided to refugees in the media? What can be done to counter this disinformation?
4. Are there any additional settlement supports that you think might work to help these particular group of newcomers and their families successfully settle in this country?

Further Information

For more information on this program, consult the following sources:

- Government of Ontario: Refugees:
  The First Year in Ontario
  www.ontario.ca/page/refugees-first-year-ontario
- Government of Canada:
  Financial Help. Resettlement Assistance Program
  www.canada.ca/en/immigration-refugees-citizenship/services/refugees/help-within-canada/financial.html
- Canadian Council for Refugees:
  Transportation Loans
  www.ccrweb.ca/en/transportation-loans

A moment in time, August 12, 2010

Tamil Sri Lankans Seek Asylum

Refugees Receive an Inhospitable Welcome

In 2010, the MV Sun Sea, a cargo ship with 492 Sri Lankan Tamils on board, was intercepted off the coast of BC. The controversy that followed led to the enactment of Bill C-31 in June 2012.

As noted throughout the chapter, when people arrive at Canadian shores via boat, they are treated with suspicion and frequently denied entry.

Examples include the arrival of the Komagata Maru in 1914 from India or the SS St. Louis carrying Jewish refugees in 1939. Both incidents resulted in subsequent government apologies (May 18, 2016 and November 7, 2018 respectively).

The MV Sun Sea

Arriving by boat means that its journey is monitored and its arrival anticipated. This frequently results in being greeted by various officials from the Canada Border Services Agency (CBSA), along with media and public attention. Concerns of human smuggling and terrorism quickly infiltrate the social discourse.

Such was the case with the arrival of the MV Sun Sea in British Columbia in 2010, only shortly after the arrival the previous fall of the MV Ocean Lady carrying 76 Tamil men. Fleeing violence in Sri Lanka and the Sri Lankan civil war, and after a three-month journey on a rickety, barely seaworthy cargo ship, all 492 men, women, and children made refugee claims on arrival.

Prior to their arrival, the then Public Safety Minister Vic Toews had already labelled some of the passengers as "suspected human smugglers and terrorists" and the media quickly picked up on this, labelling them terrorists before they had a chance to tell their story (Canadian Council for Refugees, 2015).

On arrival, Vic Toews said "Canadian officials will look at all available options to strengthen our laws in order to address this unacceptable abuse of international law and Canadian generosity" (Poynter, 2012).

Bill C-31

Most refugee claimants are not detained on arrival in Canada, and for those who are, their release is usually within a matter of days or weeks. However, for the men, women, and children on the MV Sun Sea, their detention was prolonged. Families were separated and held in various provincial prisons for months—some for over a year. At the time, the CBSA officers were directed to "use all legal means to detain the passengers as long as possible, to try to have them declared inadmissible on grounds of criminality or security, and to argue against them being recognized as refugees" (Canadian Council for Refugees, 2015, p. 3).

This incident led to long-term legislative and policy change. In 2012, amid much controversy, Bill C-31, an Act to amend the Immigration and Refugee Protection Act, was passed. Bill C-31 provides for extensive power to imprison refugee claimants and has "turned Canada into one of the only western countries that detains asylum seekers in prison facilities" (Poynter, 2012, para 4).

Under this legislation, 8,781 immigrants were detained in 2018–2019, with 69% in immigration holding centres, 16% in provincial jails, and 15% in other facilities (Canada Border Services Agency, 2019a).

As of 2017, of the MV Sun Sea passengers whose refugee applications had been finalized, two-thirds had been accepted. The MV Sun Sea incident was estimated to have cost the federal government $25 million. Yet, although six suspects (2 Canadians and 4 Sri Lankans) were criminally charged, only one man was convicted. In June 2019, BC's appeal court ordered a new trial for that person.

Chapter Review

Questions

1. What are the main theoretical explanations for migration and what do these have to do with social welfare?
2. What was the effect of the shift away from the "nationality" to the "points system" as the basis of immigrant selection after 1967?
3. Describe ways in which racial discrimination, directly or indirectly, is still a factor affecting immigrant selection and a barrier in the full integration of immigrants into Canadian society.
4. What are the three main streams under which newcomers can apply to immigrate to Canada? What are the criteria in each category?
5. In your view, what are some challenges that multiculturalism introduces into Canadian society? On the whole, do you think this policy is a good one? Why or why not?
6. Recently, there have been changes in the direction of immigration policy with respect to temporary workers. Explain what the changes have been and how they are likely to affect Canadian society in the future.
7. What are some of the barriers that new immigrants face when trying to settle themselves and their families in Canada?

Exploring Social Welfare

1. Use the Internet to find three community-based supports that assist foreign-trained professionals find and keep employment. How effective are these initiatives? How can they be improved?
2. The Conservative Party, the Liberal Party, and the New Democratic Party view immigration differently. Write a paragraph on each party summarizing their policies with respect to (1) admitting immigrants to Canada, (2) the need for social programs to help newcomers integrate successfully, and (3) the paths new immigrants should follow to gain full Canadian citizenship.

Websites

Immigration, Refugees and Citizenship Canada
www.cic.gc.ca
The Immigration, Refugees and Citizenship Canada website offers information about the process of immigration, relevant policies and regulations, and a range of research publications focused on how today's newcomers are faring socially and economically.

Canadian Council for Refugees (CCR)
www.ccrweb.ca
The Canadian Council for Refugees is a national non-profit umbrella organization committed to the rights and protection of refugees and other vulnerable migrants in Canada and around the world and to the settlement of refugees and immigrants in Canada. The membership is made up of organizations involved in the settlement, sponsorship, and protection of refugees and immigrants. The Council serves the networking, information-exchange, and advocacy needs of its membership.

Toronto Region Immigrant Employment Council (TRIEC)
www.triec.ca
Toronto Region Immigrant Employment Council (TRIEC) works to address barriers that prevent immigrants from participating in the labour market. TRIEC is especially focused on the persistent problem of immigrant underemployment — the fact that extremely highly skilled people come to Toronto from all over the world and end up in low-skilled jobs. Membership includes workers, employers, regulatory bodies, post-secondary institutions, assessment service providers, community organizations, and all levels of government in the Greater Toronto Area.

The Welfare and Well-Being of Older People

"The challenge for current policymakers will be how best to build upon the major success story of Canadian social policy in the twentieth century — the reduction of poverty among Canadian senior citizens."

– Lars Osberg. "Poverty Among Senior Citizens: A Canadian Success Story," Centre for the Study of Living Standards, 2001

Improving the Quality of Life for Positive Aging

10

There was a crisis in long-term care long before COVID–19; the pandemic cast a spotlight on it.

Over the coming 35 years, the percentage of persons over age 65 will double, and this demographic fact will place a heavy strain on the welfare of older Canadians. In particular, there remains the challenge of combatting poverty for older women, for older people with disabilities, and for older people who have had lower or precarious incomes during their working lives.

Especially worrisome is the fact that a substantial proportion of middle-income persons without an employer pension plan will face a dramatic drop in living standards during their later years. The panoply of public policies offering "voluntary" options for saving will be inadequate to address the shortcomings in declining workplace pensions and in a Canada Pension Plan with limited benefits.

Improving the Quality of Life for Positive Aging

The economic circumstances of older adults improved from the 1960s to the early 1990s, in no small part due to effective public policy. To keep the situation from getting worse, the federal government must again recalibrate public supports in the face of falling employer pension coverage and inadequate savings.

After completing this chapter, you should be able to:

- Describe the main components of the income security system for older people in Canada;
- Describe the difference between absolute and relative poverty measures and the policy implications;
- Evaluate various anti-poverty measures as to how well they accurately assess the income supports needed by older and retired Canadians;
- Describe the particular problems faced by older women with respect to income security;
- Provide an historical overview of the programs and policies related to the provision of income security for older people in Canada;
- Describe the main pillars of the federal government's National Seniors Strategy;
- Understand the important changes that are taking place with respect to Old Age Security and pension eligibility; and
- Explain the need for expanded programs that will support older people in their retirement years.

Key Concepts

- Old Age Security (OAS)
- Guaranteed Income Supplement (GIS)
- Allowance
- Provincial and territorial pension benefits.
- Canada/Québec Pension Plan (CPP/QPP)
- Occupational pension plans
- Private pension savings
- National Seniors Strategy
- Baby boom generation
- Pensionless cohorts
- Defined benefit pensions
- Defined contribution pensions
- Post-retirement health plans

10.1 Income Security Programs for Older Adults

The income security system in Canada has two primary objectives: to ensure that older people have sufficient income regardless of their pre-retirement income and to avoid a drastic reduction in standard of living upon retirement.

To accomplish these important goals, the government has devised a variety of income security measures. These can be divided into three levels:

- **Basic minimum**: Old Age Security (OAS), Guaranteed Income Supplement (GIS), the Allowance, and provincial/territorial supplements
- **Social insurance**: public pensions — CPP/QPP
- **Private plans**: occupational pensions and private savings

As the baby boom generation (born 1946–1966) retires, pension plan payouts will increase dramatically. Successive governments have anticipated this development and have attempted to ensure the sustainability of income security programs for older persons.

Unlike the OAS and GIS, which are paid out of general government revenues, the CPP/QPP payments are covered by contributions made by those who are retiring. This avoids an intergenerational transfer of wealth whereby the young are working to finance the pensions of the old who are retired. Those who are retiring have already paid contributions to the plan. The expectation is that these invested contributions will be sufficient to finance the pension benefits.

Figure 10.1

The Three Levels of Income Security for Older People

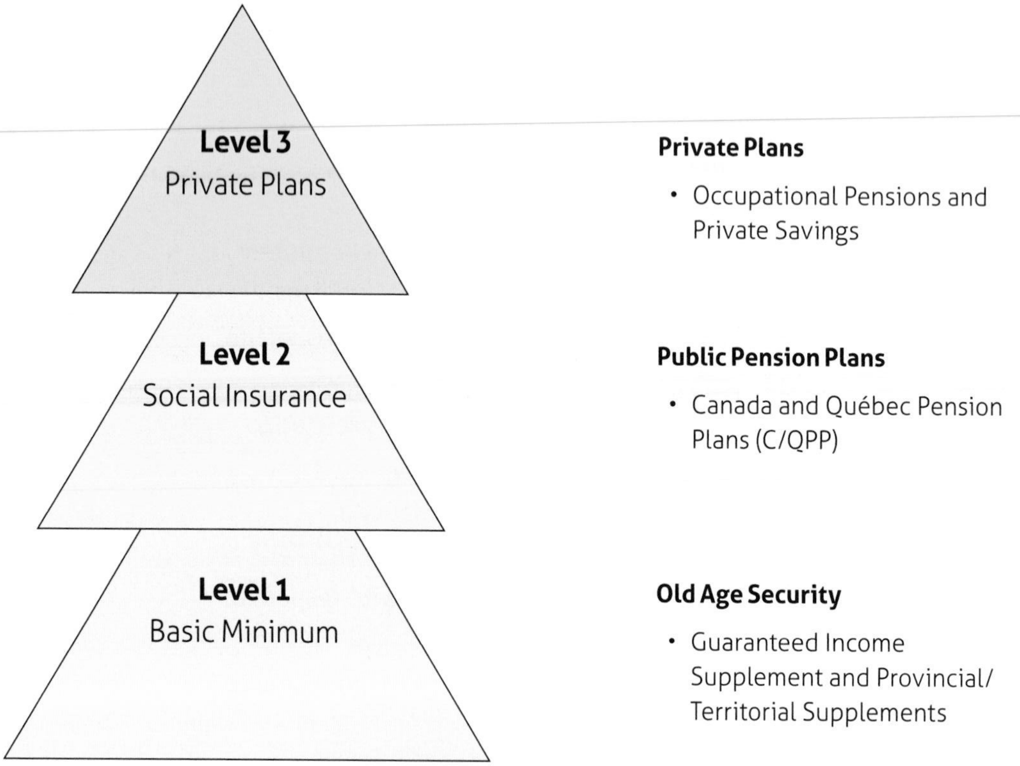

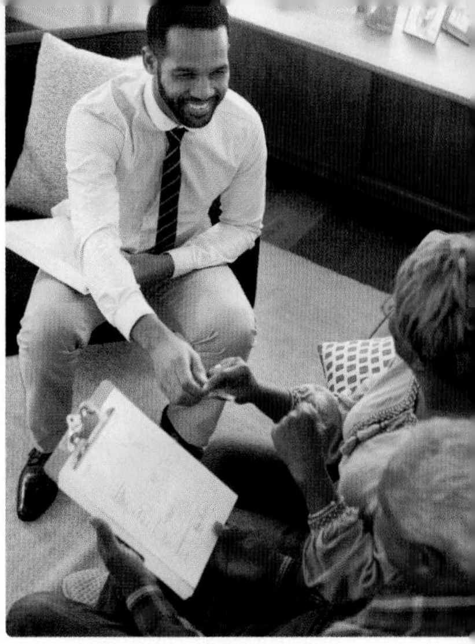

Low-Income Seniors

Supporting older Canadians to remain independent and engaged citizens involves strengthening existing and future income and savings opportunities. Great strides have been made in reducing poverty rates among older Canadians — Canada moved from one of the highest rates of poverty among older adults in Organisation for Economic Co-operation and Development (OECD) countries in the 1960s and 1970s, to one of the lowest.

Older Canadians, however, remain one of the most financially vulnerable populations, especially those who live alone, according to Canada's Federal Poverty Reduction Plan. In fact, the rate of older Canadians considered as living "in relative low income" is increasing.

(1) The Basic Minimums — OAS, GIS, SPA, and Provincial/Territorial Supplements

The first level of income security for the older persons is comprised of the following public programs:

- Old Age Security (OAS). The Old Age Security (OAS) program provides a basic pension (adjusted for inflation) to virtually everyone over 65 years of age who has lived in Canada for the required length of time. It is a universal monetary benefit (though some would argue that it is no longer universal due to the clawback for higher-income Canadians). It is an income transfer program paid out of the general revenue of the federal government. The OAS program includes the income-tested Guaranteed Income Supplement (GIS), which provides extra money to OAS recipients who have little or no other income, and the Allowance, which pays benefits to low-income spouses or partners of an OAS pensioner or widows/widowers between the ages of 60 and 64. The OAS was a universal program until 1989, when the Conservative government of Brian Mulroney introduced the clawback of benefits for people with higher incomes.
- Guaranteed Income Supplement (GIS). The Guaranteed Income Supplement (GIS) was implemented in 1966 as a targeted, income-tested benefit for OAS recipients who had no other income. It was intended as a "guaranteed annual income" program; indeed, it is one of the few guaranteed income programs operating in industrialized countries. With this program, every Canadian over the age of 65, except for those who do not meet the residency requirement, have an income that is at least equal to OAS plus the maximum GIS. With this, the program guarantees a minimum income for elderly Canadians. There has been some debate, however, as to whether the GIS, together with the OAS, actually provides an adequate income.
- Allowance. The other basic minimum income program, the Allowance (formerly the Spouse's Allowance [SPA]), was created to deal with a hardship-creating anomaly in the OAS/GIS. The 1975 SPA intended to correct the anomaly by providing an income-tested benefit to those between 60 and 65 years of age, when one spouse is over 65. The Allowance is stopped when the recipient's income reaches a certain maximum. In addition, the Allowance for the survivor provides benefits for those who are 60–64 years old and whose spouse or partner has died. The Allowance for the survivor stops when a recipient remarries or lives in a common-law relationship for at least one year.
- Provincial and territorial benefits. Federal benefits are supplemented with provincial and territorial benefits in Ontario, Manitoba, Saskatchewan, Alberta, British Columbia, Yukon, the Northwest Territories, and Nunavut. The provincial programs are generally means- or income-tested and are administered by local social assistance or welfare departments.

(2) Public Pensions — Canada/Québec Pension Plan (CPP/QPP)

The earnings-based Canada/Québec Pension Plan (CPP/QPP) makes up the second tier of income security for older persons in Canada. The CPP/QPP provides a pension upon retirement to persons who have contributed to it. It is, therefore, a insurance type of income security program — it insures the contributor against loss of income due to retirement. All employed or self-employed Canadians over the age of 18 make compulsory contributions to the plan (matched by their employer) throughout their working lives. The plan also offers disability, survivor, and death benefits, as well as inflation protection.

The CPP/QPP is a public contributory pension. Before the CPP/QPP was instituted, all pensions were administered by private insurance companies. A public contributory pension was a new way to provide income for retired persons. The basic-minimum programs (OAS and GIS) address the income needs of the retired by transferring income to the retired from taxes collected every year, that is, income is redistributed from those who are of working age to retired people. Public contributory pensions, on the other hand, help people save from their earnings during their working years and then use the accumulated funds to provide income during retirement.

As mentioned, all employed persons over the age of 18 must make compulsory CPP/QPP contributions while employed. Therefore, all those who have participated in the paid labour force, even a person with only one contribution, are eligible for benefits. Benefits can begin between ages 60 and 70. They are paid for life and are approximately 25% of average contributory earnings (the lower of actual and the maximum contributory earnings). Benefits are adjusted downward by 0.6% for each month for people who begin drawing benefits before 65 years of age, and upward by 0.7% if applying after age 65 — up to age 70. The plan is fully indexed annually to the cost of living as measured by the consumer price index (CPI).

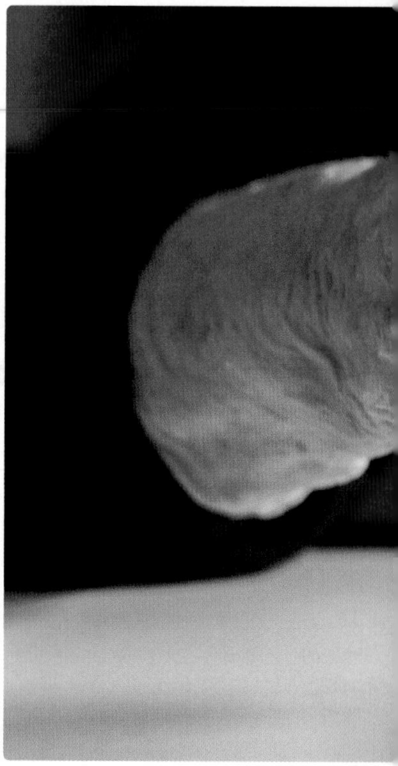

The CPP/QPP is used as a vehicle for other non-retirement-based contingencies: disability benefits, death benefits, and survivor benefits. The plan provides disability benefits to contributors only if they are unable to work due to a "severe" and "prolonged" disability — meaning that they are unable to regularly pursue any substantial gainful employment for an indefinite period. Survivor benefits are paid to the surviving spouse of a deceased contributor. Finally, a death benefit (a lump-sum benefit equal to six times the contributor's monthly pension, up to a specified maximum) is paid upon the death of a contributor.

The CPP/QPP began in 1966. The mandate at the time was to provide all members of the labour force and their families with retirement income and death and disability benefits. Although the CPP and QPP are discussed here as one plan, the Québec Pension Plan (QPP) is separately legislated by the province of Québec.

The Québec Pension Plan is closely associated with the CPP, and it is coordinated through a series of agreements between the federal government and Québec. This ensures that those who move in and out of Québec carry all the pension benefits with them. Although the option of having a separate but linked pension plan is open to all provinces, Québec is the only province to use this option.

(3) Private Plans: Occupational Pensions and Private Savings

The private pension plans component of the retirement income system consists of pensions from employers and publicly supported and regulated private savings plans such as Registered Retirement Savings Plans (RRSPs), Registered Pension Plans (RPPs), and Deferred Profit-Sharing Plans (DPSPs).

The federal government provides tax assistance on savings in RRSPs, RPPs, and DPSPs — taxes are deferred on the contributions and investment income in these plans until the savings are withdrawn or received as pension income. Private savings and assets also contribute to retirement incomes. As noted earlier, the tax-assisted private pension system accounts for an increasingly large share of retirement income system payments. Private occupational pension plans were an outcome of the escalating economy after World War II and the demand by unions for pension coverage within their collective agreements. Now, private pension capital pools are the largest in industrialized nations.

Governments increasingly rely on private forms of private pension savings and periodically raise the deductions allowed for contributors. Critics argue that these plans disproportionately benefit those with high incomes and strongly favour men over women. Over the past three decades, the proportion of seniors with private pensions, RRSPs, or CPP/QPP benefits has grown remarkably. The proportion with income from private pensions and RRSPs more than doubled between 1976 and 2009 (24% to 63%),due mostly to growth in RRSP savings; however, private pensions still cover less than a third of the labour force.

Social Welfare in Perspective

Will the CPP Be There When You Retire?

The Idea That People Retire at Age 65 Is Gone

The CPP is a mandatory savings program for employees — there's no opting out. But exactly how sustainable is the CPP? Will it still be there when you retire?

The CPP is the main source of retirement income for many who have been employed all or most of their lives. It forms one of the two major components of Canada's public retirement income system, the other component being Old Age Security (OAS).

As an employee, the government shaves a bit of money off your paycheques every year up to a certain cap. It also takes an equal amount from your employers.

When you retire — normally, for now, at age 65 — the CPP pays you a regular income that replaces a certain percentage of your past average earnings and it does so for the rest of your life. The payments are indexed to inflation.

The CPP Investment Board manages investment assets for the CPP on behalf of 20 million Canadians. It is one of the world's biggest pension funds.

The plan is administered by Employment and Social Development Canada on behalf of employees in all provinces and territories except Québec, which operates an equivalent plan, the Québec Pension Plan. The constitutional authority for pensions is shared between the provincial and federal governments; stewardship for the CPP is jointly shared. Provinces may opt out of the CPP (as Québec did in 1965), but it must offer a comparable plan to its residents. In addition, any province may establish an additional/supplementary plan anytime.

Median Retirement Age, Men and Women, 1976–2019

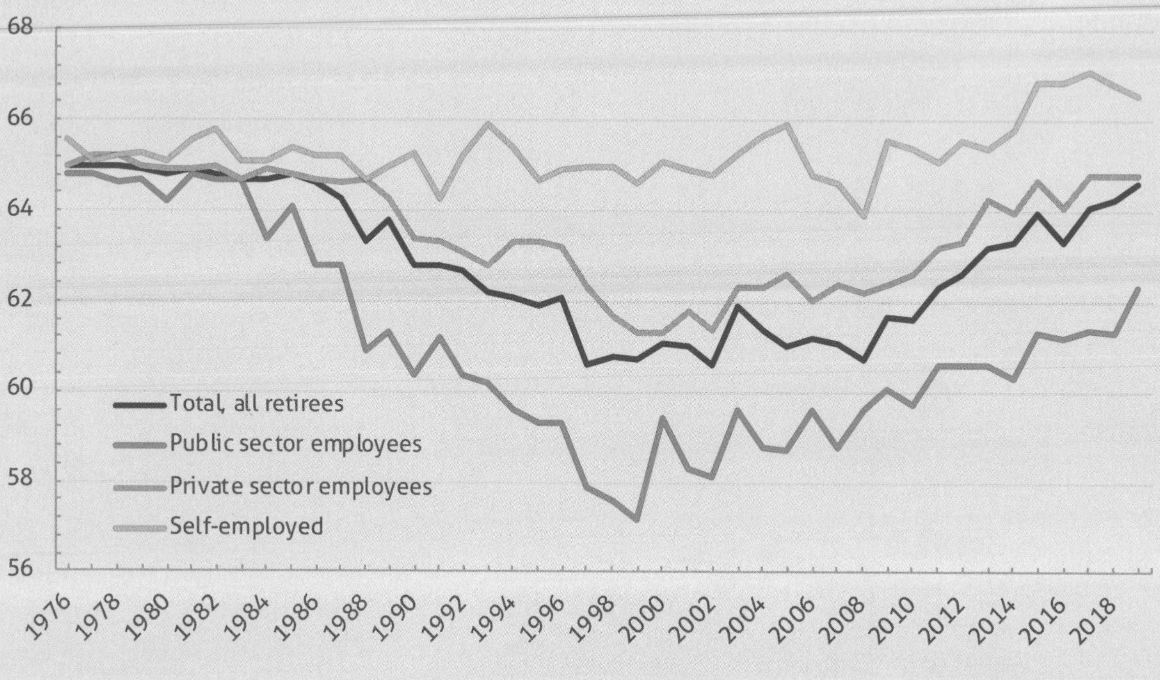

Statistics Canada. Table 14-10-0060-01 Retirement age by class of worker, annual

Age at Retirement

A big factor in the long-term funding stability of the CPP is the age at which Canadians retire. A long-run trend toward early retirement (except for the self-employed) started to reverse in the mid-1990s; more of those aged 60–64 and 65–69 stayed employed. Much of this employment is part-time or casual, but the trend remains. The number of employed older than 70+ has also increased, but the employment rate remains very low. It is not clear how long this trend will continue, but it seems unlikely to reverse. It seems clear that the historical cultural norm that people retired at age 65 is gone; average age at retirement is increasing and there is diversity in the process of retiring.

While retirement ages have been increasing, there remain a substantial number of Canadians who cannot remain employed until their late 60s or early 70s; Some have been forced to retire due to health issues or caregiving obligations. Some have worked in physically demanding jobs such as construction, which are more difficult as one ages.

So, in changing public programs one needs to be sensitive to the trends of average Canadians but also to the diverse life experiences of senior Canadians. One illustration of this is the proposal to increase the age of eligibility for OAS/GIS to age 67 from 65. Most developed countries have increased or are in the process of increasing their age of eligibility for public programs for seniors. In Canada, this proposal passed during the Harper government — premised on the increasing employment of seniors and changes in life expectancy. It would also have had a major impact on seniors unable to extend their employment to 67.

The Trudeau government reversed this decision in 2019. An alternative has been proposed to delay OAS to age 67 but leave the eligibility for GIS at 65, which would address the needs of lower-income seniors (or indeed GIS could be introduced at age 60). This would reduce benefits for average Canadians but would help to protect poorer Canadians from the adverse effects of the shift in the retirement age from 65 to 67.

Employment Rates of Men and Women in their 60s, 1976–2018

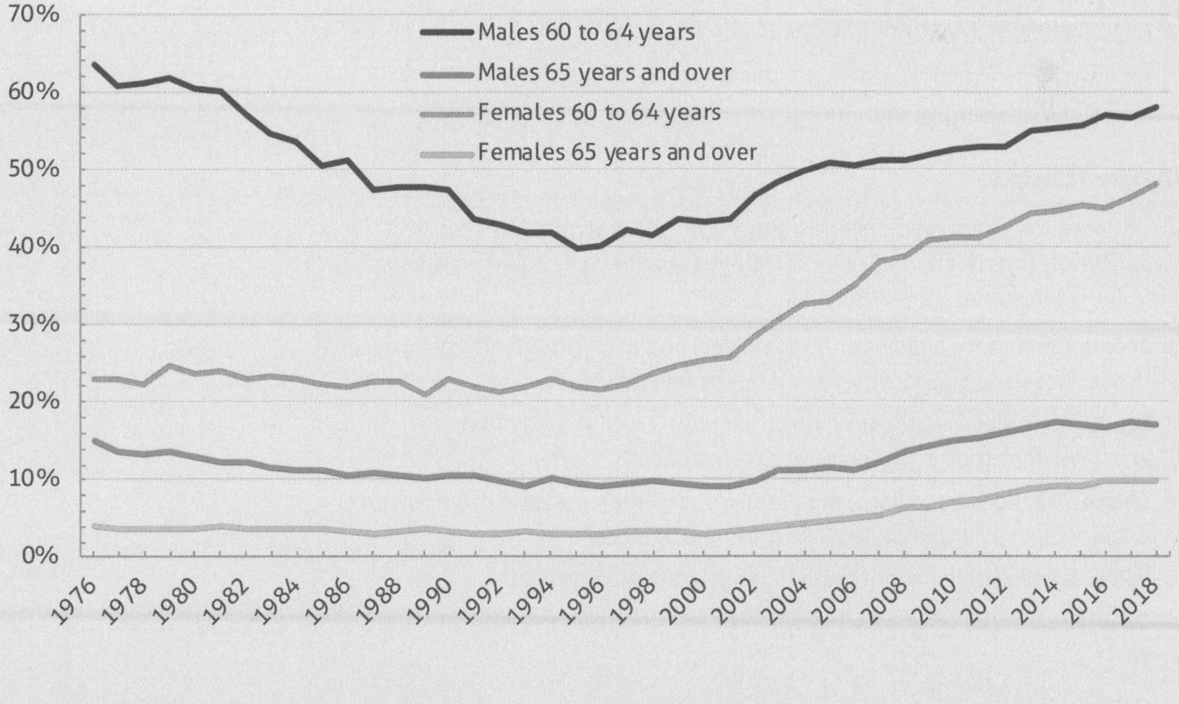

Statistics Canada. Table 14-10-0018-01 Labour force characteristics by sex and detailed age group, annual, inactive

10.2 Does Canada Need a Seniors Strategy?

Improving income security for older persons in Canada is one component of the Government of Canada's broad national seniors' agenda. Under the auspices of the Ministry of Seniors and Accessibility, the other three objectives are to (1) improve seniors' access to affordable housing, (2) promote healthy aging and improve access to health care, and (3) foster the social inclusion and engagement of seniors (Government of Canada, 2018).

The National Seniors Council (NSC) was established in 2007 to provide recommendations to the Government of Canada on matters related to the health, well-being, and quality of life of seniors. One of their four work priorities is to consider the federal and provincial strategies and initiatives that include a seniors' dimension and provide advice on gaps that could potentially be addressed in a National Seniors Strategy (Government of Canada, 2019). In 2015, the National Institute on Ageing was established at Ryerson University as the primary policy think tank on aging in Canada.

The Framework for a National Strategy

A broad alliance of organizations, including the Canadian Association of Social Workers and the Canadian Medical Association, are advocating for the development of a National Seniors Strategy involving all levels of government (Sinha et al., 2016). The framework for the strategy flowed out of five priorities identified in the World Health Organization (WHO, 2017) *Global Strategy and Action Plan on Ageing and Health*. The WHO priorities were:

- Commitment to action on healthy aging in every country
- Developing age-friendly environments
- Aligning health systems to the needs of older populations
- Developing sustainable and equitable systems for long-term care
- Improving, measuring, monitoring, and researching health and aging

The Five Principles

The Alliance for a National Seniors Strategy outlined five principles for an evidence-informed National Seniors Strategy for Canada. The five principles underlying the strategy are as follows:

- **Access.** Can older Canadians, their families, and their caregivers easily access the services and support they need in a timely way?
- **Equity.** Are older Canadians having their needs met in a way that acknowledges their socio-cultural circumstances?
- **Choice.** Are older Canadians, their families, and their caregivers empowered with the best information to make informed choices?
- **Value.** Is every dollar spent providing the best value possible?
- **Quality.** Is a focus on quality always front and centre to the work at hand?

Vational Seniors Strategy for Canada

wing Older Persons to Be Independent, Productive, and Engaged

e course of developing an overall national strategy, the planning group created ies of twelve evidence-informed policy briefs linked to the four pillars of the onal Seniors Strategy. Taken together, these policy briefs provide an up-to-date view of research findings in relation to each of the core components of the ors' strategy.

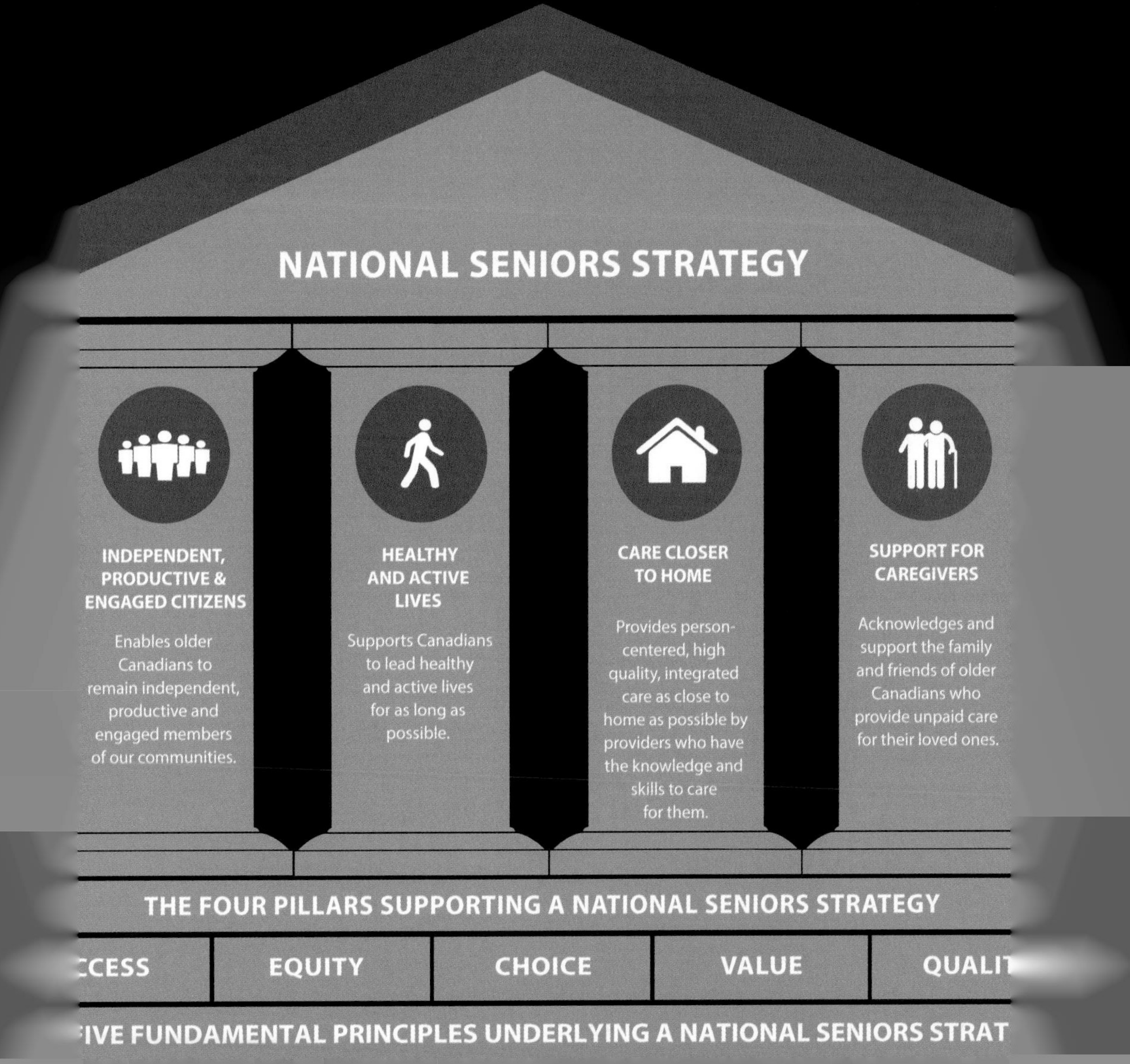

Social Welfare and Well-Being for Older Canadians

Four themes of particular interest to social workers in the evidence briefs developed by the National Seniors Strategy (NSS) are summarized below.

- **Combatting Ageism, Elder Abuse, and Social Isolation**

Ageism is multi-faceted and may include prejudicial attitudes and discriminatory practices. In recent Canadian surveys, almost two-thirds of those 66 or older indicated that "they have been treated unfairly or differently because of their age" and 80% of Canadians agree with the statement "older adults 75 and older are seen as less important and are more often ignored than younger generations" (NSS, n.d.a, para. 2).

The prevalence and severity of elder abuse is difficult to ascertain as it frequently goes unreported or unnoticed. Financial abuse is the most prevalent form of abuse, and older Canadians are the "population most at risk of suffering violence at the hand of a family member or relative" (NSS, n.d.a, para. 7). Abuse frequently occurs due to the power imbalances between older adults and their families or caregivers, and also as a result of primary caregiver stress, especially if the former depends on the latter for having their living or care needs met.

As Canadians become less likely to live in intergenerational households, less likely to participate regularly in traditional faith-based groups, more likely to have forgone a driver's licence, and more likely to experience increased physical and cognitive limitations in advanced age, the risk of becoming socially isolated increases with a significant impact on overall health and well-being.

- **A Public Health Approach to Vaccination and Fall Prevention**

Important advances in public health and health care mean that most Canadians live with fewer health problems. However, supporting healthy aging through wellness and prevention opportunities for all Canadians makes a real difference to healthy aging.

Health literacy skills — being able to access, understand, evaluate, and communicate health-related information — are critical, and yet "only 12% of older adults have adequate health literacy skills to support them in making basic health-related decisions" (NSS, n.d.,b, para. 2). Using the Internet is a typical way of accessing information, but only 60% of Canadians aged 65–74, and 29% of those over 75, have ever used the Internet (NSS, n.d.b).

Two examples of areas to increase health literacy include vaccination knowledge and fall-prevention programs. Few older Canadians receive the recommended vaccines such as influenza, pneumonia, shingles, or tetanus, and between 20% and 30% will fall, resulting in long hospital stays and reduction in independence. Occupational therapy home-assessment strategies and home renovation tax-credit programs are steps in the right direction (NSS, n.d.b).

The Crisis in Long-Term Care during COVID–19

A major report released by the Canadian Institute for Health Information (CIHI) in March 2021 found that the proportion of deaths in nursing homes from COVID–19 was significantly higher in Canada than in other wealthy countries.

Nursing home residents also received less medical care, fewer visits from doctors, and fewer hospital transfers compared with other years. The study also found that COVID–19 infections among nursing home residents actually increased in the second wave compared with the first wave.

Less crowding, increased staffing, better infection control, and greater accountability are among the steps the CIHI recommends to address the problems. Many policy experts are also advocating that the largely for-profit, long-term care system be brought under the umbrella of the Canada Health Act and our universal, publicly funded health care system.

Canadian Institute for Health Information. (2021). *The Impact of COVID-19 on Long-Term Care in Canada: Focus on the First 6 Months.*

- **Aging in Place**

Older Canadians make up about 16% of the population but account for nearly half of the health and social care costs. Although the population has changed, the health care system has not adapted to meeting the needs of an aging population.

> "The majority of Canadians now see access to supportive and palliative care in or close to their homes, and a robust home care system, as top national priorities" (Sinha et al., 2016, p. 14).

Supporting older Canadians to age in their place of choice requires having access to appropriate care services when and where they are needed (NSS, n.d.c). It is estimated that while 2.2 million Canadians receive home care, 15% have unmet needs. Furthermore, many older Canadians are prematurely institutionalized in long-term care homes due to lack of even basic home and community care support (Policy Brief #8).

Emerging policy interventions include Ontario's Home First policies, which aim to "identify individuals at high risk for institutionalization in order to provide adequate supports to enable successful transitions back to one's home or for people to remain in their homes in the first place" (NSS, n.d.c, para 6). In its first two years of implementation, both the demand for and the utilization rate for long-term care beds declined.

Home, community, and palliative services are not included in the Canada Health Act; developing best practices that enable the provision of care closer to home will not only allow more Canadians to age and die in the place of their choosing, but also enable broader system savings for its overall sustainability (NSS,n.d.c).

- **Support for Caregivers**

Family and friends are the greatest sources of care for older people. It is estimated that there are over 8 million informal caregivers in Canada, and that their economic contribution is about $30 billion. However, caregivers face an enormous toll on their own health and well-being and a loss of work and income (CARP, 2014; Sinha et al., 2016).

Providing appropriate support and recognition to meet the needs of caregivers not only keeps the health system sustainable, but also ensures that economic productivity can be improved and strengthened (Sinha et al., 2016). Currently only two federal programs — the Employment Insurance Compassionate Care Benefit and the Family Caregiver Tax Credit — provide any income relief, but both have significant limitations.

Enhancing financial support and long-term care insurance programs, providing workplace protections when providing caregiving, more funding for home care, and training and respite options for care providers all have good evidence to support their implementation (CARP, 2014; Sinha et al., 2016).

Caregiver Burnout

Caring for an older family member is often a long-term job that can become more difficult and complex over time. Exhaustion can put a great strain on family members who have the responsibility of caring for aging relatives, and can trigger frustration and resentment. For this reason, "self-care" is essential—before burnout occurs.

Moreover, women dedicate almost twice as much time to these types of tasks. Even working outside the home does not appear to reduce the amount of time women spend providing care—26.4 hours a month, versus 14.5 hours for men (Stobert & Cranswick, 2004).

There is an urgent need for social services that offer respite to informal caregivers.

What the COVID–19 pandemic has revealed ...

COVID–19: Re-Imagining Long-Term Care

Giving Long-Term Care a Prominent Place in Canadian Medicare

The COVID–19 pandemic points to the failure of the existing long-term residential care system. After COVID–19, the importance of universal, publicly funded senior care has never been clearer.

Long-term care facilities across Canada were on the front lines of the COVID–19 crisis. Across Canada, 75% of recorded deaths linked to COVID–19 happened in long-term care homes. The COVID–19 pandemic made the holes in the Canadian social safety net obvious to anyone.

The nursing homes in Ontario and Québec were especially hard hit. More than 1,800 residents and eight staff died in Ontario by the summer of 2020, making up about 64% of all deaths in the province. The numbers were even more staggering in Québec. By the summer, that province's long-term care homes experienced 4,856 deaths or about 85% of Québec's COVID–19 total (Andrew-Gee, 2020).

Re-Imagining Long-Term Residential Care

Long-term care was generally poor by any measure even before COVID–19. COVID–19 exposed these faultlines. Understaffing turned seniors' homes into danger zones. The impact of COVID–19 in long-term care homes was a horrific example of "system failure."

"Re-imagining Long-term Residential Care in the COVID–19 Crisis," authored by Pat Armstrong, Hugh Armstrong, Jacqueline Choiniere, Ruth Lowndes, and James Struthers (2020), reviewed the research on reforming long-term residential care in Canada. Their report, issued by the Canadian Centre for Policy Alternatives, outlines a full list of evidence-based recommendations.

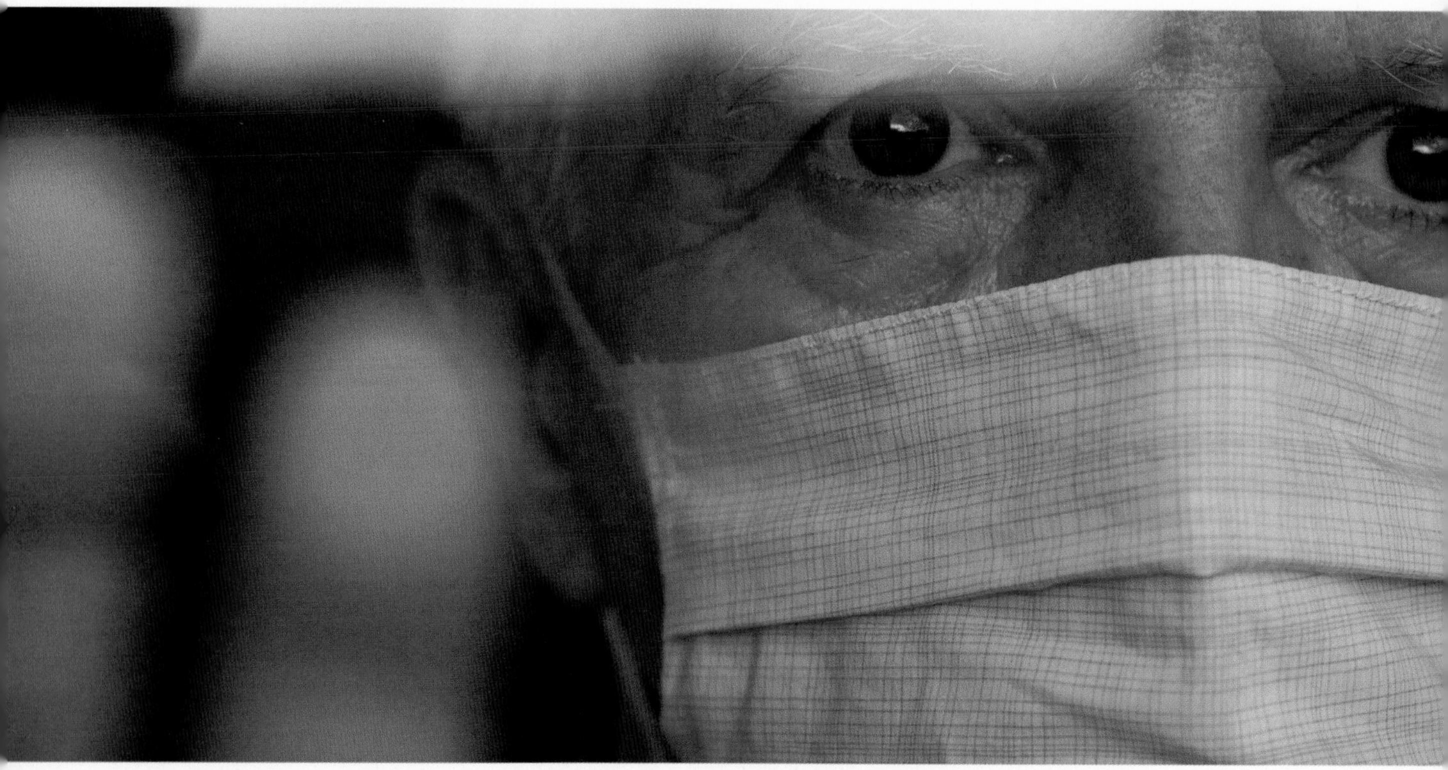

Reforming Long-Term Residential Care

The evidence shows that long-term care homes run on a for-profit basis tend to have lower staffing levels, more verified complaints, more transfers to hospitals, and higher rates for both ulcers and morbidity. Moreover, managerial practices taken directly from the business sector are designed for making a profit rather than for providing quality care.

These practices include paying low wages and hiring part-time, casual workers in order to avoid paying benefits or providing other employee protections. Contracting out services such as cleaning, laundry, food preparation, and security can also increase risk by bringing more people into homes on a daily basis.

Long-term residential care needs to be integrated into the public health care system through federal legislation. "This crisis allows us to reimagine nursing homes that are rewarding places to work, where life is worth living for residents and where visitors feel comforted about the care," observes Pat Armstrong, a distinguished research professor in sociology at York University (Armstrong et al., 2020).

The Measure of a Society

The authors of the report make the argument for a national plan for long-term care. Their short-term recommendations include:

- Making all staff permanent and limiting their work to one nursing home
- Raising staff wages and benefits, and especially providing sick leave
- Rapidly providing testing for all those living, working, or visiting in homes
- Ensuring access to protective equipment
- Severely limiting transfers from hospitals

Long-term care needs to be given pride of place in Canadian health care, argues Francine Ducharme, a professor of nursing at the University of Montréal and a co-author of *Restoring Trust: COVID–19 and the Future of Long-Term Care,* a Royal Society of Canada report on long-term care (Eastabrooks et al., 2020).

Above all, long-term care needs adequate funding. "The measure of a society can often be taken by the fate of its elderly," Ducharme said.

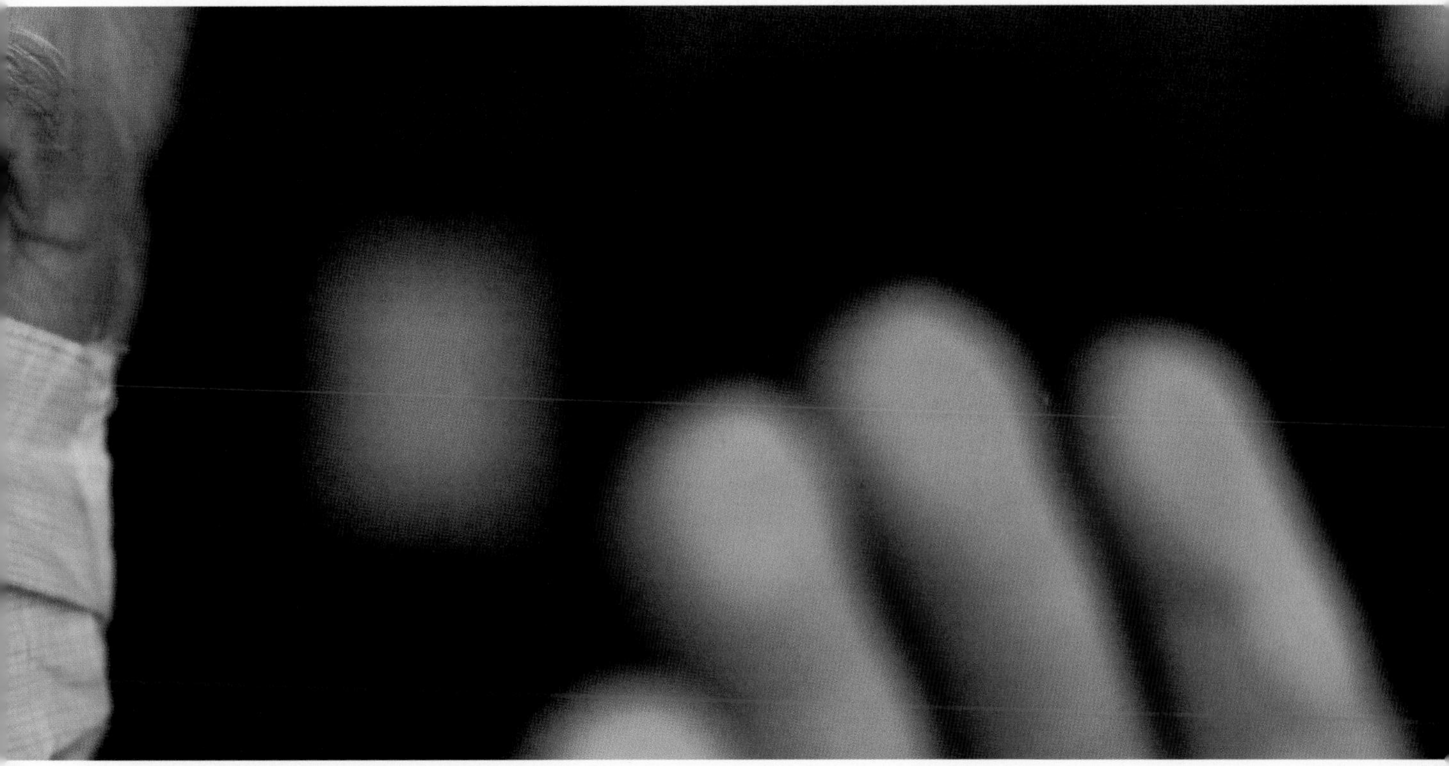

10.3 Poverty among Older Adults — Emerging Trends

The latest census puts the proportion of seniors as the highest on record — the over-65 population has surged. Four social factors currently affect the composition of the older population in Canada. These include:

- The baby boomers coming of age and beginning to retire en masse
- The improvements in health care and extension of life expectancy
- The long-term decline in the birth rate
- The changing interpretation of the retirement age

By 2030, for each person receiving income-security benefits, it is estimated that there will be only three working Canadians to support these benefits, compared to five today. As the proportion of retired persons receiving benefits keeps increasing, such expenditures will continue to rise steadily.

Baby Boomers, Universal Health Care, Birth Rates, and Retirement

The first of these factors is the demographic fact that the baby boom generation (those born between 1946 and 1966) is beginning to enter its older years. This dramatic greying of Canada has serious implications for the economy, social policy, and the overall well-being of older persons.

Second, technological improvements in health care and the effect of universal health care in Canada have resulted in a significant extension of life expectancy. In 2017, the life expectancy was 84.38 years for women and 80.65 years for men, an increase from 83 and 79 years respectively in 2011. Life expectancy is expected to continue to grow, although more slowly, reaching 86 years for women and 81 years for men in 2041.

The third factor is the long-term decline in the birth rate. Over the past 150 years, Canada has changed from a high-fertility society where women had many children during their lives to a low-fertility society where women are having fewer children overall and at increasingly older ages. Despite some fluctuations, the total fertility rate in Canada has been below the replacement level for over 40 years. In fact, 1971 was the last year the replacement-level fertility of 2.1 children per woman was reached. Combined with the extension of life expectancy, this has resulted in an increase in the proportion, or the relative size, of the older population, and these trends are expected to continue for several decades.

Finally, a long-run trend toward early retirement (except for the self-employed) reversed starting around the mid-1990s; more of those 60–64 and 65–69 stayed employed. Much of this employment is part-time or casual, but the trend remains. The number of employed older than 70 has also increased, but the employment rate remains very low. It is not clear how long this trend will continue, but it seems unlikely to reverse. It seems clear that the historical cultural norm that people retired at age 65 is gone; average age at retirement is increasing and there is diversity in the process of retiring.

Age Cohorts

A cohort is a group of people who share a statistical or demographic trait. People in the same age cohort, for example, were born during the same time frame.

As of July 1, 2014, for the first time in Canada, there were more people in the 55-to-64 age cohort than there were in the 15-to-24 cohort.

The aging of the Canadian population is due to the first of the baby boomers turning 65 in recent years, as well as increasing life expectancy and a low fertility rate.

Statistics Canada. (2014), Population Projections: Canada, the Provinces and Territories, 2013 to 2063.

Senior Poverty — Worrying Signs

Poverty rates among older persons in Canada declined noticeably in the last half of the twentieth century. Poverty for older persons is now among the lowest of all countries studied by the Organisation for Economic Co-operation and Development.

The pronounced decrease in Canada's elderly poverty rate can largely be attributed to the implementation of the Canada/Québec Pension Plan in 1966. Pensions as a proportion of disposable income among Canada's elderly more than doubled between 1980 and 1996, from 21% to 46%. The first cohort to receive full public pensions turned 65 in 1976. The generation that followed also became the first beneficiaries of private occupational pensions that had been significantly expanded between the 1950s and 1970s. Canada's system also offers a guaranteed income in the form of Old Age Security, regardless of past participation in the labour force.

However, after 20 years of dramatic reductions, Canada's elderly poverty rate measured by the Low Income Measure (LIM), has been rising since the mid-1990s. The biggest increase occurred for elderly women (Conference Board of Canada, 2015). Statistics Canada (2017) reported that there were 238,000 (3.9%) seniors living in poverty in 2017, down from 284,000 (4.9%) in 2016, and that this decline was most noticeable among unattached seniors. However, this apparent reduction may be more related to the implementation of the new Market Basket Measure used to estimate poverty levels (described on the next page).

The median age in Canada in 1941 was 26.2 years. On July 1, 2018 it was 40.8 years. By the year 2031, 20% of Canada's population — one in five — will be seniors. Will the poverty rate for Canadian seniors rise? Will older women comprise a growing share of that increase? What will be the needs of these older Canadians? How will they be taken care of?

Poverty and Intersectionality

A gender income gap exists in all generations. For example, in BC the median income of a single senior women was $24,600 compared to $26,660 for a single senior man. The gender income gap increases with age: the median income of single women over the age of 85 is $23,710, which is 19% lower than the median income of single men over the age of 84 (Ivanova, 2017, p. 6). "Low income puts these women at risk of social isolation and poverty at the very time that many of them face higher out-of-pocket health and transportation expenses due to increasing illness and disability, and the loss of social support from their spouse due to spousal illness or death" (p. 30).

A differential for seniors occurs due to the unequal access to contributory plans — women earn less than men and therefore contribute less to CPP and thus receive less benefits. Similarly, a lower wage reduces the allowable contribution to private pension plans such as RRSPs, again reducing the possible benefit in later years.

For populations that have experienced poverty continuously throughout their life course, poverty in their older years is highly likely.

Medicalization of Older Adults

Many older adults experience chronic illnesses and discomforts and, in general, healing and recovery are slower when our bodies are old . But it is a mistake to assume that all older adults are physically and cognitively impaired in some way. And cognitive impairment is not necessarily a permanent condition—it can vary from day to day.

Current social work value systems shift the emphasis away from medicalization and toward self-empowerment and social engagement, which can reduce feelings of loss and depression—mental health issues commonly faced by older adults.

Measuring Poverty Levels

What one measures and how one measures it are important in assessing seniors' poverty levels. Different measures yield different results.

There are three indicators used to measure low income in Canada: (1) Low-Income Cut-Offs (LICOs); (2) Market Basket Measure (MBM); and (3) Low Income Measure (LIM). Canada has recently adopted the MBM as the "official poverty line" — the first time that Canada has had an "official poverty line." LICOs are now an abandoned measure, although LICOs are frequently found in earlier research.

- **Low Income Cut-Offs (LICOs).** The Low-Income Cut-Offs were income thresholds below which a family devoted a larger share of its income — 20 percentage points more — to the necessities of food, shelter, and clothing than the average family. It is a *relative measure* of low income. The Low-Income Cut-Offs were adjusted for seven family sizes and five different community sizes to capture differences in the cost of living. Although now falling into disfavour, LICO data are available since 1976.
- **Market Basket Measure (MBM).** Now the "official" way of measuring poverty, the Market Basket Measure defines low income based on a specific set of goods and services that represent a basic standard of living. A family is considered low income if it does not have enough money to buy these goods and services in its community. It is an *absolute measure* of low income. This indicator is available for about 50 different communities across Canada and is more sensitive to differences in the cost of living. MBM data is available since 2002.
- **Low Income Measure (LIM).** The Low Income Measure defines low income as being below a fixed percentage of contemporary norms measured using median income. A household is considered low income if its income is below 50% of median household incomes. It is, therefore, a *relative measure* of low income. Since many countries report low income on this basis, it is frequently used for international comparisons. LIM data is also available since 1976. The United Nations Development Programme (UNDP) has an absolute and relative line ($2 per day) and LIM (roughly 50% of median income).

All poverty lines are "relative" when they are set — they reflect the time and place as to what is "decent." The difference between updating using the consumer price index (CPI) only or reflecting median incomes of the population will grow in importance over time. For example, the MBM is to be revisited every five years whereas for the LIM, a relative measure of poverty, wage growth is automatically incorporated over time.

To illustrate the difference: in 1976 the LICO for a single person in urban areas was about $3,000 per year. In 2017, after adjustments for CPI only, the equivalent would be about $17,000. In 2019, the LIM poverty line for a single person is more than $25,000 whereas the current MBM value for Toronto is about $18,000, which is similar to a standard of living from 40 years ago and much lower than contemporary incomes. Time will tell how and when the MBM reacts to "real growth" over and above CPI.

Income Support in Retirement

A 2020 National Institute on Ageing report shows that approximately 12 million working Canadians do not have access to a workplace pension plan. Canadians nearing retirement without a workplace pension plan have median savings of only $3,000.

Many of these Canadians will have no choice but to rely on available government-administered income supports in retirement.

Policy Implications

The important policy implication of how poverty is measured is the implied statement of an obligation to lower-income Canadians. The absolute poverty line means that the individual and family has enough to purchase a decent basket of goods, regardless of what is happening elsewhere. The relative poverty line, on the other hand, means that poverty reflects "social exclusion" and an inability to participate in society in a decent fashion.

To illustrate this, Figure 10.3 tells two different stories about the poverty status of seniors. The Market Basket Measure measure (an absolute measure of poverty) indicates that the circumstances of low-income of seniors have improved — that is, that their income has increased relative to a fixed basic of goods. On the other hand, the Low Income Measure result (the relative measure of poverty) shows dramatically that seniors are falling behind relative to the income of younger Canadians — that is, they are not enjoying the improving standard of living as much as other Canadians.

It should also be noted that research shows that the major factor contributing to the decline in poverty rates, by whatever measure is used, from 1976 to 1995 was the increase in CPP/QPP benefits as these pensions "matured" and were impacted by increasing female employment rates. The latter not only increased family incomes but also increased CPP benefits for retiring females. One cannot expect to see the same increases in CPP/QPP benefits in the future, as the overall participation rates of women have not increased for almost a decade.

Figure 10.3

Canadians 65+ Years of Age by Poverty Measure, 2006–2017 (Percentage)

Statistics Canada. Table 11-10-0135-01 Low income statistics by age, sex and economic family type.

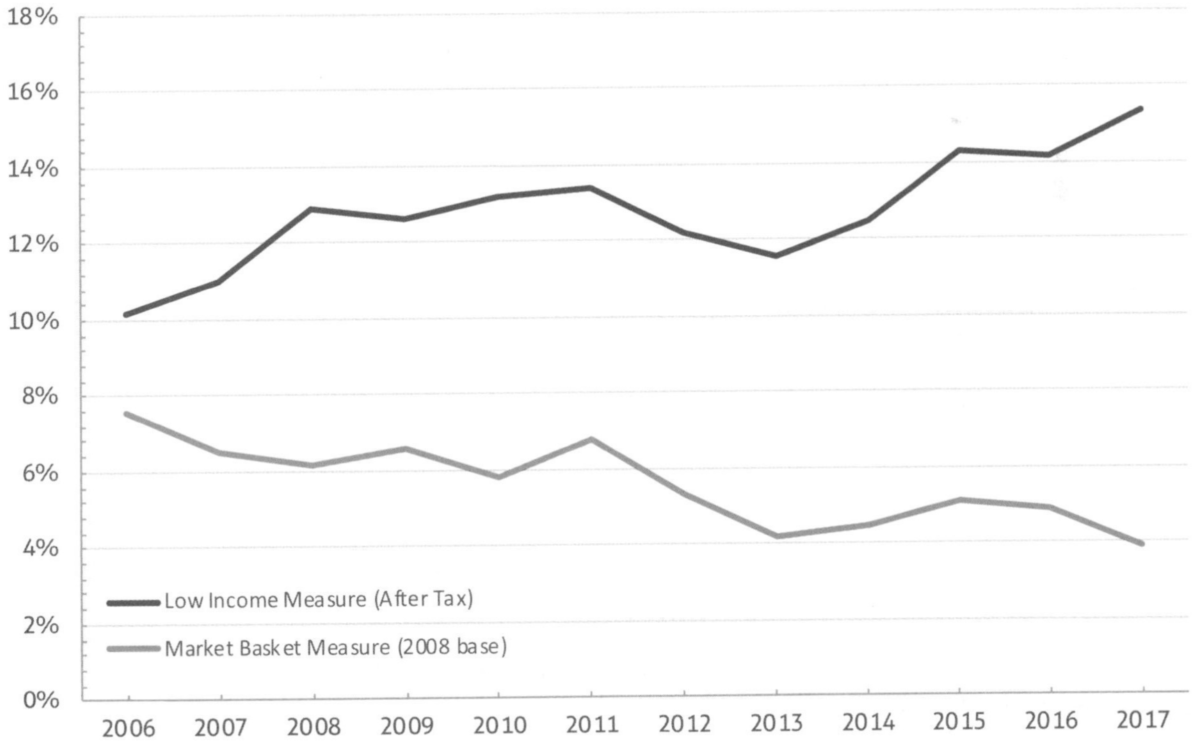

Statistics Canada. Table 11-10-0135-01 Low income statistics by age, sex and economic family type

Status and Trends in Poverty for Seniors

Figure 10.4 shows the disparity in senior poverty rates depending on family type and gender. The poverty rate for single seniors (seniors living alone who might be divorced, widowed, or never married) is much higher than for senior couples. For singles, the poverty rate for women is higher than for men. Both are unacceptably high. One should keep in mind that senior couples are usually younger than single seniors, and that they are more likely to still be employed.

The lowest rate of poverty for seniors using the LIM was in 1995. As noted earlier, the improvement up to that point reflected the maturation of the Canada/Québec Pension Plans and the retirement of more women who had participated in the labour force, yielding increased CPP/QPP pensions and benefits. Income from employer pension plans also increased, reflecting the high employer pension plan coverage in the decades before 1995. Employer pension plan coverage of the paid labour force has been falling for some time — from about 46% of paid employees in 1977 to about 38% in 2011 (Drolet and Morissette, 2014). This is due largely to a decline in private rather than public-sector coverage — and will eventually be reflected in average lower pension income at retirement.

The trends that led to higher participation rates for women (from 46% in 1976 to 62% in 2003) have stalled; overall labour force participation rates of women remained between 61% and 63% from 2003 to 2014 (Statistics Canada, Table 14-10-0018-01).

Figure 10.4

Poverty Rate of Elderly Canadians by Family Type, Low Income Measure

Statistics Canada. Table 11-10-0135-01 Low income statistics by age, sex and economic family type.

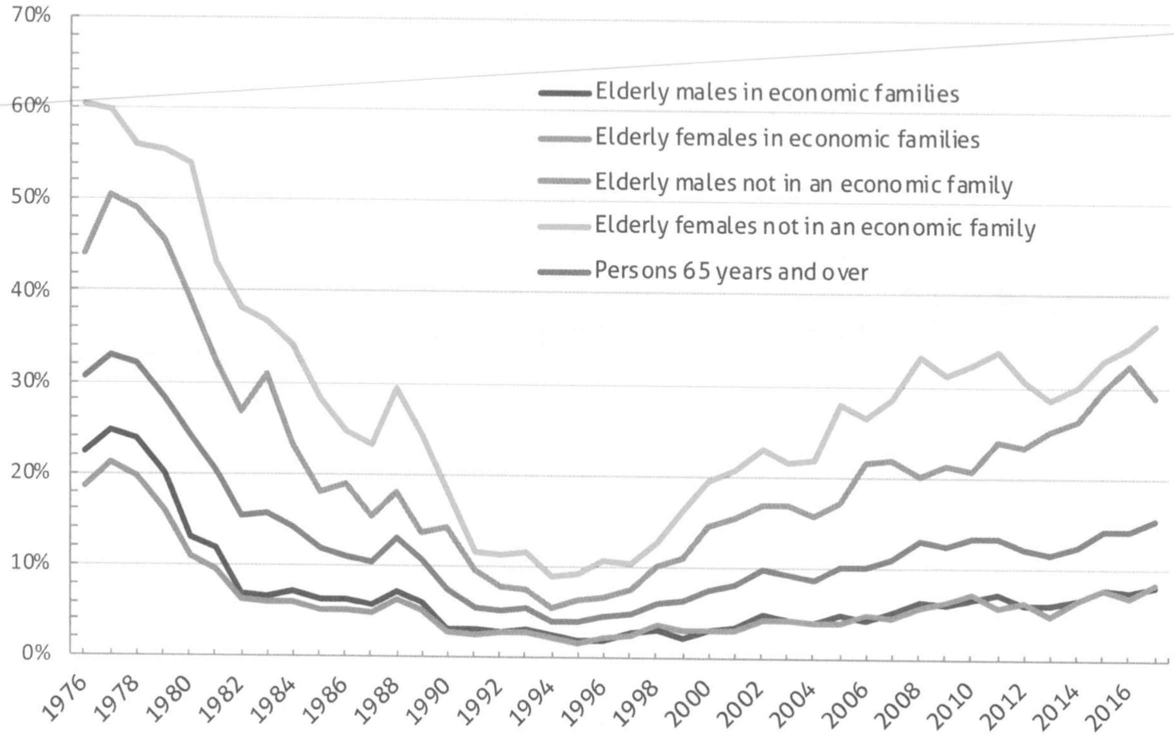

Gender Concerns — The Income Insecurity of Older Women

Differences in life expectancy and labour force experiences mean that women necessarily face different circumstances as they approach retirement.

Why are older women more likely to have low income? There are a number of reasons:

- Women are more likely to have been involved with "women's work" during their careers — caring for children, nursing the sick, looking after the home, and serving others. In addition, women have tended to work in lower-paying occupations and sectors, and more women work part-time or have had their careers disrupted for family reasons than men. These interruptions have important implications for income and pension entitlements.
- Recent decades have seen a dramatic increase in employment rates for women, particularly in the public sector which tends to have better pension coverage and pension quality, a lower gendered wage gap, and better maternity benefits. So future female retirees will be better served if they were employed in the public sector. Those retiring from the private sector will face falling pension coverage. Regardless, retired women will be disadvantaged by the wage gap, a higher rate of part-time work, and time out of the workforce taken for caregiving for children but also for other family members.
- Many women are unattached or single in old age: approximately 30% of Canadian women are widowed at age 65 and 50% are widowed by age 75. Canadian women on average must therefore fund a longer retirement period than senior men.

The policy implications of this are clear. Tying income security policymaking to seemingly gender-neutral criteria — active labour force experience — works against women. They not only have fewer sources of savings but their pension entitlements are often more limited.

"Poverty and lack of income security pose a significant barrier to quality of life for older women," notes Katherine Scott of the Canadian Centre for Policy Alternatives in Ottawa. "The high cost of housing and medications eat into even modest incomes, leaving little for food, transportation, and other needs. At age 65, women can expect to live another 21 years, and increasing numbers are living to age 90 and beyond. Many will be widowed, many will live with one or more disabilities, but most will have only limited savings and pension income to sustain them through this period of their lives" (Scott, 2019).

But age and gender are only two of many factors that affect economic security of Canadians. Other factors include race, living arrangements, education, employment, disability, sexual identity, and immigration status. The intersection of all these experiences, observes Scott, reveals the full challenges that different groups of Canadians face and what is needed by way of effective policy solutions that can meet the unique needs of these senior citizens.

Indigenous Seniors Are Respected Elders

In contrast to various mainstream Canadian cultures, Indigenous cultures tend to respect and even revere their seniors for their knowledge and experiences. Elders play an integral role in the well-being of families, communities, and nations, acting as key sources of traditional knowledge, wisdom, and cultural continuity.

Indigenous peoples comprise only 1% of the overall senior population in Canada (compared with 3% in the total population). Manitoba and Saskatchewan have the largest proportion of Indigenous peoples in their senior populations (Turcotte and Schellenberg, 2007).

10.4 Income Reduction in Retirement

There has been much concern that many future seniors will experience a major fall in their standard of living at retirement (Hamilton, 2015; Mintz, 2009; Tyler, 2015; Wolfson, 2011). But perhaps the biggest concern relates to the likelihood of pensionless cohorts — future retirees who do not have an employment pension and who earned near or above average incomes (Shillington, 2015).

A Decline in Pension Coverage

About 46% of paid employees had pension plans in 1977, and only about 38% had them in 2011 (Drolet and Morissette, 2014). The adequacy and reliability of plan benefits are also declining as employers (particularly in the private sector) shift from defined benefit to defined contribution pension plans. Two criteria can be used to assess the adequacy of income at retirement.

- **The poverty criterion.** Will incomes be adequate for a standard of living that is not too different from contemporary norms? Poverty levels using the LIM will likely increase as the OAS/GIS levels fail to keep pace with median incomes.
- **The replacement rate.** Does the retirement income allow the senior individual or couple to maintain a standard of living consistent with the lifestyle they enjoyed pre-retirement?

So, what is likely the impact of current savings levels on income after retirement for persons without income from an employment pension?

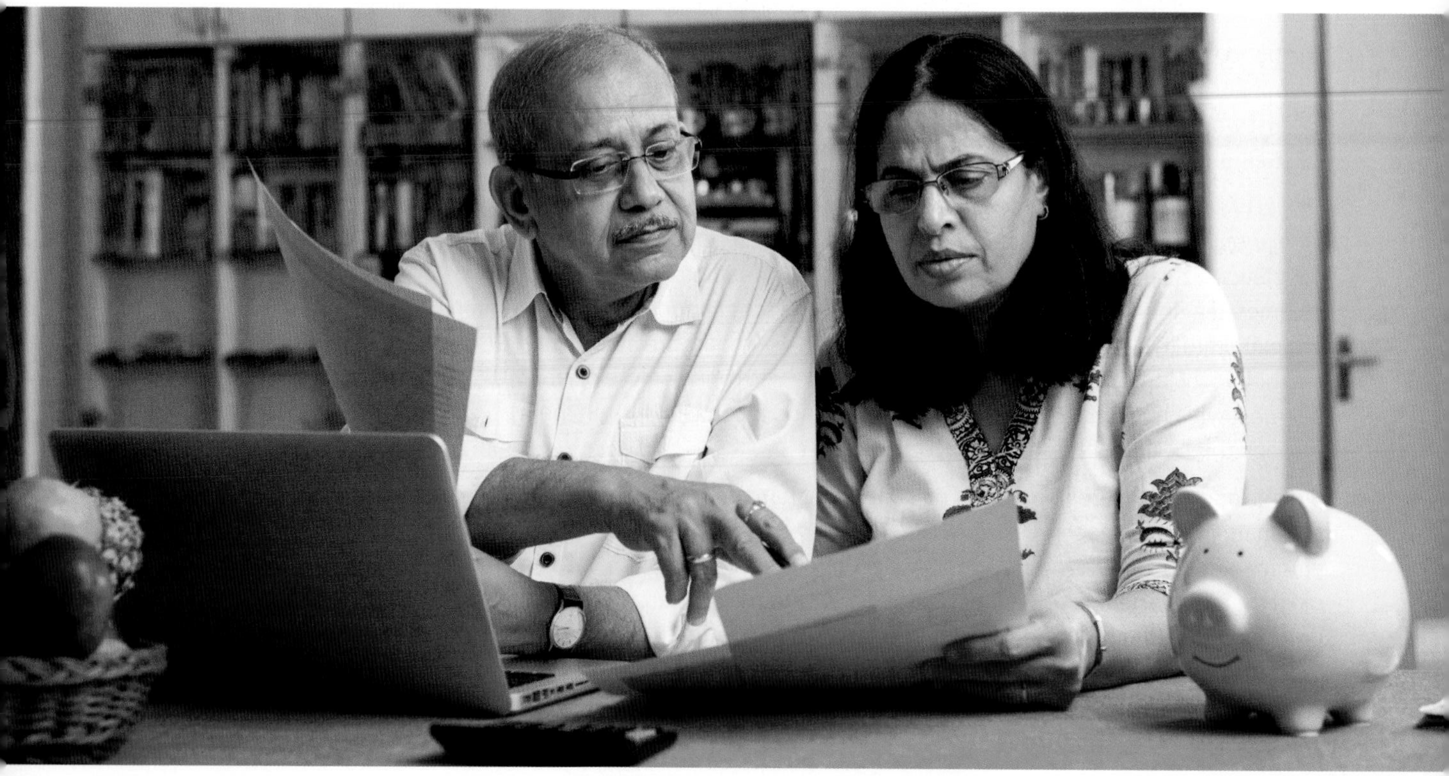

Inadequate Savings

The data in Table 10.1 come from the Survey of Financial Security, which gauges the retirement assets of economic families aged 55–64 and nearing retirement. The data are for those without employer pensions (less than $10,000 in benefits based on current or past employment). The sample size meeting these criteria is rather limited, so broad income groups are used. Of those aged 55–64, about half have essentially no accrued employer pension benefits.

Overall, about half of these families without an employer pension have virtually no savings; indeed, 78% of them have less than $100,000 in retirement savings. Table 10.1 shows the amount of retirement savings (RRSPs plus TFSAs) for families with the oldest member aged 55–64 and with virtually no assets in an employer pension plan (less than $10,000). These values highlight how little the vast majority of those nearing retirement without an employer pension plan have saved for retirement. Lower-income families eligible for OAS/GIS along with CPP/QPP may still have little or no drop in income, however inadequate that income might be.

These data demonstrate that the vast majority of these families with annual incomes of $50,000 and more will be hard pressed to save enough in their remaining period to retirement (less than 10 years) to avoid a significant fall in income. It appears that at least 25% have very limited retirement assets despite incomes of $50,000–$200,000.

One could argue that the analysis presented in Table 10.1 is somewhat simplistic because it ignores the impact of public benefits (OAS/GIS and CPP/QPP) on the amount that future seniors need to save. It is also accepted that many seniors need less income at retirement in order to maintain the standard of living that they had pre-retirement. The actual replacement rate required — the ratio of post-retirement to pre-retirement income — varies by how it is measured (pre- or post-tax). Seventy percent is commonly used, although it varies by individual circumstances and tastes; higher values are more appropriate for the poor, and lower values are more appropriate for the very wealthy. Let's next look at this problem in the context of replacement rate.

Table 10.1

Retirement Savings of Canadian Families, 55–64 Years of Age without an Employer Pension Plan

Special tabulations by the author, using the Survey of Financial Security.

	Income Group for the Economic Family				
Income 2011 ($)	**Total**	**Under $25,000**	**$25,000–$50,000**	**$50,000–$100.000**	**$100,000**
Average Income	64,000	12,600	38,000	71,000	199,000
Average Retirement Assets	85,000	17,600	57,000*	77,000	280,000
Median Retirement Assets	3,000	0	250	21,000	160,000

* Large Error +/-25%.
** Employer Pension Plan assets are less than $10,000.
Retirement Assets are RRSPs, TFSAs and Employer Pension Equity.
Families where the oldest person is 55–64.

Retirement Assets Relative to Target Income in Retirement

The analysis presented in Table 10.2 looks at retirement assets relative to target income. The calculations use a 70% pre-tax replacement rate, and the findings would not change dramatically if other reasonable replacement rates were used. Table 10.2 has adjusted the income needed at retirement from public sources available, and while this is somewhat crude, the gaps in savings make obvious the conclusion of inadequate savings.

To illustrate, a family with an income of $100,000 (pre-tax) is assumed to need $70,000 (70% of $100,000) and will get roughly $25,000 in public support. Thus, they will need to make up $45,000 per year from their private savings. The values shown in Table 10.2 are the family's retirement assets divided by the annual requirements (in this case, $45,000). That figure tells us how many years they can withdraw $45,000 ignoring any return on investment.

The last column in Table 10.2 indicates the distribution of these near-seniors by their savings. The first row indicates that 32% of these families have less than $1,000 in retirement savings. About 23% have more than $1,000 but less than one year's savings (that is, less than they need to supplement public sources to reach 70% replacement for one year). Fifteen percent have enough for 1–2.5 years, 13% have enough for 2.5–5 years, and only 18% have more than 5 years' worth of savings.

These results vary by income group, but in each income category, few have more than five years' worth of the savings needed to supplement their public income. Even those families with an income of more than $100,000 are unlikely to have more than five years' worth of the required supplemental income in their retirement savings; only 21% meet this criterion.

That is not to say that having enough savings for five years would be adequate. One might reasonably expect adequate savings to be more like 20 years' worth given a life expectancy, at age 65, of about 20 years. This is why many policy analysts argue for an expanded CPP — the only defined benefit available to all Canadians.

Table 10.2

Retirement Assets Relative to Target Income of Canadian Households, 55–64 Years of Age Who Have No Pension Assets, 2012

Special tabulations by the author, using the Survey of Financial Security.

	Family Income			
Retirement Savings Relative to Target Income*	**Under $50,000**	**$50,000–$100,000**	**$100,000+**	**Total**
Less than $1,000	54%	27%	15%	32%
Less than 100% ****	17%	27%	22%	23%
100% – 250%	7%	17%	20%	15%
250% – 500%	6%	13%	22%	13%
Greater than 500%	17%	16%	21%	18%
Total	101%	100%	100%	100%

* Note: The first category is for those with less than $1,000 of retirement assets.
Target income is the difference between 70% of current income and the public guaranteed income ($15,000/individuals; $25,000/couples).
*** Less than $10,000 of pension assets (going concern). The table only includes those who need to save privately to achieve 70% replacement.
**** 100% = enough savings for one year.

Does Home Equity Improve Income Security in Retirement?

Many who argue that there is no looming pension crisis point to home equity as an asset that could be made liquid (Hamilton, 2015; McKinsey & Company, 2015). This may be an unfair way of looking at things, however. The objective is to ensure a lifestyle comparable to that which existed pre-retirement. The foregoing analysis does not include home equity because the pre-retirement lifestyle for many middle- and moderate-income Canadians includes continued home ownership.

However, Wolfson (2015) has explored the option of including home equity in the analysis, as some researchers have argued. In fact, the inclusion of home equity does not alter the forecast of a significant drop in standard of living for a substantial number of Canadian families with moderate income but no employer pension plan. When the calculations are repeated treating family net worth as the funds available for retirement, similar to Wolfson, the fundamental policy conclusions do not change. Using net worth, the proportion of seniors (without an employer pension) who have at least five years of replacement income saved increases overall from 18% to 28%. For those with an income over $100,000, the proportion with just five years' worth of savings increases from 21% to 49%. That's still less than half.

In other words, including home equity does not change the conclusion that the overwhelming majority of families without an employer pension have inadequate savings for their retirement years.

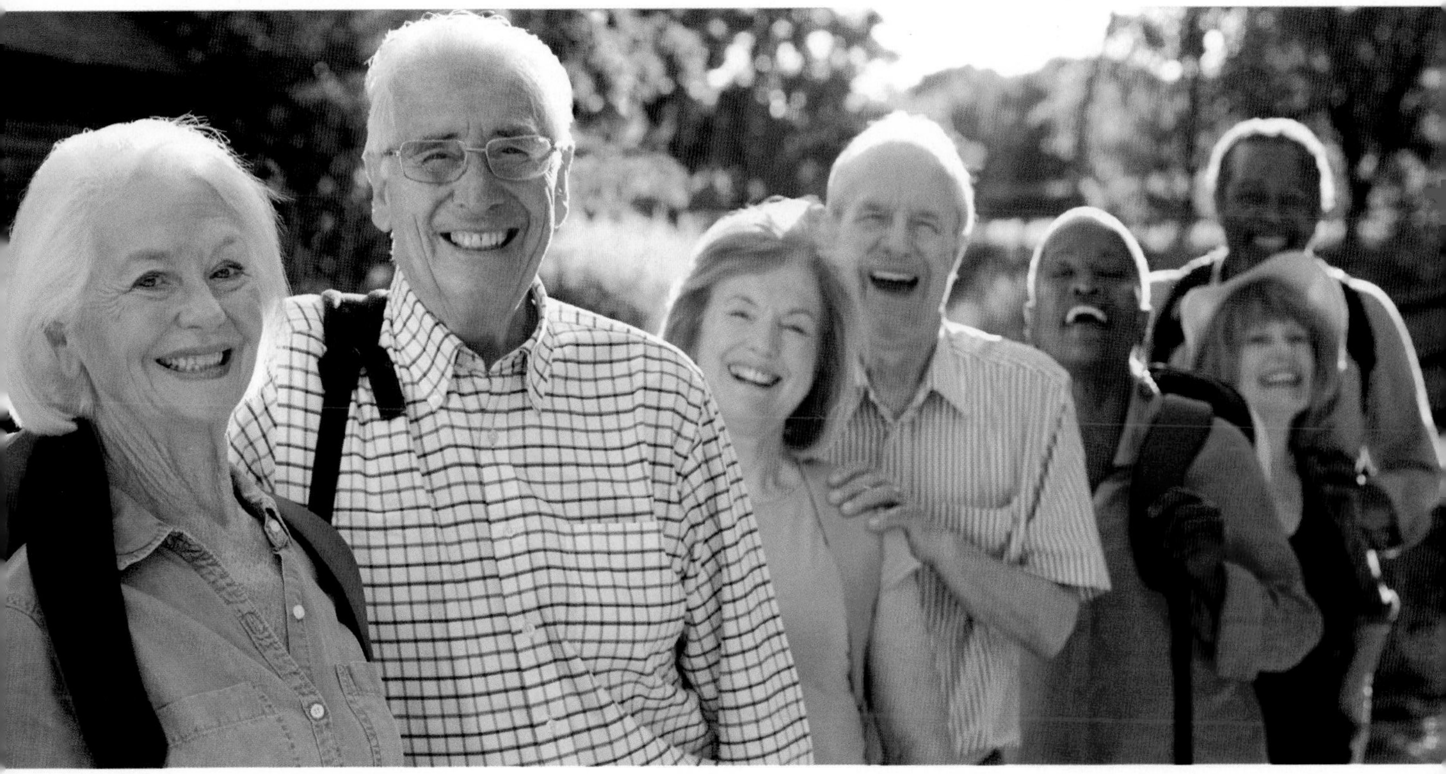

Social Welfare in Perspective

Pensionless Cohorts

A Cause for Concern

Pension coverage for the employed population is declining. The median income for seniors without pension income is just over half that for those with pension income.

Overall, workplace pension plan (WPPP) coverage has been declining. Moreover, the proportion of coverage that is defined benefit (DB), as opposed to defined contribution (DC), is declining. Indeed, we are nearing a volatile situation where DB pension plans will only exist in the public sector and will be largely unavailable in the private sector.

The first table below shows the decline in the percentage of the employed and the population ages 18 to 64 who participate in a WPPP. The second table shows the decline in DB plan members as a percentage of all WPPP members.

Table 1: Percentage of the Employed and the Population Ages 18–64 Who Participate in a WPPP

	1980	2000	2016
Employed	45%	40%	38%
Population	29%	27%	27%

Table 2: DB Plan Members as a Percentage of All WPPP Members

	1980	2000	2016
Private Sector	90%	76%	42%
Public Sector	98%	94%	91%
Both Sectors	94%	85%	67%

Author's calculations based on Statistics Canada, Tables 11-10-0106-01 (formerly CANSIM 280-0016), 14-10-0027-01 (formerly CANSIM 282-0012), and 17-10-0005-01 (formerly CANSIM 051-0001).

Income Differences

The difference in incomes at retirement between those seniors with and without a pension income is stark and cause for serious concern.

Interestingly, the difference is not all due simply to the presence or absence of an employer pension plan. Those who have had an employer pension plan are more likely to have had jobs with better pay and with health and other benefits. As well, it is possible that those who seek jobs with a pension are more likely to be those motivated to save for retirement. But certainly, participating in a pension offers advantages that make it easier to have a higher income at retirement.

For couples, those without pension income have significantly lower total incomes ($52,000) compared to those with pension income ($68,000). This is despite their higher income from earnings ($19,100 for those without pension income, compared to $7,200 for those with pension income).

For individuals, the story is very different: They are more likely than couples to be over the age of 70, and much less likely to be employed. For single women, the median incomes are $18,000 for those without a pension and $30,400 for those with a pension. For men, the medians are $19,000 and $37,300, respectively.

Generally, the median incomes for those without pension income are just over half that for those with pension income. These gaps are significant.

There are obvious societal concerns about having so many seniors at retirement age with inadequate incomes. It is also prudent to consider what future pensionless cohorts will mean for the adequacy of current programs like OAS and GIS.

10.5 Income Security for Older Adults

The retirement income security system for Canadian seniors has been described as a three-legged stool — government benefits, workplace pensions, and private savings. Today, that stool seems a lot less stable.

Pensions

While the senior population is increasing dramatically, income security provisions are not keeping up. For one thing, workplace pensions are in retreat. In 1977, nearly half of employed persons held workplace pensions; in 2014, that percentage had dropped to 33%.

The typical workplace pension has also changed. Whereas in the past most Canadians pensioners could look to defined benefit (DB) pensions as the basis of their retirement income, there has been a shift away from DB pensions toward defined contribution (DC) pensions. **Defined benefit pensions** are paid for life, and, for some, even rise along with inflation. Today, many DB plans have been closed and replaced by options like DC plans or group registered retirement savings plans where members manage their own asset allocation.

With **defined contribution pensions**, income is not guaranteed but rather is based on how well the investment selection does over time — if a person makes poor investment choices or if there is a major market downturn close to one's retirement, the individual pensioner bears the full brunt of loss in the form of reduced pension income during retirement.

Benefits

The second leg of the stool — government benefits — was designed to soften the blow in the retirement years, but increasingly this too is not enough to fill the gap. While the maximum monthly CPP payment in 2019 was $1,114, the average monthly CPP payment to pensioners was only $685. Meanwhile, Old Age Security (OAS) and the Guaranteed Income Supplement (GIS) together provide a maximum of just $15,000 per year for single seniors and $25,000 per year for seniors who live with a spouse — not enough for them to make ends meet.

Savings

Without adequate workplace or government benefits, Canadians are left to make up the shortfall through their private savings and through vehicles such as Registered Retirement Savings Plans (RRSP) and Tax-Free Savings Accounts (TFSAs). Nevertheless, a strikingly low number of Canada's lower- and middle-income earners use these vehicles. New data from Statistics Canada shows RRSP contributions steadily declined between 2000 and 2013. Canadians simply are not saving enough, either by choice or because there is too little left over after all other expenses are covered.

The result is that one in three Canadian adults is not financially prepared for retirement, according to a 2014 financial capability survey.

The Decline of Post-Retirement Health Plans

Post-retirement health plans help pay medical and dental costs and help retirees make ends meet. In the past, employers were generous. Today, the situation with post-retirement health benefits mirrors that of employment pensions.

A 2018 survey by Morneau Shepell (2018), a benefits consulting firm, found that 41% of employers offered benefit plans; a 2012 Conference Board of Canada survey found that 51% offered post-retirement benefits. Moreover, in the Morneau Shepell survey, 24% of respondents who offered such plans said they were doing little more than connecting workers to private insurance plans.

Rob Carrick, a personal finance columnist, summed it up this way:

> Benefits paid to retirees are an overlooked example of how employers are backpedalling like mad from the commitment they once had to help their workers pay for retirement. This trend demands that we stop generalizing about how well-prepared people are for retirement. There are actually three different situations to consider — those with defined benefit (DB) pension plans and post-retirement benefits, those who have second-rate pensions and post-retirement benefits and those who have no help at all because they're self-employed or working temporary jobs. (Carrick, 2018)

The upshot of all this is that fewer than half of Canadians who are retiring without an employer-sponsored pension plan have saved enough to cover themselves for a single year in retirement.

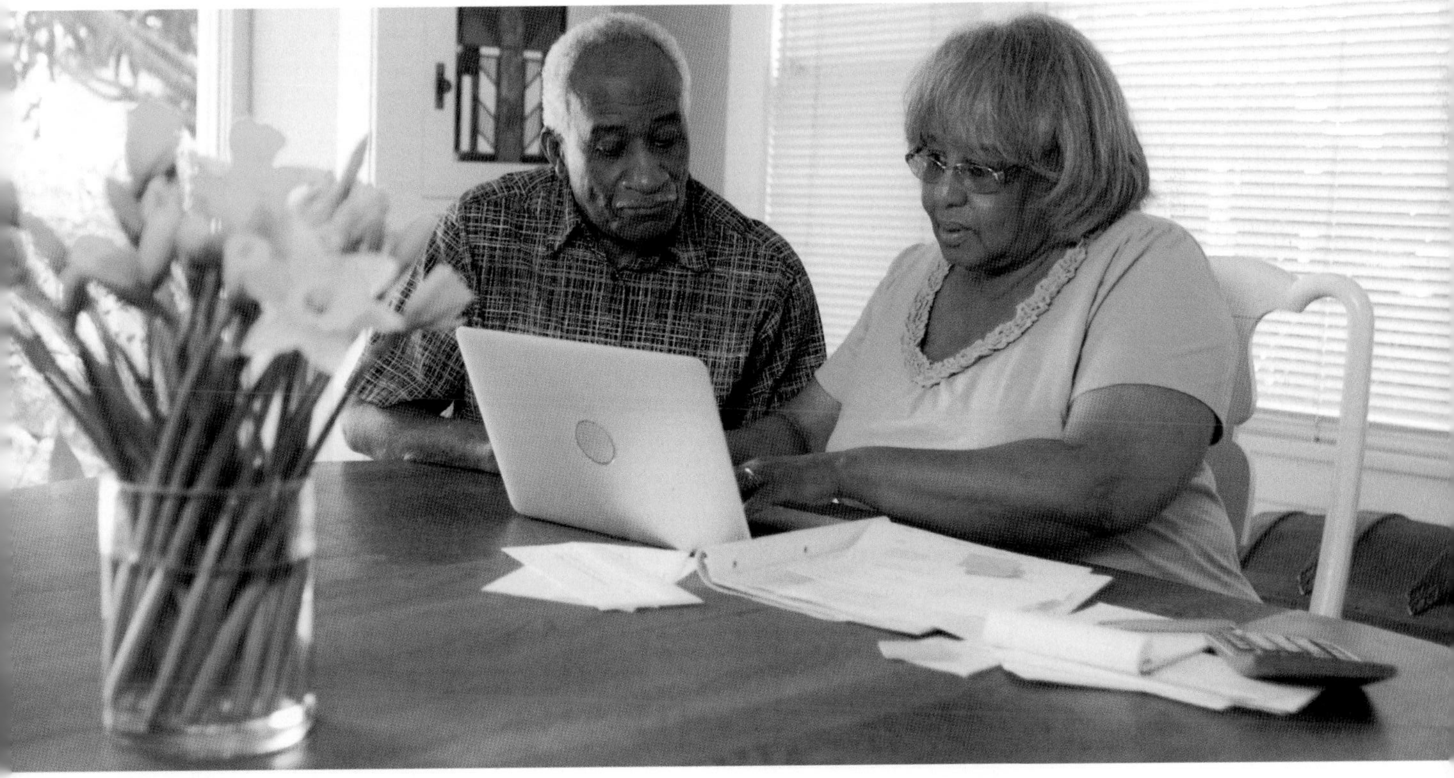

Income Security Programs Are Not Meeting the Needs of Older Adults

The issues of adequate retirement income security and seniors' poverty figure prominently in recent Canadian federal elections — as well they should. Ensuring the economic well-being of Canada's growing older adult population is an important and complex public policy challenge that the federal government must grapple with.

Few disagree with the goal of providing all persons in Canada with the means for a dignified and economically secure retirement. But there is profound disagreement about how this goal ought to be achieved and the role of different public programs in achieving it.

While there has been progress in reducing poverty among seniors over several decades, a less rosy picture arises in recent years and in projections of the future.

- Roughly half (47%) of Canadian families aged 55–64 have no accrued employer pension benefits in Canada. The vast majority of these Canadians retiring without an employer pension plan have totally inadequate retirement savings — the median value of their retirement assets is just over $3,000.
- Over half (55%) have savings that represent less than one year's worth of the resources they need to supplement government programs like OAS/GIS and CPP/QPP. And fewer than 20% have enough savings to support the supplemented resources required for at least five years.
- Even more startling: for those with annual incomes in the range of $25,000–$50,000, the median value of their retirement assets is close to just $250. For those with incomes in the $50,000–$100,000 range, the median value is only $21,000.
- Only a small minority (below 20%) of middle-income Canadians retiring without an employer pension plan have saved anywhere near enough for retirement. What this means is the vast majority of these families with annual incomes of $50,000 and more will be hard pressed to save enough in their remaining period to retirement (less than 10 years) to avoid a significant fall in income.
- A number of studies from more conservative think tanks have argued that there is no crisis in seniors' savings if one considers housing assets, and no need for expansion of public pensions. However, even when accounting for seniors' total net worth, only 28% of Canadian seniors without employer pensions have five years' worth of replacement income saved.
- In addition to tackling inadequate savings, the government also must grapple with deteriorating conditions concerning poverty. The seniors' LIM poverty rate has increased over recent years. Fully 28% of single women and 24% of single male seniors live in poverty.

Pension Reform

Canada's pension system in particular needs urgent attention, according to a report released by the Canadian Centre for Policy Alternatives (CCPA).

Old Age Security and the Canada Pension Plan provide only a modest income for people when they retire.

Not everyone has a workplace pension—about 60% of Canadians must rely on public pension programs, supplemented by their own savings.

Only about one-third of Canadians take advantage of tax-assisted private savings through RRSPs.

Almost $500 billion in unused RRSP contribution room is being carried forward.

Policy Implications for Ensuring the Income Security of Seniors

Canada should be applauded for the substantial gains made in the post–World War II period in relation to income security of seniors. Such gains were significant and were made largely as a result of public pressure by this increasingly large and vocal section of the population.

Nevertheless, there are signs that the gains seniors have made are coming under threat. As further pressure mounts, governments will have to make some difficult choices, and these may affect seniors. Do we break down a public system that has been recognized worldwide as exemplary, or do we make the necessary changes to maintain a viable and comprehensive public retirement system?

Poverty trends over the recent past depend critically on which poverty measure one uses. Using the low-income measure (LIM), we see that senior poverty has increased from a low of 3.9% in 1995 to 11.1%, or one in nine, in 2013 (Statistics Canada, Tables 11–10–0181–01 and 11–10–0135–01). The poverty rates for single seniors, particularly women (at nearly 30%), are very high and need to be addressed. Poverty rates have been rising, and savings data show that many Canadians, particularly those without an employer pension plan, have wholly inadequate retirement savings.

The challenges are many. Many older adults can still work productively past retirement age, and many want to do so. It is important that those who wish to work beyond the typical retirement age have the opportunity to do so, while ensuring that those who have put in their time and want to retire can retire without income worries. Of special concern are senior women, many of whom outlive their male counterparts and who, because of family responsibilities, may have not been able to build up sufficient pension entitlement.

These issues raise serious questions about the policy needs for future pensionless cohorts, such as the adequacy of benefits from Old Age Security, the Guaranteed Income Supplement, and the Québec and Canada Pension Plans. They also provide an invaluable baseline of evidence that the federal government must consider as it moves forward to craft policies that will address the economic security of Canada's growing population of older adults.

Social Welfare Policy in Action

Dementia: Together We Aspire

A Focus on Human Rights and Well-Being

Age is the strongest known risk factor for dementia, but dementia is not an inevitable consequence of aging. Healthy living behaviours appear to provide some protection.

Dementia is an umbrella term that describes a set of symptoms that affect the brain. It is a chronic and progressive condition that reduces independence and quality of life. It affects almost half a million Canadians aged 65 and older who are diagnosed with dementia, and their family members and caregivers.

National Legislation

The National Strategy for Alzheimer's Disease and Other Dementias Act was passed in June 2017, with the requirement to develop a national strategy.

In May 2018, a national conference on dementia discussed the challenges related to dementia and shared ideas for a national strategy. Close to 200 participants included people living with dementia, caregivers, advocacy groups, health professionals, researchers, and representatives from provincial and territorial governments. Following this conference, four stakeholder roundtables were organized across the country, and two subsequent roundtables on research and innovation occurred.

The inaugural *Dementia Strategy for Canada: Together We Aspire* stipulated common principles and objectives to guide all levels of government. The vision for the strategy is:

> A Canada in which all people living with dementia and caregivers are valued and supported, quality of life is optimized, and dementia is prevented, well understood, and effectively treated. (Public Health Agency of Canada [PHAC], 2019, p. ix)

The federal government has committed to annual reporting on the effectiveness of this strategy and a budget investment of $70 million over five years to make progress on the national objectives.

Principles Associated with the Strategy

Key to achieving the vision, the following five principles setting out core values were identified:

- Prioritize *quality of life* for people living with dementia and caregivers
- Respect and value *diversity* to ensure an inclusive approach, with a focus on those most at risk or with distinct needs
- Respect the *human rights* of people living with dementia to support their autonomy and dignity
- Engage in *evidence-informed decision making*, taking a broad approach to gathering and sharing best available knowledge and data
- Maintain *a results-focused* approach to tracking progress, including evaluating and adjusting actions as needed

National Objectives

From the vision, and guided by the principles, three national objectives and five pillars emerged. The national objectives are:

- Prevent dementia
- Advance therapies and find a cure
- Improve the quality of life of people living with dementia and caregivers

The five pillars are collaboration, research and innovation, surveillance and data, information resources, and a skilled workforce.

In the development of the national strategy, it was recognized that Indigenous communities and individuals have distinct dementia experiences and distinct needs and that further engagement with Indigenous organizations, communities, and governments would need to continue as the strategy was implemented (PHAC, 2019, p. 4).

Prevention

Currently there is an incomplete understanding of risk and protective factors for dementia. A more complete understanding requires ongoing research to identify additional risk and protective factors and the links between the two. In addition, addressing the built and social environments requires the development of age-friendly communities that can help reduce the risk of developing dementia.

Delaying the onset of dementia can significantly reduce the number of dementia cases, improve quality of life, and reduce the personal, family, and societal costs of care. Some developed countries are already beginning to see reduced incidence rates that appear to be linked to healthy living and higher education levels (PHAC, 2019, p. 12). Dementia prevention efforts include sharing knowledge about the links between the design of our environments (social, built. and environmental) and dementia risk factors.

Intervention

Improving our understanding of dementia and finding possible ways to prevent or cure this condition requires a collective international effort (PHAC, 2019, p. 19). Producing new knowledge and evaluating novel approaches for how to best intervene to improve quality of life are essential.

There is currently no cure for dementia; however, some drug therapies have been proven to have modest benefits. Other non-drug options such as music therapy, aromatherapy, pet therapy, and massage therapy show promising benefits while still requiring scientific validation. Assistive technologies, such as clocks to assist with telling time (including whether it is day or night), communication aids, electric appliances monitors, picture phones, reminder devices, as well as in-home cameras and home monitoring devices all help caregivers and support a person with dementia to maintain or improve independence (PHAC, 2019, p. 25).

The development of new evidence-informed and person-centred therapies needs to become more accessible.

Improving the Quality of Life

Improving the quality of life for people living with dementia includes eliminating stigma and creating inclusive communities so that those living with dementia can remain a part of their community and live as independently as possible. This requires ensuring that there are safe and engaging community spaces, simplified transit networks, and training for people interacting with those who have dementia.

End-of-life care for people living with dementia also needs attention as they are less likely to be referred to palliative care, are prescribed fewer palliative care medications, and have difficulty accessing end-of-life care. A framework for palliative care "can begin at the time of a dementia diagnosis and aims to reduce suffering and improve quality of life through pain and symptom management, psychological, social, emotional, spiritual and practical support, as well as support for caregivers throughout the trajectory of the condition, including after death" (PHAC, 2019, p. 36).

The quality of life for caregivers must also be addressed as they are essential members of the care team.

Questions for Reflection

You may want to look at the entire document to consider the following questions.

1. What are the social indicators that make it important to have a national dementia strategy?
2. This strategy explicitly outlines a vision statement and principles for the strategy. What principles may be missing or cause barriers for some populations?
3. Does this policy increase or decrease the opportunities for decision making, personal agency, and political engagement? How could it be improved?
4. How does this strategy address the social determinants of health and social well-being?
5. What performance indicators could be used to indicate the effectiveness (or lack thereof) of the strategy?

A moment in time: March 17, 2021

Medical Assistance in Dying (Bill C-7)

End-of-Life Options Provide Autonomy and Dignity

Medical assistance in dying (MAID) is a highly complex and deeply personal issue. On March 17, 2021, changes to the Criminal Code received Royal Assent and immediately came into force.

The new MAID law now opens the door to individuals whose deaths are not reasonably foreseeable, but who meet the other MAiD eligibility criteria, as well as those with a serious and incurable "disease, illness or disability" and those in an advanced state of decline and are suffering intolerably.

The government recognizes that issues related to MAID must still be explored fully. Concerns such as the eligibility of mature minors, advance requests, mental illness, palliative care, and the protection of Canadians living with disabilities will be examined during a parliamentary review of the legislation.

One of the main concerns is that persons with disabilities and others may be pushed toward seeking MAiD due simply to a chronic lack of supports. The Council of Canadians with Disabilities, for example, argued that legislation will have an especially negative impact on persons with disabilities and other marginalized groups.

Implications for Social Workers and Public Policy

The Canadian Association of Social Workers (CASW) advocates on behalf of the social work profession in regard to any emerging legislation. While social workers will not be directly involved in the process of assessing eligibility, CASW successfully advocated for the explicit inclusion of social workers for protection on the issue of Medical Assistance in Dying. The Criminal Code now states that "... no social worker, psychologist, psychiatrist, therapist, medical practitioner, nurse practitioner or other health care professional commits an offence if they provide information to a person on the lawful provision of medical assistance in dying."

There were 5,631 medically assisted deaths in 2019, a 26 percent increase on 2018, according to the country's first annual report on the practice. The most common underlying condition was a cancer-related illness.

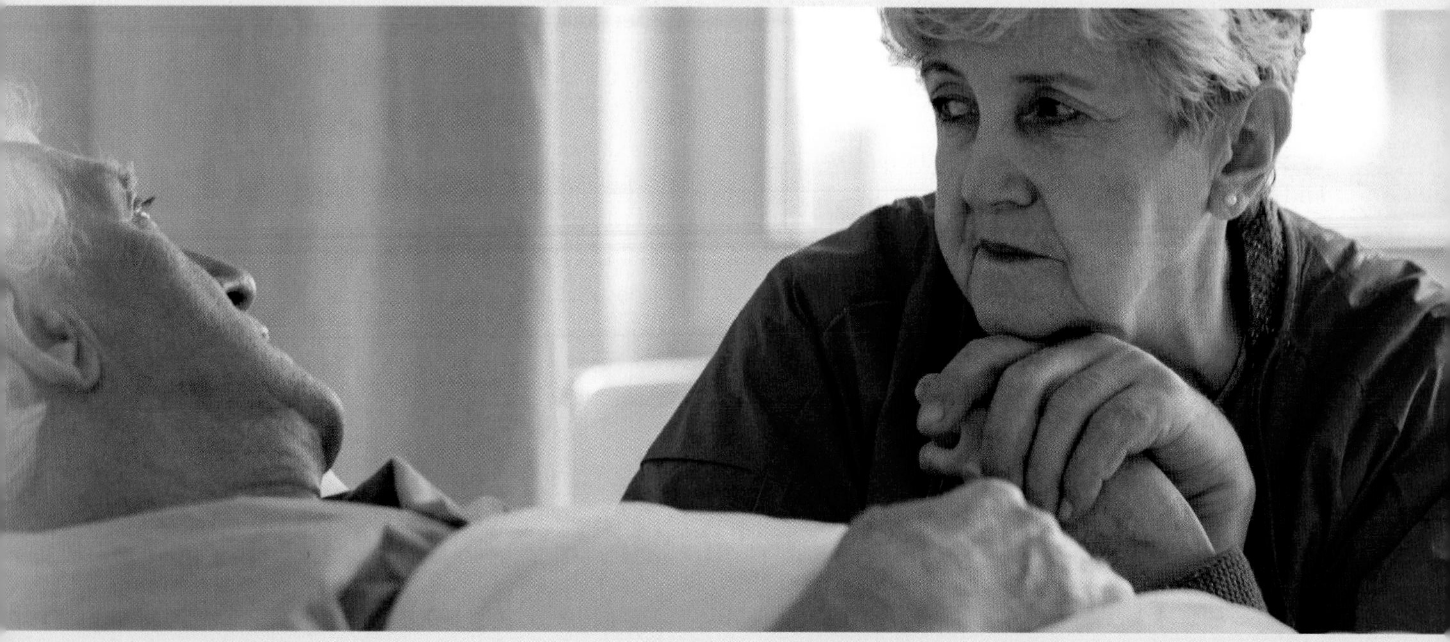

Chapter Review

Questions

1. By 2030, for each person receiving income security benefits, there will be only three working Canadians to support these benefits, What are the implications of this demographic shift for social welfare programs?
2. Briefly describe the history of income security for the elderly, beginning with the Old Age Pensions Act of 1927.
3. There is a concern that some of the income security gains that seniors have made may now be eroding. What is the evidence for this?
4. What are some of the particular issues faced by senior women in retirement? What can be done to alleviate these concerns?
5. There has been a shift away from DB pensions to DC plans. What are the disadvantages of this for employees and employers?
6. What policy steps can federal and provincial governments take today to ensure that seniors are secure in their retirement years?

Exploring Social Welfare

1. Explore the debates around mandatory retirement age. What do labour unions say about the issue, and how does this differ from the government's viewpoint?
2. Calculate your retirement year and the income security benefits you will likely be entitled to at the time. Or, if that is too far in the distance, do the same for a parent or older friend.
3. An example of a culturally appropriate and inclusive policy initiative aimed at facilitating a dignified and secure retirement for Canadian seniors is introduced at the end of this chapter. Read the policy overview provided, do some additional research on your own, then answer the "Questions for Reflection" at the end of the overview.

Websites

The Broadbent Institute
www.broadbentinstitute.ca
The Broadbent Institute champions change through the promotion of democracy, equality, sustainability, and the training of a new generation of leaders. The Institute is a non-partisan organization that brings attention to social democratic values that can help Canadians build a society that is the envy of the world. This chapter is based heavily on the author's analysis of the economic circumstances of Canadian seniors, which was released by the Broadbent Institute in 2015.

Resources for Seniors
www.seniors.gc.ca
This is the official federal government website addressing seniors' issues. Resources for Seniors provides access to a vast amount of web-based information and services across Canada. You can select your province and get up-to-date information. There are sections on finances and pensions that provide information on income security. There is also information on federal government programs related to seniors, such as combatting elder abuse and healthy living initiatives for seniors.

CARP: Canada's Association for the Fifty-Plus
www.carp.ca
Originally known as the Canadian Association for Retired Persons, CARP is an advocacy group dedicated to improving the quality of life for Canadians as they age. With an expansive membership and strong financial support, CARP presents itself as an independent voice for seniors in Canada.

The Welfare and Well-Being of Persons with Disabilities

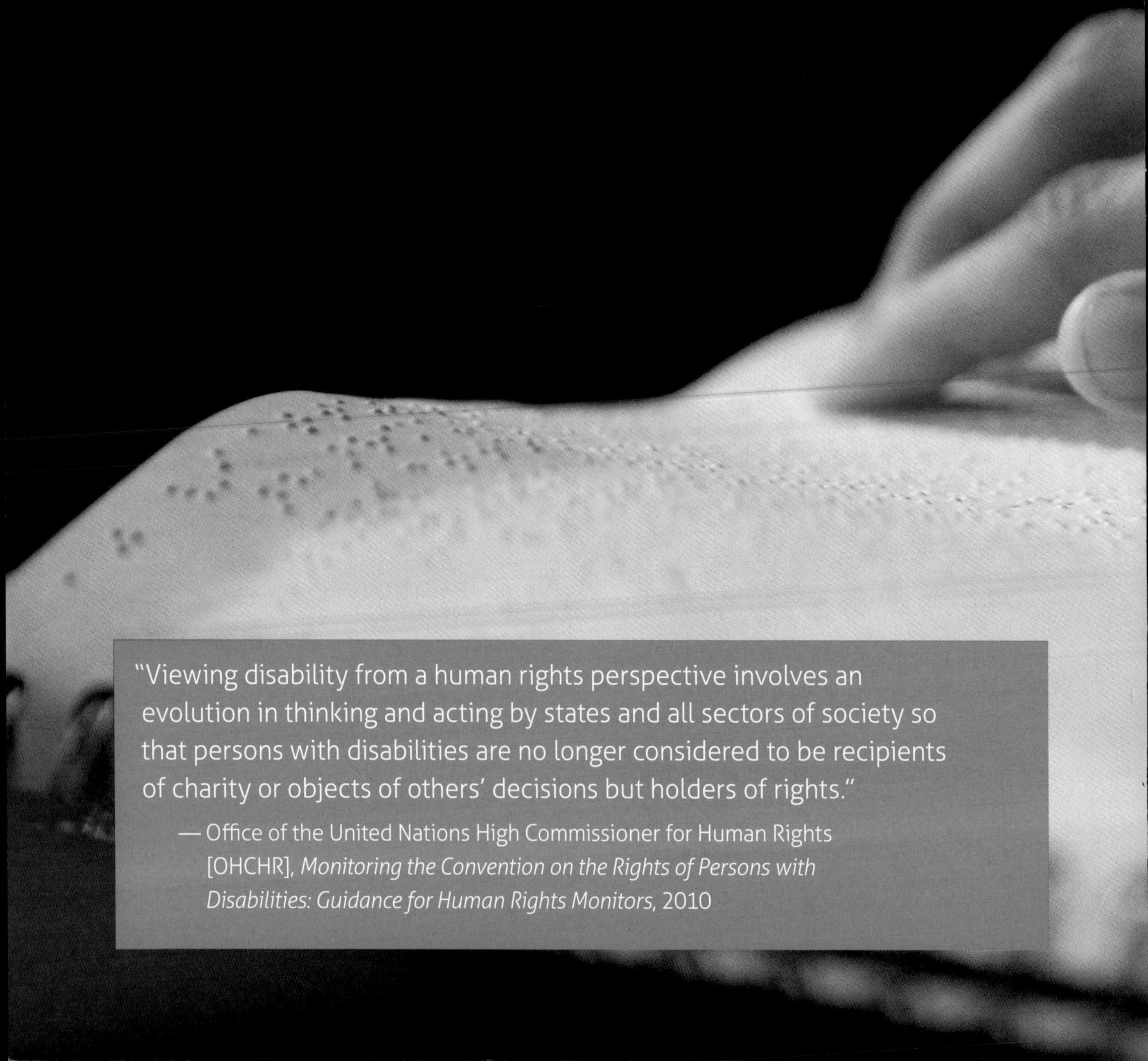

"Viewing disability from a human rights perspective involves an evolution in thinking and acting by states and all sectors of society so that persons with disabilities are no longer considered to be recipients of charity or objects of others' decisions but holders of rights."

— Office of the United Nations High Commissioner for Human Rights [OHCHR], *Monitoring the Convention on the Rights of Persons with Disabilities: Guidance for Human Rights Monitors*, 2010

Roy Hanes

11 Accessibility and Inclusion as a Human Right

Governments must ensure affordable, quality, and accessible services for people with disabilities.

Disability is a universal category that reflects the historical, cultural, religious, and economic structures of a particular society; what is defined as a disability in one society may not be defined as such in another society. The United Nations Convention on the Rights of People with Disabilities recognizes this diversity and draws attention to the fluidity of disability across the globe. It connects individual impairment to broader social arrangements that contribute to the disablement of people with impairments.

To be effective and helpful, social workers must take a holistic perspective to understand the complexities of the context in which people with disabilities live. Worldwide, most societies are designed for and by nondisabled persons; hence, the values, beliefs, structures, and systems designed to assist able-bodied persons create barriers for people with impairments. It is these barriers that disable people with impairments (UNCPR, Hanes in Robertson & Larsen, 2016).

Persons with disabilities are more likely to experience adverse socio-economic outcomes than those without disabilities. This includes less education, poorer health outcomes, lower levels of employment, and higher rates of poverty.

Accessibility and Inclusion as a Human Right

For many decades, disability advocates in Canada have argued for greater inclusion and as a result provincial, territorial, and federal governments have developed or are in the process of developing legislation that promotes greater rights and accessibility for people with disabilities. This chapter highlights the social welfare issues and challenges to ensuring full accessibility for all people.

After completing this chapter, you should be able to:

- Understand disabilities and the distribution of disabilities by age group;
- Review the history of services for people with disabilities;
- Describe the main theories for explaining disability;
- Identify the importance of the disability rights movement;
- Describe the various ways in which people with disabilities are stigmatized and stereotyped; and
- Identify federal, provincial, and territorial services and supports for people with disabilities, including income security programs.

Key Concepts

- Canadian Survey on Disability, 2017
- Medical model of disability
- Social and human rights model of disability
- Biopsychosocial model of disability
- Structural model of disability
- Stigma
- Accessible Canada Act, 2019
- Independent Living Movement (ILM)
- Council of Canadians with Disabilities (CCD)
- Immigration and Refugee Protection Act, 2001
- United Nations Declaration on the Rights of Disabled Persons

11.1 What Is a Disability?

In the early twentieth century, terms such as "crippled," "mental defect," "physical defect," "idiot," and "imbecile" were widely used to describe a person with a disability. The term "handicapped" was widely used in the mid-1900s but was replaced by the term "disability" in the 1990s. Nevertheless, even today, many social welfare programs for persons with disabilities can be traced directly to antiquated ideas dating back to the English Poor Laws of 1601. These laws defined people with disabilities as "[l]epers, bedridden creatures, people impotent to serve and people above the age of sixty-five" (Stone, 1984).

The Poor Laws were created, essentially, to separate the "deserving poor" from the "non-deserving poor" so that assistance could be provided only to those who were deemed deserving. The determination was often the responsibility of the local magistrate, who then provided legal documentation so that disabled persons could legally beg for alms or for food.

"We call on the Government of Canada to deliver a CDB that provides an adequate standard of living that recognizes the extra disability costs experienced by members of the disability community,"

Heather Walkus, Vice-Chair, Council of Canadians with Disabilities.

Needs and Means Tests

In the post–World War I period, with the rise of modern scientific medicine, the creation of workers' compensation laws, and private life insurance, physicians were gradually given more authority to determine disability. They judged whether a person with a disability would gain access to social assistance, charitable aid, compensation for work-related injuries, or personal claims from insurance.

After World War II, with the expansion of the welfare state, provincial and federal governments increasingly provided funding and assistance for people with disabilities. During this period, physicians secured control over the diagnosis of disability and, through this "medical model," became the official gatekeepers.

By the 1960s, most provinces provided some form of welfare assistance or pension for persons with disabilities. The assistance is non-contributory — meaning that people in need are provided with assistance whether or not they have paid into a specific pension plan.

Assistance programs for people with disabilities vary across provinces, but most jurisdictions assess applicants according to their "needs and means."

- **Needs assessment.** Needs assessment investigates the needs of the individual (housing, support care, equipment, personal care supplies, etc.).
- **Means assessment.** Means assessment examines the actual funding that the individual has available to pay for assessed needs (income, pension, trust funds, savings, investments, etc.).

Wherever possible, persons with disabilities are expected to pay for (or contribute to) the cost of equipment, support services, and the like. If the individual has no "means," then they may be eligible for financial assistance. To be eligible for these programs, one must first be designated as a "person with a disability (PWD)."

Keeping in Step with a More Inclusive Canada

Defining the term "disability," identifying the number of persons with disabilities, and collecting data on what impedes their full participation in society has evolved over the years. For example, the World Health Organization (WHO) draws a distinction between "impairment" and "disability." WHO (2019) defines these terms as:

- **Disabilities.** This is an umbrella term, covering impairment, activity limitations, and participation restrictions.
  - **Impairment.** This refers to a problem in body function or structure.
  - **Activity limitation.** This refers to a difficulty encountered by an individual in executing a task or actions.
  - **Participation restriction.** This refers to a problem experienced by an individual in involvement in life situations.

According to the World Health Organization,

> Disability is thus not just a health problem. It is a complex phenomenon, reflecting the interaction between features of a person's body and features of the society in which he or she lives. Overcoming the difficulties faced by people with disabilities requires interventions to remove environmental and social barriers.

Today, while no single definition is used throughout Canada, the federal government defines the term as follows:

> Disability is a complex phenomenon, reflecting an interaction between features of a person's body and mind and features of the society in which they live. A disability can occur at any time in a person's life; some people are born with a disability, while others develop a disability later in life. It can be permanent, temporary or episodic. Disability can steadily worsen, remain the same, or improve. It can be very mild to very severe. It can be the cause, as well as the result, of disease, illness, injury, or substance abuse. (Human Resources and Skills Development Canada, 2013)

In this sense, a disability is a functional limitation or restriction of an individual's ability to perform an activity. However, it is also recognized that the person always comes first and the disability comes second — that is, the person is always more important than their disability.

Today, while the term "disability" is widely and frequently used, policymakers and various levels of government are generally moving to a more inclusive understanding of the term, one that centres on the structural issues associated with inclusion and exclusion, rather than focusing on the impairment itself. This shift is occurring throughout Canadian society. For example, both the federal government and provincial governments are enacting "Accessible Acts" and municipalities are designating "Accessible Parking" areas.

Nothing About Us Without Us

A core principle underlying the UN Convention on the Rights of Persons with Disabilities is captured in the phrase "Nothing About Us Without Us."

Accordingly, the Council of Canadians with Disabilities (CCD) is asking the Government of Canada for a commitment to include the meaningful involvement of people with disabilities in the development of the Canadian Disability Benefit, the employment strategy for people with disabilities, and the process for determining eligibility for disability programs and services.

The Canadian Survey on Disability, 2017

The Canadian Survey on Disability is now the main source of data on disabilities for those aged 15 years and over. For the 2017 survey, new questions were designed to ensure better overall coverage of persons with disabilities, especially for persons with disability types that are less visible, such as mental health–related and cognitive disabilities (Statistics Canada, 2017).

An estimated one in five Canadians (or 6.2 million) aged 15 years and over have one or more disabilities that limit them in their daily activities. For many of these Canadians, challenges and obstacles in their day-to-day lives may limit their full participation in society. Understanding the challenges faced by persons with disabilities in their personal, employment, or economic situations helps inform government policy.

Prevalence and Severity of Disability

The prevalence of disabilities varies at different stages of life. Common to all age groups, however, is the prominence of pain-related disabilities, which are the most prevalent disability type among working-age adults and seniors, and the third most prevalent disability type among youth.

The most common disability types among seniors are pain, mobility, and flexibility — each affecting about one-quarter of all seniors, often in combination. Among working-age adults, 14% have a pain-related disability, and roughly half that percentage has a disability related to mental health, flexibility, or mobility (and often in combination). Mental health–related disabilities (7%) ranked fourth in prevalence among disability types for persons aged 15 years and over, and represented just over 2 million Canadians. In fact, among youth, mental health–related (8%) was the most common type of disability, followed by learning (6%) and pain-related disabilities (4%).

The prevalence of disabilities among Canadians tends to increase with age. However, more than 540,000 youths aged 15 to 24 years (13%) have one or more disabilities. This compares with 20% or 3.7 million working-age adults (25 to 64 years), and 38% or 2 million seniors aged 65 and over. Women (24%) are more likely to have a disability than men (20%) and this is the case across all age groups.

Most Canadians with a disability have more than one type of disability. Of the 6.2 million Canadians aged 15 years and over with disabilities, 29% have one type of disability, 38% have two or three disabilities, and 33% have four or more.

The severity of the disability is a major factor in the lives of those with disabilities. Persons with more severe disabilities have lower rates of employment, lower income (even when employed full-year and full-time), and a greater likelihood of living in poverty anywhere in Canada. In 2017, more than 4 in 10 Canadians with disabilities had a severe or very severe disability (Statistics Canada, 2017).

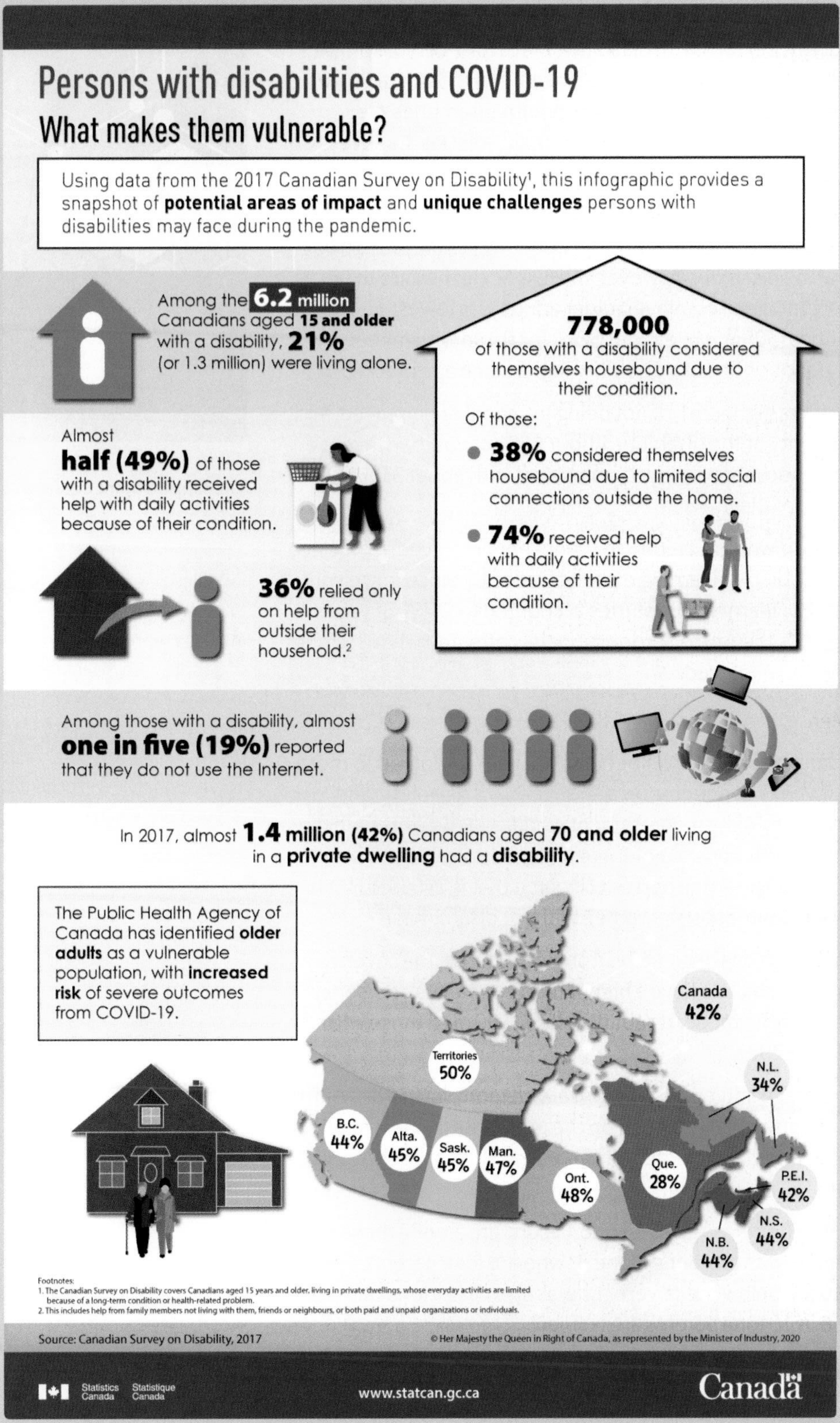

Figure 11.1: Disability in Canada during COVID–19

Just over one-fifth of the Canadian population has one or more disabilities. However, relatively little is known about their experiences during the COVID–19 pandemic. From June 23 to July 6, 2020, approximately 13,000 Canadians with long-term conditions or disabilities participated in an online questionnaire.

The survey reveals that persons with disabilities in Canada may be disproportionately impacted as they may be more likely to have underlying health conditions or to rely on outside caregivers or support to help with their daily lives.

Physical distancing measures to slow the spread of COVID–19 may also increase the overall vulnerability of people in Canada with disabilities.

Statistics Canada (2020, July 6). The vulnerability of Canadians with disabilities during the COVID–19 pandemic. *The Daily*. Statistics Canada.

Employment and Disability

According to the 2017 survey, persons with disabilities face lower employment rates, particularly Canadians with very severe disabilities, and those with lower levels of education. About 59% of working-age adults with disabilities are employed compared with around 80% of those without disabilities. As severity of disability increases, the percentage of those employed falls — from 76% among those with mild disabilities to 31% among those with very severe disabilities.

The presence of a disability does not preclude older adults (55 to 64 years) from working. The more severe the disability, however, the less likely they are to be employed. In fact, the percentage of employed older adults was lowest for those with more severe disabilities (30%), while it was 58% for those with milder disabilities and 67% for people without a disability in the same age bracket.

Youth with disabilities are at a higher risk of not being in school or employed, and this increases with the severity of the disability. About 15% of youth with milder disabilities are neither in school nor employed, compared with about 31% of youth with more severe disabilities.

Among youth with disabilities who are neither in school nor employed, 87% have a mental health–related disability, a learning disability, or both. Since those with mental health–related and/or learning disabilities accounted for 77% of youth with disabilities, this suggests they are disproportionately affected when it comes to being neither in school nor employed.

Poverty and Disability

Overall, persons with disabilities have lower personal income compared to those without disabilities and it varies depending on sex, severity of disability, and household living arrangements. Almost one-third of working-age adults with more severe disabilities live in poverty. For example, women aged 25 to 64 years with milder disabilities have median after-tax personal income that is 24% less than their male counterparts and 13% less than women without disabilities.

Among working-age adults, personal income is strongly related to the severity of disability. Those with no disabilities have a higher median after-tax personal income ($39,000) than those with milder disabilities ($34,300) and those with more severe disabilities ($19,200).

In addition, among working-age adults, 28% of those with more severe disabilities live below Canada's official poverty line (based on the Market Basket Measure), compared with 14% of those with milder disabilities and 10% of those without disabilities.

The highest rates of poverty (for those aged 15 to 64 years) are among those with more severe disabilities who are living alone or who are lone parents. For those living alone, 6 in 10 are below the poverty line, as are 4 in 10 lone parents. Regardless of disability, 8 in 10 lone parents are women.

The Employment Equity Act

The Employment Equity Act requires federal jurisdiction employers to eliminate barriers and increase representation of people with disabilities in the workforce. This also calls for employers to provide reasonable accommodations in order to remove barriers.

A Basic Income Plan for Canadians with Severe Disabilities

Today, billions of dollars are spent on a tangled system of social and economic benefits, yet many working-age Canadians with disabilities end up poor and trapped on welfare — "the dead-end default program of last resort." While there has been progress since the landmark Obstacles Report was released nearly 40 years ago by the parliamentary Special Committee on the Disabled and the Handicapped, there has been almost no improvement at all in the area of income security for persons with disabilities. What appears to be occurring is the "welfareization of disability," where social assistance becomes the main income support system for people with disabilities.

In a more recent report commissioned by the Canadian Association for Community Living and the Council of Canadians with Disabilities, the Caledon Institute outlines what is needed: a basic income plan for Canadians with severe disabilities (Mendelson et al., 2010). The basic income would offset the cost of disability to all who need it and establish a reformed system of support and services for persons with disabilities.

The basic income program would resemble the Guaranteed Income Supplement for low-income seniors. It would replace provincial/territorial social assistance for most working-age persons with severe disabilities. It would convert the existing non-refundable Disability Tax Credit into a refundable Disability Tax Credit and thereby would improve the situation of low-income persons with disabilities. With refundable tax credits, even if you don't owe any tax, the total amount of your refundable tax credits will result in a tax refund.

Figure 11.2

Comparison of Disability Benefit Expenditures, 2005–2006 and 2010–2011

Stapleton, J., Tweddle, A., & Gibson, K. (2013). *What is happening to disability income systems in Canada? Insights and proposals for further research.* Ottawa, ON: Council of Canadians with Disabilities.

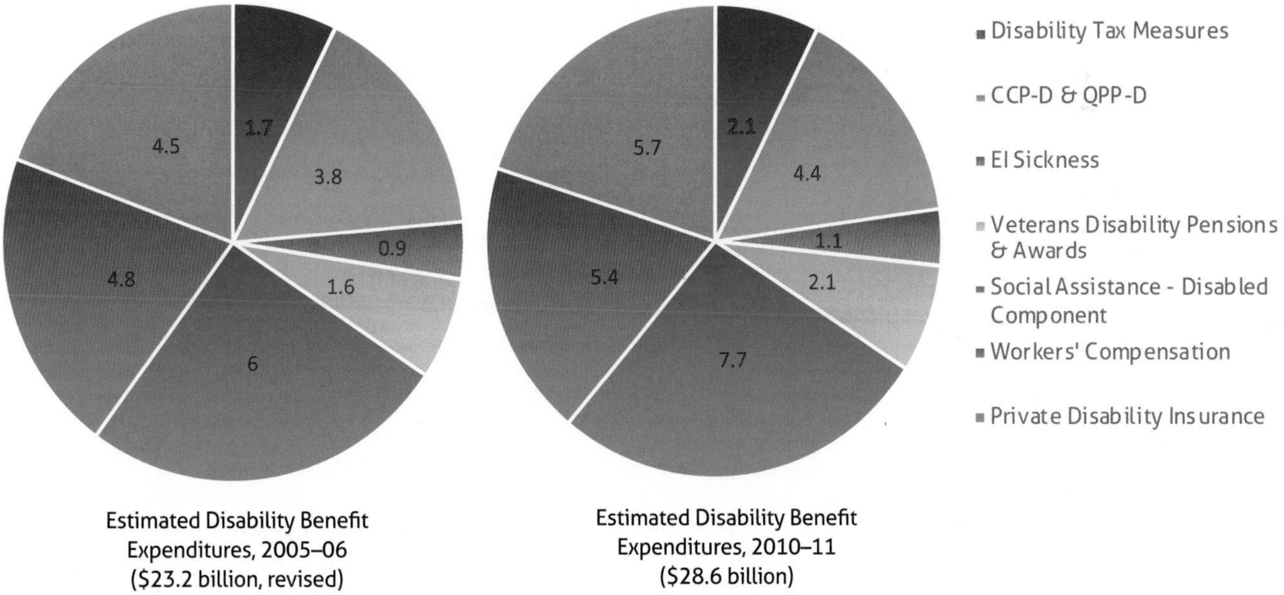

Social Welfare in Perspective

A World Where No One Is Left Behind

Fact Sheet on Persons with Disabilities

Despite millions of people escaping poverty over the last 20 years, the global situation and well-being of the majority of people with disabilities has not improved.

National disability strategies and action plans can play an important role in coordinating and guiding the implementation of the Convention on the Rights of Persons with Disabilities (CRPD) by highlighting areas to prioritize at the national level.

Disability strategies and action plans typically present measures and milestones that a country intends to reach. They also contribute toward achieving the Sustainable Development Goals (SDGs) and 2030 Agenda for Sustainable Development.

The World's Largest Minority

Around 15% of the world's population, or an estimated 1 billion people, live with disabilities. According to the World Health Organization, they are the world's largest minority (WHO, 2018).

This figure is increasing through population growth, medical advances, and the aging process, says the World Health Organization. In countries with life expectancies over 70 years, individuals spend on average about eight years, or 11.5% of their lifespan, living with disabilities, according to Disabled World, an independent health and disability news source (Disabled World, 2019).

Eighty percent of persons with disabilities live in developing countries, according to the UN Development Programme and the World Health Organization (WHO, 2018).

Disability rates are significantly higher among groups with lower educational attainment in the countries of the Organisation for Economic Co-operation and Development (OECD). On average, 19% of less educated people have disabilities, compared to 11% among the better educated (WHO, 2018).

Women, Youth, and the Poor Are Vulnerable

In most OECD countries, women report higher incidences of disability than men. Women with disabilities are recognized to be multi-disadvantaged, insofar as they experience exclusion on account of their gender and disability.

Women and girls with disabilities are also particularly vulnerable to abuse. A small 2004 survey in Orissa, India, found that virtually all of the women and girls with disabilities were beaten at home, 25% of women with intellectual disabilities had been raped, and 6% of women with disabilities had been forcibly sterilized.

According to UNICEF estimates, 30% of street youths have some kind of disability (UNICEF, 2013). Ninety percent of children with disabilities in developing countries do not attend school, says UNESCO (UNESCO, 2009).

Unemployment among persons with disabilities is as high as 80% in some countries.

Violence against Persons with Disabilities

In some countries, up to a quarter of disabilities result from injuries and violence (WHO, 2018). For every child killed in warfare, three are injured and acquire a permanent form of disability (Disabled World, 2019)

According to a British study in 2004, persons with disabilities are more likely to be victims of violence or rape. They are also less likely to obtain police intervention, legal protection, or preventive care (Simmons & Dodd, 2003). Research indicates that violence against children with disabilities occurs at annual rates at least 1.7 times greater than for their peers without disabilities (Hughes et al., 2012).

Intersecting and Compounding Problems

People with disabilities face intersecting and compounding forms of discrimination on the grounds of gender, sexuality, impairment type, age, race, ethnicity, religion or belief, and location — all of which contribute to disability-related exclusion.

Women and girls, children and youth, older people, and Indigenous people with disabilities experience a range of complex structural and institutional barriers and face multiple exclusions.

Women and girls, in particular, are disproportionately affected by disability. It is estimated that 19% of women across the world have a disability, compared to 12% of men (United Nations, 2017). Evidence across many indicators (health, sexual and reproductive health and rights, water and sanitation, and gender-based violence) demonstrates that women and girls with disabilities are marginalized and discriminated against for their gender as well as for their disability.

There has been far too little global progress to deliver on the sustainability goals and implement the UN's Convention. Business as usual will not achieve the transformational change that is needed.

The world must do more to address this and must do more to uphold the fundamental rights of all citizens, including women, girls, men, and boys with disabilities.

Adapted by the author from: United Nations (n.d.). *Fact sheet on persons with disabilities.* Department of Economic and Social Affairs. New York, NY: United Nations. Retrieved from: https://www.un.org/development/desa/disabilities/resources/factsheet-on-persons-with-disabilities.html

11.2 Approaches to Disability: Four Models

The shift to defining disability in terms of human rights instead of medical need was influenced not only by the disability rights movement but also by the development of disability theories that challenged the dominant medical model of disability. The pre-eminent British disability advocate and theorist Michael Oliver coined the terms "personal tragedy theory" and "social oppression theory" of disability to describe the differences between a medical model of disability and a socio-political model of disability (Oliver, 1990).

- The medical model of disability has its roots in rehabilitation medicine, where the focus of the intervention is on the individual. It focuses on disability as an "impairment" and a "personal tragedy" and the need of the individual to adapt or otherwise to fit within mainstream society as much as possible.
- The socio-political model, on the other hand, is concerned with the broader social and political context and the need for society as a whole to adapt and to address the needs of persons with a disability. This model includes the social and human rights model, biopsychosocial model, and structural model.

"We know from our past experiences if we are not at the table there will be negative unintended impacts, due to a lack of awareness of the complexities of how the mix of provincial and federal programs interact with each other."

Jewelles Smith, Past Chair, Council of Canadians with Disabilities.

The Medical Model of Disability

From the perspective of the **medical model of disability**, a disabling condition is viewed as an unfortunate life event where some form of professional and medical assistance is required (Oliver, 1990). This theory holds that disability is primarily a medical problem. The various forms of interventions are therefore introduced as a means of "curing" or "fixing" the individual.

According to this "personal tragedy" approach to disability, persons who become disabled, as well as their loved ones, go through various stages of psychological and emotional adjustment before they can accept themselves or their loved ones as disabled. Much of the literature pertaining to the impact of disability on the individual and on the family focuses primarily on the stages of adjustment to the disability.

Oliver (1996) argues that many of these explanations of adjustment to disability are based on psychological theories about coping with death and dying — stages of shock, denial, grief, loss, reconciliation, and acceptance. Such an approach is usually based on an interpretation of coping that involves the following assumptions:

- An individual or family must move sequentially through the coping stages to become fully adjusted.
- There is but one path through the sequence.
- An individual can be placed clearly in one stage or another by analyzing their behaviour.
- There is an optimal length of time for staying in each stage.

The Social and Human Rights Models of Disability

The social and human rights model of disability, by contrast, holds that the problems faced by people with disabilities are not the result of physical impairments alone, but also result from the social and political inequality between people with and without disabilities (Oliver, 1990). Disability Rights Promotion International (DRPI), an organization that seeks to establish international monitoring of human rights of people with disabilities, argues that:

> A human rights approach to disability acknowledges that people with disabilities are rights holders and that social structures and policies restricting or ignoring the rights of people with disabilities often lead to discrimination and exclusion.

This model of disability challenges the widely held view that disability is an individual physical or mental problem requiring individual treatment and individual solutions. Instead, external factors — such as the lack of employment opportunities, affordable housing, and accessible transportation as well as the presence of negative stereotypes and prejudicial attitudes — are identified as the primary cause of problems for people with disabilities. Disability is seen as "a form of social oppression involving the social imposition of restrictions of activity on people with impairment and the socially engendered undermining of their psycho-emotional well-being" (Thomas, 1999).

Because many social problems stem from structural and attitudinal barriers, social and political changes are required if these obstacles are to be overcome. Such systemic change requires the incorporation of a human rights focus for addressing the needs of people with disabilities. The social model has had demonstrable success for the disability movement in challenging discrimination, stigma, and marginalization. This is because it links human rights, civil rights, and political activism in pursuit of social change, placing the responsibilities on the institutions of society at large. The essential argument is that if dependency were not created, then it would disappear. It challenges the medicalization of disabled people and looks toward the social determinants of disability.

In the 1990s, the disability rights movement adopted the saying "Nothing about us without us" — that no policy should be decided by anyone without the full and direct participation of those whom the policy affects. The social and human rights model has taken different forms in different countries, depending on the political context. Common to all forms of the model, however, is the idea of persons with disabilities being active participants in shaping their own future with the full backing and support of the society in which they live.

The social and human rights model is clearly a reaction to the limitations of the medical model of disability. The latter sees disability as a problem of the individual and their bodies and resolvable by intervention by medical experts and other professionals. For the advocates of the social and human rights model, disability is a social problem caused by social oppression and prejudice rather than by impairments. "Impairments" are defective limbs or bodily functions, whereas "disability" is the exclusion from which persons with impairment suffer.

Terry Fox

In November 2004, Terry Fox was voted the second greatest Canadian of all time (after Tommy Douglas who led the fight for public health care in Canada). The nationwide contest was organized by CBC, with over 1.2 million votes being cast.

Terry Fox was an 18-year-old kinesiology student at Simon Fraser University and a member its basketball team in 1977 when he was diagnosed with bone cancer. His right leg was amputated above the knee, and he underwent chemotherapy.

While in hospital, Terry decided to run across Canada to raise money for cancer research. Since Terry's death in 1981, the Terry Fox Foundation has raised hundreds of million dollars for cancer research.

The Biopsychosocial Model of Disability

The medical and human rights models are both valid but are incomplete on their own. The latest international classification from the World Health Organization (WHO) is based on a **biopsychosocial model of disability**. This approach integrates the medical and human rights models to provide a more comprehensive framework for measuring and addressing disability at both individual and population levels.

The World Health Organization's International Classification of Functioning, Disability and Health (ICF) is part of the WHO family of international classifications, the best-known of which is the ICD-10 (the International Statistical Classification of Diseases and Related Health Problems). ICD-10 is a framework for the classification of diseases, disorders, and other health conditions. The ICF classifies functioning and disability associated with health conditions. The ICD-10 and ICF are thus complementary. The ICF creates a broader and more meaningful picture of the experience of health of individuals and populations. It was officially endorsed by all 191 WHO member states in the Fifty-fourth World Health Assembly on May 22, 2001 as the international standard to describe and measure health and disability.

The WHO approach to disability represented by the ICF is a shift in thinking—instead of emphasizing people's disabilities, the focus is more broadly on one's level of health. In other models, disability began where health ended; once you were disabled, you where in a separate category. With the biopsychosocial model, the emphasis is on health and functioning, rather than narrowly on disability. In this sense, the ICF is a more comprehensive tool for measuring functioning in society, no matter what the reason for one's impairments.

The biopsychosocial model of disability acknowledges that every human being can experience a decline in their health and thereby experience some disability — in other words, disability is not something that happens to only a minority of people. By shifting the focus from cause to impact, the ICF places all health conditions on an equal footing, allowing them to be compared using a common metric. Disability and functioning are viewed as outcomes of interactions among diseases, disorders, injuries, and contextual factors. Among contextual factors are social attitudes, legal and social structures, climate and terrain, and so forth as well as personal factors such as gender, age, coping styles, social background, education, life experiences, and other factors that influence how disability is experienced by an individual.

The International Classification of Functioning, Disability and Health identifies three levels of human functioning—(1) functioning at the level of the body or body part, (2) functioning at the level of the whole person, and (3) functioning at the level of the whole person in a social context.

Disability is viewed as dysfunction at one or more of these levels: impairments, activity limitations, and participation restrictions. The ICF is designed to be relevant across cultures as well as age groups and genders.

Canadian Disability Policy Alliance

The Canadian Disability Policy Alliance is a national collaboration of disability researchers, advocates, and policymakers aimed at creating and mobilizing knowledge to enhance disability policy in Canada. Its goals are as follows:

- **Knowledge Creation**
  To synthesize evidence and, where necessary, generate new knowledge regarding disability policy in Canada and its impact on the lives of people with disabilities
- **Knowledge Dissemination**
  To share knowledge with policymakers and other stakeholders to enhance accessibility and inclusion for people with disabilities
- **Training and Development**
  To develop capacity in the areas of policy analysis, disability studies, and collaborative research among students, staff, partners associated with the CDPA

The Structural Model of Disability

The structural model of disability builds on the earlier models and is designed to assist social workers in their daily practice (Hanes, 2016). While the medical, social and human rights, and biopsychosocial models are all useful in order to assess disability, they do not actually offer direction for social workers in their daily interactions with clients. The structural model incorporates personal and systemic assessment and intervention; it also encourages practitioners to work with clients and their families at the personal level and with organizations and advocates to bring about broader societal change (Moreau, 1979).

The structural model recognizes that individual and family counselling and support, while certainly necessary, often can be limited in their impact because of systemic issues, such as lack of housing, inaccessible transportation, financial assistance, stigma, and discrimination. To be able to intervene effectively to resolve personal and family problems their clients face, a wider range of practice skills are need on the part of the practitioner. Social workers must incorporate advocacy skills and be involved in community organizing in order to bring about lasting social change. The structural model of disability combines the medical, social and human rights, and biopsychosocial models; in addition, it seeks to provide social workers with a wide range of practice skills that can help to bring about personal as well as social change. The desired outcomes are personal empowerment, independent living, and long-term solutions.

Table 11.1

Thinking about Disability: Contrasting Approaches

	Medical	Social and Human Rights	Biopsychosocial	Structural
Nature of the Problem	• Impairment	• Social oppression	• Impairment • Social oppression	• Impairment • Social oppression
Locus of Problem	• The individual	• Social environment	• The individual • Social environment	• The individual • Social environment
Solution to Problem	• Professional intervention (physician, therapist, occupational habilitation, etc.)	• Social change initiatives	• Professional intervention (physician, occupational rehabilitation, etc.) • Social change initiatives	• Connect the personal to the socio-political and engage in social work practice that incorporates individual and societal change through individual and family counselling, group work, and community organizing
Outcome	• Resolve physical impairment	• Remove institutional barriers	• Resolve physical impairment • Remove institutional barriers	• Assist people to cope with the onset of disability through individual, family, and group counselling • Remove structural and attitudinal barriers • Support societal change and personal empowerment

Social Welfare in Perspective

Combatting Stigma and Ableism

Stereotypes Are Divisive

People with disabilities are sensitive to signs of stigmatization; building collaborative and respectful partnership and supporting the person as a whole enhance social integration.

It is widely believed that when people acquire an illness or a physical or sensory impairment, whether at birth or during their lifetime, the individual and family members go through a long period of grieving. Many losses are associated with the onset of a disabling condition; however, many people adjust and their adjustment has more to do who they were, and what resources they had prior to the onset, than with the severity of the impairment itself.

A common stereotype is that people with disabilities are psychologically damaged in some way. This stems from the belief that there is an interconnection between the physical, mental, and emotional aspects of the human body. Therefore, it is falsely assumed that if there is damage to one aspect of the system (physical disability) then there would necessarily be damage to the emotional and mental aspects as well. Of course, this is not necessarily the case.

Stereotyping

In most Western industrialized societies, there is a growing cultural emphasis on the "body beautiful." Physical attractiveness, sexuality, and desirability have become a valued cultural norm.

People with disabilities often do not meet cultural standards of physical attractiveness, and this contributes to the stigma of disability: that to have a disability is to be undesirable and unlovable.

For persons with disabilities, stigma has implications for developing new friendships and intimate relations, socializing with others, and engaging in communities and recreational activities. Stigma can also affect relationships between service users and service providers. Health care providers need to be allies with service users and help reduce the impact of stigma.

For people with disabilities, stigma can be a major barrier to participation. The Rehabilitation Research & Training Center at the University of Washington (2016) categorizes some of these barriers as follows:

- **Social Avoidance.** After developing a disability, people with disabilities may be left out of social activities or find that friends become more distant. Others may be hesitant to make eye contact or start a conversation.
- **Stereotyping.** People with disabilities may be presumed to be helpless, unable to care for themselves, or unable to make their own decisions. People with one disability, such as a speech impairment, may be presumed to have other disabilities they don't have, such as an intellectual disability.
- **Discrimination.** People with disabilities may be denied jobs, housing, or other opportunities due to false assumptions or stereotypes about disabilities. This still occurs today, despite disability rights laws.
- **Condescension.** People with disabilities may be coddled or over-protected due to a false perception that they are helpless.
- **Blaming.** People may be blamed for their disability or accused of causing their own impairment or using their disability to gain unfair benefits.
- **Internalization.** Because of social pressure, people with disabilities may themselves adopt negative beliefs about their disability and feel ashamed or embarrassed about it.
- **Hate Crimes and Violence.** People with disabilities may be targeted by hate crimes. They are more likely to be victims of physical or sexual violence.

Blaming the Victim

Sometimes the person with the disability is portrayed as deserving the impairment.

An example might be a person who became disabled as a consequence of a particular lifestyle — there tends to be little public sympathy for adults who have disabling conditions because of drug use, prostitution, or unprotected sex. Also, congenital disorders are often attributed to the risky or immoral behaviours of mothers during pregnancy. There are also examples portraying persons with disabilities as evil people in folklore, literature, TV programs, and movies.

Also, some people may feel uncomfortable and/or unsure of how to interact with people with disabilities. A good starting point is to use respectful terms when writing and speaking about issues that affect people with disabilities. Attitudes and language are the most difficult barriers to achieving equality, independence, and full participation in all aspects of Canadian society (Human Resources Development Canada, 2006).

Ableism

Students of social work and the health professions will be familiar with terms such as racism, sexism, and heterosexism, but they may be unfamiliar with the term "ableism." This is the belief in the superiority of people without disabilities. The term evolved from the persons with disabilities rights movements in the US and Britain during the 1960s and 1970s.

It is important to be aware of stigma in all its manifestations. The "PCS" acronym can be used to detect and combat the presence of ableism:

- **Personal prejudice.** Revulsion, avoidance, infantilization, condescension, and other forms of overt prejudice at the personal level
- **Cultural norms.** A negative image of being disabled (people without disabilities are valued more than those with disabilities)
- **Social division.** The many ways in which people with disabilities are kept out of the mainstream and marginalized because of structural and legal barriers

Words Matter

Human Resources and Skills Development Canada (2006) has developed some guidelines in the appropriate use of terminology. They are:

- A disability is a functional limitation or restriction of an individual's ability to perform an activity. The word "disabled" is an adjective, not a noun. People are not conditions. It is therefore preferable not to use the term "the disabled" but rather "people with disabilities."
- Avoid categorizing people with disabilities as either super-achievers or tragic figures. Choose words that are non-judgmental, non-emotional, and accurate. Avoid using "brave," "courageous," "inspirational," or other similar words to describe a person with a disability.
- Remember that the majority of people with disabilities have aspirations similar to those of the rest of the population, and that words and images should reflect their inclusion in society, except where social isolation is the focal point.
- Avoid references that cause discomfort, guilt, pity, or insult. Words like "suffers from," "stricken with," "afflicted by," "patient," "disease," or "sick" suggest constant pain and a sense of hopelessness. While this may be the case for some individuals, a disability is a condition that does not necessarily cause pain or require medical attention.
- Avoid words such as "burden," "incompetent," or "defective," which suggest that people with disabilities are inferior and should be excluded from activities generally available to people without disabilities.

11.3 The Early History of Services for People with Disabilities

At the time of Confederation, the federal government was primarily concerned with what the British North America Act identified as "peace, order, and good government." The federal government was less interested in issues such as health, education, and social relief — these were assigned to the provinces. As a result, provinces developed their own unique charitable relief programs (as well as schools and other institutions).

Because of these provincial differences, no universal support care programs were established for people with disabilities, and no comprehensive nationwide support care policy for people with disabilities exists in Canada to the present day (Hanes & Moscovitch, 2002).

Outdoor and Indoor Relief

Outdoor relief was a common form of assistance provided to persons with disabilities when their families could not take care of them. An early form of outdoor relief established in England, and later transported to British North America, was begging. Through the Poor Laws, the deserving poor, such as persons with disabilities, were given licence to beg.

As time passed, other forms of outdoor relief supplemented begging. When families could not provide for a family member (usually an elderly person or a person with a disability), these persons were housed in private homes. Funds to cover expenses for food, clothing, shelter, and medical care were often provided through municipal taxes, charitable organizations, and religious organizations. In essence, outdoor relief meant that persons with disabilities were cared for through non-institutional methods of relief and were more or less part of the community.

By the mid-nineteenth century, outdoor relief came to be seen as a mechanism that created rather than relieved dependency, and institutions such as asylums, poorhouses, and houses of industry began to replace the former methods of outdoor relief (Splane, 1965). The replacement of outdoor relief by indoor relief represented a significant shift in the philosophy regarding charitable relief.

There was a major shift in the public attitude toward social dependency and social relief as well, and the public's attitude toward the provision of relief changed. Persons with disabilities, who were once considered to be a part of the social order, were now viewed as nuisance populations. They were to be removed from society, isolated, and placed in segregated institutions. During this time, disability was often considered shameful, and many persons with disabilities were hidden away in their homes by their close family members. There are numerous examples of people with various forms of disabilities being hidden or kept at home in Canada, the US, and the UK throughout the nineteenth and twentieth centuries (Hanes, 1995).

Institutionalization of the Disabled Population

The social rejection of "defective" populations was so severe that many persons with disabilities were treated as common criminals and banned from the streets of many cities. Many were charged under vagrancy laws and even sent to jail. Many of those who were not sent to jail were sent to a local poorhouse, to a house of industry, or to an asylum. Provincial governments were reluctant to fund support programs for dependent populations, including people with disabilities, and very coercive means were used to provide for the relief of dependent populations (Hanes, 1995).

By the mid-twentieth century, many provinces had "special" residential schools for blind and deaf children and adolescents. Provincial institutions were established for people with psychiatric disabilities and, in many provinces, there were institutions for people with developmental disabilities. Specialized hospitals were established for many different disabled populations, including tuberculosis hospitals, orthopaedic hospitals, and rehabilitation hospitals.

The institutionalization of people with disabilities was so widespread that it became widely believed that this was the natural order of things (Bowe, 1978). This was to change only with the advancement of scientific medicine following World War I, when the disability category began to fall under the domain of the medical profession. Subsequently, medical professionals have made the decisions about the need for specialized care, income supports, pensions, educational supports, transportation supports, home care, and other benefits.

Photo: This provincial training school in Red Deer, Alberta, operated as an institution for mentally disabled children and adults from 1923 to 1977. Today, as the Michener Centre, it houses a service for persons with developmental disabilities, but the century-old facility has a shocking history, marked by eugenic practices like involuntary sterilization.

Rehabilitation Services

The establishment of rehabilitation services following World War II laid the foundation for the modern era of medical and social services for people with disabilities. Medical and social services were expanded to people with disabilities, including the establishment of special schools, training programs, sheltered workshops, summer camps, recreational programs, as well as the establishment of special trades and industries, and special hospitals and after-care facilities.

The post-WWII dominance of medical professionals over the lives of people with disabilities remained unchallenged until the 1970s, when the disability rights movement developed in Canada. The rise of disability rights organizations is closely linked to the rise of the consumer movement, the civil rights movement, the peace movement, the gay rights movement, and the women's movement of the late 1960s and the early 1970s.

Rather than be labelled "defective" or "handicapped," disability rights advocates argued that persons with disabilities should also be seen as members of a minority group. "Many persons with disabilities," Lex Frieden suggests, "considered themselves members of a minority group related not by colour or nationality but by functional limitation and similar need" (Frieden, 1980, p. 55).

The Canadian Charter of Rights and Freedoms

The Canadian Charter of Rights and Freedoms forms part of our constitution, which is the highest law in all of Canada.

The Charter protects a number of our rights and freedoms, including banning the discrimination of people with a mental or physical disability.

The Charter of Rights and Freedoms, 1982

The American Vocational Rehabilitation Act of 1973, which prohibited discrimination against people with disabilities, represents a pivotal point in the history of persons with disabilities. The Act states that

> No otherwise qualified handicapped individual in the United States as defined by Section 7 shall, solely by reason of his handicap, be excluded from participation in, be denied the benefits of, or be subject to discrimination under any program or activity receiving federal financial assistance.

In 1970, the Canadian government itself began to awaken to the realities of life with a disability and enacted the first law to give specific rights to people with disabilities, known as the Canadian Human Rights Act. The Act states that all Canadians have equal rights regardless of sex, race, nationality, and disability. This single step made all further advancement possible. Seven years later the Canadian Human Rights Act was passed, advancing the belief that all Canadian citizens should receive equal treatment. The law did not say much about what equal treatment should look like, but it was progress nevertheless.

Similar legislation was passed in Canada at both the provincial and territorial levels, and then in 1982, the rights of people with disabilities were fully enshrined in the Charter of Rights and Freedoms. The Canadian Charter of Rights and Freedoms is a part of the Canadian Constitution, which is a set of laws containing the basic rules about how our country operates. Section 15 of the Charter makes it clear that every individual in Canada — regardless of race, religion, national or ethnic origin, colour, sex, age or physical or mental disability — is to be considered equal.

National Strategy for the Integration of Persons with Disabilities (1991–1996)

In 1996, as part of a National Strategy for the Integration of Persons with Disabilities (1991–1996), the Federal Task Force on Disability Issues released its final report, *Equal Citizenship for Canadians with Disabilities: The Will to Act* (the Scott Report). The report was jointly commissioned by four federal ministers with policy responsibilities pertaining to disability issues: the Minister of Human Resources Development Canada, the Minister of Finance, the Minister of Justice, and the Minister of National Revenue (Government of Canada, 1996).

After public consultations across the country, the Scott Report made a number of recommendations pertaining to labour market integration, Indigenous people with disabilities, and income supports. It also called for a larger role for the federal government in disability policy and a national disability act for Canada.

The Scott Report was followed, in 1998, with the formation of the FPT Working Group on Disability Issues, which resulted in several additional landmark reports — *In Unison* in 1998 (HRDC, 1998); *Future Directions* in 1999 (HRDC, 1999); and *In Unison 2000* in 2000 (HRDC, 2000). In 2001, the Office of Disability Issues was created. The federal government also implemented the Multilateral Framework for Labour Market Agreements for Persons with Disabilities and initiated a series of bilateral agreements with provinces aimed at promoting employment for people with disabilities. In December 2004, the Working Group released its report, entitled *Supports and services for adults and children aged 5–14 with disabilities in Canada: An analysis of data on needs and gaps* (McColl et al., 2017).

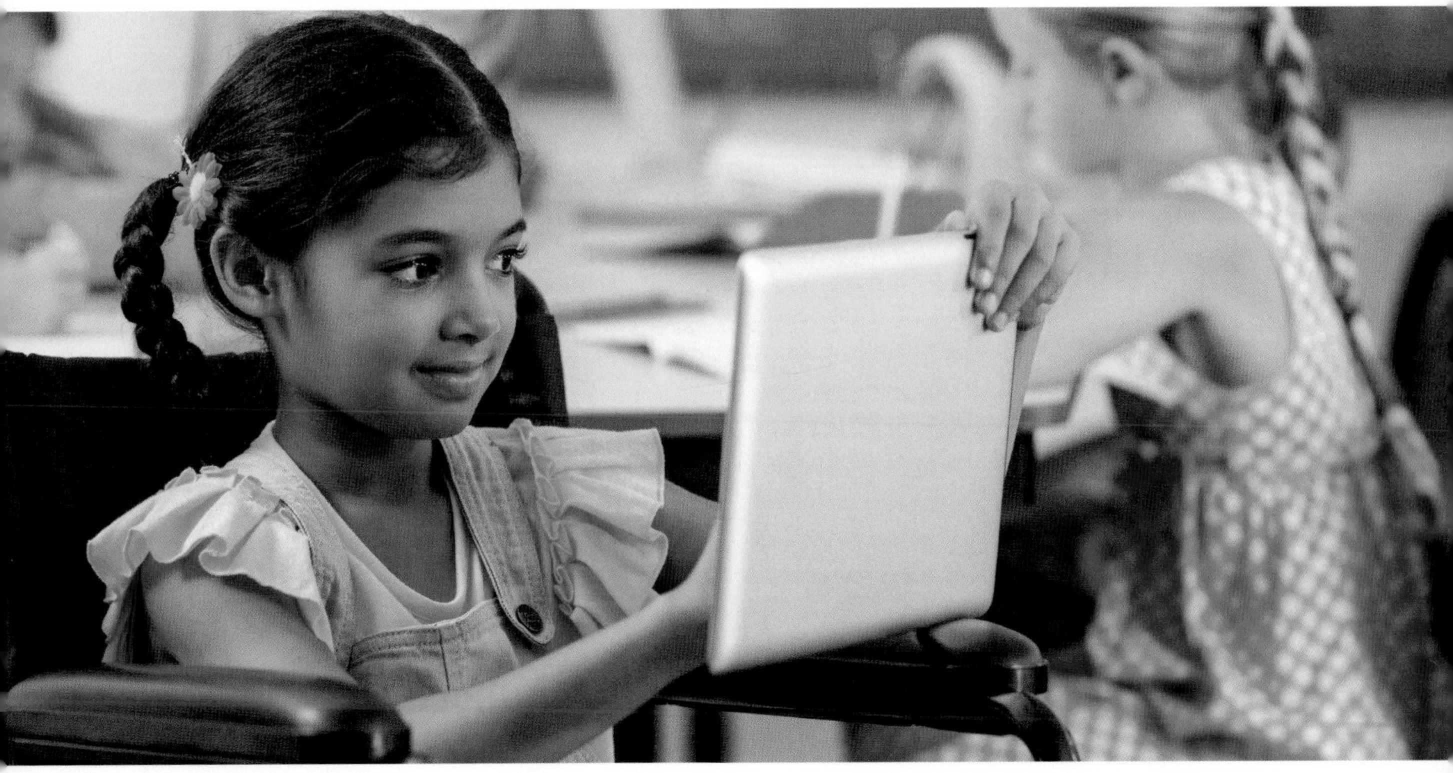

John Stapleton, Anne Tweddle, and Katie Gibson

Still Not Enough to Live On

Overview of Disability Benefits in Canada

Individuals with disabilities who do not qualify for any other public or private income security programs are left with provincially delivered social assistance programs.

Canada has eight major income support systems for persons with disabilities, as listed below.

The first five are work-triggered: that is, they are only available to those who have engaged in regular salaried or wage-paid work. These programs generally do not provide benefits to those with irregular, minimal, or contract employment, which are features of the world of work for many people with disabilities in Canada.

Social assistance disability income is not predicated on workforce attachment. The two tax measures (DTCs and RDSPs) are not work-triggered.

Employment Insurance Sickness Benefit

The Employment Insurance (EI) Sickness Benefit provides benefits for up to 15 weeks for temporary disabilities. To qualify, the worker must demonstrate that regular weekly earnings have decreased more than 40% due to sickness, injury, or quarantine, and that 600 insured hours have accumulated over the previous 52 weeks or since the worker's last claim.

The basic EI Sickness Benefit rate is 55% of a worker's average insured earnings, up to a yearly maximum insurable amount. Employment Insurance Sickness Benefits are reduced when beneficiaries receive support from workers' compensation, group insurance income, or accident compensation for lost wages.

CPP/QPP Disability Benefits

The federal government shares with the provinces jurisdiction over the Canada Pension Plan, while Québec administers the Québec Pension Plan. Employers and employees contribute to CPP or QPP, as do self-employed people.

Eligibility for the CPP-D is based on a stringent definition of disability: "severe and prolonged disability such that the person is incapable of gainful employment." The QPP-D requires a "severe and permanent disability"; the definition of severity includes an assessment of the individual's ability to engage in gainful work. Minimum contributions are also required. CPP-D is treated as a "first-payer" by private long-term disability plans, provincial social assistance programs, and provincial workers' compensation agencies. This means that any amount a person receives from CPP-D benefits will be deducted from the amount paid by the other programs. QPP-D is not necessarily treated as a first-payer.

Veterans' Disability Pensions and Awards

Veterans or members of the Canadian Armed Forces are eligible for a federal disability benefit administered by Veterans' Affairs Canada. Those eligible are Canadian Forces veterans, Merchant Navy veterans of the Second World War or Korean War, current or former members of the regular or reserve force, or civilians who served in close support of the Armed Forces during wartime.

Entitlement under the Veterans' Affairs program is based on adjudication of the attribution of disability to exposures arising from service in the Canadian Armed Forces and the severity of disability. The disability benefit is reduced if the recipient is receiving benefits from an employment-based group disability insurance plan.

Pursuant to the New Veterans Charter, which came into force on April 1, 2006, disabled veterans are now eligible for a disability award. This may be paid as a lump sum, annual payments, or a combination of the two.

Private Disability Insurance

Many employers offer employment-based short- and long-term disability plans. Typically, premiums are paid by employees and employers, although the share of premiums varies. Most plans provide a two-year period of benefits. Thereafter, benefits are only provided if the beneficiary is unable to perform any occupation for which the person is reasonably trained or educated. Plan benefits are scheduled at 50–75% of pre-disability income. Benefits are reduced dollar-for-dollar by any CPP-D or workers' compensation benefits.

Workers' Compensation

Provincial workers' compensation agencies administer income security benefits for wage losses arising from disabling disease or injury caused by work exposures. The federal government also administers a workers' compensation program for federal employees. Employers pay the premiums.

The large majority of recipients of provincial workers' compensation wage replacement benefits experience temporary disability. However, provincial workers' compensation agencies also administer benefits that acknowledge permanent impairment arising from a work-related injury or illness.

Social Assistance — Disabled Component

The social assistance programs of all provinces provide benefits to persons with a disability. In most provinces, eligibility for benefits is determined by a combination of the duration of disability and needs testing. Disability status is established by a doctor's certificate indicating the severity of disability, but the process and definition of disability for social assistance varies among provinces. Most provinces adjust benefits to account for earnings and other forms of income, including disability income security benefits.

Social assistance programs and the level of benefits paid vary between provinces. First Nations persons living on reserves receive assistance through Crown–Indigenous Relations and Northern Development Canada.

Disability Tax Credits

The primary tax measure related to disability is the Disability Tax Credit (DTC) administered by the Canada Revenue Agency. The DTC is available to persons with an impairment of physical or mental functions that has lasted or is expected to last one year, those who are blind, and those who are receiving life-sustaining therapy. This non-refundable tax credit is used to reduce the amount that the person owes on federal income tax.

Other tax measures include the Medical Expense Tax Credit, Caregiver Credit, Infirm Dependent Credit, Disability Supports Deduction, and the Refundable Medical Expense Supplement. Some of these tax measures are available to people without disabilities who have qualifying medical expenses.

Registered Disability Savings Plan

The Registered Disability Savings Plan was established in December 2008 and is administered by the Canada Revenue Agency. RDSPs are offered by financial institutions to Canadians who are eligible for the Disability Tax Credit and are under 60 years of age. The lifetime contribution limit is $200,000, but there is no annual limit. Contributions are not taxed as income. Investment income accumulates tax-free but is included in the beneficiary's income for tax purposes when paid out of the RDSP. The federal government pays a matching Canada Disability Savings Grant of up to $3,500 a year on contributions made into the RDSP and a Canada Disability Savings Bond of up to $1,000 a year into the RDSPs of low-income and modest-income Canadians, up to specified maximums.

Adapted from "What is happening to disability income systems in Canada? Insights and proposals for further research," by John Stapleton, Anne Tweddle, Katie Gibson. Ottawa, ON: Council of Canadians with Disabilities, 2013.

11.4 Accessibility Legislation

During their period in government (2006–2015), the Conservatives under Stephen Harper were not idle with respect to disability issues. However, in keeping with their overall policy outlook, their focus was on economic self-sufficiency rather than on citizenship and inclusion per se (Torjman, 2014).

The Harper government introduced a number of important initiatives, such as the Registered Disability Savings Plan (2006), the Accessibility Fund (2007), the tax-free Disability Savings Account, the Canada Student Grants for Students with Permanent Disabilities, and caregiver grants and expenses. In 2010, the federal government also contributed to the final stages of the UN Convention on the Rights of Persons with Disabilities, and ratified the agreement (McColl et al., 2017).

Human Rights

The Accessible Canada Act (ACA) builds on the Canadian Human Rights Act. It is the first national Canadian legislation on accessibility that affects all federal government departments and federally regulated agencies, including banks; interprovincial and international airlines, rail, road, and marine transportation providers; the broadcasting and telecommunications sectors; and the Canadian Forces and RCMP.

The Accessible Canada Act

In October of 2015, the newly elected Liberal government under Justin Trudeau affirmed its commitment to new legislation that would guarantee the rights of people with disabilities. The government appointed a Minister with the portfolio of disability issues and began consultations with Canadians about the type of legislation needed. In 2019, the new legislation — the Accessible Canada Act (An Act to ensure a barrier-free Canada) (ACA) — passed in both the House of Commons and the Senate of Canada with unanimous support from all parliamentarians.

The federal ACA prohibits discrimination based on disability in the federal public sector, as well as all federally regulated organizations. It covers federally regulated sectors — banking, inter-provincial and international transportation, telecommunications, and government-run services such as Canada Post. Its aim is to identify, remove, and prevent barriers for an estimated 4 million Canadians with physical, sensory, mental, intellectual, learning, communication, or other disabilities. The Canadian government earmarked $290 million over six years to implement the legislation, including penalties and fines of up to $250,000 for violations.

The ACA supports the existing rights and protections for people with disabilities, including the Canadian Charter of Rights and Freedoms, the Canadian Human Rights Act, and the United Nations Convention on the Rights of Persons with Disabilities. The Act outlines how to identify and remove accessibility barriers and prevent new barriers, including barriers in

- Built environments (buildings and public spaces)
- Employment (job opportunities and employment policies and practices)
- Information and communication technologies (digital content and technologies used to access it)
- Procurement of goods and services
- Delivering programs and services
- Transportation (by air as well as by rail, ferry, and bus carriers that operate across a provincial or international border)

Who Must Comply?

The principles underlying the ACA are a guide to how it will be interpreted and implemented. The principles are rooted in the understanding that there are barriers to accessibility that are at the heart of inequalities between Canadians with and without disabilities.

The main principles are inherent dignity, equal opportunity, barrier-free government, autonomy, inclusive design, and meaningful involvement.

The Act applies broadly to organizations under federal responsibility ("regulated entities"). This includes:

- Parliament, including the Senate, the House of Commons, the Library of Parliament, and the Parliamentary Protective Service (with some tailoring of compliance and enforcement provisions to respect parliamentary privilege)
- The Government of Canada, including government departments, Crown corporations, and agencies
- The federally regulated private sector, including organizations in the transportation sectors, broadcasting and telecommunications services, and the banking and financial sectors
- The Canadian Forces and the Royal Canadian Mounted Police (RCMP), while allowing for considerations related to bona fide occupational requirements, such as certain physical requirements necessary in order to carry out certain jobs

The Accessible Canada Act states that "all persons must have barrier-free access to full and equal participation in society."

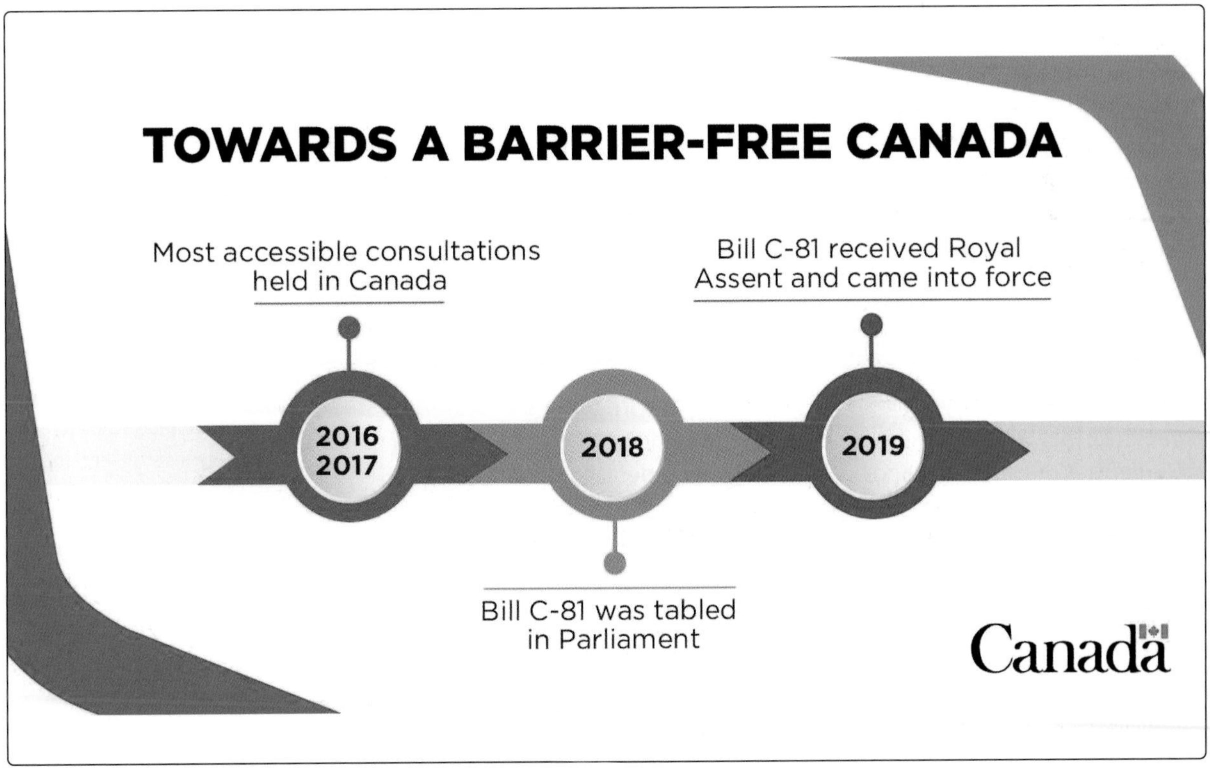

Enforcing Accessibility Standards

To make sure regulated entities meet their obligations, the Act proposes that a mix of proactive compliance activities be used. These activities include:

- **Inspections.** Officers may carry out inspections to make sure regulated entities are following the requirements of the Act and its regulations.
- **Compliance audits.** Officers may examine records and other relevant information from regulated entities to make sure they are following the Act and its regulations.
- **Compliance orders.** If an officer thinks that a regulated entity is not meeting its responsibilities, they may issue an order to the regulated entity to stop or start any activity to meet the responsibilities.
- **Notice of violation with warning.** If there is good reason to believe that a regulated entity has violated the law, officers may issue this notice with a warning to comply with the Act and its regulations.
- **Notice of violation with penalty.** If there is good reason to believe that a regulated entity has violated the law, officers may issue this notice and a fine.
- **Administrative monetary penalties.** Depending on the nature and severity of non-compliance, an officer may require that the regulated entity pay a fine (up to $250,000).
- **Compliance agreement.** Once a notice of violation has been issued, regulated entities may enter into compliance agreements to agree to address the violation in a specific way by a specific time. Entering into a compliance agreement could also reduce the fine.

Shortcomings of the Act

The purpose of the legislation is to make Canada barrier-free in areas under federal jurisdiction. The Act adds to the existing rights and protections for people with disabilities, including the Canadian Charter of Rights and Freedoms, the Canadian Human Rights Act, and Canada's approval of the United Nations Convention on the Rights of Persons with Disabilities. Member of Parliament Carla Qualtrough, who worked on the federal legislation and introduced it in Parliament in 2018, said, "What many provinces have told us is, once we do our law, they will then do a mirror image in their province" (Joannou, 2016).

Nevertheless, disability activists are concerned that there is a lack of firm timelines, that there are exemptions, and especially that the Act applies only to organizations, services, and businesses under federal control (federal agencies, broadcasting and telecommunications, banks and financial services, transportation, Parliament, the military and RCMP, and public lands).

Where there are no provincial polices in place, the Act leaves important areas untouched (hospitals and health care, social services, cities and towns, property and civil rights, civil and criminal justice, transportation (within the province), education, and housing). In these respects, it can be contrasted with the Americans with Disabilities Act, which also covers private businesses.

The Canadian Human Rights Act

Canada's human rights laws stem from the Universal Declaration of Human Rights. In 1948, John Humphrey, a Canadian lawyer and scholar, played a significant role in writing the Declaration.

The Canadian Human Rights Act of 1977 protects people in Canada from discrimination when they are employed by or receive services from the federal government, First Nations governments, or private companies that are regulated by the federal government.

Provincial and territorial human rights laws are very similar to the Canadian Human Rights Act and apply many of the same principles. They protect people from discrimination in areas of provincial and territorial jurisdiction, such as restaurants, stores, schools, housing, and most workplaces.

The Status of Provincial Legislation

It has been nearly 40 years since the Charter of Rights and Freedoms was adopted in 1982; however, as of 2020, Ontario, Manitoba, and Nova Scotia are the only provinces or territories with accessibility legislation.

- **The Accessibility for Ontarians with Disabilities Act (AODA).** The AODA became law on June 13, 2005 and applies to all levels of government, nonprofits, and private-sector businesses in Ontario that have one or more employees (full-time, part-time, seasonal, or contract). It is the oldest accessibility legislation in Canada. The legislation aims to identify, remove, and prevent barriers for people with disabilities. It makes it mandatory for the public and private sectors to follow established sets of standards when dealing with the public. The AODA includes requirements that all organizations must meet, with deadlines specific to an organization's type and size.
- **The Accessibility for Manitobans Act.** Manitoba's accessibility legislation was passed in 2013 and is similar to that of Ontario. For 2016, and every second year after that, the Act requires the Manitoba government and public-sector organizations to prepare accessibility plans that address the identification, prevention, and removal of barriers. Public-sector organizations include municipalities, public transportation organizations, colleges and universities, hospitals, and school boards. The standards address five key areas: customer service, information and communications, built environment, employment and employment practices, and transportation.
- **The Nova Scotia Accessibility Act.** With the Nova Scotia's Accessibility Act receiving Royal Assent on April 27, 2017, Nova Scotia became the third province to enact accessibility legislation. The Nova Scotia legislation aims to achieve accessibility in the whole province by 2030. The government will work with persons with disabilities and the public and the private sectors to create six standards in the areas of customer service: goods and services, information and communication, public transportation and transportation infrastructure, employment, education, and the built environment. The government also announced a grant program to help small businesses remove disability barriers.

Other provinces are following suit. British Columbia, for example, has proclaimed its vision of Accessibility 2024, with the goal of "making B.C. the most progressive province in Canada for people with disabilities by 2024" — including a fully accessible Internet. Their 10-year action plan is designed around 12 building blocks that represent the main themes that emerged through consultations: inclusive government, accessible service delivery, accessible Internet, accessible built environment, accessible housing, accessible transportation, income support, employment, financial security, inclusive communities, emergency preparedness, and consumer experience.

Other provinces and territories, including Saskatchewan and Yukon, are responding favourably to pressure by disability activists to pass similar accessibility legislation.

Web Content Accessibility

Web Content Accessibility Guidelines (WCAG) 2.2 define how to make Web content more accessible to people with disabilities.

Accessibility involves a wide range of disabilities, including visual, auditory, physical, speech, cognitive, language, learning, and neurological disabilities. These guidelines also make Web content more usable by older individuals with changing abilities due to aging and often improve usability for users in general.

WCAG 2.2 is developed in cooperation with individuals and organizations around the world, with a goal of providing a shared standard for Web content accessibility that meets the needs of individuals, organizations, and governments internationally.

What the COVID–19 pandemic has revealed ...

Canadians with Disabilities and COVID–19

Ensuring Affordable, Quality, and Accessible Services

COVID–19 has underscored the need for a federal income security program that enables the provinces to invest in personal supports and care services for Canadians with disabilities.

As a society, we've determined that seniors and children aren't expected or required to participate in the labour market, paving the pathway for federal programs like the Canada Child Benefit and the Canada Pension Plan. In a post-COVID–19 future, individuals with severe disabilities should be part of this group.

Lack of Leadership during the Pandemic

Provincial governments demonstrated a serious lack of leadership in providing financial aid to people with disabilities during the pandemic. Only three provinces offered COVID–related income support to people on social assistance.

In most provinces, people on social assistance who received the Canada Emergency Response Benefit (CERB) were no longer eligible for social assistance. Contrary to the wishes of the federal government, most provinces partially or fully clawed back CERB received by individuals on social assistance.

This means these vulnerable, low-income Canadians did not get the full support intended. Just one province, Ontario, which is applying a partial clawback, has said it will reinvest the funds into social assistance to further help those who need to access income support.

Four months into the pandemic, the federal government announced plans for a one-time, tax-free payment of up to $600 for people who are registered for the Disability Tax Credit (DTC), a non-refundable federal tax measure for those with severe disabilities. The necessary legislation for this measure did not pass, so this benefit was not forthcoming.

However, even if this one-time DTC benefit had passed, most people living with disabilities would have been left out. Significant and widespread gaps remain across the country in meeting the costs of living with a disability during the pandemic.

According to the 2017 Canadian Disability Survey, 6.2 million people aged 15 and over identify as having a disability. Of these, 2.7 million people report having a severe or very severe disability. The DTC has 1.2 million registrants, resulting in coverage for less than half of individuals living with severe disabilities. The needs for income support are evident.

Among working-age people aged 25 to 64, of those with no disability, 10% live below Canada's official poverty line. For those with severe disabilities, 28% live in poverty — and did so before the social and economic calamity of COVID–19.

In comparison to guaranteed income programs like Old Age Security for seniors, the Canada Child Benefit for families with children, and the Canada Workers Benefit for low-income workers, no federal income security program specifically provides income support or income supplementation to Canadians with disabilities.

This Wasn't Always the Case

For most of the twentieth century, the federal government did share costs with the provinces for income assistance for people with significant disabilities, supporting the development and maintenance of a national safety net for disabled Canadians.

That ended in 1996, with the cancellation of the Canada Assistance Plan and the introduction of what became the Canada Social Transfer. Interestingly, in 1996 First Ministers also identified families with children and Canadians with disabilities as collective priorities. On the income security side, much more has been done for families and children in the intervening years than for people with disabilities. The adequacy of provincial social assistance has fallen since that time.

Data from the Maytree Foundation show that from 1996 to 2018 and adjusting for inflation, the value of welfare income for a single person with a disability increased in only one province, remained more or less stable in three provinces, and declined in purchasing power in six provinces, in some jurisdictions falling by $2,000 or more. In 2018, the maximum welfare income for a person with a disability ranged from a low of just under $10,000 a year in New Brunswick to almost $20,000 in Alberta.

A Basic Income Program Is Needed for People with Severe Disabilities

It is time to address these limitations in adequacy and equity in the safety net for Canadians with disabilities and to examine major reform options moving forward.

- A Canada-wide basic income program for people with severe disabilities should be introduced. In close cooperation with the provinces, the federal government should establish a national basic income modelled along the lines of the Old Age Security/Guaranteed Income programs for seniors. The benefit would be paid monthly, indexed to the cost of living, free of social stigma, portable across the country, and the maximum benefit would be the same as for eligible low-income seniors under the OAS/GIS.
- This federal income security initiative would generate savings for provinces, potentially $2 to $3 billion overall. It would thereby free up funding for provinces because the new basic income program would replace provincial/territorial social assistance for most working-age persons with severe disabilities. This amount is large enough to justify an investment and accountability framework that would enable provinces and territories to reallocate funds to urgently needed personal supports as well as home-based and community services for those with disabilities.

As we have learned during this pandemic with long-term care facilities, there is a central role for provincial and territorial governments to ensure the availability of affordable, quality, and accessible services and supports for people with disabilities. And there is a principal role for the federal government in the provision of income security to people with disabilities through direct transfers to individuals and families.

Prince, M. (2020). COVID–19, Canadians with disabilities, and the need for major reforms. Blog (June 23). The Broadbent Institute. Reproduced by permission of the author.

Michael J. Prince is a Broadbent Policy Fellow and the Lansdowne Professor of Social Policy at the University of Victoria.

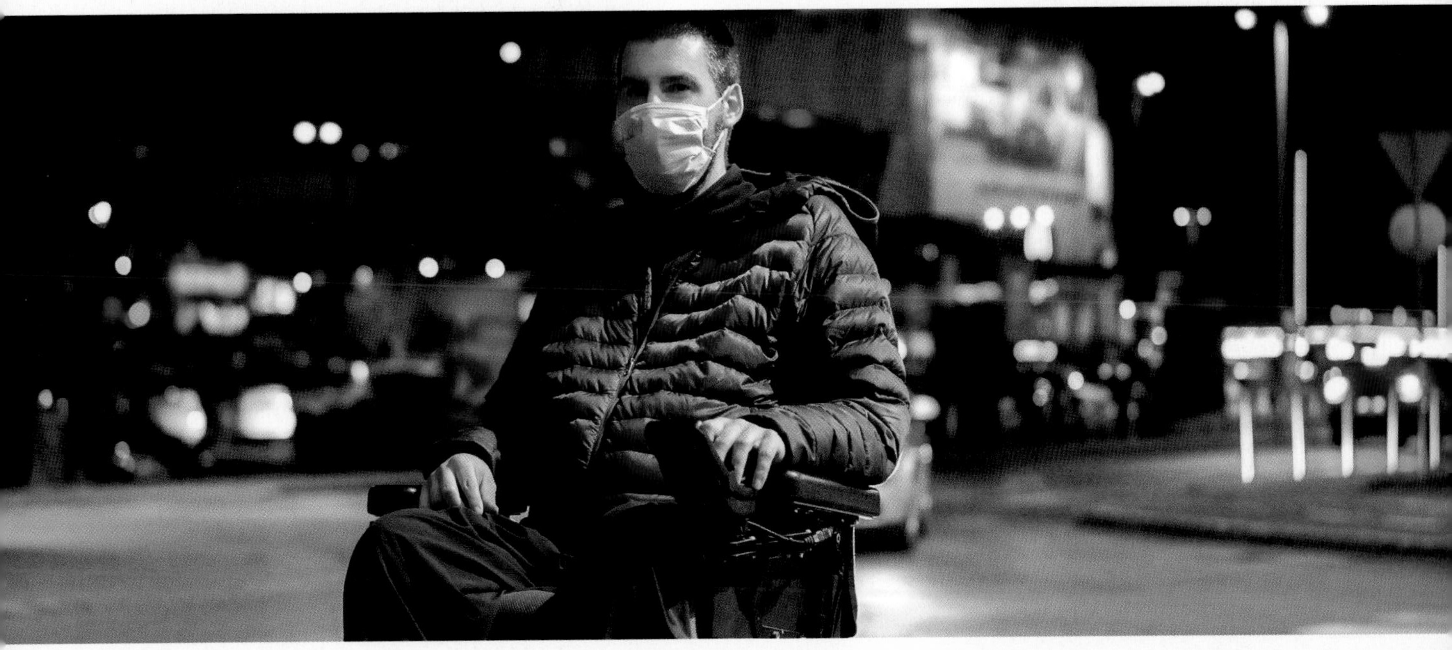

11.5 The Independent Living Movement

The Independent Living Movement (ILM) has been a key player in the struggle to achieve human rights legislation for people with disabilities. Originating in the United States during the early 1970s and introduced to Canada in 1979, the ILM has become a dominant force in disability rights activity in Canada. The objective underlying the ILM is to encourage and help persons with disabilities achieve self-direction over the personal and community services needed to attain independent living.

By 1985, Independent Living Resource Centres (ILRCs) were operating in Waterloo, Winnipeg, Thunder Bay, Calgary, and Toronto. In 1986, at the first ILM conference in Ottawa, the Canadian Association of Independent Living Centres (CAILC) was formed to act as a national coordinating body for the ILM, and the definition of a Canadian ILRC was developed. In 2008, a total of 26 ILRCs were operating across Canada.

The Independent Living Philosophy

The independent living philosophy is that persons with disabilities are citizens first and only secondarily consumers of health care, rehabilitation, or social services. As such, they have the same right to participation, the same range of options, and the same degree of freedom in everyday life that other citizens might take for granted.

The ILM philosophy empowers individuals to make the choices necessary to control their own communities and personal resources. ILRCs are governed and controlled by persons with disabilities. At least 51% of the members of each board of directors must have a disability, and each board must have a mix of people with and without a disability. ILRCs are non-profit and responsive to persons with all types of disabilities, including mobility, sensory, cognitive, emotional, psychiatric, and so forth.

The Independent Living Movement espouses the de-medicalization of disability, de-institutionalization, and cross-disability (i.e., inclusion in the ILM regardless of specific diagnoses).

A 1997 CAILC study of the effects of the ILRCs found that they succeed, in large part, not simply because they provide people an opportunity to learn skills, access information, or receive support, but because they do so in a way that is consistent with the independent living philosophy. The CAILC concluded that improvement in the quality of life for people with disabilities requires the removal of environmental, social, and economic barriers as well as skill development.

Individual empowerment was a key benefit and particularly important in improving community living skills and in developing increased confidence and self-esteem. The Association found that individuals involved with some of the programs of the ILRC have acquired knowledge of other ILM programs as well and they highly value the programs with which they are directly involved.

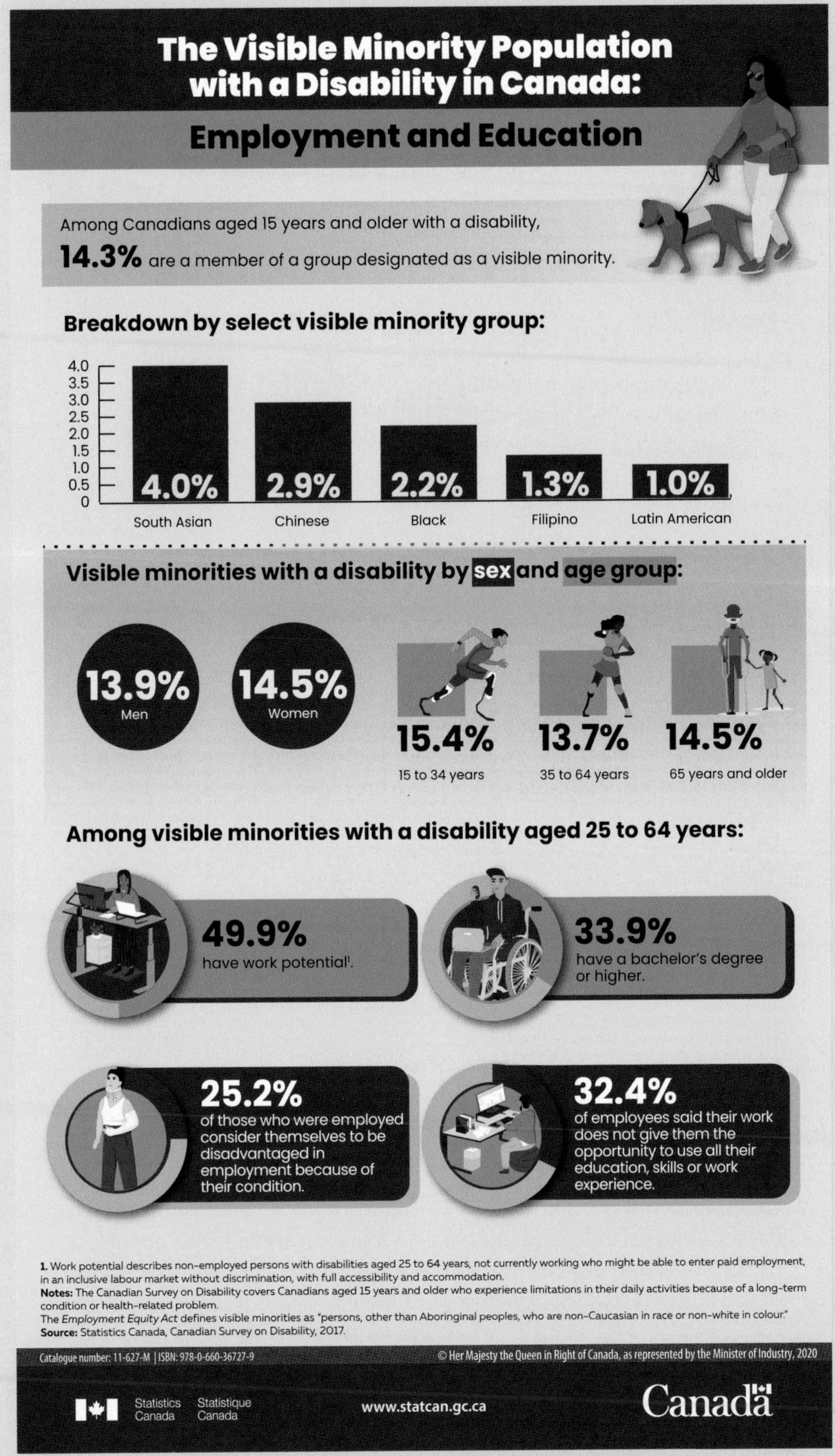

Figure 11.3: Visible Minorities with a Disability

Following the passing of the Accessible Canada Act in 2019, there has been an increased focus on removing barriers and improving accessibility for the 6.2 million Canadians with disabilities.

The COVID–19 pandemic has underscored the barriers that those with disabilities experience on a regular basis. Additionally, COVID–19 has highlighted the unique experiences and difficulties faced by certain population groups, such as groups designated as visible minorities, Indigenous people, or sexual minorities.

Results from the 2017 Canadian Survey on Disability (CSD) have shown that among population groups designated as visible minorities who have a disability, one-quarter considered themselves to be disadvantaged in employment because of their condition.

Statistics Canada (2020, July 6). *The Visible Minority Population with a Disability in Canada: Employment and Education*. Catalogue no. 11–627-M. Statistics Canada.

Table 11.2

Rehabilitation vs. Independent Living

Independent Living (IL) is more than a social movement; it is also an analytic paradigm that is reshaping the thinking of rehabilitation professionals and researchers alike. Below, the IL paradigm is contrasted with the rehabilitation paradigm that has dominated earlier disability policy, practice, and research.

	Rehabilitation	**Independent Living**
What is the problem?	The disabled person is a deficitary being whose ability to play social roles is restricted.	The disabled person is dependent on experts, rehabilitation centres, and factors such as environmental and other political conditions.
Where is the problem situated?	In the disabled person themself.	In the environment, the rehabilitation process, and in social and political circumstances.
How is the problem solved?	By the expert procedure of doctors and other specialists. The disabled person is cared for by certain organizations.	By self-help, peer counselling, self-organization of assistance, the reduction of psychological, social and other barriers, and consumer control.
What is the social role of the disabled person?	Patient, client.	Consumer.
Who is competent?	Experts.	Consumer.
What is the desired result?	Psycho-physical independence. Reduction of the "disability." Profession or institutionalization.	A self-determined life, possibly a profession, the ability to organize and to accept assistance. Assistance structures close to the consumer.

Dejong, G. (1979). Independent living: from social movement to analytic paradigm. *Arch Phys Med .Rehabil*, 60: 435–446,

Council of Canadians with Disabilities (CCD)

In Canada, one of the lead organizations behind the Independent Living Movement is the Council of Canadians with Disabilities (CCD). Formerly known as the Coalition of Provincial Organizations of the Handicapped (COPOH), the CCD was founded in 1976 by people with disabilities. In 1994, the organization adopted the name Council of Canadians with Disabilities, which was more in keeping with current disability terminology and the organization's new membership structure, which admitted national organizations of persons with disabilities as members.

The CCD is a human rights organization advocating for social justice. It advocates for an inclusive and accessible Canada, where people with disabilities have full realization of their human rights, as described in the UN Convention on the Rights of Persons with Disabilities.

The CCD contributes to an inclusive and accessible Canada by:

- **Self-representation.** Speaking out to the courts, decision makers, the media, and parliamentary committees
- **Sharing Expertise.** Working to create new policy, such as a National Action Plan on Disability
- **Knowledge Development.** Researching issues such as poverty, home supports, accessible transportation, and income support
- **Extending Disability Rights.** Pursuing litigation to effect disability-positive public policies in education, employment, health care, and transportation
- **Battling Barriers.** Working to prevent the creation of new barriers; for example, a legal case against VIA rail when it purchased inaccessible train cars
- **Law Reform.** Participating in legislative reviews; for example, the Human Rights Act, the Transportation Act, and the Employment Equity Act
- **Networking.** Collaborating with major sectors of society to promote disability rights; for example, participating in the Voluntary Sector Initiative, a joint government and community project examining technology, research, volunteerism, and policy development
- **Partnership Development.** Joining with other groups to build initiatives such as policy forums on important issues of concern to persons with disabilities

The CCD's priorities include:

- Disability-related supports
- Poverty alleviation
- Increased employment for persons with disabilities
- Promotion of human rights and civil rights
- Implementation of the UN Convention on the Rights of Persons with Disabilities (United Nations, 2006)
- Technology developed according to the principles of universal design
- Air, rail, bus and marine transport accessible to persons with all types of disabilities

Breaking Down Barriers

The Council of Canadians with Disabilities seeks to unite advocacy organizations of people with disabilities and to defend and extend human rights for persons with disabilities through public education, advocacy, intervention in litigation, research, consultation, and partnerships.

The CCD believes in:

- **Citizenship**
  People with disabilities have the same rights and responsibilities as Canadians without disabilities.
- **Consumer Control**
  People with disabilities must be involved in all stages of the development of disability services and policies and in all decision making that affects their lives.
- **Equality and Human Rights**
  All legislation must conform to the demands of the Charter of Rights and the Canadian Human Rights Act.
- **Universal Design**
  The environment should be designed to be usable by people with various disabilities.

Social Welfare Policy in Action

Equity Deferred

The Immigration and Refugee Protection Act, 2001

Legally, Canada's borders are open to most people who wish to immigrate to Canada — all, that is, except persons with disabilities and their families.

Canada's immigration policy does not discriminate against people on the grounds of race, religion, ethnicity, sexual orientation, or cultural background. Such factors are not permissible grounds for denying anyone entry. However, there is an exception for persons with disabilities under the **Immigration and Refugee Protection Act**.

Under the Act, permanent residency can be denied if a person is deemed to place an "excessive demand" on health and social services. The provision has been criticized by John Rae of the Council of Canadians with Disabilities as perpetuating "long held stereotypical views of persons with disabilities as being less deserving and a burden on society... The current law devalues Canadians with disabilities."

"What this means," observes Carolyn Zaikowski, "is families can be rejected for having deaf children and spouses can be denied because they use a wheelchair, a practice too harsh for even the United States' difficult immigration system" (Zaikowski, 2017).

While the Act does not ban people with disabilities and their families from immigrating to Canada, the excessive demand section of the Act, which maintains that potential immigrants must not place a financial burden on health, education. and social services (programs that fall under provincial and territorial jurisdiction), restricts opportunities for immigration for many people with disabilities and their loved ones.

A Possible Violation of the Charter and the UN Convention on the Rights of Persons with Disabilities

This exclusionary policy arises from an outdated idea that people with disabilities are not useful members of a society because, supposedly, they use up too many social and welfare resources:

The Immigration and Refugee Protection Act defines excessive demand as the following:

- **(a)** a demand on health services or social services for which the anticipated costs would likely exceed average Canadian per capita health services and social services costs over a period of five consecutive years immediately following the most recent medical examination required by these Regulations, unless there is evidence that significant costs are likely to be incurred beyond that period, in which case the period is no more than 10 consecutive years; or
- **(b)** a demand on health services or social services that would add to existing waiting lists and would increase the rate of mortality and morbidity in Canada as a result of the denial or delay in the provision of those services to Canadian citizens or permanent residents.
- **(c)** the disabled individual's yearly estimated health and social services costs exceeds three times the estimated costs established by the federal, provincial, and territorial governments. The threshold is based on the combined average dollar amount that the federal, provincial, and territorial governments spend on health and social services per individual per year (Immigration, Refugees and Citizenship Canada, 2018).

The law is clearly wide in scope and open to much interpretation.

Indeed, many Canadian and international immigration and disability scholars point out that an anti-immigrant policy such as this likely violates the Canadian Charter of Rights and Freedoms as well as the United Nations Convention on the Rights of Persons with Disabilities.

Recent Policy Changes

In April 2018, Immigration Minister Ahmed Hussen said that, after four decades, the federal government would be removing rules that allow permanent resident applications to be denied for serious health conditions or disabilities.

The rule changes amend the definition of social services by removing references to special education, social and vocational rehabilitation services, and personal support services. The federal government is also tripling the "cost threshold" at which an application for permanent residency can be denied on medical grounds. Such changes will allow immigrants with minor health conditions with relatively low health and social services costs, such as those with hearing or visual impairments, to be approved for permanent residency.

The rule changes have been welcomed, but they are limited in scope. Immigrant and disability organizations are demanding that the policy, which allows applicants who have a disability to be denied entry to Canada on the grounds of "excessive demand," should be repealed in its entirety.

Questions for Reflection

Look at the Immigration and Refugee Protection Act in its entirety and then give some thought to the following questions:

1. Race, religion, ethnicity, sexual orientation, or cultural background are not permissible grounds for denying an immigrant or their family from settling in Canada. Should disability be considered a legitimate criterion?
2. To what extent, if at all, should "maintenance cost" be considered when evaluating a refugee with a disability or their family for permanent residency status?
3. Research what immigrant and disability advocacy organizations are saying about this policy and about the new rule changes.
4. Do you think the new immigration rule changes go far enough? If so, why? If not, why not?

A Moment in Time: December 9, 1975

The Rights of Disabled Persons

United Nations Declaration

On December 3 every year, Canada takes part in the UN's International Day of Persons with Disabilities, raising awareness among policymakers and the wider public.

On December 9, 1975, the United Nations issued the Declaration on the Rights of Disabled Persons. The UN declaration was hailed by those advocating for new legal rights to support the advancement and protection of disabled persons in all areas of civic life, including the rights to economic security and self-reliance.

The UN International Year for Disabled Persons (IYDP) (1981) and the subsequent UN Decade of Disabled Persons (1983–1992) fostered an unprecedented level of public and political interest regarding the rights and opportunities afforded to people with disabilities. This increased general awareness and fuelled campaigns to include disability in the Charter of Rights and Freedoms.

By the turn of the century, there was a significant revival of Canadian political interest in, and public commitment to, disability rights.

On March 11, 2010, Canada ratified the UN Convention on the Rights of Persons with Disabilities (CRPD). The CRPD commits Canada to a series of measures and principles to improve the social and economic condition of people with disabilities while taking steps to improve their legal and political rights. In 2014, Canada submitted its first report to the CRPD, outlining various measures that had been taken by federal and provincial governments with respect to its commitment to improving the social and economic condition of persons with disabilities.

Chapter Review

Questions

1. How have definitions of disability changed since the nineteenth century, and what have been the implications for social policy in this area?
2. What are the medical, social/human rights, biopsychosocial, and structural models of disability? Compare.
3. Describe the main income security benefits available to people with disabilities in Canada.
4. What are the main features of the new Accessible Canada Act and what are some concerns raised by disability activists with respect to accessibility and inclusion?
5. Explain the philosophy of the Independent Living Movement.
6. Canada's immigration policies have been criticized for being highly restrictive when it comes to admitting new immigrants with disabilities. What are the restrictions?

Exploring Social Welfare

1. Only a few provinces have strong accessibility legislation in place. Provide an update on the status of accessibility legislation in your province or territory.
2. Develop a short report on the likely impact of the federal Accessible Canada Act in your province or territory.
3. The Canadian Immigration and Refugee Protection Act, 2001 contains provisions that can be used to restrict persons with disabilities from entering Canada as permanent residents. The legislation was discussed at the end of this chapter. Read the overview provided, read the legislation on your own, then answer the Questions for Reflection at the end of the feature.

Websites

Council of Canadians with Disabilities (CCD)
www.ccdonline.ca
CCD is a national human rights organization of people with disabilities working for an inclusive and accessible Canada. The CCD seeks to achieve its priorities through law reform, litigation, public education, and dialogue with key decision makers.

Independent Living Canada
www.ilcanada.ca
Founded in 1986 by the Independent Living Movement, Independent Living Canada is the national umbrella organization, representing and coordinating the network of Independent Living Resource Centres (ILRCs) at the national level.

Disabled Women's Network of Canada
www.dawncanada.net
Grounded in the lived experiences of women with disabilities and Deaf women, and using an evidence-based approach, DAWN Canada works to create change at a systemic level in order to directly improve the quality of life for women with disabilities. DAWN seeks to amplify the voice of women with disabilities and Deaf women by ensuring that they are represented at decision-making tables in the areas that matter most, including violence prevention, health equity, and access to justice.

Well-Being and Social Justice in a Global Context

"For social work today, there is an opportunity to move from the recently imposed role of picking up the debris at the bottom of the cliff, to its original role of building fences at the top — preventing disaster through work supporting communities to support themselves."

— Rory Truell, Secretary-General of the International Federation of Social Workers

Jackie Stokes

Ensuring Equitable Opportunities for All

12

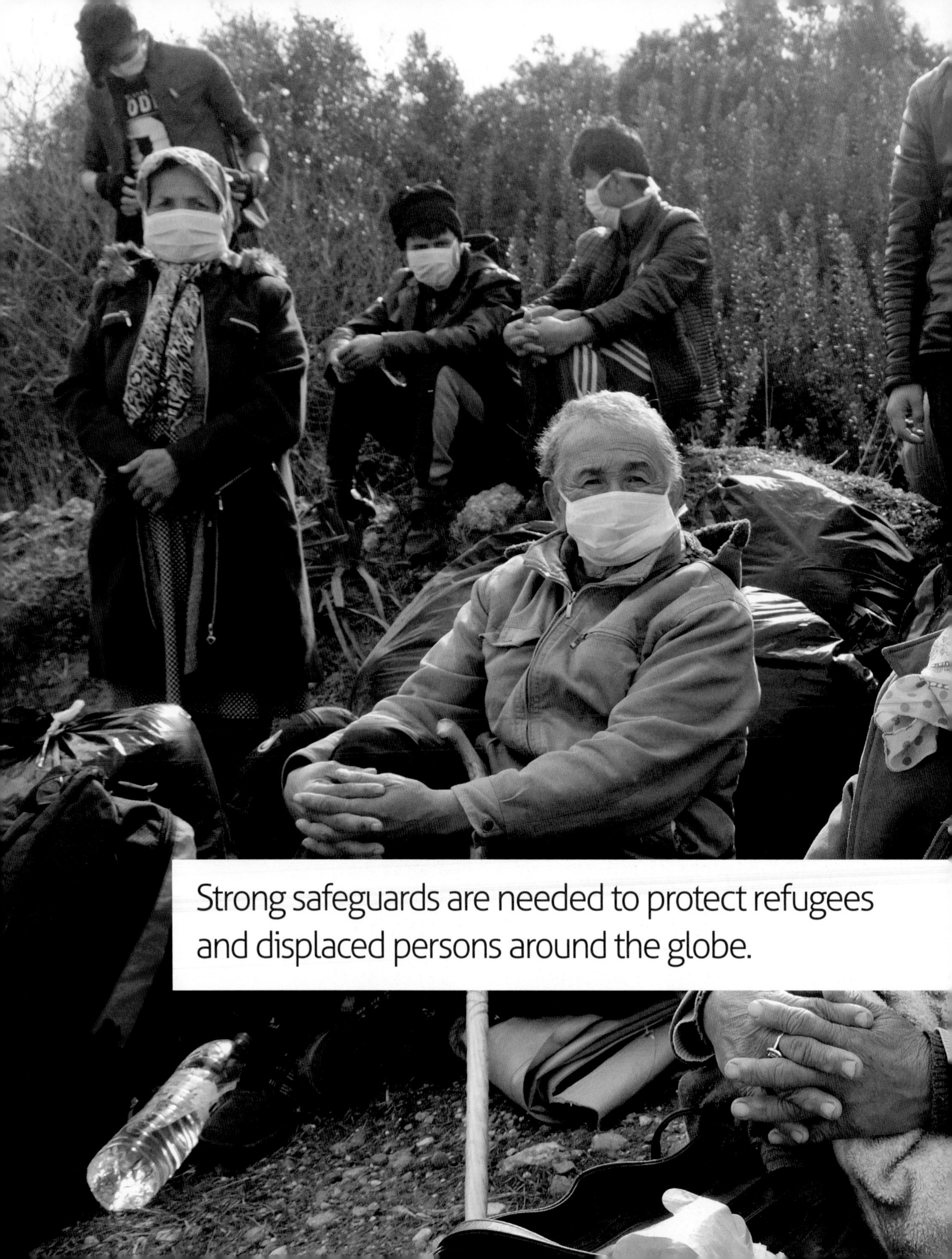

Strong safeguards are needed to protect refugees and displaced persons around the globe.

The welfare state created during the twentieth century was designed to address traditional social risks, such as old age and unemployment. Beginning in the 1980s, however, these social protections were slowly eroded through neoliberal policies that favoured market-driven solutions, giving way to visible social inequities. The global COVID–19 pandemic of 2020 exposed those weaknesses for all to see.

Social workers have an ethical responsibility to promote inclusion, equity, and social justice — not just for people living in Canada, but for all people, everywhere. This chapter examines how well-being is measured at a global level, the multidimensional aspects of globalization, and the complex problems created by rising socio-economic inequality at the global level. It then looks at how international social work organizations collaboratively address these problems through the development of a social work global agenda.

Key Concepts

- Principle of universality
- Global social work
- Human Development Index (HDI)
- Sustainable Development Goals (SDGs)
- Globalization
- The Global Agenda for Social Work and Social Development
- Global Agenda, 2020–2030
- Paris Agreement on Climate Change, 2015
- UN Declaration on the Rights of Indigenous People

Ensuring Equitable Opportunities for All

Achieving a truly just society requires universal social welfare programs that focus on investing in peoples' strengths, beginning with those who are most vulnerable. Such social programs are based on the human rights principle of shared prosperity and a commitment to an equitable distribution of wealth, both in Canada and throughout the world.

After completing this chapter, you should be able to:

- Explain what social workers mean when they stress the need for policies and programs based on principles of universality;
- Describe the thinking behind the United Nations Human Development Index (HDI) and its newer Sustainable Development Goals (SDGs), and describe why such global indicators are important;
- Describe some social and environmental challenges, regionally, nationally, and globally, for the next decade and the role for social workers in ensuring inclusion, equity, and social justice globally;
- Describe the work that is being done by international social work bodies to set out a global agenda to address the critical issues facing social workers around the world; and
- Explain each of the five themes of the 2020–2030 Global Agenda that will serve as a framework for social workers and social welfare advocates around the world over the next decade.

12.1 Toward a Modern Welfare State — Universal Investments in Equity

As social and economic inequality continued to increase well into the twenty-first century, there was growing consensus that the social protections traditionally associated with the welfare state were no longer working. Inequality was rising and well-being was not evenly distributed among Canada's diverse populations.

Equal Opportunity for All

Many scholars have drawn attention to these incontrovertible facts and called for new directions in social policy. For example, Joseph Stiglitz, an esteemed professor of economics at Columbia University and a Nobel Prize winner, has argued that, of necessity, a welfare state in the twenty-first century should be, and will need to be, different from that created in the mid-twentieth century.

A central tenet of a twenty-first–century welfare state is ensuring equality of opportunity, with a particular focus on children, their health, and their education. Ensuring equality of opportunity requires fighting against the intergenerational transmission of advantages and disadvantages and against discrimination in all of its forms. There is increasing recognition that equality of opportunity cannot occur in a society that has large disparities in income and wealth (Stiglitz, 2017).

> After decades of shaping global and national economic policies according to the dictates of neoliberal ideology, public sectors are starved, climate change is accelerating, inequality is on the rise, and democracies are confronting near-unprecedented crises. The only way forward is to leave behind the defunct economic nostrums of the past. (Stiglitz, 2020)

Stiglitz identified numerous economic and employment changes that indicate a need to reconstruct the welfare state along new lines.

> For instance, there have been marked changes in the labor market — there are no longer lifetime jobs, implying less incentive of firms to invest in their workers and less loyalty between workers and firms. Workplace-based welfarism of the mid-twentieth century variety won't work today. Matters have been made even worse because of the "sharing economy" and "innovations" in worker–employer relations — converting workers into "independent contractors."
>
> Firms that have embraced these new models are motivated in part by the desire to avoid taxes and circumvent employer regulations. At the same time, the enormous growth in inequality makes it clear that the market on its own, at least as it has been structured under neoliberalism, won't achieve anything approaching something that is socially acceptable, let alone any higher ambition, such as the just society. (Stiglitz, 2017, p. 12)

In other words, there are groups of individuals and families — women, immigrants and racialized minorities, Indigenous peoples, and persons with disabilities — whose concerns are not being addressed. If the welfare state is to be effective, it must be based on the principles of universality and equal opportunity for all.

Global Definition of Social Work

At the July 2014 IFSW General Meeting and IASSW General Assembly, the following global definition was approved:

> *Social work is a practice-based profession and an academic discipline that promotes social change and development, social cohesion, and the empowerment and liberation of people. Principles of social justice, human rights, collective responsibility and respect for diversities are central to social work. Underpinned by theories of social work, social sciences, humanities and Indigenous knowledges, social work engages people and structures to address life challenges and enhance well-being.*

Universal Public Welfare for the Twenty-First Century

The principle of universality was the fundamental idea behind the social welfare programs developed in the post–World War II period. These universal programs aimed at equality and inclusion through advancing fundamental citizenship rights, which in turn fostered a sense of belonging and national identity (Béland et al., 2019). The core idea was that everyone was entitled equally to life, liberty, and the pursuit of happiness — for themselves and their families.

Perhaps the Canadian social program most identified with this principle was the Family Allowance in 1944. At the time, every mother received the "Baby Bonus" regardless of their income or family circumstances. It was a true universal program. Canadian Medicare is another case in point. It may be inadequate in some respects, but every Canadian has access to health care under the Canada Health Act of 1968. It is universal — regardless of the shortcomings, health care is guaranteed for all. That is why Medicare has such wide support and evokes national pride.

Over time, the Baby Bonus and other universal programs like it were progressively eroded, but the notion that everyone had a human right to a decent job, decent income, decent housing, decent food, and a decent retirement never entirely disappeared. Even targeted programs, such as means-tested programs (e.g., social assistance) or clawed-back programs (e.g., Old Age Security) were based on a progressive notion of shifting the income distribution in favour of those who have less.

One can dispute whether particular targeted programs will ever result in full equality (or indeed if such programs might, in some ways, perpetuate inequality), but the guiding principle is a commitment to the universalistic idea that we are all equal.

The provision of universal public social welfare programs continues to "form a major component of the organized pursuit of social justice" (Armitage, 2003, p. 2); however, the context has changed. The postmodern challenges faced by disadvantaged and marginalized populations such as women, immigrants and racialized minorities, and Indigenous peoples call for new universal solutions.

- The feminist critique focuses on employment and pay equity, child and elder care, sexual assault, and family violence.
- The anti-racist critique centres on structural inequities experiences by Black Canadians, South Asian people, and other visible minorities.
- The Indigenous critique centres on the ongoing harm caused by colonial practices and the need for reconciliation and rethinking the relationship with Indigenous peoples (Armitage, 2003).

Going forward, there is a need to invest in providing inclusive opportunities for all. This involves a recommitment to the fundamental social welfare principle of universality in the context of equity rather than equality, and of the new problems and concerns that people in Canada face.

Intersectional Inequality

Factors such as race, ethnicity, wealth, and sex, among other characteristics, can shape individuals' life experiences and amplify poverty. However, an intersectional analysis is necessary to understand how individual experiences of poverty can result from overlapping sources of disadvantage.

Intersectional disadvantage is highly relevant for the proper design of policies and programs in order to account for the multiple interacting vulnerabilities that can create life deprivations greater than the sum of other single factors.

Social Welfare Policy in Action

Universal Strategies for Today

Addressing the New Challenges Facing Canadians

Postmodern challenges faced by vulnerable populations such as women, immigrants, racialized minorities, and Indigenous peoples call for new universal solutions.

The provision of universal public social welfare programs continues to "form a major component of the organized pursuit of social justice" (Armitage, 2003, p. 2). Indeed, the principle of universalism is embedded in the very idea of social welfare. But the modern context has changed.

Universal Strategies to Support Working Canadians

For Canadians, the world of work — and worklessness — has changed. The traditional focus of the welfare state was to protect working Canadians from the risks of unemployment (Employment Insurance) and workplace injury (workers' compensation). Today, these protections are being eroded.

The eligibility requirements for Employment Insurance (EI) are frequently rigorous and qualifying for workers' compensation often entails a bureaucratic battle. In addition, work itself is changing. Today, there are increasing demands for training and skills for a knowledge-based economy, an aging population (with the transition of baby boomers from work to retirement), worsening inequality and poverty (with the emergence of the working poor), and a gig economy (with the growth of precarious or insecure work).

While employment protections are usually linked to full-time, stable employment, a universal approach would replace this with a universal basic income to ensure income security for everyone — including the self-employed and workers who may be excluded from EI owing to the nature of their work or hours worked, etc. (Behrendt & Nguyen, 2018).

Universal labour market policies would mean broad-based income security and injury protections as well as robust legislation that would eliminate gender and other inequalities (Behrendt & Nguyen, 2018).

Universal Strategies to End Poverty

Many existing strategies to reduce poverty are residual in nature, with an underlying philosophy that the "poor" are poor of their own volition and simply need a little "shock treatment" to get back on track. Universal strategies to end poverty need to address the erosion in benefits and protections, reduced access to Employment Insurance (EI), frozen or reduced social benefits, barriers to affordable housing, lack of affordable daycare, and reliance on food banks.

On August 21, 2018, the Government of Canada released *Opportunity for All: Canada's First Poverty Reduction Strategy*. The strategic goal was a 20% reduction in poverty by 2020 and a 50% reduction in poverty by 2030, relative to 2015 levels. Any initiative aimed at poverty reduction — or, better yet, its elimination — is to be welcomed. However, there are concerns that the federal government has set a low bar, pledging to reduce poverty only by half and not until 2030. And it did not announce new funding commitments.

By contrast, the Dignity for All anti-poverty campaign, launched in 2009 by Canada Without Poverty and Citizens for Public Justice, appears more robust. Dignity for All is built on the universal principle of social justice — every citizen deserves a real and fair chance to succeed, no matter where they live in Canada or what their background is.

Whenever and wherever people are denied adequate housing, income, and food, their fundamental human rights are being violated. Rather than punitive measures, the Dignity for All plan advocates a firm commitment to universal principles of non-discrimination and equality, and a fixed focus on addressing poverty as it is experienced by the most marginalized groups.

Universal Strategies That Advance the Well-Being of Women and Families

In 1989, the Canadian Parliament pledged to eliminate childhood poverty by the year 2000. However, Canada continues to have one of the highest child poverty rates among OECD countries. In large part, this is because family policy in Canada is based on antiquated notions of the family and family relations. Canadians families have changed significantly over the past 50 years and it is time family policies were brought up to date with universal policies that are more aligned with families' needs today and guarantee equity and social justice for all.

Nowadays, most children live with working parents and a large number are raised by a lone mother. On top of that, women continue to face more duties in the home than men. Pay equity is far from universal, and even with post-secondary credentials, women "earn less than their male counterparts five years after graduating and in the vast majority of cases average gender earning differences increase from year one to year five" (Labour Market Information Council, 2020, p. x).

Canada also continues to lag behind other OECD countries in child care and parental leave provisions, with the exception of Québec. Some provinces and territories are making slow progress, but the dominant thinking at the federal level is still that of a male-breadwinner family and household (Mahon & Prince, 2019).

Universal Strategies to Guarantee Child Protection and Children's Well-Being

Children have the universal right to be protected and provided for under the 1989 Convention on the Rights of the Child; however, almost a quarter of a million Canadian children are investigated each year for child maltreatment. Enabling parents to provide for their children is important for the well-being of each individual child, but also represents a vital part of providing all children with the equal opportunities called for by the UN Convention (Sandbæk,2017).

Current approaches to child maltreatment continue to be forensic, individualized, deficit-focused, parent-blaming and, in the case of Indigenous families, fall back to colonial practices. Despite knowing the long-term consequences for children who are maltreated, child welfare systems continue to resist universal policies that could result in important gains for children and their families.

Children whose families live in poverty, who are racialized or Indigenous, or who live in impoverished communities are highly overrepresented among children who are investigated and found to have been maltreated. A universal approach through public health and early intervention is required to support families and improve all children's health and well-being.

Universal Strategies That Advance Mental Wellness for All

While mental health is a fundamental component of overall health, under current health care policy (Medicare), many mental health services do not meet the requirement of "medically necessary" under the Canada Health Act. As a result, in practice, many people do not have access to a full continuum of mental health services.

Except for mental health services that are provided to people in a hospital setting or through Medicare-covered outpatient psychiatry, such services must be paid for privately. This may be through workplace plans. However, access to mental health services is limited to either those who can afford it or those who are most seriously ill — meaning early intervention and preventive care are difficult to obtain for many.

The Mental Health Commission of Canada and the Canadian Association of Social Workers (CASW), among many others, are pressing for mental health care to become a universal program delivered under a public Medicare model.

In 2019, the Canadian Association of Social Workers released a statement calling for a new Mental Health Parity Act and a federal Minister for Mental Health and Well-Being. If implemented, this would be a major step in establishing mental health as a universal right and help bring an end to the stigma and barriers to service experienced by Canadians with mental health concerns.

Universal Strategies That Facilitate Reconciliation with Indigenous Peoples

Indigenous peoples in Canada have been subjected relentlessly to settler-colonial policies that have involved seizing ancestral lands and keeping them, first for the settlers themselves and more recently for purposes of resource extraction. Government policies aimed at "assimilating" Indigenous peoples have led to immeasurable harms. Still today, many communities experience poverty and housing conditions resembling those in the Third World.

Countering all this is the demand for Indigenous self-determination — Indigenous control of Indigenous affairs in ways that go beyond narrow "self-government" agreements. Indigenous peoples are asserting a nation-to-nation relationship with the Crown as a first step in the process of reconciliation. Everything follows from acceptance of this as a way forward.

A recent positive development is Canada's commitment to the UN Declaration on the Rights of Indigenous Peoples and the principle of free, prior and informed consent. The new policy means that Canadian governments must now secure the prior agreement of Indigenous groups before making decisions that affect their lives.

Universal Strategies That Foster Multiculturalism and Eliminate Racial Discrimination

Recent years have seen tightened rules for obtaining citizenship, and larger numbers of temporary workers. Immigrants entering Canada under the economic stream (those who have wealth, desirable skills, or other credentials) are likely to gain permanent residency relatively quickly. They are thus eligible for social protections much earlier than immigrants entering as temporary workers or those admitted under the family stream or refugee and humanitarian stream. As well, under the Immigration Refugee Protection Act of 2001, immigrants or family members who are disabled must first demonstrate they do not present an "excessive demand." Uneven entitlements such as these create a second-class citizenship for immigrants (Béland et al., 2019).

Immigrants offer a net advantage to Canada and to its economy. A universalist approach would not pit immigrant against immigrant, nor immigrant against non-immigrant. Instead, such measures would facilitate inclusion for all newcomers and send a clear message to all Canadians about the benefits of multiculturalism policy, encouraging them to extend a welcoming hand (Béland et al., 2019).

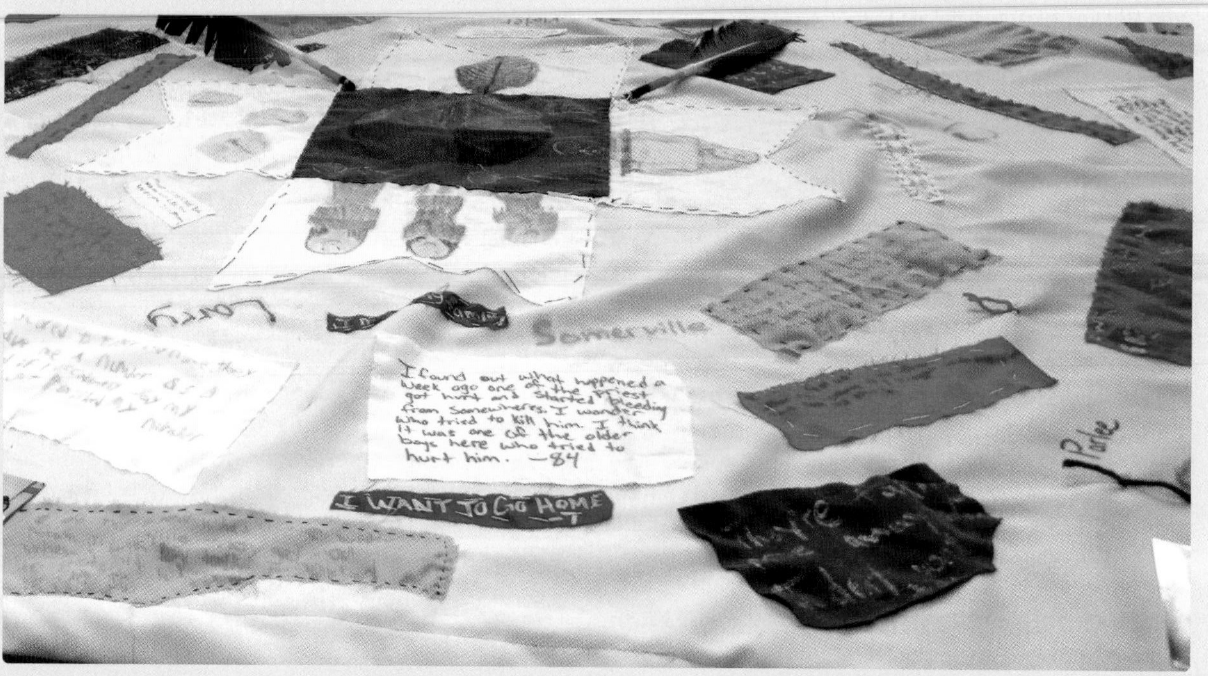

Universal Strategies That Advance the Well-Being of Older Canadians

In general, the postwar welfare state worked well for elderly and retired people in Canada — income security programs substantially reduced poverty for older populations. But there are signs that those gains are being eroded.

In part, this is due to funding and program cutbacks. However, in addition, a series of new risks have emerged. Among these are the implications of a large baby boom generation entering retirement, longer life expectancies, the erosion of occupational pensions, and mounting elder care needs.

Ensuring the well-being of Canada's older adult population is a complex public policy challenge. Protecting and expanding these near-universal income security programs remain key (Béland & Marier, 2019). Ongoing clawbacks to OAS, GIS, and CPP are eroding the universality of these programs.

It is important that those who wish to work beyond the typical retirement age are able to do so, while ensuring that those who want to can retire without income worries. It is important, too, that employees have secure pensions that will ensure comfortable post-work lives. And it is important that home care and other services are in place to support older adults with everyday living.

A good start has been made with the development of a National Seniors Strategy. This strategy is a universal approach focused on protecting income programs while helping older people in Canada remain independent, productive, and engaged. The federal government could pass legislation to make these universal principles a reality so the older population can live with dignity and greater security in their later years.

Universal Strategies That Advance the Well-Being of Persons with Disabilities

Disability rights is an area of social policy where progress has been made, albeit slowly. The Accessible Canada Act, 2019 (An Act to ensure a barrier-free Canada) was introduced by the Liberal government and eventually passed with unanimous support. The ACA is an important landmark in the long struggle for the rights of persons with disabilities in Canada.

The principles underlying the ACA are the universal principles of inclusion, equity, and social justice. The next steps involve expanding the legislation to include the private sector and addressing outstanding inequities in supports and services.

People with disabilities have the same rights and responsibilities as those without disabilities and all legislation must conform to the Charter of Rights and Freedoms and the Human Rights Act. The physical environment should be designed to be usable by people with various disabilities and these individuals and their representatives must be involved in all stages of decision making that affects their lives.

In addition, the social environment needs to adapt to the needs of people with invisible disabilities, including neuro-developmental problems and other chronic conditions.

Advocacy organizations like the Canadian Council on Disability lead the way in defending existing programs and extending them while adhering to universal principles of inclusion, equity, and social justice for all.

Photo: A memory blanket created for display at the final Truth and Reconciliation Commission event in Ottawa on June 2, 2015.

12.2 The Well-Being of the World's Population

Social workers are interested in resolving social problems such as poverty, violence, homelessness, mental health, substance use, and environmental degradation while ensuring that all Canadians have an opportunity to prosper and be healthy. As a practice-based profession and an academic discipline, social work promotes social change and human development, social cohesion, the empowerment and liberation of people, and environmental justice. These same core principles of social justice, human rights, collective responsibility, respect for diversities , and care of the planet also underlie global social work.

Global Social Well-Being Indicators

We know that certain countries are more economically developed than others but there is less agreement on how to measure human development. The World Bank's annual World Development Report classifies countries as "low," "lower-middle," "upper-middle," and "high" using Gross National Income (GNI) per capita. With a GNI of $46,370 in 2019, Canada would be considered a high-income economy. Other typologies simply categorize countries as "developed" or "developing." Still others divide the world into First World (Western capitalist countries), Second World (the former Soviet Union, China), and Third World (previously colonized countries in Asia, Africa, the Middle East, and Central and South America) (Midgley, 2017). Although these classifications can help facilitate comprehension, it is important to keep in mind that the categories themselves are subject to change. Some researchers even argue that attempts to classify the world's nation states are futile and each country should be given equal prominence (Midgley, 2017).

The research agencies of the United Nations take human development and global inequality seriously. The United Nations consists of 193 nation states and accounts for the vast majority of the world's population. Established after the Second World War, its purpose is "to achieve international co-operation in solving international problems of an economic, social, cultural, or humanitarian character."

Two UN indices developed by the United Nations Development Programme (UNDP) are widely used to gauge human development at the global level. These indicators are (1) the Human Development Index (HDI), which considers health and education along with GNI, and (2) the Sustainable Development Goals (SDGs). Both the HDI and SDGs place less emphasis on narrow economic factors such as GNI or Gross National Product (GNP). The two indices are regarded as more accurate and useful indicators of social well-being because "some countries with high GNP levels lag behind on indicators of social well-being" (Midgley, 2017, p. 27).

Of course, health and well-being varies within countries, too (Midgley, 2017). The levels of social well-being are highest in Western countries (the Global North), while the lowest are found in the developing countries of the Global South; the highest levels of well-being are in Europe, North America, and Australasia. While these countries generally experience a low incidence of absolute poverty and high standards of health, nutrition, literacy, education, and housing, many inequities exist within and between these economically advanced nations (Midgley, 2017).

Globalization and De-Globalization

Today, the well-being of nation states is being shaped by global economic forces that seem largely to be beyond each country's control. "Globalization" is the term used to capture this free flow of investment, people, and information.

The pace of economic globalization has ebbed and flowed over the years. Recently, as tensions have increased over trade, more protectionist measures have emerged, marking what has been dubbed "de-globalization." The "Make America Great Again" slogan of the Trump presidency in the United States and Britain's withdrawal from the European Union (Brexit) are examples.

The shocks of the COVID-19 pandemic accelerated "nearshoring" as governments and businesses sought to reduce their reliance to a handful of countries.

(1) Human Development Index (HDI)

The UN's Human Development Index (HDI) is a composite index that focuses on people's capabilities through the measurement of three basic dimensions of human development: (1) a decent standard of living (measured by GNI), (2) knowledge (measured by expected years of schooling and mean years of schooling), and (3) a long and healthy life (measured by life expectancy at birth).

As with all indexes, the HDI is a simplification. For example, the HDI does not reflect quality-of-life factors such as political empowerment or personal security. However, in the period since the first HDI report, three additional sub-indexes have been developed by the UN: the Inequality-Adjusted Human Development Index (IHDI), the Gender Inequality Index (GII), and the Multidimensional Poverty Index (MPI). These three sub-indexes shed even further light on the state of human well-being in countries across the world.

The Human Development Report (UNDP, 2019) explored inequalities in human development; while "the first two decades of the 21st century have seen remarkable progress in reducing extreme deprivations, gaps remain unacceptably wide for a range of capabilities — the freedoms for people to be and do desirable things such as go to school, get a job, or have enough to eat" (p. 1). Further, inequalities are taking different forms as the climate crisis and technological changes sweep the world. While global inequalities in life expectancy at birth have declined, the inequalities that shape opportunities later in life are increasing.

Figure 12.1

The Main Components of the UN's Human Development Index (HDI)

It is necessary to look beyond income if global inequity is to be tackled in all its forms.

UNDP & OPHI (2020).

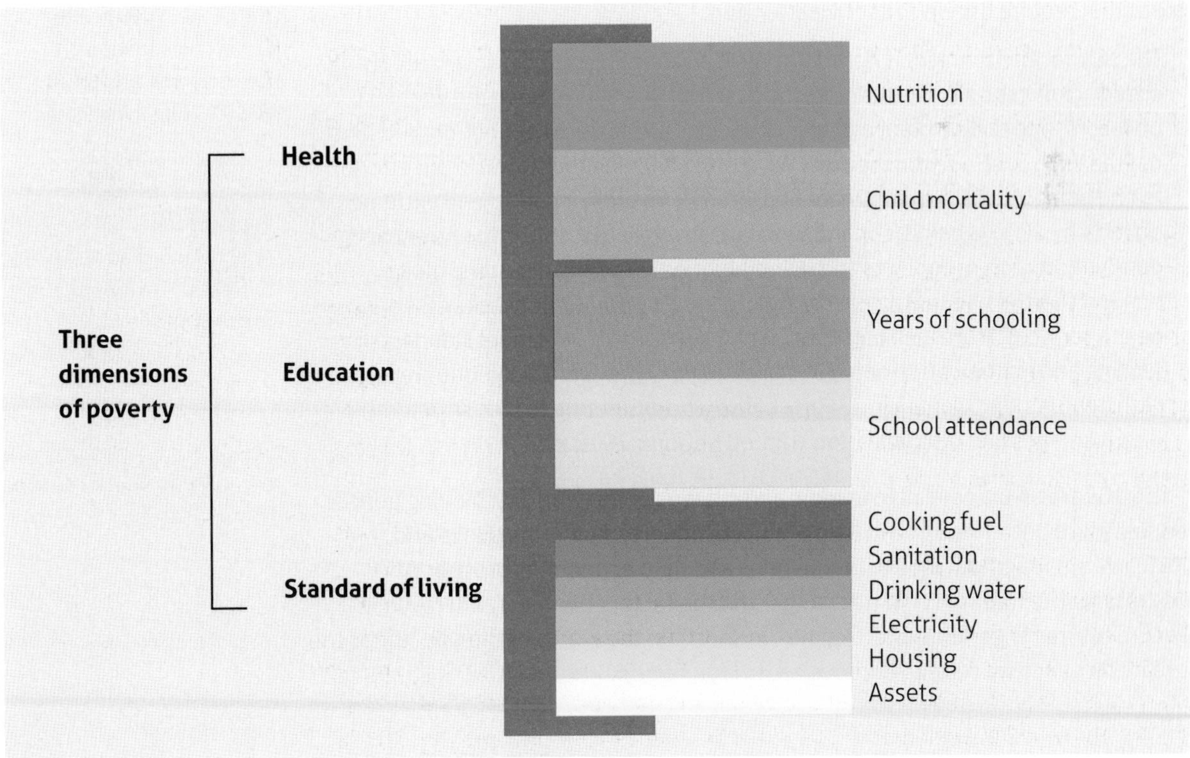

(2) Sustainable Development Goals (SDGs)

The HDI focuses on what a person can be or do and focuses on individual outcomes (Stewart, 2013). However, research shows that a diverse set of structural obstacles to human development exist. These systemic barriers go beyond an individual's control and they affect inequality between individuals and groups (United Nations, 2019). Both socio-economic and political inequality need to be addressed if full human development is to occur.

The Sustainable Development Goals (SDGs) were adopted by all UN member states in 2015 to address precisely this problem. They were part of a call to end poverty permanently, to protect the planet, and to ensure that all people enjoy peace and prosperity. The premise underlying the SDGs is that economic development must balance social, economic, and environmental sustainability. Through the UN's pledge to "leave no one behind," the member states also committed to fast-track those furthest behind. The SDGs pledged several life-changing "zeros" — including *zero poverty, zero hunger, zero AIDS,* and *zero discrimination against women and girls* — and all by 2030.

Implementing the Global Goals

In order to make the 2030 Agenda a reality, there must be a strong commitment to implementing the global goals.

The Division for Sustainable Development Goals (DSDG) in the UN Department of Economic and Social Affairs provides support and capacity-building for the SDGs and related thematic issues — water, energy, climate, oceans, urbanization, transport, science and technology, the Global Sustainable Development Report, partnerships, and Small Island Developing States.

DSDG also plays a key role in evaluating the implementation of the 2030 Agenda and in advocacy and outreach activities relating to the SDGs.

The SDGs set out an ambitious agenda. They seek to eliminate (rather than reduce) poverty and they include demanding targets on health, education, and gender equality. The SDGs are universal, applying to all countries and all people and address issues that were not included in earlier targets, such as climate change, sustainable consumption, innovation, and the importance of peace and justice (UNDP, n.d.). Notwithstanding the progress to date, the Sustainable Development Goals Report for 2019 (written before the COVID–19 pandemic) identified many areas that require urgent collective attention.

> The natural environment is deteriorating at an alarming rate: sea levels are rising; ocean acidification is accelerating; the past four years have been the warmest on record; one million plant and animal species are at risk of extinction; and land degradation continues unchecked. We are also moving too slowly in our efforts to end human suffering and create opportunity for all: our goal to end extreme poverty by 2030 is being jeopardized as we struggle to respond to entrenched deprivation, violent conflicts and vulnerabilities to natural disasters. Global hunger is on the rise, and at least half of the world's population lacks essential health services. More than half of the world's children do not meet standards in reading and mathematics; only 28% of persons with severe disabilities received cash benefits; and women in all parts of the world continue to face structural disadvantages and discrimination. (United Nations, 2019, p. 5)

The SDGs are an urgent call to leaders and citizens of the world. Achieving gender equality and better health will help eradicate poverty. Fostering peace and inclusive societies will reduce inequalities and help economies prosper. And addressing the threat of climate change, and the factors behind it, will result in a secure future for generations to come. "In short," in the words of the UN, "this is the greatest chance we have to improve life for future generations" (UNDP, 2015).

The Sustainable Development Goals

The 17 Sustainable Development Goals are:

1. No poverty
2. Zero hunger
3. Good health and well-being
4. Quality education
5. Gender equality
6. Clean water and sanitation
7. Affordable and clean energy
8. Decent work and economic growth
9. Industry, innovation and infrastructure
10. Reduced inequality
11. Sustainable cities and communities
12. Responsible consumption and production
13. Climate action
14. Sustainable life below water
15. Sustainable life on land
16. Peace and justice strong institutions
17. Partnerships to achieve the goals

United Nations (2015). Transforming Our World: The 2030 Agenda for Sustainable Development. New York, NY: United Nations. Development Programme.

12.4 Taking Global Responsibilities Seriously

Social workers in Canada and around the world have a responsibility to advocate for, participate in, and pay attention to global social justice. These professional responsibilities are supported by the National Schools of Social Work accrediting body (Canadian Association for Social Work Educators [CASWE]) and through ethical codes and standards of practice developed by the Canadian Association of Social Workers (CASW). These national organizations participate as members in the International Federation of Social Workers (IFSW), and the CASWE has representation on the International Association of Schools of Social Work (IASSW). Through these collaborations, social workers in Canada can stay informed about, and contribute to, multiple international and global issues.

The persistence of extreme poverty, civil war and conflict, and climate change calls for a shared understanding of our moral connections (Brown, 2016). Global citizenship requires an understanding of the interconnectedness of human beings and the environment, a respect for cultural diversity and human rights, and a commitment to attaining social justice for people around the world (Sherman, 2016).

The Global Agenda for Social Work and Social Development

At the 2010 Joint World Conference on Social Work and Social Development in Hong Kong, the IFSW, the IASSW, and International Council on Social Welfare (ICSW) held their first fully integrated, joint conference in recent times. The consultation culminated in a framework for action entitled *The Global Agenda for Social Work and Social Development.*

The Global Agenda for Social Work and Social Development identified four pillars (or themes). They were:

- Promoting social and economic equalities
- Promoting the dignity and worth of peoples
- Promoting community and environmental sustainability
- Strengthening recognition of the importance of human relationships

The Global Agenda energized and united social work and social development efforts around the world and guided the work of these global bodies throughout the 2010s decade. It was a framework to "address the worldwide dynamics that perpetuate poverty, inequality of opportunities and access to resources, and oppression, to give major prominence to the key contributions of social work and social development" (IASSW, ICSW, IFSW, 2014, p. 3).

Reports on the first two pillars were launched at the world conferences in 2014 and 2016; the third report was launched at the 2018 world conference in Dublin. The final report was launched at the Virtual World Conference held in 2020 (originally scheduled to be in Calgary).

A summary of these four reports is provided on the following pages.

Gender equality is not only a fundamental human right, but a necessary foundation for a peaceful, prosperous, and sustainable world.

There has been progress over the last decades: More girls are going to school, fewer girls are forced into early marriage, more women are serving in Parliament and positions of leadership, and laws are being reformed to advance gender equality.

Despite these gains, many challenges remain: discriminatory laws and social norms remain pervasive, women continue to be underrepresented at all levels of political leadership, and 1 in 5 women and girls between the ages of 15 and 49 report experiencing physical or sexual violence by an intimate partner within a 12-month period.

The effects of the COVID–19 pandemic could reverse the limited progress that has been made on gender equality and women's rights. The coronavirus outbreak exacerbates existing inequalities for women and girls across every sphere — from health and the economy, to security and social protection.

Women play a disproportionate role in responding to the virus, including as frontline health care workers and carers at home. Women's unpaid care work has increased significantly as a result of school closures and the increased needs of older people. Women are also harder hit by the economic impacts of COVID–19, as they disproportionately work in insecure labour markets. Nearly 60 % of women work in the informal economy, which puts them at greater risk of falling into poverty.

The pandemic has also led to a steep increase in violence against women and girls. With lockdown measures in place, many women are trapped at home with their abusers, struggling to access services that are suffering from cuts and restrictions. Emerging data shows that, since the outbreak of the pandemic, violence against women and girls — and particularly domestic violence — has intensified.

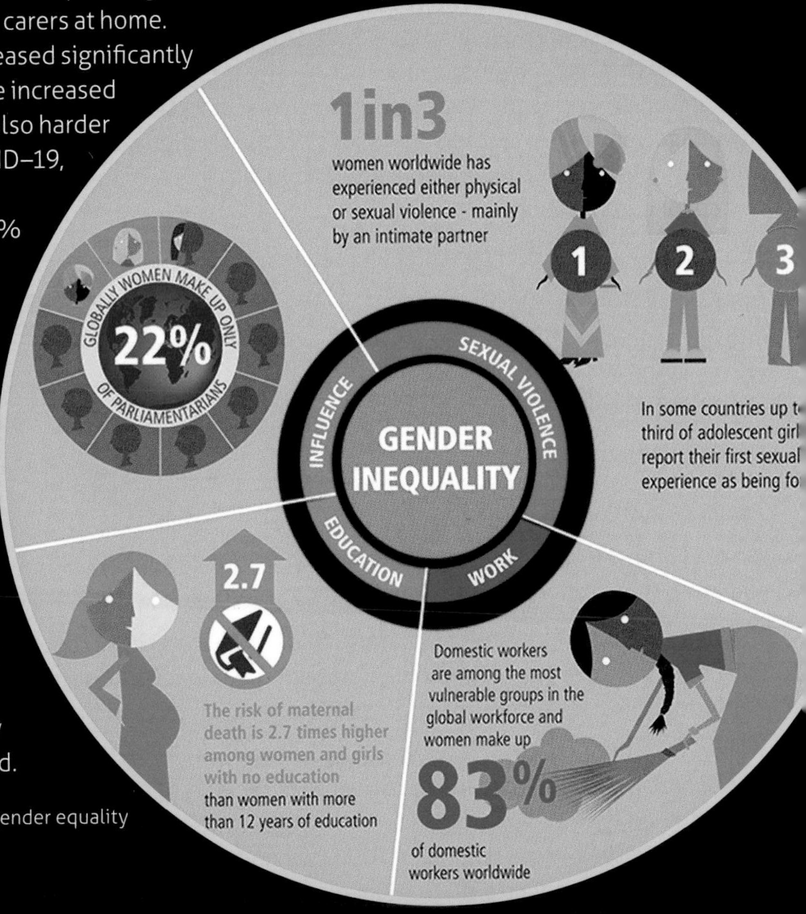

GENDER INEQUALITY
INFLUENCE
SEXUAL VIOLENCE
EDUCATION
WORK
1in3
women worldwide has experienced either physical or sexual violence - mainly by an intimate partner
1
2
3
In some countries up t
third of adolescent girl
report their first sexual
experience as being fo
GLOBALLY WOMEN MAKE UP ONLY
22%
OF PARLIAMENTARIANS
2.7
The risk of maternal death is 2.7 times higher among women and girls with no education than women with more than 12 years of education
Domestic workers are among the most vulnerable groups in the global workforce and women make up
83%
of domestic workers worldwide

Sustainable Development Goal 5: Achieve gender equality and empower all women and girls.

8
MARCH
HAPPY WOMEN'S DAY

International Women's Day

Report 1 (2014): Promoting Social and Economic Equalities

The first report in 2014 addressed the problems of social and economic inequality. Social workers recognize that, for many people, "the opportunities for social mobility and full realization of their potential are beyond their own efforts; family inheritance and place of birth (be it locality, community, or country) and access to resources are determining factors for many" (IASSW, ICSW, IFSW, 2014, p. 3). The widening social and economic inequality within and across most countries is well-documented. It not only affects the poor, but is also detrimental to growth, stability, and well-being in general.

There is a global consensus on the need to bridge the divide between the "haves" and the "have-nots" as evidenced by the groundswell of support for the International Labour Conference Recommendation 202 (June 2012) concerning National Floors of Social Protection that every country should establish and maintain. These guarantees should ensure, at a minimum, that "over the life cycle, all in need have access to essential health care and to basic income security" (IASSW, ICSW, IFSW, 2014).

A just and fair social environment is required in order for people, families, and communities to have access to choices for well-being. Inequality constrains opportunities and keeps people in poverty and disadvantage. It is also demonstrable that "growing inequalities can be arrested by integrated policies that are universal in principle while paying particular attention to the needs of disadvantaged and marginalized populations" (United Nations, 2013. p.21). In order to promote socio-economic equalities, advocacy in the following areas was identified for urgent action:

- The realization of human rights for all peoples
- A socially just international economy
- The development of socio-economic structures that ensure environmental sustainability
- The recognition that social cohesion and institutional solidarity must be at the forefront of policy and government decisions

- **Canada's Contribution**

Toward this end, the Canadian Association of Social Workers (CASW) commissioned two reports on social and economic rights.

- The *Canada Social Transfer Project: Accountability Matters* (2012) critically examined the inconsistent implementation of the Canada Social Transfer (CST), the primary source of federal funding that supports provincial and territorial social welfare programs.
- The *Canada Social Transfer and the Social Determinants of Health* (2013) examined policies and practices in relation to social service funding and delivery, and their impacts on social determinants of health. The authors conclude that "economic and social inequalities are exacerbated by the inadequacy of (financial) benefits" (p. 2).

Global Poverty

COVID–19, the newest and most immediate threat to poverty reduction worldwide, has unleashed socio-economic shock waves that have long-term implications.

The latest research from the World Bank suggests that the effects of the COVID-19 pandemic will almost certainly be felt in most countries through to 2030. The World Bank reckons that the original goal of bringing the absolute poverty rate to less than 3% globally by 2030 is now beyond reach without swift and substantial policy action.

Report 2 (2016): Promoting the Dignity and Worth of People

Poverty, or extreme inequality, is one of the most undignified experiences for millions of people. It not only creates economic vulnerabilities, but also pushes people to live a life devoid of dignity and self-worth. The IFSW, the IASSW, and the ICSW describe the aims of this pillar in the Global Agenda to:

> shape environments in which people can live without fear, give expression to their identity and personality as they wish whilst showing respect to others, care for their family and community members, practice their beliefs and religions, participate in and shape their communities through social as well as political engagement and have access to the resources needed for a dignified and secure life. (IASSW, ICSW, IFSW, 2016, p. 5)

For people living in poverty, there are frequent threats to health and safety, sanitation facilities are seriously inadequate, and thousands resort to begging and homelessness. Lack of respect for dignity and worth of peoples is evident worldwide, sometimes as a consequence of age, race, or gender, but also for minority groups such as people with disabilities and certain health conditions and LGBTQ+ people.

The large numbers of the world population who lack access to safe living and working environments, clean water, and certainty for their futures experience a lack of dignity and worth (Mukherjee et al., 2011). Respect for the dignity and worth of peoples is therefore a profound and practical challenge in a divided world (IASSW, ICSW, IFSW, 2016).

- **Canada's Contribution**

Toward this end, in 2015, the Canadian Association of Social Workers (CASW, 2015) released a policy paper proposing a new Social Care Act for Canada that called for a guaranteed annual income for all Canadian citizens and proposed principles of public administration, comprehensiveness, universality, portability, accessibility, and fairness in ways similar to how the Canada Health Act ensures that all citizens have access to the same quality of health care.

In June 2020, in the midst of the COVID–19 pandemic, the CASW also released a statement recognizing and strongly condemning the rise in racist incidents directed at people of Chinese and Asian descent. The release drew attention to all forms of racism, including anti-Black and anti-Indigenous racism. It called upon the media to cease minimizing language around racism, to encourage the public to actively intervene and prevent racism incidents, and for governments to participate and promote actions that condemn discrimination and promote inclusion, respect, and diversity (CASW, 2020).

Dignity and Worth

Respecting the "dignity and worth of peoples" is the second pillar of The Global Agenda for Social Work and Social Development and is at the heart of CASW's Code of Ethics. Value 1 of the Code of Ethics states:

> *Social work is founded on a long-standing commitment to respect the inherent dignity and individual worth of all persons* (CASW, 2005, p. 4).

This principle is also embedded in the Canadian Charter of Rights and Freedoms, in the Universal Declaration of Human Rights, and in the UN's Human Development Index and Sustainable Development Goals.

Report 3 (2018): Promoting Community and Environmental Sustainability

Social work has always been concerned with the health and well-being of people in the communities and the environments within which they live and move. However, historically, little attention has been paid to the physical and natural environment or to environmental sustainability. This was the focus of the 2018 Global Agenda report.

A number of social problems relating to community and environmental sustainability were identified as affecting social work practice in each region of the world in different ways and to different degrees.

> The growing awareness of the impact of environmental changes on people includes concerns about food insecurity, water shortages, vulnerability to natural disasters, rising sea levels, desertification, and housing pressures, including the rapid growth of urban informal settlements (slums). Environmental pressures are stimulating and sustaining major conflicts and wars and contributing to the largest migration of peoples in the history of the world. (IASSW, ICSW, IFSW, 2018, p. 8)

The contemporary social work focus on environmental justice is critical to the well-being and survival of both people and the planet. By exploring sustainable community themes, the profession is also rediscovering its roots — and the reality that social work must take a holistic approach if we wish to understand people and support them in responding to their circumstances and difficulties.

Neoliberal shifts in budgets have reduced funding to community organizations. This impacts environmental public health research on issues such as the impact of urban design on improving the health of residents by encouraging and maximizing active lifestyles. Additionally, the production of inexpensive goods has led to an increase in consumption (i.e., the "replace it, don't fix it" cycle). Increased consumption puts stress on the environment and impacts the ecological cycle.

- **Canada's Challenges**

For Canada, the environmental challenges are immense. For example, despite an election promise to eliminate boil-water advisories by 2021, the current investment by the federal government in improving water systems has been estimated to be insufficient to end all advisories. For most communities, at issue is a lack of modern water treatment systems and problematic water storage and delivery systems.

In the CASW scope of practice, the global vision of social work is a world consistently working toward social justice and well-being for all citizens with a person-in-environment focus. Social justice is a focus of CASW's code of ethics, and the next revision will focus on reconciliation with Canada's Indigenous peoples as a tenet of social work in Canada.

Sustainable Communities

Throughout the world, most people want the same things. They want access to clean air and water; opportunities to succeed; a safe and healthy community to raise their children; shelter; lifelong learning; a strong sense of community; and the ability to have a say in the decisions that affect their everyday lives.

A sustainable community addresses these multiple human needs. It is a place where persons of diverse backgrounds and perspectives are welcome and safe and where opportunity and prosperity are shared.

Report 4 (2020): Recognition of the Importance of Human Relationships

The fourth and final pillar of the Global Agenda was focused on the importance of human relationships. In this respect, it returned to the origin and heart of social work practice — relationships between people.

Social workers know that healthy relationships promote healing and well-being. Fractured relationships cause conflict and pain (IASSW, ICSW, IFSW, 2020). This final report reviewed how improved human relationships can lead to human betterment and social progress in the period of global challenges ahead. The final report identified the following themes:

- **Relationships in work.** A significant concern for many social workers around the globe is the challenges arising from poorly resourced and unhelpful working environments. This includes negative managerial relationships that appear to value procedures, data, financial calculations, and efficiency over human relationships. There is growing evidence that positive attitudes and relationships in the workplace result in higher staff morale and stronger commitment. The resulting more stable workforce creates positive outcomes, user satisfaction, and even efficiency and cost savings.
- **Relationship-based practice.** Professional discussions in recent years have referred to the "rediscovery" of relationship-based social work practice: "which broadly emphasizes 'capabilities,' 'strengths,' 'emotions,' and 'expertise' of service users based on lived experience alongside the practitioners' 'use of self' within relationships to ... support a process of discovery and transformation" (p. 17).
- **Relationships with service users and co-production.** Engaging with service users to work jointly and equally together to "co-produce" and achieve agreed outcomes is gaining recognition in policy development. Involving people with lived experience as trainers and assessors "enables oppressed social groups to represent the world as their own and on their own terms, since only then can they change it according to their own aspirations" (p. 18).
- **Relationships to secure resources and funding.** Effective relationships with like-minded professional and grassroots organizations to bring pressure to bear on governments and to influence public opinions was an important highlight from various global regions.
- **Digital relationships through social media.** Advocating for social media organizations to implement policies that protect children and vulnerable people and seek to influence governments to enact appropriate legislation was raised globally.

Developed in collaboration by IFSW, IASSW, and ICSW, this final report answers the question: What do the people (clients, service users, citizens, beneficiaries) with whom social workers interact want to see improved? The conclusion: "The regional reports imply that people who use services tend to want the same things as the practitioners, namely adequate resources, quality services, respectful relationships and a positive working environment" (p. 19).

"Relationships are one of the most important aspects of our lives. Nevertheless, building positive and meaningful relationships can be very challenging for many people. Technology is changing relationships as we know them. Online hate speech is a growing problem. Fake news is dominating minds and headlines.

"In this atmosphere and culture, building sustainable human relationships becomes an important part of the work of social workers.

"Only when we are willing to value and promote relationships that are based on mutual trust, then we are in the way to reduce destructive dynamics in our society.

"Social workers, offering relationship in a professional context, give people a chance to grow and a way to define who are they and what they can do to improve their lives."

Ana Radulescu, President of the International Federation of Social Workers, Europe.

12.5 The New Global Agenda, 2020–2030

Beginning in 2018, the three sister organizations — International Association of Schools of Social Work (IASSW), International Council on Social Welfare (ICSW), and International Federation of Social Workers (IFSW) — began the consultation process to develop the Global Agenda themes for the 2020 decade.

Building on the themes of the 2010–2020 agenda, the two-year consultation commenced with an online process enabling individuals to submit proposals. This was followed by national and regional workshops and culminated in discussions at the virtual world conference in 2020 (IFSW, 2020).

Ethical Obligations of Canadian Social Workers

The Canadian Association of Social Workers' Code of Ethics, Section 8.0, stipulates that "social workers advocate for change in the best interests of clients and for the overall benefit of society, the environment and the global community."

CASW, 2005.

The 2020–2030 Themes

In the consultation phase, the IASSW President, Annamaria Campanini, challenged social workers and the social justice community to reimagine a new world that critically interrogates and challenges the pervasive influences of neoliberal capitalist globalization, new public management, and the indiscriminate adoption of science of the logical positivist tradition.

Further, she identified pervasive social ills that individuals and families across the globe experience, such as "ongoing human rights abuses, poverty and inequality, hunger, environmental disasters linked to climate change and global warming, wars and conflict, drug and human trafficking, xenophobia, migration, and gender-based violence" (IASSW, ICSW, IFSW, 2019, p. 5).

Campanini stated:

> A new world is only possible if social work and social development educators and practitioners unite in protecting people who are in vulnerable positions, but at the same time building their agency to engage in challenging and undoing oppression, discrimination, marginalization and exclusion, generally based on intersecting social criteria such as race, class, gender, caste, disability, sexual orientation, geographic location, religion and language. (p. 5)

The culminating conversation about the 2020–2030 agenda occurred at the virtual world conference where more than 20,000 participants from 185 countries from all parts of the social work system came together — political leaders, people who have experienced care, community leaders, educators, social service leaders, and social workers.

The Global Agenda 2020–2030 sets the framework for the global efforts of social workers and social welfare advocates over the next decade. IFSW Secretary-General Dr. Rory Truell concluded the world conference by highlighting the importance of social work "in advocating that formal social protection systems need to change focus from providing services for people in crisis to becoming agencies of social transformation that prevent social crisis" (IFSW, 2020, para 5).

The Global Agenda highlights the importance of co-building and co-designing alongside communities, as well as underscoring the message that social work is essential for every country´s economic and social development.

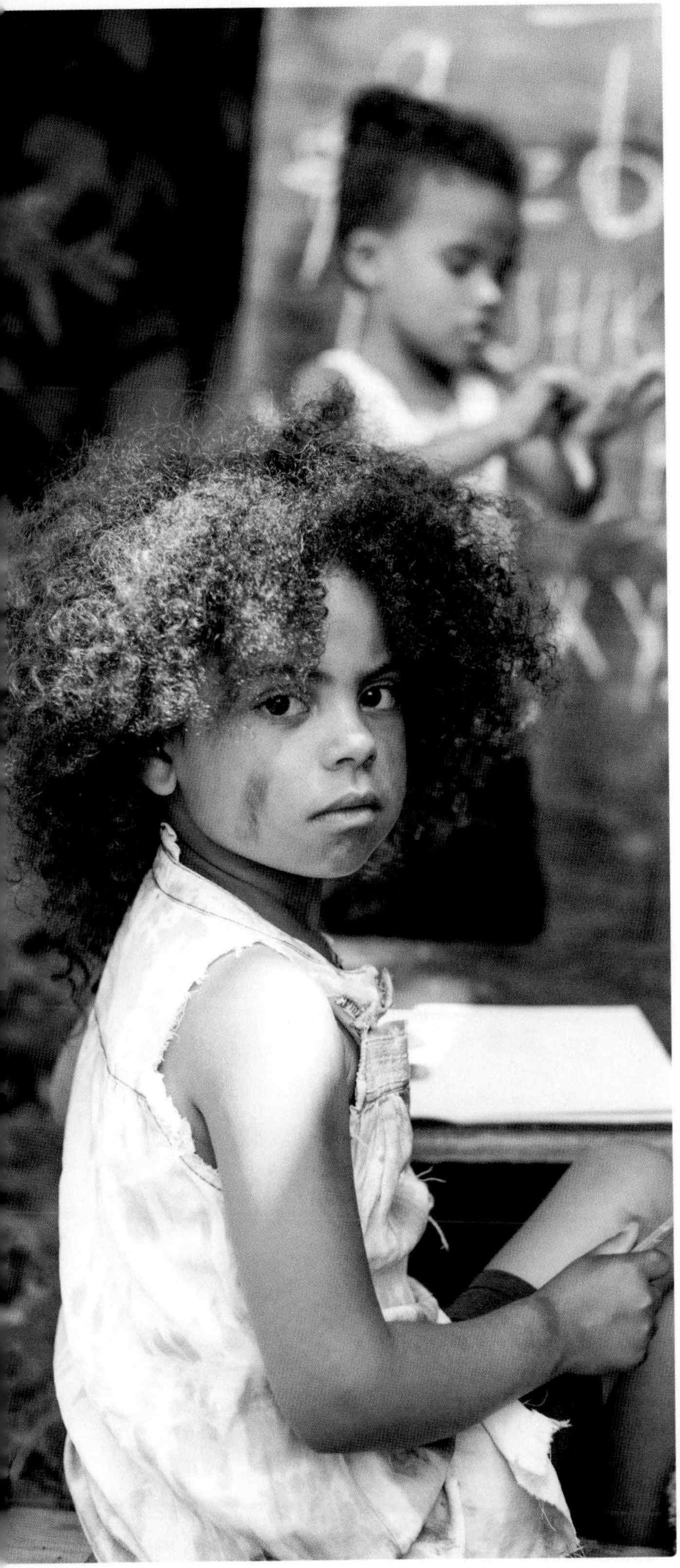

The Global Agenda

The five new themes for the 2020–2030 agenda were presented at the end of the 2020 virtual conference:

1. **Valuing Social Work as an Essential Service**
   - Realizing the essential role of the social work profession to connect people, communities, and systems; to co-build sustainable communities; and to contribute to liveable futures
   - Resourcing the profession with legal recognition, respectful working conditions, education, and continuing professional development and supporting professional associations
2. **Co-Building Inclusive Social Transformation**
   - Co-building with people, families, communities, social movements, and governments to achieve inclusive social transformation locally, nationally, regionally, and globally
   - Promoting participatory democracy, gender equality, and action to address racism, economic sustainability, and climate justice
3. **Ubuntu: "I am because we are"**
   - Making nurturing relationships central to the social work profession in all aspects of our work
   - Promoting Indigenous knowledge and the decolonization of the social work profession
4. **Transforming Social Protections Systems**
   - Transforming social protections systems to secure the human dignity and rights of all peoples
   - Strengthening connections for security and change. Promoting harmony in relationships and a way of living between peoples, communities, and mother earth
5. **Promoting Diversity and the Power of Joint Social Action**
   - Celebrating the strengths of all people and their active role in leading social development
   - Working together to co-design and co-build thriving communities and societies for people and the environment

Social Welfare in Perspective

It's Time to Listen to the Inuit

It Is Time to Humanize Climate Change Issues

The Inuit and the world's Indigenous peoples live with the impacts of climate change every day, even after the news cycle moves on.

When other regions of Canada and world are struck with major environmental and natural disasters, communities, first responders, and the media rush to their aid. Not so for the Inuit and other Indigenous peoples of our country, who have already experienced life-threatening emergencies on many levels, and are now at the front lines of the slow, multifaceted disaster that is climate change.

Because temperatures in the Arctic are rising faster than anywhere else in the world, we must look to the experiences of Inuit as a harbinger of what is to come, and seek their guidance on how to live more sustainably.

Virtually every community across the North is now struggling to cope with extreme coastal erosion, thawing permafrost, and rapid destructive runoff, which particularly affects coastal communities in Alaska and in northern and western Canada. Despite our cold northern winters, sea ice continues to rapidly decline. Glacial melt, long relied on for drinking water, is now unpredictable. In one stunning case, the Kaskawulsh Glacier in the Yukon has receded so far that its meltwater has changed direction, flowing south toward the Gulf of Alaska and the Pacific Ocean instead of north toward the Bering Sea. Ice that used to serve as our winter highways is giving way and invasive species are travelling much farther north than ever before. While the impact and extent of each change varies across the North, the trends are consistent. The change is not just coming, it is already here.

Melting Arctic ice has also attracted the attention of foreign governments, researchers, and corporations who see an opportunity to access the North's wealth of resources. But this interest has to be better informed by awareness of what is happening to Indigenous communities, who are trying to cope with the grave reality of their changing environment.

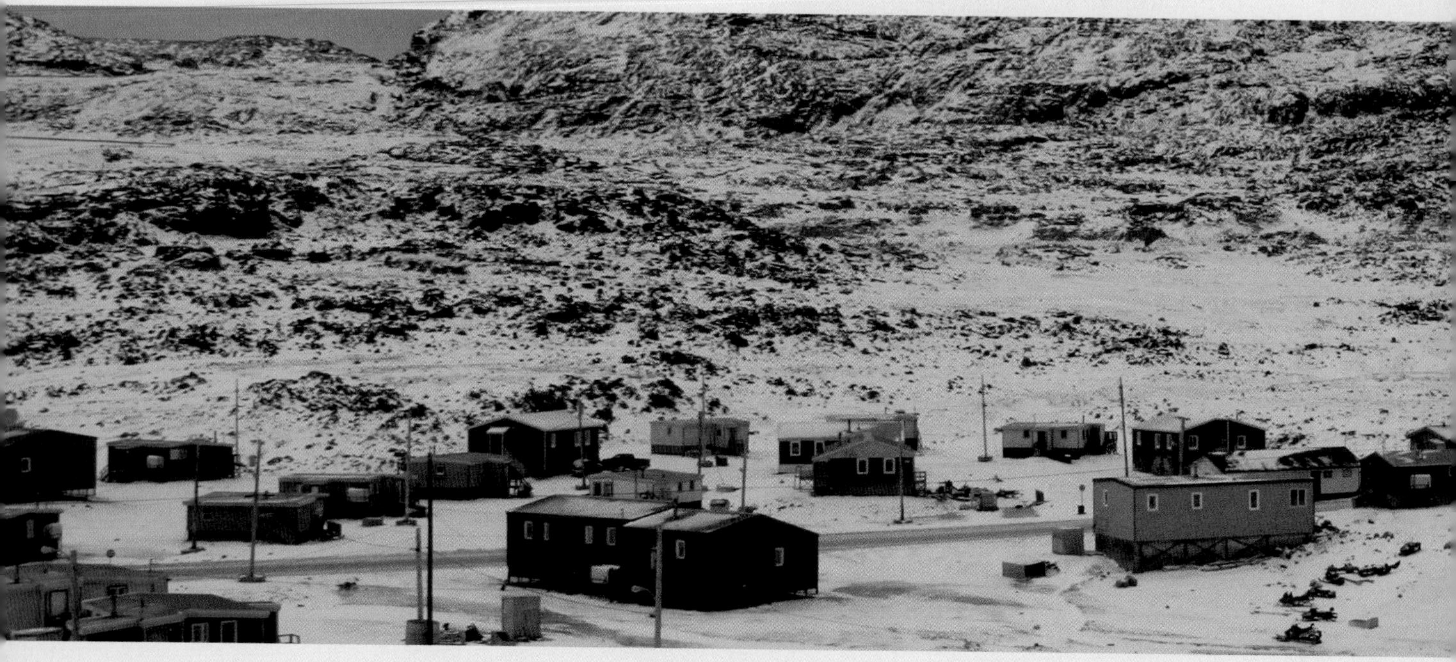

Recently, the United Nations Intergovernmental Panel on Climate Change (IPCC) issued a special report on the impacts of global warming 1.5°C above pre-industrial levels. The report paints a stark picture: humans have already caused approximately 1.0°C of global warming and without an immediate and concerted effort to reduce greenhouse gas emissions, the 1.5°C threshold will be reached sometime between 2030 and 2052.

In order to arrest this dangerous trajectory, the world must take note of what is happening in the Arctic — because what happens in the Arctic does not stay in the Arctic. Arctic ice is the planet's air conditioner; as it melts, that air conditioner is breaking down, creating havoc around the world.

Environmental advocates around the world have sought to protect human rights affected by dangerous climate change through various kinds of legal proceedings. Given that governments have been slow to act, recent cases in the Netherlands, Colombia, and the United States suggest that climate litigation may increasingly be seen as an essential tool to protect human rights and to safeguard the environment.

Although it can be hard for individuals to grasp the urgency of the situation, make no mistake: climate change will negatively impact our quality of life. Asserting this human perspective could help to spur action where other approaches — such as highlighting only the impact on wildlife like polar bears and coral reefs — have not yet achieved sufficient results. Inuit have much wisdom to share with the world about living sustainably, in harmony with nature — all while coping with the effects of climate change.

Inuit and Indigenous peoples provided life-saving guidance to early European visitors unfamiliar with the severe conditions of this land, which they ignored at their peril. The whole planet benefits from a frozen Arctic and Inuit still have much to teach the world about the vital importance of Arctic ice, not only to our culture, but to the health of the rest of the planet.

Sheila Watt-Cloutier, "It's Time to Listen to the Inuit on Climate Change," *Canadian Geographic*. November 19, 2018. Reproduced by permission. © 2018 Sheila Watt-Cloutier / *Canadian Geographic*.

Sheila Watt-Cloutier is an Inuit environmental and human rights advocate, author of *The Right to Be Cold* (2015), and Nobel Prize nominee.

12.6 Global Challenges, 2020–2030

Rarely has any year been as tumultuous as 2020 for the social welfare and well-being of the global population. As the global social and economic conditions changed because of the COVID pandemic, "governments introduced social control measures (such as physical distancing) and economic interventions at a global scale never before seen and the role of multi-lateral institutions suddenly became central to politics, especially the World Health Organization and UN development agencies. This showed clearly that there is no truth in the political rhetoric that there are limits to the possibilities of government intervention and international co-operation" (IASSW, ICSW, IFSW, 2020, p. 5).

This section looks at ongoing global challenges that will shape the opportunities for a decent standard of well-being for the world's population over the foreseeable future. If the COVID pandemic has taught us anything about social welfare, it is that the world's priorities can change rapidly — and the government's ability to pivot and use resources to ensure social well-being for its population depends on core principles of inclusion, equity, and social justice for all.

COVID–19

The global experience of the COVID–19 pandemic affected all parts of the world, social and political consequences were profound, and social problems and tensions became visible and exacerbated. Those who are poorest suffer the most in a pandemic (IASSW, ICSW, IFSW, 2020). There is little doubt that through the recovery and into the post COVID–19 world, social relationships will be disrupted, the number of people in extreme poverty will increase, and unemployment will make the SDGs virtually impossible to achieve.

Although the consequences cannot be predicted, the pandemic will likely result in increased inequality. Rather than emphasizing closing borders, building walls, increasing separation, and reinforcing nationalism and racism, social workers will advocate for international solidarity, strengthening of multilateral organizations, and nurturing mutual respect.

- **A Role for Social Workers**

Many of the ways that social workers provided services prior to COVID–19 were no longer effective during the pandemic. COVID–19 pushed social workers into a crisis-management role, and prompted them to become creative and think of new ways of providing services (Truell & Crompton, 2020). For example, in Wuhan, Chen Lanlan, then Director of Wuhan Yifei Social Work Service Centre, described gathering an online group of colleagues using the WeChat app as the best way to organize people quickly. Although they were quickly overwhelmed as residents worried about what to do, the social work community in Wuhan managed to establish order by dividing the day into two shifts focused on simultaneously helping existing clients while expanding services to meet new needs — all through telephones and online networks rather than face-to fact contact (Truell & Crompton, 2020).

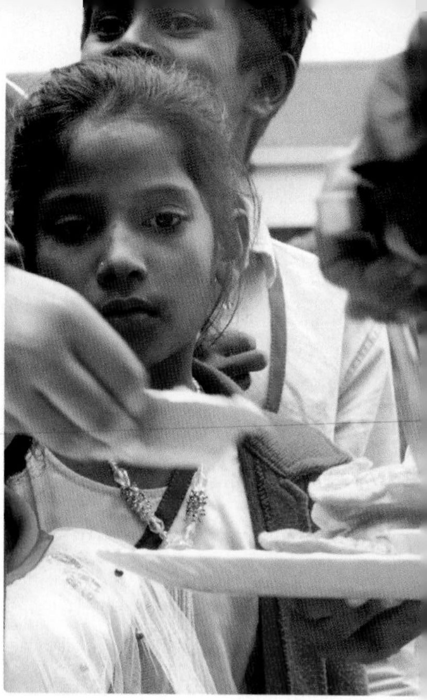

Global Food Insecurity

The United Nations Food and Agricultural Organization (FAO) has warned of "a looming food crisis," stating that the pandemic could have a devastating impact on global hunger and poverty — especially on the poorest and most vulnerable populations.

David Beasley, Executive Director of the United Nations World Food Programme, said that the world "could be facing multiple famines of biblical proportions." (USGLC, 2020).

USGLC (2020, July 7). COVID–19 Brief: Impact on food security. U.S. Global Leadership Coalition. https://www.usglc.org/coronavirus/global-hunger/

- **Dramatically Increased Global Poverty**

The devastating effects of the COVID–19 pandemic on world poverty requires emphasizing. In the first year of the pandemic, according to a World Bank study, COVID–19 likely pushed between 88 million and 115 million people into "extreme poverty" (Lakner et al., 2020). This translates into a global poverty rate — the share of the world's population living on less than $1.90 per day — between 9.1% and 9.4% in 2020. According to the World Bank, these estimates are close to the global poverty rate of 9.2% in 2017, implying a three-year setback in its own previously projected poverty reduction targets.

The World Bank study goes on to make projections for the remainder of the decade, and calculates that the upshot of COVID–19 is a 6- to 7-year setback in its global poverty reduction goal relative to their projections without the pandemic. It is important to stress that even these World Bank projections are almost certainly on the conservative side — they are estimates only of "extreme poverty" and represent "hypothetical scenarios" of what would happen if all countries from 2022 onwards grew in accordance to what occurred before COVID–19.

Either way, the implications of these estimates for the world's poorest poor are staggering. "Tallying the new poor for the whole decade (i.e., 2020–2030)," the World Bank report notes, "would result in between 831 million and 1.16 billion additional years spent in poverty due to COVID–19" (Lakner et al., 2020).

Figure 12.2

World Bank Projections of "Extreme Poverty" Globally Due to the COVID–19 Pandemic

Lakner, C. et al. (2020, June). *How Much Does Reducing Inequality Matter for Global Poverty?* World Bank Global Poverty Monitoring Technical Note.

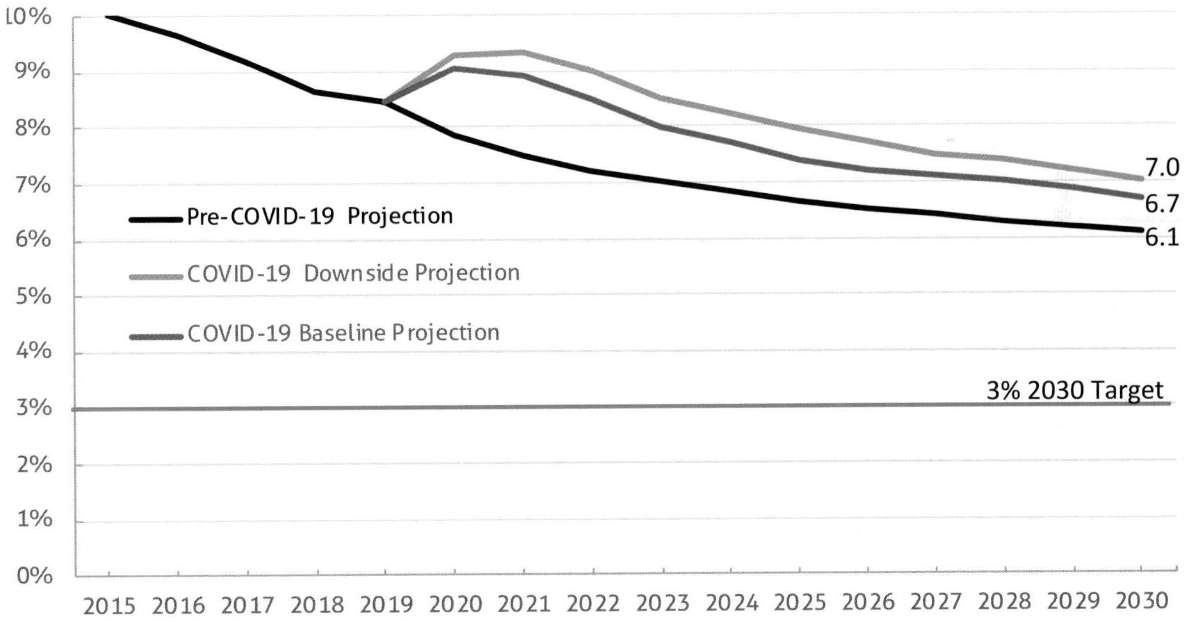

Note: Extreme poverty is defined as those living under $1.90 a day. 2017 is the last year with official global poverty rates. COVID–19 projections use June 2020 *Global Economic Prospects* (GEP) growth forecasts for 2019–2021 and country-specific historical (2008–2018) annual growth rates thereafter; Pre-COVID–19 projection uses June 2020 GEP forecast for 2019, January 2020 GEP forecast for 2020–2021, and historical growth rates thereafter.

Racial Inequity and the Anti-Racism Response

International migration significantly benefits and enriches Canada and international communities. However, some leaders seek to divide communities through politicization, which undermines democracy and inclusive civic engagement. Migrants may be targets of violence, and the climate of hostility makes it more difficult for agencies to secure funding and for newcomers to find a settled environment (IASSW, ICSW, IFSW, 2018).

Amid growing awareness of racial inequities in the number and intensity of cases of COVID–19 among Black people in the United States, the violent killing of George Floyd in May 2020 aroused rage around the world. Hundreds of thousands of people from different backgrounds across dozens of countries cried out that "Black Lives Matter." The Canadian Nurses Association president stated that "anti-Black racism is a public health emergency in Canada" and that longstanding and negative structural determinants of health have created and continue to reinforce serious health and social inequities for Black people in Canada (CNA, 2020).

Although Black Lives Matter focuses on anti-Black racism, Indigenous racism within the health system in Canada came to the forefront with the death of 37-year-old Joyce Echaquan in a Québec hospital as she livestreamed the racist tirade she experienced from staff. In the same month, health workers in BC were allegedly betting on Indigenous patients' blood alcohol levels. These recent events are further examples of the well-known and documented accounts of how racism contributes to poorer health outcomes for people of colour and Indigenous people in Canada (Godin, 2020).

- **A Role for Social Workers**

In a profession premised on pursuing social justice, the rise of anti-immigrant, Islamophobic, and racist narratives poses critical challenges to addressing the structural roots of social and power inequities (Ladhani & Sitter, 2020). "Social workers are one of the key professional groups engaging with displaced people, helping to build better relationships between local people and migrants, working to foster better mutual understanding and supporting migrants to find forms of employment" (IASSW, ICSW, IFSW, 2020, p. 11).

Since the late 1990s, schools of social work and practising social workers across Canada have shifted their focus from anti-racism to anti-oppressive practice as a way to avoid creating a hierarchy of oppressions. However, embedding anti-racism language within the language of diversity and multiculturalism may be insufficient in attending to the complexities of racial inequities.

Awakening to the extent and deep embeddedness of racism and racial realities can be overwhelming, but is necessary in order to move forward with meaningful actions in a world where racism permeates social, political, and economic life (Ladhani & Sitter, 2020).

Black Lives Matter

Black Lives Matter (BLM) is a political and social movement that advocates non-violent civil disobedience to protest police brutality and all forms of racially motivated violence against Black people.

BLM rose to prominence on social media in 2013 with the use of the hashtag #BlackLivesMatter after the acquittal of George Zimmerman in the 2012 shooting death of Black American teen Trayvon Martin.

The BLM movement gained widespread popular support in 2020 following the killing of George Floyd by Derek Chauvin, a Minneapolis police officer.

In the midst of a global pandemic, an estimated 15 million to 26 million people participated in the 2020 Black Lives Matter protests, making it one of the largest movements in United States history. Similar large protests took place in support of BLM in major and minor cities throughout the world.

Photo: A Black Lives Matter protest march in downtown Vancouver on June 19, 2020 to mark Juneteenth, a holiday celebrating the emancipation of those who had been enslaved in the United States.

Climate Change and Environmental Justice

As with combatting inequality and social injustice, minimizing the impact of environmental change is recognized as a core component of the UN's Sustainable Development Goals. Environmental concerns entered into public debate with Rachel Carson's publication *Silent Spring* in 1962. Since then, US Vice-President Al Gore's documentary *An Inconvenient Truth* (Gore, 2006) and many other reports on the risks of global climate change have raised alarms about global warming and the need for action to meet environmental challenges (McKinnon, 2008). More recently, the world was captivated by Swedish teenager Greta Thunberg, who has sparked young people around the world to undertake actions to bring attention to the climate crisis.

Severe weather events alone result in loss of income, property damage, lower productivity, the relocation of people, increased stress for families, and higher costs for health care and social services. The Government of Canada estimated that the 1998 ice storm in Ontario and Québec was responsible for 28 deaths, affected over 1.6 million Canadians due to electrical power failure, and stopped 2.6 million people from working. Economic losses amounted to $5.4 billion (Natural Resources Canada, 2004). In 2018, insured damage associated with severe weather events across Canada reached $1.9 billion (IBC-BAC, 2020). These are staggering numbers.

Worldwide, the United Nations reported that between 1995 and 2015, 6,457 weather-related disasters (floods, storms, droughts, heat waves, wildfires) claimed the lives of 600,000 people and affected an additional 4.2 billion people (United Nations, 2016). However, the human impact is not equal — low-income countries suffer the greatest losses.

Environmental justice is the principle that all people and communities are entitled to equal protection under environmental and public health laws and regulations. It involves fair treatment and meaningful involvement of all people regardless of race, colour, national origin, or income with respect to the development, implementation, and enforcement of environmental laws, regulations, and policies (EPA, 2020).

• A Role for Social Workers

For the most part, the social work profession has been slow to address the issues of sustainability and environmental justice (Drolet et al., 2015; McKinnon, 2008). In addition to protecting vulnerable individuals and communities affected by environmental change, the social worker's role may include critiquing laws, using mass media, facilitating workshops and public forums to raise consciousness, researching alternatives, informing public debate, advising decision makers, lobbying, contributing to policy formulation, and participating in social action, protests, and civil disobedience and facilitating others to join such actions (Ramsay & Boddy, 2017).

Schools of social work can facilitate making environmental justice and disaster interventions core elements in the social work repertoire of knowledge, skills, capacity building, and curriculum (Dominelli & Ku, 2017).

Environmental Justice

Environmental justice is the principle that all people and communities are entitled to equal protection under environmental and public health laws and regulations.

The principle involves fair treatment and meaningful involvement of all people regardless of race, colour, national origin, or income with respect to the development, implementation, and enforcement of environmental laws, regulations, and policies (EPA, 2020).

Migration, Population Movement, and COVID–19

Global climate change and the frequency of extreme weather events contribute to humanitarian migration. Sometimes this may be voluntary mobility as individuals with resources relocate, while in other situations an entire community may have no option but to relocate (IOM, 2020a). Migration and mobility are related to broader globalization processes associated with economic, social, political,and technological transformations (IOM, 2020a).

In the two years between 2018 and 2020, there were major migration and displacement events that caused great hardship and trauma as well as loss of life. Foremost were the displacements of millions of people due to conflict (such as within and from the Syrian Arab Republic, Yemen, the Central African Republic, the Democratic Republic of the Congo, and South Sudan), extreme violence (such as inflicted upon Rohingya people forced to seek safety in Bangladesh) or severe economic and political instability (such as faced by millions of Venezuelans) (IOM, 2020a).

Many migrants have increased vulnerability associated with COVID–19 due to personal, social, situational, and structural factors (IOM, 2020b). Travel restrictions to "flatten the curve" and to contain the virus have also greatly affected mobility. "Labour migration has been temporarily suspended in some countries while, in others, migration processing and assistance to asylum seekers are being slowed down" (IOM, 2020b).

Another consequence of the COVID–19 pandemic has been the exposure of the poor living and working conditions of migrant workers, making social distancing impossible, and the lack of health care services for them. This has resulted in a much higher incidence of the virus (IASSW, ICSW, IFSW, 2020). Fake news, misinformation, and politicization of issues lead to stigmatizing and exclusion, which carry higher risk for migrant populations as they hide potential symptoms rather than seeking treatment (IOM, 2020b).

- **A Role for Social Workers**

The global movement of people affects social work practice in many ways, both personally and professionally. Social workers can themselves be migrants, or can become involved with migration issues for reasons of personal interest or employment or as members of communities forced into migration (IASSW, ICSW, IFSW, 2018).

Social work experience throughout the world has highlighted that not all refugees seek the same futures and that policy and agency responses must take into account the differing needs and aspirations of the refugees and their communities (IASSW, ICSW, IFSW, 2016). Refugees are not helpless, as is often portrayed by the media and by some politicians. Refugees have significant resources, skills, strengths, and education and can make positive contributions to their new environments (IASSW, ICSW, IFSW, 2016).

A Global Refugee Crisis

"A dramatic increase in conflict coupled with environmental degradation as the result of climate change have now created a crisis affecting tens of millions, further exacerbating impacts on vulnerable populations. These numbers include refugees, particularly women and girls, including female-headed households, as well as internally displaced persons.

"These vulnerable people live in refugee camps, large urban settings, small towns, and in the countryside and are prone to facing marginalization due to their status, coupled with their intersecting identity factors including but not limited to, their gender and race."

Rae, B. (2020). *A global crisis requires a global response.* Report by Hon. Bob Rae, Special Envoy of Prime Minister of Canada on Humanitarian and Refugee Issues.

Populist Governments

Since the financial crisis of 2008, there has been a resurgence of ideas and movements that can be collectively termed nationalist or populist. In Europe, the rise of populism shifted the centre-left/centre-right duopoly that existed since the end of World War II, fragmenting the centre left and shifting support to the right (Galston, 2018).

In the late 20th century this shift appeared to reflect a response to economic distress; however, "it is now evident that populism draws strength from public opposition to mass immigration, cultural liberalization, and the perceived surrender of national sovereignty to distant and unresponsive international bodies" (Galston, 2018, para 2). Galston argues that "left unaddressed, the rise of anti-immigrant, anti-internationalist sentiment, which has shifted the political balance within Europe, could have grave consequences for liberal democracy itself" (para 3).

In the United States, Donald Trump entered the White House as a populist leader; joining other populist leaders around the world such as Erdogan in Turkey, Orban in Hungary, and Duterte in the Philippines. These leaders gain support from people who are experiencing rising inequality and feel that they have been "left behind" due to mass immigration and globalized economies (Champion, 2019). Unlike many other political ideologies, populism is not inherently left or right. Populists say they are rescuing democracies that have been hijacked by elites and are pushing back against liberal forms of democracy (Champion, 2019).

In general, Canada is considered a liberal-democratic country; however, Canada is not immune to the economic and demographic forces and populism dividing the United States. According to Graves and Valpy (2018), both associated with public policy faculties at Canadian universities, populism is the "biggest force reshaping democracy, our economies and public institutions" (para 2), and it has emerged due to economic despair, inequality, racism, and xenophobia. Further, it is very much alive in Canada, with an EKOS research survey in 2017 suggesting that 30 to 40% of adult Canadians are drawn to it (Graves & Valpy, 2018).

- **Role for Social Workers**

Some forms of populism embrace public services as a way to build support from the populace, as seen in Italy in the 1930s, but more frequently such movements do not recognize structural inequality, preferring to blame individuals for their own misfortunes. The result is resistance to financing services for minorities and those who are perceived as weak. This appears to describe the context for social work practice in much of the Western world and contrasts with the internationalist and more left-leaning political movements seen in the twentieth century (IASSW, ICSW, IFSW, 2018).

The divisiveness of populism is it opposition to humanitarian values, the idea of inclusive societies, and the need to protect the vulnerable — principles that are embedded in social work values and agendas.

Xenophobia

Xenophobia, the denigration of certain groups and populations, is frequently associated with viral outbreaks. It is for precisely this reason that the World Health Organization (WHO) opted against using a geographic location when officially naming the new coronavirus early in 2020.

"Stigma, to be honest, is more dangerous than the virus itself," Tedros Adhanom Ghebreyesus, the WHO director-general, stated recently. Nevertheless, many media outlets and US leaders, particularly former President Trump, referred to the disease as the "China virus" or the "Wuhan virus."

Technological Change and Social Media

Widespread access to social media and digital technologies presents both challenges and opportunities. "The increased flows and volumes of information and the ability to transport people and things to all corners of the earth are speeding up many social dynamics in the twenty-first century. The way cell phones impact personal interactions, the reality of presidential candidates whose idea of politics is sending out 140-character tweets, the rapidly shrinking attention spans of our children or students staring into their devices — are all illustrative and telling" (Smith, 2017, p. 8).

On the other hand, technology has opened up great potential, such as the spotlight that the Black Lives Matter movement has shone on the value of cell phone cameras to record events that previously may have been ignored, the usefulness of social media in organizing a range of social movements, the ability of poor people in areas of Africa with poor infrastructure to have access to modern banking and finance, and so on.

Technology has also become increasingly important in the migration process. The use of digital technology by migrants to gather information and advice in real time has raised interest and, at times, concern. For example, the use of apps "to share the latest information, including to support clandestine border crossings, together with the consolidation of social media platforms to connect geographically dispersed groups with common interests, has raised valid questions concerning the extent to which technology is used to support irregular migration, as well as to enable migrants to avoid abusive and exploitative migrant smugglers and human traffickers" (IOM, 2020a, p. 26).

On the other hand, access to emerging technology at low cost has provided migrants with better supports and integration in receiving countries, while maintaining social links and financial support to their families and societies back home, including through the increasing prevalence of "mobile money" apps (IOM, 2020a).

The New Normal

Use of video-conferencing software increased enormously as the coronavirus pandemic forced millions to work, learn, and socialize remotely. At its peak, Zoom reportedly counted more than 300 million daily participants in virtual meetings.

While video conferencing is sometimes confusing and its behavioural norms are still developing, many have become adept and look forward to a new normal where video conferencing and other technology provide multiple choices for accessibility.

- **A Role for Social Workers**

Social media is increasingly a tool for social work and community development and was increasingly used during COVID–19 to ensure physical distancing. However, while a benefit to many, social media presents many ethical challenges. To this end, CASW, along with other social work professional groups, have identified key ethical considerations.

On a broader scale, both individuals and government are becoming more able and adept at manipulating information on the Internet, while ethicists raise concerns about rights to privacy and free expression (IASSW, ICSW, IFSW, 2014).

12.7 Transformative Social Welfare

The welfare states created during the post–World War II period were aimed at reducing economic risks through universal health care, education, and income security. However, by the end of century, neoliberal polices essentially had undermined the notion that the state should be responsible for all citizens, and governments reduced social spending accordingly (Midgley, 2017). Subsequently, structural risks have left groups of individuals marginalized and discriminated against, with seemingly little being done to address chronic poverty. The 2020 COVID–19 pandemic highlighted the apparent inability of both traditional "safety net" and neoliberal policies to protect ordinary citizens.

Expanding Social Protections

Devereux & Sabates-Wheeler (2004) have conceptualized a "transformative social protections" framework that moves beyond the narrow "safety net" approach to social welfare. They advance a multi-faceted approach in which "strategies to deal with problems of social vulnerability require a transformative element, where 'transformative' refers to the need to pursue polices that relate to power imbalances in society that encourage, create and sustain vulnerabilities" (p. 9).

In this social protections model, the full range of social interventions can be grouped under four categories:

- **Protective measures.** Protective measures are narrowly targeted safety-net measures in the conventional sense — they aim to provide relief from deprivation and poverty. These programs include social assistance programs, disability benefits, old age security programs, etc.
- **Preventive measures.** Preventive measures seek to avert deprivation. This is similar to traditional social safety-net measures and includes programs such as the Canada Pension Plan, health insurance, maternity and paternity benefits, and Employment Insurance.
- **Promotive measures.** Promotive measures aim to enhance incomes and capabilities through a range of livelihood-enhancing programs such as school feeding programs, early childhood education, and training programs.
- **Transformative measures.** Transformative measures seek to address social equity and exclusion. They include upholding human rights for minority ethnic groups and changing regulatory frameworks to protect socially vulnerable groups against discrimination and abuse. This includes national anti-stigma campaigns to transform public attitudes and behaviour and enhance inclusion and social equity

While the COVID–19 pandemic has exposed the dire consequences of inequality, "the post-pandemic world could experience even greater inequalities unless governments do something" (Stiglitz, 2020). By broadening the scope of social policy interventions, the social protections framework is useful in helping to map out the new tasks ahead for governments and policymakers.

The transformative social protections framework is illustrated in Figure 12.3.

Figure 12.3 presents the social protections framework in graphic form. It can be read as follows:

- The solid black line indicates a direct relationship between preventive and promotive policies. For example, risk-reduction programs such as early childhood education provide opportunities that people would not otherwise have.
- The dashed line indicates a less obvious relationship. For example, minimum wage legislation can be both promotive and transformation as it enhances incomes.
- The thin dotted line indicates a weak relationship between protective and promotive aspects of social protection.
- Finally, the very thick dashed line indicates that many protective measures can have the unfortunate effect of reinforcing inequalities and patterns of exclusion.

Figure 12.3

A Conceptual Framework for Transformative Social Protections

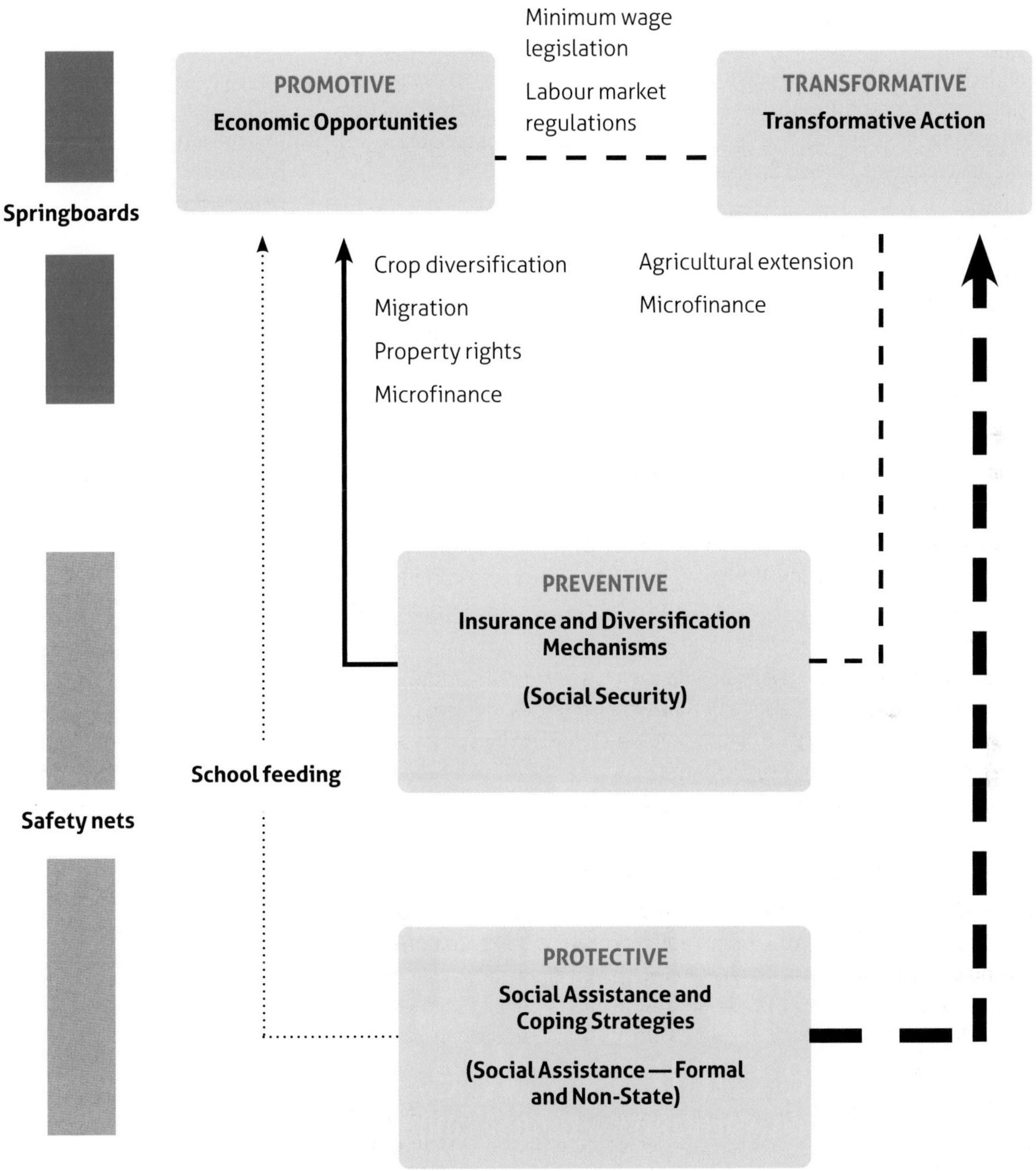

Devereux, S. & Sabates-Wheeler, R. (2004). *Transformative social protection.* IDS Working Paper 232. Institute of Development Studies.

Promoting Capacity Building

Social work's central role is to respond to people in their local environment — to support, protect, and transform. Change happens locally; however, local transformational change contributes significantly to the wider society and economies:

> As people become empowered they become engaged in economic activity and this leads to increased social and economic outcomes. A comprehensive social protection system contributes to the reduction of poverty, reduces inequalities, contributes to social cohesion, and lays the base for a socially sustainable economic development. (Basu & Strickler, 2013 cited in Stark, 2019, p. 15)

In the developing world and the developed world, the "aid" model has failed to provide sustainable change (Mansaray et al, 2020). Rather, the "trade, not aid" model is proving more effective in reducing poverty. It is also a model that "recognizes and reflects on Indigenous knowledge with its emphasis on the knowledge of intra-dependence of people and environment, which results in the balance of social equilibrium" (Mansarey et al., 2020, p. 13).

As we move into a post COVID–19 era, opportunities abound to promote creative and innovative practices that can ensure sustainable communities while protecting the future of the planet. The focus on social transformation centres on "working with people so that the vulnerable become strong; instead of being recipients of care from the community they become contributors to their community" (Mansarey et al., 2020, p. 45).

"I Am Because We Are"

The word and concept "Ubuntu" originates from the Indigenous peoples of South Africa and was popularized across the world by its president, Nelson Mandela.

"Ubuntu" is a philosophy that resonates with the social work perspective of the interconnectedness of all peoples and their environments. It speaks to the need for international solidarity and it also highlights the relevance of Indigenous knowledge and wisdom.

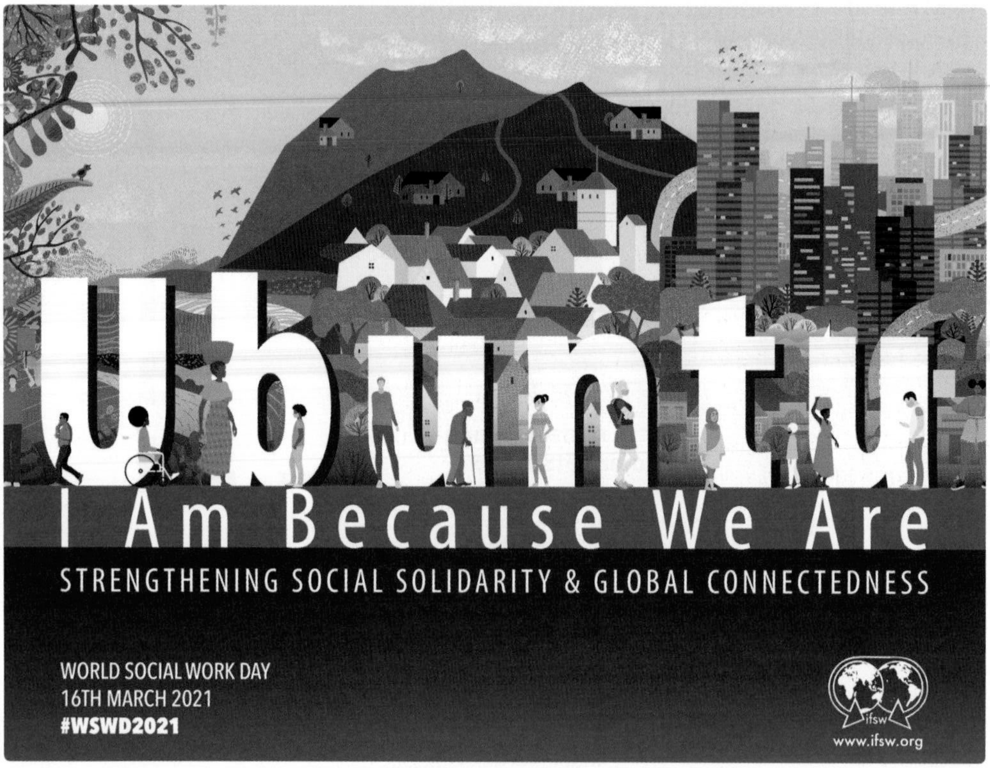

World Social Work Day

On the third Tuesday of March every year social workers all over the world celebrate the contributions of the profession to individuals, families, communities and wider society.

Developing Universal Social Opportunities

The five themes introduced earlier in this chapter were informed by IFSW's 90-plus years of global social work experience. They are built on the principles of inclusivity, participation, and the co-creation of meaningful social responses to build a thriving, sustainable, and just society of interconnected communities.

In light of the COVID–19 pandemic, social workers around the world are re-evaluating how they can do social work differently and better. Many of the traditional ways of working are being questioned and rejected as attention is paid to decolonizing the social work profession. The pandemic recovery period will provide new opportunities to contribute skill, knowledge, and expertise to ensure that the strengths of all people are acknowledged in order to fight inequality, and promote environmental and social justice.

The new working arrangements brought about by the lockdowns have already given rise to a re-evaluation of many social work practices. Social media, Skype, Zoom, and Microsoft Meetings are suddenly in the toolbox of the social worker. Adjusting to interviewing and meeting on screens and by telephone conversations rather than in face-to-face meetings has upended some social work practices. To be sure, not all the innovation has been welcomed, but some has taken people by pleasant surprise and will become commonplace.

The pandemic may have given momentum to new ideas and new ways of working, but it also continues to devastate people's lives. The redevelopment of social services will occur in the context of a gruelling global recovery process (Truell & Crompton, 2020, p. 39). Implementing transformative social change will not be easy. It will occur in the context of a protracted recovery from a major health and economic crisis resulting from the COVID–19 pandemic. However, there is an opportunity within this context to revisit the balance between collective responsibility for each other (social determination) and the right to self-determination, the balance of rights and responsibilities (Stark, 2019).

Achieving a just society requires universal social welfare programs that focus on fostering economic and social opportunities, especially for those who are most vulnerable. Over the next ten years, the international social work profession and its national affiliates will be pushing for state and NGO social protections to be developed *with* people rather than *for* them.

Canada and the world are stronger when we collaborate to strengthen all people and global communities and the environment we live in through supportive protections and inclusive opportunities.

Social Welfare Policy in Action

The Paris Agreement, 2015

Canada's Pan-Canadian Framework on Climate Change

The Paris Agreement on Climate Change of 2015 not only charted a new course in the global climate effort but represented a significant milestone in international cooperation.

The UN's 2015 Sustainable Development Goals coincided in time with another historic agreement. The Paris Agreement on Climate Change of December 12 brought all of its signatory nations into a common cause to undertake ambitious efforts to combat climate change and intensify the investments needed for a low-carbon future.

Meeting Global Warming Targets

Greenhouse gases (GHGs) trap heat in the Earth's atmosphere, so when more heat is trapped, the temperature of the planet increases. The Paris Agreement's aim is to keep the rise in global temperature this century less than 2° Celsius above pre-industrial levels and to pursue efforts to limit the increase to 1.5° Celsius.

The Agreement requires that all parties report regularly on their efforts at implementing the Agreement. All members of the UN Framework Convention on Climate Change (UNFCCC) have signed the agreement and 189 parties (of 197 parties) have ratified it. The only significant emitters who did not sign were Iran and Turkey.

Of course, there are also those who deny climate change or minimize its importance. In June 2017, US President Donald Trump announced the US's intention to withdraw from the Paris Agreement, and did so on November 4, 2020, shortly before the end of President Trump's 2016 term. President Biden renewed the US commitment to the Paris Agreement as one of his first executive orders in January 2021.

In 2020, the world was not on track to limit warming to 1.5°C and meet the Paris Agreement goals. The Climate Action Tracker (CAT) estimates that under current policies, the world will exceed 1.5°C of warming around 2035, 2°C around 2053, and 3.2°C by the end of the century.

The Pan-Canadian Framework on Clean Growth and Climate Change

Canada ratified the Paris Agreement on Climate Change on October 5, 2016 by a vote in Parliament. The Paris Agreement entered into force on November 4, 2016.

Under the Paris Agreement, Canada committed to reducing its GHG emissions by 30% below 2005 levels by 2030. The Government of Canada also announced that it will develop a plan to set Canada on a path to achieve a prosperous net-zero emissions future by 2050. These commitments will have an impact on Canada's future emissions projections, including for 2030, as new measures associated with this plan are developed and implemented.

To help guide its climate-change agenda, the federal government has developed the Pan-Canadian Framework on Clean Growth and Climate Change. The Framework was developed with the provinces and territories and in consultation with Indigenous peoples to help Canada meet its emissions reduction targets, grow the economy, and build resilience to a changing climate.

Canada is committed to implementing the Pan-Canadian Framework while strengthening existing and introducing new GHG-reducing measures to exceed Canada's 2030 emissions reduction goal, and begin work so that Canada can achieve net-zero emissions by 2050.

The Pan-Canadian Framework is Canada's collective plan for the country in relation to the Paris Agreement of 2015. It outlines a transition to a strong and competitive economy that will foster job creation, create clean technologies and exports, and provide a healthy environment for our children and grandchildren.

The Four Pillars of the Pan-Canadian Framework

The Pan-Canadian Framework on Clean Growth and Climate Change has four main pillars. Together, these interrelated pillars form an emissions-reduction plan.

1. **Price carbon pollution.** Pricing carbon pollution is an efficient way to reduce emissions, drive innovation, and encourage people and businesses to pollute less. However, relying on a carbon price alone to achieve Canada's international target would require a very high price.
2. **Additional measures to reduce emissions.** The second pillar involves removing barriers where pricing alone is insufficient. For instance, tightening energy-efficiency standards and codes for vehicles and buildings reduces emissions and help consumers save money.
3. **Adapt to climate change and build resilience.** Third, communities must be adequately prepared for climate risks like floods, wildfires, droughts, and extreme weather events, especially vulnerable regions like Indigenous, northern, coastal, and remote communities.
4. **Accelerate innovation for clean technology.** Finally, positioning Canada as a global leader on clean technology will lead to new good jobs across the country. Such investments will improve mitigation measures and equip Canada's workforce with the knowledge and skills to succeed.

The Rights of Indigenous Peoples

The Pan-Canadian Framework also reiterates Canada's commitment to nation-to-nation, government-to-government, and Inuit-to-Crown relationships with First Nations, the Métis Nation, and Inuit.

This commitment is in line with the United Nations Declaration on the Rights of Indigenous Peoples, including free, prior and informed consent. On May 9, 2016, Canada officially removed its "objector status" to the UN Declaration.

Questions for Reflection

Locate at the Pan-Canadian Framework on Clean Growth and Climate Change in its entirety on the Internet and give some thought to the following questions:

1. In your opinion, does the Framework adequately align Canada with the goals of the Paris Agreement?
2. It appears that Canada and the world are falling short of the targets set by the Paris Agreement. In your opinion, what additional measures might bring things back into alignment?
3. One of the difficult tasks for the various levels of government is to balance climate concerns with maintaining economic growth. In your opinion, how is this task possible?
4. A key principle underlying the UN Declaration on the Rights of Indigenous Peoples is that of free, prior and informed consent. Is this human rights principle adequately reflected in the Pan-Canadian Framework and actions of the federal government to date?
5. Are there additional steps in relation to climate change that Canada can take that would show leadership to the rest of the world?

A Moment in Time, May 9, 2016

Declaration on the Rights of Indigenous Peoples

Free, Prior and Informed Consent

On May 9, 2016, to standing applause at the UN General Assembly, Canada officially removed its "objector status" to the UN Declaration on the Rights of Indigenous Peoples.

The new policy means that Canadian governments must now secure the prior agreement of Indigenous groups before making decisions that affect their lives.

The UN itself had adopted the Declaration in 2007 — with only Australia, New Zealand, the US, and Canada opposing. Canada endorsed the UNDRIP in 2010, but the Conservative government under Stephen Harper called it only an "aspirational document" and therefore it was not legally binding.

In 1982, Canada had amended its constitution to enshrine the rights of Indigenous peoples. The amendment states: "The existing Aboriginal and treaty rights of the Aboriginal peoples of Canada are hereby recognized and affirmed."

Historic Step Forward

The adoption of UNDRIP has been a long time coming and is another step forward but there are disagreements about what the ramifications of implementing such a "framework" declaration will be. In international law, declarations are non-binding.

Disputes over access to land, natural resources, and water, for example, lie at the heart of recent clashes between Indigenous peoples and federal and provincial governments.

Following the 2016 policy change, the former national chief of the Assembly of First Nations, Ovide Mercredi, called for Canada to honour and fulfill its existing treaty obligations with Indigenous peoples in Canada.

Chapter Review

Questions

1. What is globalization? Why do many analysts, rightly or wrongly, associate the decline of the welfare state with the rise of globalization?
2. What was the vision of those who advocated expansion of the welfare state after World War II? What's different today?
3. Itemize the core principles underlying social work and social welfare advocacy at the international level?
4. Compare and contrast the HDI and SDG with the Canadian Index of Wellbeing.
5. Explain some initiatives that social workers can undertake to advance the cause of environmental justice.
6. The climate change debate often aligns with the "left-right" political divide. Why might this be the case?
7. The principle of universalism in the social welfare context aligns closely with the ideas of inclusion, equity, and social justice and with a social investment framework. Explain why.

Exploring Social Welfare

1. Some analysts have argued that the world needs "fair trade," not "free trade," to address poverty. Does free trade necessarily contribute to income inequalities? If so, how does this happen? Write a short report or discuss in class.
2. Populism is a political ideology and movement that seeks to rally ordinary people against society's elites and others whom they blame for their troubles. Draw up a list of political leaders in the world today who might be called populist and indicate the main groups that they single out for criticism.

Websites

International Forum on Globalization (IFG)
www.ifg.org
The International Forum on Globalization is a North-South research and educational institute providing analysis and critiques on the cultural, social, political, and environmental impacts of economic globalization. Its goals are to expose the multiple effects of economic globalization in order to stimulate debate about its effects and to encourage ideas and activities that revitalize local economies and communities and ensure long-term ecological stability.

Canadian Public Health Association
www.cpha.ca
Founded in 1910, the Canadian Public Health Association is the independent voice for public health in Canada with links to the international community. CPHA is the only Canadian non-governmental organization focused exclusively on public health and is uniquely positioned to advise decision makers about public health system reform and to guide initiatives to help safeguard the personal and community health of Canadians and people around the world.

The Council of Canadians
www.canadians.org
Since 1985, the Council of Canadians has brought Canadians together to act for social, economic, and environmental justice in Canada and around the world. Its work is built on a strong foundation of timely and strategic campaigns to fight for the values, social programs, and progressive policies that Canadians believe in. Look to the Council's website for valuable information on free trade, globalization, and their effects on Canada and the world.

Credits

1. Social Welfare and Social Well-Being in Canada

3, © The Canadian Press/Frank Gunn (Photo ID: CP112034328); 4, © MaxAch, Shuttersstock (Photo ID: 1759706840); 7, © Garrick Tremain./National Library of New Zealand, Wellington, NZ (H-150-021); 8, © The Canadian Index of Wellbeing, reproduced by permission: www.uwaterloo.ca/canadian-index-wellbeing; 9, © Meunierd, Shutterstock (Photo ID: 1684044883); 11, © The Canadian Index of Wellbeing, reproduced by permission: www. uwaterloo.ca/canadian-index-wellbeing; 13, © Jessi Zou, Shutterstock (Photo ID: 134458168); 14, © Art Babych, Shutterstock (Photo ID: 379357762); 17, © JHVEPhoto, Shutterstock (Photo ID: 1733736623); 18, © Rawpixel.com, Shutterstock (Photo ID: 374588935); 20, © Lucian Coman, Shutterstock (Photo ID: 37934509); 23, © Blvdone, Adobe Stock (Photo ID: 1233213955); 29, © Boris Spremo/The Globe and Mail; Reprinted by permission of The Canadian Press (Photo ID: CP111664378); 40, © Zstock, Adobe Stock (Photo ID: 333938100)

2. The Rise and Fall of the Welfare State

43, Library and Archives Canada; 44, Photo: Glenbow Library and Archives, Calgary, AB (pending); 47, Illustration of an irish workhouse, published 1901, artist unknown; 49, © GilbertScott. org, pending; 51, © SimonP, Wikimedia Creative Commons, public domain; 53, © Alina Reynbakh, Shutterstock (Photo ID: 451005517); 54, J.S. Woodsworth, The Canadian Museum of History (historymuseum.ca); 55, © Arthur G. Racey (1870-1941), Bibliothèque et Archives nationales du Québec (Photo ID: P600,S5,PDEN59); 57, Library and Archives Canada; 58, Library and Archives Canada; 59, Wikimedia Creative Commons, public domain; 60, The Valiant Five statue in Calgary, AB (Thivierr, Wikimedia CC); 63, Library and Archives Canada (Photo ID: e010999987); 64, © The Canadian Press/Andrew Vaughan (Photo ID: CP2642026); 66, Provincial Archives of Saskatchewan, R-PS62-229-25; 69, Sir William Beveridge, British Government; Leonard Marsh, City of Vancouver Archives; 71, © The Canadian Press/Ryan Remiorz (Photo ID: CP17364); 72, Reagan White House Photographs, 1/20/1981 – 1/20/1989, White House Photographic Collection; 75, PMO photo by Jason Ransom; 77, © Rj_k, Shutterstock (Photo ID: 374150659); 78, Wikipedia Creative Commons [public domain]; 81, © Stacey Newman, Shutterstock (Photo ID: 291935885); 82, © Marc Bruxelle, Shutterstock (Photo ID: 1736550203); 85, © Derek Robbins, Shutterstock (Photo ID: 1745870363); 88, Virtual Museum.ca

3. Canadian Labour Market Policies and Programs

91, © Engel.ac, Adobe Stock (Photo ID: 185470031); 92, © Iakov Filimonov, Shutterstock (Photo ID: 1593889381); 95, © Gorodenkoff, Shutterstock (Photo ID: 761907082); 96, © Daniele COSSU, Shutterstock (Photo ID: 1751227352); 101, © Iryna Imago, Shutterstock (Photo ID: 1845304078); 111, © The Canadian Press/Giordano Ciampini (Photo ID: CP18567343); 117, © Oleg Golovnev, Shutterstock (Photo ID: 289804415); 119, © Monkey Business Images, Shutterstock (Photo ID: 126648689); 121, © Olesia Bilkei, Shutterstock (Photo ID: 223604782); 124, © Myboston, Shutterstock (Photo ID: 700198537); 128, © The Canadian Press/ Andrew Vaughan (Photo ID: CP13224446)

4. The Welfare and Well-Being of People in Poverty

131, © The Canadian Press/Darryl Dyck (Photo ID: CP17487229); 132, © The Canadian Press/Chris Young (Photo ID: CP17247136); 136, © Canada without Poverty (www.cwp-csp.ca); 138, © Halfpoint, Shutterstock (Photo ID: 1850300899); 140, © Shawn Goldberg, Shutterstock (Photo ID: 1863343018); 142, © Icatnews, Shutterstock (Photo ID: 610527113); 151, © Angelina Bambina, Shuttterstock (Photo ID: 1658813662); 153, © Rawpixel.com, Shutterstock (Photo ID: 254867587); 155, © The Canadian Press/ Nathan Denette (Photo ID: CP144720); 159, © Mikeledray, Shutterstock (Photo ID: 1430654129); 160, © GTS Productions, Shutterstock (Photo ID: 1466354693); 162, © Mostofa Mohiuddin, Shutterstock (Photo ID: 1852282969); 165, © Food Banks Canada, reproduced by permission; 167, © Meunierd, Shuttterstock (Photo ID: 1078419095); 169, Library and Archives Canada; 171, © Toronto Star; 173, © Meunierd, Shutterstock (Photo ID: 1743632969); 178, © Shawn Goldberg, Shutterstock (Photo ID: 1863389116)

5. The Welfare and Well-Being of Women and Families

181, © Fizkes, Shutterstock (Photo ID: 1667120917); © Vadim. Petrov, Shutterstock (Photo ID: 311255735); © Fizkes, Shutterstock (Photo ID: 1354297568); © rSnapshotPhotos, Shutterstock (Photo ID: 74719702); © Michaeljung, Shutterstock (Photo ID: 297418070); 182, © Vancouver Heritage Foundation; 190, © Robert Kneschke, Shutterstock (Photo ID: 182289416); 193, © Catherine Zibo, Shuttterstock (Photo ID: 1369010915); 196, © Velour Noire, Shutterstock (Photo ID: 1855922989); 199, © Santypan, Shutterstock (Photo ID: 543939718); 200, © Miriam Doerr Martin Frommherz, Shutterstock (Photo ID: 1688780239); 209, © Steve Nease, Neasecartoons.com; 216, © Everett Collection, Shutterstock (Photo ID: 94202290); 218, © ValeStock, Shutterstock (Photo ID: 123551527); 222, © Aivoges Shutterstock (Photo ID: 114029434)

6. The Welfare and Well-Being of Canadian Children

225, © Iakov Filimonov, Shutterstock (Photo ID: 1855243849); 226, © 2xSamara.com Shutterstock (Photo ID: 83407198); 231, © The Canadian Press/Adrian Wyld (Photo ID: CP14710175); 233, © AP Group of Photographers, Shutterstock (Photo ID: 1173655255); 237, © 2020 Canadian Institute of Child Health, pending; 238, © Ontario Human Rights Commission; 239, © Monkey Business Images, Shutterstock (Photo ID: 116494735); 244, © 2xSamara.com, Shutterstock (Photo ID: 150544307); 253, © Vectortwins, Shutterstock (Photo ID: 412735153); 255, © ESB Professional, Shutterstock (Photo ID: 307383305); 256, © Monkey Business Images, Shutterstock (Photo ID: 280358093); 260, © Tuzemka, Shutterstock (Photo ID: 108189845)

7. Social Welfare and Mental Well-Being in Canada

263, © Agsandrew, Shutterstock (Photo ID: 278514176); 264, © Eldar Nurkovic, Shutterstock (Photo ID: 1709102869); 267, © Cherries, Shutterstock (Photo ID: 1717327240); 268, © Spasic - nef, Shutterstock (Photo ID: 1697483893); 271, Unknown source; 272, © Trevor Hagan/Winnipeg Free Press Files, pending; 273, © Michelangeloop, Shutterstock (Photo ID: 691299277); 277, © Art Babych, Shutterstock (Photo ID: 494511457); 280, © Evgeny Atamanenko, Shutterstock (Photo ID: 1022465209); 283, © WavebreakMediaMicro, Adobe

Stock (Photo ID: 336571521); 286, © Wikimedia Creatve Commons (public domain); 291, © Utlanof, Adobe Stock (Photo ID: 53199184); 297, © Avgust Avgustus, Shutterstock (Photo ID: 1161695500); 298, © Expatpostcards, Shutterstock (Photo ID: 1557595463)

8. The Welfare and Well-Being of Indigenous Peoples

301, © The Canadian Press/Darryl Dyck (Photo ID: 127087); 302, © The Canadian Press/Nathan Denette (Photo ID: CP111169511); 305, © Bing Wen, Shutterstock (Photo ID: 1119397259); 314, © J. C. Jackson/Department of Indian Affairs and Northern Development/Library and Archives Canada; 318, © The Canadian Press/Jeff McIntosh (Photo ID: CP13303654); 321, © Alexfan32, Shutterstock (Photo ID: 1089146540); 323, © The Canadian Press/Shaney Komulainen (Photo ID: CP16966621); 325, © Arindambanerjee, Shutterstock (Photo ID: 178122623); 327, © David Jackson, 2020.; 328, © Corona Borealis Studio, Shutterstock (Photo ID: 1642467388); 330, © Quinn Dombrowski, Wikimedia Creative (public domain); 332, © Colin Temple, Shutterstock (Photo ID: 1667165335); 335, © Arindambanerjee, Shutterstock (Photo ID: 566434015); 337, © The Canadian Press/Andrew Vaughan (Photo ID: 19377637); 339, © Margarita Young, Shutterstock (Photo ID: 1524833549); 342, © Truth and Reconciliation Commission of Canada

9. The Welfare of Immigrants and Temporary Residents

345, © The Canadian Press/Deborah Baic (Photo ID: 02324418); 346, © The Canadian Press/Sean Kilpatrick, (Photo ID: 180074); 348, © Rob Crandall, Shutterstock (Photo ID: 1173501802); 355, © The Canadian Press/Graham Hughes (Photo ID: CP17491402); 356, © The Canadian Press/Jason Scott (Photo ID: CP2747501); 360, © James Kirkikis, Shutterstock (Photo ID: 790107520); 365, © The Canadian Press/Rob Gurdebeke (Photo ID: CP110166970); 366, © The Canadian Press/Ryan Remiorz, (Photo ID: CP17090544); 368, © Gvictoria, Shutterstock (Photo ID: 95233180); 377, © Pat Lauzon, Shutterstock (Photo ID: 1850756851); 378, © The Canadian Press/Galit Rodan (Photo ID: CP17841770); 379, © Arindambanerjee, Shutterstock (Photo ID: 366262412); 380, © The Canadian Press/Ryan Remiorz (Photo ID: CP140332)

10. The Welfare and Well-Being of Older People

387, © Photoshooter2015, AdobeStock (Photo ID: 55632850); 388, © The Canadian Press/Ryan Remiorz (Photo ID: CP17289357); 391, © Monkey Business Images, Shutterstock (Photo ID: 1125901487); 393, © Matej Kastelic, Shutterstock (Photo ID: 1086254576); 399, © Wavebreakmedia, Shutterstock (Photo ID: 1313234774); 400, ©Cryptographer, Shutterstock (Photo ID: 1698306562); 402, © AJuice Flair, Shutterstock (Photo ID: 1807086568); 403, © Deyan Georgiev, Shutterstock (Photo ID: 1507753340); 404, © Elena_Alex_Ferns, Shutterstock (Photo ID: 1840640113); 407, © Bing Wen, Shutterstock (Photo ID: 667578115); 408, © StockImageFactory.com, Shutterstock (Photo ID: 1346799779); 411, © Monkey Business Images, Shutterstock (Photo ID: 765977281); 413, © Phovoir, Shutterstock (Photo ID: 86775760); 415, © Rocketclips, Inc., Shutterstock (Photo ID: 1195914484); 416, © The Canadian Press/Fred Chartrand (Photo ID: CP2871663); 420, © Photographee.eu, Shutterstock (Photo ID: 1032185266)

11. The Welfare and Well-Being of Persons with Disabilities

423, © Elasimson, Shutterstock (Photo ID: 1494060542); 424, © Ronnie Chua, Shutterstock (Photo ID: 1716062461); 427, © Wavebreakmedia, Shutterstock (Photo ID: 1476863489); 430, © Photodiem, Shutterstock (Photo ID: 95101282); 433, © Roman Chazov, Shutterstock (Photo ID: 1814841908); 435, © Meunierd, Shutterstock (Photo ID: 1076735525); 441, © Michener Centre, 2013.; 443, © Wavebreakmedia, Shutterstock (Photo ID: 464169620); 447, © Fizkes, Shutterstock (Photo ID: 1463201225); 449, © Olesia Bilkei, Shutterstock (Photo ID: 521324719); 451, © Grejak, Shutterstock (Photo ID: 1670317450); 456, © Aleutie, Shutterstock (Photo ID: 383760118); 458, © Likeyellow, Shutterstock (Photo ID: 1857528883)

12. Well-Being and Social Justice in a Global Context

461, © Sdecoret, Shutterstock (Photo ID: 566877226); 462, © Alexandros Michailidis, Shutterstock (Photo ID: 1675341478); 465, © Arindambanerjee, Shutterstock (Photo ID: 1090762163); 468, © Susan G. Enberg, Shutterstock (Photo ID: 1550136422); 473, © Derick Hudson, Shutterstock (Photo ID: 190525038); 475, © Aleksandrs Bondars, Shutterstock (Photo ID: 371900104); Bottom: Unknown source; 476, © Clicksabhi, Shutterstock (Photo ID: 1435184768); 478, © 9387388673, Shutterstock (Photo ID: 246680374); 481, © LightField Studios, Shutterstock (Photo ID: 1786015253); 482, © Sophia Granchinho, Shutterstock (Photo ID: 1052270816); 484, © Sandeep Jeengar, Shutterstock (Photo ID: 1697304613); 487, © MaxAch, Shutterstock (Photo ID: 1759706768); 488, © Roschetzky Photography, Shutterstock (Photo ID: 766204174); 490, © Christopher Penler, Shutterstock (Photo ID: 1606480828); 494, © 2020 International Federation of Social Workers; 498, © Aliaksandr Antanovich, Shutterstock (Photo ID: 1032417775)

References

Chapter 1

Accessible Canada Act, S.C., C-10 (2019). https://www.canlii.org/en/ca/laws/astat/sc-2019-c-10/152117/sc-2019-c-10.html

Allin, S., & Rudoler, D. (2016). *The Canadian health care system.* https://international.commonwealthfund.org/countries/canada/

APTN National News. (2018). *"No answers for me:" Chief says First Nations left out of Fort McMurray fire response.* https://aptnnews.ca/2018/10/30/no-answers-for-me-chief-says-first-nations-left-out-of-fort-mcmurray-fire-response

Armitage, A. (2003). *Social welfare in Canada.* Oxford University Press.

Balajee, S., et al., (2012). *Equity and empowerment lens (racial justice focus).* Multnomah County. https://multco.us/diversity-equity/equity-and-empowerment-lens

BC Teachers' Federation. (2019). *A social justice lens.* https://bctf.ca/uploadedFiles/Public/SocialJustice/Publications/SJLens.pdf

Brown, M. R. G., Agyapong, V., Greenshaw, A. J., et al. (2019). After the Fort McMurray wildfire there are significant increases in mental health symptoms in grade 7–12 students compared to controls. *BMC Psychiatry, 19,* 18.

Canada. (2014). *Action for seniors report.* https://www.canada.ca/en/employment-social-development/programs/seniors-action-report.html

Canada. (2019a). *Budget of Canada: Investing in the middle class 2019.* https://www.budget.gc.ca/2019/home-accueil-en.html

Canada. (2019b). *Canada's Youth Policy.* https://www.canada.ca/content/dam/y-j/documents/YP-ENG.pdf

Canada Health Act, R.S.C., C-46 (1985). https://laws-lois.justice.gc.ca/eng/acts/c-6/FullText.html

Canadian Association for Social Work Education. (2014). *Standards for accreditation.* https://caswe-acfts.ca/commission-on-accreditation/coa-standards/

Canadian Index of Wellbeing. (2016). *How are Canadians really doing? The 2016 CIW National Report.* Canadian Index of Wellbeing and University of Waterloo. https://uwaterloo.ca/canadian-index-wellbeing/sites/ca.canadian-index-wellbeing/files/uploads/files/c011676-nationalreport-ciw_final-s.pdf

Canadian Social Enterprise Fund. (2017). *What is a social entrepreneur?* http://www.csef.ca/what_is_a_social_entrepreneur.php

Caputo, R. (2014). *Policy analysis for social workers.* Sage.

Carrasco-Campos, Á., Moreno, A., & Martínez, L.-C. (2017). Quality of life, well-being and social policies in European countries. *IntechOpen.* https://www.intechopen.com/books/quality-of-life-and-quality-of-working-life/quality-of-life-well-being-and-social-policies-in-european-countries1

Chappell, R. (2014). *Social welfare in Canadian society* (5th ed.). Nelson.

Conference Board of Canada. (2018). *The value of volunteering in Canada.* https://volunteer.ca/vdemo/Campaigns_DOCS/Value%20of%20Volunteering%20in%20Canada%20Conf%20Board%20Final%20Report%20EN.pdf

Dunlop, J. (2006). Privatization: How government promotes market based solutions to social problems. *Critical Social Work, 7*(2).

Estes, R. J., & Zhou, H. (2015). A conceptual approach to the creation of public-private partnerships in social welfare. *International Journal of Social Welfare,* 24(4), 348–363. https://doi.org/10.1111/ijsw.12142

Imagine Canada. (2018). *30 years of giving in Canada: Who gives, how, and why?* https://www.imaginecanada.ca/en/360/30-years-giving-canada-who-gives-how-and-why-infographic

Marshall, T. H. (1950). *Citizenship and social class, and other essays.* Cambridge University Press.

McCarten, J. (2020, April 14). Compared to U.S., Canada's COVID–19 response a case study in political civility. *CTV News.* The Canadian Press.

Moscovitch, A. (2015). Welfare state. In *The Canadian encyclopedia.* https://www.thecanadianencyclopedia.ca/en/article/welfare-state

Organisation for Economic Co-operation and Development. (2006). *Starting strong II: Early childhood education and care.*

Organisation for Economic Co-operation and Development. (2017). *Government at a glance.* https://doi.org/10.1787/gov_glance-2017-en

Ornston, D. (2020, June 26). Learning from Denmark's socially inclusive approach to COVID–19. *Policy Options.* https://policyoptions.irpp.org/magazines/june-2020/learning-from-denmarks-socially-inclusive-approach-to-covid/

Osberg, L. (2001). Poverty among senior citizens. In P. Grady & A. Sharpe (Eds.), *The state of economics in Canada: Festschrift in honour of David Slater* (pp. 151–181). Queen's University Press.

Pew Research Centre (2020). *Americans stand out in belief that their country is more divided now than before coronavirus outbreak.* Pew Research Centre: Global Attitudes & Trends (August 26). Washington, DC. https://www.pewresearch.org

Phillips, S., & Echenberg, H. (n.d.). *Simon says "take a giant step forward:" Advancing the National Children's Agenda (A discussion paper for the National Children's Alliance).* National Children's Alliance. https://web.archive.org/web/20160911200922/http:/www.nationalchildrensalliance.com/nca/pubs/simon/index.htm

Rice, J. J., & Prince, M. J. (2000). *Changing politics of Canadian social policy.* University of Toronto Press.

Shookner, M. (2002). *An inclusion lens: Workbook for looking at social and economic exclusion and inclusion.* Health Canada.

Statistics Canada. (2017). *The Canadian families of today and yesteryear* (Child Care Canada). https://www.childcarecanada.org/documents/child-care-news/17/08/2016-census-canadian-families-today-and-yesteryear

Statistics Canada. (2018, November 28). Canadian survey on disability, 2017. *The Daily.*

Statistics Canada. (2019a, February 26). Canadian Income Survey, 2017. *The Daily.* https://www150.statcan.gc.ca/n1/daily-quotidien/190226/dq190226b-eng.htm

Statistics Canada. (2019b). *Dimensions of poverty hub.* https://www.statcan.gc.ca/eng/topics-start/poverty/

Swift, J., Davies, J., Clarke, R., & Czerny, M. (2003). *Getting started on social analysis in Canada* (4th ed.). Between the Lines.

UNICEF Canada. (2017). *UNICEF report card 14: Oh Canada! Our kids deserve better.* https://www.unicef.ca/en/unicef-report-card-14-child-well-being-sustainable-world

Vaalavuo, M. (2013). The redistributive impact of "old" and "new" social spending. *Journal of Social Policy,* 42, 513–539. https://doi.org/10.1017/S0047279413000251

Walmsley, C. (2019). Ideas and social policy. In R. Harding & D. Jeyapal (Eds.), *Canadian social policy for social workers* (pp. 30–48). Oxford University Press.

Zaidi, A. (2006, August). *Poverty of elderly people in EU25* (Policy brief). https://www.euro.centre.org/publications/detail/247

Chapter 2

Aiello, R. (2019, July 15). Here's how Canada changed under Justin Trudeau. *CTV News.* https://www.ctvnews.ca/politics/here-s-how-canada-changed-under-justin-trudeau-1.4494319

Ballingall, A. (2019, July 20). Justin Trudeau made reconciliation a top priority. Four years later, what's changed. *Toronto Star.* https://www.thespec.com/news-story/9512154-justin-trudeau-made-reconciliation-a-top-priority-four-years-later-what-s-changed-/

Beattie, S. (2020, June 3). The coronavirus crisis exposed gaps in Canada's social programs. Now's the time to fill them. *HuffPost Canada.* https://www.huffingtonpost.ca/entry/canada-social-programs-coronavirus_ca_5ed516dfc5b63bc4db6bd017

Belshaw, J. (2015). *Canadian history: Pre-Confederation.* https://opentextbc.ca/preconfederation/chapter/2-4-the-millennia-before-contact/

Brooks, N., & McQuaig, L. (2015). *Robbing the poor to give to the rich.* https://canadiandimension.com/articles/view/robbing-the-poor-to-give-to-the-rich

Bryden, J. (2014, December 22). Trudeau promised he's be accessible PM, unmuzzle bureaucrats. *Maclean's.* https://www.macleans.ca/politics/ottawa/trudeau-promises-hed-be-accessible-pm-unmuzzle-bureaucrats/

Campbell, B. (2011, December 12). *Rising inequality, declining democracy.* Canadian Centre for Policy Alternatives. https://www.policyalternatives.ca/publications/commentary/rising-inequality-declining-democracy

Canada. (2012). Jobs growth and long-term prosperity [budget plan]. https://www.budget.gc.ca/2012/plan/toc-tdm-eng.html

Canada. (2016). *Pan-Canadian framework on clean growth and climate change: Canada's plan to address climate change and grow the economy.* http://publications.gc.ca/collections/collection_2017/eccc/En4-294-2016-eng.pdf

Canada. (2018). *Persons Day.* https://cfc-swc.gc.ca/commemoration/whm-mhf/persons-personne-en.html?wbdisable=true

Canadian Council on Social Development. (2005, Spring). *Fast facts: The disappearing just society.* Perception.

CBC News. (2015, October 20). Canada votes 2015: Post-election day coverage. *CBC News.* https://www.cbc.ca/news/politics/canada-votes-2015-election-justin-trudeau-prime-minister-1.3279606

Choi, K., Zajacova, A., Haan, M., & Denice, P. (2020, May 21). New COVID–19 hotspots predicted by data linking race and health. *Western News.* London, ON: Western University. https://news.westernu.ca/2020/05/new-covid-19-hotspots-predicted-by-data-linking-race-and-health/

Conference Board of Canada. (2011). *Hot topic: Canada inequality—Is Canada becoming more unequal?* https://www.conferenceboard.ca/Files/hcp/pdfs/hot-topics/caninequality.pdf

Conference Board of Canada. (2020). *Canadian income inequality: Is Canada becoming more unequal?* https://www.conferenceboard.ca/hcp/hot-topics/canInequality.aspx

Council of Canadians. (2011). *Budget cuts to Environment Canada and how they affect Canada's water sources.* https://canadians.org/fr/node/3623

Courtney, J. C. (2007). Right to vote in Canada. *The Canadian Encyclopedia.* https://www.thecanadianencyclopedia.ca/en/article/franchise

Dion, J. (2017). *Falling through the cracks: Canadian Indigenous children with disabilities.* International Human Rights Internships Program – Working Paper Series. https://www.mcgill.ca/humanrights/files/humanrights/ihri_wps_v5_n12_dion.pdf

Elections Canada. (2020). *A history of the vote in Canada.* https://www.elections.ca/content.aspx?section=res&dir=his&document=chap2&lang=e

Finkel, A. (2006a). Paradise postponed, 1939–50: The Second World War and its aftermath. In A. Finkel (Ed.), *Social policy and practice in Canada: A history* (pp. 125–147). Wilfrid Laurier University Press.

Finkel, A. (Ed.). (2006b). *Social policy and practice in Canada: A history.* Wilfrid Laurier University Press.

First Nations Health Authority. (2020). Our history, our health. https://www.fnha.ca/wellness/our-history-our-health

Goldi Productions. (2007). *Canada's First peoples: First peoples before European contact.* https://firstpeoplesofcanada.com/fp_groups/fp_groups_overview.html

Government of Alberta. (n.d.). *Walking together: First Nations, Metis and Inuit perspectives in curriculum.* http://www.learnalberta.ca/content/aswt/kinship/documents/traditional_social_organization.pdf

Government of Canada. (2006). *Prime Minister Stephen Harper marks GST reduction.* https://www.canada.ca/en/news/archive/2006/06/prime-minister-stephen-harper-marks-gst-reduction.html

Guest, D. (1980). *The emergence of social security in Canada.* UBC Press.

Hadas, E. (2020, May 13). Welfare states will be big COVID–19 winners. *Breaking News.* https://www.reuters.com/article/us-health-coronavirus-welfare-breakingvi/breakingviews-hadas-welfare-states-will-be-big-covid-19-winners-idUSKBN22P25E

Hayward, J. (2012, April 29). Harper government most secretive, journalists say. *The Globe and Mail.* https://www.theglobeandmail.com/news/politics/harper-government-most-secretive-journalists-say/article4103406/

Healy, T., & Trew, S. (Eds.). (2015). *The Harper record 2008–2015.* Canadian Centre for Policy Alternatives. https://www.policyalternatives.ca/sites/default/files/uploads/publications/National Office/2015/10/The_Harper_Record_2008-2015.pdf

Héroux, G. (2015). The stone yard. In Lorinc, J., McClelland, M., & Scheinberg, E., *The ward: The life and loss of Toronto's first immigrant neighbourhood.* Coach House Press.

Hummel, M. (2016). Environmental and conservation movements. T*he Canadian Encyclopedia.* https://www.thecanadianencyclopedia.ca/en/article/environmental-and-conservation-movements

Johnson, A. (1975). Canada's social security review 1973–75: The central issues. *Canadian Public Policy, 1*(4), 456–472.

Lenard, P. (2015). Stephen Harper's abhorrent record on refugees and immigration. *The Broadbent Blog.* https://www.broadbentinstitute.ca/pattitamaralenard/harper_dimal_record_refugees_immigration

Marx, P (2020, July 7). Jean Chrétien's austerity made Canada less prepared for COVID–19. *Canadian Dimension.* https://canadiandimension.com/articles/view/jean-chretiens-austerity-made-canada-less-prepared-for-covid-19

McQuillan, K. (2013). *All the workers we need: Debunking Canada's labour shortage fallacy.* https://www.policyschool.ca/wp-content/uploads/2016/03/labour-shortages-mcquillan.pdf

Morris, C. (2006). Royal Commission on the Status of Women in Canada. [Updated March 22, 2016, by Anne-Marie Pedersen, Calina Ellwand, Maude-Emmanuelle Lambert.] *The Canadian Encyclopedia.* https://www.thecanadianencyclopedia.ca/en/article/royal-commission-on-the-status-of-women-in-canada

Moscovitch, A., & Albert, J. (1987). The benevolent state: The growth of welfare in Canada. In *Labour (Committee on Canadian Labour History), 21,* 332.

National Collaborating Centre for Aboriginal Health. (2009–2010). *Poverty as a social determinant of First Nations, Inuit, and Métis health.* https://www.ccnsa-nccah.ca/docs/determinants/FS-PovertySDOH-EN.pdf

Nelson, J. (2013). *The Harper government's war on science.* Canadian Center for Policy Alternatives. https://www.policyalternatives.ca/publications/monitor/harper-governments-war-science

Newitt, M., & Silnicki, A. (2015). The need for federal leadership in public health care. In T. Healy and S. Trew (Eds.), *The Harper record 2008–2015* (pp. 255–264). Canadian Centre for Policy Alternatives. https://www.policyalternatives.ca/sites/default/files/uploads/publications/National Office/2015/10/The_Harper_Record_2008-2015.pdf

O'Neill, M (2020, June 12). Canada has a long, documented history of racism and racial discrimination. Don't look away. *The Globe and Mail.* https://www.theglobeandmail.com/opinion/article-canada-has-a-long-documented-history-of-racism-and-racial/

Picard, A. (2012, April 9). Harper's disregard for Aboriginal health. *The Globe and Mail.*

Ramsay, S., & Boddy, J. (2016). Environmental social work: A concept analysis. *British Journal of Social Work, 47*(1), 68–86. https://doi.org/10.1093/bjsw/bcw078

Richmond, C. A. M., & Cook, C. (2016). Creating conditions for Canadian Aboriginal health equity: The promise of healthy public policy. *Public Health Review, 37*(2). https://doi.org/10.1186/s40985-016-0016-5

Sandher, J., & Kleider, H. (2020, June 24). Coronavirus has brought the welfare state back, and it might be here to stay. *The Conversation.* https://theconversation.com/coronavirus-has-brought-the-welfare-state-back-and-it-might-be-here-to-stay-138564

Senate of Canada. (1971). *Poverty in Canada — Report of the Special Senate Committee on Poverty.* Senator David A Croll, Chair. Canada.

Senate of Canada. (2008). *Poverty, housing and homelessness: Issues and options.* https://sencanada.ca/Content/SEN/Committee/392/soci/rep/repfinaljun08-e.pdf

Senate of Canada. (2012, June 21). 1st Session, 41st Parliament, Volume 150, Issue 99 (2130). Hon. Lillian Eva Dyck.

Shajahan, P. K., & Sharma, P. (2018). Environmental justice: A call for action for social workers. *International Social Work, 61*(4), 476-480.

Smardon, B. (1995). The federal welfare state and the politics of retrenchment in Canada. In R. Blake and J. Keshen (Eds.), *Social welfare policy in Canada: Historical readings* (pp. 344 -365). Copp Clark.

Trudeau, J. (2018). Statement by the prime minister on the 100th anniversary of women winning the right to vote in federal elections. https://pm.gc.ca/en/news/statements/2018/05/24/statement-prime-minister-100th-anniversary-women-winning-right-vote

Trudeau, J. (2020, April 1). Daily Update for April 1, 2020. Reproduced in *Maclean's*: "Canada hasn't seen this type of civic mobilization since the Second World War." https://www.macleans.ca/news/canada/trudeau-coronavirus-update-april-1-full-transcript/

Truell, R., & Jones, D. N. (Ed). (2018). *Global agenda for social work and social development: Third report. Promoting community and environmental sustainability.* International Federation of Social Workers, International Association of Schools of Social Work, and International Council of Social Welfare.

Watt-Cloutier, S. (2020). Upirngasaq (Arctic Spring). *Granta, Essays & Memoir,* Issue 153. https://granta.com/upirngasaq-arctic-spring/?fbclid=IwAR0jrqteJhAjxn08RG5APA-KrrGWRbzZj3SkZIv74ULovzuYc_Ze8LAbufY

Wernick, M. (2016). *Twenty-third annual report to the Prime Minister on the Public Service of Canada.* Privy Council Office.

Wernick, M. (2019). *26th annual report to the Prime Minister on the Public Service of Canada.* Privy Council Office.

Zhang, S. (2017, January 26). Looking back at Canada's political fight over science. *The Atlantic.* https://www.theatlantic.com/science/archive/2017/01/canada-war-on-science/514322/

Chapter 3

ACORN Canada. (2017). *EI: It's time to modernize and fix EI!* https://acorncanada.org/its-time-modernize-and-fix-ei

Angus Reid (2020, June 18). *As COVID–19 rewrites playbook on social safety net, majorities support idea of basic income of up to 30K.* Angus Reid Institute. http://angusreid.org/universal-basic-income-covid19/

Bedard, E. (2014a). *Across Canada, worker compensation systems are in crisis.* https://rabble.ca/news/2014/12/across-canada-worker-compensation-systems-are-crisis

Bedard, E. (2014b). *Democracy gone astray.* http://democracyastray.blogspot.com/2014/12/across-canada-worker-compensation.html

Beland, L-F., Brodeur, A., Mikola, D., & Wright, T. (2020, May 20). Here's how the coronavirus is affecting Canada's labour market. *The Conversation.* https://theconversation.com/heres-how-the-coronavirus-is-affecting-canadas-labour-market-137749

Block, S., Galabuzi, G.-E., & Tranjan, R. (2019). *Canada's colour-coded income inequality.* Canadian Centre for Policy Alternatives. https://www.policyalternatives.ca/publications/reports/canadas-colour-coded-income-inequality

British Columbia. (2019, December 8). Reducing injuries for health-care workers focus of new safety organization [Press release]. https://news.gov.bc.ca/releases/2019HLTH0160-002372

Brophy, J., Keith, M., & Hurley, M. (2019). Breaking point: Violence against long-term care staff. *New Solutions*, 29(1), 10–35.

Brückner, M., & Lederman, D. (2015). *Effects of income inequality on economic growth.* VOX CEPR Policy Portal. https://voxeu.org/article/effects-income-inequality-economic-growth

Brunet, S. (2019, July 5). The transition from school to work: The NEET (not in employment, education or training) indicator for 20- to 24-year-olds in Canada. *The Daily.* Statistics Canada. https://www150.statcan.gc.ca/n1/pub/81-599-x/81-599-x2019001-eng.htm

Canadian Centre for Occupational Health and Safety. (2019). *Workplace health and well-being — Comprehensive workplace health and safety program.* https://www.ccohs.ca/oshanswers/psychosocial/mentalhealth_work.html

Canadian Centre for Policy Alternatives. (2018). *Getting there: Alternative Federal Budget 2018.* https://www.policyalternatives.ca/sites/default/files/uploads/publications/National%20Office/2018/02/Alternative_Federal_Budget2018.pdf

Canadian Women's Foundation (2020). *Resetting normal: Women, decent work and Canada's fractured care economy.* (With the Canadian Centre for Policy Alternatives, Ontario Nonprofit Network, and Fay Faraday.) https://canadianwomen.org/wp-content/uploads/2020/07/ResettingNormal-Women-Decent-Work-and-Care-EN.pdf

CEIC Data. (2019). Canada GDP per Capita. https://www.ceicdata.com/en/indicator/canada/gdp-per-capita

Clemens, J., Palacios, M., & Li, N. (2020, July). Distribution of CERB: Estimating the number of eligible young people living with parents. *Fraser Research Bulletin.* The Fraser Institute. https://www.fraserinstitute.org/sites/default/files/distribution-of-CERB.pdf

Conference Board of Canada. (2019). *Income per capita.* https://www.conferenceboard.ca/hcp/provincial/economy/income-per-capita.aspx

Dinan, S., & Béland, D. (2020, June 10). COVID–19 and support for the unemployed. *Policy Options.* https://policyoptions.irpp.org/magazines/june-2020/covid-19-and-support-for-the-unemployed/

Drewes, T., & Meredith, T. (2015). *If at first you don't succeed: Toward an adult education and training strategy for Canada.* Institute for Research on Public Policy. https://irpp.org/research-studies/if-at-first-you-dont-succeed/

Dubreuil, B. (2014). Westray disaster. *The Canadian Encyclopedia.* https://www.thecanadianencyclopedia.ca/en/article/westray-disaster

Dungan, P., & Murphy, S. (1995). *The UI system as an automatic stabilizer in Canada.* Human Resources Development Canada.

Dungan, P., & Murphy, S. (2012). *The stabilization impact of the Employment Insurance program.* Human Resources Development Canada.

Employment and Social Development Canada. (2016). *Engagement on the future of Indigenous labour market programming* — May 2016 to December 2016, thematic summary. https://www.canada.ca/en/employment-social-development/corporate/reports/indigenous/engagement-future-labour-market-programming.html

Employment and Social Development Canada. (2018a). Backgrounder: Proactive pay equity. https://www.canada.ca/en/employment-social-development/news/2018/10/backgrounder-pay-equity.html

Employment and Social Development Canada. (2018b, October 29). Government of Canada introduces historic proactive pay equity legislation [Press release]. https://www.canada.ca/en/employment-social-development/news/2018/10/government-of-canada-introduces-historic-proactive-pay-equity-legislation.html

Employment and Social Development Canada. (2018c, December 13). Historic proactive pay equity legislation receives royal assent [Press release]. https://www.newswire.ca/news-releases/historic-proactive-pay-equity-legislation-receives-royal-assent-702728262.html

Employment and Social Development Canada. (2019a, September 10). Government of Canada appoints Canada's first federal Pay Equity Commissioner [Press release]. https://www.newswire.ca/news-releases/government-of-canada-appoints-canada-s-first-federal-pay-equity-commissioner-810248902.html

Employment and Social Development Canada. (2019b, October 4). *Employment Insurance monitoring and assessment report for the fiscal year beginning April 1, 2017 and ending March 31, 2018.* https://www.canada.ca/en/employment-social-development/programs/ei/ei-list/reports/monitoring2018/chapter2/regular-benefits.html

Fang, T., & Gunderson, M. (2019). *Poverty dynamics among vulnerable groups in Canada.* Institute for Research on Public Policy. https://irpp.org/research-studies/poverty-dynamics-among-vulnerable-groups-in-canada/

Finnie, R., & Gray, D. (2011). *Labour-force participation of older displaced workers in Canada: Should I stay or should I go?* Institute for Research on Public Policy. https://irpp.org/research-studies/labour-force-participation-of-older-displaced-workers-in-canada/

Flanagan, R. (2019, March 26). Violence in long-term care homes prompts fears of staffing crisis. *CTV News.*

Government of Ontario. (2019). *Workplace violence prevention in health care: A guide to the law for hospitals, long-term care homes and home care.* Ministry of Labour, Training and Skills Development. https://www.ontario.ca/page/workplace-violence-prevention-health-care-guide-law-hospitals-long-term-care-homes-and-home-care

Guest, D. (1980). *The emergence of social security in Canada.* UBC Press.

Halliwell, C. (2013). *No shortage of opportunities: Policy ideas to strengthen Canada's labour market in the coming decade.* Institute for Research on Public Policy. https://irpp.org/research-studies/no-shortage-of-opportunity/

Hardy, V., Lovei, M., & Patterson, M. (2018). *Labour statistics at a glance: Recent trends in Canada's labour market: A rising tide or a passing wave?* Statistics Canada. https://www150.statcan.gc.ca/n1/pub/71-222-x/71-222-x2018001-eng.htm

Institute for Research on Public Policy. (2015). *Sickness benefits in Canada.* http://irpp.org/wp-content/uploads/2015/09/infographic-report-2015-09-03.png.

International Insurance Society. (n.d.). William Meredith. https://www.insurancehalloffame.org/laureateprofile.php?laureate=132

Kapsalis, C. (2010, February 6). *Financial impacts of receiving Employment Insurance (final report).* Data Probe Economic Consulting.

Law Commission of Ontario. (2012). *Quick facts about vulnerable workers and precarious work.* https://www.lco-cdo.org/en/our-current-projects/vulnerable-workers-and-precarious-work/vulnerable-workers-interim-report-august-2012/quick-facts-about-vulnerable-workers-and-precarious-work/

Macdonald, D. (2020). Canadian workforce unevenly protected from COVID–19. *Behind the Numbers* (March 16). Ottawa, ON.: Canadian Centre for Policy Alternatives. https://behindthenumbers.ca/2020/03/16/canadian-workforce-unevenly-protected-from-covid-19/

Makarenko, J. (2009). *Employment insurance in Canada: History, structure and issues.* Health, Education and Social Welfare. https://www.mapleleafweb.com/features/employment-insurance-canada-history-structure-and-issues.html

Manitoba Collaborative Data Portal. (2018). *Median vs average household income: What is the difference between these indicators, and how to interpret them.* http://www.mbcdp.ca/blog/median-vs-average-household-income-what-is-the-difference-between-these-indicators-and-how-to-interpret-them

Mendelson, M., Battle, K., Torjman, S., & Caledon Institute of Social Policy. (2009). *Canada's shrunken safety net: Employment Insurance in the great recession.* Caledon Institute of Social Policy.

Meredith, T., & Chia, C. (2015). *Leaving some behind: What happens when workers get sick.* Institute for Research on Public Policy. https://irpp.org/wp-content/uploads/2015/09/report-2015-09-03.pdf

Meredith, W. R. (1913). *Meredith Report.* Legislative Assembly of Ontario.

Moyser, M. (2017). *Aboriginal people living off-reserve and the labour market: Estimates from the Labour Force Survey, 2007–2015.* Statistics Canada Catalogue no. 71-588-X. Statistics Canada.

National Association of Social Workers. (2013). *Guidelines for social worker safety in the workplace.* https://www.socialworkers.org/LinkClick.aspx?fileticket=60EdoMjcNC0%3d&portalid=0

Ontario Public Service Employees Union. (2017, January 31). Understanding basic income: A position paper from the Ontario Public Service Employees Union.

Organisation for Economic Co-operation and Development. (2015). *Inequality.* http://www.oecd.org/social/inequality.htm

Organisation for Economic Co-operation and Development. (2018a). *Employment rate.* https://data.oecd.org/emp/employment-rate.htm

Organisation for Economic Co-operation and Development. (2018b). *Labour force participation rate.* https://data.oecd.org/emp/labour-force-participation-rate.htm#indicator-chart

Organisation for Economic Co-operation and Development. (2019). *Under pressure: The squeezed middle class.*

Palme, J., & Cronert, A. (2015). *Trends in the Swedish social investment welfare state: "The enlightened path" or "the third way" for "the lions"?* ImPRovE Working Papers, 15/12. https://ideas.repec.org/p/hdl/improv/1512.html

Parliamentary Budget Office (2020, July 7). *Costing a guaranteed basic income during the covid pandemic.* Ottawa, ON.: Office of the Parliamentary Budget Officer. https://www.pbo-dpb.gc.ca/web/default/files/Documents/Reports/RP-2021-014-M/RP-2021-014-M_en.pdf

Patterson, M. (2018). *Labour statistics at a glance: Who works part time and why?* Statistics Canada. https://www150.statcan.gc.ca/n1/pub/71-222-x/71-222-x2018002-eng.htm

Pay Equity Commission. (2018). *An overview of pay equity in various Canadian jurisdictions.* http://www.payequity.gov.on.ca/en/GWG/Pages/overview_pe.aspx

Perkins, D. (2010). Activation and social inclusion: challenges and possibilities. *Australian Journal of Social issues, 45*(2), 267–287.

Prince, M. (2016). *Inclusive employment for Canadians with disabilities: Toward a new policy framework and agenda.* Institute for Research on Public Policy. https://irpp.org/wp-content/uploads/2016/08/study-no60.pdf

Public Health Agency of Canada. (2018). *Key health inequalities in Canada: A national portrait.* Infographic. https://www.canada.ca/en/public-health/services/publications/science-research-data/inequalities-working-poor-canadians-infographic.html

RBC Economics. (2011). *Immigrant labour market outcomes in Canada: The benefits of addressing wage and employment gaps.* RBC Economics Research. http:http://www.rbc.com/newsroom/pdf/1219-2011-immigration.pdf

Regehr, C. (2018). *Stress, trauma, and decision-making for social workers.* Columbia University Press.

Richard, K. P. (1997). *The Westray story: A predictable path to disaster.* Westray Mine Public Inquiry (N.S.).

Risk, R. C. B. (2012). "This nuisance of litigation": The origins of workers' compensation in Ontario. In D. Flaherty (Ed.), *Essays in the history of Canadian law* (Vol. 2, pp. 418–491). University of Toronto Press.

Robson, J. (2017). *Parental benefits in Canada: Which way forward?* Institute for Research on Public Policy. https://irpp.org/research-studies/parental-benefits-in-canada-which-way-forward/

Ryan, S. (2016). Violence and harassment in health and social services. *Table Talk*. Canadian Union of Public Employees. https://cupe.ca/violence-and-harassment-health-and-social-services

SafetyLine. (n.d.). *History of workplace safety: A look at over 200 years of safety developments in the workplace*. https://safetylineloneworker.com/blog/history-of-workplace-safety/

Smith, D. (2014). Workers' compensation. *The Canadian encyclopedia*. https://www.thecanadianencyclopedia.ca/en/article/workers-compensation

Statistics Canada. (2016b). *Canadian Community Health Survey: Unmet health care needs*. Health fact sheets.

Statistics Canada. (2018a, March 22). Distributions of household economic accounts for income, consumption, saving and wealth of Canadian households, 2017. *The Daily*. https://www150.statcan.gc.ca/n1/daily-quotidien/180322/dq180322b-eng.htm

Statistics Canada. (2018b). *Guide to the Labour Force Survey*. https://www150.statcan.gc.ca/n1/pub/71-543-g/71-543-g2018001-eng.htm

Statistics Canada. (2019a). *Aboriginal identity of person*. https://www23.statcan.gc.ca/imdb/p3Var.pl?Function=DECI&Id=246617

Statistics Canada. (2019b). *Income of individuals by age group, sex and income source, Canada, provinces and selected census metropolitan areas*. https://www150.statcan.gc.ca/t1/tbl1/en/tv.action?pid=1110023901

Statistics Canada. (2020, March). *The impact of COVID–19 on the Canadian labour market*. Ottawa, ON. https://www150.statcan.gc.ca/n1/en/pub/11-627-m/11-627-m2020028-eng.pdf?st=pfRWn9nd

Trading Economics. (n.d.). *Canada unemployment rate*. https://tradingeconomics.com/canada/unemployment-rate

Van Santvoort, A. (2017). *B.C. leads country for underemployment*. Business in Vancouver. https://biv.com/article/2017/09/bc-leads-country-underemployment

Vancity. (2019). *Recognizing the problem: Workplace credential and the newcomer experience in BC*. https://www.vancity.com/AboutVancity/News/MediaReleases/WorkplaceCredentials_Jun26_2019/Vancity_Newcomers-Report.pdf

Vanzo, R. (2020, July 11). CERB update: Will Canada adopt universal basic income? *The Motley Fool*. https://www.fool.ca/2020/07/11/cerb-update-will-canada-adopt-universal-basic-income/

Weise, R. (1972). *Social security abroad: Canada's new unemployment act*. Bulletin. https://www.ssa.gov/policy/docs/ssb/v35n2/v35n2p31.pdf

Wood, D. E. (2019). *Employment Insurance: Next steps on the road to renewal*. Atkinson Foundation. https://atkinsonfoundation.ca/site/uploads/2019/02/Atkinson_EI-Report_13019-FINAL.pdf

Zietsma, D. (2010, February). *Immigrants working in regulated occupations. Perspectives on labour and income*. https://www150.statcan.gc.ca/n1/pub/75-001-x/2010102/article/11121-eng.htm

Chapter 4

Aivalis, C. (2018, August 13). Conservatives end "basic income" program in Ontario, afraid to be proved wrong. *Washington Post*.

Anderson, J. E. (2012). *Public finance: Principles and policy* (2nd ed.). Cengage Learning.

Angus Reid Institute. (2018). *Poverty in Canada: Most say governments are doing too little, but disagree on what should be done*. Angus Reid Institute. http://angusreid.org/poverty-in-canada-part-2/

Baldwin, B., & Shillington, R. (2017, June 14). *Unfinished business: Pension reform in Canada*. Institute for Research on Public Policy (IRPP). https://irpp.org/research-studies/unfinished-business-pension-reform-in-canada/

Barnes, S., Abban, V., & Weiss, A. (2015). *Low wages, no benefits: expanding access to health benefits for low-income Ontarians*. The Wellesley Institute. https://www.wellesleyinstitute.com/wp-content/uploads/2015/02/Low-Wages-No-Benefits-Wellesley-Institute-Feb-2015.pdf

Bechtel, B. (2013). Food banks. *The Canadian encyclopedia*. https://www.thecanadianencyclopedia.ca/en/article/food-banks

Beedie, N., Macdonald, D., & Wilson, D. (2019). Towards justice: Tackling Indigenous child poverty in Canada. *Upstream*. https://www.afn.ca/wp-content/uploads/2019/07/Upstream_report_final_English_June-24-2019.pdf

Bird, F. (1970). *Report of the Royal Commission on the Status of Women in Canada*. http://epe.lac-bac.gc.ca/100/200/301/pco-bcp/commissions-ef/bird1970-eng/bird1970-eng.htm

Brown, D. (2019, October 1). Poverty costs Ontario up to $33B annually, new report says. *CBC News Toronto*. https://www.cbc.ca/news/canada/toronto/ontario-poverty-costs-billion-annually-report-1.5302882

Buist, S. (2015, November 27). Researchers link poverty and shorter life expectancy. *Hamilton Spectator*. https://www.thespec.com/news-story/6140009-researchers-link-poverty-and-shorter-life-expectancy/

Campaign 2000. (2018). *Bold ambitions for child and family poverty eradication: 2018 report card on child and family poverty in Canada*. https://campaign2000.ca/wp-content/uploads/2018/11/C2000NationalEnglishReportCardNov2018.pdf

Campaign 2000. (2020a). *Child and family poverty 30 years later: 2020 setting the stage for a poverty-free Canada*. https://campaign2000.ca/wp-content/uploads/2020/01/campaign-2000-report-setting-the-stage-for-a-poverty-free-canada-updated-january-24-2020.pdf

Campaign 2000. (2020b). *Our story*. https://campaign2000.ca/about-us/our-story/

Canada Without Poverty. (2018, August 21). Canadian poverty reduction strategy [Press release]. http://www.cwp-csp.ca/2018/08/countrys-first-national-poverty-strategy-acts-as-a-foundation-for-a-canada-without-poverty/

Canada Without Poverty, & Citizens for Public Justice. (2015). *Dignity for all: A national anti-poverty plan for Canada*. https://dignityforall.ca/wp-content/uploads/2017/02/DignityForAll_Report.pdf

Canadian Public Health Association. (n.d.). *What are the social determinants of health?* https://www.cpha.ca/what-are-social-determinants-health

Conference Board of Canada. (2011). *Canadian income inequality: Is Canada becoming more unequal?* https://www.conferenceboard.ca/hcp/hot-topics/canInequality.aspx

Conference Board of Canada. (2013). *Elderly poverty*. https://www.conferenceboard.ca/hcp/Details/society/elderly-poverty.aspx?AspxAutoDetectCookieSupport=1

Conference Board of Canada (2018, July 30). *Poverty*. https://www.conferenceboard.ca/hcp/provincial/society/poverty.aspx

Crocker, G. (2015). *The economic necessity of basic income*. Munich Personal RePEc Archive. https://mpra.ub.uni-muenchen.de/62941/1/MPRA_paper_62941.pdf

Culhane, D. (2018). *Chronic homelessness*. Homeless Hub. https://www.homelesshub.ca/resource/chronic-homelessness-0

Dachner, N., & Tarasuk, V. (2017, October 23). *Food waste and food insecurity in Canada — Diverting food waste to charitable food programs will not address food insecurity in Canada*. Proof: Food insecurity policy research. https://proof.utoronto.ca/food-waste-and-food-insecurity-in-canada/

Dej, E., & Ecker, J. (2018, July 18). Homelessness & precarious housing in Canada: Where we have been & where we are going. *Public Sector Digest*. https://publicsectordigest.com/article/homelessness-precarious-housing-in-canada-where-we-have-been-where-we-are-going

Duong, D. (2020, June 2). A crisis within a crisis: Race and income determine COVID–19 outcomes. *Healthing*. https://www.healthing.ca/diseases-and-conditions/coronavirus/a-crisis-within-a-crisis-race-and-income-determine-covid-19-experience

Early Years Study. (2020). *Early years study 4: Thriving kids, thriving society*, the fourth landmark study, led by the Honourable Margaret McCain. https://earlyyearsstudy.ca/

Edmonton Gleaners Association. (2020). *Our humble beginnings and present work.* https://www.edmontonsfoodbank.com/about/history/

Employment and Social Development Canada. (2019, October 4). *Employment Insurance monitoring and assessment report for the fiscal year beginning April 1, 2017 and ending March 31, 2018.* https://www.canada.ca/en/employment-social-development/programs/ei/ei-list/reports/monitoring2018/chapter2/regular-benefits.html

Feed Ontario. (2019). *Cost of poverty in Ontario 2019.* https://feedontario.ca/cost-of-poverty-2019/

Flavo, N. (2017). *Ten things to know about social assistance in Canada.* The Canadian Observatory on Homelessness/Homeless Hub. https://homelesshub.ca

Food and Agriculture Organization of the United Nations. (2003). Food security: Concepts and measurement (Chapter 2). http://www.fao.org/3/y4671e/y4671e06.htm

Food Banks Canada. (2019). *HungerCount 2019.* https://hungercount.foodbankscanada.ca/assets/docs/FoodBanks_HungerCount_EN_2019.pdf

Food Banks Canada. (2020). *Hunger facts.* https://www.foodbankscanada.ca

Forget, E. (2011). The town with no poverty: The health effects of a Canadian guaranteed annual income field experiment. *Canadian Public Policy, 37*(3), 283–305.

Fortin, P., Godbout, L., & St-Cerny, S. (2012). *Impact of Québec's universal low-fee childcare program on female labour force participation, domestic income and government budgets.* Université de Sherbrooke.

Gardner, B., Barnes, S., & Social Assistance Review Health Working Group. (2011). *Towards a social assistance system that enables health and health equity.* The Wellesley Institute. https://www.wellesleyinstitute.com/wp-content/uploads/2011/11/Towards-a-Social-Assistance-System-that-Enables-Health-and-Health-Equity-Brief-to-the-Commission-for-the-Review-of-Social-Assistance-in-Ontario2.pdf

Goering, P., Veldhuizen, S., Watson, A., Adair, C., Kopp, B., Latimer, E., Nelson, G., MacNaughton, E., Streiner, D., & Aubry, T. (2014). *National at home/chez soi final report.* Mental Health Commission of Canada. http://www.mentalhealthcommission.ca

Gold, K. (2019, May 2). "They've taken baby steps": Professor slams Ottawa's housing strategy. *The Globe and Mail.*

Government of Canada. (2018a). *Canada's first National Housing Strategy: A place to call home.* https://www.placetocallhome.ca/

Government of Canada. (2018b). *Opportunity for all — Canada's first poverty reduction strategy.* http://www.psdssab.org/?wpfb_dl=251

Government of Canada. (2019). *On-reserve income assistance program.* https://www.sac-isc.gc.ca/eng/1100100035256/1533307528663

Gunaseelan, V. (2018, March 23). Let's lift all Canadians out of poverty: Canada needs a dialogue about a national basic income program. *Hamilton Spectator.* https://www.toronto.com/opinion-story/8345150-let-s-lift-all-canadians-out-of-poverty/

Handler, J., & Babcock, A. S. (2006). The failure of workfare: Another reason for a basic income guarantee. *Basic Income Studies, 1*(1). https://doi.org/10.2202/1932-0183.1000

Herd, D., Mitchell, A., & Lightman, E. (2005). Rituals of degradation: Administration as policy in the Ontario Works programme. *Social Policy & Administration, 39*(1), 65–79. https://doi.org/10.1111/j.1467-9515.2005.00425.x

Homeless Hub. (n.d.). *Housing first.* https://www.homelesshub.ca/solutions/housing-accommodation-and-supports/housing-first

Hughes, J. (2012). *Homelessness closing the gap between capacity and performance.* Mowat Centre for Policy Innovation. https://munkschool.utoronto.ca/mowatcentre/wp-content/uploads/publications/56_homelessness.pdf

Jackson, A. (2014). *How the Conservatives have failed on child poverty.* Broadbent Institute. https://www.broadbentinstitute.ca/en/blog/how-conservatives-have-failed-child-poverty

Krueger, L., Accles, L., & Wernick, L. (1997, July). *Workfare: The real deal II.* https://www.researchgate.net/profile/Laura_Wernick/publication/307133992_Workfare_The_Real_Deal_II/links/57c4916808ae5e5a8191bc59/Workfare-The-Real-Deal-II.pdf

Laidley, J., & Aldridge, H. (2020). *Welfare in Canada 2019.* Maytree Foundation. https://maytree.com

Liberto, D. (2019, August 23). What is the poverty gap? *Investopedia.* https://www.investopedia.com/terms/p/poverty-gap.asp

Macdonald, D., & Friendly, M. (2019). *Developmental milestones: Child care fees in Canada's big cities 2018.* Canadian Centre for Policy Alternatives. https://www.policyalternatives.ca/publications/reports/developmental-milestones

Macdonald, D., & Wilson, D. (2016). *Shameful neglect: Indigenous child poverty in Canada.* Canadian Centre for Policy Alternatives. https://www.policyalternatives.ca/sites/default/files/uploads/publications/National%20Office/2016/05/Indigenous_Child%20_Poverty.pdf

McIntyre, L., Kwok, C., Emery, J. H., & Dutton, D. J. (2016). Impact of a guaranteed annual income program on Canadian seniors' physical, mental and functional health. Canadian Journal of Public Health, 107(2), e176–e182. https://doi.org/10.17269/cjph.107.5372

McIsaac, E. (2017). *Focusing on rights can help us eliminate poverty.* Maytree. https://maytree.com/publications/focusing-rights-can-help-us-eliminate-poverty/

Montgomery, M. (2019, February 6). Food bank need in Canada: Unacceptably high. *Radio Canada International.*

Native Women's Association of Canada. (2017). *Poverty reduction strategy: The Native Women's Association of Canada engagement results.* http://www.nwac.ca/wp-content/uploads/2018/08/Poverty-Reduction-Strategy-Revised-Aug23.pdf

Office of the United Nations High Commissioner for Human Rights. (2014). *The right to adequate housing.* United Nations Fact Sheet No. 21. https://ohchr.org/Documents/Publications/FS21_rev_1_Housing_en.pdf

O'Leary, D., & Majic, L. (2018, July 18). *Here's what Canada's first national anti-poverty plan needs. Dignity for All.* https://dignityforall.ca/heres-what-canadas-first-national-anti-poverty-plan-needs

Organisation for Economic Co-operation and Development. (2019). *Poverty gap.* https://data.oecd.org/inequality/poverty-gap.htm

Pasma, C., & Citizens for Public Justice. (2010). *Bearing the Brunt: How the 2008–2009 recession created poverty for Canadian families.* https://cpj.ca/wp-content/uploads/Bearing_the_Brunt.pdf

Peck, J. (2001). *Workfare states.* Guilford Press.

Peck, J., & Theodore, N. (2000). Commentary. "Work first": Workfare and the regulation of contingent labour markets. *Cambridge Journal of Economics, 24*(1), 119–138. https://doi.org/10.1093/cje/24.1.119

Raphael, D. (2014). Social determinants of children's health in Canada: Analysis and implications. *International Journal of Child, Youth and Family Studies,* 5(2), 220–239.

Riches, G., & Tarasuk, V. (2014). Canada: Thirty years of food charity and public policy neglect. In G. Riches & T. Silvasti (Eds.), *First world hunger revisited* (pp. 42–56). Palgrave Macmillan.

Scott, K. (2018, August 27). Canada's new poverty reduction strategy: Strong on accountability, short on action. *Behind the Numbers.* Canadian Centre for Policy Alternatives.

Segal, H. (2016). *Finding a better way: A basic income pilot project for Ontario: A discussion paper by Hugh D Segal.* Ontario Ministry of Community and Social Services. https://files.ontario.ca/discussionpaper_nov3_english_final.pdf

Smith-Carrier, T., & Green, S. (2017). Another low road to basic income? Mapping a pragmatic model for adopting a basic income in Canada. *Basic Income Studies, 12*(2), 1–25.

Smith-Carrier, T., & Lawlor, A. (2016). Realizing our (neo-liberal) potential? A critical discourse analysis of the poverty reduction strategy in Ontario, Canada. *Critical Social Policy, 37*(1), 105–127. https://doi.org/10.1177/0261018316666251

Smith-Carrier, T., Ross, K., Kirkham, J., & Decker Pierce, B. (2017). "Food is a right ... Nobody should be starving on our streets": Perceptions of food bank usage in a mid-sized city in Ontario, Canada. *Journal of Human Rights Practice, 9*(1), 29–49. https://doi.org/10.1093/jhuman/hux010

Statistics Canada. (2011). *Table: 11-10-0185-01. Persistence of low income.* https://www150.statcan.gc.ca/t1/tbl1/en/tv.action?pid=1110018501

Statistics Canada. (2017a). Canadian Income Survey, 2017. *The Daily.* https://www150.statcan.gc.ca/n1/daily-quotidien/190226/dq190226b-info-eng.htm

Statistics Canada. (2017b)). *Dictionary, census of population, 2016: Core housing need.* https://www12.statcan.gc.ca/census-recensement/2016/ref/dict/households-menage037-eng.cfm

Statistics Canada. (2019a). *Distributions of household economic accounts for income, consumption, saving and wealth of Canadian households, 2018.* https://www150.statcan.gc.ca/n1/daily-quotidien/190327/dq190327b-eng.htm

Statistics Canada. (2019b). The population living in shelters: Who are they? *The Daily* (April 15). https://www150.statcan.gc.ca/n1/daily-quotidien/190415/dq190415a-eng.htm

Statistics Canada. (2020a). *Table 11-10-0020-01. After-tax low income status of census families based on Census Family Low Income Measure (CFLIM-AT), by family type and family composition.* https://doi.org/10.25318/1110002001-eng

Statistics Canada. (2020b). *Table 11-10-0134-01. Gini coefficients of adjusted market, total and after-tax income.* https://doi.org/10.25318/1110013401-eng

Statistics Canada. (2020c). *Table 11-10-0135-01. Low income statistics by age, sex and economic family type.* https://doi.org/10.25318/1110013501-eng

Tarasuk, V., Germain, A.-A. F., & Loopstra, R. (2019, January 31). The relationship between food banks and food insecurity: Insights from Canada. *International Journal of Voluntary and Nonprofit Organizations.* https://link.springer.com/article/10.1007%2Fs11266-019-00092-w

Tweddle, A., & Aldridge, H. (2019). *Welfare in Canada, 2018.* Maytree. https://maytree.com/welfare-in-canada/

United Church of Canada. (2018, August 22). National anti-poverty strategy welcomed. *News.* https://www.united-church.ca/news/national-anti-poverty-strategy-welcomed

Uppal, S. (2019, August). Homeownership, mortgage debt and types of mortgage among Canadian families. *Insights on Canadian Society.* Statistics Canada Catalogue no. 75-006-X. https://www150.statcan.gc.ca/n1/pub/75-006-x/2019001/article/00012-eng.htm

Uppal, S., & LaRochelle-Côté, S. (2015, June). Changes in wealth across the income distribution, 1999 to 2012. *Insights on Canadian Society.* Statistics Canada Catalogue no. 75-006-X. https://www150.statcan.gc.ca/n1/pub/75-006-x/2015001/article/14194-eng.htm

von Rueden, U., Gosch, A., Rajmil, L., Bisegger, C., & Ravens-Sieberer, U. (2006). Socioeconomic determinants of health related quality of life in childhood and adolescence: Results from a European study. *Journal of Epidemiology and Community Health, 60*(2), 130–135.

World Health Organization. (n.d.). *Poverty and social determinants.* http://www.euro.who.int/en/health-topics/environment-and-health/urban-health/activities/poverty-and-social-determinants

Zon, N. (2018, September 18). The Poverty Reduction Act tootless but not pointless. *Policy Options.* https://policyoptions.irpp.org/magazines/november-2018/poverty-reduction-act-toothless-not-pointless/

Chapter 5

Adamson, P. (2008). The child care transition: A league table of early childhood education and care in economically advanced countries. *Innocenti Report Card 8.* UNICEF Innocenti Research Centre.

Armstrong, P., & Armstrong, H. (2010). *The double ghetto: Canadian women and their segregated work.* Wynford Project Edition. Oxford University Press.

Baker, M., Gruber, J., & Milligan, K. (2008). Universal child care, Maternal labor supply, and family well-being. *Journal of Political Economy, 116*(4).

Bezanson, K. (2019). Feminism, federalism and families: Canada's mixed social policy architecture. *Journal of Law and Equality, 14*(1), 188.

Blau, F., & Kahn, L. (2003). Understanding international differences in the gender pay gap. *Journal of Labor Economics, 21*(1), 106–144.

Block, S., & Galabuzi, G-E (2018). *Persistent inequality: Ontario's colour-coded labour market.* Canadian Centre for Policy Alternatives. https://www.policyalternatives.ca/sites/default/files/uploads/publications/Ontario%20Office/2018/12/Persistent%20inequality.pdf

Blum, S., Koslowski, A., Macht, A., & Moss, P. (2018). *International review of leave policies and research 2018.* https://doi.org/10.13140/RG.2.2.18149.45284

Budig, M., Misra, J., & Boeckmann, I. (2012). The motherhood penalty in cross-national perspective: The importance of work–family policies and cultural attitudes. *Social Politics, 19*(2).

Burton, P., & Phipps, S. (2017). Economic well-being of Canadian children. *Canadian Public Policy, 43*(4).

Campaign 2000. (2018). *Bold ambitions for child and family poverty eradication.* Report card on child and family poverty 2018. https://campaign2000.ca/wp-content/uploads/2018/11/C2000NationalEnglishReportCardNov2018.pdf

Campaign 2000. (2020). *Setting the stage for a poverty-free Canada: Report card on child and family poverty in Canada 2019.* https://campaign2000.ca/wp-content/uploads/2020/01/campaign-2000-report-setting-the-stage-for-a-poverty-free-canada-january-14-2020.pdf

Canada. (2014). *Family tax cut.* Canada Revenue Agency. https://www.canada.ca/en/revenue-agency/programs/about-canada-revenue-agency-cra/federal-government-budgets/budget-2014-road-balance-creating-jobs-opportunities/family-tax-cut.html

Canada. (2018). *Indigenous early learning and child care framework.*

Canadian Gender Budgeting Act, SC 2018 c. 27, s. 314.

Canadian Health Coalition and Ontario Health Coalition. (2017). *Health accord break down: Costs & consequences of the failed 2016/17 negotiations.*

Canadian Health Coalition. (2018). *Ensuring quality care for all seniors, policy brief.*

Catalyst. (2019). *Quick take: Women in energy — Gas, mining, and oil.* https://www.catalyst.org/research/women-in-energy-gas-mining-oil/

Cranswick, K., & Dosman, D. (2008). Eldercare: What we know today. *Canadian Social Trends, 86*(1), 49–57.

De Henau, J., Himmelweit, S., Santos, C., & Soobedar, Z. (2011). Comparing welfare regimes by their effects on intra-household inequalities. ESPANET conference proceedings (September 8–10). Valencia, Spain.

Department of Finance Canada. (2015). *Update of the economic and fiscal projections.* https://www.budget.gc.ca/efp-peb/2015/pub/chap02-en.html

Department of Finance Canada. (2018a). *Backgrounder: Canada's new parental sharing benefit.* https://www.canada.ca/en/department-finance/news/2018/04/backgrounder-canadas-new-parental-sharing-benefit.html

Department of Finance Canada. (2018b). *Gender results framework (Chapter 5). Budget 2018.* https://www.budget.gc.ca/2018/docs/plan/chap-05-en.html

Department of Finance Canada. (2019a). *Gender report. Budget 2019.* http://publications.gc.ca/site/eng/9.870212/publication.html

Department of Finance Canada. (2019b). *Report on federal tax expenditures — Concepts, estimates and evaluations 2019*. https://www.canada.ca/en/department-finance/services/publications/federal-tax-expenditures/2019.html

Dirk, A., Fitzenberger, B., & Sommerfeld, K. (2010). *Rising wage inequality, the decline of collective bargaining, and the gender wage gap*. Institute for the Study of Labor, Discussion Paper No. 4911,

Drolet, M. (2002). Can the workplace explain Canadian gender pay differentials? *Canadian Public Policy/Analyse de Politiques, 28* (Suppl.), S41–S63.

Eichler, M. (1997). *Family shifts: Families, policies and gender equality*. Oxford University Press.

Ekberg, J., Eriksson, R., & Friebel, G. (2013). Parental leave — A policy evaluation of the Swedish "Daddy-Month" reform. *Journal of Public Economics, 97*(C), 131–143.

Employment and Skills Development Canada. (2017). *Multilateral Early Learning and Child Care Framework*. https://www.canada.ca/en/employment-social-development/programs/early-learning-child-care/reports/2017-multilateral-framework.html

Employment and Skills Development Canada. (2018). *Backgrounder: Proactive pay equity*. https://www.canada.ca/en/employment-social-development/news/2018/10/backgrounder-pay-equity.html

Employment and Skills Development Canada. (2019). *Canada's Poverty Reduction Strategy — An update*.

Evans, J. (2002). Work/family reconciliation, gender wage equity and occupational segregation: The role of firms and public policy. *Canadian Public Policy, 28*, S187–S216.

Fairholm, R. (2009). *Literature review of socioeconomic effects and net benefits*. Child Care Human Resource Sector Council.

Family Caregiver Alliance. (2006). *Caregiver health*. National Centre for Caregiving.

Fast, J. (2015). *Caregiving for older adults with disabilities: present costs, future challenges*. Institute for Research on Public Policy.

Fast, J., Lero, D., DeMarco, R., Ferreira, H., & Eales, J. (2014). Combining care work and paid work: Is it sustainable? *Fact sheets: Research on Aging Policies and Practice*. University of Alberta.

Fast, J., Williamson, D. L., & Keating, N. C. (1999). The hidden costs of informal elder care. *Journal of Family and Economic Issues, 20*(3), 301–326.

Ferragina, E. (2017). Does family policy influence women's employment? Reviewing the evidence in the field. *Political Studies Review, 17*(1), 65–80.

Fortin, P., Godbout, L., & St-Cerny, S. (2012). *Impact of Québec's universal low-fee childcare program on female labour force participation, domestic income and government budgets*. https://www.homelesshub.ca/resource/impact-quebecs-universal-low-fee-childcare-program-female-labour-force-participation

Fortin, P., Godbout, L., & St-Cerny, S. (2013). Emploi et inégalités sociales: L'impact des services de garde à contribution réduite du Québec sur le taux d'activité féminin, le revenu intérieur et les budgets gouvernementaux. *Revue Interventions économiques, 47*.

Fox, D.,, & Moyser, M. (2018). *The economic well-being of women in Canada: Women in Canada: A gender-based statistical report*. Statistics Canada Catalogue no. 89-503-X. https://www150.statcan.gc.ca/n1/pub/89-503-x/2015001/article/54930-eng.htm

Friendly, M., Larsen, E., Feltham, L., Grady, B., Forer, B., & Jones, M. (2018). *Early child care and education in Canada 2016* (11th ed.). Childcare Resource and Research Unit.

Gaspard, H., & Woolner, E. (2019, August). Because it's 2019: Checking in on gender budgeting in Canada. *Policy Magazine*. https://policymagazine.ca/because-its-2019-checking-in-on-gender-budgeting-in-canada/

Gouvernement du Québec. (2020). *Québec Parental Insurance Plan*. https://www.rqap.gouv.qc.ca/en/home

Government of Nova Scotia. (2020). *Caregiver benefit*. https://novascotia.ca/dhw/ccs/FactSheets/Caregiver-Benefit.pdf

Guest, D. (2006). Family allowance. *The Canadian encyclopedia*. (Updated by Julia Skikavich, December 18, 2013). https://thecanadianencyclopedia.ca/en/article/family-allowance

Gunderson, M. (1998). *Women and the Canadian labour market: Transitions towards the future*. Statistics Canada/ITP Nelson.

Hegewischa, A., & Gornick, J. (2011). The impact of work-family policies on women's employment: A review of research from OECD countries. *Community, Work and Family, 14*(2), 119–138.

Heisz, A., Jackson, A., & Picot, G. (2002). *Winners and losers in the labour market of the 1990s*. Statistics Canada, Analytical Studies Branch Research Paper Series No. 184. Statistics Canada Catalogue no. 11F0019. https://www150.statcan.gc.ca/n1/en/catalogue/11F0019M2002184

Hill, N., Alook, A., & Hussey, I. (2017). *How gender and race shape experiences of work in Alberta's oil industry*. Parkland Institute.

Hurteau, P. (2018). *Combien coûterait la transformation des garderies privéeesen CPE?* Institute de research et d'informations socioéconomiques (Graphique 11).

Hussey, I., & Jackson, E. (2017). Gendering the downturn: Is the NDP doing enough for Alberta women? Parkland Institute. https://www.parklandinstitute.ca/gendering_the_downturn

International Monetary Fund. (2017). *Gender budgeting in G7 countries*. https://www.imf.org/~/media/Files/Publications/PP/pp041917gender-budgeting-in-g7-countries.ashx

Jacobs, J. C., Lilly, M. B., Ng C., & Coyte P. C. (2013). The fiscal impact of informal caregiving to home care recipients in Canada: How the intensity of care influences costs and benefits to government. *Social Science and Medicine, 81*, 102–109.

Jenson, J. (2013). Historical transformations of Canada's social architecture. In K. Banting & J. Myles, (Eds.), *The fading of redistribution* (Chapter 2). UBC Press.

Keefe, J. (2011). *Supporting caregivers and caregiving in an aging Canada*. Institute for Research and Public Policy.

Kröger, T., & Yeandle, S. (2013). *Combining paid work and family care: Policies and experiences in international perspective*. Policy Press.

Lahey, K. (2015). Uncovering women in taxation: The gender impacts of detaxation, tax expenditures and joint tax/benefit units. *Osgoode Hall Law Journal, 52*(2), 451.

Lahey, K. (2016). Tax units in Canada and gender: Ability to pay, equity or keeping women in their place? In J. Li, B. Wilkie, & L. Chapman (Eds.), *Income Tax at 100 Years: Reflections on the Income War Tax Act*. Canadian Tax Foundation.

Laurin, A., & Kesselman, J. R. (2011). *Income splitting for two-parent families: Who gains, who doesn't, and at what cost?* CD Howe Institute.

Lavoie, A., Gringas, L., & Aude, N. (2015). *La qualité educative dans les garderies non subventionnées. Faits saillants, Enquête Québécoise sur la qualité des services de garde éducatifs 2014*. Institut de la statistique du Québec.

Lefebvre, P., & Merrigan, P. (2008). Child-care policy and the labor supply of mothers with young children: A natural experiment from Canada. *Journal of Labor Economics, 26*(3).

Lero, D., & Joseph, G. (2007). *A systematic review of the literature on combining work and eldercare in Canada*. University of Guelph and The Homewood Foundation.

Liberal Party. (2019). *More time and time to help families raise their kids*. https://www.liberal.ca/wp-content/uploads/2019/09/Backgrounder-More-time-and-money-to-help-families-raise-their-kids.pdf

Lindahl, B. (2018). Paternal leave extremely important to reach gender equality. *Nordic Labour Journal*. http://www.nordiclabourjournal.org/i-fokus/in-focus-2018/nordic-working-life/article.2018-06-14.5410895249

Living Wage Canada (2020). *Calculating a living wage*. http://livingwagecanada.ca

Macdonald, D. (2014). *Income splitting in Canada: Inequality by design*. Canadian Centre for Policy Alternatives.

Macdonald, D., & Friendly, M. (2020). *In Progress: Child care fees in Canada 2019.* Canadian Centre for Policy Alternatives. https://www.policyalternatives.ca/sites/default/files/uploads/publications/National%20Office/2020/03/In%20progress_Child%20care%20fees%20in%20Canada%20in%202019_march12.pdf

Mandel, H. (2012). Winners and losers: The consequences of welfare state policies for gender wage inequality. *European Sociological Review, 28*(2), 241–262.

Margolis, R., Hou, F., Haan, M., & Holm, A. (2019). Use and sharing of parental benefits in Canada. *Journal of Marriage and Family, 81*, 450–467.

Marshall, K. (2008). Fathers' use of paid parental leave. *Perspectives on Labour and Income, 9*(6).

McInturff, K., & Tulloch, P. (2014). *Narrowing the gap: The difference that public sector wages make.* Canadian Centre for Policy Alternatives.

McKay, L., Mathieu, S., & Doucet, A. (2016). Parental-leave rich and parental-leave poor: Inequality in Canadian labour market based leave policies. *Journal of Industrial Relations, 58*(4), 11–12.

Milan, A. (2015). *Families and living arrangements: Women in Canada: A gender-based statistical report.* Statistics Canada Catalogue no. 89-503-X.

Milligan, K. (2016). The tax recognition of children in Canada: Exemptions, credits, and cash transfers. *Canadian Tax Journal, 64*(3), 601–618.

Milligan, K., & Stabile, M. (2007). The integration of child tax credits and welfare: Evidence from the Canadian National Child Benefit program. *Journal of Public Economics, 91*(1–2), 305–326.

Milligan, K., & Stabile, M. (2008). Do child tax benefits affect the well-being of children? Evidence from Canadian Child Benefit Expansions. *NBER Working Paper No. 14624.*

Ministers Responsible for Social Services (1997). *The National Child Benefit: Building a better future for Canadian children.* Queen's Printer.

Mirabelli, A. (2018). *What's in a name? Defining family in a diverse society.* Originally published as a *Transition* article in December 2015. The Vanier Institute of the Family.

Moscovitch, A., & Falvo, N. (2017). The introduction and evolution of child benefits in Canada. *Behind the Numbers.* Centre for Policy Alternatives.

Moyser, M., & Burlock, A. (2018). *Time use: Total work burden, unpaid work, and leisure.* Statistics Canada Catalogue no. 89-503-X.

Moyser, M., & Milan, A. (2018). Fertility rates and labour force participation among women in Québec and Ontario. *Insights on Canadian Society,* Catalogue no. 75-006-X. Statistics Canada. https://www150.statcan.gc.ca/n1/pub/75-006-x/2018001/article/54976-eng.pdf

Office of the Auditor General of Canada. (2009). *2009 Spring report of the Auditor General of Canada (Chapter 1: Gender-based analysis).* https://www.oag-bvg.gc.ca/internet/English/parl_oag_200905_01_e_32514.html

Office of the Auditor General of Canada. (2015). *2015 Fall reports of the Auditor General of Canada. Report 1 — Implementing gender-based analysis.* https://www1.oag-bvg.gc.ca/internet/English/parl_oag_201602_01_e_41058.html

Organisation for Economic Co-operation and Development. (2011). *Help wanted: Providing and paying for long-term care.*

Organisation for Economic Co-operation and Development. (2018). Starting close, growing apart: Why the gender gap in labour market income widens over the working life. *Employment Outlook 2018.*

Organisation for Economic Co-operation and Development. (2019a). *Family benefits public spending (indicator).* https://data.oecd.org/socialexp/family-benefits-public-spending.htm

Organisation for Economic Co-operation and Development. (2019b). *Gender pay gap (indicator).*

Pasolli, L. (2019). *An analysis of the Multilateral Early Learning and Child Care Framework and the Early Learning and Child Care Bilateral Agreements.* Child Care Now (Child Care Advocacy Association of Canada).

Pedwell, T. (2018, September 20). Arbitrator awards rural Canada Post carriers pay hike of up to 25 percent. *The Globe and Mail.*

Revenu Québec. (2020). *Tax credit for caregivers.* https://www.revenuquebec.ca/en/citizens/tax-credits/tax-credit-for-caregivers/

Robson, J. (2017). Parental benefits in Canada: Which way forward? *IRPP Study, No. 63*, 13–14.

Samman, E., & Lombard, J. (2019). *Childcare and working families: New opportunity or missing link? An evidence brief.* UNICEF.

Scott, K. (2019a). Action on equity: Does Canada's new legislation deliver? *Behind the Numbers.* Canadian Centre for Policy Alternatives.

Scott, K. (2019b). *The promose and reality of gender budgeting.* https://www.policyalternatives.ca/publications/monitor/promise-and-reality-gender-budgeting

Scott, K. (2020). A feminist recovery plan for a gender-just future. *Monitor, 27*(3). Canadian Centre for Policy Alternatives.

Sinha, M. (2013). *Portrait of caregivers, 2012. Spotlight on Canadians: Results from the General Social Survey.* Statistics Canada Catalogue no. 89-652-X.

Spence, J. C., Holt, N. L., Dutove, J. K., & Carson, V. (2010). Uptake and effectiveness of the Children's Fitness Tax Credit in Canada: The rich get richer, *BMC Public Health, 10*, 356.

Standing Committee on the Status of Women. (2016). *Implementing gender-based analysis plus in the Government of Canada.* Parliament of Canada.

Statistics Canada. (2015a). *Statistical units: Census family.* https://www23.statcan.gc.ca/imdb/p3Var.pl?Function=Unit&Id=32746

Statistics Canada. (2015b). The shift to small*er households over the past century.* Canadian Megatrends. Statistics Canada Catalogue no. 11-630-X. https://www150.statcan.gc.ca/n1/daily-quotidien/180313/dq180313a-info-eng.htm

Statistics Canada. (2016a). *Data tables, 2016 census: Families, households and marital status.* Statistics Canada Catalogue No. 98-400-X2016392; *2016 census of population.* Statistics Canada Catalogue No. 998-400-X2016304. https://www150.statcan.gc.ca/n1/en/catalogue/98-400-X2016304

Statistics Canada. (2016b). *Median employment income of men and women aged 25 to 64 years by educational attainment status.* Data tables, 2016 census. Statistics Canada Catalogue no. 98-400-X2016261.

Statistics Canada. (2016c). *Data tables, 2016 census: Occupation — National Occupational Classification (NOC) 2016 (693A), Highest Certificate, Diploma or Degree (15), Labour Force Status (3), Age (13A) and Sex (3) for the Labour Force Aged 15 Years and Over in Private Households of Canada, Provinces and Territories, Census Metropolitan Areas and Census Agglomerations, 2016 Census - 25% Sample Data.* Statistics Canada Catalogue No. Catalogue no. 98-400-x2016295

Statistics Canada. (2017a). Same-sex couples in Canada in 2016. *Census in brief.* Statistics Canada Catalogue no. 98-200-X2016007.

Statistics Canada. (2017b). Young adults living with their parents in Canada in 2016. *Census in brief.* Statistics Canada Catalogue no. 98-200-X2016008.

Statistics Canada. (2018a). *Canadian Income Survey, 2016.*

Statistics Canada. (2018b). Employment Insurance coverage survey, 2017. *The Daily.* https://www150.statcan.gc.ca/n1/daily-quotidien/181115/dq181115a-eng.htm

Statistics Canada. (2018c). *Employment Insurance coverage survey — Public use microdata file.* https://www150.statcan.gc.ca/n1/en/catalogue/89M0025X

Statistics Canada. (2020). Caregivers in Canada, 2018, *The Daily* (January 8). https://www150.statcan.gc.ca/n1/en/daily-quotidien/200108/dq200108a-eng.pdf?st=LqPzKSWN

Statistics Canada. (2019, April 10). Survey on early learning and child care arrangements, 2019. *The Daily.*

Statistics Canada. (n.d.a). Table 11-10-0135-01. *Low income statistics by age, sex and economic family type. Poverty rate based on the after tax low income measure (LIM-AT).*

Statistics Canada. (n.d.b). Table 11-10-0136-01. *Low income statistics by economic family type. Estimates calculated using the Low Income Measure After Tax.*

Statistics Canada. (n.d.c). Table 11-10-0143-01. *Average female and male earnings and female-to-male earnings ratio.*

Statistics Canada. (n.d.d). Table 11-10-0191-01. *Income statistics by economic family type and income source.*

Statistics Canada. (n.d.e). Table 11-10-0239-01. *Income of individuals by age group, sex and income source, Canada, provinces and selected census metropolitan areas.*

Statistics Canada. (n.d.f). Table 11-10-0240-01. *Distribution of employment income of individuals by sex and work activity, Canada, provinces and selected census metropolitan areas.*

Statistics Canada. (n.d.g). Table 13-10-0418-01. *Crude birth rate, age-specific fertility rates and total fertility rate (live births).*

Statistics Canada. (n.d.h). Table 14-10-0007-01. *Employment insurance benefit characteristics by class of worker, monthly, unadjusted for seasonality.*

Statistics Canada. (n.d.i). Table 14-10-0009-01. *Employment insurance beneficiaries by type of income benefits, monthly, unadjusted for seasonality.*

Statistics Canada. (n.d.j). Table 14-10-0018-01. *Labour force characteristics by sex and detailed age group, annual, inactive (x 1,000).*

Statistics Canada. (n.d.k). Table 14-10-0023-01. *Labour force characteristics by industry, annual (x 1,000).*

Statistics Canada. (n.d.l). Table 14-10-0120-01 (formerly CANSIM 282-0211). *Labour force characteristics by family age composition, annual 1.*

Statistics Canada. (n.d.m). Table 14-10-0327-01. *Labour force characteristics by sex and detailed age group, annual. Labour force participation of women 25-54 years.*

Statistics Canada. (n.d.n). Table 17-10-0060-01. *Estimates of population as of July 1st, by marital status or legal marital status, age and sex.*

Statistics Canada. (n.d.o). Table 17-10-0134-01. *Estimates of population (2016 Census and administrative data), by age group and sex for July 1st, Canada, provinces, territories, health regions (2018 boundaries) and peer groups.*

Statistics Canada. (n.d.p). Table 37-10-0012-01. *Postsecondary graduates, by program type, credential type, Classification of Instructional Programs, Primary Grouping (CIP_PG) and sex.*

Statistics Canada. (n.d.q). Table 42-10-0005-01. *Type of child care arrangement, household population aged 0 to 5 years.*

Statistics Canada. (n.d.r). Table 44-10-0005-01. *Population providing care to a family member or friend with a long-term illness, disability or aging needs by sex and relationship between respondent and primary care receiver.*

Statistics Canada. (n.d.s). Table 45-10-0014-01. *Daily average time spent in hours on various activities by age group and sex, 15 years and over, Canada and provinces. Women aged 15 years and older.*

Status of Women Canada, Privy Council Office, & Treasury Board of Canada Secretariat. (2016). *Action plan on gender-based analysis (2016–2020).*

Status of Women Canada. (n.d.). *Gender-based analysis plus.* https://cfc-swc.gc.ca/gba-acs/index-en.html

Thévenon, O. (2011). Family policies in OECD countries: A comparative analysis. *Population and Development Review,* 37(1), 57–87.

Turcotte, M. (2013). Family caregiving: What are the consequences? *Insights on Canadian Society.* Statistics Canada Catalogue no. 75-006-X.

Turner, A., & Findlay, L. (2008). Informal caregiving for seniors. *Health Reports, 23*(3). Statistics Canada Catalogue no. 82-003-X.

Uppal, S. (2015). *Employment patterns of families with children. Insights on Canadian society.* Statistics Canada Catalogue no. 75-006-X.

van Belle, J. (2016). *Paternity and parental leave policies across the European Union.* RAND Europe.

Women in Mining Canada. (2010). *Ramp up: A study on the status of women in canada's mining and exploration sector (Final Report).*

Wright, T. (2019, February 2). Internal docs shows many federal departments not meeting gender analysis targets. *The Canadian Press.*

Zossou, C. (2021). *Sharing household tasks: Teaming up during the COVID-19 pandemic.* Statistics Canada. www150.statcan.gc.ca/n1/pub/45-28-0001/2020001/article/00081-eng.htm

Chapter 6

Afifi, T. O., McTavish, J., Turner, S., MacMillan, H. L., & Wathen, C. N. (2018). The relationship between child protection contact and mental health outcomes among Canadian adults with a child abuse history. *Child Abuse & Neglect, 79,* 22–30.

Albert, J., & Herbert, M. (2013). Child welfare. *The Canadian encyclopedia.* https://www.thecanadianencyclopedia.ca/en/article/child-welfare

Alliance for Child Protection in Humanitarian Action (2019, March). *Technical note: Protection of Children during the coronavirus pandemic, version 1.* https://alliancecpha.org/en/system/tdf/library/attachments/the_alliance_covid_19_brief_version_1.pdf?file=1&type=node&id=37184

Armitage, A., & Murray, E. (2007). Thomas Gove: A commission of inquiry puts children first and proposes community governance and integration of services. In L. Foster & B. Wharf (Eds.), *People, Politics and Child Welfare in British Columbia* (pp. 139–157). UBC Press.

Badgley, R. (1984). *Report of the Committee on Sexual Offences against Children and Youth.* Government of Canada.

Baiden, P., & Fallon, B. (2018). Examining the association between suicidal behaviors and referral for mental health services among children involved in the child welfare system in Ontario, Canada. *Child Abuse & Neglect, 79,* 115–124.

Bill C-78: An Act to amend the Divorce Act, the Family Orders and Agreements Enforcement Assistance Act and the Garnishment, Attachment and Pension Diversion Act and to make consequential amendments to another Act. First reading. House of Commons of Canada. First session, 42nd Parliament (2019, February 28). https://www.parl.ca/LegisInfo/BillDetails.aspx?billId=9868788&Language=E

Bill C-92: An Act Respecting First Nations, Inuit and Métis Children, Youth and Families. First reading. House of Commons of Canada. First session, 42nd Parliament (2019, September 11). https://www.parl.ca/DocumentViewer/en/42-1/bill/C-92/first-reading

Bimman, A. (2018, December 4). I love you, daddy, my heart cracked: How the opioid crisis affects children left behind. *Global News.* https://globalnews.ca/news/4726775/opioid-crisis-children-left-behind/

Black, T. (2009). *Children's exposure to intimate partner violence (IPV): Challenging asumptions about child protection practices* (PhD dissertation, Factor-Inwentash Faculty of Social Work, University of Toronto).

Bounajm, F., Beckman, K., & Thériault, L. (2014). *Success for all: Investing in the future of Canadian children in care.* The Conference Board of Canada.

Brehaut, J., & Juzwishin, D. (2005). *HTA Initiative #18 — Bridging the gap: The use of research evidence in policy development.* Alberta Heritage Foundation for Medical Research.

Bross, D., & Mathews, B. (2013). The battered-child syndrome: Changes in the law and child advocacy. In R. Krugman & J. Korbin (Eds.), *C. Henry Kempe: A 50-year legacy to the field of child abuse and neglect. Child maltreatment (Contemporary Issues in Research and Policy)* (Vol. 1, pp. 39–50). Springer.

Browne, R. (2020, May 9). Children in Ontario group homes and foster care test positive for coronavirus. *Global News*. https://globalnews.ca/news/6924993/coronavirus-ont-group-home-foster-care/

Callahan, M., & Swift, K. (2007). Great expectations and unintended consequences: Risk assessment in child welfare in British Columbia (pp. 158–183). In L. Foster & B. Wharf (Eds.), *People, politics and child welfare in British Columbia*. UBC Press.

Campaign 2000 (2020). *Setting the stage for a poverty-free Canada: Report card on child and family poverty in Canada 2019*. https://campaign2000.ca/wp-content/uploads/2020/01/campaign-2000-report-setting-the-stage-for-a-poverty-free-canada-january-14-2020.pdf

Canada. (2014). *Budget 2014 — The road to balance: Creating jobs and opportunities*. https://www.canada.ca/en/revenue-agency/programs/about-canada-revenue-agency-cra/federal-government-budgets/budget-2014-road-balance-creating-jobs-opportunities/family-tax-cut.html

Canada. (2019). Bill C-92: An act respecting First Nations, Inuit and Métis children, youth and families. https://www.canada.ca/en/indigenous-services-canada/news/2019/06/an-act-respecting-first-nations-inuit-and-Métis-children-youth-and-families-receives-royal-assent.html

Children First Canada. (2020). *Raising Canada 2020: Top 10 threats to childhood in Canada and the impact of COVID–19*. Children First Canada. https://static1.squarespace.com/static/5669d2da9cadb69fb2f8d32e/t/5f51503d5ceab254db134729/1599164484483/Raising+Canada+Report_Final_Sept.pdf

Choate, P. W., & Engstrom, S. (2014). The "good enough" parent: Implications for child protection. *Child Care in Practice, 20*(4), 368–382.

Coles, E., Cheyne, H., Rankin, J., & Daniel, B. (2016). Getting it right for every child: A national policy framework to promote children's well-being in Scotland, United Kingdom. *The Milbank Quarterly, 94*(2), 334–365.

Collier, L. (2018). Young victims of the opioid crisis. *Monitor on Psychology, 49*(1). https://www.apa.org/monitor/2018/01/opioid-crisis

Commission to Promote Sustainable Child Welfare. (2012). *Realizing a sustainable child welfare system in Ontario: Final report*. Minister for Children and Youth Services.

De Cao, E., & Sandner, M. (2020, May 12). The potential impact of the COVID–19 on child abuse and neglect: The role of childcare and unemployment. *Vox*. https://voxeu.org/article/potential-impact-covid-19-child-abuse-and-neglect

Edwards, K. (2018, January 16). Terrible consequences. Jane Philpott on Indigenous children in foster care. *Macleans*. https://www.macleans.ca/politics/terrible-consequences-jane-philpott-on-indigenous-children-in-foster-care

Feder, K., Letourneau, E. J., & Brook, J. (2019). Children in the opioid epidemic: Addressing the next generation's public health crisis. *Pediatrics, 143*(1). https://doi.org/10.1542/peds.2018-1656

Fluke, J., Chabot, M., Fallon, B., MacLaurin, B., & Blackstock, C. (2010). Placement decisions and disparities among Aboriginal groups: An application of the decision making ecology through multi-level analysis. *Child Abuse & Neglect, 34*, 57–69.

Freud, A., Goldstein, J., & Solnit, A. J. (1979). *Before the best interests of the child*. The Free Press.

Frioux, S., Wood, J. N., Fakeye, O., Luan, X., Localio, R., & Rubin, D. M. (2014). Longitudinal association of county-level economic indicators and child maltreatment incidents. *Maternal and Child Health Journal, 18*(9), 2202–2208. https://doi.org/10.1007/s10995-014-1469-0

Gough, P. (2006). *Kinship care*. Centre of Excellence for Child Welfare. https://cwrp.ca/sites/default/files/publications/en/KinshipCare42E.pdf

Gove, T. (1995). *Report of the Gove Inquiry into child protection in British Columbia — Volume one: Matthew's story*. British Columbia Ministry of Communication and Social Services.

Government of British Columbia, Government of Alberta, Government of Manitoba, Government of Saskatchewan, Government of New Brunswick, Government of Newfoundland and Labrador, Government of Nova Scotia, Government of Prince Edward Island, Government of Northwest Territories, Government of Nunavut, Government of Yukon, & Government of Ontario. (2016). *Provincial/Territorial Protocol on Children, Youth and Families Moving between Provinces and Territories*. https://cwrp.ca/sites/default/files/publications/en/pt_protocol_-_children_-_families.pdf

Guedes, M. A., & Mikton, C. (2013). Examining the intersections between child maltreatment and intimate partner violence. *Western Journal of Emergency Medicine, 14*(4), 377–379.

Gupta, A. (2017). Poverty and child neglect — The elephant in the room? *Families, Relationships and Societies, 6*(1), 21–36

Gypen, L., Vanderfaeillie, J., De Maeyer, S., Belenger, L., & Van Holen, F. (2017). Outcomes of children who grew up in foster care: Systematic review. *Children and Youth Services Review, 76*, 74–83.

Hadland, S., Wood, E., Dong, H., Marshall, B., Kerr, T., Montaner, J., & DeBeck, K. (2015). Suicide attempts an dchilhood maltreatment among street youth: A prospective cohort study. *Pediatrics, 136*(3), 440–449.

Houston, S., & Griffiths, H. (2000). Reflections on risk in child protection: Is it time for a shift in paradigms? *Child and Family Social Work, 5*, 1-10. DOI: 10.1046/j.1365-2206.2000.00145.x.

Hughes, R., & Rycus, J. (2006). Issues in risk assessment in child protective services. *Journal of Public Child Welfare, 1*(1), 85–116.

Humphreys, C., & Stanley, N. (Eds.). (2006). *Domestic violence and child protection: Directions for good practice*. Jessica Kingsley Publishers.

Hyslop, I. (2017). Child protection in New Zealand: A history of the future. *British Journal of Social Work, 47*(6), 1800–1817. https://doi.org/10.1093/bjsw/bcx088

Jones, A., Sinha, V., & Trocmé, N. (2015). *Children and youth in out-of-home care in the Canadian provinces. CWRP information sheet #167E*. Centre for Research on Children and Families, McGill University.

Jones, C., Henderson, G., & Woods, R. (2019). Relative strangers: Sibling estrangements experienced by children in out-of-home care and moving towards permanence. *Children and Youth Services Review, 103*, 226–235. https://doi.org/10.1016/j.childyouth.2019.05.038

Jonson-Reid, M., Drake, B., & Zhou, P. (2013). Neglect subtypes, race, and poverty: Individual, family, and service characteristics. *Child Maltreatment, 18*, 30–41.

Kendall, P., & Turpel-Lafond, M. (2007). *Joint special report: Health and well-being of children in care in British Columbia: Educational experience and outcomes*. Representative for Children and Youth

King, B., Fallon, B., Boyd, R., Black, T., Antwi-Boasiako, K., & O'Connor, C. (2017). Factors associated with racial differences in child welfare investigative decision-making in Ontario, Canada. *Child Abuse & Neglect, 73*, 89–105. https://www.ncbi.nlm.nih.gov/pubmed/28950215

King, H., & Pasternak, S. (2018). *Canada's emerging Indigenous rights framework: A critical analysis (A special report)* Yellowhead Institute.

Kovarikova, J. (2017). *Exploring youth outcomes after aging-out of care*. Office of the Provincial Advocate for Children and Youth.

Lee, B., Fuller-Thomson, E., Fallon, B., Trocmé, N., & Black, T. (2017). Asian-Canadian children and families involved in the child welfare system in Canada: A mixed methods study. *Child Abuse & Neglect, 70*, 342–355. https://doi.org/10.1016/j.chiabu.2017.06.022

Lindo, J., Schaller, J., & Hansen, B. (2018). Caution! Men not at work: Gender-specific labor market conditions and child maltreatment. *Journal of Public Economics, 163*, 77–98.

Luther, I. (2015). On the "poverty of responsibility" A study of the history of child protection law and jurisprudence in Nova Scotia. (PhD dissertation, Dalhousie University). https://dalspace.library.dal.ca/bitstream/handle/10222/61015/Luther-Ilana-PhD-Law-August-2015.pdf?sequence=1)

Malakieh, J. (2019, May 9). Adult and youth correctional statistics in Canada, 2017/18. *The Daily*. Ottawa, ON: Statistics

Canada. https://www150.statcan.gc.ca/n1/pub/85-002-x/2019001/article/00010-eng.htm

Martin, M., Dykxhoorn, J., Afifi, T. O., & Colman, I. (2016). Child abuse and the prevalence of suicide attempts among those reporting suicide ideation. *Social Psychiatry and Psychiatric Epidemiology, 51*(11), 1477–1484.

Mosher, J., & Hewitt, J. (2018). Reimagining child welfare systems in Canada (Part I). *Journal of Law and Social Policy, 28*, 1–9. https://digitalcommons.osgoode.yorku.ca/jlsp/vol28/iss1/1

Mulcahy, M., & Trocmé, N. (2010). *Children and youth in out-of-home care in Canada: CECW information sheet #78E*. McGill University, Centre for Research on Children and Families.

National Collaborating Centre for Aboriginal Health. (2017). Indigenous children and the child welfare system in Canada. *Child, Youth and Family Health*. https://www.ccnsa-nccah.ca/docs/health/FS-ChildWelfareCanada-EN.pdf

Ontario Association of Children's Aid Societies. (n.d.). *Permanency*. http://www.oacas.org/data-results/permanency/

Ontario Association of Children's Aid Societies. (2018a). *2018–2019 OACAS operational plan*. http://www.oacas.org/wp-content/uploads/2018/07/Plan-OACAS-Operational-Plan-2018-2019-FINAL.pdf

Ontario Association of Children's Aid Societies. (2018b). *Strategic Pplan*. https://www.oacas.org/who-we-are/strategic-plan/

Ontario Human Rights Commission. (2017). *Under suspicion: Research and consultation report on racial profiling in Ontario*. http://www.ohrc.on.ca/en/under-suspicion-research-and-consultation-report-racial-profiling-ontario

Ontario Ministry of Children, Community and Social Services (2019). http://www.children.gov.on.ca/htdocs/English/professionals/childwelfare/societies/index.aspx

Ontario Ministry of Children, Community and Social Services. (2018). *Policy directive: CW 003-18 — Protection services for 16–17 year olds*. http://www.children.gov.on.ca/htdocs/English/professionals/childwelfare/CYFSA/policy_directive_CW003-18.aspx

Ontario Ministry of Children, Community and Social Services. (n.d.). *Your voice matters*. http://www.children.gov.on.ca/htdocs/English/professionals/childwelfare/modern-legislation.aspx

Paré, M. (2017). Children's rights are human rights and why Canadian implementation lags behind. *Canadian Journal of Children's Rights, 4*(1). https://ojs.library.carleton.ca/index.php/cjcr/article/view/1163/1130

Public Health Agency of Canada. (2010). *Canadian Incidence Study of Reported Child Abuse and Neglect – 2008: Major findings*. http://cwrp.ca/sites/default/files/publications/en/CIS-2008-rprt-eng.pdf

Public Health Agency of Canada. (2018). *Provincial and territorial child protection legislation and policy 2018: Protecting and empowering Canadians to improve their health*. https://www.canada.ca/en/public-health/services/publications/health-risks-safety/provincial-territorial-child-protection-legislation-policy-2018.html

Public Health Agency of Canada. (2019). *Opioid-related harms in Canada*. https://health-infobase.canada.ca/datalab/national-surveillance-opioid-mortality.html

Representative for Children and Youth. (2017). *Room for improvement: Toward better education outcomes for children in care*. https://www.rcybc.ca/sites/default/files/documents/pdf/reports_publications/rcy-education-support-final.pdf

Resolutions Consultancy. (2012). *Signs of safety workbook and signs of safety comprehensive briefing paper*. Resolutions Consultancy Pty Ltd.

Schumaker, K. (2012). *An exploration of the relationship between poverty and child neglect in Canadian child welfare* (PhD dissertation, University of Toronto).

Signs of Safety. (2019). *What is the Signs of Safety?* http://www.aascf.com/pdf/What_is_the_Signs_of_Safety.pdf

Sinha, V., Trocmé, N., Fallon, B., & MacLaurin, B. (2013). Understanding the investigation-stage overrepresentation of First Nations children in the child welfare system: An analysis of the First Nations component of the Canadian Incidence Study of Reported Child Abuse and Neglect 2008. *Child Abuse & Neglect, 37*(10), 821–831.

Sistovaris, M., Fallon, B., Miller, S., Birken, C., Denburg, A., Jenkins, J., Levine, J., Mishna, F., Sokolowski, M., & Stewart, S. (2020). *Child welfare and pandemics: Literature scan*. Policy Bench, Fraser Mustard Institute of Human Development, University of Toronto.

Spratt, T., Nett, J., Bromfield, L., Hietamäki, J., Kindler, H., & Ponnert, L. (2015). Child protection in Europe: Development of an international cross-comparison model to inform national policies and practices. *British Journal of Social Work, 45*(5), 1508–1525.

Statistics Canada (2007). *The south Asian community in Canada*. https://www150.statcan.gc.ca/n1/pub/89-621-x/89-621-x2007006-eng.htm

Statistics Canada (2011). *Ethnic diversity and immigration*. https://www150.statcan.gc.ca/n1/pub/11-402-x/2011000/chap/imm/imm-eng.htm

Statistics Canada. (2019). *Diversity of the Black population in Canada*. https://www150.statcan.gc.ca/n1/pub/89-657-x/89-657-x2019002-eng.htm

Taylor, G. (2016). *A focus on family violence in Canada : The chief public health officer's report on the state of public health in Canada*. Public Health Agency of Canada.

Taylor, J., Baldwin, N., & Spencer, N. (2008). Predicting child abuse and neglect: Ethical theoretical and methodological challenges. *Journal of Clnical Nursing, 17*(9), 1193–1200. https://doi.org/10.1111/j.1365-2702.2007.02192.x

Taylor, J., Lauder, W., Moy, M., & Corlett, J. (2009). Practitioner assessment of "good enough" parenting: Factorial survey. *Journal of Clinical Nursing, 18*(8), 1180–1189. https://doi.org/10.1111/j.1365-2702.2008.02661.x

Trocmé, N., Fallon, B., Sinha, V., Van Wert, M., Kozlowski, A., & MacLaurin, B. (2013). Differentiating between child protection and family support in the Canadian child welfare system's response to intimate partner violence, corporal punishment, and child neglect. *International Journal of Psychology, 48*(2), 128–140.

Truth and Reconciliation Commission of Canada. (2015). *Final Report of the Truth and Reconciliation Commission of Canada: Summary: Honouring the truth, reconciling for the future*. http://caid.ca/TRCFinExeSum2015.pdf

Turner, T. (2016). *One vision one voice: Changing the Ontario child welfare system to better serve African Canadians. Practice framework part 1: Research report*. Ontario Association of Children's Aid Societies.

United Nations. (1990). *Convention on the rights of the child*. https://www.ohchr.org/en/professionalinterest/pages/crc.aspx

Until the Last Child. (2014). *The history of child welfare in Canada*. https://untilthelastchild.com/the-history-of-child-welfare-in-canada/

van Miert, C. (2015). Dealing to child neglect. *Nursing New Zealand, 21*, 32–33.

Waite, D., Greiner, M., & Laris, Z. (2018). Putting families first: How the opioid epidemic is affecting children and families, and the child welfare policy options to address it. *Journal of Applied Research on Children: Informing Policy for Children at Risk, 9*(1). https://digitalcommons.library.tmc.edu/childrenatrisk/vol9/iss1/4

Winkworth, G., & Mcarthur, M. (2006). Being "child centred" in child protection. What does it mean? *Children Australia, 31*(4), 13–21

World Health Organization. (2016). *Child maltreatment*. https://www.who.int/news-room/fact-sheets/detail/child-maltreatment

Chapter 7

Abacus Data. (2019). Abacus national public opinion poll. https://abacusdata.ca/tag/polling/

Arsenault-Lapierre, G., Kim, C. & Turecki, G. (2004). Psychiatric diagnoses in 3275 suicides: A meta-analysis. *BMC Psychiatry* 4(37). https://doi.org/10.1186/1471-244X-4-37

Bartram, M. (2017). Making the most of the federal investment of $5 billion for mental health. *Canadian Medical Association Journal,189*(44), E1360–E1363. doi: 10.1503/cmaj.170738

Bartram, M. (2019). Toward a shared vision for mental health and addiction recovery and well-being: An integrated two-continuum model. *Journal of Recovery in Mental Health, 2*(2–3), 55–72. https://jps.library.utoronto.ca/index.php/rmh/article/view/32749

Bartram, M. (2020). Mental health, substance use and COVID19: Getting ahead of a perfect storm. *Behind the Numbers*. Canadian Centre for Policy Alternatives.

Bartram, M., & Lurie, S. (2017). Closing the mental health gap: The long and winding road? *Canadian Journal of Community Mental Health*, 36, 1–14.

Bartram M. (2019). Expanding access to psychotherapy in Canada: Building on achievements in Australia and the United Kingdom. *Healthcare Management Forum, 32*(2), 63–67. doi:10.1177/0840470418818581

Bell Canada (2016). *Bell Let's Talk Day 2016 is January 27: Join the growing global conversation and support Canada's mental health!* https://letstalk.bell.ca/en/news/92/its-bell-lets-talk-day-lets-talk-text-tweet-and-share-about-mental-health

Bowleg, L. (2012). The problem with the phrase women and minorities: Intersectionality—an important theoretical framework for public health. *American Journal of Public Health 102*(7), 1267–1273. https://doi.org/10.2105/AJPH.2012.300750

Canada, House of Commons, 1957. 22nd Parliament, 5th Session. *Hansard*. Available at https://parl.canadiana.ca/browse/eng/c/debates/22-5

Canadian Centre on Substance Use and Addiction. (2017a). *Moving toward a recovery-oriented system of care: A resource for service providers and decision makers*. https://www.ccsa.ca/sites/default/files/2019-04/CCSA-Recovery-Oriented-System-of-Care-Resource-2017-en.pdf

Canadian Centre on Substance Use and Addiction (2017b). *Life in recovery from addiction in Canada: Communications toolkit*. https://www.ccsa.ca/life-recovery-addiction-canada-communications-toolkit

Canadian Centre on Substance Use and Addiction (2017c). *Life in recovery from addiction in Canada: Technical report*. https://www.ccsa.ca/sites/default/files/2019-04/CCSA-Life-in-Recovery-from-Addiction-Report-2017-en.pdf

Canadian Institute for Health Information (2019). *Common challenges, shared priorities: Measuring access to home and community care and to mental health and addictions services in Canada*. https://www.cihi.ca/sites/default/files/document/shp-companion-report-en.pdf

Canadian Institute for Substance Use Research (2018). *Canadian substance use costs and harms 2007–2014*. https://www.ccsa.ca/sites/default/files/2019-04/CSUCH-Canadian-Substance-Use-Costs-Harms-Report-2018-en.pdf

Canadian Mental Health Association. (1964). *More for the mind*. Toronto: Author.

Canadian Mental Health Association (2018). *Mental health in the balance: Ending the health care disparity in Canada*. https://cmha.ca/wp-content/uploads/2018/09/CMHA-Parity-Paper-Full-Report-EN.pdf

Chandler, M. J., & Lalonde, C. (1998). Cultural continuity as a hedge against suicide in Canada's First Nations. *Transcultural Psychiatry, 35*(2), 191–219. https://doi.org/10.1177/136346159803500202

Chiu, M., Amartey, A., Wang, X., & Kurdyak, P. (2018). Ethnic differences in mental health status and service utilization: A population-based study in Ontario, Canada. *The Canadian Journal of Psychiatry, 63*(7), 481–491. doi: 10.1177/0706743717741061. Epub 2018 Mar 7. PMID: 29514512; PMCID: PMC6099776.

Chiu, M., Lebenbaum, M., Newman, A. M., Zaheer, J., and Kurdyak, P. (2018). Ethnic differences in mental illness severity: A population-based study of Chinese and South Asian patients in Ontario, Canada. *Journal of Clinical Psychiatry, 77*(9), e1108–e1116.

Francis, D. (1977). The development of the lunatic asylum in the Maritime provinces. *Acadiensis, 6*(2). https://journals.lib.unb.ca/index.php/Acadiensis/article/view/11437/12187

Frank, R. G. (2018). Reflections on the Mental Health Parity and Addiction Equity Act after 10 years. *The Milbank Quarterly, 96*(4), 615–618.

Gilmour, H. (2014). Positive mental health and mental illness. *Health Reports, 25*(9), 82-003-x. Ottawa, ON: Statistics Canada.

Government of Canada. (2019a). *Supervised consumption sites: Status of applications*. https://www.canada.ca/en/health-canada/services/substance-use/supervised-consumption-sites/status-application.html

Government of Canada. (2019b). *About reaching home: Canada's homelessness strategy*. https://www.canada.ca/en/employment-social-development/programs/homelessness.html

Health and Welfare Canada. (1986). *Achieving health for all: A framework for health promotion*. http://www.hc-sc.gc.ca/hcs-sss/pubs/system-regime/1986-frame-plan-promotion/index-eng.php

Health Canada. (2004). *A 10-year plan to strengthen health care* [First Ministers meeting 2003]. www.scics.gc.ca/CMFiles/800042005_e1JXB-342011-6611.pdf

Health Canada (2016). *Pillars of the Canadian drugs and substances strategy: A comprehensive, collaborative, compassionate and evidence-based approach to drug policy*. https://www.canada.ca/en/health-canada/services/publications/healthy-living/pillars-canadian-drugs-substances-strategy.html

Health Canada. (2018). *Background document: Public consultation on strengthening Canada's approach to substance use issues*. http://publications.gc.ca/collections/collection_2018/sc-hc/H14-266-2018-eng.pdf

Institute for Health Metrics and Evaluation. (2018). *Findings from the Global Burden of Disease Study 2017*. http://www.healthdata.org/policy-report/findings-global-burden-disease-study-2017

Inuit Tapiriit Kanatami. (2016). *National Inuit Suicide Prevention Strategy*. https://www.itk.ca/wp-content/uploads/2016/07/ITK-National-Inuit-Suicide-Prevention-Strategy-2016.pdf

Jesseman, R., & Payer, D. (2018). *Decriminalization: Options and evidence*. https://www.ccsa.ca/sites/default/files/2019-04/CCSA-Decriminalization-Controlled-Substances-Policy-Brief-2018-en.pdf

Keyes, C. L. M. (2007). Promoting and protecting mental health as flourishing: A complementary strategy for improving national mental health. *American Psychologist, 62*(2), 95–108. http://www.midus.wisc.edu/findings/pdfs/380.pdf

Khan, S. (2017). Concurrent mental and substance use disorders in Canada. *Health Reports: Concurrent Mental and Substance Use Disorders in Canada*. https://www150.statcan.gc.ca/n1/pub/82-003-x/2017008/article/54853-eng.htm

Lim, K-L, Jacobs, P., & Dewa, C. (2008). *How much should we spend on mental health?* https://www.ihe.ca/advanced-search/how-much-should-we-spend-on-mental-health-

McQuaid, R. J., Malik, A., Moussouni, K., Baydack, N., Stargardter, M., & Morrisey, M. (2017). *Life in recovery from addiction in Canada*. https://www.tandfonline.com/doi/abs/10.1080/07347324.2018.1502642?journalCode=watq20

Mental Health Commission of Canada. (2011). *Mental health first aid Canada* (2nd ed.). www.mentalhealthfirstaid.ca.

Mental Health Commission of Canada. (2012). *Changing directions, changing lives: The mental health strategy for Canada*. https://www.mentalhealthcommission.ca/sites/default/files/MHStrategy_Strategy_ENG.pdf

Mental Health Commission of Canada. (2013). *Making the case for investing in mental health in Canada*. https://www.mentalhealthcommission.ca/sites/default/files/2017-03/case_for_investment_eng.pdf

Mental Health Commission of Canada. (2015). *Guidelines for recovery-oriented practice: Hope. Dignity. Inclusion*. https://www.mentalhealthcommission.ca/sites/default/files/MHCC_RecoveryGuidelines_ENG_0.pdf

Mental Health Commission of Canada. (2017). *Strengthening the case for investing in Canada's mental health system: Economic considerations*. https://www.mentalhealthcommission.ca/sites/default/files/2016-06/Investing_in_Mental_Health_FINAL_Version_ENG.pdf

Mental Health Foundation. (2019). *Parity of esteem.* https://www.mentalhealth.org.uk/a-to-z/p/parity-esteem

Mitchell, A. J., Hardy, S., & Shiers, D. (2017). Parity of esteem: Addressing the inequalities between mental and physical healthcare. *BJPsych Advances, 23*(3), 196–205.

Mulvale, G., & Bartram, M. (2015). No more "us" and "them": Integrating recovery and well-being into a conceptual model for mental health policy. *Canadian Journal of Community Mental Health, 34*(4), 31-67.

National Aboriginal Health Organization. (2008). *Cultural competency and safety: A guide for health care administrators, providers and educators.* http://www.multiculturalmentalhealth.ca/wp-content/uploads/2013/10/culturalCompetency1.pdf

National Native Addiction Partnership Foundation. (2011). *Honouring our strengths: A renewed framework to address substance use issues among First Nations People in Canada.* (In association with the Assembly of First Nations and Health Canada).

Organisation for Economic Co-operation and Development (OECD). (2012). *Sick on the job? Myths and realities about mental health and work.* https://doi.org/10.1787/9789264124523-en

Organisation for Economic Co-operation and Development (OECD). (2014). Making mental health count. *Focus on Health.* www.oecd.org/els/ health-systems/Focus-on-Health-Making-Mental-Health-Count.pdf

Public Health Agency of Canada. (2015). *Chronic diseases: Mental illness.* https://www.canada.ca/en/public-health/services/chronic-diseases/mental-illness.html

Public Health Agency of Canada. (2019). *National report: Apparent opioid-related deaths in Canada* (January 2016 to March 2019). Special Advisory Committee on the Epidemic of Opioid Overdoses. https://health-infobase.canada.ca/datalab/national-surveillance-opioid-mortality.html

Rush, B. R. & Ogborne, A .C. (1992). Alcoholism treatment in Canada: History, current status and emerging trends. In Klingemann, H., Takala, J. P. & Hunt, G. (eds.), *Cure, Care or Control: Alcoholism Treatment in Sixteen Countries*, pp. 253-267. New York: State University of New York Press.

Schibli, K. (2019). *Mental health parity in Canada: Legislation and complementary measures. 2019 Position Statement.* https://www.casw-acts.ca/sites/default/files/attachements/Mental_Health_Parity_-_Final_Paper.pdf

Spadorcia, L. (2020, October 7). Fix the mental health system as part of an inclusive recovery. *Policy Options.*

Statistics Canada. (2013). *Canadian community health survey: Mental health, 2012*.

Statistics Canada. (2017). *Canadian survey on disability, 2017.*

Statistics Canada. (2018). *Canadian tobacco, alcohol and drugs survey, 2017.* https://www150.statcan.gc.ca/n1/en/daily-quotidien/181030/dq181030b-eng.pdf

Stergiopoulos, V., O'Campo, P., Hwang, S., Gozdzik, A., Jeyaratnam, J., Misir, V., Nisenbaum, R., Zerger, S., & Kirst, M. (2014). *At Home/Chez Soi Project: Toronto site final report.* http://www.mentalhealthcommission.ca

Stuart, H., Patten, S. B., Koller, M., Modgill, G., & Liinamaa, T. (2014). Stigma in Canada: Results from a rapid response survey. *Canadian Journal of Psychiatry*, 59(October), Supplement 1.

Supreme Court of Canada. (2011). *Canada (Attorney General) v. PHS Community Services Society.* In Canada SCo, editor. [2011] 3 SCR 134, vol. 33556. Ottawa: Canada.

Sutherland, G., & Stonebridge, C. (2016). *Healthy brains at work: Estimating the impact of workplace mental health benefits and programs.* https://www.conferenceboard.ca/e-library/abstract.aspx?did=8242&AspxAutoDetectCookieSupport=1

World Health Organization (2008). *Closing the gap in a generation: Health equity through action on the social determinants of health.* https://www.who.int/social_determinants/final_report/csdh_finalreport_2008.pdf

Chapter 8

Blackstock, C. (2010, June 15). First Nations children. *Canadian Medical Association Journal, 182*(9), 941. https://doi.org/10.1503/cmaj.110-2029

Blackstock, C. (2014). *Reconciliation means not having to say sorry a second time: Conversation with Cindy Blackstock, First Nations Child and Family Caring Society.* Amnesty International Canada. https://www.amnesty.ca/blog/reconciliation-means-not-having-to-say-sorry-a-second-time-conversation-with-cindy-blackstock-f

Bui, V. (2020). *Fighting COVID–19 starts with universal access to water and sanitation.* The Council of Canadians. https://canadians.org/analysis/fighting-covid-19-starts-universal-access-water-and-sanitation

Canadian Human Rights Tribunal. (2016). *Canadian Human Rights Tribunal on First Nations Child Welfare.* https://cwrp.ca/canadian-human-rights-tribunal-first-nations-child-welfare

Castelo, M. (2020, April 9). Continuing remote learning for students without internet. *EdTech.* https://edtechmagazine.com/k12/article/2020/04/continuing-remote-learning-students-without- internet

Coburn, V. (2018). *Splitting INAC: Coercive fiscal federalism in the disguise of "reconciliation."* Yellowhead Institute.

DeBruin, D., Liaschenko, J., & Marshall, M. F. (2012). Social justice in pandemic preparedness. *American Journal of Public Health, 102*(4), 586-591.

Government of Canada. (1969). Statement of the Government of Canada on Indian policy (The White Paper, 1969). Presented to the First Session of the Twenty-eighth Parliament by the Honourable Jean Chrétien, Minister of Indian Affairs and Northern Development. https://www.aadnc-aandc.gc.ca/eng/1100100010189/1100100010191#chp1

Government of Canada. (1983). *Penner report.* House of Commons. http://caid.ca/PennerRep1983.pdf

Government of Canada. (1985). *Indian Act* (R.S.C., 1985, c. I-5). https://laws-lois.justice.gc.ca/eng/acts/i-5/

Government of Canada. (1996). *Report of the Royal Commission on Aboriginal Peoples.* Royal Commission on Aboriginal Peoples.

Government of Canada. (2006). *Indian Residential Schools Settlement Agreement (IRSSA).* Indigenous and Northern Affairs Canada. http://www.residentialschoolsettlement.ca/settlement.html

Government of Canada. (2017). *Principles respecting the Government of Canada's relationship with Indigenous peoples.* Minister of Justice. https://www.justice.gc.ca/eng/csj-sjc/principles.pdf

Government of Canada. (2018). *Recognition and implementation of Indigenous Rights Framework (RIIRF).* Crown–Indigenous Relations and Northern Affairs Canada. https://www.rcaanc-cirnac.gc.ca/eng/1536350959665/1539959903708

Government of Manitoba. (1983). *No quiet place: Review committee on Indian and Métis adoptions and placements: Interim report.* Manitoba: Ministry of Community Services and Corrections and Ministry of Community Services and Corrections. https://digitalcollection.gov.mb.ca/awweb/pdfopener?smd=1&did=24788&md=1

Indian Chiefs of Alberta. (1970). *Citizens plus.* http://caid.ca/RedPaper1970.pdf

Joannou, A. (2020, March 30). "We have overcrowding": Alberta chief wants housing to deal with COVID-19. *Edmonton Journal.*

Krishna, P. (2020). How Native Americans are fighting a food crisis. *New York Times.* https://www.nytimes.com/2020/04/13/dining/native-americans-coronavirus.html

Lafontaine, A. (2018, March 19). Close the gap between Indigenous health outcomes and the rest of Canada. *CBC News.* https://www.cbc.ca/news/indigenous/opinion-indigenous-health-alika-lafontaine-1.4547798

Metallic, N., Friedland, H., & Morales, S. (2019a, July 4). *The promise and pitfalls of C-92: An act respecting First Nations, Inuit, and Métis children, youth and families.* Special Report (July 4). Yellowhead Institute.

Metallic, N., Friedland, H., Morales, S., Hewitt, J., & Craft, A. (2019b). *An act respecting First Nations, Inuit, and Métis children, youth and families: Does bill C-92 make the grade?* Special Report (March 21). Toronto, ON: Yellowhead Institute.

Nassif-Pires, L., De Lima Xavier, L., Masterson, T., Nikiforos, M., & Rios-Avila, F. (2020). *Public policy brief: Pandemic of inequality.* Annandale-on-Hudson, NY: Levy Economics Institute of Bard College.

National Inquiry into Missing and Murdered Indigenous Women and Girls. (2019). *Reclaiming power and place: The final report of the National Inquiry into Missing and Murdered Indigenous Women and Girls.* https://www.mmiwg-ffada.ca

Ngabo, G. (2020, March 31). Indigenous northern communities are short on hand sanitizer. Small breweries are answering the call. *The Star.* https://www.thestar.com/news/canada/2020/03/31/indigenous-northern- communities-are-short-on-hand-sanitizer-small-breweries-are-answering-the-call.html

Noonoo, S. (2020, March 20). Here's what schools can do for the millions of students without internet access. *EdSurge.* https://www.edsurge.com/news/2020-03-20-here-s-what-schools-can-do-for-the-millions-of- students-without-internet-access

PAHO. (2020). *Considerations on Indigenous Peoples, Afro-descendants, and other ethnic groups during the COVID–19 pandemic.* https://www.paho.org/en/documents/considerations-indigenous-peoples-afro-descendants-and-other-ethnic-groups-during-covid

Preston, T. J. (2014). *Inquest report in the matter of The Fatality Inquiries Act and in the matter of Brian Lloyd Sinclair, deceased.* The Provincial Court of Manitoba.

Saint-Girons, M., Joh-Carnella, N., Lefebvre, R., Blackstock, C., & Fallon, B. (2020). *Equity concerns in the context of COVID–19 — A focus on First Nations, Inuit, and Métis communities in Canada.* Toronto, ON: Canadian Child Welfare Research Portal.

Shield, D., & Martell, C. (2020, May 12). RCMP "had no understanding" of sun dance ceremony that was interrupted, dancer says. *CBC News.* https://www.cbc.ca/news/canada/saskatoon/beardys-okemasis-sun-dance- 1.5566551

Sinclair, R. (2016). The Indigenous child removal system in Canada: An examination of legal decision-making and racial bias. *First Peoples Child and Family Review, 11*(2), 8–18.

Stollery, B. (2018, May 3). *Canada's digital divide: Preserving Indigenous communities means bringing them online.* Friends of Canadian Broadcasting. https://friends.ca/explore/article/canadas-digital-divide- preserving-indigenous-communities-means-bringing-them-online/

Truth and Reconciliation Commission of Canada. (2015). *Calls to action.* http://nctr.ca/assets/reports/Calls_to_Action_English2.pdf

United Nations. (2007, September 13). *United Nations declaration on the rights of Indigenous Peoples.* https://www.un.org/development/desa/indigenouspeoples/wp-content/uploads/sites/19/2018/11/UNDRIP_E_web.pdf

Wilson, D., & Macdonald, D. (2010). *The income gap between Aboriginal Peoples and the rest of Canada.* Canadian Centre for Policy Alternatives. https://www.policyalternatives.ca/sites/default/files/uploads/publications/reports/docs/Aboriginal%20Income%20Gap.pdf

Wood, S. (2020, April 14). Adapting to coronavirus: How B.C. First Nations balance food security and conservation. *The Narwhal.* https://thenarwhal.ca/adapting-to-coronavirus-how-b-c-first-nations-balance-food- security-and-conservation/

Chapter 9

Alboim, A., & Cohl, K. (2012). *Shaping the future: Canada's rapidly changing immigration policies.* Maytree.

Ansari, S. (2020, July 7). Pick our fruit, get COVID–19. *Macleans.* https://www.macleans.ca/opinion/coronavirus-exposing-canada-exploitative-immigration-practices/

Arango, J. (2004). Theories of international migration. In J. Daniele (Ed.), *International migration in the new millennium. Global movement and settlement* (pp. 15–35). Ashgate Publishing Company.

Atak, I., Hudson, G., & Nakache, D. (2017). *Making Canada's refugee system faster and fairer: Reviewing the stated goals and unintended consequences of the 2012 refugee reform.* CARFMS Working Paper No. 2017/3, Toronto. http://carfms.org/wp-content/uploads/2017/05/CARFMS-WPS-No11-Idil-Atak.pdf

Aydemir, A., Chen, W., & Corak, M. (2013). Intergenerational education mobility among the children of Canadian immigrants. *Canadian Public Policy / Analyse De Politiques, 39*(Supplement 1), S107–S122. https://doi.org/10.3138/CPP.39.Supplement1.S107

Balakrishnan, A. (2019, August). Challenges continue for legal aid practitioners despite funding boost from Ottawa. *Law Times* (August). https://www.lawtimesnews.com/practice-areas/human-rights/challenges-continue-for-legal-aid-practitioners-despite-funding-boost-from-ottawa/287329

Banerjee, R., Reitz, J. G., & Oreopoulos, P. (2018). Do large employers treat racial minorities more fairly? An analysis of Canadian field experiment data. *Canadian Public Policy, 44*(1), 1.

Bauder, H. (2008). Foreign farm workers in Ontario (Canada): Exclusionary discourse in the newsprint media. *The Journal of Peasant Studies, 35*(1), 100–118.

Beiser, M. (2005). The health of immigrants and refugees in Canada. *Canadian Journal of Public Health, 96*(Supplement 2), S30–S44.

Berry, J. W. (2003). Conceptual approaches to acculturation. In K. Chung, P. Balls-Organista, & G. Marin (Eds.), *Acculturation: Advances in theory, measurement, and applied research* (pp. 17–37). Washington: American Psychological Association Press.

Bhuyan, R., Valmadrid, L., Panlaqui, E. L., Pendon, N. L., & Juan, P. (2018). Responding to the structural violence of migrant domestic work: Insights from participatory action research with migrant caregivers in Canada. *Journal of Family Violence, 33*(8), 613–627. https://doi.org/10.1007/s10896-018-9988-x

Britneff, Beatrice. (2018, October 30). One-quarter of Ottawa's homeless are refugees and immigrants, survey suggests. *Global News.* https://globalnews.ca/news/4611416/one-quarter-of-ottawas-homeless-are-refugees-and-immigrants-survey-suggests/

Canada Border Services Agency. (2019a). *Annual detention statistics 2012–2019.* Ottawa, ON: Government of Canada. https://www.cbsa-asfc.gc.ca/security-securite/detent/stat-2012-2019-eng.html

Canada Border Services Agency. (2019b, September). *Transportation company obligations: Guide for transporters.* https://www.cbsa-asfc.gc.ca/trans/guide-eng.html?wbdisable=true

Canadian Council for Refugees. (2014, February). *Cessation — basic information.* https://ccrweb.ca/en/cessation-basic-information

Canadian Council for Refugees. (2014). *Government overhaul of temporary foreign worker program: CCR response to 2014 changes.* http://ccrweb.ca/en/TFWP-ccr-response-2014-changes

Canadian Council for Refugees. (2015). *Sun Sea: Five years later.* https://ccrweb.ca/sites/ccrweb.ca/files/sun-sea-five-years-later.pdf

Canadian Council for Refugees. (2016). *Excluded family members: Brief on R. 117 (9) (d) (May).* https://ccrweb.ca/sites/ccrweb.ca/files/excluded-family-members-brief-may-2016.pdf

Cheng, S-J. A. (1999). Labor migration and international sexual division of labor: A feminist perspective. In G. A. Kelson, & D. L. DeLaet (Eds.), *Gender and immigration.* New York: New York University Press.

Chow, L. (2000). *Chasing their dreams,* Prince George, BC: Caitlin Press.

Citizenship and Immigration Canada. (2012, November 2). *An immigration system that works for Canada's economy.* http://www.cic.gc.ca/english/department/media/releases/2012/2012-11-02.asp

Corak, M. R. (2011). *Age at immigration and the education outcomes of children.* Ottawa, ON: Statistics Canada. https://www150.

statcan.gc.ca/n1/en/pub/11f0019m/11f0019m2011336-eng.pdf?st=reFPLn5a

Corbett, D. C. (1957). *Canada's immigration policy*. Toronto, ON: University of Toronto Press.

Dam, H., Chan, J., & Wayland, S. (2018). Missed opportunity: International students in Canada face barriers to permanent residence. *Journal of International Migration & Integration, 19*, 891.

Daniel, D. (2005). The debate on family reunification and Canada's Immigration Act of 1976. *The American Review of Canadian Studies* (Winter), 683–703.

Dangzalan, L. J. (2020, November 3). Canada needs a permanent fix for its abuse-prone caregiver programs. *The Globe and Mail*.

Department of Justice (2019, September). *Legal aid program*. https://www.justice.gc.ca/eng/fund-fina/gov-gouv/aid-aide.html

Dirks, G. E. (1977). *Canada's refugee policy: Indifference or opportunism*? Montréal, QC: McGill-Queen's University Press.

Draaisma, M. (2019). Police in Ontario free 43 Mexicans brought to Canada by alleged human traffickers. *CBC News*. https://www.cbc.ca/news/canada/toronto/human-trafficking-bust-barrie-1.5014269

Drolet, J. L., & Teixeira, C. (2019). Fostering immigrant settlement and housing in small cities: Voices of settlement practitioners and service providers in British Columbia, Canada. *The Social Science Journal*. https://doi.org/10.1016/j.soscij.2019.07.010

Employment and Social Development Canada. (2014). *Improving clarity, transparency and accountability of the Temporary Foreign Worker Program*. https://www.canada.ca/en/employment-social-development/services/foreign-workers/reports/overhaul.html

Employment and Social Development Canada. (2020, March). *Temporary Foreign Worker Program 2012–2019*. https://open.canada.ca/data/en/dataset/76defa14-473e-41e2-abfa-60021c4d934b

Frank, A. G. (1967). *Capitalism and underdevelopment in Latin America: Historical studies of Chile and Brazil*. New York: Monthly Review Press.

Government of Canada. (2008). *Budget Implementation Act, 2008* (S.C. 2008, c. 28). Ottawa, ON.: Author. https://laws-lois.justice.gc.ca/eng/AnnualStatutes/2008_28/page-13.html

Government of Canada (2019). *How long will I have to repay my loan?* Otttawa, ON: Author. http://www.cic.gc.ca/english/helpcentre/answer.asp?qnum=1403&top=11

Griffith, A. (2018). What the census tells us about citizenship. *Policy Options*. http://policyoptions.irpp.org/magazines/march-2018/what-the-census-tells-us-about-citizenship/

Guo, S. and Wong, L. (Eds.). (2015). *Revisiting multiculturalism in Canada: Theories, policies and debates* (1st ed.). Rotterdam, The Netherlands and Boston, MA: Sense Publishing. https://doi.org/10.1007/978-94-6300-208-0

Harris, K. (2018, January 7). Liberals relaunch family reunification lottery despite angry backlash around "immigration fiasco." *CBC News*. https://www.cbc.ca/news/politics/immigration-parents-grandparents-sponsorship-1.4442456

Hawkins, F. (1988). *Canada and immigration* (2nd ed.). Kingston, ON: McGill-Queen's University Press;

Hyman, I. (2011). The mental health and well-being of immigrant and refugee women in Canada. In D. L.Spitzer (Ed.), *Engendering migrant health. Canadian perspectives* (pp. 99–117). Toronto, ON: University of Toronto Press.

Immigration, Refugees and Citizenship Canada. (2016). *Evaluation of the resettlement programs (GAR, PSR, BVOR and RAP)*. Evaluation Division (July). https://www.canada.ca/content/dam/ircc/migration/ircc/english/pdf/pub/resettlement.pdf

Immigration, Refugees and Citizenship Canada (2018, December 21). *Medical inadmissibility*. https://www.canada.ca/en/immigration-refugees-citizenship/services/immigrate-canada/inadmissibility/reasons/medical-inadmissibility.html#excessive-demand

Immigration, Refugees and Citizenship Canada. (2019). *How express entry works*. https://www.canada.ca/en/immigration-refugees-citizenship/services/immigrate-canada/express-entry/works.html

Immigration, Refugees and Citizenship Canada. (2019). *Work in Canada temporarily*. http://www.cic.gc.ca/english/work/apply-who.asp

Joly, Y., Salman, S., Ngueng Feze, I., Granados Moreno, P., Stanton-Jean, M., Lacey, J., & Love, R. (2016). DNA testing for family reunification in Canada: Points to consider. *Journal of International Migration & Integration, 1*, 1–14. https://doi.org/10.1007/s12134-016-0496-7

Kelley, N., & Trebilcock, M. (2000). *The making of the mosaic* (2nd ed.). Toronto ON: University of Toronto Press.

Keung, N. (2012, January 29). Exploitive rent demands "a norm" for newcomers. *Toronto Star*. https://www.thestar.com/news/investigations/2012/01/29/exploitive_rent_demands_a_norm_for_newcomers.html

Khan, A. M., Urquia, M., Kornas, K., Henry, D., Cheng, S. Y., Bornbaum, C., & Rosella, L. C. (2017). Socioeconomic gradients in all-cause, premature and avoidable mortality among immigrants and long-term residents using linked death records in Ontario, Canada. *Journal of Epidemiology and Community Health, 71*(7), 625–632. https://doi.org/10.1136/jech-2016-208525

Knowles, V. (2007). *Strangers at our gates: Canadian immigration and immigration policy, 1540–2006* (Revised edition, p. 111). Toronto, ON: Dundurn Press.

Koopowitz, L., & Abhary, S. (2004). Psychiatric aspects of detention: Illustrative case studies. *Australia and New Zealand Journal of Psychiatry, 38*, 495–500.

Kymlicka, W. (1994). *Multicultural citizenship: A liberal theory of minority rights*. Oxford, UK: Oxford University Press.

Levitz, S. (2017, October 2). Loan program blamed for leaving refugees in financial trouble to be reworked. *CTV News*. https://www.ctvnews.ca/canada/loan-program-blamed-for-leaving-refugees-in-financial-trouble-to-be-reworked-1.3615275

Luck, S. (2019, January 22). Abdoul Abdi's case changes N.S. policies on children in care. *CBC News*. https://www.cbc.ca/news/canada/nova-scotia/abdoul-abdi-child-welfare-nova-scotia-policy-change-1.4979208

Macklin, A. (2003). Dancing across borders: "Exotic dancers," trafficking, and Canadian immigration policy. *International Migration Review, 37*(2): 464–499.

Magalhaes, L., Carrasco, C., & Gastaldo, D. (2010). Undocumented migrants in Canada: A scope literature review on health, access to services, and working conditions. *Journal of Immigrant and Minority Health, 12*(1), 132–151. https://doi.org/10.1007/s10903-009-9280-5

Mahtani, M. (2004, March). Interrogating the hyphen-nation: Canadian multicultural policy and "mixed race" identities. *Social Identities 8*(1), 67–90. https://doi.org/10.1080/13504630220132026

Mansouri, F., & Cauchi, S. (2007). A psychological perspective on Australia's asylum policies. *International Migration, 45*(1), 123–150.

Martin, B. (2017). *A stone in the ocean: A mixed methods investigation into the experiences of families trying to reunite in Canada*. 1–376 [PhD dissertation]. Toronto, ON: Ryerson University.

Massey, D. S., Arango, J., Hugo, G., Kouaouci, A., Pellegrino, A., and Taylor, J. E. (1998). Contemporary theories of international migration. In D. S. Massey et al. (Eds.), *Worlds in motion. Understanding international migration* (pp. 17–59). Oxford: Clarendon Press.

Mojtehedzadeh, S. (2019, October 14). Snakes, rats, bedbugs, abuse. Complaints filed by Mexican migrant workers expose underside of Canada's seasonal agriculture program. *The Toronto Star*.

Ng, E., Pottie, K., & Spitzer, D. (2011). Official language proficiency and self-reported health among immigrants to Canada. *Health Reports, 22*(4), A1.

Peutz, N. (2006). Embarking on an anthropology of removal. *Current Anthropology, 47*(2), 217–241

Potocky, M. (2008) Immigrants and refugees. In *Encyclopaedia of social work*. http://www.oxford-naswsocialwork.com/entry?entry=t203.e193

Poynter, B. (2012, November 29). Canada accused of treating Tamil asylum seekers like prisoners. *The Guardian*. https://www.

theguardian.com/world/2012/nov/29/canada-accused-tamil-asylum-prisoners

Ravanera, Z., Esses, V., & Lapshina, N. (2014). The integration of immigrants of differing official language ability and use in Canada: Analysis of the 2006 census and the 2007–2008 *Canadian Community Health Survey*. Ottawa, ON: Citizenship and Immigration Canada.

Redmond, M., & Martin, B. (n.d.). *All in the (definition of) family: How restrictive Canadian immigration law denies the right to family to migrant parents and their children* (unpublished).

Refugee Sponsorship Training Program. (2017). *Start-up costs for all provinces (excluding Québec)*. http://www.rstp.ca/wp-content/uploads/2019/03/Start-up.pdf

Refugee Sponsorship Training Program. (2019a). *Ontario Resettlement Assistance Program (RAP) rates*. http://www.rstp.ca/wp-content/uploads/2019/10/Ontario-new-rates-effective-Nov-012019.pdf

Refugee Sponsorship Training Program. (2019b). *Alberta Resettlement Assistance Program (RAP) rates*. http://www.rstp.ca/wp-content/uploads/2019/10/Alberta-RAP-Rate-New-Rates-effective-Nov-01-2019.pdf

Reitz, J. (2001). Immigrant skill utilization in the Canadian labour market: Implications of human capital research. *Journal of International Migration and Integration, 2*(3), 347–378.

Rousseau, C., Mekki-Berrada, A., & Moreau, S. (2001). Trauma and extended separation from family among Latin American and African refugees in Montréal. *Psychiatry, 64*(1), 40–59.

Sá, C. M., & Sabzalieva, E. (2018). The politics of the great brain race: Public policy and international student recruitment in Australia, Canada, England and the USA. *Higher Education, 75*(2), 231–253. https://doi.org/10.1007/s10734-017-0133-1

Samers, M. (2010). *Migration*. New York, NY: Routledge

Silove, D. (1999). The psychosocial effects of torture, mass human rights violations, and refugee trauma: Toward an integrated conceptual framework. *The Journal of Nervous and Mental Disease, 187*(4), 200–207.

Silove, D., Steel, Z., & Watters, C. (2000). Policies of deterrence and the mental health of asylum seekers. *Journal of the American Medical Association, 284*(5), 604–611.

Spitzer, D. L. (2011). Work, worries and weariness: Towards an embodied and engendered migrant health. In D. L.Spitzer (Ed.). *Engendering migrant health. Canadian perspectives* (pp. 23–39). Toronto, ON: University of Toronto Press.

St. Denis, V. (2011). Silencing Aboriginal curricular content and perspectives through multiculturalism: "There are other children here." *Review of Education, Pedagogy, and Cultural Studies, 33*(4), 306–317. https://doi.org/10.1080/10714413.2011.597638

Stark, O. (1991). *The migration of labor*. Cambridge, MA: B. Blackwell

Stasiulus, D., & Jhappan, R. (1995). The fractious politics of a settler society: Canada. In D. Stasiulus & N. Yuval-Davis (Eds.), *Unsettling settler societies* (pp. 95–131). Thousand Oaks, CA: Sage Publications.

Taylor, C. (1994). The politics of recognition. In A. Gutmann (Ed.), *Multiculturalism: Examining the politics of recognition* (pp. 25–73). Princeton, NJ: Princeton University Press.

Taylor, K. (1991). Racism in Canadian immigration policy, *Canadian Ethnic Studies, 23*(1), 1–20.

Todaro, M. P., & Maruszko, L. (1987). Illegal migration and US immigration reform: A conceptual framework. *Population & Development Review, 13*(1), 101–114.

UFCW Canada and the Agriculture Workers Alliance. (2020). *The status of migrant farm workers in Canada, 2020: Marking three decades of advocacy on behalf of Canada's most exploited workforce*. www.ufcw.ca | www.ufcw.ca/awa.

UNHCR. (2011). *The 1951 convention relating to the status of refugees and its 1967 protocol*. http://www.unhcr.org/4ec262df9.html

UNHCR. (2019). *Global trends: Forced displacement in 2018*. https://www.unhcr.org/globaltrends2018/

United Nations. (2017). *International migration report*. https://www.un.org/en/development/desa/population/migration/publications/migrationreport/docs/MigrationReport2017_Highlights.pdf

Yalnizyan, A. (2018, May 15). Immigration policy should foster new Canadians, not temporary workers. *The Globe and Mail* (originally published July 6, 2015).

Wallerstein, I. (1974). The rise and future demise of the world capitalist system: Concepts for comparative analysis. *Comparative Studies in Society and History, 16*(4), 387–415.

Whitaker, R. (1987). *Double standard: The secret history of Canadian immigration*. Toronto, ON: Lester & Orpen Dennys Ltd.

Chapter 10

Andrew-Gee, E., & Stone, L. (2020, August 10). Understaffing turned seniors' homes into COVID–19 danger zones, health workers say. What can be done to fix that? *The Globe and Mail*. https://www.theglobeandmail.com/canada/article-understaffing-turned-seniors-homes-into-COVID–19-danger-zones-health/

Armstrong, P., Armstrong, H., Choiniere, J,, Lowndes, R., & Struthers, J. (2020). *Re-Imagining long-term residential care in the COVID–19 crisis*. Canadian Centre for Policy Alternatives. https://www.policyalternatives.ca

CARP (2014). *CARP's new vision for caregiver support*. Canadian Association for Retired Persons. https://www.carp.ca/wp-content/uploads/2014/02/Caregiver-Brief-Feb-2014.pdf

Carrick, R. (2018, October 23). Health benefits for retirees are steadily disappearing. *The Globe and Mail* (originally published in 2016).

Conference Board of Canada. (2015). *Benefits benchmarking 2015*. https://www.conferenceboard.ca/e-library/abstract.aspx?did=7364

Drolet, M., & Morissette, R. (2014). *New facts on pension coverage in Canada*. Catalogue no. 75-006-X. Statistics Canada.

Dying with Dignity Canada. (2019). *Get the facts: Bill C-14 and assisted dying law in Canada*. https://www.dyingwithdignity.ca/get_the_facts_assisted_dying_law_in_canada

Estabrooks, C.A., Straus, S., Flood, C. M., Keefe, J., Armstrong, P., Donner, G., Boscart, V., Ducharme, F., Silvius, J.,, & Wolfson, M. (2020). *Restoring trust: COVID–19 and the future of long-term care*. Royal Society of Canada. https://rsc-src.ca/sites/default/files/LTC%20PB%20%2B%20ES_EN.pdf

Government of Canada. (2019). *National Seniors Council work priorities*. National Seniors Council. https://www.canada.ca/en/national-seniors-council/corporate/priorities.html

Hamilton, M. (2015). Do Canadians save too little? *Commentary* (No. 428). C. D. Howe Institute.

Health Canada. (2018). *Third interim report on medical assistance in dying in Canada*. Government of Canada. https://www.canada.ca/en/health-canada/services/publications/health-system-services/medical-assistance-dying-interim-report-june-2018.html

Ivanova, I. (with Shannon Daub, Marcy Cohen and Julie Jenkins). (2017). *Poverty and inequality among British Columbia's seniors*. Canadian Centre for Policy Alternatives.

McKinsey & Company. (2015). *Building on Canada's strong retirement readiness*. McKinsey & Company, Financial Services Practice. www.mckinsey.com/clientservice/financial_services

Mintz, J. (2009). *Summary report on retirement income adequacy research*. Prepared for the Research Working Group on Retirement Income Adequacy of Federal-Provincial-Territorial Ministers of Finance. Department of Finance.

Morneau Shepell. (2018, October). *Human resources trends for 2019. Insights on what HR leaders are expecting in the coming year: Summary report*. https://www.morneaushepell.com/permafiles/91423/hr-trends-2019-summary-report.pdf

National Seniors Strategy. (n.d.a). *NSS evidence briefs: Ageism, elder abuse and social isolation*. http://nationalseniorsstrategy.ca/the-four-pillars/pillar-1/addressing-ageism-elder-abuse-and-social-isolation

National Seniors Strategy. (n.d.b). *NSS evidence briefs: Wellness and prevention activities.* http://nationalseniorsstrategy.ca/the-four-pillars/pillar-2/wellness-and-prevention

National Seniors Strategy. (n.d.c). *NSS evidence briefs: Home, community, long-term care, and end-of-life services.* http://nationalseniorsstrategy.ca/the-four-pillars/pillar-3/access-to-services

Public Health Agency of Canada. (2019). *A dementia strategy for Canada: Together we aspire.* Health Agency of Canada.

Scott, K. (2019, April 4). Submission to the House of Commons Standing Committee on the Status of Women regarding the challenges faced by senior women. Canadian Centre for Policy Alternatives.

Shillington, R. (2015). *An analysis of the economic circumstances of Canadian seniors.* The Broadbent Institute. http://www.broadbentinstitute.ca/an_analysis_of_the_economic_circumstances_of_canadian_seniors.

Sinha, S. K., Griffin, B., Ringer, T., Reppas-Rindlisbacher, C., Stewart, E., Wong, I., Callan, S., & Anderson, G. (2016). *An evidence-informed National Seniors Strategy for Canada* (2nd ed.). Alliance for a National Seniors Strategy.

Statistics Canada. (2017, February 26). Canadian Income Survey, 2017. *The Daily.* https://www150.statcan.gc.ca/n1/daily-quotidien/190226/dq190226b-eng.htm

Statistics Canada. Table 11-10-0135-01 (formerly CANSIM Table 206-0041). Low income statistics by age, sex and economic family type.

Statistics Canada. Table 11-10-0181-01 (formerly CANSIM Table 202-0802). Low income statistics by age, sex and economic family type.

Statistics Canada. Table 14-10-0018-01 (formerly CANSIM 282-0002). Labour force characteristics by sex and detailed age group, annual, inactive (x 1,000).

Stobert, S. & Cranswick, K. (2004). Looking after seniors: Who does what for whom? *Canadian Social Trends.* No. 74. Statistics Canada Catalogue no. 11-008-XIE. p. 2-6.

Turcotte, M. & Schellenberg, G. (2007). *A Portrait of Seniors in Canada: Introduction.* Statistics Canada. Catalogue no. 89-519-X.

Tyler, M. (2015). *Lower risk, higher reward: Renewing Canada's retirement income system.* Mowat Centre.

Wolfson, M. (2011). *Projecting the adequacy of Canadians' retirement income: Current prospects and possible reform options.* IRPP Study, No. 17. Institute for Research on Public Policy.

Wolfson, M. (2015). *What, me worry?* Canadian Centre for Policy Alternatives.

World Health Organization. (2017). *Global strategy and action plan on ageing and health (2016–2020).*

Chapter 11

Bowe, F. (1978). *Handicapping America: Barriers to disable people.* Harper and Row.

Disabled World. (2019). Disability statistics: Information, charts, graphs and tables. Disabled World. https://www.disabled-world.com/disability/statistics

Frieden, L. (1980). Independent living program models. *Rehabilitation Literature.,41,* 169–173.

Government of Canada. (1996). *Equal citizenship for Canadians with disabilities: The will to act (The Scott report).* Federal Task Force on Disability Issues. Human Resources Development Canada.

Government of Canada. (2001). *Immigration and Refugee Protection Act* (S.C. 2001, c. 27). https://laws.justice.gc.ca/eng/acts/i-2.5/

Government of Canada. (2019). *Accessible Canada Act (An Act to ensure a barrier-free Canada) (ACA).* S.C. 2019, c. 10. https://laws-lois.justice.gc.ca/eng/acts/A-0.6/

Hanes, R. (1995, Spring). Persons with disabilities: Social policy research and the need for inclusion. *Canadian Review of Social Policy,* 35.

Hanes, R. (2016). Critical disability theory: Developing a post social model of disability (Chapter 7). In Jeanette Robertson and Grant Larsen (Eds.), *Disability and social change: A progressive Canadian approach.* Fernwood Press.

Hanes, R., & Moscovitch, A. (2002). Disability supports in the social union. In Allan Puttee (Ed.), *Social union and disability policy.* Institute for Intergovernmental Relations.

Hughes, K., Bellis, M. A., Jones, L., Wood, S., Bates, G., & Eckley, L. (2012, April 28). Prevalence and risk of violence against adults with disabilities: A systematic review and meta-analysis of observational studies. *Lancet, 379*(9826), 1621–1629. https://doi.org/10.1016/S0140-6736(11)61851-5

Human Resources and Skills Development Canada. (2013). *Federal disability reference guide.* https://www.canada.ca/content/dam/esdc-edsc/migration/documents/eng/disability/arc/reference_guide.pdf

Human Resources Development Canada. (1998). *In unison: A Canadian approach to disability issues, a vision paper.* (Issued by the Federal/Provincial/Territorial Ministers Responsible for Social Services.) Ottawa, ON: Office for Disability Issues.

Human Resources Development Canada. (1999). *Future directions to address disability issues for the Government of Canada : Working together for full citizenship.* Office for Disability Issues.

Human Resources Development Canada. (2000). *In unison 2000: Persons with disabilities in Canada.* Issued by the Federal/Provincial/Territorial Ministers Responsible for Social Services. Office for Disability Issues.

Human Resources Development Canada. (2006). *A way with words and images: Suggestions for the portrayal of people with disabilities.* https://www.canada.ca/content/dam/esdc-edsc/migration/documents/eng/disability/arc/way_with_words.pdf

Immigration, Refugees and Citizenship Canada. (2018). *Excessive demand: Calculation of the cost threshold.* Cat. No. Ci4-181/2018E-PDF. https://www.canada.ca/content/dam/ircc/migration/ircc/english/pdf/pub/excessive-demand-report-eng.pdf

Joannou, A. (2016, September 23). Federal minister launches consultations on new accessibility rules. *Yukon News.*

McColl, M-A., Jaiswal, A., Jones, S, Roberts, L., & Murphy, C. (2017). *A review of disability policy in Canada* (3rd ed.). Canadian Disability Policy Alliance. http://www.disabilitypolicyalliance.ca/wp-content/uploads/2018/01/A-Review-of-Disability-Policy-in-Canada-3rd-edition-Final-1-1.pdf

Mendelson, M., Battle, K., Torjman, S., & Lightman, E. (2010). *A basic income plan for Canadians with severe disabilities.* The Caledon Institute of Social Policy. https://maytree.com/wp-content/uploads/906ENG.pdf

Moreau, M. (1979). A structural approach to practice. *Canadian Journal of Social Work Education, 5,* 78–94.

Office of the United Nations High Commissioner for Human Rights. (2010). *Monitoring the Convention on the Rights of Persons with Disabilities: Guidance for Human Rights Monitors.* Professional Training Series No. 17.

Oliver, M. (1990). *The politics of disability: A sociological approach.* Macmillan.

Oliver, M. (1996). *Understanding disability: From theory to practice.* St. Martin's Press.

Simmons, J., & Dodd, T. (2003). *Crime in England and Wales 2002/2003.* Home Office Statistical Bulletin.

Splane, R. (1965). Review: The role of public welfare in a century of social welfare development. In Meilicke, C. A. and Storch, J. L. (Eds.). *Perspectives on Canadian health and social services policy: History and emerging trends.* Health Administration Press.

Stapleton, J., Tweddle, A., & Gibson, K. (2013). *What is happening to disability income systems in Canada? Insights and proposals for further research.* Council of Canadians with Disabilities. http://www.ccdonline.ca/en/socialpolicy/poverty-citizenship/income-security-reform/disability-income-systems#sec-foreward

Statistics Canada. (2017). *Canadian survey on disability, 2017.*

Stone, D. (1984). *The disabled state.* Temple University Press.

Thomas, C. (1999). *Female forms: Experiencing and understanding disability.* Open University Press.

Torjman, S. (2014). *Disability policy highlights.* Caledon Institute for Social Policy.

UNESCO. (2009). *Towards inclusive education for children with disabilities: A guideline.* UNESCO (United Nations Educational, Scientific and Cultural Organization).

UNICEF. (2013, May). Children and young people with disabilities fact sheet. United Nations Children's Fund. http://www.unicef.org/disibilities

United Nations. (2006). *UN Convention on the Rights of Persons with Disabilities.* https://www.un.org/development/desa/disabilities/convention-on-the-rights-of-persons-with-disabilities.html

United Nations. (2017). *Situation of women and girls with disabilities and the status of the Convention on the Rights of Persons with Disabilities and the optional protocol thereto.* Report of the Secretary-General.

United Nations. (n.d.). *Fact sheet on persons with disabilities.* Department of Economic and Social Affairs. https://www.un.org/development/desa/disabilities/resources/factsheet-on-persons-with-disabilities.html

University of Washington. (2016). *Disability stigma and your patients.* Aging Well with a Physical Disability Factsheet Series. http://agerrtc.washington.edu

WHO. (2018, January 16). *Disability and health. Key facts.* https://www.who.int/en/news-room/fact-sheets/detail/disability-and-health

WHO. (2019). *Health topics: Disabilities.* https://www.who.int/topics/disabilities/en/

Zaikowski, C. (2017, January 12). Canada is a progressive immigration policy dream — unless you have a disability. *Washington Post.* https://www.washingtonpost.com/posteverything/wp/2017/02/03/canada-is-a-progressive-immigration-policy-dream-unless-you-have-a-disability/

Chapter 12

Armitage, A. (2003). *Social welfare in Canada.* Don Mills, ON: Oxford University Press.

Behrendt, C., & Nguyen, Q. (2018). *Innovative approaches for ensuring universal social protection for the future of work.* Geneva, Switzerland: International Labour Organization. https://www.ilo.org/wcmsp5/groups/public/ — -dgreports/ — -cabinet/documents/publication/wcms_629864.pdf

Béland, D., Blomqvist, P., Andersen, J.G., & Palme, J. (2014). The universal decline of universality? Social policy change in Canada, Denmark, Sweden and the UK. *Social Policy & Administration, 48* (7). https://doi.org/10.1111/spol.12064

Béland, D., & Marier, P. (2019). Universality and the erosion of old age security. In Beland, Machildon, & Prince (Eds.), *Universality and social policy in Canada.* (pp. 103-120). Toronto, ON: University of Toronto Press.

Béland, D., Marchildon, G., & Prince M. (Eds.). (2019). *Universality and social policy in Canada.* Toronto, ON: University of Toronto Press.

Brown, G. (2016). *The universal declaration of human rights in the 21st century: A living document in a changing world.* Open Book Publishers. https://doi.org/10.11647/OBP.0091

Canadian Association of Social Workers (CASW). (2005). *Code of ethics, 2005.* Ottawa, ON: Canadian Association of Social Workers.

Canadian Association of Social Workers (CASW). (2015). *A new social care act for Canada.* https://www.casw-acts.ca/sites/casw-acts.ca/files/a_new_social_care_act_for_canada.pdf

Canadian Association of Social Workers (CASW). (2020). *Statement on anti-asian racism amid the COVID–19 pandemic.* https://caswe-acfts.ca/casw-acfts-statement-on-anti-asian-racism-amid-COVID–19-pandemic/

Canadian Nurses Association (CNA). (2020, June 11). *Anti-black racism is a public health emergency in Canada.* https://www.cna-aiic.ca/en/news-room/news-releases/2020/anti-black-racism-is-a-public-health-emergency-in-canada#sthash.HCOyPXLn.dpuf

Champion, M. (2019). *The rise of populism.* Bloomberg. bloomberg.com/quicktake/populism

Coffey, C., Revollo, P. E., Harvey, R., Lawson, M., Butt, A. P., Piaget, K., Sarosi, D., & Thekkudan, J. (2020). *Time to care: Unpaid and underpaid care work and the global inequality crisis.* Oxfam. https://oxfamilibrary.openrepository.com/bitstream/handle/10546/620928/bp-time-to-care-inequality-200120-en.pdf

Cohen, M., Morrison, J., & Smith, D. (1995). Dismantling social welfare: Chronology of federal government cutbacks, 1985–1995. *CCPA Monitor,* (November). http://www.sfu.ca/~mcohen/publications/Polecon/dismantl.pdf

Davy, B., Davy, U., & Leisering, L. (2013). The global, the social and rights. New perspectives on social citizenship. *International Journal of Social Welfare, 22,* S–S14. https://doi.org/10.1111/ijsw.12041

Devereux, S. & Sabates-Wheeler, R. (2004). *Transformative social protection.* IDS Working Paper 232. Institute of Development Studies.

Dominelli, L., & Ku, H-B. (2017). Green social work and its implications for social development in China. *China Journal of Social Work, 10* (1), 3–22. https://doi.org/10.1080/17525098.2017.1300338

Dominelli, L., & Ioakimidis, V. (2016). The challenges of realising social justice in 21st century social work. *International Social Work, 59*(6), 693–696.

Drolet, J., Wu, H., Taylor, M., & Dennehy, A. (2015). Social work and sustainable social development: Teaching and learning strategies for "green social work"curriculum. *Social Work Education, 34*(5), 528–543.

Environmental Protection Agency (EPA). (2020). *Environmental justice.* Washington, DC: United States Environmental Protection Agency.

Galston, W. (2018). The rise of European populism and the collapse of the centre-left. *Bloomberg* (March 8). https://www.brookings.edu/blog/order-from-chaos/2018/03/08/the-rise-of-european-populism-and-the-collapse-of-the-center-left/

Godin, M. (2020, October 9). She was racially abused by hospital staff as she lay dying. Now a Canadian Indigenous woman's death is forcing a reckoning on racism. *Time.* https://time.com/5898422/joyce-echaquan-Indigenous-protests-canada/

Gore, A. (2006). *An inconvenient truth: The planetary emergency of global warming and what we can do about It.* New York, NY: Rodale Press.

Government of Canada (n.d.). *Climate change and health: Populations at risk.* Ottawa, ON: Author. https://www.canada.ca/en/health-canada/services/climate-change-health/populations-risk.html

Graves, F., & Valpy, M. (2018, December 3). Canada is a tinderbox for populism. The 2019 election could spark it. *Maclean's.* https://www.macleans.ca/politics/canada-is-a-tinderbox-for-populism-the-2019-election-could-spark-it/

Hanes, R. (2016). Challenging critical disability theory: Developing a post social model of disability. In J. Robertson and G. Larsen (Eds.), *Disability and social change: A progressive Canadian approach* (pp. 65–80). Fernwood Press.

IASSW, ICSW, IFSW. (2014). *Global agenda for social work and social development: First report. Promoting social and economic equalities.* David N Jones (Ed.). Rheinfelden, Switzerland: IFSW.

IASSW, ICSW, IFSW. (2016). *Global agenda for social work and social development: Second report. Promoting the dignity and worth of peoples.* David N Jones (Ed.). Rheinfelden, Switzerland: IFSW.

IASSW, ICSW, IFSW. (2018). *Global agenda for social work and social development: Third report. Promoting community and environmental sustainability.* David N Jones (Ed.). Rheinfelden, Switzerland: IFSW.

IASSW, ICSW, IFSW. (2019). *Reflections on the next global agenda: Volume 1. Contributions from IASSW, ICSW and IFSW.* Rheinfelden, Switzerland: IFSW.

IASSW, ICSW, IFSW. (2020). *Global agenda for social work and social development: Fourth report. Strengthening recognition of the importance of human relationships*. David N Jones (Ed.). Rheinfelden, Switzerland: IFSW.

Insurance Bureau of Canada. (n.d.). *Severe weather caused $1.3 billion in insured damage in 2019*. Toronto, ON: Author. http://www.ibc.ca/on/resources/media-centre/media-releases/severe-weather-caused-1-3-billion-in-insured-damage-in-2019

International Federation of Social Workers (IFSW). (2020). *IFSW conference concludes: A new era for social work*. https://www.ifsw.org/ifsw-conference-concludes-a-new-era-for-social-work/

International Federation of Social Workers (IFSW). (2014, August 6). *Global definition of social work*. https://www.ifsw.org/global-definition-of-social-work/

International Organization for Migration (IOM). (2020a). *World migration report 2020*. Intrenational Organization for Migration.

International Organization for Migration (IOM). (2020b). Migration factsheet no. 6 — The impact of COVID–19 on migrants. https://www.iom.int/sites/default/files/our_work/ICP/MPR/migration_factsheet_6_COVID–19_and_migrants.pdf

Midgley, J. (2016). *Social welfare for a global era: International perspectives on policy and practice*. Los Angeles, CA: Sage Publications, Inc.

James, H. (2020, March 4). *Could coronavirus being about the "waning of globalization"?* World Economic Forum. https://www.weforum.org/agenda/2020/03/globalization-coronavirus-covid19-epidemic-change-economic-political/

Labour Market Information Council. (2020). *How much do they make? New evidence on the early career earnings of a Canadian post-secondary education grade rates by credential & field of study*. Ottawa, ON: Author. https://lmic-cimt.ca/wp-content/uploads/2020/01/How-Much-Do-They-Make-Executive-Summary.pdf

Ladhani, S., & Sitter, K. C. (2020). The revival of anti-racism. *Critical Social Work, 21*(1). doi 10.22329/csw.v21i1.6227

Lakner, C., Gerszon, D., Mahler, D. G., Mario Negre, M., & Prydz, E. B. (2020, June). *How much does reducing inequality matter for global poverty?* World Bank Global Poverty Monitoring Technical Note.

Landwehr, C., & Schäfer, A. (2020). *Populist, technocratic, and authoritarian responses to COVID–19*. Social Sciences and Research Council. https://items.ssrc.org/COVID–19-and-the-social-sciences/democracy-and-pandemics/populist-technocratic-and-authoritarian-responses-to-COVID–19/

MacDonald, F. F., & Midgley J. (2007). Introduction: Globalization, social justice and social welfare. *Journal of Sociology and Welfare, 34*(2). https://scholarworks.wmich.edu/jssw/vol34/iss2/2/

Mahon R., & Prince, M. (2019). From family allowances to the struggle for universal childcare in Canada. In Bleand, Machildon, & Prince (Eds.), *Universality and social policy in Canada* (pp.83–102). Toronto, ON: University of Toronto Press.

Mansaray, A., Mansaray, G., & Stark, R. (2020). *Social work beyond borders volume 2: Paths through change — the power of social determination*. International Federation of Social Workers.

McKinnon, J. (2008). Exploring the nexus between social work and the environment. *Australian Social Work, 61*(3), 256–268. https://doi.org/10.1080/03124070802178275

Midgley, J. (2017). *Social welfare for a global era: International perspectives on policy and practice*. Sage.

Mukherjee, A., Waring, M., et al. (2011). *Who cares? The economics of dignity*. London, UK: Commonwealth Secretariat.

Murphy, M., & McGann, M. (2020). *Renewing welfare through universal entitlement: Lessons from COVID–19*. https://www.socialeurope.eu/renewing-welfare-through-universal-entitlement-lessons-from-COVID–19

Natural Resources Canada. (2004). *Climate change impacts and adaptation: A Canadian perspective*. http://adaptation.nrcan.gc.ca/perspective/index_e.php

Oxfam. (2020, January 20). *World's billionaires have more wealth than 4.6 billion people*. https://www.oxfam.org/en/press-releases/worlds-billionaires-have-more-wealth-46-billion-people

Ramsay, S., & Boddy, J. (2017). Environmental social work: A concept analysis, *British Journal of Social Work, 47* (1), 68–86. https://doi.org/10.1093/bjsw/bcw078

Sandbæk, M. (2017). European policies to promote children's rights and combat child poverty. *International Journal of Environmental Research and Public Health, 14*, 837. https://doi.org/10.3390/ijerph14080837

Sherman, P. (2016). Preparing social workers for global gaze: Locating global citizenship within social work curricula. *Social Work Education, 35* (6), 632–642. https://doi.org/10.1080/02615479.2016.1190328

Smith, D. (2017). Globalizing social problems: An agenda for the twenty-first century. Presidential address. *Social Problems, 64*, 1–13. https://doi.org/10.1093/socpro/spw032

Stark, R. (2019). *Social work beyond borders. The importance of relationships*. The International Foundation of Social Workers.

Stewart, F. (2013, March). *Capabilities and human development: Beyond the individual — the critical role of social institutions and social competencies*. United Nations Development Programme. http://hdr.undp.org/sites/default/files/hdro_1303_stewart.pdf

Stiglitz, J. (2017). *The welfare state in the twenty-first century*. New York, NY: Roosevelt Institute. https://rooseveltinstitute.org/wp-content/uploads/2017/06/Welfare-Chapter-JS.pdf

Stiglitz, J. (2020). Solidarity now. *On Point*. New York, NY: Project Syndicate. https://www.project-syndicate.org/onpoint

Truell, R., & Crompton, S. (2020). *To the top of the cliff: How social work changed with COVID–19*. International Federation of Social Workers.

United Nations. (2013). *Inequality matters: Report on the world social situation 2013*. Department for Economic and Social Affairs.

United Nations. (2015). *Transforming our world: The 2030 agenda for sustainable development*. New York, NY: United Nations. Development Programme.

United Nations. (2016). *World economic and social survey 2016: Climate change resilience: An opportunity for reducing inequalities*. New York, NY: Department of Economic and Social Affairs.

United Nations. (2019). The future is now: Science for achieving sustainable development. *Global Sustainable Development Report*. https://sustainabledevelopment.un.org/content/documents/24797GSDR_report_2019.pdf

United Nations. (2019). *The sustainable development goals report, 2019*. New York, NY: United Nations Development Programme. https://unstats.un.org/sdgs/report/2019/The-Sustainable-Development-Goals-Report-2019.pdf

United Nations Development Programme (UNDP). (n.d.). *What are the sustainable development goals?* Oslo, Norway: Oslo Governance Centre. https://www.undp.org/content/oslo-governance-centre/en/home/sustainable-development-goals.html

United Nations Development Programme (UNDP). (2015). *Sustainable development goals: Background on the goals*. New York, NY: United Nations Development Programme. https://www.undp.org/content/undp/en/home/sustainable-development-goals/background.html

United Nations Development Programme (UNDP). (2019c). *Human development report 2019: Beyond income, beyond averages, beyond today*. New York, NY: United Nations. Development Programme. http://hdr.undp.org/sites/default/files/hdr2019.pdf

United Nations Development Programme (UNDP). (2020). *Charting pathways out of multidimensional poverty: Achieving the SDGs*. United Nations Development Programme and Oxford Poverty and Human Development Initiative. http://hdr.undp.org/sites/default/files/2020_mpi_report_en.pdf

Watt-Cloutier, S. (2018). It's time to listen to the Inuit on climate change. *Canadian Geographic* (November 19). © Sheila Watt-Cloutier / *Canadian Geographic*. https://www.canadiangeographic.ca/article/its-time-listen-inuit-climate-change

Index